Listen to This

MARK EVAN BONDS

Custom Edition for Penn Foster

PENN FOSTER

Taken from:

Listen to This
by Mark Evan Bonds

Learning Solutions

New York   Boston   San Francisco
London   Toronto   Sydney   Tokyo   Singapore   Madrid
Mexico City   Munich   Paris   Cape Town   Hong Kong   Montreal

Pearson Learning Solutions, 501 Boylston Street, Suite 900, Boston, MA 02116
A Pearson Education Company
www.pearsoned.com

Printed in the United States of America

1 2 3 4 5 6 7 8 9 10 XXXX 14 13 12 11 10 09

000200010270568571

DC

ISBN 10: 0-558-65615-3
ISBN 13: 978-0-558-65615-7

Table of Contents

THE ELEMENTS OF MUSIC: A Brief Introduction 1

Melody 2
SCI-TECH The Acoustics of Melody 6
Rhythm 7
Harmony 8
CULTURAL CONTEXT Illegal Harmony? 10
Texture 10
Timbre 11
SCI-TECH The Acoustics of Timbre 13
Dynamics 12
Form 14
Word-Music Relationships 14
Genre 15

PART 1 THE MIDDLE AGES 17
The Middle Ages: At a Glance 21

1 Hildegard von Bingen
Play of Virtues (excerpt) 22
Listening Guide 28
BIOGRAPHY Visions Through Music 27
THE COMPOSER SPEAKS Hildegard Defends the Practice of Music 30
CULTURAL CONTEXT The Morality Play 23
EXPAND YOUR PLAYLIST Chant 30

2 San Ildefonso Indians of New Mexico
Eagle Dance 31
Listening Guide 35
CULTURAL CONTEXT The Powwow 33
EXPAND YOUR PLAYLIST Native American Music 36

3 Francesco Landini
"Behold, Spring" 37
Listening Guide 41
BIOGRAPHY The Composer as Poet 40
THE MONEY TRAIL Producing a Manuscript 42
EXPAND YOUR PLAYLIST Medieval Polyphony 42

4 Alfonso el Sabio
Songs to the Virgin Mary no. 249,
"He Who Gladly Serves" 43
Listening Guide 46
BIOGRAPHY The King Gets All the Credit 47
MAP Islam in Europe 44
SCI-TECH Reed Instruments 47
EXPAND YOUR PLAYLIST Instrumental Music of the Middle Ages 48

MUSIC OF THE MIDDLE AGES: A Summary 49
IN REVIEW: Medieval Style 49

PART 2 THE RENAISSANCE 50
The Renaissance: At a Glance 53

5 Josquin des Prez
"The Cricket" 54
Listening Guide 58
BIOGRAPHY "Master of the Notes" 57
MAP Stations in a Career 57
MUSIC IN PERFORMANCE Playing and Singing 59
EXPAND YOUR PLAYLIST The Music of Sounds 59

6 Thomas Weelkes
"Since Robin Hood" 60
Listening Guide 64
BIOGRAPHY A Shakespearean Composer 63
CULTURAL CONTEXT Musicians as Spies 65
EXPAND YOUR PLAYLIST The Italian Madrigal 65

7 William Byrd
"Sing Joyfully" 66
Listening Guide 70
BIOGRAPHY A Catholic Composer at a Protestant Court 71
THE COMPOSER SPEAKS Eight Reasons for Learning How to Sing 72
MUSIC IN PERFORMANCE The Sound of the All-Male Choir 69
EXPAND YOUR PLAYLIST Sacred Music of the Renaissance 72

8 Rhyming Singers of the Bahamas
"My Lord Help Me to Pray" 73
Listening Guide 76
CULTURAL CONTEXT Bob Marley and the Birth of Reggae 74
EXPAND YOUR PLAYLIST Music of the Caribbean 78

WEB BONUS CHAPTER 1
Tielman Susato: *Moorish Dance* WB1-1
Listening Guide WB1-6
BIOGRAPHY The Composer as Publisher WB1-5
THE MONEY TRAIL The Business of Music Publishing WB1-7
EXPAND YOUR PLAYLIST Instrumental Music of the Renaissance WB1-8

MAKING CONNECTIONS: Music of the Middle Ages
    and the Renaissance 79
IN REVIEW: Renaissance Style 80

PART 3 THE BAROQUE ERA 81
The Baroque: At a Glance 86

9 Claudio Monteverdi
Orpheus, selection from Act II 88
Listening Guide 92
BIOGRAPHY Master of Old and New Styles 91
THE MONEY TRAIL Monteverdi Turns Down a Job Offer 94
EXPAND YOUR PLAYLIST Old and New Practices in the
    Seventeenth Century 94

10 Henry Purcell
Dido and Aeneas: Overture and Act I, nos. 1–4 95
Listening Guide 98
BIOGRAPHY Inspired by the Stage 100
MUSIC IN PERFORMANCE Opera in English 101
EXPAND YOUR PLAYLIST Baroque Opera 101

11 Mbuti Pygmies
"Marriage Celebration Song" 102
Listening Guide 106
CULTURAL CONTEXT Do I Repeat Myself? 103
EXPAND YOUR PLAYLIST Singing in the Rain (Forest) 108

12 Barbara Strozzi
"Revenge" 109
Listening Guide 112
BIOGRAPHY "Secure from the Lightning Bolts of Slander" 114
CULTURAL CONTEXT Female Composers in the Baroque Era 115
EXPAND YOUR PLAYLIST Baroque Chamber Music 116

13 Johann Sebastian Bach
Fugue in G Minor, BWV 578 ("Little") 117
Listening Guide 121
BIOGRAPHY New Jobs, New Genres 123
MAP Bach's World 124
MUSIC IN PERFORMANCE Changing the Sound, but Not the Notes 120
EXPAND YOUR PLAYLIST Baroque Organ Music 124

WEB BONUS CHAPTER 2
Hmong People of Laos: *Gaeng School Song* WB2-1
Listening Guide WB2-4
EXPAND YOUR PLAYLIST The *Gaeng's* All Here! WB2-7

14 Antonio Vivaldi
The Four Seasons, "Winter," first movement 125
Listening Guide 128
BIOGRAPHY Composing for Orphans 130
SCI-TECH Trade Secrets: Building the Perfect Violin 131
EXPAND YOUR PLAYLIST Program Music 131

15 Johann Sebastian Bach
Brandenburg Concerto no. 2 in F Major, BWV 1047,
    finale 132
Listening Guide 136
MUSIC IN PERFORMANCE The Art of Trumpet Playing,
    Lost and Found 135
EXPAND YOUR PLAYLIST The Baroque Concerto 138

16 George Frideric Handel
Water Music, selections 139
Rigaudon I 140
Hornpipe 141
Listening Guide 143
BIOGRAPHY The Well-Traveled Composer 146
MAP Handel's World 146
CULTURAL CONTEXT The Composer as Cultural Hero 147
EXPAND YOUR PLAYLIST Baroque Suites 147

17 Johann Sebastian Bach
Cantata 140: *Awake, a Voice Calls to Us,* selections 148
Listening Guide 154
THE MONEY TRAIL Bach's Working Conditions 153
EXPAND YOUR PLAYLIST Sacred Music of the Late Baroque 153

18 George Frideric Handel
Messiah, selections 156
He that dwelleth in heaven (recitative) 157
Thou shalt break them (aria) 157
Hallelujah (chorus) 159
Listening Guide 162
CULTURAL CONTEXT Why Stand? 161
EXPAND YOUR PLAYLIST Covering the "Hallelujah" Chorus 166

MAKING CONNECTIONS: Music of the Renaissance
    and Baroque 167
IN REVIEW: Baroque Style 168

PART 4 THE CLASSICAL ERA 169
The Classical Era: At a Glance 173

19 Joseph Haydn
String Quartet in C Major, op. 76, no. 3, second movement 174
Listening Guide 180
BIOGRAPHY Writing to Order 179
CULTURAL CONTEXT Musical Appropriation 182
EXPAND YOUR PLAYLIST Chamber Music and Solo Keyboard Music of the
  Classical Era 182

20 Master Musicians of the Ikuta-ryu
Cherry Blossom 183
Listening Guide 188
THE MONEY TRAIL Geisha in Japanese Life 184
EXPAND YOUR PLAYLIST Zither-Dee-Dee 187

21 Joseph Haydn
Symphony no. 102 in B-flat Major, third and fourth
movements 190
Minuet 192
Rondo 193
Listening Guide 194
MAP Haydn's Travels 198
CULTURAL CONTEXT Concerts and Concert Manners
  in the Classical Era 199
THE COMPOSER SPEAKS Haydn in London 198
EXPAND YOUR PLAYLIST Haydn's Symphonies 199

22 Wolfgang Amadeus Mozart
Symphony no. 40 in G Minor, K. 550, first movement 200
Listening Guide 206
BIOGRAPHY The Composer as Chameleon 208
MAP Mozart's Travels 208
CULTURAL CONTEXT The Drama of Sonata Form 205
CULTURAL CONTEXT Mozart's Sister 209
EXPAND YOUR PLAYLIST Mozart's Symphonies 209

23 Wolfgang Amadeus Mozart
Piano Concerto in A Major, K. 488, first movement 210
Listening Guide 216
THE MONEY TRAIL Mozart's Concerts: The Bottom Line 214
MUSIC IN PERFORMANCE Mozart on Modern Instruments 215
EXPAND YOUR PLAYLIST The Classical Concerto 218

24 Wolfgang Amadeus Mozart
The Marriage of Figaro, Act I, selection "Cosa sento" 219
Listening Guide 224
EXPAND YOUR PLAYLIST Opera in the Classical Era 223

25 Lisa Lu and the Beijing Opera Company
The Reunion 228
Listening Guide 232
CULTURAL CONTEXT *Jingju* and the Cultural Revolution 231
EXPAND YOUR PLAYLIST Traditional Chinese Music 234

MAKING CONNECTIONS: Music of the Baroque
  and Classical Eras 235
IN REVIEW: Classical Style 236

PART 5 THE NINETEENTH CENTURY 237
The Nineteenth Century: At a Glance 242

26 Ludwig van Beethoven
Symphony no. 5 in C Minor, op. 67, first movement 244
Listening Guide 248
BIOGRAPHY Composing through Deafness 250
CULTURAL CONTEXT Fate? 247
EXPAND YOUR PLAYLIST Beethoven's Other Symphonies 251

27 Franz Schubert
"Erlkönig", D. 328 252
Listening Guide 256
BIOGRAPHY Turning Poetry into Music 254
EXPAND YOUR PLAYLIST Schubert's Songs 255

28 Felix Mendelssohn
Overture to A Midsummer Night's Dream 260
Listening Guide 264
BIOGRAPHY The Cosmopolitan Composer 263
THE COMPOSER SPEAKS Mendelssohn Reflects on his *Overture to
  A Midsummer Night's Dream* 266
EXPAND YOUR PLAYLIST Shakespeare in Music 266

29 Hector Berlioz
Symphonie fantastique, fourth movement
("March to the Scaffold") 267
Listening Guide 270
BIOGRAPHY Music as Autobiography 271
SCI-TECH How Loud Is Too Loud? 272
EXPAND YOUR PLAYLIST The Music of Dreams 272

30 Fanny Mendelssohn Hensel
Piano Trio in D Minor, op. 11, third movement 273
Listening Guide 276
BIOGRAPHY Overcoming Obstacles 275
CULTURAL CONTEXT Women Composers of the Nineteenth
  Century 277
EXPAND YOUR PLAYLIST Chamber Music of the Nineteenth
  Century 278

WEB BONUS CHAPTER 3
Robert Schumann: "Dedication" WB3-1
Listening Guide WB3-6
BIOGRAPHY The Composer as Critic WB3-5
EXPAND YOUR PLAYLIST The Song in the Nineteenth
    Century WB3-8

31 Clara Wieck Schumann
"Forward!" 279
Listening Guide 282
BIOGRAPHY Independent Spirit 281
CULTURAL CONTEXT Music and Politics 284
EXPAND YOUR PLAYLIST Political Music 284

32 Frédéric Chopin
Mazurka in B-flat, op. 7, no. 1 285
Listening Guide 290
BIOGRAPHY A Polish Composer in France 289
MUSIC IN PERFORMANCE Speeding Up and Slowing Down:
    Robbed Time 291
EXPAND YOUR PLAYLIST Piano Music of the Nineteenth Century 292

33 Louis Moreau Gottschalk
Union 293
Listening Guide 296
BIOGRAPHY The Musician as Showman 297
MAP Gottschalk's Concert Tour, Spring 1862 297
CULTURAL CONTEXT Music in the Civil War 295
EXPAND YOUR PLAYLIST The Nineteenth-Century Virtuoso 298

34 Ravi Shankar
Raga Sindhi-Bhairavi 299
Listening Guide 304
CULTURAL CONTEXT Meet the Sitar 301
EXPAND YOUR PLAYLIST Raga 303

35 Giuseppe Verdi
La Traviata, Act I, selection 306
Listening Guide 310
BIOGRAPHY The Composer as Social Reformer 309
MAP Verdi's Premieres 308
CULTURAL CONTEXT The Diva 314
EXPAND YOUR PLAYLIST The Art of the Diva 314

36 Richard Wagner
The Valkyrie, Act III, selection ("Wotan's farewell") 315
Listening Guide 320
BIOGRAPHY The Composer as Radical 322

MAP Wagner's life 323
CULTURAL CONTEXT Wagner and Tolkien: A Tale
    of Two Rings 319
EXPAND YOUR PLAYLIST Opera in the Nineteenth Century 323

37 Johannes Brahms
Symphony no. 4 in E Minor, op. 98, finale 324
Listening Guide 328
BIOGRAPHY The Composer as Hedgehog 327
MUSIC IN PERFORMANCE The Conductor 326
EXPAND YOUR PLAYLIST The Art of the Conductor 332

38 Antonin Dvořák
String Quartet in F Major, op. 96 ("American"),
third movement 333
Listening Guide 336
BIOGRAPHY In Search of National Sounds 337
MAP Dvořák: The Summer of 1893 328
THE COMPOSER SPEAKS The Sources of an American
    Musical Style 338
MUSIC IN PERFORMANCE How to Make a Quartet 339
EXPAND YOUR PLAYLIST Nationalism in Nineteenth-Century
    Music 339

MAKING CONNECTIONS: Music of the Classical Era
    and the Nineteenth Century 340
IN REVIEW: Nineteenth-Century Style 341

PART 6 THE TWENTIETH CENTURY 342
The Twentieth Century: At a Glance 346

39 Claude Debussy
Voiles from *Preludes,* book 1 350
Listening Guide 356
BIOGRAPHY The Path Less Taken 358
CULTURAL CONTEXT Impressionism 359
EXPAND YOUR PLAYLIST Impressionism 359

40 Gamelan Gong Kebyar of Belaluan
Kebyar Ding III, "Oncang-oncangan" 360
Listening Guide 364
CULTURAL CONTEXT Gotta Minimalist? 363
EXPAND YOUR PLAYLIST Gamelan Music 367

41 Charles Ives
The Unanswered Question 368
Listening Guide 372
BIOGRAPHY Against the Grain 373
EXPAND YOUR PLAYLIST Tonal versus Atonal 373

42 Arnold Schoenberg
"Columbine" from *Pierrot lunaire* 374
Listening Guide 378
BIOGRAPHY The Composer as Outsider 377
CULTURAL CONTEXT Expressionist Film 379
EXPAND YOUR PLAYLIST Expressionism 379

43 Igor Stravinsky
The Rite of Spring, Part One (excerpt) 380
Listening Guide 386
BIOGRAPHY "Modernsky" 385
MAP Stations in Stravinsky's Life 385
THE MONEY TRAIL The Business of Dance 388
MUSIC IN PERFORMANCE The Audience Riots 389
EXPAND YOUR PLAYLIST Ballet Music 389

44 Berta Waza
Greetings by Aba Musa! 390
Listening Guide 394
CULTURAL CONTEXT Polytonality in Jazz 393
EXPAND YOUR PLAYLIST Come Blow Your Horn! 396

45 Scott Joplin
Maple Leaf Rag 397
Listening Guide 402
BIOGRAPHY The King of Ragtime 401
MUSIC IN PERFORMANCE Should You Play the Notes in the Score? 403
THE MONEY TRAIL Making Money on a Hit 404
EXPAND YOUR PLAYLIST Rooted in Ragtime 404

46 Robert Johnson
"Terraplane Blues" 405
Listening Guide 410
BIOGRAPHY A Deal with the Devil 412
MUSIC IN PERFORMANCE Who Wrote the Blues? 413
EXPAND YOUR PLAYLIST The Blues in Different Styles 413

47 Duke Ellington
Cotton Tail 414
Listening Guide 418
BIOGRAPHY Composing Jazz and Beyond 422
CULTURAL CONTEXT The Swing Revival 423
EXPAND YOUR PLAYLIST Rhythm Changes in Jazz 423

48 Charlie Parker
Ornithology 424
Listening Guide 428
BIOGRAPHY The Self-Destructive Artist 430
MUSIC IN PERFORMANCE Improvisation 427
EXPAND YOUR PLAYLIST From Bebop to Free Jazz 430

49 Ruth Crawford
Piano Study in Mixed Accents 431
Listening Guide 436
BIOGRAPHY Modernist Composer and Folksong Arranger 435
CULTURAL CONTEXT Twelve-Tone Composition 437
EXPAND YOUR PLAYLIST Women Composers of the Twentieth Century 437

WEB BONUS CHAPTER 4
Germaine Tailleferre:
Concertino for Harp and *Orchestra,* finale WB4-1
Listening Guide WB4-4
BIOGRAPHY One of Six WB4-5
CULTURAL CONTEXT Using the Past to Send a Message WB4-6
EXPAND YOUR PLAYLIST Neoclassicism WB4-6

50 William Grant Still
"A Black Pierrot" from *Songs of Separation* 438
Listening Guide 442
BIOGRAPHY A Career of Firsts 441
EXPAND YOUR PLAYLIST Twentieth-Century African American Composers in the Western Classical Tradition 443

51 Aaron Copland
"Hoe-Down" from *Rodeo* 444
Listening Guide 448
BIOGRAPHY Populist Modernist 447
CULTURAL CONTEXT "Are You Now or Have You Ever Been . . .?" 449
CULTURAL CONTEXT Using "Hoe-Down" 447
EXPAND YOUR PLAYLIST The Sound of the American West 449

52 Leonard Bernstein
"Tonight" from *West Side Story* 450
Listening Guide 454
BIOGRAPHY Four Lives in One 458
EXPAND YOUR PLAYLIST Broadway's Social Conscience 458

53 John Cage
4'33" 459
Listening Guide 462
BIOGRAPHY What is a Composer? 461
THE COMPOSER SPEAKS John Cage on *4'33"* 462
CULTURAL CONTEXT Paying for Silence 463
EXPAND YOUR PLAYLIST Experimental Composers of the Twentieth Century 463

54 Philip Glass
"Knee Play 1" from *Einstein on the Beach* 464
Listening Guide 467
BIOGRAPHY Prolific Minimalist 468
EXPAND YOUR PLAYLIST Minimalism 469

55 Chuck Berry
"School Day" 470
Listening Guide 476
BIOGRAPHY Musical Recipe for Rock 'n' Roll 473
SCI-TECH Television and the Rise of Rock 'n' Roll 475
EXPAND YOUR PLAYLIST Styles of Early Rock 'n' Roll 475

WEB BONUS **CHAPTER 5**
Mahalia Jackson: "It Don't Cost Very Much" WB5-1
Listening Guide WB5-6
BIOGRAPHY A Divine Collaboration WB5-5
CULTURAL CONTEXT Gospel in Black and White WB5-8
EXPAND YOUR PLAYLIST Southern and Black Gospel WB5-8

56 The Marvelettes
"Please, Mr. Postman" 478
Listening Guide 482
BIOGRAPHY An Orchestrated Collaboration 484
THE MONEY TRAIL Reading Labels 485
EXPAND YOUR PLAYLIST Close Harmony in Different Styles 485

57 Beach Boys
"Good Vibrations" 486
Listening Guide 490
BIOGRAPHY Making the Album that Never Was 492
CULTURAL CONTEXT The Summer of Love 493
EXPAND YOUR PLAYLIST Psychedelia 493

WEB BONUS **CHAPTER 6**
Sex Pistols: "God Save the Queen" WB6-1
Listening Guide WB6-6
BIOGRAPHY The Original British Punks WB6-8
MUSIC IN PERFORMANCE The "Do It Yourself" Aesthetic WB6-9
EXPAND YOUR PLAYLIST Punk and New Wave WB6-9

58 Public Enemy
"Fight the Power" 494
Listening Guide 498
BIOGRAPHY Politics and Music 500
CULTURAL CONTEXT Hip Hop's Elements 501
EXPAND YOUR PLAYLIST Musical References in "Fight the Power" 501

59 Tania León
A la Par, second movement ("*Guaguancó*") 502
Listening Guide 506
BIOGRAPHY Resisting Labels 505
CULTURAL CONTEXT Postmodern Architecture 507
EXPAND YOUR PLAYLIST Postmodern Music 507

60 Tan Dun
"Farewell" from *Crouching Tiger, Hidden Dragon* 508
Listening Guide 511
BIOGRAPHY Composer in Two Worlds 512
SCI-TECH Matching Images with Sound 513
EXPAND YOUR PLAYLIST Film Music 513

MAKING CONNECTIONS: Music of the Nineteenth and Twentieth Centuries 514
IN REVIEW: The Twentieth Century 515

PART 7 MUSIC TODAY 516
Data Collection: Listen First 517
What Are the Words? 517
Doing the Research 520
Data Collection: Melody, Rhythm, Harmony 522
Data Collection: Texture, Timbre, Dynamics 524
Form 525
Word-Music Relationships 527
Creating Your Own Analysis 530

Glossary 532
Index 536

Dear Reader,

Music is a form of energy: we can't see it, but we can feel the way it moves our spirits. Yet how often do we listen—really *listen*—to music? Listening is one of those things we already know how to do, but it's also one of those things we can all do better. Smart listening can help us enjoy whatever music we like even more: The better we know how a piece works, the more deeply it will move us.

This is a book that will help you learn how to listen to music. All music. It does that by putting listening first. The focus throughout this book is on the basic elements of music—**melody, rhythm, harmony, form, texture, timbre, dynamics, form, word-music relationships,** and **genre**—which provide the fundamental building blocks of music everywhere. In the process, you'll get to know some wonderful music, from plainchant to Gospel, from Beethoven to Chuck Berry, from symphonies to hip hop. And lots more in between.

Enjoy!

Evan Bonds

Mark Evan Bonds

MARK EVAN BONDS is the Boshamer Distinguished Professor of Music at the University of North Carolina at Chapel Hill, where he has taught since 1992. He received his B.A. from Duke University and earned his Ph.D. at Harvard. He has written several books and numerous essays on music, including *Music as Thought: Listening to the Symphony in the Age of Beethoven* and *A History of Music Western Culture*, now in its third edition. *Listen to This* reflects his experience and dedication to teaching music appreciation to undergraduates for almost 20 years.

Listen to the music. Hear the elements. Expand your playlist.

Informed by over 300 instructor and student reviews, *Listen to This* was created for today's students. It will expand your students' playlist with its listening-oriented approach and the integration of the musical elements. For the professor, it provides a customizable, modular format that gives you the flexibility to design your ideal music appreciation course. *Listen to This* encourages students to explore history, culture, and musical styles through active listening, not just through passive reading. This text will instill a life-long appreciation of music in your students by expanding their playlist today!

Listen to the music

What's the first thing you do in class?

Putting Listening First
We listen to music all the time, on our iPods, at our computers, and in our cars. But do we really actively listen? Are we opening our ears to different styles of music? How can we build these skills? *Listen to This* addresses this central issue for every Music Appreciation student: **It expands listening skills with a dynamic, fresh approach.**

◀ Each Era Plays its Part
The book is structured **chronologically,** with each part focusing on a single era of music. Part openers begin each significant musical era and set the stage for active listening. "At a Glance" contents help students frame the information to follow.

◀ *Listen to This* Chapter Opener
Just as each class begins with listening to a musical work, *Listen to This* begins each chapter with a **guided listening exercise,** focusing on three or four key elements that will provide the focus for a deeper discussion.

Listening Guides

Detailed Listening Guides focus on the key elements in the chapter, increasing understanding and retention of key information.

Expanding on the traditional Listening Guide, these visual guides walk students through the piece while tying the listening experience to the chapter material.

Student FAQs

Based upon real questions from students, Student FAQs encourage students to think about listening more critically and at the same time raise issues that are often asked in class.

Modular Format

Each chapter covers a single work, to keep the act of listening in the foreground. This **modular approach gives instructors added flexibility to choose the works of music** that best suit the needs of their students, the curriculum, and add their own instructional material. In addition, MyMusicLab offers 6 Web Bonus Chapters for students and professors to use to further enrich the course.

Hear the elements

What tools can you give your students to expand their listening skills?

Elements Up Front

The elements of music—**melody, rhythm, harmony, texture, timbre, dynamics, form, word-music relationships,** and **genre**—link all types of musical expression around the world. Understanding these elements empowers students for a lifetime of informed listening. These elements of music are introduced in the book's first section, and then consistently presented at the beginning of each chapter.

 Melody   **Rhythm**   **Harmony**   **Texture**   **Timbre**   **Dynamics**   **Form**   **Word-Music Relationships**   **Genre**

Each part closes with a quick review of the elements.

The Elements of Music: A Brief Introduction

Using the well-known piece, "The Star-Spangled Banner," this section highlights each fundamental element in sequence. Different arrangements and performances of this work are offered to highlight specific elements as they are introduced. The *Listen to This* chapter opener reintroduces the elements.

Expand Your Playlist

What is your main goal for your music appreciation course?

Encouraging Broader Listening

World Music Coverage Professors have the option of covering world music with examples that show how the same musical elements found in classical styles can be heard around the world. These concrete connections help students better understand the full range of musical expression.

Real World Connections Students absorb and retain abstract ideas far better when they can relate them directly to specific examples. Few students have seen a Medieval morality play but most have seen at least one episode of *Star Wars*. *Listen to This* is written in engaging, concise prose with real world examples that help students directly relate to the content and master basic concepts.

Saves Time, Improves Results

ISBN 0205651011 www.mymusiclab.com

◄ MyMusicLab is a central part of the learning process, and it engages students throughout the course. MyMusicLab is a dynamic online resource that provides opportunities for practice, assessment, and instruction. Key components include:

- Complete, **page-fidelity ebook**, with hyperlinks to musical examples.
- **Full streaming audio** for *all* the listening examples. These are the *same* performances as on the CD set in their entirety.

◄ - **Automated listening guides** to build student listening skills.
- **Web Bonus Chapters** feature related repertory for further study.
- Robust, self-grading **student assessment activities**, providing instant feedback, for practice, self-study, or homework.
  - **Listening activities** that help students identify key musical styles and composers
  - **Pre- and post-assessment questions** for each chapter of the book
  - **Flashcards** for review of key concepts and terminology many with pronunciations and musical examples
- Cultural Connections through **online documentaries and videos**
- Interactive **introduction to the orchestra and its instruments**

◄ - **Music Primer** reviews the basic elements for students

5 CD set

ISBN 013183827X

The complete recordings referenced in the text are available online in streaming audio, and also—in identical versions—on an optional five-CD set for those who prefer to have the music examples on disc.

Resources for Teaching and Learning

Instructor's Manual and Test Bank—Our Instructor's Manual and Test Bank written by Patricia Cox, Harding University, is an invaluable resource for new and experienced faculty alike. Contents include chapter outlines, chapter summaries, class projects, and a lecture outline as well as essay questions for each chapter of *Listen to This*. The Test Bank contains hundreds of sample test questions in various formats, including multiple choice, true/false, and fill-in-the-blank.

mypearsontest ☑

MyPearsonTest—This powerful assessment generation program by Karen Dale, Cleveland State Community College, contains hundreds of sample test questions.

PowerPoint Slides—PowerPoint slides by Nancy Hadsell, Texas Women's University—These pre-made PowerPoint slides include illustrations and photos from the text, as well as content from a variety of other sources that highlight key points in the text. Also includes easy-to-follow notes on how to customize and enhance your presentations.

Theme and Variations Form

- Very popular in Classical Era
- Theme presented and then altered in several ways
- Examples of variation techniques:
  - Change of key
  - Change of mode (major to minor/minor to major)
  - Change of tempo or meter
  - Change of timbre (i.e., instrumentation)
  - Change in texture (homophony/polyphony)

Listen to This
By Mark Evan Bonds   4-8   PRENTICE HALL
                                                    ©2010 Pearson Education, Inc.
                                                    Upper Saddle River, NJ 07458

Clicker Response Resources by Linda Ferguson, Valparaiso University (Indiana)—PowerPoint slides with multiple choice questions appropriate for use with Classroom Response Systems are available for instructor classroom use.

Five CD set

ISBN 013183827X

The complete recordings referenced in the text are available online in streaming audio, and also—in identical versions—on an optional five CD set for those who prefer to have the music examples on disc.

Custom Publishing Opportunites

Listen to This is available in a custom version specifically tailored to meet your needs. You may select the individual works that you want to study or add your own original material. The book's modular format and chapters focusing on a single work of music allows great flexibility to you to create your ideal Music Appreciation text. See your local publisher's representative for further information.

Acknowledgements

From the very start, this book has been a collaborative effort. I am particularly grateful to my co-contributors, Jocelyn Neal, Joe Kaminski, and Scott Robinson for their outstanding work on chapters dealing with popular music and non-Western music. At Pearson-Prentice Hall, I am grateful to Richard Carlin, Executive Editor, and Christopher Johnson, my original editor; Sarah Touborg, Editor-in-Chief for the Arts; Rochelle Diogenes, Director of Development; Mary Rottino, Senior Managing Editor; Barbara Taylor-Laino, Project Manager; Laura Gardner, Art Director for Design Development Services; Wendy Gordon, Executive Marketing Manager; Kate Mitchell, Senior Marketing Manager; Sarah Holle, Editorial Project Manager; and Emma Gibbons, Editorial Assistant. For their work on MyMusicLab, thanks to David Alick, Senior Media Editor and Rich Barnes, Media Project Manager. On the permissions front, Francelle Carapetyan (Image Research Editorial Services) and Tom Laskey (Sony) made the extraordinary routine. I owe a special debt of gratitude to Teresa Nemeth, my development editor, whose keen eye and intellect helped improved the text at every stage of the process.

I wish also to thank the Supplement Authors: Patricia Cox, Harding University, for writing the Instructor's Manual; Karen Dale, Cleveland State Community College, for the MyTest Software; Nancy Hadsell, Texas Women's University, for authoring the PowerPoint slides, and Linda Fergusson, Chair, Music Department, Valparaso University (Indiana), for creating the Clicker Response System PowerPoint Slides.

For their assistance creating and authoring MyMusicLab, I wish to thank: Anthony Paul De Ritis, Ph.D., Chair, Music Department, Northeastern University; Candace Bailey, North Carolina Central University; Dan Brown; Dr. Vicki Curry, James Madison University; Maureen Ton, Website Maintenance, Music Department, Northeastern University; Matt Baumer, Indiana University of Pennsylvania; Mathew E. E. Rippere, Westfield State College; Michael Condouris, Amber Digital LLC; and Nora Farrell, Virtual Instruments.

I am also grateful to students in my Music 141 and 142 classes at the University of North Carolina at Chapel Hill, who over the past few years "test-drove" earlier versions of a number of chapters. Their feedback has been invaluable. I would also like to thank Tim Carter, Chair of the Music Department, for his consistent encouragement and support of this project. Thanks, too, to Alicia Levin, who kindly recorded several piano examples for the "Elements of Music" section of the book, and to Paul Cole, who contributed his expert skills as a recording engineer.

Finally, I would like to thank the many colleagues at a variety of institutions who provided consistently thoughtful suggestions for improving earlier versions of the text, beginning with Edward Eanes of Kennesaw State University, who was particularly helpful in the early stages of this project.

Developing *Listen to This*

Listen to This is the result of an extensive development process involving the contributions of over 160 instructors, as well as their students. Student reviews have sharpened the clarity of the writing style and the value of in-text learning tools, examples, and assessment features. We are grateful to all who have provided feedback on the manuscript, design, and ancillary package, including the following:

Thomas W. Acord, California State University Eastbay, Hayward Campus
Mary Kay Adams, James Madison University
Francisco Albo, Georgia State University

Gerard Aloisio, Minnesota State University
Bill Alves, Harvey Mudd College
Alison Arnold, North Carolina State University
Candace Bailey, North Carolina Central University

Matthew Balensuela, DePauw University
Audrey L. Barksdale, Morris College
Michael Barta, Southern Ilinois University
Laura Basini, Sacramento State

Sharyn Battersby, Clayton State University

Dr. Matthew Baumer, Indiana University of Pennsylvania

Nora Beck, Lewis & Clark Community College

Barbara Bennett, University of California, Riverside

Michael Berry, Texas Tech University

Andrew Bishko, Ozarks Technical Community College

Bradford Blackburn, Truman State University

La Wanda J. Blakeney, Louisiana State University

Lloyd Bone, Glenville State College

Jeri Bonnin, The University of Montana Western

Katharine Boyes, Saint Augustine's College

William Briegel, Indiana Tech

Mary Brown-Bonacci, Westfield State College

David Bubsey, East Tennessee State University

Robert Busan, San Francisco State University

Ken Cardillo, Chattanooga State

Charles Carson, Lone Star College-Montgomery

Marva Carter, Georgia State University

Vincent Cee, University of Massachusetts, Amherst

David Chapman, Modesto Junior College

Ting-Lan Chen, University of Nebraska at Kearney

Jonathan Chenoweth, University of Northern Iowa

Linda Christensen, Wayne State University

Meng Chun-Chi, Southern Illinois University Carbondale

Stephen Clark, Austin Peay State University

Keith Clifton, Central Michigan University

Richard Scott Cohen, Ferris State University

Peter Coll William, Paterson University

Steve Cooper, Northwest Arkansas Community College

Vanessa Cornett-Murtada, University of St. Thomas

Patricia Cox, Harding University

Sandra Cox, Northwest Mississsippi Communty College

Norval Crews, Midwestern State University

Vicki Curry, James Madison University

Fred Dade, Shippensburg University

Karen McCall Dale, Cleveland State Community College

Michael Day, North Carolina A&T State

Michelle Debruyn, Columbus State University

Gene Ditch, St. Charles Community College

Edward Eanes, Kennesaw State University

Diane Earle, Kentucky Wesleyan College

Dr. Jeffrey Emge, University of Texas at Tyler

Ron Emoff, Ohio State University at Newark

Norman Engstrom, Illinois Valley Community College

Gary Evans, Ferrum College

Gary Fair, Modesto Junior College

Beth Farber, Southern Polytechnic State University

Laura Feo-Fernandez, University of Memphis

Linda C. Ferguson, Valparaiso University

Paul K. Fessler, Wilmington University

Gail Fleming, Southwestern Illinois College

Alan Flowers, University of North Alabama

Scott Fogelsong, San Francisco Conservatory of Music

Hugh Foley, Rogers State University

Eric Fried, Texas Tech University

Cliff Ganus, Harding University

Jonathan Gibson, James Madison University

Fern Glass, University of Montana

Betsy Glesner, Metropolitan State College of Denver

Karen Goodman, Montclair State University

Todd Guy, Indiana Wesleyan University

David Haas, University of Georgia

Christopher Hahn, Black Hills State University

Patricia Hales, Purdue University Calumet

Dennis Harrington, Thomas College

Robert L. Harris, Amstrong Atlantic State College

Larisa Hart Ozarks, Technical Community College

William P. Hayden, University of South Florida-Tampa

Marianne Henry, Texas A&M University

Dr. Daniel M. Heslink, Millersville University of PA

Julie Hill, University of Tennessee at Martin

Shulamit Hoffmann, College of San Mateo

Stephen Hopkins, Penn State University

Ronald Horner, Indiana University of Pennsylvania

Glen Hosterman, Lock Haven University

Luke Howard, Brigham Young University

Timothy Howard, California State University Northridge

John Husser, Virginia Tech

Sr. Mary Karita Ivancic, Notre Dame College

Ed Jacobs, Southwestern Illinois College

Miriam Jenkins, University of Massachusetts, Amherst

David Johansen, Southeastern Louisiana University

Celeste Johnson, Oklahoma State University

Lise Keiter-Brotzman, Mary Baldwin College

Andrew Kosciesza, Montgomery County Community College

Richard Scott Kravchak, California State University, Dominguez Hills

Nancy Kudlawiec, University of West Alabama

Jonathan Kulp, University of Louisiana at Lafayette

Lynn Lamkin, University of Houston

Zoe Lang, University of South Florida-Tampa

Stephanie Lawrence-White, Bennett College for Women

Mark Lee, Columbia State Community College

Gary Lewis, Midwestern State University

Max Lifchitz, The State University of New York at Albany

Milton Lites, Pulaski Technical College

Margaret Lucia, Shippensburg University of Pennsylvania

Mary Macklem, University of Central Florida

Josh Martin, Chipola College

Francis Massinon, Austin Peay State University

Steven Maxwell, Kansas State University

Prudence McDaniel, Texas A&M University

Cynthia McGregor, Southwestern College

Gary McRoberts, Fullerton College

Valerie Meidinger, Marian College

Carole Miklos, Indiana University Northwest

Paul Moulton, The College of Idaho

Aleesa J. Naish, University of Alabama at Birmingham

Jocelyn Nelson, East Carolina University

Ronald Noble, University of Texas at San Antonio

Seow-Chin Ong, University of Louisville

Jeremy Owens, Blue Mountain College

John Packard, Penn State University

David Patterson, University of Massachusetts, Boston

Laura Peterson, St. Bonaventure University

Heather Platt, Ball State University

Maurice Poe, Sacramento State

Linda Pohly, Ball State University

Glendora Powell, Louisburg College

James Randall, University of Montana

Matt Rippere, Westfield State College

Stephanie Robinson,San Diego City College

Barry Salwen, University of North Carolina, Wilmington

Carolyn Sanders, University of Alabama in Huntsville

Peter Schimpf, Metropolitan State University

Aric Schneller, Idaho State University

Pamela Shannon, Northwest Missouri Community College

Steve Shearon, Middle Tennessee State

Reeves Shulstad, Salem College

James Sifferman, Southeast Missouri State University

Margaret Skidmore, Eastern Michigan University

Cecilia Smith, South Texas College

Drew Stephen, University of Texas, San Antonio

James Stepleton, Stevens Institute of Technology

Ann Stokes, Bloomsburg University

Jonathan Sturm, Iowa State University

Anne Swartz, Baruch College of the City University of New York

James Syler, University of Texas at San Antonio

Robert Tanner, Morehouse College

Cynthia Thompson, Carrell Harding University

Kristen Todd, Oklahoma Baptist University

Andrew Tomasello, Baruch College of the City University of New York

William Toutant, California State University Northridge

Victor Vallo Jr., Immaculata University

Bertil van Boer, Western Washington University

Lori Wacker, East Carolina University

Jeanine Wagner, Southern Illinois University, Carbondale

Betsy Wahl, Ozarks Technical Community College

John Walker, St. Charles Community College

Scott Warfield, University of Central Florida

Lee Weimer, Lambuth University

Karen Werner, Moberly Area Community College

Ran Whitley, Campbell University

Donna Gwyn Wiggins, Winston-Salem State University

Brenda Witmer, James Madison University

Elizabeth Wollman, Baruch College of the City University of New York

Eric Wood, University of the Pacific

Chris Woods, Greenville College

Katrina Zook, University of Wyoming

Rudolf Zuiderveld, Illinois College

THE ELEMENTS OF MUSIC: A Brief Introduction

Melody

Melody: The Tune. Melody is a single line of notes heard in succession as a coherent unit. A melody has shape, moving up or down in ways that capture and hold our attention over a span of time. A melody is like a story: it has a beginning, a middle, and an end.

Rhythm

Rhythm: The Time. Rhythm is the ordering of music through time. Not all music has a melody, but all music has rhythm. A drum solo, for example, makes its effect primarily through rhythm. Rhythm can operate at many levels, from a repetitive, underlying pulse or beat to rapidly changing patterns of longer and shorter sounds.

Harmony

Harmony: Supporting the Melody. Harmony is the sound created by multiple voices playing or singing together. Harmony enriches the melody by creating a fuller sound than can be produced by a single voice.

Texture

Texture: Thick and Thin. Texture is based on the number and general relationship of musical lines or voices. Every work of music has a texture from thick (many voices) to thin (a single voice). Sometimes one line or voice is more important; at other times, all the lines or voices are of equal importance.

Timbre

Timbre: The Color of Music. Timbre is the character of a sound. The same melody sounds very different when performed by a violin, a clarinet, a guitar, or a human voice. These sources can all produce the same pitch, but what makes the same melody sound different is the timbre of each one.

Dynamics

Dynamics: Loud to Soft. The same music can be performed at many degrees of volume, from very soft to very loud. Dynamics determine the volume of a given work or passage in a work of music.

Form

Form: The Architecture of Music. A single melody is usually too short to constitute a complete work of music. Typically, a melody is repeated, varied, or contrasted with a different melody. The way in which all these subunits are put together—the structure of the whole—is musical form. Form is based on repetition (**A A**), variation (**A A'**), contrast (**A B**), or some combination of these three possibilities.

Word-Music Relationships

Word-Music Relationships: How Words Shape What We Hear. If there is a text to be sung, we must consider the relationship of the words to the music. How does the music capture the meaning and spirit of its text? And even if there is not a text to be sung, many works have titles that suggest how we might hear them. Titles like *Winter*, *Rodeo*, and *The Rite of Spring* strongly influence the way in which we hear these works. Some composers have even written detailed descriptions of what a particular work is about in what we call "program music."

Genre

Genre: Great Expectations. When we get into a car, we imagine what kind of a trip we are about to take and where we are going: business, pleasure, across town, across the state. When we listen to a work of music, we have similar expectations. Symphony, opera, and song are all examples of genres. Each one tells us in advance how long it is likely to be, what kinds of instruments or voices we will hear, and what kinds of forms we might hear. Genre also tells us about the function of a work. Dance music, for example, serves a different purpose from music to be used in a service of worship.

No matter what the period or style, all music grows out of some combination of these basic elements.

In any given work, these elements all work together quite closely. But by isolating and examining the nature and function of each separately, we can better appreciate their specific contributions to the music we hear.

We can best isolate the functions of these various elements by considering how each of them operates within a single, well-known work. We all know "The Star-Spangled Banner" from having heard it countless times, but how often have we actually *listened* to it? We can hear and recognize the tune easily enough, but listening demands that we focus on its various elements and the ways they work together. Let's look at each of the basic elements of music to see how it functions in this song.

Melody

Melody is a single line of notes heard in succession as a coherent unit. A *note* is the smallest unit of music, the building block out of which larger structures are created. So what makes the notes of a melody hang together? How is the melody of "The Star-Spangled Banner" organized, and how do we know it's over, other than by having heard it so often? Think about how we sing this melody and where we draw a breath:

> O, say can you see (breath) by the dawn's early light (breath)
> What so proudly we hailed (breath) at the twilight's last gleaming? (breath)

These breaths correspond to the ends of **phrases** in both the poetry and the music. The first line of the text breaks down into two phrases (O, say can you see / by the dawn's early light), which make up a larger phrase (the entire line). Together they constitute a complete unit of thought, a question. But do we feel a sense of closure when we sing "dawn's early light"? Not really. The phrase sounds as if it hasn't quite finished yet, which indeed it has not. Only when we get to the end of the second line ("twilight's last gleaming") do we feel anything approaching a sense of musical completeness. The second line is organized on the same principle as the first (two sub-phrases), and together, these two phrases make a still larger unit that is self-contained. By the time we sing "at the twilight's last gleaming," we feel as if we have reached a goal of sorts. This is the end of a still larger phrase, a complete musical statement. When we hear a point of arrival like this, we are hearing what is called a **cadence**. A cadence is like a period in a sentence: it signals the end of a unit. We sense a point of resolution, of closure.

The melody of "The Star-Spangled Banner" is typical of the way melodies in general are constructed: smaller units (sub-phrases) combine into larger units (phrases), which combine into still larger units (complete statements), which end with a cadence. These complete statements—musical sentences, in effect—combine to create an entire musical work. Sometimes it is helpful to listen to the structure of the smallest units; at other times, it is helpful to listen to the medium- and large-scale units. In the end, we can listen to how all these units operate together to form a complete and satisfying whole.

Another important component of melody is the nature of the **melodic motion**. Do the notes move smoothly in stepwise fashion (as in "land of the free")? Or do they make big leaps (as in "What so *proud*ly we hailed")? Smooth, stepwise motion is called **conjunct motion**; motion by leaps, especially large leaps, is called **disjunct motion**. Most melodies consist of a combination of both kinds of motion. "The Star-Spangled Banner" alternates between the two. It opens with disjunct motion ("O, say can you see by") followed by a brief passage of conjunct motion ("by the dawn's"), followed in turn by a large leap downward (between "dawn's" and "early") followed by more conjunct motion. Graphically, this variety of motion can be represented in such a way that even if you cannot read music, you can see the relationship between the downward or upward movement of the notes and the distances between them.

mymusiclab

CD I · **Track 1**
Melodic motion in the opening phrase of "The Star-Spangled Banner"

The opening of "The Star-Spangled Banner" with a line indicating steps and leaps

Very few melodies are entirely conjunct or disjunct. The national anthem is typical in combining both kinds of motion, and in balancing downward and upward movement.

The notes of any given melody typically derive from the notes of a **scale**. The familiar "do-re-mi-fa-so-la-ti-do" is a scale, a series of notes that moves stepwise and covers a complete span called an **octave** (so-called because it covers eight notes). The distance between each note is called an **interval**. The intervals in the standard scale are mostly whole steps, with two strategically placed half steps. Every adjacent note on the keyboard, whether it is a white key or a black key, is a half step apart.

CD I · Track 2
The C major scale

A scale by itself is not particularly interesting as a melody, but a scale provides the notes—the essential building blocks—of a melody:

CD I · Track 3
The opening of "The Star-Spangled Banner"

The opening of "The Star-Spangled Banner" in the key of C major

The upward or downward movement of notes is conveyed graphically in music notation. A melody that moves downward also moves downward on the staff (the system of parallel horizontal lines). Again, even if you cannot read music, you can see that higher notes appear higher on the staff than lower notes. This kind of visual aid can help reinforce what we hear.

CD I · **Track 4**
Lower and higher notes

Scales can begin and end on any pair of notes. The diagrams on page 4 show a scale that begins and ends on the note "C," and a melody that centers on this same note (on "O, *say* can you *see*"). Because C is the central note of the scale on which this melody is based, we would say that this melody is in the **key** of C. But the same melody can be played in any key. Thus "The Star-Spangled Banner" can also be performed in the key of D, or the key of A-flat, or any other key.

In the standard system in use in Western music since about 1600, there are 12 keys, one on each of the 12 half steps in any octave (see the scale diagram above). In notation, the sharp sign (♯) indicates that a note is raised a half step, while a flat sign (♭) indicates that a note is lowered a half step. For each of these keys, whether it is E-flat or F-sharp or A, there are two modes, major and minor. The **major mode** corresponds to the scale produced by singing "do-re-mi-fa-so-la-ti-do." Melodies using these notes tend to sound brighter and somehow happier. "The Star-Spangled Banner" is in the major mode. Like all national anthems, it seeks to convey a mood of optimism and joy, and it does this in part through its use of melody derived from a major-mode scale.

The **minor mode**, by contrast, strikes most listeners as darker, more somber, and less optimistic. Most of the notes in the minor mode are also in the major. But two of the seven notes—the third ("mi") and sixth ("la")—are slightly lower, and this creates a very different kind of sound. Listen to what "The Star-Spangled Banner" would sound like in the minor mode; all the notes are the same as in the original except for "mi" and "la."

CD I · **Track 5**
"The Star-Spangled Banner" in minor mode

Clearly, the minor mode is not well suited for a national anthem: it sounds too pessimistic, too dark, too sad. A national anthem might have a brief phrase in the minor mode somewhere in the middle, but not across the board. The minor mode is perfect, however, for songs expressing grief or anguish. And many musical works move back and forth between the major and minor modes to create contrasting moods. (In fact, "mode" and "mood" come from the same root word in Latin.)

The Acoustics of Melody

What makes the notes in a melody move up or down and sound different from one another? What makes some parts of a melody louder than others? **Acoustics** is the science of sound—how it is produced, transmitted, and perceived—and a few basic principles of acoustics help explain the most basic elements of melody.

From a technical point of view, sound is vibrating air. Musicians can cause air to vibrate in three basic ways:

- By striking a surface (drums, cymbals, xylophones, and any other percussion instrument)
- By plucking or stroking a taut string (guitar, banjo, violin, and any other plucked or bowed instrument)
- By blowing air (flute, clarinet, trumpet, and any other wind instrument, including the human voice)

The patterns of vibration set in motion by these actions determine the pitch and volume of the sound. **Pitch** is the position of a sound on a range from very low (the bass register) to very high (the soprano register). Through an oscilloscope, we can "see" the shape of the **sound wave** of any sustained pitch. In its simplest form, the sound wave of a single pitch looks like this:

The distance between the peak of each wave is known as the **wavelength**, and the number of wavelengths in one second—the **frequency**—determines the pitch of the sound. The higher the frequency, the higher the pitch. The pitch to which most North American orchestras tune their instruments is an "A" played at a frequency of 440 cycles per second (cps, also known as hertz or Hz, named after Gustav Hertz, the nineteenth-century German physicist who studied sound waves). The lowest note on the standard modern piano is also an "A," but at a frequency of only 27.5 cps; the highest note, a "C," vibrates at 4,186 cps. The normal human ear can perceive frequencies in a range from approximately 20 cps (extremely low) to 20,000 cps (extremely high). Some animals have a far wider range of hearing: dogs, for example, can respond to frequencies as high as 50,000 cps, even though the sound of the dog whistle producing this frequency is inaudible to us.

What makes sounds loud or soft? **Dynamics**—the volume of sound—is determined by the size of each wave, its **amplitude**: The same pitch—440 cps—at softer volume would look like this:

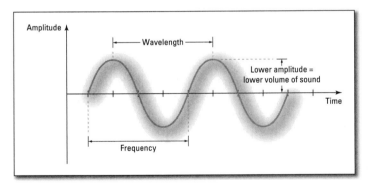

The same pitch as the previous sound wave, with a smaller amplitude, producing a lower volume of sound

The frequency—the distance between the peaks of each wave—is the same, but the amplitude is smaller; thus the same pitch sounds softer. The wavelengths in a louder version of this same pitch would have the same frequency, but the amplitude would be higher.

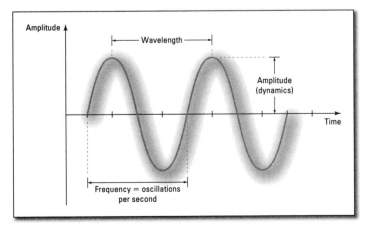

The structure of a sound wave

Rhythm

Rhythm is the ordering of music through time. The most basic framework of this temporal ordering is **meter**. In music, as in poetry, meter is an underlying pattern of beats that maintains itself consistently throughout a work. If we slowly read aloud the first line of "The Star-Spangled Banner," we can hear that it falls into a regular pattern of three-beat units: LONG-short-short, LONG-short-short, etc., with the long syllables accented (emphasized), the short ones unaccented (— = long; ˘ = short):

˘ — ˘ ˘ — ˘ ˘ — ˘ ˘ —

O, | say can you | see, by the | dawn's early | light?

In poetry, this meter is known as *dactylic* (LONG-short-short). In music, this meter corresponds to what is known as **triple meter**: one accented (strong) beat followed by two unaccented (weak) beats. The rhythm of the music to "The Star-Spangled Banner" is thus organized within the framework of triple meter (**1**-2-3, **1**-2-3, **1**-2-3, etc.), following the meter of its poetry. (The "O" at the very beginning of the text stands outside the first unit: both rhythmically and textually, its function is to get us started, without actually saying much of anything.)

3 | **1** 2 3 | **1** 2 3 | **1** 2 3 | **1** 2 3 | **1** 2 3 | **1** etc.

O, | *say* can you | *see* by the | *dawn's* early | *light* What so | *proud*-ly we | *hailed* . . . etc.

In music, each of these rhythmic units is known as a **measure**. Ordinarily, the first note of each measure receives a relatively strong accent, which helps project the pattern of the meter, just as you would emphasize certain words ("say," "see," "dawn's," "light") if you were reading the text out loud without singing it.

But meter is only one aspect of rhythm. Not every note of "The Star-Spangled Banner" is simply accented or unaccented, strong or weak. Some notes are noticeably longer in duration than others ("say can you SEE," "the rockets' red GLARE"), while others are extremely brief (the word *the* in "and the rockets' red glare," for example).

mymusiclab

CD I · **Track 6**
Accented notes

Rhythmic values

These longer and shorter notes function flexibly within the broader framework of the underlying meter. So long as the basic pattern of the rhythmic unit is maintained (**1**-2-3), the actual number and duration of the notes within each unit can vary considerably. A melody in which all the notes were exactly the same length would be quite monotonous. Here is what the beginning of "The Star-Spangled Banner" would sound like if all the notes were of equal value:

The opening of "The Star-Spangled Banner," with notes in all the same rhythmic values.

The meter is still triple (**1**-2-3), but the individual notes have lost all rhythmic differentiation.

What would "The Star-Spangled Banner" sound like in a different meter? An American composer named E. E. Bagley (1857–1922) actually worked the opening of the melody into a march he called *National Emblem*. Here, the music moves in **duple meter**, with only two beats to each measure (**1**-2 | **1**-2 | **1**-2 | etc.). This corresponds to the function of the music, to help soldiers or band members march in step (**Left**-right | **Left**-right | **Left**-right | etc.).

Notice how the pitches (the notes) are the same as the tune we know as "The Star-Spangled Banner." But the meter—the framework of the rhythm—is fundamentally different: LONG-short | LONG-short instead of LONG-short-short | LONG-short-short. Could we march to the standard version of "The Star-Spangled Banner"? Not really, because it's in triple meter, and with two legs, it's much easier to march to duple meter.

Harmony

Harmony is the sound created by multiple notes played or sung simultaneously. Whether we realize it or not, we've all heard "The Star-Spangled Banner" performed in many different harmonizations. The melody stays the same, but the notes underneath the tune are different. The resulting harmony can change the character of the work, sometimes subtly, sometimes radically. There is no official version of the harmony of "The Star-Spangled Banner." (Indeed, there is not even an official version of the melody itself.)

If we think of music in terms of space, then melody can be said to be horizontal, harmony vertical. Just as melodies can outline selected notes of a scale through time, harmony presents notes drawn from a scale simultaneously, sounding together. When we hear three or more notes played at the same moment, we often speak of these as a **chord**. A melodic line can be accompanied by a series of chords that change as the melody progresses. A melody as rich as "The Star-Spangled Banner" would sound monotonous—and downright wrong—if it were harmonized with a single chord from beginning to end. The most common harmonization of the tune supports the melody with a variety of different chords:

E. E. Bagley's *National Emblem* sheet music
Courtesy BenCar Archives

Melody

Harmony: C Major   A Minor   A Minor   D Major   G Major

C Major   G Major   D Minor   C Major   G Major   C Major

A harmonized version of "The Star-Spangled Banner," with the melody in the upper staff and the harmony in the lower staff

CD I · Track 9
Harmonized version of the opening of "The Star-Spangled Banner," Marvin Gaye, vocals

We all know what a melody without harmony sounds like (just think of the early stages of contestants performing on *American Idol*). But what about harmony without melody? Here is one harmonization of "The Star-Spangled Banner" without the melody.

A single melody can always be harmonized in more than one way, and "The Star-Spangled Banner" is no exception. And some harmonizations are more unconventional than others. Consider, for example, this harmonization of the melody by the American composer Louis Moreau Gottschalk (see chapter 36), from a piece for piano entitled *Union,* written shortly after the beginning of the Civil War.

Even today, almost 150 years later, musicians are still coming up with new ways of harmonizing this same melody. South City Voices, an Atlanta-based vocal jazz ensemble, recently recorded their own version of the tune. The melody is the same as the one we hear all the time, but the harmonies are not.

Harmony works on a larger scale as well. If a melody is in the key of C major, its primary harmony also centers on C major, establishing this key at the beginning as a kind of home base and returning to it at the end to create a sense of closure. We call this primary key area the **tonic**. A piece that began in one key but ended in another would sound somehow open-ended and incomplete. "The Star-Spangled Banner" begins and ends in the same key, no matter what key is used in performance.

CD I · Track 10
Harmony of "The Star-Spangled Banner" without melody

CD I · Track 11
Louis Moreau Gottschalk, excerpt from *Union*

CD I · Track 12
South City Voices. A version of "The Star-Spangled Banner" with extremely unusual harmonies

Illegal Harmony?

The Russian-born composer Igor Stravinsky (1882–1971) emigrated to the United States in 1939 and became an American citizen in 1945. In honor of his new homeland, he made an arrangement of the national anthem that many contemporaries found offensive.

He performed the work in public only once, at the beginning of a concert by the Boston Symphony Orchestra on January 14, 1944. When word got out about the unusual harmonies in his arrangement, the police moved in and confiscated the music on the grounds of a Massachusetts state law forbidding "tampering" with state property. Threatened with arrest, Stravinsky withdrew the work from subsequent programs.

Jimi Hendrix's rendition of "The Star-Spangled Banner" on his electric guitar at the Woodstock Festival in August 1969 aroused controversy as well, but there was no suggestion that he be arrested for adding dissonances and feedback to the melody.

CD I · Track 13
Igor Stravinsky's harmonization of "The Star-Spangled Banner."

Igor Stravinsky leads an orchestra rehearsal at the Hollywood Bowl, ca. 1955. He lived in Los Angeles for most of the last three decades of his life. When word got out about his unconventional harmonization of "The Star-Spangled Banner" in Boston in 1944, Stravinsky was threatened with arrest.

Music Division, The New York Public Library for the Performing Arts, Astor, Lenox, and Tilden Foundations

Marvin Gaye sings "The Star-Spangled Banner." The texture is decidedly homophonic: the focus is entirely on the melody, while the accompaniment (a drum set) stays very much in the background.

Mike Segar/Reuters/Corbis/Reuters America LLC

Texture

Texture is a function of the number and general relationship of musical lines to one another. Textures can range from thick (many voices) to thin (a single voice).

- When "The Star-Spangled Banner" is performed as a single melodic line, with no accompaniment at all, the texture is **monophonic** (*mono* = "single"; *phonic* = "sounding"). This may be a single soloist, or it may be a group of performers all playing or singing the same melody. When multiple performers are singing or playing a single melody together, we call this kind of monophonic texture **unison**.

- When the melody is performed with a supporting accompaniment, the texture is **homophonic** (*homo* = "same," as in "sounding at the same time"). This is the most common form of performance of this particular song whenever there is a soloist. The soloist sings the melody, while an instrumental ensemble or backup chorus provides musical support. The previous example showing the harmonized "Star-Spangled Banner" is what homophonic texture can look like in musical notation.

- When the melody is performed against another line of equal importance, the texture is **polyphonic** (*poly* = "many"). In polyphonic texture, every line is, in effect, a melody. Think about the children's song "Row, Row, Row Your Boat," for example: every voice is singing the same music, so we can't say that one voice has the melody and others don't. And yet all the voices work together to create a satisfying sound.

Here is what the opening of "The Star-Spangled Banner" would look and sound like in a polyphonic texture:

mymusiclab
CD I · Track 14
Homophonic version of "The Star-Spangled Banner"

mymusiclab
CD I · Track 15
Polyphonic version of "The Star-Spangled Banner," opening phrase

Opening of "The Star-Spangled Banner" in polyphonic texture

Polyphonic realizations of "The Star-Spangled Banner" in its entirety are rare, but they do exist. John Knowles Paine's *Concert Variations on "The Star-Spangled Banner,"* for organ, which he wrote at the height of the Civil War, features an extended passage in which the principal melody is played against other lines that are melodic in their own right and not mere accompaniment. Listen to the melody at the beginning in a single voice, all by itself. Then notice how the same melody enters later, in a second voice (at 0:11), later again in a third voice (at 0:34), and so on. In the end, no one voice is subordinate to any other. Polyphonic texture can also consist of melodies that are different but sound good when played or sung together.

mymusiclab
CD I · Track 16
John Knowles Paine's *Concert Variations on "The Star-Spangled Banner,"* Variation 5, in which the principal melody is played against itself

Timbre

Timbre is the color of music, the character of sound. The same melody can sound very different depending on who is singing or what instruments are playing. At one time or another, "The Star-Spangled Banner" has been performed by probably just about every instrument or combination of instruments imaginable, from a solo kazoo to a large symphony orchestra. And even when performed on the same instrument, it can sound very different.

mymusiclab
CD I · Track 17
"The Star-Spangled Banner," Kevin Gaffney, trumpet

CD I · Track 18
"The Star-Spangled Banner,"
Louis Armstrong, trumpet

The range of musical timbres is enormous, extending from a single instrument or a single voice to an entire orchestra or an entire chorus—or both together. As we examine timbres in individual pieces, we will look at the instruments that create those timbres.

Louis Armstrong playing the trumpet, 1964
JAN PERSSON/Lebrecht Music & Arts Photo Library

Dynamics

Dynamics is a term used to indicate the volume of sound, ranging from very soft to very loud. We have all heard "The Star-Spangled Banner" played at a single (loud) volume by a military band. We have also heard it performed at a level only slightly above a whisper, often by an ensemble of unaccompanied voices. And we have heard performances that move from the one extreme to the other. Dynamics can change suddenly, or they can change gradually. Volume is a relative quality: what seems loud to one listener might be barely audible to another, and vice versa.

The Acoustics of Timbre

What makes different instruments sound different? The answer to this question goes to the heart of what timbre is—the quality of a sound, apart from its pitch or volume. The pitch "A" played at 440 cps sounds quite different on an oboe than on a violin, a guitar, or a saxophone. The basic wavelength of the sound produced by these instruments on this one pitch will all be the same, but the shape of these wavelengths varies considerably.

Just as individual colors blend different light waves, any naturally produced sound is the product of a mixture of many different sound waves. The basic sound wave is known as a fundamental. When produced by a machine (as in the case of a midi file), we hear *only* the fundamental: the sound is pure, but for that very reason it is unnatural. This is what makes midi files sound so mechanical. When produced by a musical instrument like a violin, guitar, or piano, the sound wave of the fundamental is enhanced by the addition of many partials, frequencies that resonate with the fundamental to create a richer quality of sound.

You can hear an example of how some of these partials sound by doing a simple experiment on the piano. With one hand, depress the keys C and G in the octave above middle C, but do not actually play the notes: just push these keys down very slowly and hold them in place. Now, with the other hand, strike the note middle C forcefully. What you hear is mostly middle C, but if you listen carefully, you can also hear the higher notes as well. If you play middle C again, normally this time, without the additional held-down notes, you can recognize these partials in what is known as the spectral content of middle C on the piano—the full range of sounds produced in and around a given wavelength. The most prominent of the partials are known as overtones. The timbre of all acoustic instruments results from a mixture of fundamentals and partials. Instruments that create their sound digitally (such as a keyboard synthesizer) can often mimic these instruments by adding partials to the fundamentals.

(a)   (b)   (c)   (d)   (e)

The look of different sounds: Oscilloscope readings of the same pitch (A = 440 cps) played by (a) a flute, (b) a trumpet, (c) a soprano saxophone, (d) a violin, and (e) a bassoon. Notice that the wavelength—the distance between each peak—are the same (producing the same pitch), but the shape of the vibrating air column is different in each instrument (producing contrasting timbres).

Cengage Learning

In music, it is common to use Italian terms to refer to volume:

pianissimo *(pp)* — very soft

piano *(p)* — soft

mezzo piano *(mp)* — medium soft

mezzo forte *(mf)* — medium loud

forte *(f)* — loud

fortissimo *(ff)* — very loud

Form

Form is the structure of a musical work, the way in which its individual units are put together. Form is based on three and only three possible strategies: repetition, variation, and contrast. When we say something, we can then do only one of three things: say once again exactly what we have just said, word-for-word (repetition); repeat what we have just said in a slightly different manner (variation); or say something altogether different (contrast). These three strategies apply to music as well.

In "The Star-Spangled Banner," the opening phrase of the music is repeated literally for the second phrase:

> Phrase 1: O, say can you see by the dawn's early light what so proudly we hailed at the twilight's last gleaming?

> Phrase 2 (same melody, repeated): Whose broad stripes and bright stars through the perilous fight, o'er the ramparts we watched were so gallantly streaming?

If we call the opening phrase of music "A," then the first half of "The Star-Spangled Banner"—the music, independent of the text—can be diagrammed as:

A A

What happens next? Do we hear yet another repetition of **A,** a variation of **A,** or something completely different? "And the rockets' red glare . . ." is, of course, completely different from what we have heard before. For that reason, we can call this phrase "B." And the concluding phrase of "The Star-Spangled Banner" ("Oh, say does that star-spangled banner yet wave . . .") is different yet again ("C"). So the form of the song as a whole can be represented as:

A A B C

This form happens to be extremely common in songs from many times and places (Martin Luther's famous hymn "A Mighty Fortress Is Our God," Stephen Foster's "Oh, Susanna," Radiohead's "Black Star," and even "Dixie," the unofficial anthem of the Confederate States of America during the Civil War). Forms can also be expanded (**AABCA**) or contracted (**ABA**) in an almost infinite variety of combinations.

Word-Music Relationships

Word-music relationships are many and diverse. The most obvious intersection of words and music occurs in works with a text to be sung. How do the notes relate to the words? So far, we have examined only the music of "The Star-Spangled Banner," not the words. Let's look now at the text and see how it fits the music.

Structurally, the text (or at least its first stanza) consists of three questions, interrupted by a statement. (The second, third, and fourth stanzas of the text provide answers to all these questions, but no one ever sings them, and for purposes of brevity, we will focus here on the first stanza.)

First Question

O, say can you see by the dawn's early light
What so proudly we hailed at the twilight's last gleaming?

Second Question

Whose broad stripes and bright stars through the perilous fight,
O'er the ramparts we watched were so gallantly streaming?

Statement

And the rockets' red glare, the bombs bursting in air,
Gave proof through the night that our flag was still there.

Third Question

Oh, say does that star-spangled banner yet wave
O'er the land of the free and the home of the brave?

If we consider the overall structure of the melody—the tune—we can see how well it fits the words:

Music	**A**	**A**	**B**	**C**
Text	Question 1	Question 2	Statement	Question 3

The opening two questions are sung to the identical music (**A**), but the statement presents a very different melodic idea in a very different range. With the words "And the rockets' red glare . . . ," the music moves into a different theme (**B**) and a higher range, which helps set the stage for a return to the opening range of the song (and one last question) in the concluding section (**C**).

Notice, too, how the range of the melody corresponds to the content of the text. The voice moves into a very high register at the words "And the rockets' red glare," appropriately enough. And it hits this same high note—the highest one in the entire melody—again just before the end, on "free" in "o'er the land of the free."

Genre

Genre is the category of a given work (symphony, sonata, song), determined by a combination of its performance medium and its social function. Knowing the genre of a work we are about to hear tells us a great deal about what to expect. Let's suppose you're at the Olympics, witnessing a medals ceremony. The athlete who has won the gold medal has just received her medal, but you've never heard of the country she represents, and you certainly have never heard its national anthem, which is about to play. Yet based on your knowledge of the genre of national anthem, you can actually anticipate a fair amount about this piece of music you've never heard before. You can reasonably expect a work of fairly short duration—probably between one and two minutes—that is lively in tone and has a bright sound, and that will probably be performed by a wind band (trumpets, trombones, clarinets, and the like), possibly with a drum. These expectations are based on the principal function of a national anthem: to arouse in citizens a sense of national pride. Long-winded works do not fit the bill here, and slow, mournful music is not likely to instill a sense of enthusiasm in a crowd. There are exceptions to this rule, of course, just as there are exceptions to generic expectations in all kinds of music, but knowing the typical nature and function of the work we are about to hear can help us relate the unknown (the new work) to its archetype (the genre, or works we know from that genre).

"The Star-Spangled Banner" certainly fits the pattern of the genre of national anthem. It is short (about a minute-and-a-half to two minutes, depending on how slowly or quickly it is performed), in major mode, and is performed in its "standard" version—the one played at the Olympics, for example—by a wind band with drums.

When we listen, we normally do not think about all these elements—melody, harmony, rhythm, texture, timbre, dynamics, form, word-music relationships, and genre—separately. This is because they work together to create a satisfying whole. To isolate any one of them from the others, in a particular work, we need to make a special effort to listen only to the melody, or only to the texture, or only to the form. Yet this kind of listening can help us raise our awareness of the role that these individual elements can play. For this reason, we have a separate column for each element in the listening guides that accompany the music in this book. It may require listening a few times through to hear what is going on with each element. As we internalize these building blocks of music, we can better appreciate the complexity and beauty of the art. Do we need to be conscious of all these elements as we listen? No. But our understanding and enjoyment of a piece of music will increase the more we are aware of all that goes into music in general. The more we know, the better we can listen. And the better we listen, the more we can enjoy the experience.

PART 1 The Middle Ages

What we now think of as the Middle Ages, or the medieval era, covered almost a thousand years, between the fall of the Western Roman Empire in 476 CE and the beginning of the Renaissance in the early fifteenth century. The people of this time did not think of themselves as being in the "middle" or "between" anything at all, of course. Only later did historians see this span of time as a period lying between antiquity and the Renaissance.

The music of the Middle Ages reflects its many and varied social functions, both sacred and secular. The church dominated intellectual and cultural life in the Middle Ages. Music, along with all the other arts, was perceived as a means of serving God. Over the course of several hundred years, generations of anonymous composers—most of them monks or priests—developed an enormous repertory of plainchant (also known as *Gregorian chant*), which consisted of monophonic, unaccompanied melodies sung by a single voice or by a choir in unison. Plainchant projected the words of the sacred liturgy in a manner that was at once clear and moving. Secular courts also needed music for their ceremonies and entertainments, and composers provided a steady stream of songs, settings of poems that tell of love, pain, heroism, and all the other emotions that make up the human condition. Polyphony—multiple independent voices sung or played together—became increasingly important for both sacred and secular music from the tenth century onward.

The sounds of medieval music, both sacred and secular, may at first seem unfamiliar to us today: the scales on which they based their melodies differ from ours, and most of their instruments are no longer in common use. But the more we listen to this music, the more we can hear in it the same basic elements we still use today. Above all, we can recognize in this music the effort of medieval composers to heighten the expressivity of the texts they set and to elevate music beyond language. This basic urge connects us with music that is a thousand years old.

◀ According to legend, Pope Gregory (ca. 540–604) received the melodies of plainchant from the Holy Spirit, which appeared to him in the form of a dove. This repertory of music would later come to be known as Gregorian chant.
Antiphonary of Hartker of St. Gall, Cod. Sang. 390, p.13. Stiftsbibliothek St. Gallen

Music for Sacred Spaces

By far the largest and most imposing structures of the Middle Ages were its churches, monuments to God and physical testimonies to the power of the church itself. This was the era of the great Gothic cathedrals, buildings of unprecedented size, grace, and light. These structures did more than provide a space for worship: they were meant to inspire, to lift the eye heavenward, to instruct mortals about their relationship to the divine. The stained glass windows in these churches were similarly instructive, depicting biblical scenes in ways that could be understood even by those who could not read or write.

Sacred music fulfilled a similar function. Its purpose was to enhance the texts being sung and inspire worshippers with the beauty of their sound. Plainchant was the perfect vehicle for projecting sacred texts with great clarity across enormous spaces. All the services of the church were provided with their appropriate melodies. And there were many services: the typical monk or nun attended church nine times a day. Eight of these services were devoted to the reading and singing of prayers, psalms, and hymns. The most important service of each day was Mass, a ritual reenactment of Christ's Last Supper with his disciples. The anonymous composers of the early Middle Ages devoted special efforts to the many chants of the Mass. Morality plays like Hildegard von Bingen's *Play of Virtues* (*Ordo virtutum*) combined plainchant with newly composed poetry to convey the teachings of the church and help the faithful learn the differences between good and evil.

▲ Gothic architecture: The interior of Chartres Cathedral (France). By the 13th century, technological advances had allowed builders to construct high, vaulted ceilings meant to draw both the eye and the spirit upward, toward the heavens. Plainchant was perfectly crafted to fill these immense spaces.

Roger Moss Photography

Music for Entertainment

As the great cathedrals were symbols of divine power, medieval castles were symbols of secular, worldly power. Their stone walls and moats reflect the constant threat of attack from the outside. Medieval Europe was divided into a series of kingdoms, duchies, and fiefdoms of widely varying sizes, each ruled by a lord to whom subjects paid their allegiance—and taxes. Medieval courts used the arts as a means of projecting their

◀ Caerphilly Castle, Wales, dates from the 13th century. Its daunting exterior was a defense against invaders.

Adina Tovy/Getty Images—Robert Harding World Imagery

cultural power and impressing subjects and visitors alike. Rulers competed for the services of the best poets, singers, and dancers.

Courtly life demanded courtly entertainments. Wandering minstrels passed from town to town and castle to castle providing poetry, song, acrobatics, and juggling—sometimes combining all at once. Poet-composers known variously as *troubadours* (in the south of present-day France), *trouvères* (in the north), and *minnesingers* (in what is now Germany) sang and played songs about love, heroism, and the pastoral life. Other courts employed their own full-time musicians and composers. Music featured prominently at nearly every courtly gathering. Medieval listeners, like listeners of today, enjoyed music that captured the simple pains and pleasures of being human. "Behold, Spring" ("Ecco la Primavera"), by the prolific blind composer Francesco Landini, welcomes spring as a season of lightheartedness, beauty, and love. Its flowing melody and resonant harmonies still speak to us today.

Literary works like Giovanni Boccaccio's *Decameron* and Geoffrey Chaucer's *Canterbury Tales*, both from the fourteenth century, remind us that medieval song texts could be as bawdy and explicit as any today. In each, travelers must take turns entertaining their companions, and song plays an important role throughout. Significantly, Boccaccio (1313–75) and Chaucer (ca. 1342–1400) both wrote in the vernacular languages of their respective regions (present-day Italy and England), rather than in Latin, the language of the church. Similarly, a good deal of medieval secular music was sung to texts in the language of the people.

▲ An acrobat balances on a pair of swords, accompanied by two musicians. The one on the left plays the pipe and tabor (a small drum), while the one on the right plays a double flute.

By permission of The British Library

▼ Five couples in a line dance, accompanied by a drummer (left) and a bagpipe player (right). This image is from a medieval manuscript of the *Roman de la Rose*, an allegorical poem written in France in the 13th century. The gold paint actually contains a high percentage of finely ground gold.

British Library, London, UK/The Bridgeman Art Library

Music for Dancing

In an era when relationships with the opposite sex outside of marriage were closely regulated, dance was a highly significant social activity. We have no detailed descriptions of medieval dance, but we do have images of dancing as well as actual works of dance music that have survived from this time. Most dances appear to have been group activities, somewhat similar to present-day line dancing. And almost every image of dancing comes with a drummer providing the basic beat.

When thinking about medieval art and life today, we should consider not only what it looked like, but what it sounded like. The instruments of the Middle Ages were for the most part quite different from those of today. The shawm used in Alfonso el Sabio's "He Who Gladly Serves" ("Aquel que de volontade"), for example, was an early wind instrument that would eventually be replaced by the modern oboe. Yet this work would sound very different if played on an oboe, for the shawm's more open and raspy sound belongs as much to the medieval world as the era's great churches and castles.

Information Technology 1.0

The earliest medieval music was not notated. The picture on page 17 of Pope Gregory taking dictation from the Holy Spirit is symbolic but contains a historical inaccuracy: until about the tenth century, music was transmitted orally, not in written form. The earliest chant manuscripts show simple symbols above the texts, indicating motion of the pitch up or down. These served essentially as memory aids for singers already familiar with the melodies. Later chant, such as that of Hildegard in the twelfth century, adds lines for the pitches and some symbols for rhythm (see illustration p. 24). By the time Landini was writing in the later fourteenth century, an even more precise system of notation had developed (see illustration p. 41).

Written music remained hard to come by, even after the development of notation. Printing did not emerge until the middle of the fifteenth century, and so music (like all other texts) had to be written out by hand, one copy at a time. Making a manuscript was a time-consuming and costly process: ink and parchment were expensive (paper did not become widely available until the Renaissance), and scribes had to work slowly and carefully. Manuscripts, moreover, are not always entirely accurate. Scribes were only human, and anyone who has ever hand-copied a text of any complexity will know how easy it is to leave out, repeat, or garble words or even whole passages of text. Even in the hands of the most skilled medieval scribes, these manuscripts were not always entirely faithful to the original.

Many manuscripts were in themselves works of art whose purpose went beyond the mere transmission of words or music. The scribes who produced these documents were often monks of great artistic talent. Every larger church or monastery had its own *scriptorium,* a workshop that produced manuscripts, reminding us once again of the church's power over what could—and could not—be reproduced and distributed.

Elaborate initial "B," the first letter in the first word of the chant.

The notation shows only the relative position of the notes—their rising and falling—not exact pitches.

These early forms of notes are called neumes.

The words of the liturgy were written onto the parchment first, the notes added later.

▲ A 12th-century plainchant manuscript prepared in a monastery in what is now northern Germany. The J. Paul Getty Museum, Los Angeles. From the *Stammheim Missal* (97.MG.21, Folio 58).

The Middle Ages: AT A GLANCE

| chapter 1 | chapter 2 | chapter 3 | chapter 4 |

ca. 1150
HILDEGARD VON BINGEN
Play of Virtues (excerpt)
GENRE: Plainchant

Chapter Highlight:
Christian Plainchant
Plainchant was monophonic music ideally suited for projecting words across the vast spaces of medieval churches. Anonymous composers devoted special attention to chants for the Mass, the most important Christian worship service. Plainchant was later extended to morality plays and liturgical dramas.

KEY CONCEPTS
Chant, Monophony, conjunct and disjunct motion, cadences, free vs. metered rhythm, melismatic and syllabic text-setting, medieval modes.

chapter 2

SAN ILDEFONSO INDIANS OF NEW MEXICO
Eagle Dance
GENRE: Native American music

Chapter Highlight:
Chant Around the World
Jewish, Buddhist, Hindu, Islamic, Native American, Shamanic, and other traditions all employ some form of chant that projects sacred texts using more melodic and rhythmic elements than are found in the patterns of everyday speech.

KEY CONCEPTS
Chant, vocables, terraced melody, ceremonial dance.

ca. 1350 - 1400
FRANCESCO LANDINI
"Behold, Spring"
GENRE: Secular song

Chapter Highlights:
Secular Song
A variety of monophonic and polyphonic song types flourished in the Middle Ages, including **ballatas, caccias,** and **virelais.** Typical texts extolled courtly love or heroism. The layering of new melodies on top of chants produced songs with as many as three different texts. Machaut and Lorenzo da Firenze were two other song composers.

Polyphony
The earliest polyphony consisted of new melodies superimposed on plainchant. Polyphony soon extended to music of all kinds, sacred and secular. The composer Perotin wrote an early form of polyphony called organum. One of the most famous medieval composers, Machaut, wrote numerous works for two and three parts, including the earliest known complete setting of the Mass.

KEY CONCEPTS
Polyphony, metered rhythm, conjunct and disjunct motion, cadences, form based on large-scale repetition, variation, contrast.

LATE 13TH CENTURY
ALFONSO EL SABIO
Songs to the Virgin Mary
no. 249, "He Who Gladly Serves"
GENRE: Instrumental arrangement of vocal music

Chapter Highlight:
Instrumental Music
Musicians of the Middle Ages often performed vocal music on instruments alone. Much instrumental music was for dance. Two popular medieval dances were the saltarello, a "leaping" dance, and the estampie, a "stomping" dance.

KEY CONCEPTS
Medieval instruments, heterophony, form based on large-scale repetition, variation, contrast.

476
Western Roman Empire ceases to exist

800
Charlemagne crowned emperor by Pope Leo III

936
Otto I establishes what comes to be known as the Holy Roman Empire

1066
The Normans conquer England

1095
First Crusade begins

1215
King John of England signs the Magna Carta

1348-1350
The Black Death ravages Europe

Historical Events

1

Berlin •

BINGEN

GERMANY

• Frankfurt

Munich •

Hildegard von Bingen
Play of Virtues (excerpt)

Listen to This

Texture

Listen for the sound of a single voice, or multiple voices singing together. This is **monophonic** texture.

Melody

Listen for occasional leaps in the otherwise smooth and flowing melodies. Listen, too, for the cadences—brief resting points—throughout.

Word-Music Relationships

Note that most characters sing their lines, but one speaks (or shouts) his. Notice how clearly the singers project the Latin words, mostly with one note per syllable, but occasionally with many notes drawn out over a single syllable. Listen also for the climax of the drama, when the pitches move into a very high range.

Rhythm

Listen to the way the rhythm is free for the most part, reflecting the irregular rhythms of the words being sung. But feel the regular **1**-2-**3**-4 | **1**-2-**3**-4 pulse that appears briefly about halfway through.

Music exerts a powerful pull on the human spirit, and medieval composers put this power to good use. Hildegard von Bingen recognized that the words of her *Play of Virtues* (*Ordo virtutum*), while moving in their own right, could be made even more expressive set to music. The combination of text and music continues to move audiences even today.

Hildegard's *Play of Virtues* is a morality play, a dramatized allegory of Good versus Evil struggling over the fate of a single soul. The plot centers on a series of disputes between Satan and 16 Virtues. Each of the Virtues—Charity, Obedience, Humility, Chastity, and so on—is represented by a different singer. When the Virtues sing together as a single chorus, they all sing exactly the same melody. Satan, however, never sings at all: he simply shouts his lines. In the medieval period, music was widely perceived as a divine gift of heaven, and it seems only fitting that the Devil should have no music at all. The contrast between the spoken part of Satan and the sung part of the Virtues is immediate and striking.

In setting this morality play to music, Hildegard was building on a long tradition of liturgical plainchant, the music used in the daily services of the church. This repertory of chant had developed slowly over many centuries. It grew out of the chants of Jewish services of worship, particularly the melodic recitation of the Psalms. Over time, many of the texts of the Christian liturgy were set to music by a series of anonymous composers, presumably monks

---

CULTURAL CONTEXT

The Morality Play

How do we learn the difference between good and evil, and how do we learn to choose between them? In the Middle Ages, morality plays like Hildegard von Bingen's *Play of Virtues* offered a way of dramatizing such questions literally. But morality plays did not end with the Middle Ages. Popular works today like the Star Wars, Harry Potter, and Lord of the Rings series are built on the same basic plot outline: an innocent figure struggles between the forces of good and evil.

In a scene from *The Empire Strikes Back*, Luke Skywalker (Mark Hamill) and Darth Vader (David Prowse) carry out the battle between good and evil.

Lucasfilm/20th Century Fox/The Kobal Collection

Work	Evil	Innocent Soul	Good
Hildegard, *Play of Virtues*	Satan	The Soul, Penitent	The Virtues
Tolkien, *Lord of the Rings*	Sauron	Frodo	Gandalf
Lucas, *Star Wars*	Darth Vader	Luke Skywalker	Jedi Knights
Rowling, *Harry Potter*	Voldemort	Harry Potter	Dumbledore

In each case, the embodiment of evil was once good: Sauron began as a good spirit; Darth Vader was once a Jedi knight; Voldemort was originally an innocent boy named Tom Marvolo Riddle; and Satan himself was a fallen angel.

Music plays a powerful role in the works that began as dramas (*Play of Virtues*, Star Wars) and in the film adaptations of the two that began as novels (Lord of the Rings, Harry Potter). Think, for example, of the difference in sound between the darkness of Darth Vader's music and the stirring march that symbolizes the Jedi Knights. These aural cues reinforce the essence of the good and evil characters.

and priests. The melodies were transmitted orally and did not begin to be put down in writing until they already had been circulating for many centuries. Hildegard's style of chant is similar to the more florid kinds of plainchant found in the services of worship. The most important service of worship—the Mass—was itself a ritual reenactment of Christ's last supper with his disciples, with the celebrant priest (a representative of Christ) distributing bread and wine to his followers. The idea of a bodily reenactment of past events gradually extended to readings from scripture as well: dramatized performances of such events as the two Marys finding the empty tomb of Christ on Easter morning became increasingly common from the eleventh century onward. Hildegard's setting of a play about the struggle for an innocent soul extends this practice.

The Clarity of Monophonic Texture

The monophonic texture of this music—whether sung by one singer or by a group of singers in unison—allows the performers to project the text with great clarity. In the performance here, the musicians have taken the liberty of adding a few instruments—a harp, a drum, and at one point, bells—to the vocal line from time to time. Although the written score is for voices alone, it seems likely that performers in the Middle Ages would have added these and other instruments to give variety to the music's timbre. But these instruments are entirely independent of the words and music: in no way do they carry or even support the melodic line or affect the structure of the whole. The music remains essentially monophonic, with no instruments at all for long stretches at a time.

The earliest preserved music from the Middle Ages was monophonic. In the church, this repertory came to be known as **plainchant** because of the simplicity of its texture. (Later, it would also be called **Gregorian chant** on the grounds that Pope Gregory I was said to have written the bulk of it in the late sixth century.) Plainchant fulfilled its function perfectly: it projected its text—the main focus of attention for worshippers—with wonderful clarity and a melodic beauty that enhanced the meaning of the words. It was particularly well suited for performance in the large, resonant spaces of medieval churches. The beauty of the melodies and words together, echoing off the stone walls, must have made an enormous impact on worshippers.

Medieval Melody

Hildegard's flowing melodies move primarily by step (conjunct motion), but the occasional leaps (disjunct motion) provide variety and give each phrase of text a clear profile. Many of the melodic phrases begin with a leap upward and then descend gradually through a series of steps, cadencing on the same note with which the phrase began. This kind of melodic contour and cadencing is typical of plainchant in general and is always related to the structure of the text being sung: a sentence of text almost invariably ends with a cadence.

What has sometimes been described as the "otherworldly" sound of plainchant—the quality that makes plainchant sound different from other kinds of music—is due in part to the

Hildegard von Bingen's *Play of Virtues*, in a manuscript prepared in the scriptorium of Hildegard's own cloister in the 12th century.

Wiesbaden Hessische Landesbibliothek

Melodic contour: rising, then falling

The opening of the present excerpt, represented in modern notation. The melodic phrase starts and ends on D, rising and then falling to a cadence.

scales on which these melodies are based. Whereas today we have only two modes (major and minor), medieval composers had four additional modes, each of which uses a sequence of whole steps and half steps different from the pattern found in the standard scale of today. The easiest way to imagine (and hear) the full range of medieval modes is to play a series of notes upward on the piano using only the white keys starting and ending on D, then another series on E, then another on F, and finally another on G. Each of these scales sounds slightly different from the others, and each also sounds different from the standard major and minor scales of today. (The major scale is found on the white keys from C to C, and the minor scale on the white keys from A to A.) In the Middle Ages, each of these scales (modes) was given its own Greek name, based on the mistaken belief that these corresponded to the modes of ancient Greek music. The medieval modes are Dorian (on D), Phrygian (on E), Lydian (on F), Mixolydian (on G), Aeolian (on A), and Ionian (on C). The opening of this particular excerpt is based on the Dorian mode, beginning and cadencing on the note D.

Projecting Words Through Music

A composer has two basic choices in setting words to music: she can set each syllable to a single note or she can set each syllable to multiple notes. The first style—one note per syllable—is called **syllabic**, and it ensures that the words will be heard with special clarity. The second style—more than one note per syllable—is called **melismatic**. A **melisma** is a syllable sung to many notes. This kind of setting provides variety and emphasizes key words in a text, such as the word *regina* ("queen") after 0:56 or the word *curre* ("hasten" or "run") after 1:26. An entirely melismatic setting might make it difficult for listeners to understand every word, whereas an entirely syllabic setting might not provide sufficient musical variety. By mixing syllabic and melismatic settings, Hildegard provides musical variety, even while providing for a clear projection of the text.

Note, too, how certain passages are sung in a very high **register** or range. When Satan has been bound—the climactic moment of the drama (3:18 in the Listening Guide)—Victory sings in an extremely high register. The effect is thrilling.

Contrasting Rhythms

No one is absolutely certain exactly how plainchant was performed. There are two general approaches, free or measured. The performance here presents the music in a relatively free rhythm, with the individual notes lengthened or shortened according to the length of the syllables in the words being sung. A measured performance would adhere to a consistent meter, such as **duple meter** (**1**-2-**3**-4 | **1**-2-**3**-4 | etc.).

Now listen to this excerpt again, using the Listening Guide.

Hildegard von Bingen (1098–1179)

VISIONS THROUGH MUSIC

We can securely attribute more compositions to Hildegard von Bingen than to any other musician, male or female, who worked before the early fourteenth century. In spite of her impressive output, Hildegard did not consider herself a professional composer or musician. Born into a noble family in what is now western Germany, she entered a Benedictine convent at the age of 7 and took vows when she was 16. In her early 30s, she began to experience visions and revelations, which she recorded in a series of books. She considered herself a channel through which the Holy Spirit transmitted its message to humankind, sometimes in the form of prose, sometimes in the form of poetry, sometimes in the form of poetry with music. Hildegard was the first woman to receive explicit permission from a pope to write on theology. She also wrote on such diverse subjects as medicine, plants, and the lives of the saints, all while directing the life of a thriving convent.

Hildegard von Bingen shown in a contemporary manuscript. She looks heavenward for inspiration as she records what she called her "visions," which included both words and music.

Codex Lucca 1942. Biblioteca Statale, su concessione del Ministero per i Beni e le Attivita' Culturali. Photo: Studio Foto Ghilardi.

PLAYLIST: HILDEGARD

Nuns and monks in Hildegard's time attended church services not just once a week, or even once a day, but usually nine times a day. Hildegard wrote many chants for these services of worship. Here are some examples:

"Lord, Have Mercy" (*Kyrie eleison*) is one of five sections of the Mass, the ritual reenactment of Christ's Last Supper with his disciples. *Hildegard von Bingen: Heavenly Revelations*. Oxford Camerata, Naxos.

"O Blessed Infancy" (*O beata infantia*) is an antiphon, a short piece sung before and after a psalm is sung in church. *The Complete Hildegard von Bingen, Volume Three: O Nobilissima Viriditas*. Celestial Harmonies B00005.

"Honor Be to the Holy Spirit" (*Spiritui sancto honor sit*) is a responsory, a type of chant sung after the reading of scriptures in church. This type of chant takes its name from the fact that a chorus of singers responds to the singing of a soloist. *Hildegard von Bingen: 11,000 Virgins*. Anonymous 4. Harmonia Mundi Fr. B0000B003O.

"Hail, Generous One" (*Ave generosa*) is a hymn, a devotional chant to a freely composed text, often with many strophes or stanzas. *Hildegard von Bingen: Heavenly Revelations*. Oxford Camerata, Naxos.

Listening Guide

CD I · Track 19
GO TO PEARSON mymusiclab for the Automated Listening Guide

Hildegard von Bingen *Play of Virtues* (excerpt)

Time	Character	Latin Text	English Translation
0:00	The Devil (speaks, does not sing)	Que es, aut unde venis? Tu amplexata es me, et ego foras eduxi te. Sed nunc in reversione tua confundis me; Ego autem pugna mea diciam te!	Who are you, and where do you come from? You have embraced me, and I have led you forth. But now, in your turning back, you confuse me; But I will hurl you down with my assault!
0:23	The Soul, Penitent	Ego omnes vias meas malas esse cognovi et ideo fugi a te; modo autem, o illusor pugno contra te. Inde tu, o regina Humilitas, tuo medicamine adiuva me.	I knew all my ways to be evil, and therefore I ran away from you; now, however, O deceiver, I fight against you. Thence, you, O Queen Humility, help me with your medicine.
1:22	Humility (to Victory)	O Victoria, que istum in celo superasti, curre cum militibus tuuis, et omnes ligate diabolum hunc.	O Victory, who conquered that one [the Devil] in heaven, hasten with your knights, and all of you bind that Devil.
1:52	Victory (to the Virtues)	O fortissimi et gloriosissimi milites, venite, et adiuvate me istum fallacem vincere.	O you most brave and glorious knights, come and help me to conquer that deceitful one.
2:21	The Virtues	O dulcissime bellatrix, in torrente fonte qui absorbuit, lupum rapacem! O gloriosa coronata, nos libenter militamus tecum contra illusorem hunc.	O fairest warrior, who swallowed the greedy wolf in the torrent! O glorious crowned one, we willingly fight with you against that deceiver.
2:53	Humility	Ligate ergo istrum, o virtutes preclare!	Bind him, then, o shining Virtues!
3:14	The Virtues (binding Satan here)	O regina nostra, tibi parebimus et precepta tua in omnibus adimplebimus.	O our queen, to you we will be obedient, and we will fulfill your precepts in all things.
3:36	Victory	Gaudete, o socii, quia antiquus serpens libatus est.	Rejoice, O companions, because the old serpent has been bound.
4:04	The Virtues	Laus tibi Christe, rex angelorum!	Praise to you, O Christ, King of the Angels!

Rhythm	**Word-Music Relationships**	**Texture**
Free, corresponding to length of syllables	The Devil's shouting reflects the medieval belief that hell is a place with no music	(Spoken)
	Melisma on *regina* ("queen") suggests her importance	Monophonic
	Melisma on *curre* ("run")	
	Notes in extremely high register—climax of the drama	

Student FAQs

Why are there only women's voices singing?

Two reasons: (1) During the Middle Ages, the Virtues personified in this work—Chastity, Love, Obedience, Mercy, Humility, Discretion, Patience, and so on—were almost all associated with the female gender. (2) Hildegard wrote this work to be performed in her own convent— that is, by her fellow nuns.

If it was performed by nuns, who spoke the part of the Devil?

Only priests—thus only males—could celebrate the Mass, and so each convent had assigned to it a priest to administer the sacraments. In all likelihood, this priest— a monk from a nearby monastery—would have played the role of the Devil.

Is plainchant still used in churches?

In some churches on some occasions, yes. Pope Benedict XVI recently announced that the Vatican choir would begin using plainchant once again on a regular basis. But chant is no longer the principal vehicle for singing texts in the Roman Catholic Church. It is still possible to hear special plainchant services from time to time, however.

THE COMPOSER SPEAKS

Hildegard Defends the Practice of Music

Over 850 years ago, Hildegard von Bingen was embroiled in a debate that continues today: what is the impact of music on the human mind and spirit? Does it support the religious experience, or does it serve as a sensual distraction from religion? To the present day, some religions embrace music, some limit or even shun it.

Hildegard landed in the center of this controversy when church authorities forbade her nuns from singing in church: they were only allowed to speak the words of the services. The authorities wanted to punish Hildegard because she was alleged to have allowed excommunicated individuals—barred from receiving Communion because of a grave offense against the church—to be buried on the consecrated ground of her convent's cemetery. In a lengthy letter to the church authorities, Hildegard eloquently defended the practice of music. Church officials eventually relented and allowed Hildegard's convent to resume its singing.

❖

In obedience to you we have until now given up the singing of the Divine Office, celebrating it only by quiet reading—and I heard a voice coming from the living light, telling of those various kinds of praise concerning which David speaks in the Psalms: "Praise him with the sound of the trumpet, praise him with the psaltery and the cithara, praise him with the tympanum and the chorus, praise him with strings and the organ, praise him with the well-sounding cymbals, praise him with the cymbals of jubilation. Let every spirit praise the Lord" [Psalm 150: 3–6]. In these words we are taught about inward concerns by external objects, how according to the makeup of material things (the properties of musical instruments) we ought best to convert and to refashion the workings of our interior man to the praise of the Creator. . . .

Thus it is just that God be praised in everything. And since man sighs and moans with considerable frequency upon hearing some song, as he recalls in his soul the quality of celestial harmony, the prophet David, considering with understanding the nature of what is spiritual (because the soul is harmonious) exhorts us in the psalm, "Let us confess the Lord on the cithara, let us play to him on the psaltery of ten strings" [Psalm 32:1], intending that the cithara, which sounds from below, pertains to the discipline of the body; that the psaltery, which sounds from above, pertains to the striving of the spirit; and that the ten strings refer to the contemplation of the Law. Thus they who without the weight of sure reason impose silence upon a church in the matter of songs in praise of God, and thereby unjustly deprive God of the honor of his praise on earth, will be deprived themselves of the participation in the angelic praises heard in Heaven, unless they make amends by true regret and humble penitence.

Source: "Epistle 47: To the Prelate of Mainz," in *Source Readings in Music History,* Oliver Strunk, ed.; rev. edition, Leo Treitler, ed. (New York: Norton, 1998), pp. 183–86.

 EXPAND YOUR PLAYLIST

Chant

Christianity is only one of many faiths that use monophonic chants in sacred rituals. Jewish, Buddhist, Hindu, Islamic, Native American (see Chapter 2), and other traditions employ some form of chanting.

Buddhist chant
Tibetan Mantras and Chants. Buddhist Monks of Maitri Vihar. Sounds of the World B00000IXHK. A selection of Buddhist chants from a contemporary Tibetan monastery.

Christian plainchant
Chant. The Benedictine Monks of Santo Domingo de Silos. Angel B000002. A selection of different types of plainchant sung in the Catholic Church. This recording became a triple-platinum album when it was released on CD in the mid-1990s, selling more than 3 million copies in the U.S. alone.

Hindu chant
Sacred Hindu Chants and Mantras. Retro Music B000BS6XYS. A wide range of meditative Hindu chants.

Islamic chant
Music of Islam, Vol. 10: *Qur'an Recitation.* Celestial Harmonies B0000007Z5. Selections from the *Qur'an.*

Jewish chant
Chants Mystique: Hidden Treasures of a Living Tradition. Musical Heritage Society 514284Y. A wide range of chants from various branches of Judaism.

2

GLOBAL CONNECTION

San Ildefonso Indians of New Mexico
Eagle Dance

 Listen to This

 Texture	Notice that all voices sing one melodic line together, throughout the song.
 Word-Music Relationships	Listen for repeated syllable groups. Notice the way the voices function like musical instruments.
 Form	How many sections can you identify? Are these sections repeated or contrasted?
 Melody	Do the melodies have a general upward or downward contour?

Chant is a universal phenomenon. It appears in some form in many, if not all, cultures of the world, and across all historical epochs. Many Christians and Jews still incorporate chant in their religious services. The Hindu Vedas, Tibetan chants, Thai and Vietnamese Buddhist chants, as well as Confucian, Buddhist, Taoist, and shamanic chants in China, Korea, and Japan still occur in their cultural contexts.

Chant is the predominant form of music in Native North American Indian culture. Where it has not died out from the effects of the nineteenth-century wars with Euro-American settlers, it survives on reservations. American popular music has not adopted Native American music as it has European and African musical traditions, although there are cases of Native American music absorbing the influences of rock and blues. Native American chanting can be heard today at **powwows**, intertribal gatherings where Native Americans of mixed tribes express their mutual bond and identity.

The *Eagle Dance* was once part of an ancient rain ceremony in times of drought. Today, it is performed in many Native American Indian cultures, always accompanied by chant. The dance portrays the life cycle of the eagle, a creature regarded as the connecting link between heaven and earth. Two men in eagle feathers dance movements that imitate eagles turning, flapping, and swaying in the air. The eagle's feathers bear prayers and are not allowed to touch the ground. It is relatively easy to locate online video clips of Hopi and Pueblo Indians performing this graceful dance, which has been compared to the most delicate ballet.

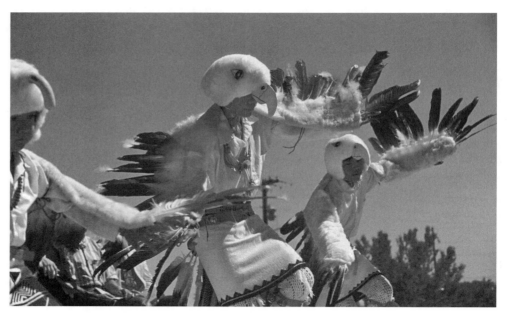

Eagle Dancers from the San Juan Pueblo, New Mexico
Jack Kurtz/The Image Works

Texture: Monophony

Like the other forms of chant we have heard, the *Eagle Dance* consists of one melodic line. It is sung by male voices in unison. Even the percussion instruments are conceived as singing the chant; their sounds punctuate the rhythm of the chant rather than furnishing a contrasting and independent rhythmic line. Nearly all Native American music is monophonic, and most often, it is accompanied by percussion. In this case, the drumming is done with a single drumstick. If a larger drum is used, several players strike the rhythm together.

The Powwow

Originally, every Native American tribe had its own culture and traditions. However, after the European discovery of America, the Native American tribes were either eradicated or forcibly resettled, with many tribes and cultures mixed together on reservations. Eventually, individual tribal traditions gave way to a pan-Indian culture, at the heart of which is the annual pow-wow, or gathering.

The powwow is a means of celebrating Native American culture and preserving it against outside influences. Over the decades, powwows have become fairly standardized, including dancing, singing, traditional storytelling and crafts, and general socializing. Contests are held for best performances, with significant prizes to be won.

Each powwow begins with a "Grand Entry," a procession of all the participants into the arena where the event is to be held. After all have entered, flags are brought into the arena, including various tribal flags and the U.S. flag, carried by military veterans. Next to enter are the tribal elders and honored guests, followed by the dancers, men first, then women. A round dance usually ends the opening ceremonies.

Then, various groups perform dances that range from war dances to religious and ceremonial dances. Each group competes for the best performance. Singers perform the traditional songs to accompany these dances, along with other musicians, primarily drummers. Some of the traditional dances performed include the gourd dance, fancy feather or eagle dance, grass dance, and jingle dance.

At this contemporary powwow held in California, men perform the Grass Dance.

Spencer Grant/PhotoEdit Inc.

The powwow is usually organized by a committee that solicits the participants and organizes their performances. An emcee hosts the event itself, to make sure it runs smoothly.

Powwows have proven to be popular attractions for Native Americans, as well as others who are interested in learning more about Native American culture. They have also become profitable for their organizers, so they have grown in number, particularly in the western and midwestern United States. Annual listings of regional powwows can be found on the Web and in publications catering to Native Americans.

Word-Music Relationships: Beyond Language

In Native American culture, songs are believed to come from the spirit world. A song is transmitted through a person who hears it in a dream or revelation and then teaches it to others. Because songs are not about worldly matters, the words of humans have no place. Native American chant thus makes use of **vocables**: meaningless sung syllables, the sound of which serves like a melodic instrument. Some syllables are more accented than others, and all syllables are sung as prescribed, for they are part of the song. This requires careful memorization.

Form: ABA

The chant for the *Eagle Dance* is in three sections, **ABA**, with a brief introduction. Each section has its own melody, built of smaller, repeating units (see also "A Terraced Melody"). Varied vocable order at the end of each melody group creates contrast within each section.

A Terraced Melody

Although the **A** and **B** sections contrast in their rhythms and sung syllables, they are similar in the overall downward contour of their melodies. Both gradually descend the scale in what are known as **terraced** stages, eventually resolving on a low tone. This is typical of North American Indian chant melodies.

The **A** melody consists of two phrases with identical vocables:

A

(Ya hey ya ha ye ya hey ye) (ya hey ya ha ye ya hey ye)

This melody occurs three times, on slightly different pitches, but with the same terraced downward contour. After the third time, vocables are sung in a varied order, creating a tapered ending for the **A** section.

The essential **B** melody consists of the shorter vocable set "*Hey le ya,*" likewise sung twice:

B

(Hey le ya) (hey le ya)

This melodic phrase is repeated. The third time, it varies slightly at the end and concludes with different vocables (*hey ya ay*):

(Hey le ya) (hey ya ay)

This is followed by a compressed version of what has been sung so far:

(Hey le ya) (hey le ya) (hey le ya)

Varied syllables bring this set of phrases to a close, and the music slows briefly. Then the entire pattern repeats, once again tapering off with a succession of varied syllables that bring the entire **B** section to a close.

Now listen to this chant again, following the Listening Guide.

Listening Guide

San Ildefonso Indians of New Mexico *Eagle Dance*

Time	Form	Text (vocables)	Melody
0:00	Free introduction	*Hyo hey ya* *hyo hey ya hey ya* *hwey ye ya* *hya hey ya* *hey hey hey he* *hya hey ya* *hey hey ya*	Non-metered chant with rapid drum pulsations
0:23	Metered part of the introduction	*Hey ye hey ya* *hey ye hey ye* *hey ya hey ye ye ye*	The chant becomes metered: slow groups of four beats.
0:31	A	*Ya hey ya ha ye ya hey ye* *ya hey ya ha ye ya hey ye* (three times, followed by vocables in varied order, tailing off the section)	The **A** melody is sung three times: slightly different pitches, but with the same terraced downward contour. After the third time, the vocables and melodic fragments are sung in a varied order.
1:03	B	*Hey le ya, hey le ya* (twice) *Hey le ya, hey ya ay* *Hey le ya, hey le ya, hey ya ay*	Contrasting terraced melody. Faster meter of four beats, more than double the speed of **A**.
1:16	The first half of **B** concludes	(Varied vocables)	Varied vocables and melodic fragments. The chant slows to a halt
1:19	Resumed tempo of **B**	*Hey le ya, hey le ya* (twice) *Hey le ya, hey ya ay* *Hey le ya, hey le ya, hey ya ay*	The **B** melodic pattern repeats.
1:32	Slowing down	(Varied vocables)	The chant slows to a halt again.
1:35–end	A	*Ya hey ya ha ye ya hey ye* *ya hey ya ha ye ya hey ye* (three times, followed by vocables in varied order, tailing off the section)	The slow meter of the **A** unit returns with the first terraced melody.

Student FAQs

Why do traditional Native American chants often move from a higher to a lower tone?
Descending melodies are typical of many forms of traditional vocal music. The descending tone mirrors the exhalation of breath.

Why is this dance performed by men only?
Traditionally, only males were allowed to participate in the ceremonial songs and dances of Native Americans. At today's powwows, the Eagle Dance is still usually performed by men. The eagle is a strong symbol of virility to Native Americans, and in this dance, it is associated with maintaining the fertility of the land and thus the survival of the tribe.

Why do Native American songs feature vocables instead of words?
There are different theories. Many of the songs have a sacred or ceremonial meaning, the actual texts transcend language. The meaning cannot be expressed in words, so vocables stand in for them. Another theory is that, as Native American tribes were combined on reservations, they needed to find a way to sing together. Using vocables allowed everyone to sing.

EXPAND YOUR PLAYLIST

Native American Music

Creation's Journey: Native American Music. Smithsonian Folkways Recordings SFW40410.
Anthology of North American Indian and Eskimo Music. Folkways Records FW04541.
Cry from the Earth: Music of the North American Indians. Folkways Records FW37777.
These are all good anthologies that give an overview of Native American musical styles.

An Historical Album of Blackfoot Indian Music. Folkways Records FW34001.
These historic recordings are from cylinder recordings made in the 1920s and 1930s; while the sound quality is not the best, the performances are rare and interesting.

Hopi Sunshield Singers. *Pow-Wow Songs Live!* Canyon CR-6180.
Intertribal powwow songs recorded live.

Blackfire. *One Nation Under.* Canyon CR-7049.
Blackfire is a group of Native American siblings who play what they describe as "fireball alternative punk." Joey Ramone makes a guest appearance on this disc. Political lyrics comment on the plight of Native Americans.

3

Francesco Landini
"Behold, Spring"

Listen to This

Texture

Listen to how the two voices—one high, one low—relate to each other. They are similar, yet each retains its own distinct shape. Listen through the piece once, focusing your attention on the top voice; then listen through it again, focusing on the lower voice. Finally, listen through it a third time, noting how the two combine to create a harmonious whole.

Rhythm

Feel the regular pulse of three beats, the first accented (**1**-2-3 | **1**-2-3 |).

Melody

Listen for the stepwise motion in both voices. Notice the brief stopping points that subdivide the melody of each strophe into smaller units.

Form

Listen for the repetition of large-scale units. The poetry is in three verses, with the first repeated at the end. Notice that the music for verses 1, 3, and 4 is identical; the music for verse 2 is different.

Word-Music Relationships

Notice the largely syllabic text setting—one note per syllable. Occasionally you will hear a melisma—multiple notes over a single syllable.

Music was already the food of love in the Middle Ages, long before Shakespeare coined the phrase. Poets were inspired to write love poetry, and composers were inspired to set those poems to music to make them even more moving. Francesco Landini's "Behold, Spring" ("Ecco la primavera") is a setting of one such poem. It is a ballata for two voices. The ballata was one of many genres of secular song in the Middle Ages, and in the patterned rhythms of "Behold, Spring," we can hear the origins of the genre in dance (in Italian, *ballata* means "danced"). Landini's setting captures the feeling of bodies in motion.

The repertory of secular song in the Middle Ages is enormous. This was the age of courtly love, a highly stylized form of love in which a knight declares himself as the servant of the lady he is wooing. All his heroic deeds are done in her honor, and his love for her ennobles him, even if—especially if—she rejects his advances. Some songs describe the lady's beauty, others the knight's suffering (caused by her rejection of him), still others the pleasures of love. In the *Decameron*, the poet Giovanni Boccaccio—who lived in Florence at the same time as Landini and undoubtedly knew him—describes how a small group of lords and ladies, fleeing the plague in a group, sings "Behold, Spring" and songs like it "in amorous tones" to "divert their minds with music."

The Richness of Polyphonic Texture

This brief work uses a new kind of musical texture that had been emerging slowly for several centuries: **polyphony**. In polyphony, two or more voices of equal importance combine in such a way that each voice retains its own identity (*poly* = "many"; *phon* = "sound"). Here, the upper and lower voices are of equal importance, and while our ear is drawn to the upper line for acoustical reasons (higher pitches always tend to stand out more), the lower line is every bit as melodious.

Composers created the earliest polyphonic works sometime around the eighth or ninth century by adding new lines above or below existing plainchant melodies. These new melodic lines were crafted in such a way as to embellish what was already present, and church authorities sanctioned this new kind of music on the grounds that it was, in effect, a gloss or commentary on a well-known passage of text and music (the chant). Some of the earliest works of polyphony are extraordinarily long and intricate, but they were always based on an existing liturgical melody. A twelfth-century cleric named Perotin, who worked at the Cathedral of Notre Dame in Paris, wrote immensely long and intricate works known as organum (see Expand Your Playlist). These used plainchant melodies in long note values in the lowest voice, with faster-moving voices layered above the plainchant. These polyphonic works thus preserved the plainchant (in the lowest voice) even while embellishing it (in the upper voices). Gradually, composers began writing polyphony against new, original melodies, extending the technique beyond sacred music to include secular music as well. Landini's "Behold, Spring" is one of these entirely new secular compositions.

Rhythm: The Pulse of Meter

When two (or more) parts are moving closely together, rhythmic freedom is not possible the way it is in monophony—where there is only one line and no other parts need be considered. If you are a composer writing for two or more voices, you need to consider how to make the parts mesh properly and stay together. Landini organizes "Behold, Spring" around a steady pattern of **triple meter** (**1**-2-3 | **1**-2-3 | etc.). The lengths of the individual notes vary, but the music falls into consistent units of three beats.

Units of Melody

The mostly conjunct (stepwise) melodic lines are subdivided into smaller units, each of which ends with a **cadence**, a brief stopping point at which the music pauses (or, in the case of the final cadence, ends). Cadences are to music as periods are to verbal expression: when we are writing, we indicate the ends of units of thought with commas or periods, and when we speak, we make correspondingly briefer or longer pauses. By breaking our speech into units (sentences) and subunits (clauses), we make it easier for listeners to understand what we are saying. Music operates on the same principle. Here, Landini inserts a brief cadence at the end of the second and fourth lines in each four-line strophe. In this particular work, Landini always cadences on the **unison**—that is, both voices sing exactly the same note. The rhythms of the two voices also emphasize the arrival on each cadence. At times the two voices move in the same rhythmic pattern, while at other times their rhythms diverge, but the rhythms always coincide just before each cadence.

Form: Turning Poetry into Music

In most vocal music, the form of the text shapes the form of the work. "Behold, Spring" is no exception. The poetry consists of three verses, known as **strophes** (or **stanzas**—the terms are interchangeable), with the first repeated at the end. The music of the second strophe contrasts with the others. Landini thus uses both repetition and contrast to create a musical form that can be diagrammed as **ABAA:**

Strophe	1	2	3	4 (=1, repeated)
Music	**A**	**B**	**A**	**A**

This combination of repetition, variation, and contrast is basic to all musical forms. Once an idea is presented (in this case, the text and music of the first strophe, "1/**A**"), only one of three things can happen:

1. It can be repeated.
2. It can be varied.
3. It can be contrasted through the introduction of a new idea.

Landini uses all three of these devices:

1. He contrasts 1/**A** by presenting both a new text and new music in 2/**B**.
2. He varies 1/**A** by presenting the same music with a new text in 3/**A**.
3. He repeats both the text and music of 1/**A** in strophe 4/**A**.

Word-Music Relationships: Syllabic vs. Melismatic

Landini sets the text in a manner that is largely syllabic. He uses melismas only occasionally, as on "temp'è" (line 3 of the first strophe) and again on "tempo" in the third line of the second strophe. This creates a welcome degree of variety: listening to an entirely syllabic setting might be a bit monotonous. But the syllabic setting allows the text to be projected quite clearly, even though the two voices are not always singing together in exactly the same rhythm.

Now listen to this ballata again, using the Listening Guide.

Francesco Landini (ca. 1325–97)

THE COMPOSER AS POET

Blinded by smallpox at an early age, Landini was the most famous and prolific Italian composer of the fourteenth century. He served as organist at a church in Florence for many years and also won renown as a poet. The phenomenon of the poet-composer was not unusual in the Middle Ages: many of the songs from this era are settings of poetry written by the composer himself. Landini is believed to have written more than 150 secular songs, which together represent about one-third of all Italian music that has survived from the fourteenth century.

One fourteenth-century contemporary praised Landini so lavishly as a composer, performer, and poet that he acknowledged that readers might think he was exaggerating about the abilities of any one individual in so many diverse fields. But this contemporary seemed certain that everyone would agree that

> [no one] ever played the organ so well. All musicians grant him that. And thus recently [i.e., 1364], at Venice, he was publicly crowned with laurel by His Majesty the King of Cyprus. In just this manner, once upon a time, poets were crowned by the Emperors of Rome.
>
> Source: Leonard Wood (ed.), The Works of Francesco Landini (Cambridge, Mass.: The Medieval Academy of America, 1939), 301–303; translation modified slightly.

This image of Francesco Landini is from the *Squarcialupi Codex*, a richly illuminated manuscript of polyphonic music from the 14th century. Landini is shown playing a small portative (or portable) organ.

Courtesy of Firenze, Biblioteca Medicea Laurenziana/Ministry for Cultural Affairs/Med. Palat. 87, c. 121v

PLAYLIST: LANDINI

"I feel the flame of love" (Sento d'amor la fiamma). Another ballata.

"My dear lady" (Cara mia donna). A ballata for three voices.

"Farewell, farewell sweet lady" (Adieu, Adieu, dous dame). A virelais (a genre of French song) that exists in two versions: one for two voices, one for three.

"Thus thoughtful" (Così pensoso). A caccia or hunting song for three voices.

Listening Guide

Francesco Landini   "Behold, Spring"

Time	Strophe	Italian Text	English Translation	Form	Melody
0:00	1	Ecco la primavera che 'l cor fa rallegrare; temp'è da 'nnamorare e star con lieta cera.	Behold, Spring, which makes the heart rejoice; it's the time to fall in love and to be of good cheer.	Music can be labeled as **A**.	Melisma on *primavera*. Cadence on *rallegare*. Melisma on **temp'è**. Cadence on *cera*.
0:17	2	No' vegiam l'aria e 'l tempo che pur chiama allegreza in questo vago tempo ogni cosa ha vagheza.	We see the air and weather bringing about gladness; in this lovely time every thing has loveliness.	Contrasting music (**B**)	Melisma on **tempo**. Cadence on *allegreza*. Melisma on **tempo**. Cadence on **vagheza**.
0:38	3	L'erbe con gran frescheza e fiori copron prati e gli alberi adornati sono in simil maniera.	The meadows are covered with fresh grass and with flowers; and the trees are adorned in a similar manner.	Same music as strophe 1, (**A**), different words	Melisma on **fresc**he. Cadence on *prati*. Melisma on **e**. Cadence on *maniera*.
0:54	4	Ecco la primavera che 'l cor far allegrare; temp'è da 'nnamorare e star con lieta cera.	Behold, Spring, which makes the heart rejoice; it's the time to fall in love and to be of good cheer.	Text and music (**A**) of strophe 1 repeated	[Same as Strophe 1]

Modified from text *HMWC 2/e Anthology I*, p. 41, which is credited (p. 310) to Giovanni Carsaniga from *I am Music: Works by Francesco Landini*, Move Records, Carlton, South Australia, 1997.

Student FAQs

The words are about spring and flowers and falling in love. Why doesn't the music sound happier?
What makes music sound "happy" differs widely according to place and time. Our notions of what makes music sound lively or optimistic today (major mode, a "bright" sound, fast rhythmic motion) are culturally conditioned and did not emerge in Western music until roughly the sixteenth century.

Was this written for women's voices?
This recording features women's voices, but the piece could be performed just as easily by men's voices, or by men's and women's together.

Producing a Manuscript

Music today is distributed primarily through recordings and through print: best-selling CDs are reproduced in millions of copies, music files can be put online, and sheet music printed. But in the Middle Ages, every document had to be written by hand. "Manuscript" means literally "handwritten" (*manu* = "hand"; *scriptus* = "that which is written"), so each manuscript was by its very nature unique.

These manuscripts could be extraordinarily expensive to produce. The one known today as the *Squarcialupi Codex* (a *codex* is a manuscript of many pages bound together) is an unusually elaborate example. Its material alone represented an enormous investment:

- **Parchment.** This codex consists of more than 216 leaves of parchment, the prepared skin of a sheep or goat, cleaned, dried, and stretched to form a smooth surface for writing. Parchment is more durable than paper (which scarcely existed at the time) but also far more expensive to produce.

- **Gold leaf.** Many of the painted miniatures within the codex are decorated with gold leaf, actual pieces of gold beaten very thin.

- **Miniature Portraits.** Whoever commissioned this codex must have asked that all works by a given composer be gathered together in the manuscript. Thus all 146 of Landini's works in the *Squarcialupi Codex* appear in one continuous section, with his portrait at the beginning.

We know where the *Squarcialupi Codex* was made—the monastery of Santa Maria degli Angeli, in Florence (present-day Italy)—but we do not know who commissioned it or paid for it. The music of the *Squarcialupi Codex* is largely secular (worldly), not sacred, and thus it was probably commissioned by an

The ornamental instruments are overlaid with gold leaf.

By the 14th century, staff lines had become standard, and note-forms more closely resemble those in use today.

Francesco Landini, the composer, is shown playing a portative organ.

The *Squarcialupi Codex*
Courtesy of Firenze, Biblioteca Medicea Laurenziana/Ministry for Cultural Affairs/Med. Palat. 87, c. 121v

affluent individual. At some later point in the fifteenth century, this manuscript came into the possession of the Florentine organist Antonio Squarcialupi (1416–80), after whom it is now named. There was no commercial market for a manuscript like this: it was created for, funded, and enjoyed by a single individual.

 EXPAND YOUR PLAYLIST

Medieval Polyphony

Perotin, "All the Ends of the Earth Have Seen" ("Viderunt omnes"). The three upper voices weave in and around each other over a slow-moving fourth voice, derived from plainchant. The effect is mesmerizing.

Anonymous, "In Paris/It Is Said / Fresh Strawberries" ("À Paris/On parole/Fraise nouvele"). One of many thirteenth-century polyphonic works with multiple texts: each of the three voices sings its own text, the upper two about the virtues of life in Paris, the third a street vendor's cry selling fresh fruit.

Guillaume de Machaut, "Mass of Our Lady" ("Messe de Notre Dame"). The earliest known setting of the complete Mass by an individual composer, from the mid-fourteenth century.

Guillaume de Machaut, "My Beginning Is My End" ("Ma fin est mon commencement"). A secular song for three voices, in which the two upper voices are retrograde images of each other, that is, one part is the same as the other, only in reverse.

Lorenzo da Firenze, "All in Their Places" ("A poste messe"). A fourteenth-century Italian caccia, a stylized hunting song that imitates the sounds of horns and dogs.

4

Alfonso el Sabio
Songs to the Virgin Mary no. 249, "He Who Gladly Serves"

Listen to This

Timbre

Listen for the contrast between the **percussion** instruments (two drums) and the **wind** instruments (two shawms).

Form

Listen for the two basic units that make up the melody. They begin in the same way, but the second one moves into a higher range. Notice the way these units are repeated and varied.

Texture

Listen for three distinct textures on the shawms:

1. Both instruments play the same notes together (monophony).
2. One instrument plays the melody while the other holds a long, single note (homophony).
3. Both instruments play the same melody at the same time, but one of them plays a more elaborate and embellished form of it (**heterophony**).

We sometimes think of the Middle Ages as the "Dark Ages," but there was nothing dark about the sound of their instruments. The penetrating sound of the shawm, featured on this recording of "He Who Gladly Serves" ("Aquel que de volontade"), offers a good example of just how vivid and intense medieval timbres could be.

Relatively little music written specifically for instruments survives from the Middle Ages. But we know from numerous accounts that composers and musicians rarely made sharp distinctions between vocal and instrumental music, and that they often performed vocal lines on instruments if not enough singers happened to be available for a performance. So while the

The Iberian Peninsula in the Middle Ages

A modern performer in medieval garb plays the shawm, the wind instrument heard in this performance of "He Who Gladly Serves." Today's musicians have reconstructed medieval instruments, like the shawm, that had fallen out of use over time.

Richard E York; John A Howells Photography

original version of "He Who Gladly Serves" is for voices, with a text to be sung, the performance here reflects the common medieval practice of performing music with whatever was at hand. Jazz musicians still commonly arrange songs with words for instruments alone. When the great jazz saxophonist John Coltrane performed "My Favorite Things" (from *The Sound of Music*) on his saxophone, he was carrying on a tradition that had begun in the Middle Ages.

"He Who Gladly Serves" is one of the *Songs to the Virgin Mary (Cantigas de Santa Maria)* attributed to Alfonso el Sabio ("Alfonso the Wise"), who ruled the Kingdom of Castile and León on the Iberian peninsula between 1252 and 1284. The *Cantigas* is a collection of more than 400 songs preserved in several different manuscripts. One of these sources, now housed in the library of the monastery in Escorial, Spain, is full of miniatures showing a great variety of medieval instruments, lending further support to the idea that this music was not meant exclusively for voices.

Timbre: The Sound of Double Reeds

The shawm is a double-reed instrument: the player blows through a pair of cane strips, and the vibrating air resonates down a long, open-ended tubular base made of wood. This produces a reedy, slightly nasal sound. Although the shawm is still widely used in northern Africa and the Middle East, it had largely disappeared from western Europe by the end of the Renaissance. The closest relative of this instrument in the modern-day orchestra is the oboe, but the oboe's sound is more refined and not as delightfully raucous.

Form: Repetition and Contrast

The form of this piece arises out of the repetition and contrast of two fairly short melodic units. These two units (which we can label as **A** and **B**) begin in a similar manner, but **B** soon moves into a higher register. In this performance, a passage on the drums alone introduces two complete statements of the melody (that is, **ABA ABA**). The **A** section alone is repeated twice at the end to close out the work.

Three Kinds of Texture

In this piece, we hear three different textures:

1. **Monophony:** Both instruments play the same notes together, in unison.

Monophonic texture (0:27)

2. **Homophony:** One instrument plays the melody, the other a **drone bass**—that is, a single long note held underneath the melodic line. The effect is very much like that of a bagpipe, another instrument widely used in medieval times.

Homophonic texture (0:54)

3. **Heterophony:** Both instruments play the same melody at the same time, but one of them plays a more elaborate and embellished form of it. The two lines are thus similar (but not as similar as in unison texture) and at the same time different (but not as different as in homophonic texture).

Heterophonic texture (1:12)

Now listen to this work again, using the Listening Guide.

Listening Guide

Alfonso el Sabio *Songs to the Virgin Mary* no. 249, "He Who Gladly Serves"

Time	Form	Texture	Timbre
0:00	Introduction		Drums only. Rhythm continues throughout entire work.
0:27	First statement of the melody as a whole: Section **A**	Unison	Shawms 1 and 2 in unison
0:36	Section **B**	Unison	
0:45	Section **A**	Unison	
0:54	Second statement of the melody as a whole: Section **A**	Homophonic	Shawm 1: melody Shawm 2: drone bass
1:03	Section **B**	Heterophonic	Shawm 1: melody Shawm 2: embellished version of melody played simultaneously
1:12	Section **A**	Heterophonic	Shawm 1: melody Shawm 2: embellished version of melody played simultaneously
1:22	Closing: Section **A**	Homophonic	Shawm 1: melody Shawm 2: drone bass
1:30	Section **A**	Alternates between unison and heterophonic	Shawms 1 and 2 at times in unison, at times with one of the instruments playing an embellished version of the melody

Student FAQs

Why shawms?
Why not? The performers in this recording could have used almost any instrument and still been in keeping with medieval attitudes toward performing vocal music without singing.

Are the drum parts really that lively?
Drum parts were never notated in the Middle Ages, but we know from paintings that they were central to many instrumental ensembles, so we must assume that musicians used the notated music as a baseline, adding and embellishing as they saw fit. The sources of the *Cantigas* that include music transmit only the melodic line. In this respect, medieval instrumental music was probably very much like today's jazz: a melody provides the basis of a more elaborate performance that takes liberties with the original tune.

Alfonso el Sabio (1221–84)

THE KING GETS ALL THE CREDIT

The manuscripts preserving the music and poetry known as the *Songs to the Virgin Mary (Cantigas de Santa Maria)* ascribe these works to Alfonso el Sabio ("Alfonso the Wise"), who ruled the Kingdom of Castile and León (in what is now central and northwestern Spain) during the thirteenth century. Scholars now believe that if Alfonso wrote any of the words or music at all, he probably wrote only a relatively small number of them. We can be certain, however, that Alfonso was the moving force behind the creation and compilation of these songs: he commissioned many works in a wide variety of areas, including literature, philosophy, theology, and even chess.

The real composer of this particular song is in all likelihood anonymous, as is the case with so many medieval artists. After all, we often do not even know the names of the architects who designed the great Gothic cathedrals and churches being built around this same time, in the thirteenth century. Many of these composers were monks, priests, or nuns; others were employed as musicians at courts; still others were troubadours, trouvères, and minnesingers, who traveled widely.

Alfonso el Sabio (center) listens to musicians performing a song in praise of the Virgin Mary (right). This image is from one of the several 13th-century manuscripts that preserve the *Songs to the Virgin Mary*.
Archivo Fotográfico Oronoz, Madrid

SCI-TECH

Reed Instruments

If you've ever created a sound by blowing on a blade of grass, you've applied the basic principle common to all reed instruments. These range from the medieval shawm (heard here) to the modern-day saxophone. By blowing into a reed instrument's mouthpiece, the player sets in motion two thin strips of cane that have been specially shaped and dried. This vibrating piece of cane, known as a *reed,* creates a resonance that produces the instrument's distinctive sound.

Finding good reeds is a challenge for musicians. More advanced players often make their own reeds, buying the raw material—strips of thin cane, specially grown and processed—and then shaving them down to just the right degree of thickness. A reed that is too thick will produce a "wooly" sound, but if it is too thin, it will break after only a short time.

There are two subfamilies of reed instruments:

A close-up of the mouthpiece of a shawm, with its double reed
Richard E. York

- **Double-reed instruments:** The mouthpiece consists of two reeds opposed to one another. One reed thus vibrates initially against the other reed, which tends to produce the slightly "buzzy" sound heard here on the shawm. The two main double-reed instruments in use today are the oboe and the bassoon.

- **Single-reed instruments:** The mouthpiece consists of a single reed secured to a hard surface. The principal single-reed instruments today are the clarinet and the saxophone.

A clarinet mouthpiece, showing a single reed
Cleve Bryant/PhotoEdit Inc.

King David plays the psalter with a plectrum (pick).

Vielle, a forerunner of the violin

Lute

Tambourine

Clappers (castanets)

Saint Cecilia, the patron saint of music, plays a portative (portable) organ.

Bagpipes and shawm

Trumpets

Drums

This 14th-century illustration shows a number of different instruments surrounding Saint Cecilia, the patron saint of music, who plays a portative (portable) organ.

Scala/Art Resource, N.Y.

EXPAND YOUR PLAYLIST

Instrumental Music of the Middle Ages

Kyrie cunctipotens genitor. An arrangement, for organ, of a liturgical vocal composition from the Mass, with a chant melody in the slow-moving lower voice and a free embellishment in the upper voice. Ensemble Unicorn, *Codex Faenza: Instrumental Music of the Early 15th Century.* Naxos 8.553618, Track 16.

Palästinalied. An arrangement of a German song from the time of the Crusades ("Palestine Song"), performed here on a recorder (a flute-like instrument) and a small drum. *The World of Early Music.* Naxos 8.554770, Track 5.

La quinte estampie real. The *estampie* was an energetic type of dance that involved stamping of the feet, as its name suggests. This performance is by an ensemble of wind and percussion instruments. Dufay Collective, *A Dance in the Garden of Mirth.* Chandos CHAN 9320, Track 9.

Saltarello. Another type of dance, this one involving leaping (*saltare* in Italian means "to jump"). This recording is for hurdy-gurdy, vielle, and drum. St. George's Canzona, *A Medieval Banquet.* ASV Living Era, Track 1.

PART 1 Summary

MUSIC OF THE MIDDLE AGES: A Summary

 Texture — Both monophonic and polyphonic

 Harmony — A by-product of counterpoint

 Melody — Flowing, largely conjunct, divided into sections by cadences; melodies based on scales of the medieval modes

 Form — Based on repetition, variation, and contrast

 Rhythm — Free (plainchant) and metrically structured

 Word-music relationships — Syllabic settings to project texts clearly; melismatic settings to emphasize key words

IN REVIEW: Medieval Style

Monophony. A single melodic line, whether sung by a solo voice or by a choir in unison. This was the essential texture of plainchant, the earliest music of Christian worship.
- Hildegard von Bingen, *Play of Virtues* (Chapter 1)
- San Ildefonso Indians, *Eagle Dance* (Chapter 2)

Polyphony. Two or more different melodic lines performed simultaneously. This texture was used in both sacred and secular music.
- Francesco Landini, "Behold, Spring" (Chapter 3)

Heterophony. Two voices singing the same melody simultaneously, but with different embellishments.
- Alfonso el Sabio, *Songs to the Virgin Mary* no. 249, "He Who Gladly Serves" (Chapter 4)

Syllabic and melismatic text-setting. Text set to one note per syllable or multiple notes per syllable.
- Hildegard von Bingen, *Play of Virtues* (Chapter 1)
- Franceso Landini, "Behold, Spring" (Chapter 3)

Metered rhythm. Rhythm structured around a fixed metrical pattern allowed polyphonic voices to coordinate.
- Francesco Landini, "Behold, Spring" (Chapter 3)

Instrumental music. Medieval performers could and did play vocal music on a variety of different instruments, such as the shawm.
- Alfonso el Sabio, *Songs to the Virgin Mary* no. 249, "He Who Gladly Serves" (Chapter 4)

PART 2 The Renaissance

The Renaissance—a period extending from roughly 1425 to 1600—witnessed the recovery of many of the arts and sciences from antiquity that had been lost or forgotten during the Middle Ages. "Renaissance" is the French word for "rebirth," and what was reborn in this era was the spirit of **humanism**, an intellectual and cultural movement that explored human interests and values through the pursuit of science, philosophy, literature, painting, sculpture, and music, particularly vocal music.

Renaissance composers brought the spirit of humanism to their art by setting both sacred and secular texts in ways that united words and music more directly than ever before. Composers devoted special attention to both the rhythm of the poetry and the meanings of individual words. They created a sound based on the ideal of equal-voiced parts in three, four, five, and eventually even six voices. The typical Renaissance vocal composition features a full, rich sound, intricate in both its texture and rhythm yet always attentive to the text being sung.

Music for Catholics, Music for Protestants

As a Catholic, composer William Byrd had to watch his step in an England ruled by a Protestant monarch. While maintaining his own faith, he cultivated favor with Queen Elizabeth I in part by writing large quantities of music for Protestant church services, including the brilliant choral anthem *Sing Joyfully*. The rift among Christians had begun in 1517, when an obscure German monk named Martin Luther nailed a long list of complaints on the doors of a church in Wittenberg. Luther was responding to what a number of people saw as growing corruption and a weakening spirituality in the church. He set in motion a revolution, known as the Reformation, that would establish Protestantism as a new branch of Christianity. From that point onward, the Western church would remain divided into two main branches, Protestant and Catholic. The faith of any European monarch—Catholic or Protestant—would determine the faith and the politics of his or her realm. Composers responded to these changes by writing new music for the Protestant liturgy in languages other than Latin. Catholic composers, in what became known as the Counter-Reformation, redoubled their efforts to write music that would move the souls of the faithful.

Music for Growing Markets

Renaissance composers and musicians benefited from the enormous economic growth throughout Europe that began in the fifteenth century. The Italian peninsula and the area known as the Low Countries (present-day Belgium and the Netherlands) led the way in this new era of economic

◀ Martin Luther, 1529. Luther was a composer as well as a theologian: he wrote both the words and the music to the Protestant hymn "A Mighty Fortress Is Our God" ("Ein' Feste Burg ist Unser Gott"). This portrait is by the famed German artist Lucas Cranach the Elder.

Erich Lessing/Art Resource, NY

expansion. The discovery of the New World—Christopher Columbus lived his entire life in the Renaissance—swelled royal and private coffers still more. As kingdoms, duchies, and city-states expanded both in population and in wealth, the demand for music and the arts in general became greater and greater. The best composers and musicians could command high salaries.

The ideal "Renaissance man" was someone who cultivated knowledge and experience in the full range of arts and sciences, not just one. In his famous handbook of noble behavior, *The Book of the Courtier,* the Italian courtier and writer Baldassare Castiglione recommended that every would-be nobleman learn the basic arts of singing and playing an instrument such as the lute. Music-lovers entertained themselves and their listeners with such whimsical songs as

▲ Hans Holbein the Younger's *The Ambassadors* (1533) shows two courtly gentlemen with the symbols of their status: a globe and navigational instruments, and, on the bottom shelf of the table behind them, a lute, a set of four flutes, and an open hymnal. (The odd object in the foreground is a distorted rendering of a skull, a reminder of human mortality.)

©National Gallery, London

▲ Musicians playing the drum and flute (right foreground) accompany a lord and lady in dance. Compare this painting from the 1520s with the medieval painting of dancing couples from 100 years before (see p. 19). The strong sense of perspective (depth), considerable detail in the faces, and realistic portrayal of the individual figures show Renaissance art's inspiration from newly rediscovered classical Greek models.

By permission of The British Library

Josquin des Prez's "The Cricket" ("El grillo"), about a cricket, or with madrigals such as Thomas Weelkes's "Since Robin Hood," using whatever instruments or voices were on hand.

The New Individuality

The Renaissance was an age of growing confidence in the powers of human reason and the distinctiveness of every individual. Art became more personal. The contrasts between drama in the Middle Ages and in the Renaissance provide a revealing example of this new sense of individuality. Medieval drama had tended toward allegory: the Innocent Soul in Hildegard von Bingen's *Ritual of Virtues (Ordo Virtutum)* is a symbolic figure torn between other symbolic figures, the Virtues and the Devil. By the end of the Renaissance, playwrights like William Shakespeare and Christopher Marlowe were writing dramas and comedies with flesh-and-blood characters. Hamlet may be a prince, but his emotions are very human. Renaissance painting and sculpture also reflect this newfound sense of individuality. Compare, for example, the facial expressions of the figures in the Renaissance dance scene shown here with the faces in a corresponding dance scene from the Middle Ages on page 19. Each Renaissance face bears the stamp of a distinct personality.

In a similar fashion, Renaissance composers captured human emotions in ways that seem far more personal in tone to us today. Josquin's "The Cricket," for example, conveys a sense of genuinely playful humor with its imitation of cricket song, and Thomas Weelkes's "Since Robin Hood" is full of unexpected rhythmic shifts that match its fanciful text at every turn.

Information Technology 2.0

The invention of printing by movable metal type in the mid-fifteenth century changed forever the way information could be transmitted. What had once circulated in scarce and enormously expensive manuscripts could now be disseminated rapidly and relatively cheaply through print. Music printing had become an established business by 1500, and individuals could now buy music for their own personal use at a reasonable price. Some composers achieved international renown, thanks in no small part to the unprecedented speed with which their works could circulate across the entire continent. Tielman Susato was both a composer and a publisher, and his *Moorish Dance (La Moresca)* could be purchased in music shops throughout Europe.

Proofreading the first "pulls" off the press. Obvious errors could be corrected at once.

Delivering fresh paper to the shop.

Applying ink to the set typeface.

Pulling the press itself. The screw mechanism exerts enormous pressure between the blank paper and the inked typeface, thereby affixing the ink to the page.

▸ A 16th-century printing press workshop in operation

Art Resource/The New York Public Library for the Performing Arts

Setting the pieces of movable type into a text to be printed. The manuscript to be set is taped to the wall.

Returning used type back to its case for use on the next page of type.

The Renaissance: AT A GLANCE

chapter 5

ca. 1500
JOSQUIN DES PREZ
"The Cricket"
GENRE: Secular song

Chapter highlight:
Counterpoint

Renaissance composers used counterpoint to create polyphonic textures. Word-painting was a way to capture the spirit of the text, sometimes even by imitating the sounds of nature.

KEY CONCEPTS
Four-voice polyphonic texture, counterpoint, word-painting, ternary form.

chapter 6

1608
THOMAS WEELKES
"Since Robin Hood"
GENRE: Madrigal

Chapter highlight:
The Madrigal

The madrigal, usually written for three to six voices, is the most important type of secular song in the Renaissance. The genre became popular in Italy (Arcadelt, de Rore, Luzzaschi, Marenzio), then found its way to England in the closing decades of the sixteenth century (Byrd, Farmer, Gibbons, Morley, Wilbye). Madrigals featured word painting and subtle parallels between poetic and musical meter.

KEY CONCEPTS
Three-voice texture, poetic meter and musical meter, shifting meters, syncopation, word-painting.

chapter 7   **chapter 8**   **WEB BONUS** **chapter 1**

1590
WILLIAM BYRD
"Sing Joyfully"
GENRE: Anthem

Chapter highlight:
Sacred polyphony

The anthem and the motet were the two most important genres of Renaissance choral music. By the end of the sixteenth-century, six-voice a cappella texture had become the norm. Imitative counterpoint and word-painting brought texts alive. Tallis, Luther, Palestrina, and Victoria are noted composers of sacred polyphony in the sixteenth century.

KEY CONCEPTS
Polyphony, a cappella choral music, six-voice texture, imitative counterpoint, word-painting, elided cadence.

1965
RHYMING SINGERS
OF THE BAHAMAS
"My Lord Help Me to Pray"
GENRE: Bahamian music

Chapter highlight:
Polyphony

Polyphony, the singing or intoning of many parts, is a worldwide phenomenon. In much African and African-influenced music, polyphony is created as parts overlap.

KEY CONCEPTS
Polyphony, call-and-response, syncretism, polytextuality, intonation.

ca. 1550
TIELMAN SUSATO
Moorish Dance
GENRE: Dance music

Chapter highlight:
Instrumental Music

Dance music is rhythmically clear and consistent to match the repeated steps of the dancers. Pavanes, galliards, allemandes, sarabandes, and gigues are some of the dances that flourished in the Renaissance. Important composers of instrumental music in the Renaissance include Giovanni Gabrieli, William Byrd, and Antonio de Cabezón.

KEY CONCEPTS
Renaissance instruments, dance music, binary form, music publishing in the Renaissance.

1455
Gutenberg Bible, first printed book

1492
Christopher Columbus makes first voyage to New World

1508–1512
Michelangelo paints the ceiling of the Sistine Chapel

1517
Martin Luther's 95 theses begin the Protestant Reformation

1543
Nicholas Copernicus publishes his treatise placing the sun at the center of the solar system

1558–1603
Reign of Elizabeth I of England

1594
William Shakespeare: *Romeo and Juliet*

Historical Events

5

Josquin des Prez
"The Cricket"

Listen to This

Texture

Listen for the polyphony of four distinct voices, all of equal importance. Listen for the difference between those passages in which the voices sing together in the same rhythm and those in which they go their own separate ways.

Word-Music Relationships

Listen for the examples of **word painting:** the long notes on the words "hold a long line" (at 0:08) and the chirping sounds (at 0:14, 0:21, and elsewhere) that imitate the sound of a cricket.

Form

Listen for the contrasting section in the middle (starting at 0:29), when the notes sound longer and more drawn out, and for the return of the opening section toward the end (at 0:55).

Why do composers write songs? Why set poetry to music? The answer, at one level, is quite simple: good music makes the meaning of a text more vivid and memorable. The poem inspires the composer, and the composer's melding of words and music inspires us as listeners. Think how much easier it is to remember verses that have been set to melody than it is to remember a poem all by itself. This was as true in the Renaissance as it is today, for composers throughout history have been drawn to the challenge of setting words to music.

When Josquin sat down to compose "The Cricket" ("El grillo"), he faced the challenge of writing music that would be as humorous as the poem itself. The text praises the singing of crickets over that of birds. It lauds the insect's versatility as a singer: he can sing long notes and stay in one place for long periods of time, unlike birds, who flit from place to place. The cricket can sing drinking songs, and when the weather turns warm in May, he sings of love. Josquin uses catchy, clever rhythms to imitate the sound of the cricket. His melodic lines enhance the spirit of the poem, and his textures bring out the meaning of key words.

Josquin's setting is typical of Renaissance song in general, in that it speaks a musical language that seems contemporary to us even today. Its melodies, rhythms, and textures certainly strike us as more familiar than those of the Middle Ages. Hildegard von Bingen (chapter 1) and Francesco Landini (chapter 3) were equally inspired by the texts they set, yet their musical language is somehow less direct, more hauntingly austere. Medieval and Renaissance musical styles might be said to differ in the way that Old English differs from Modern English. It is a not a matter of one language being better than the other. Medieval and Renaissance song create their own distinct kinds of beauty by using the same basic elements of music in different ways.

Texture: Polyphony in Four Voices

The four voice parts of "The Cricket" correspond to the four registers of the human voice:

- Soprano (highest range)
- Alto (second-highest range)
- Tenor (second-lowest range)
- Bass (lowest range)

In Josquin's setting, these four voices are essentially equal, and they move together in step for most of the work. Only occasionally does Josquin differentiate among the voices rhythmically, and the words we hear at those moments stand out from the rest of the song. The most striking of these moments occur at the words *longo verso* ("long verse") at 0:07–0:13, and at *amore* ("love") at 0:50–0:54, when each voice momentarily goes its own way, setting these key words apart from all others in the text.

Equal-voice texture—polyphony—is the norm for Renaissance music in general, as opposed to monophony (a single melodic line) or homophony (a melodic line accompanied by other voices of lesser importance). Composers took great pride in their skill at **counterpoint**, a system of rules and procedures governing the composition of multiple melodies that are not only satisfying when played alone but that sound good when played together. "Counterpoint" takes its name from the Latin word *contrapunctum*, or "note-against-note" (the Latin word for "note" is *punctum*). Counterpoint is a demanding art and one that aspiring composers still learn today in almost exactly the same manner as in the Renaissance: by writing first one new melody against an existing one, then adding a third, and a fourth, and so on.

A woodcut image of the composer
Lebrecht Music & Arts Photo Library

Medieval and Renaissance scribes often inserted humorous vignettes into otherwise very serious manuscripts. Here, the scribe seems to be commenting on the parallels between human singers and the noises animals make.

MS 127. *Chansonnier Zeghere Van Male*, 1542, f. 4r. Courtesy Mediatheque Municipale de Cambrai

Word-Music Relationships: Music Imitates Nature

When the text speaks of the cricket's ability to "hold a long line" of music (*longo verso*, at 0:07), the top and bottom voices sing very long notes, while the inner voices weave around each other in the middle. Josquin is also playing on a pun in the text here: in Italian, *verso* can mean a line of verse, or it can also mean the noise an animal makes. So what we hear at this point is both a long-held note and the sound of the cricket.

When the text tells us that the cricket also sings about drinking (*dalle beve*, at 0:14), we hear a cricket-like chirping sound a little like the hiccups of someone who has had a bit too much to drink. The music then repeats these same words to a series of rapid-fire notes with all four voices singing together in exactly the same rhythm, repeating each word nonsensically ("Of of drinking drinking cricket cricket sings," at 0:21). Finally, when the cricket sings of love (*amore*, at 0:50), we hear all four voices break into an extended melisma. Here, on this one word, the music is at its most complex and intense, in keeping with the spirit of the text.

Ternary Form

As is almost always the case in vocal music, the form of the text shapes the form of the music. The text of "The Cricket" falls into two broad sections:

1. How the cricket can hold a long note and can sing of drinking;
2. How the cricket is different from birds, who also sing.

Josquin gives distinctive music to each of these two sections (labeled **A** and **B** in the Listening Guide). By repeating the opening section of the text and music (**A**) at the end, however, he creates what is known as **ternary form**, which consists of three parts, **ABA.** Ternary form uses the basic principles of contrast (**B** contrasts with **A**) and return (**A** comes back at the end).

Now listen to this piece again, using the Listening Guide.

Josquin des Prez (ca. 1450–1521)

"MASTER OF THE NOTES"

Josquin was an international celebrity in his time. Even nonmusicians knew who he was: the famed theologian Martin Luther declared that "Josquin is the master of the notes, which must do as he wishes, while other composers must follow what the notes dictate." And music publishers were eager to put Josquin's name on the music they wanted to sell, regardless of whether he had written it or not. Josquin knew his own worth, too. An agent of the Duke of Ferrara, who was seeking to hire a new composer for his court, reported to his master that the two best available composers were Josquin and Heinrich Isaac. "It is true that Josquin composes better," the agent wrote, "but he composes when he wants to, and not when one wants him to, and he is asking 200 ducats in salary while Isaac will come for 120." To the duke's credit, he hired Josquin anyway.

Though Josquin is generally considered the greatest composer of the early Renaissance, much of his life is shrouded in mystery. He was born and died somewhere in an area on the border between what is now France and Belgium, but he spent much of his life working in Italy, including St. Peter's in Rome. Scholars have recently discovered that there were several composers going by the name of "Josquin" in the late fifteenth and early sixteenth centuries, and it may be one of these "other" Josquins who wrote "The Cricket." For the moment though, no one can be absolutely certain.

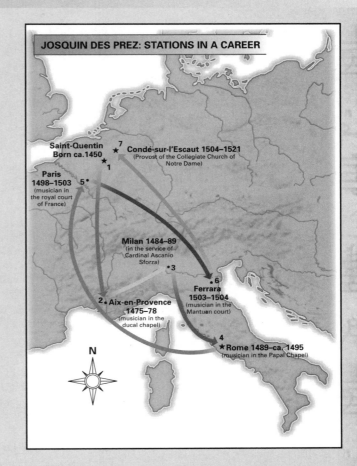

JOSQUIN DES PREZ: STATIONS IN A CAREER

Saint-Quentin Born ca.1450
Condé-sur-l'Escaut 1504–1521
(Provost of the Collegiate Church of Notre Dame)
Paris 1498–1503
(musician in the royal court of France)
Milan 1484–89
(in the service of Cardinal Ascanio Sforza)
Ferrara 1503–1504
(musician in the Mantuan court)
Aix-en-Provence 1475–78
(musician in the ducal chapel)
Rome 1489–ca. 1495
(musician in the Papal Chapel)
N

PLAYLIST: JOSQUIN

Missa Pange Lingua. A setting of the Ordinary of the Mass (those portions said or sung at every Mass, regardless of the occasion). The work takes its name from the medieval plainchant hymn melody that provides the basis for many of Josquin's themes.

Missa La Sol Fa Re Mi. Another setting of the Mass Ordinary, this one based on a series of notes that corresponds to a scale descending from "La" (A) to "Mi" (E). Josquin challenged himself to give variety to such a basic and simple idea repeated over and over.

"Hail Mary . . . Serene Virgin" (*Ave Maria . . . virgo serena*). A motet (sacred song) for four voices, one of Josquin's most famous compositions.

"Virgin Nurse of God, Undefiled" (*Illibata Dei virgo nutrix*). Another motet in praise of the Virgin Mary, for five voices. The first letter of each line spells out "Josquin des Prez."

Josquin des Prez   "The Cricket"

Time	Form (Musical Section)	Original Italian Text	English Translation	Word-Music Relationship	Texture
0:00	A	El grillo è buon cantore Che tienne longo verso.	The cricket is a good singer Who can hold a long line.	Word painting with long notes on *longo verso* ("long line" or "long noise")	Polyphonic (4 equal voices)
0:14		Dalle beve grillo canta El grillo è buon cantore.	Of drinking the cricket sings The cricket is a good singer.	Back-and-forth between upper and lower voices imitates the chirping of the cricket.	
0:29	B	Ma non fa come gli altri uccelli, Come li han cantato un poco, Van' de fatto in altro loco Sempre el grillo sta pur saldo.	But he doesn't do what birds do: After they've sung a bit, They go somewhere else; The cricket always stays put.	Contrasting section, slightly lower in register, slightly darker in sound	
0:43		Quando la maggior è 'l caldo Al'hor canta sol per amore.	And when the weather is hottest He sings solely for love.	Elaborate melismas make the word *amore* ("love") stand out.	
0:55	A	El grillo è buon cantore Che tienne longo verso. Dalle beve grillo canta El grillo è buon cantore.	The cricket is a good singer Who can hold a long line. Of drinking the cricket sings The cricket is a good singer.	Work ends as it began, with text and music repeated, suggesting that the cricket goes on singing just as before.	

Student FAQs

I hear only one melody here, in the top voice. How can there be more than one melody going on at the same time?

For acoustical reasons, our ear tends to be drawn to the highestsounding voice within a group of voices. But if you listen to the lower voices—isolate them, in effect— you will hear three other well-shaped melodic lines as well.

Are the two higher voices here sung by men or women?

Normally, the soprano and alto parts are sung by women, for these ranges lie naturally within the range of the female voice. But in this recording, as in many recent recordings of earlier music (pre-1700), the two upper parts are sung by men, reflecting the performing practice of earlier times. The higher of these—the soprano part—is sung by a man singing *falsetto*, a technique by which the voice bypasses the larynx, which is the part of the throat that otherwise gives men's voices a deeper register. Many male groups or singers still use this technique today (such as the Beach Boys, Marvin Gaye, Coldplay). For more on this style of singing, see chapter 7.

At the very end, it doesn't sound as if the music is quite finished. Why is that?

Like most music written before 1600, the melodic lines are derived from one of the medieval modes—in this case, the mode on D (Dorian). Modal writing of this kind did not call for a work to end on what we might think of today (somewhat anachronistically) as the tonic (see p. 9). So to Josquin's contemporaries, the final cadence of this work would have sounded quite normal and not incomplete at all.

Playing and Singing

Today's songwriters know that any big hit is likely to be performed in many different ways: with words, without words, and arranged for all kinds of instruments and instrumental ensembles. Josquin almost certainly felt the same way. Even though he clearly wrote "The Cricket" with a specific text—and insect—in mind, he knew it would become popular in different arrangements: for four wind instruments, for four stringed instruments, for some combination of winds and strings, or for a solo lute.

Josquin, like almost all Renaissance composers, wrote music in such a way that it could be either sung (with a text) or played (without a text), and played on many different kinds of instruments. Indeed, a great deal of the vocal repertory from this time has come down to us in manuscripts that have no vocal texts at all. We know what words to sing only because the texts have survived in other manuscripts. Renaissance musicians were resourceful, and they used whatever combination of voices or instruments might have been available at any given moment. In the case of "The Cricket," listeners might lose the witty connections between the text and the music (the chirping sounds, for one), but this did not prevent them from enjoying vocal music on instruments, or allowing instruments to fill in one or more of the vocal lines.

In this image, created during Josquin's lifetime, a mixed group of instrumentalists and a vocalist perform a piece that was written as a vocal composition. The figure on the left sings; another, on the right, plays the lute, and in the center, yet another plays the flute. The painting is so clear that we can even recognize the music. Presumably, the lutenist is also singing.

Master of Female Half Lengths (ca. 1490–ca. 1540) "The Concert"/Bridgeman Art Library

 EXPAND YOUR PLAYLIST

The Music of Sounds

All music may be sound, but are all sounds music? There are no easy answers, but sounds from the outside world have found their way into the music of almost every culture, time, and place.

Birds

Clément Janequin's "The Song of the Birds" ("Le chant des oiseaux," early sixteenth century), imitates the songs of thrushes, robins, nightingales, and cuckoos.

The music of the Kaluli of Papua New Guinea is modeled on the sounds of the rainforest, including frogs, insects, and birds. *Voices of the Rainforest: A Day in the Life of the Kaluli People* (Rykodisc 10173).

The French composer Olivier Messiaen incorporated birdsong into many of his works. His "Awakening of the Birds" ("Réveil des oiseaux," 1953), consists almost entirely of imitated bird songs.

Monkeys

The *Cecak* or *Ketjak*, also known as the "Ramayana Monkey Chant," from Bali (Indonesia), features a group of 100 or more men who imitate, through gesture and song, a group of legendary fighting monkeys. *Audio*: Nonesuch H-72028. *Video*: http://www. maniacworld.com/baraka-ramayana-monkey-chant.htm or http://ramayana.magnify.net/item/QPJ1WLXJCJ NMTG3L.

Trains

Artur Honegger named his orchestral work *Pacific 231* (1923) after a type of steam locomotive. The piece builds slowly in momentum before reaching full speed.

Billy Strayhorn's *Take the "A" Train* (1941), made famous by Duke Ellington's big band recording, imitates the driving rhythms of the New York City subway line running from Manhattan to Harlem.

Battle

Clément Janequin's *La bataille* (early sixteenth century) imitates battle noises, trumpet calls, cannon fire, and the cries of the wounded.

Ludwig van Beethoven's *Wellington's Victory* (1813) imitates the firing of cannon, using bass drums.

Pyotr Ilich Tchaikovsky's *1812 Overture* (1882) imitates cannon fire through the use of bass drums. Some orchestras, including the Boston Pops in their outdoor performances on the Fourth of July, use fireworks. Now and then, performances even use the real cannons Tchaikovsky called for in the score.

6

Thomas Weelkes
"Since Robin Hood"

 Listen to This

Texture

Listen to the three distinct voices, each of equal weight. This texture is polyphonic.

Rhythm

Listen for the shift in rhythm in the middle of the piece from duple to triple meter.

Word-Music Relationships

Listen to the descriptive nature of the music with certain words, such as "to skip" and "trip it."

What seems simple on the surface can often be quite intricate. On first listening, Thomas Weelkes's "Since Robin Hood" strikes most people as a fairly straightforward setting of a lightweight and rather odd, almost nonsensical text. But with careful listening, we can begin to hear the many and remarkable ways in which Weelkes has captured the spirit of the text.

"Since Robin Hood" is a **madrigal**, a musical setting of a text in a single strophe (stanza), and the text of this madrigal is a poem about dancing. "Kemp" is the English actor William Kemp, who was a friend of Shakespeare and an original shareholder in London's Globe Theatre. (Among his many roles, Kemp played the role of the nurse in *Romeo and Juliet* in an age when women were not allowed onstage.) What Kemp later called his "Nine-Day Wonder" was a feat of shameless self-promotion: he danced all the way from London to Norwich, a distance of about 140 miles, over a period of nine days. Like any good self-promoter, Kemp wrote a book about his exploits.

The dance that Kemp performed over these nine days was the Morris dance, a traditional English dance of obscure origins whose name is probably a corruption of "Moorish dance." Tielman Susato's *Moorish Dance (La Moresca)* belongs to this same tradition (see Web Bonus Chapter 1). It is a group dance, with stock characters that include a hobby horse (a dancer wearing the costume of a horse's body from his waist down) and Maid Marian (a male dressed in women's clothing). The dancers—all male in Kemp's time—wore small bells on their calves. The group nature of the dance made Kemp's feat all the more unusual, for as the lyrics of the song tell us, he "did dance alone," with the other figures (Robin Hood, Maid Marian, Little John, and the hobby horse) all absent ("forgot").

A famous portrayal of Kemp on his nine-day Morris dance tour, accompanied by a pipe-and-tabor player

© Dorling Kindersley

Texture: Polyphony in Three Voices

The texture is polyphonic throughout, which is typical of the Renaissance madrigal. No one voice predominates, and all three contribute equally to the whole. The three voices move together in more or less the same rhythm, creating a declamatory style of singing. This makes the text easier to understand, for it is as if all the voices are reciting the text together—in song.

The melody in the uppermost voice of Weelkes's setting would have been familiar to Shakespeare's contemporaries, for this was a tune already well known by the end of the sixteenth century and one closely associated with Morris dancing. (It is even called "The Morris Tune" in various sources of the time.) But the lines in the two lower voices have their own distinctive melodic profiles as well.

Poetic Rhythm in Music

To understand the rhythm of the music, we must first consider the rhythm of the poetry. The **meter** of a poem is its basic rhythmic unit. Most metrical poems stick to a single meter from beginning to end. But "Since Robin Hood" is unusual because it keeps shifting from one meter to another.

Read the text out loud and exaggerate the rhythmic patterns of the accented (long) syllables. The pattern that emerges at the beginning is **iambic**: short-LONG, short-LONG, short-LONG, short-LONG, which can be represented by the symbols ˘ (=short) and / (=LONG):

˘　/　˘　/　　˘　　/　˘　/
Since **Rob**in **Hood**, Maid **Mar**ian,

˘　　/　˘　/　　˘　　/
And **Little John** are **gone**,

˘　　/　˘　/　　˘　　/　˘　/
The **hob**by **horse** was **quite** for**got**,

˘　　/　　˘　/　　˘　/
When **Kemp** did **dance a**lone.

But in the second section of the poem, the meter changes. Read this part out loud, again emphasizing the natural stresses within the words:

/ ˘ / ˘ / ˘ / ˘
He did **la**bour **af**ter the **ta**bor.

/ ˘ / ˘ /˘ /
For to **dance** then **in**to **France**.

If you try to read these lines in the iambic meter of the opening (short-LONG), you'll realize at once that it just doesn't work: the accents are all wrong, because these lines are in **trochaic** meter (LONG-short, LONG-short, etc.).

In the third and final section of the poem, the meter becomes quite jumbled, moving briefly back to iambic (short-LONG) for one line:

˘ / ˘ /
In **hope** of **gains**

before shifting to yet another kind of meter, **anapestic** (short-short-LONG):

˘ ˘ / ˘ ˘ /
He did **trip** it on the **toe**,
Diddle **did**dle diddle **doe**.

Now that you've read the text with an eye (and ear) to its meter, listen to how these shifts in the meter of the poetry are reflected in the shifting meters of the music.

1. The opening lines (iambic) are in **duple meter**, and the note lengths are fairly even:

˘ / ˘ / ˘ / ˘ / ˘ / ˘ / ˘ /
Since | **Rob**-in **Hood**, Maid |**Mar**-i-**an**, and | **Lit**-tle **John** are | **gone**
(4) | **1** 2 3 4 |**1** 2 3 4 | **1** 2 3 4 | **1**

With four beats to each musical measure, beats **1** and **3** and especially **1** are the beats that are normally emphasized, and the poetry fits this scheme quite nicely.

2. The second section (trochaic) shifts to **triple meter** to accommodate the new trochaic meter of the poetry (LONG-short):

/ ˘ / ˘ / ˘ / ˘
He did | **la**-bour | **af**- ter the | **ta**- bor
1-2 3 1-2 3 1-2 3 1-2 3

The accented syllables on "1" are longer: they get two beats, whereas the unaccented syllables (or groups of syllables) get only one beat.

3. Even though the text remains in trochaic meter ("He took pains to skip it . . ."), Weelkes returns to duple meter, like at the beginning. But here, the notes are **syncopated**— that is, they run against the regular pulse of the musical meter, with accents on beats other than "1" and "3." This allows Weelkes to present the words "to skip" in almost graphic fashion, with the voices tossing these two words back and forth among themselves. In this way, we lose any strong sense of metrical pulse, just at that moment when the text talks about skipping.

Word Painting in the Renaissance Madrigal

As noted previously, certain words ("to skip," "did trip it") are set quite graphically, instances of **word painting**. These are among the few passages in the entire madrigal in which the voices are not singing in rhythm together. Instead of declaiming these words in a clear fashion, the voices in effect "skip" ahead of themselves. Word painting is a device that is well suited to the Renaissance madrigal. Composers used whatever musical elements they could to enhance the meaning and pleasure of the poetry, and word painting is so common in this repertory that it is sometimes called a *madrigalism*.

Now listen to this piece again, using the Listening Guide.

Thomas Weelkes (ca. 1575–1623)

A SHAKESPEAREAN COMPOSER

Weelkes belonged to that generation of English composers who lived during the age of Shakespeare, a period of great cultural achievements under the reigns of Elizabeth I and James I. Like Shakespeare, Weelkes and his contemporaries were fascinated by Italian poetry and music (many of Shakespeare's plays, it should be remembered, take place in Italy). The Italian madrigal came to England toward the end of the sixteenth century, and Weelkes lost no time imitating these Italian models. In an era of great poets and playwrights—Shakespeare, Ben Jonson, Christopher Marlowe, and Philip Sydney, among others—English composers had no difficulty finding new texts to set to music.

Like most composers of his day, Weelkes was a professional musician. He received a Bachelor of Music degree from New College, Oxford, served as organist at Chichester Cathedral, and wrote a great deal of sacred music in addition to madrigals. His career ended badly, however, when he was dismissed from his position for drunkenness and blasphemy. No likeness of him survives.

PLAYLIST: THE ENGLISH MADRIGAL

William Byrd, "This Sweet and Merry Month of May"

John Farmer, "Fair Phyllis I Saw Sitting All Alone"

Orlando Gibbons, "The Silver Swan"

Thomas Morley, "Now Is the Month of Maying"

Thomas Weelkes, "As Vesta Was from Latmos Hill Descending"; "Hark, All Ye Lovely Saints"

John Wilbye, "Weep, Weep, Mine Eyes"

Listening Guide

Thomas Weelkes   "Since Robin Hood"

Time	Text	Poetic Meter	Musical Meter	Word-Music Relationships	Texture
0:00 (repeats at 0:09)	Since Robin Hood, Maid Marian, And Little John are gone, The hobby horse was quite forgot, When Kemp did dance alone.	Iambic (short-LONG)	Duple (**1**-2-3-4)		Polyphonic (three equal voices)
0:18 (repeats at 0:40)	He did labour after the tabor. For to dance then into France.	Trochaic (LONG-short)	Triple (**1**-2-3)	Music changes meter when the text changes meter, following— "laboring after"—the rhythm of the imaginary drum to which Kemp is dancing	
0:27 (repeats at 0:49)	He took pains to skip it	Trochaic (LONG-short)	Duple (with syncopation, that is, accents off the normally accented beats)	Syncopation reflects "skipping"	
0:31 (repeats at 0:53)	In hope of gains.	Iambic (short-LONG)	Duple (with syncopation, that is, accents off the normally accented beats)	Syncopation (in a different meter now) reflects striving, the "hope of gains"	
0:34 (repeats at 0:56)	He did trip it on the toe, Diddle diddle diddle doe.	Anapestic (short-short-LONG)	Duple (no syncopation)	"Did trip it on the toe" is an old-fashioned way of saying "danced elegantly," and a steady beat returns here, without syncopation	

Student FAQs

I can't hear the shift in meters in the music. What should I do?

Try beating time, as if you were playing a drum to back up the singers. The opening section is fairly regular (1-2, 1-2, 1-2, etc.). When you get to the shift at 0:18, shift to three beats, with the heavy beat on "1" (**1**-2-3, **1**-2-3, **1**-2-3, etc.). At 0:27, shift back to **1**-2, **1**-2, etc. This physical pattern may help you hear the shifting meters.

Is that a man or a woman singing the highest voice?

As in the recording of Josquin's "The Cricket," this is a man singing *falsetto*, a technique by which a singer bypasses the voice box (larynx), thereby creating a sound in the very high range. In the 1960s, the Beach Boys became famous for this kind of singing.

Musicians as Spies

Being a musician and a spy might seem an odd combination, but in Elizabethan England at the end of the sixteenth century, playing an instrument provided the perfect cover for gathering intelligence. Over the course of the sixteenth century, England had gone back and forth between Protestant monarchs (Henry VIII) and Catholic monarchs (Mary I). Throughout the long reign of Elizabeth I (1558–1603), a Protestant, England was awash in rumors and actual plots to overthrow the monarchy and invade the country. As in today's global struggles, good intelligence about the intentions and resources of one's enemies carried a very high value. A coded message, intercepted by a spy, led to the arrest and eventual execution of Mary, Queen of Scots, in 1587.

Musicians were in an ideal position to carry secret messages between households, to eavesdrop on conversations, and to observe the comings and goings of the great households in which they were engaged. And good musicians were always in demand: no large-scale entertainment of the landed gentry was complete without dancing, and dancing required musicians, who were able to pass easily between the servants (who always knew about comings and goings) downstairs and the lords and ladies upstairs. Musicians at the royal court were routinely loaned out to loyal supporters of the queen, with the understanding that these employees would also report on any events or rumors they had witnessed; they presumably received an extra tip for particularly useful information. For an underpaid musician, then, spying provided a good source of supplementary income.

A group of musicians—or perhaps musician-spies?—playing at a masked ball in Elizabethan England

National Portrait Gallery, London

 EXPAND YOUR PLAYLIST

The Italian Madrigal

The English madrigal, which blossomed at the end of the sixteenth century, was directly indebted to the Italian madrigal, which had been flourishing for more than half a century earlier. Indeed, the earliest English-language madrigals were direct translations from the Italian. Here are some of the composers that were admired (and imitated) by the English:

Jacob Arcadelt (ca. 1505–68). "The White and Gentle Swan" ("Il bianco e dolce cigno"). Judging from the number of published editions, this was one of the most popular of all Italian madrigals in the sixteenth century. The text is about the swan, a bird who is mute throughout its life, yet according to legend sings just before dying.

Cipriano de Rore (1516–65). "Once Again in Parting" ("Ancor che col partire"). A four-voice madrigal about the pain of parting lovers, a favorite subject of Renaissance madrigalists.

Luzzascho Luzzaschi (1545–1607). "I Love You, My Life" ("T'amo mia vita"). This madrigal, for three women's voices, was written for the celebrated Consort of Ladies ("Concerto delle donne"), a group of extraordinarily talented women musicians at the court of Ferrara, in northern Italy.

Lucca Marenzio (1553 or 1554 to 1599). "Alone and Pensive" ("Solo e pensoso"). For five voices, with lyrics by the fourteenth-century poet Petrarch, this madrigal expresses loneliness and despair.

Claudio Monteverdi (1567–1643). "I Love You, My Life" ("T'amo mia vita"). A setting of the same text as Luzzaschi's earlier madrigal, but in the new style of the Baroque (see Part 3 of this book), with instrumental accompaniment an essential element of this five-voice work.

7

William Byrd
"Sing Joyfully"

Listen to This

Texture

Try to hear the six distinct voices, all of equal weight. Listen also for passages in which one voice presents a musical idea that the other voices then imitate in quick succession.

Form

Notice how each new section of the text receives its own new musical idea.

Word-Music Relationships

Listen to how Byrd captures in music the feeling of the text's key words, such as "joyfully" and "sing loud." Note the word painting on certain phrases, such as "Blow the trumpet," which imitates the sound of the trumpet.

Words and music seem made for each other, but their marriage is not always a happy one. What creates verbal clarity—monophonic texture and syllabic text setting—does not always coincide with what creates musical beauty. Long, lyrical melodies, melismatic text setting, and rich polyphonic textures, although musically satisfying, run the risk of obscuring the text to be sung.

This potential problem had grown particularly acute by the end of the Renaissance, when compositions for six voices, like William Byrd's "Sing Joyfully," had become the norm. The musical effect of this full-bodied sound can be irresistible. Reverberating off the high ceilings and stone walls of the large churches and cathedrals for which this work was written, Byrd's music is rich and luxuriant. Even if we did not understand the words at all, the music alone is capable of moving us, of giving us a heightened sense of spirituality. Yet Byrd and other composers of his time were deeply committed to setting music in a manner that projected the words clearly. His challenge was to do this in a way that also exploited the potentials of six-part polyphony.

Byrd's "Sing Joyfully" takes as its text the first four verses of Psalm 81. He called his setting an **anthem**, the English equivalent of what composers writing for the Roman Catholic Church called a **motet**, a sacred choral work (see Expand Your Playlist). It is an example of **a cappella choral music**: choral music because there is more than one singer to a part, and a cappella (Italian for "in the church style") because it is meant to be sung without instrumental accompaniment of any kind.

Texture: Polyphony in Six Voices

One of the ways in which Byrd projected the text to be sung even while writing for six independent parts was to use a technique known as **imitative counterpoint**. Counterpoint, as noted before, is basic to all polyphony, for it is a style of writing in which all voices are of equal importance. Imitative counterpoint is a particular type of counterpoint in which one voice, entirely by itself for a short time, introduces each new theme and is answered (imitated) by other voices that enter in succession shortly afterward, even as the first voice continues to sing. Imitative counterpoint, or simply **imitation**, as it is often called, has been of great importance for composers of all eras from the Renaissance onward.

The composer Palestrina (right) presents his First Book of Masses to Pope Julius III (1554). Palestrina lived at approximately the same time as Byrd, in what is Italy today (see Expand Your Playlist).

At the very beginning of this work, only four voices enter in imitation, and two of them (Soprano 1 and Alto 2) enter together (at 0:05). But by the time even only four voices have entered (0:10), we would be hard put to say exactly what words they are singing, for at no given point are they all singing the same word, at least not here in the opening. At the point marked with an asterisk in the example above, for example, one of the voices is singing the word "God," another the "un-" syllable of the word "unto," and the third the"-to" syllable in "unto." If this were three or four different people all talking at the same time, it would be a complete jumble. Fortunately, each voice is differentiated by its range, so they do stand out from one another, even when they are singing together. And because the first voice began by itself, we are able to hear this first full statement of the opening text as a unit; when we hear the other voices enter with the same words, we know that they are singing the same text even if we cannot make out every word in every voice at all times. Finally, like other composers of his era, Byrd liberally repeats the text in all the parts several times before moving on, to help impress upon us the words being sung.

Sectional Form

The form of the music follows the form of the text. Each new line of the text receives its own melodic idea, which is shared to at least some extent by all the voices. Each line of text, in turn, ends with a cadence, marking the end of a section. Some of the cadences are **elided**—that is, a new line of text and music begins before the previous one has come to a complete stop (as between lines 1 and 2)—while other cadences bring the music to a full (if brief) stop (as at the end of line 6).

Word-Music Relationships: The Music Paints the Words

Byrd sets the opening phrase—"Sing joyfully"—to a lively, upward-moving musical motive. And at "Blow the trumpet" (1:06), we hear a clear instance of word painting, with the voices imitating the kind of fanfare-like figure associated with that instrument, complete with echoes. A more subtle instance of word painting can be found toward the end (1:53) on the words "For this is a statute for Israel." After a brief pause, all the voices sing the words "For this" in exactly the same rhythm, which creates the kind of declamatory sound fitting the public proclamation of a law or statute.

Now listen to this piece again, using the Listening Guide.

MUSIC IN PERFORMANCE

The Sound of the All-Male Choir

With few exceptions, women were not permitted to sing in church choirs until well into the eighteenth century, and in some locales even into the nineteenth. It was feared that women might create a distraction; many choruses, moreover, used students from a church or cathedral school, and the pupils at such schools were almost invariably boys. In any event, the sound of an all-male chorus, with boys singing the soprano and alto lines and men singing the tenor and bass lines, became a sound ideal that has persisted in some churches down to the present day. Listen in particular for the different quality of the upper voices.

There are some excellent albums offering examples of the all-male chorus. One that features Byrd's "Sing Joyfully" is *An English Chorister's Songbook,* by the Salisbury Cathedral Choir (Metronome MET 1016). Other all-male choirs that have recorded extensively include the Choir of King's College (Cambridge), Christ Church Cathedral Choir (Oxford), and New College Choir (Oxford).

The Choir of New College, Oxford. This ensemble of 16 men and 12 boys has provided music for daily services since the 14th century.

Thomas Photos, Oxford. Courtesy New College Choir

Listening Guide

CD I · Track 25
GO TO PEARSON mymusiclab for the Automated Listening Guide

William Byrd "Sing Joyfully"

Time	Text	Form	Texture	Word-Music Relationships
0:00	1. Sing joyfully unto God our strength,	Musical idea **A**.	Imitation among the voices	Lively, upward-moving motif for "joyfully"
0:22	2. Sing loud unto the God of Jacob.	Musical idea **B**. Elided cadence: **B** music begins before **A** music ends		Long notes on "Sing loud"
0:37	3. Take the song and bring forth the timbrel,*	Musical idea **C**.	Imitation again	
0:51	4. The pleasant harp and viol.*	Musical idea **D**.		Lyrical, flowing melody matches the sound of these two soft instruments
1:06	5. Blow the trumpet in the new moon,	Musical idea **E**.		Fanfare-like theme on the word "trumpet"
1:26	6. Ev'n in the time appointed, and at our feast day,	Musical idea **F**. Section ends with a strong cadence.		
1:52	7. For this is a statute for Israel,	Musical idea **G**.		All voices sing in the same rhythm on the words "For this," as suits a public proclamation.
2:03	8. And a law of the God of Jacob.	Musical idea **H**. Strongest cadence at the very end of the work.		

*A timbrel could mean either a small drum or a tambourine. A viol is a bowed string instrument.

Student FAQs

I still can't understand the words. Is that a problem?

Many listeners in Byrd's time complained about the same thing—not just for his music, but for a great many works of polyphony. Even with imitative counterpoint and the exposed declamation of certain passages, the words do tend to get lost at points. This is one of the issues that composers of the early Baroque era were keen to address (see chapters 9 and 10).

Are those boys' voices in the upper range?

No, those are women singing in a style meant to imitate boys' voices, which is what choirs in Byrd's time would have used. The sopranos and altos in this particular recording are singing with very little vibrato (vibration) in their voices, which creates a sound quality similar to that produced by boys. For an illustration of what an all-male choir sounds like, see "Music in Performance."

William Byrd (1542–1623)

A CATHOLIC COMPOSER AT A PROTESTANT COURT

As a Roman Catholic in England, William Byrd had to negotiate his way carefully through the intrigues in and around the court of the Protestant queen, Elizabeth I. This was the same queen, after all, who had ordered the execution of her Catholic cousin, Mary Queen of Scots, in 1587. Byrd was harassed at various times because of his faith: authorities searched his house on at least one occasion and kept him under varying degrees of surveillance for years on the suspicion that he was harboring "papists"—the catch-all term of the day for Catholics disloyal to the Crown. Byrd's talent as a composer seems to have provided him sufficient protection from serious persecution, however. He even managed to secure a monopoly on the printing of music in England for a short time. The fact that he also wrote large quantities of music to be performed in Anglican (Protestant) services—including the anthem "Sing Joyfully"—certainly helped Byrd avoid the fate of many other Catholics in Protestant England.

Widely regarded as the greatest English composer of the Renaissance, Byrd was also the most important English music publisher of his time.

Abigail Lebrecht/Lebrecht Music & Arts Photo Library

Queen Elizabeth I being carried through the streets of London by her courtiers.

PLAYLIST: BYRD

Mass for Four Voices. A setting of the Mass Ordinary, in Latin.

O Lord, Make Thy Servant Elizabeth. A motet for the Anglican service of worship, which included a prayer for the monarch.

Sadness and Anxiety (*Tristitia et anxietas*). A motet with powerful settings of its key words.

"This Sweet and Merry Month of May." One of Byrd's many madrigals, a secular song (see chapter 6).

THE COMPOSER SPEAKS

Eight Reasons for Learning How to Sing

In his *Psalmes, Sonets, & Songs* of 1588, the English composer William Byrd offered eight reasons why people should learn how to sing. Byrd was not completely objective on the matter—if more people learned to sing, more would buy his published music—but his reasons nevertheless resonate with what many others of the time said about the value of making music.

Reasons briefly set downe by th'auctor, to perswade every one to learne to sing.

1. *First it is a Knowledge easely taught, and quickly learned where there is a good Master, and an apt Scoller.*
2. *The exercise of singing is delightfull to Nature & good to preserve the health of Man.*
3. *It doth strengthen all the parts of the brest, & doth open the pipes.*
4. *It is a singular good remedie for a stuttering & stammering in the speech.*
5. *It is the best meanes to procure a perfect pronunciation & to make a good Orator.*
6. *It is the onely way to know where Nature hath bestowed the benefit of a good voyce: which gift is so rare, as there is not one among a thousand, that hath it: and in many, that excellent gift is lost, because they want Art to expresse Nature.*
7. *There is not any Musicke of Instruments whatsoever, comparable to that which is made of the voyces of Men, where the voyces are good, and the same well sorted and ordered.*
8. *The better the voyce is, the meeter it is to honour and serve God therewith: and the voyce of man is chiefly to be imployed to that ende.*

Omnis spiritus laudet Dominum ["Let every spirit praise the Lord"*]*

   Since singing is so good a thing,

   I wish all men would learne to sing.

EXPAND YOUR PLAYLIST

Sacred Music of the Renaissance

In an age of spiritual strife, Catholics and Protestants alike recognized the power of music to sway the hearts and minds of the faithful. The intense spirituality of the age gave rise to some of the most moving sacred music ever written. While the Roman Catholic Church retained a liturgy entirely in Latin, Protestant denominations called for services to be conducted primarily in their native language of English.

England
Thomas Tallis (ca. 1505–1585). "I Have Never Put My Hope in Any Other but You" ("Spem in alium"). This sacred Latin motet, for 40 different voices (eight choirs, each with five voices), is one of the monumental works of Renaissance vocal music.

Tallis. "Verily I Say Unto You." A much more modest anthem, for four voices, written for a typical Anglican church choir.

Germany
Martin Luther (1483–1546). "A Mighty Fortress Is Our God" ("Ein' feste Burg ist unser Gott"). Luther wrote both the words and music of what would come to be known as the anthem of the Protestant Reformation.

Johann Walter (1496–1570). "A Mighty Fortress Is Our God" ("Ein' feste Burg ist unser Gott"). One of many elaborate settings of Luther's hymn. Walter, like many other Protestant composers, used this well-known melody as a basis for a more extended work.

Italy
Giovanni Pierluigi da Palestrina (1525 or 1526 to 1594). *Mass in Honor of Pope Marcellus* (*Missa Papae Marcelli*) and *Missa brevis*. Palestrina was the leading composer of sacred music in Italy in the sixteenth century, and church leaders applauded his music for the clarity of its text settings.

Spain
Tomás Luis de Victoria (ca. 1549–1611). "O Great Mystery" ("O magnum mysterium"). A sacred motet for six voices, written for services on Easter Monday by the greatest Spanish composer of the Renaissance.

8

MORES ISLAND

THE BAHAMAS

•Nassau

Rhyming Singers of the Bahamas
"My Lord Help Me to Pray"

Listen to This

Texture

Identify the lead part and the way the other parts respond to it. How many voices are there? In what ways do they seem dependent on each other, and in what ways independent?

Melody

Try to determine the distinctive upward, downward, or up-and-down motion of each voice.

Word-Music Relationships

Which words remain constant? Notice how the singers change and add words while maintaining the basic textual framework.

Form

Listen for the call (lead vocalist) and response (chorus) form.

Polyphony, the singing or intoning of many parts, is a worldwide phenomenon. In the Bahamas, sometime during the nineteenth century, sponge fishermen passing time on their boats developed a genre known as *rhyme singing*. Rhyme songs, based on gospel texts, are sung in three parts, each with different words. In this way, rhyme songs resemble the polytextual works that originated in the thirteenth century in Paris, at the Cathedral of Notre Dame (see Expand Your Playlist, chapter 3).

Sponging was done in shallow water off the west coast of Andros Island. The men sang on their boats on Sunday nights and when they brought their sponges to Nassau. The tradition may be almost gone and in need of revival among younger generations. "My Lord Help Me to Pray" is performed by Bruce Green (lead singer, or **rhyme**), his cousin Clifton Green (bass), and his friend Tweedie Gibson (treble). The men are from Mores Island, Bahamas, and this example was recorded in 1965.

Texture: Call-and-Response Polyphony

At the beginning of "My Lord Help Me to Pray," it is easy to hear the alternation between the rhyme singer and the other two parts (treble and bass), which function together. This alternation is known as **call-and-response:** the lead singer calls and the other parts respond. As the rhyme song progresses, the calls and responses overlap to an increasing degree, creating a thick polyphonic texture.

Call-and-response and the overlap of parts are important structural elements of African music, as well as of African-derived music in the Americas. Rhyme singing is an African American **syncretism,** which means that it combines different forms of belief and practice. The songs are mostly Christian spirituals, but they are mixed with local Bahamian cosmology: the rhyme part is associated with the wind, the treble part with the sky, and the bass part with the earth. In the same way, rhyme singing combines Christian gospel texts with African call-and-response.

CULTURAL CONTEXT

Bob Marley and the Birth of Reggae

Caribbean music is as rich and varied as the many islands that dot the ocean from Cuba and Haiti to Barbados and Aruba. Over the past few decades, American popular styles—particularly rock and roll—have been heard throughout the Caribbean thanks to radio stations and recordings reaching the islands. Local styles have evolved that take elements of American pop and wed them with local rhythms and concerns. One of the most popular of the styles to emerge in this cultural melting pot has been reggae, and its greatest star was Bob Marley (1945–81).

Reggae is closely associated with the Rastafarian religion. Marley was a Rasta and practiced its beliefs. The Rastafarians combine elements of Western and African religious beliefs and venerate as their leader Haile Selassie I, who led Ethiopia from the 1930s through the mid-1970s. Its emphasis on black liberation, culture, and artistic expression had strong appeal in Jamaica, the impoverished nation where Marley lived and worked.

Bob Marley was a performer, composer, and political activist, and he embodied for many the best of reggae music. Marley and his group, the Wailers, set the basic style of reggae, with its loping rhythm and topical lyrics. Among Marley's best-known songs are "I Shot the Sheriff" (popularized in a cover by Eric Clapton), "One Love" (used as a theme song on Jamaican tourism commercials), "No Woman, No Cry," and "Jammin'."

Marley died of skin cancer in 1981; however, his recordings and message continue to resonate in world popular music today.

Bob Marley, songwriter, performer, and political activist, who popularized reggae music around the world in the mid-1970s

Intoning the Melody

What we may hear as singing in "My Lord Help Me to Pray," Bahamian culture actually considers "intoning," referring more specifically to the act of "saying words in tones." While those outside Bahamian culture have come to call these pieces "songs," Bahamians call them "rhymes." Thus, the melodic lines sung by each of the three singers are called **intonations**.

Each line has its own intonation model:

- **Rhyme line.** Varied and often improvised, but always descending in motion. Each phrase ends on its lowest tone.

- **Treble line.** Consists of two halves, *a* and *b*. The *a* ascends and pauses on the highest tone of the phrase, sounding like an unresolved question. The *b* descends and resolves on the lowest tone of the phrase, giving finality.

- **Bass line.** Varied slightly, but primarily two essential tones that provide the basic harmonic support. At times, the bass line occurs under the rhyme line as additional support.

Here is a graphic representation of each:

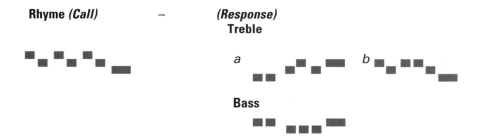

Rhyme *(Call)* – *(Response)*
Treble

a *b*

Bass

Word-Music Relationships

The actual rhyming occurs in the couplets (pairs of metered lines) intoned by the rhyme part. After a spoken introduction of the title, the first couplet begins:

Oh Lord, what a faithful soul
(My Lord, help me to pray)
Oh Lord, what a faithful soul
(My Lord, help me to pray)

Subsequent couplets use different text for each line, but always with "My Lord, help me to pray" as the response.

Later, at 0:43, the rhyme part breaks the couplet pattern and sings an embellished version of "The Lord's Prayer" ("Our Father, who art in heaven, hallowed be Thy name . . ."). The other voices likewise embellish their parts with added words. Listen particularly at 0:31 and at 0:56, where the bass begins to improvise words around his part. The treble continues to sing the response, less altered. By the song's end, the parts have become very polyphonically and textually independent and complex.

Now listen to this piece again, following the Listening Guide.

Rhyming Singers of the Bahamas "My Lord Help Me to Pray"

Time	Form	Texture	Melody
0:01	Introduction	Spoken	Introduction
0:05	Call and response	Responsorial. The treble and bass are in harmony.	Phrase 1 by rhyme singer, phrase 2 by his partners; pause on highest note Phrase 3 by the rhyme singer, phrase 4 by his partners, treble resolving on its lowest tone
0:31	Metered song set by the rhythm of the treble and bass. Overlapping call and response.	Polyphonic—the call and response overlap to create a thick texture.	The couplet rhyme phrases continue to alternate with the treble and bass phrases to construct complete melodies.
0:43		Polyphonic overlapping maintains the sense of thick texture.	"The Lord's Prayer" melodically embellished.
0:56		Polyphonic overlapping maintains the sense of thick texture.	The bass improvises as the treble stabilizes.

Word-Music Relationships

A singer states the title.

The first called rhyme, "Oh Lord what a faithful soul," followed by the response, "My Lord help me to pray."

Followed by different rhymes in call and response with the treble and bass.

Rhyming becomes improvised words. The treble adds words.

The bass improvises new words and rhythms.

The rhyme singer improvises words and rhythms around the text of "The Lord's Prayer."

The rhyme singer improvises rhymes until the end.

The bass improvises more words.

Why are many work songs set in call-and-response style?

Call-and-response is one way of structuring a large group of people to work together. The rhythm of the song and the repeated structure help facilitate finishing a heavy job, such as loading cartons onto a ship, laying railroad track, or lifting heavy nets. The "call" by the leader usually coincides with the first part of a movement (such as the lifting of hammers to lay railroad track) and the "response" with its culmination (the banging of the hammer down onto the spike).

Is rap related to Bahamian rhyme songs?

Rhyming or intoning is found in many African-influenced cultures around the world. Rap has many roots, including the African American practice of the "dozens" (in which rhymed insults are traded between two or more people) and the practice of mobile Jamaican deejays who traveled in sound trucks, setting up impromptu dances in public spaces, using rhymed introductions to attract a crowd.

Is call-and-response heard in other religious song traditions?

Call-and-response is quite common in religious singing, and there are many examples of it found throughout the world. "Lining out" a hymn in American shape note singing is one form of call-and-response: a leader sings a line, and then the congregation repeats it. This is a way of learning the song, and eventually the leader may just sing a guiding word or two—between the actual lines of the hymn—to remind the congregation of what is coming next.

Music of the Caribbean

Music of the Caribbean
Caribbean Party. *Putamayo 132.*
A good, short collection of representative dance recordings from throughout the Caribbean.

Jamaica
Bongo, Backra & Coolie. *Jamaican Roots, Vol. 1,* Folkways 4231.
Bongo, Backra & Coolie. *Jamaican Roots, Vol. 2,* Folkways 4232.
Roots music from various different Jamaican cultural groups recorded by Kenneth Bilby in the early 1970s.

Reggae
Bob Marley:
Natty Dread, Tuff Gong 422-846204-2.
Considered by many to be Marley's finest studio album.

Babylon by Bus, Tuff Gong 422-846197-2.
Influential live album recorded during Marley's European tour in 1978.

Bahamas
The Real Bahamas, Vols. 1 and 2, Nonesuch Explorer 72013 and 72078.
Recordings of various performers, including legendary guitarist Joseph Spence, made in 1965.

Calypso
Lord Invader. *Calypsos in New York,* Smithsonian Folkways 40454.
Calypso was very popular in the 1950s in New York, and many island musicians made their home there working at local clubs. This gathers recordings of Lord Invader, one of Calypso's major stars, made from the 1940s through the 1950s.

PART 2 Summary

	Middle Ages	Renaissance
Texture	Monophonic and polyphonic	Polyphonic, including imitative counterpoint
Melody	Flowing, largely conjunct, divided into sections by cadences; melodies based on scales of the medieval modes	Flowing, but with greater use of disjunct motion; divided into sections by cadences; melodies based on scales of the medieval modes
Rhythm	Free (plainchant) and metrically structured	Relatively smooth and flowing rhythms within a metrically structured framework
Timbre	No sharp distinction between instrumental and vocal music	No sharp distinction between instrumental and vocal music; a growing number and variety of instruments
Harmony	A byproduct of counterpoint	A byproduct of counterpoint
Form	Based on repetition, variation, and contrast	Based on repetition, variation, and contrast; primarily sectional; binary form for dance music
Word-music relationships	Syllabic settings to project texts clearly; melismatic settings to emphasize key words	Limited use of word painting

IN REVIEW: Renaissance Style

Polyphonic texture. Although monophonic plainchant continued to be used in sacred services, new music is almost entirely polyphonic. Imitative counterpoint becomes increasingly important (Byrd). Four-voice texture is the norm at the beginning of the Renaissance (Josquin); six-voice texture is the norm by the end (Byrd).

- Josquin, "The Cricket" (Chapter 5)
- Weelkes, "Since Robin Hood" (Chapter 6)
- Byrd, "Sing Joyfully" (Chapter 7)
- Rhyming Singers of the Bahamas, "My Lord Help Me to Pray" (Chapter 8)
- Susato, *Moorish Dance* (Web Bonus Chapter 1)

Melody. Greater use of disjunct motion; melodies still based on medieval modes.

- Josquin, "The Cricket" (Chapter 5)
- Weelkes, "Since Robin Hood" (Chapter 6)
- Byrd, "Sing Joyfully" (Chapter 7)
- Susato, *Moorish Dance* (Web Bonus Chapter 1)

Rhythm. Metrical structure provides a framework for rhythms that are usually fluid (Josquin, Weelkes, Byrd), though in the case of dance music these rhythms are more repetitive (Susato).

- Josquin, "The Cricket" (Chapter 5)
- Weelkes, "Since Robin Hood" (Chapter 6)
- Byrd, "Sing Joyfully" (Chapter 7)
- Susato, *Moorish Dance* (Web Bonus Chapter 1)

Word painting. Setting specific words to music that imitates the meaning of those words.

- Josquin, "The Cricket" (Chapter 5)
- Byrd, "Sing Joyfully" (Chapter 7)

Binary Form. The most common form for dance movements, consisting of two sections, each repeated in performance.

- Susato, *Moorish Dance* (Web Bonus Chapter 1)

PART 3 The Baroque Era

The Baroque era in music spans a period between roughly 1600 and 1750. The name was first applied to this era long after it was over by historians who wanted to characterize the period between the Renaissance and the Classical Era. By using the term "baroque," historians were calling attention to the extravagant and even bizarre qualities of the music. And indeed, harmonies, textures, and forms tend to be more free and unpredictable in Baroque music than in the music of the Renaissance. The standard texture of polyphony now made room for homophony as well, in which one voice was clearly more important than the others. Putting one voice in the musical foreground meant that a solo singer could portray onstage the thoughts and actions of a single dramatic character. The new use of homophony beginning around 1600 thus made possible the emergence of opera. Composers extended the expressive possibilities of solo singing into sacred music as well, creating the genre of the oratorio, which was nothing less than an unstaged opera on a sacred topic. The new texture of homophony also made possible the instrumental genre of the concerto, in which a soloist or small group of soloists could stand out against the backdrop of a larger ensemble. Singers and instrumentalists alike began to display their virtuosity with pride, improvising and embellishing their parts as never before, always with exuberance and often quite elaborately.

The Baroque era was a period of energy and motion, of ornamentation and extremes. New contrasts between light and dark appeared in painting; similarly, musical compositions exhibited bold contrasts in sounds, between high and low, soft and loud. Painting and sculpture gained a new sense of motion; music, likewise, propelled itself forward by the continuous unfolding of small groupings of notes. Architecture was highly ornate; musical lines, too, were decorated by ornamental flourishes and trills (notes next to each other that are played in alternation very rapidly). In all the arts, the

◄ *A Musical Interlude,* by the Dutch painter Jan Verkolje (ca. 1674). Like a work of Baroque music, this painting uses a strong sense of movement to depict a single "affect," or emotion. The gentleman has turned, in a sudden moment of passion, and grasped the hand of his musical partner, a woman playing a viol.
Private Collection/Photo © Christie's Images/The Bridgeman Art Library

expression of one particular emotion, known as an *affect,* became all-important. Baroque composers and performers were committed to representing the passions through music. These passions are not to be understood as personal self-expression, though. Like good actors, Baroque musicians tried to move their audiences by the artful imitation of emotion.

Projecting Cultural Power Through Music

One summer night in 1717, a festive collection of barges floated down the Thames River. Grand orchestral sounds filled the air: brass, strings, and wind instruments, playing music majestic enough for a king but rhythmic enough to suggest the spirit of a dance. The king on board was an absolute monarch, a ruler who believed in his divine right to govern and in the totality of his power. He was King George I of Britain, and he wanted the world to know it. For his party on the Thames, he hired the finest musicians to play and the most accomplished composer to write and conduct. The composer was George Frideric Handel, and the work he composed was called, appropriately, *Water Music.* One contemporary newspaper reported that the king was so pleased with Handel's music that he had it repeated three times. Another account tells us that "the number of additional boats filled with people desirous of hearing was beyond counting," and that the party did not end until 4:30 in the morning.

▲ Louis XIV styled himself as "The Sun King," the royal center of the solar system. He even danced the part in the "Ballet of the Night," performed at his court in 1653. He spent lavish amounts of the state's money on the creation of new operas and ballets.
Lebrecht Music & Arts Photo Library

▼ Louis XIV's palace at Versailles, west of Paris, depicted in 1722 by Jean-Baptiste Martin. The grounds included a magnificent opera house.
Topham/The Image Works

During the Baroque era, a nation's splendor was measured in cultural terms as well as political and economic terms. Rulers vied with one another for the best court poets, the best court composers, the best court musicians. Art was an important means of projecting power and authority. Across the English Channel from George I, Louis XIV, who ruled France from 1643 until his death in 1715, also insisted on the divine right of kings and the absolute nature of his power. Using state funds, he built an enormous palace at Versailles and ruled with single-handed authority. "I am the state," he is alleged to have declared. Louis XIV spared no expense on the arts and was particularly passionate about music and dance, sponsoring such composers as Jean-Baptiste Lully, Antonia Bembo, and Elisabeth Jacquet de la Guerre.

The Splendor of the Church

The arts served also to project the power of the church, and the same theatricality and intense artistic expression designed to arouse earthly passions could awaken passion for religious subjects as well. Churches spent large sums of money on lavish decoration that would both convey the church's authority and inspire religious fervor. Filling these brilliant interiors was the sound of the Baroque organ, an instrument whose powerful resonance and striking variety of timbre was unsurpassed in creating awe. Churches invested small fortunes in their organs, and it was in the Baroque era that organ building enjoyed its golden age. The renowned organist Johann Sebastian Bach, whose Fugue in G Minor we will hear, made frequent trips to towns and cities around central Germany to test the craftsmanship of newly installed instruments.

Music also served as an important means of conveying the teachings of the church, and sacred music could be every bit as elaborate as sacred architecture. The first movement of J. S. Bach's Cantata no. 140 ("Awake, A Voice Calls to Us") is based on a relatively simple and well-known hymn tune, but Bach constructed an intricate and extended structure around it, even while leaving the melody itself

▲ The organ loft of the 18th-century Augustinian Monastery church in Herzogenburg, Austria. Scarcely a square inch of surface is left unadorned. In a similar manner, Baroque musicians embellished composers' works.

Hannes Sallmutter

Horns

Basso continuo for the orchestra

Audience members following the text being sung, with a libretto.

Soloists

Chorus

Basso continuo for recitatives (see chapter 10)

The bailiff maintains order in the theater

A merchant sells refreshments to members of the audience

▲ Opera became a big business during the Baroque era. This 1740 painting depicts an opera performed at the Teatro Reale in Turin (present-day northern Italy).

Museo Civico, Turin, Italy/The Bridgeman Art Library

▲ Stefano Dionisi in the title role of the 1994 film *Farinelli*. Carlo Broschi (1705–82), who used "Farinelli" as his stage name, was the most celebrated castrato of The 18th century. The producers of *Farinelli* re-created his singing voice by blending two separate recordings—one by a woman, one by a man—onto a single soundtrack.

more or less intact. Listeners of all levels could thus easily follow the course of this intricate movement and be uplifted by its glorious sound.

Opera, Oratorio, and the Entrepreneurial Spirit

The earliest operas, including Claudio Monteverdi's *L'Orfeo*, were performed in private theaters at the courts of the nobility and royalty. But societal changes soon affected the development of opera in profound ways. In various outposts around Europe—most notably Venice and England—a growing spirit of entrepreneurship made the arts increasingly accessible to the public. The first public opera houses opened in Venice in 1637, and by the early eighteenth century, even some theaters under the control of ruling monarchs began opening their doors to paying customers. By 1700, opera had become big business: fortunes could be made and lost on the success or failure of operatic productions. Impresarios (producers) invested heavily in new productions and paid enormous sums to the singers who could ensure the success of a new work. When the church prohibited performances of operas during the penitential season of Lent (the period preceding Easter), these same impresarios filled their opera houses by hiring the same singers and instrumentalists to perform oratorios. The oratorio was essentially identical to opera in its musical form, but it was unstaged, and the libretto was usually based on a sacred subject. The oratorio we will hear, Handel's *Messiah*, moves audiences today as it did in 1742 when it was first performed.

Not all productions of opera and oratorio were successful, however. In fact, arson became a serious problem in the opera world for a time during the Baroque era: in an attempt to recoup losses, unscrupulous investors were known to set fire to opera houses to collect insurance money.

The Virtuoso

The Baroque era was an age of opulence, and that opulence extended to the world of sound. Virtuoso singers and instrumentalists were coveted by rulers and the public alike. As soloists, these musicians were expected to embellish the parts written for them. What is preserved in the notated score today is by many accounts only an outline of what these skilled soloists actually performed. In Barbara Strozzi's song "Revenge," we will hear a soprano soloist of today re-create the highly ornamented, improvisatory style of the early eighteenth century. Antonio Vivaldi's violin concerto "Winter," from his *Four Seasons*, places extraordinary demands on the soloist. And in his Brandenburg Concerto no. 2, J. S.

Bach created a vehicle by which not one but four different soloists—on trumpet, oboe, violin, and recorder—can display their talents.

Castrati—singers who had been castrated as young boys so as to preserve the high range of their voices—were in especially high demand. Through their art, the most successful castrati became the equivalent of millionaires. They possessed both the high range of a woman's voice and the physical power of a man's voice, and the effect could be stunning. The castrato was an entirely unnatural phenomenon, of course, and barbaric by today's standards, but for Baroque audiences, the pursuit of vocal beauty justified even the most drastic measures.

The Baroque: AT A GLANCE

chapter 9

1607
CLAUDIO MONTEVERDI
Orpheus, **selection from Act II**
GENRE: Early Baroque Opera

Chapter highlight:
Early Baroque Opera
Early opera featured homophony, enabling one singer to portray one character. Polyphony remained popular, however. Gabrieli, Schütz, and Cavalli were significant in bridging the gap between the two.

KEY CONCEPTS
Homophony, basso continuo, recitative, word painting.

chapter 10

1689
HENRY PURCELL
Dido and Aeneas: **Overture and Act I, nos. 1-4**
GENRE: Baroque Opera

Chapter highlight:
Baroque Opera
English, Italian, and French operas unfolded through a series of numbers in different musical formats. Lully and Charpentier represent French opera; Handel, though German, wrote operas in the Italian style, featuring the da capo aria.

KEY CONCEPTS
Ostinato, Overture, French overture, aria.

chapter 11

MBUTI PYGMIES
Marriage Celebration Song
GENRE: Ostinato

Chapter highlight:
Ostinato
Ostinato—the repetition of one pattern of notes and rhythms—provided a simple unifying structure. Ostinato is also used widely in musical traditions around the world.

KEY CONCEPTS
Ostinato, polyphony, rhythmic interlock, hocket, call-and-response, heterophony.

chapter 14

1720
ANTONIO VIVALDI
Four Seasons, **"Winter," first movement**
GENRE: Concerto

Chapter highlight:
Program Music
Program music is instrumental music explicitly connected in some way with a story, person, or idea.

KEY CONCEPTS
Concerto, Ritornello, violin, program music.

chapter 15

1720
JOHANN SEBASTIAN BACH
Brandenburg Concerto no. 2 in F Major, BWV 1047, finale
GENRE: Concerto grosso

Chapter highlight:
The Baroque Concerto
The concerto highlights contrasts among instruments and performing forces, and became a vehicle for virtuosic displays. Among the best-loved concertos were composed by Corelli, Vivaldi, Handel, and Bach.

KEY CONCEPTS
Concerto, Ritornello, fugal texture, harmonic basis of form.

chapter 16

1717
GEORGE FRIDERIC HANDEL
Water Music, **selections**
GENRE: Suite

Chapter highlight:
The Baroque Suite
Suites are collections of popular dances. The variety of dances—fast vs. slow, lively vs. stately, duple vs. triple—creates contrasting moods. De la Guerre, Couperin, Bach, and Handel wrote suites for orchestra and for keyboard.

KEY CONCEPTS
Binary form, modulation, orchestration.

chapter 12

1651

BARBARA STROZZI
"Revenge"

GENRE: Baroque Song

Chapter highlight:
Baroque Chamber Music

Chamber music is intimate and requires only a few performers. Two other women who composed songs were Francesca Caccini and Antonia Bembo. The sonata was a very popular instrumental genre, with Corelli a notable composer of these.

KEY CONCEPTS

Embellishment, chamber music, trio-sonata texture, contrasting timbres.

chapter 13

1705

JOHANN SEBASTIAN BACH
Fugue in G minor, BWV 578
("Little")

GENRE: Fugue

Chapter highlight:
Baroque Organ Music

The fugue represents the era's fascination with polyphonic texture. The fantasia, prelude, and toccata, which took advantage of the organ's timbral range, were also popular. Sweelinck and Buxtehude were other notable composers of organ works.

KEY CONCEPTS

Counterpoint, Organ, imitative, timbre, arrangements.

WEB BONUS
chapter 2

HMONG PEOPLE OF LAOS:
Gaeng School Song

GENRE: Laotian Music

Chapter highlight:
Counterpoint

In counterpoint, equal melody lines run counter to one another. It has been a popular European compositional technique since the Renaissance and is found in musical traditions from other continents as well.

KEY CONCEPTS

Counterpoint, free reeds, circular breathing.

---

chapter 17

1731

JOHANN SEBASTIAN BACH
Cantata 140 ("Awake, a Voice
Calls to Us"), selections

GENRE: Cantata

Chapter highlight:
Sacred Music of the Late Baroque

Cantatas range from a single movement for a vocalist to a cycle of movements for soloists, chorus, and orchestra. The Mass is the central liturgical service of the Catholic Church. Motets, similar to cantatas, were used in both services. Composers include Bach, Delalande, A. Scarlatti, and Handel.

KEY CONCEPTS

Chorale, ritornello principle, song form (AAB).

chapter 18

1747

GEORGE FRIDERIC HANDEL
Messiah, selections

GENRE: Oratorio

Chapter highlight:
Oratorio

A large work performed by orchestra, choir, and soloists, usually on a religious theme. Unlike an opera, it is not staged, but performed as a concert work. Handel's *Messiah* is perhaps the most famous oratorio.

KEY CONCEPTS

Word-music relationships, fugue, ritornello principle.

1607
Jamestown Colony established in Virginia

1616-48
30 Years' War

1619
First African slaves land in Virginia

1642-46
Puritan Revolution in England

1643-1715
Louis XIV of France reigns

1733
Georgia established as last English colony in North America

Historical Events

9

Claudio Monteverdi
Orpheus, selection from Act II

Listen to This

Texture

Listen for homophony at the beginning: the solo singer carries the melody, while a small group of instruments provides support. Toward the end, when the chorus enters, listen for the change to polyphonic texture: all voices have equal importance.

Word-Music Relationships

Listen to the way in which Monteverdi uses the music to enhance the text and heighten the expressive emotion of what the characters say. Notice how the soloist's singing style differs from that of the chorus.

While the idea of a sung drama with one singer for each character may seem perfectly obvious to us today, it was the object of a concerted musical and intellectual search in the early years of the Baroque era. The monophonic dramas of the Middle Ages, like Hildegard von Bingen's *Play of Virtues* (chapter 1), had long since been forgotten. It was not until the decades around 1600 that a small group of philosophers, musicians, and poets began meeting in Florence (in present-day Italy) to consider how they might revive the synthesis of music and drama they knew had been practiced by the ancient Greeks. The result was **opera**, a drama sung from beginning to end. For all its changes over the ensuing centuries, the genre of opera has remained devoted to its original purpose: to convey a story onstage through characters who express their thoughts and emotions by singing.

Monteverdi's *Orpheus (L'Orfeo)* was not the very first opera, but it was among the earliest works in this new genre and remains the most frequently performed of all early operas.

The music is richly varied, with elaborate songs and choruses for the singers and lively instrumental music for the dancers. And while the story itself is based on myth, the music makes the characters seem very human, their emotions very real.

Orpheus, the legendary singer of Greek mythology, learns from a messenger that his beloved Euridice has died from the bite of a serpent. The selection here, from Act II, begins just after the messenger has delivered this terrible news. Orpheus is stunned; the chorus echoes his grief. Later in the opera, Orpheus uses the power of music to persuade the guardians and gods of the underworld (Hades) to allow him to cross the River Styx and bring Euridice back from the dead to "see the stars once more." He is allowed to do so, on the condition that he not look behind him on his ascent out of the underworld. But he cannot resist the temptation to look back, and Euridice is lost to him once again. Monteverdi's setting of the myth has a bittersweet ending, in which Euridice herself takes her place among the stars as a constellation.

Homophonic Texture:
One Character, One Voice

The texture of homophony—a single principal voice with subordinate accompaniment (see Elements, p. 8)—is essential in opera, for it allows one singer to represent a single character onstage. The group of instruments accompanying the singer here is known collectively as the **basso continuo** ("continuous bass"). This small ensemble, as its name suggests, plays continuously and provides an underlying bass line and harmonies. The basso continuo typically consists of two instruments: one that can sustain long notes (such as a bass viol, a cello, or a bassoon), and one that can play chords (such as a lute or a harpsichord). The organ was one of the few instruments that could sustain a sound *and* play chords. In the recording here, the basso continuo part is performed by a combination of organ and lute. In practice, musicians of the Baroque era used whatever number and combination of instruments were available.

Homophonic texture also made it much easier to understand the text. A single singer carrying the melodic line, with a subordinate accompaniment (the basso continuo), could articulate the words clearly without competing with other voices. The rich sound of polyphonic texture came at the expense of textual clarity. Listen again to William Byrd's "Sing Joyfully" (chapter 7), without following the text in the book, and see how well you can understand the words. Even the best choirs cannot project every word with equal clarity: this kind of writing for four, five, or six voices is simply too thick.

The new homophonic texture restored a greater sense of balance between text and music. Indeed, composers who used this new manner of writing argued that the text should determine the nature of the music and not vice versa—even if the expressive portrayal of certain words meant occasionally breaking long-standing musical rules about harmony and counterpoint. Composers who believed in the text as a driving force called this new way of writing the *seconda prattica* ("second practice"). This newer compositional style came to be seen in opposition to the *prima prattica* ("first practice"), the older style (see Expand Your Playlist).

Word-Music Relationships: Between Speech and Song

The selection opens with an extended **recitative** by Orpheus. The word "recitative" derives from the same root word as "recite," and this style of singing in fact lies somewhere between singing and speaking. It is still singing—we hear sustained pitches and definite rhythms—but the syllabic setting of the text makes it closer to speech than the more melodic, lyrical kind of singing we hear more frequently. The great advantage of recitative over more conventional styles of singing is that it allows the words to be projected with special clarity: melody is less important. In this sense, recitative is rather like plainchant (discussed in chapter 1), but with the addition of supporting instruments underneath the vocal line.

The chorus that follows is written in the polyphonic style of the *prima prattica*. As in the sung dramas of Greek antiquity, the chorus—here, the gathering of nymphs and shepherds—comments from time to time on what has just occurred. The texture is necessarily polyphonic because the chorus represents the reactions of those witnessing the drama onstage and, by extension, those witnessing the drama from the audience. The textures in Monteverdi's *Orpheus* thus include both homophony and polyphony; this coexistence of old and new styles is typical of music throughout the Baroque era.

Now listen to the excerpt again, following the Listening Guide.

Claudio Monteverdi (1567–1643)

MASTER OF OLD AND NEW STYLES

Claudio Monteverdi's career straddled the Renaissance and the Baroque era, and he mastered both the old and new approaches to composition. The madrigal "Luci serene e chiare," featured in the playlist, is a good example of the earlier polyphonic style. The "Lamento della ninfa," on the other hand, reveals his shift to the new homophonic way of writing. He served for many years at the court of Mantua, where he produced *Orpheus* (1607), the first opera to win widespread acclaim. In 1613 he became director of music at St. Mark's Basilica in Venice, where he lived the rest of his life. Monteverdi was constantly trying new styles and new genres. In addition to operas for an elite audience at court, he also wrote works for the new public opera houses that began to open in Venice at the end of the 1630s. His music remained a touchstone for all subsequent seventeenth-century composers.

PLAYLIST: MONTEVERDI

Coronation of Poppea (L'incoronazione di Poppea). This opera is based on the historical figures of the Emperor Nero (who fiddled while Rome burned) and his lover, Poppea, who schemes and plots to eliminate everyone who stands in her way of becoming Empress of Rome.

The Return of Ulysses to His Homeland (Il ritorno d'Ulisse in Patria). The libretto of this opera draws on the end of Homer's *Odyssey.*

Psalm 100 (Confitebor tibi). Written for soloist, chorus, and orchestra, this piece is one of many sacred works Monteverdi wrote at San Marco in Venice.

"Serene and clear eyes" ("Luci serene e chiare"). This madrigal is composed in the earlier polyphonic style.

"The Western Wind Returns" ("Zefiro torna"). This is an Italian-language madrigal for two tenors and basso continuo, to a text by the fourteenth-century Italian poet Petrarch.

"Lament of the Nymph" ("Lamento della Ninfa"). Here is an extended madrigal for vocal soloists, chorus, and basso continuo.

This portrait of Monteverdi dates from around 1613, when he was appointed music director at St. Mark's in Venice, one of the most prestigious musical positions in all Italy.

Landesmuseum Ferdinandeum, Innsbruck, Austria/© Photograph by Erich Lessing/Art Resource, NY

Vespers in Honor of the Blessed Virgin Mary (*Vespro della Beata Vergine*). Monteverdi wrote this work when he was music director at the Basilica of San Marco in Venice. Its various movements present both old and new styles, the *prima prattica* and the *seconda prattica.*

Listening Guide

Claudio Monteverdi *Orpheus,* selection from Act II

Time	Singer	Italian Text	English Translation
0:00	Orpheus	Tu se' morta, mia vita, ed io respiro? Tu se' da me partita Per mai più non tornare, ed io rimango? No, che se i versi alcuna cosa ponno, N'andrò sicuro a' più profondi abissi; E intenerito il cor del Re dell'ombre, Meco trarrotti a riveder le stelle. O, se ciò negherammi empio destino, Rimarrò teco in compagnia di morte. Addio terra, addio cielo e sole, addio.	Thou art dead, my life, and I still breathe? Thou art departed from me, Never to return, and I remain? No, if my verses still hold any power, I shall descend to the deepest depths; And I shall soften the heart of the king of shadows And bring thee back with me to see the stars again. Or if impious fate denies me this, I shall remain there in the company of the dead. Farewell, earth, farewell, sky and sun, farewell.
2:54	Chorus of nymphs and shepherds	Ahi caso acerbo, ahi fat'empio e crudele. Ahi stelle ingiuriose, ahi cielo avaro. No si fidi uom mortale Di ben caduco e frale, Che tosto fugge, e spesso A gran salita il precipizio è presso. (Alessandro Striggio)	Ah, bitter event! Ah, impious and cruel fate! Ah, misaligned stars! Ah, voracious heaven! Let no mortal trust in transient and frail happiness, for it soon flies away, and often the great height is close to the precipice. (Transl. MEB)

 Texture	 Word-Music Relationship
Homophonic (voice and accompanying basso continuo)	Recitative (syllabic). Word painting on *abissi* ("depths"): melody descends; rises up to the word *stelle* ("stars") and sinks down again on *morte* ("the dead").
Polyphonic (chorus of five parts, all equal)	Lyrical singing. Word painting on *acerbo* ("bitter"), with sharp dissonance (conflicting notes). Word painting on *fugge* ("flies"), with rapid rhythms, and on *salita* ("height"), with rising melodic line.

Student FAQs

If recitative makes it so much easier to understand the words, why isn't the whole opera written in recitative?

So far as text intelligibility is concerned, recitative has definite advantages over lyrical singing. However, if an opera consisted entirely of recitative, we would likely miss the more musical elements that lyrical singing has to offer. Composers of opera typically use a combination of different singing styles and instrumental and vocal combinations to create a wide variety of timbres and textures.

Does the basso continuo play when the chorus sings?

Yes it does, though it is not as noticeable because the alto, tenor, and bass voices provide the necessary harmonic support to the upper line. Once the basso continuo took hold in the early seventeenth century, it was used for homophonic and polyphonic textures alike.

Monteverdi Turns Down a Job Offer

Noble families competed not only among themselves for the best and brightest artists and musicians, they also competed with the church. When Monteverdi became music director at St. Mark's, in Venice, he received not only a higher salary than he had in Mantua (where he had first presented *Orpheus*) but also a staff of paid assistants, which allowed him the luxury of accepting commissions to write secular music—madrigals and operas—for venues outside the church. When the rulers of Mantua tried to lure Monteverdi back to their court, he declined the offer diplomatically but firmly.

I shall . . . submit for Your Lordship's consideration the fact that this Most Serene Republic [Venice] has never before given to any of my predecessors—whether it were Adriano [Willaert] or Cipriano [de Rore], or [Gioseffo] Zarlino, or anyone else—but 200 ducats in salary, whereas to me they give 400. . . . Nor, having done this for me, have they ever regretted it: on the contrary they have honored me, and honor me continually in such manner, that no singer is accepted into the choir until they ask [my] opinion . . . nor do they take on organists or an assistant director unless they have [my] opinion . . . nor is there any gentleman who does not esteem and honor me, and when I am about to perform either chamber or church music, I swear to Your Lordship that the entire city comes running.

Next, the duties are very light. . . . Moreover, [the Director of Music's] allowance is assured until his death: neither the death of a procurator nor that of a doge interferes with it, and . . . if he does not go at the appointed time to pick it up, it is brought round to his house. . . . [T]hen there is occasional income, which consists of whatever extra I can easily earn outside St. Mark's of about 200 ducats a year . . . because whoever can engage the director to look after their music—not to mention the payment of 30 ducats, and even 40, and up to 50 for two vespers and a mass—does not fail to take him on, and they also thank him afterwards with well-chosen words.

Source: Claudio Monteverdi, *The Letters of Monteverdi.* Rev. ed., ed. and trans. Denis Stevens. (Oxford: Clarendon Press, 1995), pp. 190–91.

EXPAND YOUR PLAYLIST

Old and New Practices in the Seventeenth Century

The music of the early Baroque encompasses both old *(prima prattica)* and new *(seconda prattica)* styles, sometimes in the same work. These composers bridged the gap between Renaissance polyphony and Baroque homophony.

Giovanni Gabrieli (ca. 1554/57–1612) was the most celebrated composer working in Venice in the decades before Monteverdi's arrival. His *Oh Great Mystery (O magnum mysterium)* is a sacred piece for chorus, brass ensemble, and solo vocalist, combining elements of the old and new practice in a single work.

Heinrich Schütz (1585–1672) was the leading German composer of the seventeenth century. He studied composition in Venice, possibly with Monteverdi.

"Sing Unto the Lord a New Song" ("Cantate domino canticum novicum"), a setting of Psalm 96, in Latin, is written in the *prima prattica* for four-part chorus.

"Sing Unto the Lord a New Song ("Singet dem Herren ein neues Lied") is a version of the same psalm in German. It is written in the newer *seconda prattica,* for solo voice, two violins, and basso continuo. The vocal and instrumental parts are quite florid and virtuosic.

Pier Francesco Cavalli (1602–1676) was Monteverdi's successor as music director at St. Mark's in Venice. Like Monteverdi, he composed in many genres, including operas and sacred music. *Dido (La Didone)* is an opera based on the same plot as Purcell's *Dido and Aeneas* (see chapter 10), a story taken from Virgil's *Aeneid*.

10

Henry Purcell
Dido and Aeneas: Overture and Act I, nos. 1–4

Form

Listen for the variety of forms within the span of only a few minutes of action. Following the instrumental **overture**, we hear a vocal **recitative** answered by a **chorus**, then an **aria** ("song"), then another recitative, and finally another chorus.

Word-Music Relationships

Listen specifically for the difference between those passages that are recitatives (more speech-like) and those that are arias (more lyrical).

Henry Purcell's *Dido and Aeneas* is one of the first operas ever written in English. Its early performance history is shrouded in mystery. The first documented production was sometime before 1689 at a school for young ladies in Chelsea (west of London at the time, now a part of the city), but it may have been performed as early as 1685. The work seems to have disappeared from the stage shortly afterward, and it was not revived until 1700, almost five years after the composer's death, in a drastically altered version. *Dido and Aeneas* may have been suppressed for political reasons, either by Purcell himself or by the Crown, on the grounds that it could have been perceived as an unflattering commentary on the dual reign of King William, a foreigner, and Queen Mary, daughter of Charles I. The opera's plot, after all, deals with a foreign prince (Aeneas) who promises to marry the Queen of Carthage (Dido), but then abandons her, driving her to suicide.

The chief characters of the opera are the following:

- Dido, the Queen of Carthage (soprano; the highest vocal range)
- Aeneas, a Trojan prince (baritone; the middle-low male voice)
- Belinda, Dido's maidservant (soprano)

Aeneas is a refugee from Troy, which has just fallen to the Greeks and their Trojan Horse. Fulfilling a promise from the gods, Aeneas and his companions are now on their way from Troy to the Italian peninsula, where he is destined to establish the city of Rome. On the coast of northern Africa (what is now Tunisia), they land at Carthage, ruled by the widowed Queen Dido. True to operatic convention, Dido and Aeneas immediately fall in love. He pledges to abandon his mission to found Rome, but when a witch disguised as Mercury, the messenger of the gods, orders him to leave, he obeys and departs. Dido dies, disconsolate, but not before singing a long lament at the very end of the opera. The excerpt here is from the very beginning of the opera.

Form by the Numbers

Purcell moves the plot forward through a series of brief, self-contained units known as "numbers," as follows:

1. **Overture**. There had to be some way to get the audience to settle down and be quiet. Far from the well-trained classical audiences of today, who file in respectfully to hear an esteemed musical work, audiences in Purcell's time (and, indeed, for the century and a half that followed) could be quite boisterous and noisy. For one thing, the music they were about to hear was new and had not yet entered the ranks of cherished masterworks. For another, people regarded the opera as a supreme social event, as many people still do today. A purely instrumental opening, or **overture**, signaled to the audience that it was time to leave the socializing and direct attention to the stage, where the singers would soon appear.

    The form of this particular overture—a slow introduction followed by an imitative fast section—was very common in French operas of the time and for that reason is known as a **French overture**. We hear two typical characteristics of the French overture here:
    a. The slow introduction features a consistent alternation between long and short notes (a "LONG-short-LONG-short" pattern).
    b. The fast section begins with **imitation** among the voices: the same theme introduced by different instruments of the orchestra in succession.

2. **Scene and Chorus**. An aria, sung by Belinda to Queen Dido ("Shake the cloud from off your brow"). "Aria" is Italian for "air" or "melody," and is used to describe any lyrical movement or piece for solo voice, usually with some kind of instrumental accompaniment. The chorus then joins in, reinforcing this same sentiment with different words ("Banish sorrow, banish care").

3. **Song**. Another aria, this one more elaborate. Dido laments her state ("Ah! Belinda"). She sings her melody over an **ostinato** pattern in the bass, a short array of nine notes repeated over and over. ("Ostinato" comes from the same root word as "obstinate.") This kind of pattern is also known as a **ground bass** or simply a **ground**.

4. **Recitative.** Belinda and Dido in dialogue ("Grief increases by concealing"). The recitative, as we saw in chapter 9, provided a way of delivering text quickly and clearly in a singing style similar to speech. The accompaniment is a simple basso continuo (see p. 89), played by harpsichord and cello in this case.

5. **Chorus.** In the manner of the chorus in an ancient Greek tragedy, the chorus comments on what has just happened on the stage, reinforcing Belinda's advice that Troy and Carthage join forces in the union of Dido and Aeneas ("When monarchs unite").

Purcell was influenced by composers of both French opera (especially Lully; see Expand Your Playlist) and Italian opera (including Alessandro Scarlatti, among others), who had begun moving more and more toward a clear division between recitative and aria.

Word-Music Relationships: Speaking, Expressing, Commenting

When Purcell's characters need to talk to each other, he gives them something between speech and song: the recitative. When his characters need to convey some deeper feeling, he gives them lyrical arias in which they can linger expressively over individual words. The chorus, observing and feeling for us at closer range, punctuates these longer melodic expressions with comments communicated clearly and intelligibly, with one syllable per note. Each unit of the opera is dominated by a single *affect,* or emotion. Belinda is agitated in her opening number: she sings in uneven (dotted) rhythms, particularly on the word "shake." Dido, in turn, sings her first lament (no. 3) to a repeated bass pattern that mirrors her state of constant sorrow. The chorus "When monarchs unite," with its lively, dance-like rhythms and major mode, injects a note of optimism into the musical narrative.

Now listen to the piece again, following the Listening Guide.

Henry Purcell *Dido and Aeneas:* Overture and Act I, nos. 1–4

The Overture

Time	Number	Form: Section	Texture
0:00	1. Overture	Slow introduction (**A**)	Melody in the uppermost voice; prominent basso continuo part below
0:53		Literal repeat of slow introduction (**A**)	
1:35		Fast section (**B**)	Begins with imitative entries
2:03		Literal repeat of fast section (**B**)	

Act I

When the curtain goes up on Act I, we see the Palace of Carthage, with Queen Dido, accompanied by Belinda, her maidservant and confidante, and other members of the court. Dido laments her current state: her husband has died, she has not remarried, and her kingdom, as a result, is vulnerable and unstable.

Time	Number	Character(s) Singing	Text
2:39	2. Scene and Chorus	Belinda	Shake the cloud from off your brow, Fate your wishes does allow; Empire growing, pleasures flowing, Fortune smiles and so should you.
3:11		Chorus	Banish sorrow, banish care, Grief should ne'er approach the fair.
3:39	3. Song (Aria)	Dido	Ah! Belinda, I am pressed With torment not to be confessed, Peace and I are strangers grown. I languish till my grief is known, Yet would not have it guess'd.
7:28	4. Recitative	Belinda and Dido	**Belinda:** Grief increases by concealing. **Dido:** Mine admits of no revealing. **Belinda:** Then let me speak; the Trojan guest Into your tender thoughts has pressed; The greatest blessing Fate can give Our Carthage to secure and Troy revive.
8:05	5. Chorus	Chorus	When monarchs unite, how happy their state, They triumph at once o'er their foes and their fate.

Rhythm

Dotted rhythms featured prominently

Theme consists of notes of equal value
(not dotted)

**Word-Music
Relationships**

Rapid dotted rhythms on "shake," as if
to mimic the act of shaking

Ground bass (ostinato), a brief pattern
repeated in the bass line throughout the
entire number, reflecting the unceasing
nature of Dido's torment

The first part of the dialogue stands
between speech and song; Belinda's
last two lines stand out because they
are more lyrical and because she
repeats these words.

The syllabic setting helps make the
words more intelligible.

Student FAQs

Why is there so much repetition of the words?

Text repetition is common in many operas from
different times and places. Repeating the words
gives listeners a better chance of understanding
them, and altering the music with each statement
of the words allows the composer to bring out
ever-deeper levels of meaning in them.

How long is this opera?

For an opera, it's very short:
most performances run
somewhere between 50
minutes and an hour. Most
operas, by contrast, run at
least two hours and often
three or more, not including
intermissions.

Henry Purcell (ca. 1659–95)

INSPIRED BY THE STAGE

Henry Purcell contributed songs and instrumental music to dozens of plays but wrote only one true opera, *Dido and Aeneas*. The English public was largely hostile to opera during the seventeenth century, in part because of England's strong tradition of spoken theater. Shakespeare had called for songs or instrumental music at many points in a number of his plays, but the idea of singing an entire drama from beginning to end was something most English theatergoers considered absurd. Not until the early eighteenth century would opera take hold in England, and when it did, the rage was for opera sung in Italian, not English. It would be another 50 years before audiences would begin to accept the idea of English-language opera. Purcell, in short, was far ahead of his time. When *Dido and Aeneas* was rediscovered in the late eighteenth century, it helped establish his eventual reputation as the greatest of all seventeenth-century English composers.

Purcell was born into a family of musicians and served in his early years as a composer and organist at the English court and later at Westminster Abbey, where he is buried near the organ. Although he wrote many semi-operas—works combining song and spoken dialogue—and a great deal of sacred music, he remains best known for a work that is unique for its time.

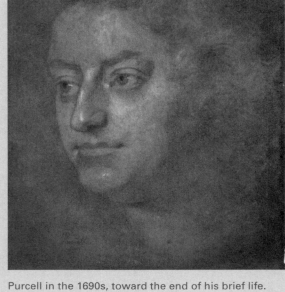

Purcell in the 1690s, toward the end of his brief life.
National Portrait Gallery, London

Michele Serrano-Möritz as Dido (left) and Elizabeth Hillebrand as Belinda in the opening scene of Purcell's *Dido and Aeneas*, from a production by the Bronx Opera Company in 2006.
Heidi Schumann

PLAYLIST: PURCELL

Chaconne in G minor, Z. 730. A purely instrumental ground bass (ostinato) for four stringed instruments and basso continuo.

"Sound the Trumpet" from *Ode for Queen Mary's Birthday.* A duet for tenors and basso continuo, with the voices imitating trumpets.

"One Charming Night" from *The Faerie Queen.* An aria from a semi-opera, set to a libretto by Sir Edmund Spenser.

"Lord, What Is Man?" A song for solo voice and basso continuo.

My Heart Is Inditing. A full anthem (see chapter 7) in the tradition of English sacred music, for chorus and string orchestra.

MUSIC IN PERFORMANCE

Opera in English

Why aren't there more operas in English? Most of the works in the operatic repertory were written in other languages, particularly Italian (opera began on the Italian peninsula, after all), but also French and German. From the very start, opera was slow to gain a foothold in England because of the strong tradition of spoken drama. With playwrights like Shakespeare, who needed opera?

Some claim that English is not a singable language. Italian, it is true, has more vowels, which can be sustained and therefore lend themselves well to singing. But the enormous repertory of English-language songs offers compelling evidence that English words lend themselves to singing just as well. In our day, many operas are being written in English, partly because it has become a language of worldwide significance—much as Italian was, in the seventeenth and eighteenth centuries. Benjamin Britten's operas from the 1940s and 1950s (*Peter Grimes, The Turn of the Screw*) are staples of the repertory. More recent contributors include Thea Musgrave (*Mary, Queen of Scots*), John Adams (*Nixon in China*), and Philip Glass (*Einstein on the Beach*; see chapter 54).

Should foreign-language operas be sung in English? The advantage is obvious: audiences could easily understand what's being sung onstage. But there are drawbacks, too. It's difficult to create translations that retain the sense of the original and still mesh well with the composer's music. A composer might write a melodic phrase in such a way as to reach the highest note on one particular word, and a good translation must take that into account. Finally, English is a challenging language when it comes to rhyme: French, German, and especially Italian offer many more possibilities for rhymed words, and rhyme often plays an important role in opera texts.

One recent development to address these challenges has been the use of super-titles. Listeners who want to follow the text can see the translations projected above the stage. Many opera houses now use this system for operas sung in foreign languages. More recently, a few opera houses have begun trying out personalized screens on individual seats. With the growing ease of international travel, one can't always assume that someone watching an Italian-language opera in Berlin necessarily understands German. He or she might want the text translated into English, French, Mandarin, or any number of other languages.

 EXPAND YOUR PLAYLIST

Baroque Opera

The most important repertories of later Baroque opera were in Italian and French. Italian opera enjoyed international acclaim; French opera was limited to France. Today, both repertories are performed.

Italian Opera
George Frideric Handel (1685–1759), although German by birth, wrote many Italian operas during his years in London. These operas were often based on subjects from Classical history (Roman emperors, for example) or myth.

The aria "Or la tromba" ("Now the trumpet") from *Rinaldo* is a **da capo aria**, which is very typical of **opera seria** (or "serious opera"), as Italian opera of this kind was called. A da capo aria opens with two contrasting sections, **A** and **B**; at, the end of the **B** section, the singer return to the beginning of the **A** section, following the direction in the score of *da capo*—literally, "from the head," or as we would say, "from the top." When the singer performs this **A** section a second time, he or she embellishes it heavily. The typical opera seria consists of an alternation of recitatives, which move the action forward, and da capo arias, in which the singers reflect on what has just happened on the stage.

"Piangerò," a lament by Cleopatra from *Giulio Cesare*, is also a da capo aria. The **A** section is slow, the **B** section fast.

French Opera
Jean-Baptiste Lully (1632–87) was the favorite composer of King Louis XIV of France. The aria "Enfin, il est en ma puissance" from the opera *Armide,* is a stirring monologue by the sorceress Armida, who contemplates murdering the sleeping Renaud (Rinaldo) but cannot bring herself to do it because of his beauty.

Marc-Antoine Charpentier (1643–1704) was another French composer who lived during the reign of Louis XIV. Charpentier's *Andromède* provides instrumental music for a play based on the Greek myth of Andromeda. In the aria "Quelle est lente, cette journée" you hear the very fluid rhythms typical of Baroque French homophony.

Jean-Philippe Rameau (1683–1764) was the greatest composer of French opera in the eighteenth century. In "Rossignols amoureux" ("Amorous nightingales"), an aria from the opera *Hippolyte et Aricie,* both voice and instruments imitate the song of the nightingale.

11

DEMOCRATIC
REPUBLIC
OF THE
CONGO
Kinshasa
ITURI
FOREST
Lubumbashi

Mbuti Pygmies
"Marriage Celebration Song"

Listen to This

Texture

How many different vocal lines can you identify? Compare how they function independently and work together. How do the inner voices support each other on the same part?

Rhythm

Listen to how the parts are arranged rhythmically. Do the parts seem to function rhythmically as individuals, or do they work together?

Form

Listen for the repetition of one basic unit. How is this unit constructed?

Ostinato, such as we heard in Dido's aria "Ah! Belinda," was a very popular musical feature during the Baroque period. The repetition of one pattern of notes and rhythms throughout an entire piece provided a simple unifying structure above which a variety of melodies could be constructed. Because of the ease with which an ostinato can be understood and remembered, this organizational technique has been used widely in **oral traditions**—those passed down without the aid of written music—throughout the world.

Do I Repeat Myself?

The use of an ostinato bass—a repeating bass part—onto which a melody line is overlaid is common in many different forms of music. A great example in American popular music is the doo wop vocal music of the 1950s.

How does doo wop work? In the vocal quartet, each voice has its own role. The bass singer handles the repeated foundation part, often in the form of a short phrase of nonsense syllables. Think of the classic "Sh'Boom" by the Chords. The bass part is a simple repeated part:

Sh'boom, sh'boom, sh' falalala sh' falalala

Above this floats the melody:

Life could be a dream . . .

Between melody and bass, the other two voices fill in by also singing short melodic fragments. These four parts—fairly simple and seemingly independent—actually fit together to form one musical experience. We don't hear the individual parts as separate (although we can listen for them if we want) but instead experience the piece as a coherent whole.

How is this similar to the Pygmy music that we're hearing in this chapter?

The Chords, a 1950s doo wop group, famous for their recording of "Sh-Boom."
Michael Ochs Archives Ltd./Getty Images Inc.—Los Angeles

Mbuti Pygmies making music. The pipes they are blowing into are made of leaves; each member of the group plays a single note.
Nick Greaves/Alamy Images

The Mbuti Pygmies from the northeastern region of the Democratic Republic of the Congo (DRC, formerly known as Zaire) use ostinatos as the basis for complex musical structures involving polyphony, interlocking rhythms, and the alternation of voices to create a melody. In recent years, the music of the Pygmies has found growing interest among Western audiences, and its influence has extended to various pop, jazz, and world beat genres.

The Mbuti Pygmies inhabit the Ituri Forest, which borders Uganda to the east, Sudan to the north, and the DRC to the south and west. Although they are citizens of the DRC, the majority of Pygmy groups maintain a semiautonomous hunting-and-gathering existence. The Mbuti Pygmies are nomads, camping for a few weeks at a time in different locations of the forest in search of game. The hunt is a communal affair in which men string nets in semicircles and women and children beat the brush to scare game into the nets. Food is shared. A political hierarchy is absent because survival depends on cooperation and not competition. In the same way, musical parts in Pygmy songs are distributed equally and coordinated carefully. The contribution of each separate part reflects every member's contribution to food gathering in the rainforest.

Texture: Layers upon Layers

The ostinato in this song is made of multiple layers that overlap and interlock in intriguing ways. The most obvious textural layer is the **call-and-response**, in which one group of voices sings an opening motive, and three different groups in succession sing their answers (see the top line of the diagram below).

Beneath the call-and-response structure, two heterophonic lines are stacked. **Heterophony** is the simultaneous playing or singing of two or more versions of a melody. Thus, the line marked "Heterophonic voice 1" in the diagram below actually consists of multiple voice lines all singing similar melodies but not identical pitches. (The same is true of the line marked "Heterophonic voice 2.") Heterophony is a basic way of creating harmonic support without using harmony built from chords. It gives a thicker texture to the polyphony.

The two heterophonic lines are further layered by a **hocket** construction. Hocket is a form of polyphony consisting of two or more rhythmically **interlocking** voices. When voices interlock, one voice fills the spaces left by another's rests to complete a melodic unit. In other words, the melody is distributed throughout the parts, and each part contains only its constituent notes, sounded at the precise time. Hockets were also particularly popular in medieval France (see chapter 3).

Think of a game where each player can speak only one word. Each person would then have to say this word at precisely the right moment to fit into a sentence; for example:

Voice I:	I		
Voice II:		am	
Voice III:		a	
Voice IV:			girl.

Now imagine that each person sings just one note in a melody. The same effect would be created by having them chime in when their note was needed:

Voice I:	Hap-py	day		
Voice II:		Birth-		
Voice III:			to	
Voice IV:				you.

In Pygmy hocketing, this is made more complicated by the fact that each singer may sing two or three different notes, but the basic challenge of fitting these notes together into a melody remains.

In the following diagram, you can see the spaces left by some parts and filled by others; imagine vertical lines to make this clear. When you listen to the song, you can hear the interesting alternation of parts—identifiable by their slightly different timbres—to create one melody.

The melodic-rhythmic fragments also overlap: a singer sustains a tone over the entrance tone of the singer that follows, which fills what would otherwise be a slight gap of sound between phrases. Sounds of crickets form the background to the singing voices, adding another interesting textural element.

Here is a representation of the interlocking melodic-rhythmic fragments that create the hocket, which continues throughout the song as an ostinato:

Interlocking Rhythms

The rhythmic complexity of African hocket comes partly from the number of different parts that interlock and partly from the complexity of each individual part. No single line stands on its own. Each response in the call-and-response construction is built from interlocking subunits. The hocket thus occurs on many levels, as shown in the diagram.

Form: A Call-and-Response Ostinato

The call-and-response may be represented as four phrases, **ABBB**, covering a total of eight beats. This essential melodic unit repeats over and over to create the ostinato. The five basic lines remain consistent. The pitches used to create the heterophony vary each time, however, as do the melody lines and vocalizations that are improvised to embellish the ostinato.

Now listen to this song again, following the Listening Guide.

Listening Guide

Mbuti Pygmies "Marriage Celebration Song"

Time	Form	Texture	Rhythm
0:00	The song is already in progress.	Polyphonic throughout, with heterophony in each phrase subunit. The hocket is already established.	Eight beats per cycle, built of four interlocking phrases. Each phrase in itself is built from interlocking voices.
0:01	Ostinato cycle 1. **A:** the call.	Thick throughout	A long sung tone followed by two shorter sung tones, descending
0:02	**B, B, B:** the responses. One singer sets the intonation for the first response voices.	Thinner than the call. Voices overlap.	The first of the three interlocking responses is sung. The next two follow until up to the second cycle. All responses are constructed of interlocking subunits.
0:07	Ostinato cycle 2, beginning once again with the call	Texture remains the same: polyphonic	A long sung tone followed by two shorter sung tones, descending
0:09	**B, B:** first two responses, sung by separate singers	Thinner than accented call. Voices overlap.	Interlocking responses continue after call throughout.
0:12	**B:** third response; different from previous two, tapering the phrase cycle.	Voices overlap.	The same throughout
0:13	Ostinato cycle 3	Polyphonic throughout	
0:20	Ostinato cycle 4. The lead singer of the call is heard over the group for the first time on this recording.		
0:26	Cycle 5		
0:32	Cycle 6		
0:38	Cycle 7		
0:44	Cycle 8		
0:51	Cycle 9		
0:57	Cycle 10		

Note: The selection begins midway through the song, and the lead singer is absent in the first three cycles but rejoins the song on the fourth cycle. Thus, in the early seconds of the excerpt, a different singer leads the response and sets the intonation.

Student FAQs

How do Pygmies learn and remember these songs if there is no written notation?

Traditional singers and musicians around the world have developed a way of learning music without using any system of notation. Often, master musicians of one generation will teach students, either formally or informally, passing on their knowledge. Of course, with no recordings or written documentation, songs may change as they are sung over time. This is called "oral transmission" by ethnomusicologists because the music is learned orally.

Why do Pygmies sing?

They sing for the same reason that most people do. However, many Pygmy songs have associations with specific rituals. For instance, the song featured in this chapter is linked to the wedding ceremony. Singing is a group activity in which everyone takes part, rather than one where a professional performs and others merely listen (as in many Western cultures).

How hard is it to sing in a hocketing style?

Try it with a group of friends! It's not that hard to learn your individual part, but synchronizing your singing with everyone else is very difficult if you've never tried it before. Add the idea that different melodies are occurring simultaneously (perhaps in different rhythms), and you'll get some sense of the skill of these Pygmy singers.

EXPAND YOUR PLAYLIST

Singing in the Rain (forest)

Mbuti Pygmies of the Ituri Rainforest. Smithsonian Folkways Recordings SFW40401.

Colin Turnbull was among the first Western anthropologists to spend considerable time studying and recording the Mbuti Pygmies in Africa. His landmark book, *The Forest People,* published in 1960, is considered a classic study of these people and helped introduce their culture to Western audiences. These recordings were made in the late 1950s and include many examples of the hocketing vocal style that we've studied in this chapter.

Heart of the Forest: The Music of the Baka Forest People of Southeast Cameroon. Hannibal HNCD 1378.

The Baka Forest people have their own unique form of vocal and instrumental hocketing. This recording includes a wide range of music, including performances on the single-string musical bow, and the distinctive vocal "yodeling" practiced by this tribe.

Centrafique: Anthologle de la Musique des Pygmees Aka. Ocora C559012 13.

Recorded by Pierre Toureille for UNESCO, this two-CD set documents the music of the Aka Forest peoples. Along with Turnbull's earlier recordings, this is considered a classic collection for those who love this musical style.

The Spirit Cries: Music from the Rainforests of South America & the Caribbean. Rykodisc RCD 10250.

Edited by percussionist Mickey Hart of the Grateful Dead, this collection of field recordings goes beyond Africa to trace related musical styles found across the ocean in South America and the Caribbean. The mixture of European and African influences is striking in these recordings.

12

Barbara Strozzi
"Revenge"

 Listen to This

 Melody

Listen for the contour of the melodic lines and the way in which the singer embellishes these lines. Many of the longer notes are ornamented with shorter ones before or after.

 Form

Notice the alternation of the two contrasting melodies, one in a lively duple meter, the other in a slower triple meter.

Timbre

Listen for the relationship of the two violins to the voice. The instruments echo the last phrase of each line of the text. Listen, too, for the way in which the instruments in the basso continuo (harpsichord, cello, and lute) support the vocal line.

A poetic text that expresses a jilted lover's thirst for revenge demands energetic, extroverted music, and that is exactly what Barbara Strozzi gave "Revenge" ("La Vendetta"). She called this setting, which we today might designate simply as a song, an *arietta* or "little aria." It allows the singer to display great vocal agility, and it makes effective use of contrasting timbres. The music is intimate and requires only a few performers: one singer, two violinists, and a basso continuo of two instrumentalists. Music like this was meant to be performed for private gatherings in relatively small rooms or "chambers," hence the term **chamber music**. In chamber music, we hear only one performer on each part, in contrast to orchestral music, which features multiple players on a part.

Decoration of the Melody

In this performance of "Revenge," the singer adds extra notes to the melody line, decorating it more elaborately as the piece progresses. The opening melody returns twice (at 0:54 and at 1:47) and becomes more florid with each appearance. Listeners of the Baroque era expected soloists to add this kind of ornamentation; the melodic lines written by the composer were only a starting point for performance. Music of the Baroque era is in many respects like jazz today: musicians embellish a basic tune in a highly individual and often quite spontaneous manner.

Homophonic texture made this kind of improvisation possible. With two or more independent melody lines, players would have to agree in advance just how their embellishments would work together.

Form: Contrast and Repetition

Strozzi alternates the two contrasting melodies—the first in duple meter, the second in triple meter—to create a large-scale structure that can be diagrammed in this way:

A	**B**	**A**	**B**	**A**
Duple	Triple	Duple	Triple	Duple

The contours and rhythms of the two melodies differ markedly: the first moves mostly downward, with short, quick notes, while the second moves mostly upward, using longer notes. The return of each melody creates a sense of coherence for the piece. This combination of contrast and return is basic to a great deal of Baroque music. The opening melody (**A**) gives the work an anchor, while the contrasting melody provides variety.

The **A** melody

The **B** melody

The words to the **A** melody do not change. This device—bringing back the same words with the same basic melody at regular intervals over the course of a work—is called a **refrain**. Refrains had been used in song since the Middle Ages, and they continue to be used today. Many popular songs rely on the use of refrains. Here are a few examples:

- All the lonely people, where do they all belong? (The Beatles, "Eleanor Rigby")
- With a knick-knack paddywhack give the dog a bone/This old man came rolling home ("This Old Man")
- The answer, my friend, is blowin' in the wind, The answer is blowin' in the wind (Bob Dylan, "Blowin' in the Wind")

Timbre: Contrast and Punctuation

In addition to the basso continuo (see p. 89), Strozzi uses two violins to great effect. They punctuate the end of every line in the refrain (the **A** section), each time providing an echo to what the soprano has just sung. This kind of back-and-forth between instruments and voices is another new element in Baroque music and has remained a basic compositional technique to the present day. The violins drop out entirely during the **B** sections of the work, further emphasizing the contrast between the **A** and **B** sections. The basso continuo part also participates in this interplay between instruments and voices. In the middle of the **B** section (at 0:38), you can hear the roles of voice and instruments reversed: the cello introduces the basic thematic idea before the soprano picks it up.

The sonority of the purely instrumental passages of this song—two violins and basso continuo—was a favorite in the Baroque era. Many works of chamber music from this time feature two high instruments (violins, flutes, oboes, recorders, or any mixture of these various instruments) and basso continuo. Such a combination produced what is known as **trio-sonata texture**, with three main voices: two in the soprano and one in the bass (the basso continuo). Arcangelo Corelli, J.S. Bach, and Handel all wrote trio sonatas (see Expand Your Playlist).

Now listen to this arietta again, following the Listening Guide.

Barbara Strozzi "Revenge"

Time	Original Italian Text	English Translation	Timbre
0:00	La vendetta è un dolce affetto, il dispetto vuol dispetto, Il rifarsi è un gran diletto.	Vengeance is a sweet emotion; spite desires spite, and getting even is a great pleasure.	Soprano, basso continuo, two violins
0:26	Vane son scuse e ragioni per placar donna oltraggiata, non pensar che ti perdoni! Donna mai non vendicata pace ha in bocca e guerra in petto.	Excuses and reasons are useless in placating an outraged woman; do not think that she will pardon you! A woman who has never avenged herself has peace on her lips and war in her heart.	Soprano, basso continuo
0:54	La vendetta è un dolce affetto il dispetto vuol dispetto, il rifarsi è un gran diletto.	Vengeance is a sweet emotion; spite desires spite, and getting even is a great pleasure.	Soprano, basso continuo, two violins
1:19	Non perdona in vendicarsi all'amante più gradito che l'adora e vuol rifarsi quand'il fiero insuperbito verso lei perd'il rispetto.	She does not pardon, when taking vengeance, even the most agreeable lover who adores her and wants to make up with her when the proud and arrogant man loses respect for her.	Soprano, basso continuo
1:47	La vendetta è un dolce affetto il dispetto vuol dispetto Il rifarsi è un gran diletto.	Vengeance is a sweet emotion; spite desires spite, and getting even is a great pleasure.	Soprano, basso continuo, two violins

Meter	Form (melodic idea)	Melody
Duple	A	Moves primarily downward in short, rapid notes
Triple	B	Moves primarily upward in longer, sustained notes
Duple	A'	Embellished further
Triple	B' (embellished)	Embellished further
Duple	A''	Embellished still further

Student FAQs

How do performers know how to embellish this music?

At least some performance practices of the Baroque era are documented in the books that taught musicians how to sing or play instruments. But these are really only start-ing points. Now, as then, musicians must use artistic judgment and embellish the music as they see fit. Opinions about what constitutes too much or too little embel-lishment vary widely.

If chamber music is performed by one musician to a part, is there a limit on the number of parts for it to still be considered chamber music?

Nine different parts—a nonet—is generally considered to be the largest number of performers in a work of chamber music. With more than nine musicians, the "chamber" becomes rather crowded.

Barbara Strozzi (1619–77)

"SECURE FROM THE LIGHTNING BOLTS OF SLANDER"

Being a female composer—and a supremely talented one, no less—was not an easy proposition in the seventeenth century. When Barbara Strozzi published her first work in 1644, a collection of madrigals, she anticipated the criticism against her sex:

> To the august name of Your Highness I do reverently consecrate this first work, which I, as a woman, send forth into the light all too anxiously, so that under an oak tree of gold it may rest secure from the lightning bolts of slander prepared for it.

Her anticipation of "slander" was not without foundation. Rumors surrounded Strozzi's life. She had been adopted by the poet Giulio Strozzi and may in fact have been his natural daughter, born out of wedlock. She grew up in a family at the center of Venice's intellectual and cultural life and attended meetings of poets and philosophers that did not normally include women. Her chastity seems to have been a source of repeated satire and jest in the late 1630s. One source accused her of having an affair with a castrato; another noted, "It is a fine thing to distribute the flowers after having already surrendered the fruit."

Strozzi's achievements as a composer are all the more impressive in this light. By the end of her life, she had published eight volumes of music, including about 125 individual works of music, more than all but a few of her male contemporaries. And she accomplished all this without benefit of a secure professional position in music and without extended support from any one patron.

PLAYLIST: STROZZI

"With New Bad News, I Cannot Sing" ("Con male nuove, non si puo' cantare") is a lament for soprano and basso continuo.

The Gamba Player, by Bernardo Strozzi, ca. 1640. The woman depicted here may be Barbara Strozzi.

Erich Lessing/Art Resource, NY

"Proud Eyes" ("Gl' occhi superbi") is a love song for soprano and basso continuo.

"Betrayal!" ("Tradimento!") is a song from the perspective of a jilted lover for soprano and basso continuo.

"Between Hope and Fear" ("Tra le spiranze e 'l timore"). This is a dialogue—for a single voice and basso continuo—between hope and fear.

Female Composers in the Baroque Era

Barbara Strozzi was one of a relatively small number of women in the Baroque era who were able to publish their own compositions. The success of countless women composers in more recent times may make us wonder why there were so few in the past.

While many women received musical training as performers—particularly as singers or as keyboard players—very few enjoyed the benefit of instruction in composition. Francesca Caccini (1587–ca. 1641) and Elisabeth Jacquet de la Guerre (1665–1729), two accomplished composers of the Baroque period, were both daughters of musicians and learned harmony and counterpoint at home. Others, like Barbara Strozzi, grew up in highly cultured households in which musicians and composers circulated freely. But for the most part, women simply did not have access to the kind of rigorous instruction needed to learn the art of composition.

Part of the reason for this is that there were virtually no professional prospects for women composers. Of the women who published music on the Italian peninsula between 1566 and 1700, more than half were nuns. Isabella Leonarda (1620–1704) was easily the most prominent and prolific of this latter group, publishing some 20 volumes of her own compositions, mostly sacred vocal music but also some instrumental works as well. Unless they worked in convents, women could not hold positions associated with composing. Even Barbara Strozzi, with all her talents, struggled to make ends meet in the later years of her life. In spite of her prowess as a composer, she would never have been considered as a potential successor to Monteverdi as Music Director of St. Mark's Basilica in Venice. That honor went instead to Monteverdi's pupil (and Strozzi's teacher) Francesco Cavalli. From a strictly economic point of view, then, there was no reason for parents to encourage their daughters in this direction. Without an appointment at a church or court or some other institution, it was just not possible for a composer to earn a decent living.

These conditions would change little over the next two centuries. So while there are many examples of women performers from the Renaissance onward, including many noted virtuosos, the number of women composers in relation to men remained disproportionately small until well into the twentieth century. Only with the advent of compulsory public education and the broadening of career options to women did the phenomenon of the female composer cease to be unusual.

The first woman to write an opera in French, Elisabeth Jacquet de la Guerre was also widely admired for her abilities on the harpsichord. Here she is depicted in the act of composing at the harpsichord, with a sheet of paper in one hand, a quill pen in the other.

Private Collection, London.

A sonata for three violins and basso continuo. The basso continuo group here consists of a harpsichordist and a cellist (right). A delineation between a leading voice or voices and supporting instruments (the basso continuo) marks a decisive break with the predominantly polyphonic style of the Renaissance.

Courtesy of the Cultural Affairs Bureau of the Macao S.A.R. Government

EXPAND YOUR PLAYLIST

Baroque Chamber Music

Baroque composers wrote unprecedented quantities of chamber music, both for voices and instruments and for instruments alone. One genre they cultivated with special intensity was the **sonata**, a word whose literal meaning is "that which is played" (as opposed to the **cantata**, "that which is sung": see chapter 17). Composers wrote sonatas for many combinations of instruments; the most popular variety involved two high-ranged instruments (such as two violins, two oboes, or two flutes) and basso continuo. This combination was known as the **trio sonata**. Sonatas could be performed as in the home (the **sonata da camera**, or "chamber sonata") to provide entertainment, or in the church (the **sonata da chiesa**, or "church sonata") during sacred services to provide devotional music.

- **Arcangelo Corelli** (1653–1713) wrote many trio sonatas of both kinds. His Trio Sonata in A Major, op. 3, no. 12, a chamber sonata, features much interplay between the two solo violins over a basso continuo. His Trio Sonata in F Major, op. 1, no. 1, is a church sonata. His Sonata in D Major, op. 5, no. 1, is for a single violin and basso continuo and allows the violinist ample opportunity to display virtuosity on the instrument.

- **Johann Pachelbel** (1653–1706). The Canon and Gigue in D Major, for three violins and basso continuo, is one of the best-known works of the entire Baroque era. This piece features three violins that play a canon over an ostinato bass. A canon is another word for round, in which each voice sings or plays exactly the same melody with staggered entries (as in "Row, row, row your boat").

- **Marin Marais** (1656–1728) composed much virtuosic music for the viola da gamba, a forerunner of today's cello. The second book of his *Pièces de violes* (*Works for Viol*) contains several suites for viol and basso continuo. Marais and his music were featured in the 1991 film *All the Mornings of the World* (*Tous les matins du monde*).

13

Johann Sebastian Bach
Fugue in G Minor, BWV 578 ("Little")

Listen to This

Timbre

Listen for the variety of sounds from this one instrument. Every "voice" (melodic line) in the work has its own distinctive sound. The organ is not only the largest and loudest of all instruments, it is capable of producing the greatest variety of timbres.

Melody

There is only one real theme in this work, and we hear it many times. It appears all by itself at the very beginning. Listen to how it begins slowly and then picks up speed.

Texture

Listen for the way in which the theme is first presented by a single voice, then imitated in a second voice, then imitated yet again with the entrances of the third and fourth voices. See how many of these iterations of the main theme your ear can pick out: in the high voice, the low voice, and (perhaps most difficult of all) the middle voices.

A **fugue** is a polyphonic work based on a central theme. Fugues are easy to recognize: they typically begin with the theme in one voice, which is imitated by all the other voices in succession, each presenting its own statement of the theme. "Fugue" comes from the same root word as "fugitive" and refers to the tendency of voices to "chase" one another: a theme presented in one voice is "pursued," as it were, by a second (and often third or fourth) voice that brings in the same theme but slightly later. The fugue represents the continuing fascination of composers and listeners alike with the intricacies of polyphonic texture. Many composers of the Baroque regarded the fugue as the touchstone of a composer's art, for it demanded more than just the invention of a good tune. That tune also had to be capable of being played against other, independent voices derived from the tune itself.

This particular fugue for organ is an early work by Bach, written when he was only about 20 years old. He probably composed it during his years in Arnstadt, where he was the organist of the town's church.

One Instrument, Many Timbres

The organ is sometimes called the "King of Instruments" because of its size, power, and variety of tone. No other acoustic (that is, nonelectric) instrument possesses the range of volume and timbre found in the organ. Every organ consists of a keyboard (called a *manual*), and pipes through which wind is forced. The keys control the flow of air to the pipes: when an organist pushes down on a key, air flows into the pipe connected to that key, creating a musical note. The largest pipes, which can be up to 16 feet high, produce the lowest notes; while the smallest pipes, some as small as a pencil, produce the highest notes. Most organs also have a pedal board, which allows the organist to play notes with his or her

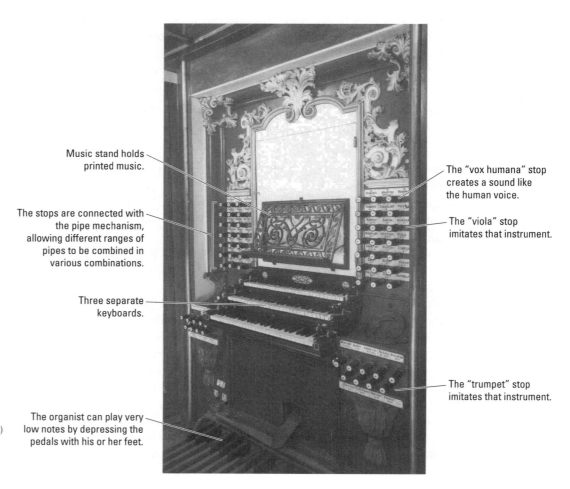

Music stand holds printed music.

The stops are connected with the pipe mechanism, allowing different ranges of pipes to be combined in various combinations.

Three separate keyboards.

The "vox humana" stop creates a sound like the human voice.

The "viola" stop imitates that instrument.

The "trumpet" stop imitates that instrument.

The organist can play very low notes by depressing the pedals with his or her feet.

Organ console of Sint Jans (Grote Kerk) in Gouda, Netherlands.

Used with permission from Rizzoli International Publications, Inc.

feet. Notes played from the pedal board tend to be quite low. There is no standard size or configuration for the organ: the number of keys and pipes can vary considerably.

In this particular piece, the variety in timbre results largely from the varying registers of the voices. High voices have a particular sound—perhaps a bit reedy—middle voices have a more rounded tone, and the lowest voices blast forth like brass instruments. The organ has a tremendous range from the lowest notes (played by the feet) to the highest notes (played on the manual; see image to left). The organist can choose the particular combination of pipes for any work or section of a work and give each different line its own distinctive sound. The number of possible combinations of registers on a large organ can range well into the hundreds.

A Distinctive Melody

The theme of this work appears many times, and its slow and stately entrance (section **A,** below) stands out even among a welter of fast-moving voices. After its slow beginning, the theme begins to accelerate, moving in shorter note values (section **B,** below). Finally, it kicks into high gear and moves very rapidly (section **C**). This rhythmic progression—slow to faster to fastest—gives the theme a strong sense of forward progression. And because this is the only real theme in the work, this sense of constant rhythmic motion extends to the work as a whole.

Fugal Texture

A fugue typically begins with the central theme, also known as a **subject**, in one voice alone. This subject is often quite catchy or attention-grabbing, particularly its first few notes. Some characteristic feature—a melodic leap, a distinctive rhythm—typically makes the subject stand out as it enters in the second voice, then the third, and so on, even as the other voices continue their independent lines. The type of polyphony used in a fugue is known as **imitative counterpoint**. The voices "imitate" one another, each sounding against ("counter") the others at the same time.

Fugue has more to do with texture—the way the voices relate to each other—than with form. Still, most fugues tend to unfold according to a conventional pattern. The opening entry of all the voices on the main subject is known as a **fugal exposition** because it "exposes" the main idea of the work. Beyond this exposition, the only formal convention is that the main theme must reappear at some point (and it usually reappears at many points) within the later course of the movement. These later entries of the subject are known as **middle entries**. Passages in which the main subject (the main theme) is absent are called **episodes**, though not every fugue has them. But the typical fugue, including this one, consists of a fugal exposition and a series of middle entries, interspersed with episodes.

0:00

Subject begins in soprano

a
(slow)

b
(faster)

Fugues—for all kinds and combinations of instruments and voices—were extremely common throughout the Baroque era in many different genres. The finale of Bach's Brandenburg Concerto no. 2 (see chapter 15) is a fugue for solo instruments and orchestra; portions of the "Hallelujah Chorus" (see chapter 18) are, in effect, brief fugues for chorus and orchestra. In the centuries following the Baroque era, composers continued to take up the challenge of writing fugues, both as practice exercises in composition and as works for performance. Fugal writing still turns up today in music of varying styles and genres.

Now listen to Bach's fugue again, following the Listening Guide.

Johann Sebastian Bach Fugue in G Minor, BWV 578 ("Little")

Time	Form: Section	Melody: Fugue Subject
0:00	Exposition	0:00 in highest voice (soprano) 0:20 in next-highest voice (alto) 0:45 in next-lowest voice (tenor) 1:05 in lowest voice (bass)
1:23	Episode 1	(Subject is absent)
1:35	Middle Entry 1	In tenor voice
1:57	Episode 2	(Subject is absent)
2:07	Middle Entry 2	In alto voice
2:25	Episode 3	(Subject is absent)
2:38	Middle Entry 3	In bass voice
2:56	Episode 4	(Subject is absent)
3:16	Middle Entry 4	In soprano voice
3:34	Episode 5	(Subject is absent)
4:08	Final Entry	In bass voice

Student FAQs

What forces air through the organ pipes?

Nowadays, the airflow in an organ is generated by an electric pump. In Bach's day, someone—usually a small boy—had to tread on a large set of bellows that operated somewhat like a stair-climber machine in a modern-day gym. This produced a steady flow of air through the pipes. Even older organs that have been restored now use an electronically generated airflow.

So the modern organ is electronic?

Only the airflow is generated electronically. What we call the electronic organ is really a different instrument altogether. It looks and sounds like a manual organ, but it produces sound through a system of electromagnetic currents, an amplifier, and speakers. Laurens Hammond (1895–1973), an American inventor, created the first mass-market, portable electronic organ in the 1930s.

Johann Sebastian Bach Fugue in G Minor, BWV 578 ("Little")

Leopold Stokowski's Orchestral Transcription (1940)

Time	Form: Section	Melody: Fugue Subject	Orchestral Timbre
0:00	Exposition	0:00 in highest voice (soprano) 0:15 in next-highest voice (alto) 0:32 in next-lowest voice (tenor) 0:46 in lowest voice (bass)	0:00 solo oboe 0:15 English horn 0:32 bassoon 0:46 bass trombone
0:59	Episode 1	(Subject is absent)	Flutes enter.
1:08	Middle Entry 1	In tenor voice	Subject = clarinets, then flutes
1:23	Episode 2	(Subject is absent)	Winds
1:30	Middle Entry 2	In alto voice	Subject = violas
1:42	Episode 3	(Subject is absent)	Violas, then various winds
2:52	Middle Entry 3	In bass voice	Subject = double basses
2:04	Episode 4	(Subject is absent)	Strings
2:18	Middle Entry 4	In soprano voice	Subject = violins
2:30	Episode 5	(Subject is absent)	Various winds, then full orchestra
2:56	Final Entry	In bass voice	Subject = trombones

MUSIC IN PERFORMANCE

Changing the Sound, but Not the Notes

Leopold Stokowski (1882–1977) ranks among the most influential conductors of the twentieth century. After emigrating to the United States from his native England in 1905, he helped develop the Philadelphia Orchestra into one of the world's leading ensembles. He also played a key role in bringing classical music to Hollywood. When he appeared with Mickey Mouse in Walt Disney's *Fantasia* in 1940, Stokowski was already a celebrity himself. Musical purists looked down on Stokowski's many orchestral transcriptions of works originally written for other instruments, but countless listeners have admired the way in which his arrangements illuminate the workings of the inner voices, particularly in a densely contrapuntal work like Bach's Fugue in G Minor.

Mickey Mouse congratulates Leopold Stokowski in Walt Disney's *Fantasia* (1940). The film includes a sequence in which Stokowski conducts his orchestral arrangement of another organ work by J.S. Bach, the Toccata and Fugue in D Minor.
©Walt Disney/Courtesy: Everett Collection

Johann Sebastian Bach (1685–1750)

NEW JOBS, NEW GENRES

Born into a family of musicians, Johann Sebastian Bach earned his living through music one way or the other throughout his entire life. He changed jobs often between the ages of 18 and 38, and with every new position, he wrote whatever music was required of him. When he was a church organist, early in his career, he wrote the majority of his organ works, including the Fugue in G Minor discussed in this chapter. Later, as violinist and concertmaster at a court orchestra (Weimar) and as music director (Cöthen), he wrote the bulk of his orchestral music, including the Brandenburg Concerto no. 2 (see chapter 15). And when Bach became cantor of St. Thomas's Church in Leipzig in 1723, he began writing new cantatas for use in the services there (see chapter 15). By the time he died, Bach had written at least one work in virtually every genre of music except for opera. Why no opera? The reason is simple: Bach never held a job that required him to write one.

Bach's two marriages—his first wife died in 1720—produced 20 children, 10 of whom survived into adulthood. Several of the sons became renowned composers in their own right. Indeed, Carl Philipp Emanuel Bach (1714–88) would become more famous than his father during the elder Bach's lifetime. Johann Christian Bach (1735–82), sometimes called the "London Bach" because of his eventual home, was one of Mozart's favorite composers. Wilhelm Friedemann Bach (1710–84), said to be perhaps the most musically gifted of all Bach's sons, met repeated misfortunes in his career and died in poverty.

Bach in the 1740s. Proud of his abilities as a composer, Bach chose to have himself portrayed holding a particularly complex work of imitative counterpoint of his own invention.
Lebrecht Music & Arts Photo Library

PLAYLIST: BACH

St. Matthew Passion, BWV 244.
An extended work for vocalists and orchestra, with choral movements, recitatives, and arias. This three-hour work narrates the betrayal and crucifixion of Christ and is built around texts from the Gospel of St. Matthew.

Partita no. 2 for Violin, BWV 1004: Chaconne.
Bach's self-imposed challenge was to write a contrapuntal work for an instrument—the violin—that is essentially melodic and normally plays only one musical line at a time.

The Well-Tempered Clavier, Book 1, BWV 846–69.
Two sets of keyboard preludes and fugues in all 24 major and minor keys. Bach wrote these works for teaching purposes.

A Musical Offering, BWV 1079.
In 1747 Bach visited his son Carl Philipp Emanuel Bach, who was a musician at the court of King Frederick II of Prussia. Frederick—himself a composer and flute player—gave Bach a particularly difficult theme on which to improvise. Later, Bach composed and sent Frederick an enormous set of different works, all based on this same theme, a "musical offering" to the king.

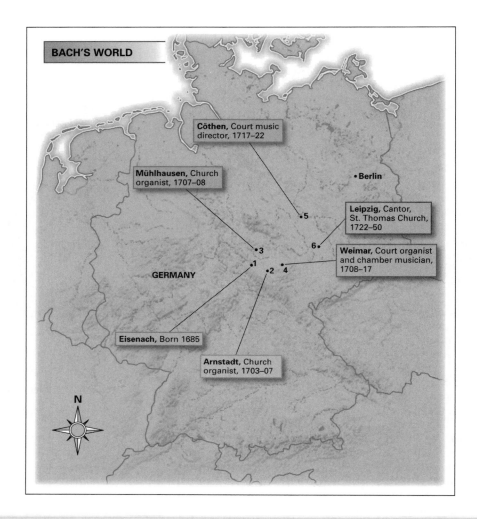

BACH'S WORLD

Cöthen, Court music
director, 1717–22

Mühlhausen, Church
organist, 1707–08

• Berlin

Leipzig, Cantor,
St. Thomas Church,
1722–50

•5

•3

•6

Weimar, Court organist
and chamber musician,
1708–17

•1   •2   4

GERMANY

Eisenach, Born 1685

Arnstadt, Church
organist, 1703–07

N

Bach moved within a small orbit. The
cities and towns in which he worked
encompassed an area roughly the size
of southern New Jersey.

EXPAND YOUR PLAYLIST

Baroque Organ Music

Jan Pieterszoon Sweelinck

"Echo" Fantasia (Ionian) (early seventeenth century). A native of
what is now the Netherlands, Sweelinck wrote a great deal of organ
music. A fantasia is a freely constructed work, meant to sound improvised, as if it were being thought up on the spot. This is one of
several fantasias in which Sweelinck uses special echo effects.

Dietrich Buxtehude

Praeludium in G Minor, BuxWV 149 (ca. 1675–89). Buxtehude was
the greatest organist in the generation before Bach. This prelude
("praeludium" is the Latin term) is a multisectional work: parts of
it are free, parts of it are fugal.

Johann Sebastian Bach

Toccata and Fugue in D Minor, BWV 565 (ca. 1705?). Perhaps the

most famous work of organ music ever written, this has been used
in countless horror movies to provide "scary" music. A toccata is a
"touch piece," one that calls for a light and rapid touch on the keys.

"Jig" Fugue, BWV 577. This work is no longer believed to be an
authentic work of Bach, but whoever wrote it certainly knew how
to write fugues. The rhythm is so compelling that audiences
have been known to clap along with it.

Chorale Prelude (Wachet auf, ruft uns die Stimme), BWV 645. An
organ version of one of the movements from the Cantata 140 (see
chapter 17). Bach wrote many organ arrangements of chorale
(hymn) tunes. These works are called chorale preludes because
they were performed before the congregation sang the chorale.

14

Antonio Vivaldi
The Four Seasons, "Winter," first movement

Listen to This

Timbre

Listen for the contrast in sound between the solo instrument (the violin) and the ensemble (a small orchestra of stringed instruments, plus basso continuo). Notice how the soloist plays with the orchestra at some points and not at others.

Form

Listen for the way in which long sections with the soloist alternate with long sections without the soloist.

Word-Music Relationships

This work is entitled "Winter." Do you hear any sounds that might suggest this season of the year?

A **concerto** is an instrumental work for a soloist (or sometimes more than one soloist) and a larger ensemble. This particular concerto is for a solo violin and an orchestra of stringed instruments, plus basso continuo. It is the last of four concertos for this same combination of instruments that Vivaldi designated collectively as *The Four Seasons.* Although each of these concertos—"Spring," "Summer," "Fall," and "Winter"—stands on its own, the four together represent the cycle of the seasons, a favorite theme of painters and poets alike. "Winter," like most other concertos of its time, consists of three movements in the sequence Fast-Slow-Fast. The movement here is the first of the three.

Contrasting Timbres

The concerto emerged as a particularly thrilling genre for Baroque audiences because it featured a sharp contrast between the sound of a solo instrument and the combined sound of all the other instruments. In this way, it was a perfect manifestation of the Baroque love of extremes. The concerto also became a vehicle for virtuosic displays, another Baroque fascination. Vivaldi in particular, both as a composer and as a player, took the art of the virtuoso violin to new levels. He worked in both a time (the early eighteenth century) and a place (northern Italy) where violin making and violin playing were at their very peak: to this day, the best violins are from the era and region in which Vivaldi worked.

The appeal of the concerto's contrasting timbres, dialogue between soloist and orchestra, and virtuosity lasted beyond the Baroque period and into the present day. The concerto has undergone changes over the centuries but remains a popular genre among composers and audiences alike. Nearly every modern symphony concert program features a concerto—from the Baroque or from a later period—and Vivaldi's masterful opposition of solo and large-group string timbres has given *The Four Seasons* lasting popularity.

Form: The Ritornello Principle

This movement consists of a series of alternating sections between the orchestra (also known as the **tutti**, Italian for "all") and the soloist. Each statement and return of the full ensemble is known as the **ritornello** (Italian for "little [i.e., brief] return"). This formal design of alternating ritornello and solo sections is known as the **ritornello principle** and is basic to almost all concerto movements of the Baroque era. The form of this movement, based on the ritornello principle, can be represented graphically in this way:

Ritornello 1   Solo 1   Ritornello 2   Solo 2   Ritornello 3   Solo 3   Ritornello 4

The form of the movement is also structured around large-scale changes of key area. A *key area* is a set of harmonies that all have a distinctive relationship to one particular note, known as the **tonic**. At the beginning and end of this movement, that tonic note is F, and because the mode is minor, this central key area is called "F minor." F minor acts as the "home" key, and it is by definition the key in which the movement begins and ends. (If it closed in a different key, the ending would not sound as conclusive.) But if the entire movement were in a single key, it would sound monotonous, and so Vivaldi moves the music to key areas other than the tonic—including some in the major mode. These other key areas provide a sense of harmonic variety.

The ritornello principle is found not only in concertos, but in almost every Baroque work that contrasts a soloist or group of soloists against a larger ensemble. Operatic arias, for example, routinely open with an instrumental ritornello (Ritornello 1), followed by the entrance of the voice (Solo 1), a brief return of the orchestra without the voice (Ritornello 2), a reentry of the voice (Solo 2), and so on. Composers and audiences of the Baroque relished the sound of contrasting forces, and the ritornello principle provided the perfect means by which to present such contrasts.

Section	Ritornello 1	Solo 1	Ritornello 2	Solo 2	Ritornello 3	Solo 3	Ritornello 4
Key Area	F minor	C minor	F minor	F minor	E♭ Major	E♭ Major → C minor	F minor

Variety: Modulates to different (non-tonic) keys

Unity: Begins and ends in F minor (the tonic key) and re-establishes F minor in the middle

Word-Music Relationships: Program Music

The form of this particular concerto is also shaped by its relationship to a poem ("Winter") that Vivaldi appended to the first publication of the score in 1725. He indicated quite precisely which lines of the following poem relate to which points of the concerto. This concerto is thus an example of **program music**, an instrumental work that is in some way associated with a story, event, or idea. A composer can indicate such connections by a suggestive title, a prose or poetic narrative, or both. A listener may choose to listen to the piece with the program in mind—in the case of Vivaldi's "Winter," hearing the strings shaking as if with cold in Ritornello 1, a stamping of feet in Ritornello 2, and a chattering sound in the Solo 3—or simply listen to the piece as music that does not represent anything besides itself. Indeed, some composers (for example, Berlioz—see chapter 29), have gone back and forth about whether their audiences should be aware of a program or simply be allowed to hear the music as it unfolds.

"Winter"

First movement: To tremble from cold in the icy snow
In the harsh breath of a horrid wind
To run, stamping our feet every moment
Our teeth chattering in the extreme cold.

Second movement: Before the fire to pass peaceful, contented days,
While the rain outside pours down.

Third movement: To walk on the ice and, at a slow pace
For fear of falling, move carefully.
To make a bold turn, slip, fall down.
To go on the ice once more and run hard
Until the ice cracks and breaks up.
To hear the Sirocco [the north wind], Boreas [the south wind], and all
The winds at war leave their iron gates:
This is winter, but even so, what joy it brings!

Antonio Vivaldi, *The Four Seasons,* op. 8, nos. 1–4, ed. Eleanor Selfridge-Field. New York: Dover, 1999, p. xiii.

Now listen to the movement, using the Listening Guide.

Antonio Vivaldi *The Four Seasons*, "Winter," first movement

Time	Melody	Harmony: Key Area	Form	Word-Music Relationships (1): The Poetry
0:00	1	F minor	Ritornello 1	To tremble from cold in the icy snow
0:37	2	C minor	Solo 1	In the harsh breath of a horrid wind
0:59_1:12	1_____3	F minor	Ritornello 2	To run, stamping our feet every moment
1:26	4	F minor→ unstable	Solo 2	
2:05	1	E♭ major	Ritornello 3	
2:25	5	E♭ major→ C minor	Solo 3	Our teeth chattering in the extreme cold
3:04	3	F minor	Ritornello 4	

Word-Music Relationships (2): The Music

Repetitive figure in the strings suggests trembling

The solo violin also "trembles" and moves from high to low, like the wind.

Faster tempo ("running"); the music begins to "stamp" at 1:12.

The soloist bounces the bow very rapidly against the string, creating a "chattering" sound (2:35_3:03).

Student FAQs

I can't hear the difference in key areas between the sections. How can I learn to hear these changes?

With digital technology, it's easy to make side-by-side comparisons. Using the Listening Guide, start the music at 0:37. The long note to which the solo violinist keeps returning is C, the tonic of C minor. Let the music run through 1:00. Vivaldi again and again emphasizes this new key area of C minor. Now go back to the beginning, which is in F minor. Hear the difference? The main note at the beginning is F, the root of the tonic key of F minor. Now let the music run through and listen for the change of key between the opening and 0:37. This may take some time at first, but once you start listening for changes of key, it gets easier to recognize them. And even if you don't always hear the key changes consciously, you will appreciate that they affect the way the music sounds by providing both harmonic unity (the tonic) and variety (all other keys).

What does the violin soloist do during the tutti sections?

The soloist plays with the first violin section of the orchestra. But because the sound of the solo instrument blends into the sound of the orchestra, the soloist cannot be heard as a separate, distinct voice.

Which is more important, the musical or the programmatic form?

The two work in tandem and reinforce each other. We do not know if Vivaldi began with the poem and wrote a concerto around it, or if he began with a concerto and wrote a poem around it. It's also possible that the two processes took shape simultaneously.

Antonio Vivaldi (1678–1741)

COMPOSING FOR ORPHANS

Known as the "Red Priest" because he was red-haired and ordained, Antonio Vivaldi served for many years as director of music at Venice's Ospedale della Pietà ("Hospice of Compassion"), a large orphanage for girls. Being the music director of an orphanage might strike us today as a strange job for one of the most famous composers of his time, but to judge from the music Vivaldi wrote for the young women at this particular institution, they must have been quite talented indeed. Later in his life Vivaldi moved to Vienna, where he worked at the court of Charles VI, but he wrote most of his concertos while in service to the orphanage in Venice.

Vivaldi was extremely prolific. He wrote almost 350 solo concertos (about two-thirds of which are for solo violin) and 45 double concertos (more than half of which are for two violins). His music was widely published and admired throughout Europe during his lifetime. J.S. Bach arranged several of his concertos for the organ and in the process taught himself how to write concertos "in the Italian style." Bach and Handel may have had greater facility at counterpoint, but Vivaldi was a master of melodic invention and formal novelty. Almost every one of his concertos contains some unusual twist that makes it different from all the rest.

Antonio Vivaldi was famous both as a composer and as a violinist during his lifetime. His red hair is covered by his wig.

Lebrecht Music & Arts Photo Library

PLAYLIST: VIVALDI

The Four Seasons: "Spring." The opening theme (Ritornello 1) is now a popular ringtone for cell phones.

The Four Seasons: "Summer." The finale depicts a violent thunderstorm.

The Four Seasons: "Fall." The finale depicts a hunting scene.

Concerto for Mandolin, RV 532. More typically associated with bluegrass music, the mandolin was already a popular instrument in the Baroque.

Gloria, RV 589, for chorus and orchestra. A thrilling setting of the Gloria portion of the Mass Ordinary.

Concerto for Flute, Strings, and Basso Continuo, op. 10, no. 1. Nicknamed "The Tempest at Sea" because of its stormy sound.

Trade Secrets: Building the Perfect Violin

From the Middle Ages onward, instrument makers maintained a wall of silence around the secrets of their crafts, passing them on only to their apprentices (often their children) by word of mouth. We no longer know exactly how the great violin makers of the seventeenth and eighteenth centuries produced instruments that remain unsurpassed even today.

The most famous of these makers was Antonio Stradivari (or "Stradivarius," to use the Latinized form of his name), who worked in Cremona, a small city in what is now northern Italy. No two of his instruments are exactly alike. Like all makers, Stradivarius (1644–1737) was constantly tinkering with the precise dimensions of the instruments—the angle and length of the fingerboard, the thickness and placement of the bass-bar underneath the upper surface of the instrument, and the shape of the f-holes. He took many of his trade secrets with him to the grave.

In the last 50 years, however, historians, musical instrument curators, and scientists have begun to penetrate those secrets, using sophisticated techniques of chemical analysis and radiography to analyze surviving instruments. We now know that key factors included an instrument's shape, the quality of the wood from which it was made, the techniques used for carving the wood, and the characteristics of the varnish that protected it. With the recovery of at least some of this ancient craft, it is now possible to produce very good copies of these instruments, but the originals remain superior. The chief reason

Front and rear view of a "Strad." A Stradivarius violin sold for $2.03 million in 2005, the highest price ever paid for a musical instrument.

Royal Academy of Music/Lebrecht Music & Arts Photo Library

for this probably lies in the nature of the wood. Because even the best trees today have been affected by air pollution, it is no longer possible to find wood of the same quality.

   EXPAND YOUR PLAYLIST

Program Music

Program music—instrumental music explicitly connected in some way with a story, person, or idea outside the music itself—has long fired the imaginations of composers and listeners.

Johann Kuhnau, *Six Biblical Sonatas* (1700). Each of these six sonatas, for harpsichord, depicts a famous story from the Bible. When David defeats Goliath, we "hear" the stone hurled toward the giant and the enormous thud when he falls to the ground.

Marin Marais, *An Image of Abdominal Surgery* (1725). A lengthy work for solo viola da gamba, it depicts in great detail the removal of a gallstone. The score includes such comments as "The Incision," "Blood Flows," and "The Stone Is Removed."

Ludwig van Beethoven, *Wellington's Victory*, op. 91 (1813). Depicts the victory of the English general over Napoleon's forces

at the Battle of Vittoria (Spain). The opening mimics the trumpet calls of the armies, and the percussion simulate the sounds of cannon and musket fire.

Hector Berlioz, *Symphonie fantastique* (1830). See chapter 29.

George Gershwin, *An American in Paris* (1928). This work recreates, in sound, impressions of Paris, including honking horns of the traffic, French speech, and an American's homesickness for his native country.

John Adams, *A Short Ride in a Fast Machine* (1986). The title suggests the acceleration and tremendous speed of this work for large orchestra. As the composer said: "You know how it is when someone asks you to ride in a terrific sports car, and then you wish you hadn't?"

15

CÖTHEN → Berlin
GERMANY Leipzig
Frankfurt
Munich

Johann Sebastian Bach
Brandenburg Concerto no. 2 in F Major, BWV 1047, finale

Listen to This

Timbre

Listen for the contrasting sounds of the four solo instruments, which enter in this order:
- The trumpet, a brass instrument, has a loud, bright sound.
- The oboe, a woodwind instrument, has a piercing, slightly nasal sound.
- The violin, a stringed instrument, has a resonant, lyrical sound.
- The recorder, another woodwind instrument, has a soft, gentle sound similar to that of a flute.

Also listen for the way in which the sound of the four solo instruments as a group contrasts with the sound of the larger ensemble, which is a small orchestra of stringed instruments (violins, violas, cellos, basses) and basso continuo.

Form

Listen for the alternation between the soloists as a group and the orchestra as a whole. Like all concertos of the Baroque era, this one is built around the ritornello principle, in which sections played by the soloists alone (accompanied only by the basso continuo) alternate with sections played by the full orchestra.

Texture

Listen for the way in which the melody is presented successively by each of the soloists at the beginning and then taken up by each voice in turn repeatedly over the course of the movement. This entire movement is a fugue.

Not all concertos are for only one soloist. Baroque composers also cultivated the genre of the **concerto grosso**—in Italian, this means literally "big concerto"—with multiple soloists. Bach's Brandenburg Concerto no. 2 is one of six such works dedicated to the Margrave of Brandenburg (a region in what is now eastern Germany) in 1721. Bach's six Brandenburg Concertos feature unique instrumental combinations and contain three or four movements each. The movement here is the last of three.

Extreme Timbres

Central to the solo concerto and concerto grosso is timbral contrast: soloist(s) vs. orchestra. In this particular work, the solo instruments provide unusual contrast among themselves. The trumpet is one of the loudest and most penetrating of all instruments, while the recorder is one of the softest and gentlest. The oboe and violin lie between these two extremes. Bach clearly relished the challenge of combining such a wide spectrum of solo instruments in the same concerto. It was a new and bold measure to group such different instrumental timbres together.

Form: The Ritornello Principle Returns

As in Vivaldi's concerto for solo violin and orchestra (see chapter 14), this movement is based on the **ritornello principle**: sections for the soloists (Solo 1, Solo 2, etc.) alternate with sections for the full orchestra (Ritornello 1, Ritornello 2, etc.). The soloists—or at least some of them—also play along with the full orchestra during the ritornello sections. The basso continuo instruments—harpsichord and cello—live up to their name, playing continuously throughout the movement.

   Like Vivaldi in his solo concerto "Winter," Bach uses different key areas to establish a sense of a beginning, a contrasting middle, and an ending that brings harmonic closure to the whole. The movement opens and closes in the key of F major; in between, it moves through a variety of different key areas. If the movement did not **modulate**—that is, move to a different key area—the theme would not sound as fresh as it does each time it comes back (and it comes back often). If it ended in a key other than the tonic—its primary key area, the one in which it began—it would sound open-ended and inconclusive.

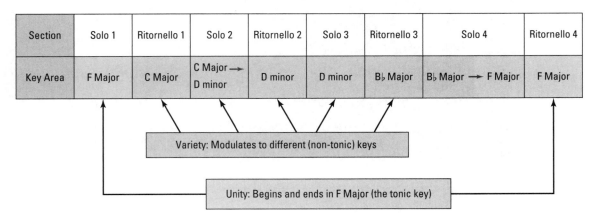

Section	Solo 1	Ritornello 1	Solo 2	Ritornello 2	Solo 3	Ritornello 3	Solo 4	Ritornello 4
Key Area	F Major	C Major	C Major → D minor	D minor	D minor	B♭ Major	B♭ Major → F Major	F Major

Variety: Modulates to different (non-tonic) keys

Unity: Begins and ends in F Major (the tonic key)

Fugal Texture

Although Bach did not label it as such, this entire movement is a fugue. The texture, as with any fugue, is polyphonic. As we have seen (chapter 13), fugue is more a function of texture than of form. But as in Bach's Fugue in G Minor, BWV 578, the fugal finale of Bach's Brandenburg Concerto no. 2 employs some of the most common structural features, to wit:

- **Fugal exposition.** It gets this name from the fact that it "exposes" the theme in each of the solo instruments in turn.
- **Middle entries.** These are passages (throughout the movement) that reintroduce the subject, often in imitation with other instruments.
- **Episodes.** Here the subject does not appear at all. In this movement, the episodes happen to coincide with the tutti sections, in which all the instruments of the orchestra play.

Now listen to this movement again, following the Listening Guide.

An outdoor evening instrumental concert in the town square of Jena in the 1740s. The large orchestra includes trumpets and timpani. J.S. Bach led a similar ensemble in nearby Leipzig for a time.
Museum für Kunst und Gewerbe, Hamburg, Germany

The Art of Trumpet Playing, Lost and Found

When Bach died in 1750, most of his music soon disappeared from the active repertory. Keyboard performers still knew and played some of the works that he had written for harpsichord and for organ, but the choral and orchestral music was largely forgotten. When performers began rediscovering Bach's music in the nineteenth century, they were baffled by how to perform some of it, including the very difficult trumpet part of Brandenburg Concerto no. 2.

Both trumpets and the art of trumpet playing had changed drastically in the meantime. In the nineteenth century, the instrument began to be produced with valves and keys that allowed players to produce a wider range of notes with a more uniform quality of sound. But the art of playing the "natural"—valveless—trumpet gradually disappeared. In Bach's time, and

for centuries before that, trumpet playing had been strictly regulated: the trumpet was an aural symbol of military and political power, and not just anyone could pick up the instrument. Trumpeters had to join guilds to practice their art, and the secrets of the art, as in all guilds, were transmitted largely by word of mouth. When restrictions on trumpet playing began to be lifted in the late eighteenth century, the guilds soon disappeared, and with them the knowledge of how to perform the kinds of high, rapid passagework so prevalent in Bach's Brandenburg Concerto no. 2.

In the late nineteenth century, a few trumpet players began experimenting with specially designed instruments (so-called Bach trumpets) that would allow them to play this earlier music. Over time, more and more musicians became interested in using original instruments or accurate reproductions of them. Today, the lost art of playing the high range of the Baroque trumpet has been recovered, and we can hear Bach's Brandenburg Concerto no. 2 in a manner that more closely resembles the sound of what Bach himself heard when he conducted it.

Binding
The bell and tubing sections are kept separate by a wooden block. Heavy woolen cord holds them together.

Bell
Often has an embossed rim, bearing the maker's name, the name of the town, and the date.

Back bow

Knop
Strengthens the joint between bell and tube.

The Baroque ("natural") trumpet. There are no keys or valves, only one long piece of coiled tubing. Bach wrote his Brandenburg Concerto no. 2 for a smaller trumpet that could reach a higher range but which similarly lacked keys or valves.

GRAHAM SALTER/Lebrecht Music & Arts Photo Library

Mouthpiece   Valves   Bell

First valve tube   Second valve tube   Third valve tube   Water key   Tuning slide

The modern trumpet. Notice the valves and multiple coils of tubing, both of which allow the trumpeter to lengthen or shorten the column of air, thereby making it easier to produce a wider range of notes.

© Dorling Kindersley

Johann Sebastian Bach Brandenburg Concerto no. 2 in F Major, BWV 1047, finale

Time	Form: Ritornello/Solo	Timbre	Texture: The Fugue
0:00	Solo 1	0:00 Trumpet alone 0:08 Oboe enters 0:26 Violin enters 0:33 Recorder enters 0:51 Trumpet reenters	Fugal exposition
0:59	Ritornello 1	Tutti and soloists	Episode 1
1:11	Solo 2	Recorder and violin; subject in oboe at 1:23	Middle Entry 1
1:31	Ritornello 2	Tutti and soloists	Episode 2
1:47	Solo 3	Oboe and violin together, then recorder, then trumpet	Middle Entry 2
2:03	Ritornello 3	Tutti and soloists	Episode 3
2:15	Solo 4	Trumpet and oboe together, subject in oboe; recorder at 2:23	Final Entry
2:30	Ritornello 4	Tutti and soloists	Final Entry (cont'd.)

**Harmony:
Key Areas**

F major
C major
C major → D minor
D minor
D minor
B♭ major
B♭ major → F major
F major

Student FAQs

Did Bach ever write programs for his concertos the way Vivaldi did?

No. In fact, very few of Bach's instrumental works give any hint at a story or idea outside the music. He did write a work for harpsichord he called *Capriccio on the Departure of a Beloved Brother,* BWV 992, and he labeled individual sections with such titles as "Friends gather and try to dissuade him from departing," "They imagine the dangers which might befall him," and "The Friends' Lament," but on the whole, these verbal cues are the exception rather than the rule in Bach's music.

Is the basso continuo part of the ritornello or the solo group?

Both. Its function is to support whatever other instruments are playing at the moment, so it plays in both the solo and ritornello sections.

The Baroque Concerto

Baroque listeners responded enthusiastically to the emergence of a genre highlighting contrasts among instruments and performing forces. Here are some of the best-loved concerto composers and their works, all of which are still performed regularly today.

Arcangelo Corelli (1653–1713). Corelli was one of the first composers to write large-scale concertos, all with two violins and basso continuo as soloists, accompanied by a string orchestra.

- Concerto Grosso in G Minor, op. 6, no. 8, known as the "Christmas Concerto" because it ends with a pastoral-like movement thought to depict the shepherds and their flocks who came to see the infant Jesus in the manger.

Antonio Vivaldi (1678–1741). In addition to his *Four Seasons* (see chapter 14), Vivaldi wrote literally hundreds of concertos, both for solo instruments and for groups of solo instruments. Like Bach, Vivaldi seems to have been attracted to the idea of writing for unusual instruments and unusual combinations of instruments.

- Concerto in C Major for Mandolin and Strings, RV 425. The first movement of this work has been used in several movie soundtracks, including *Casanova* (2005) and *The Royal Tenenbaums* (2001), as well as for a 2005 episode of *The Sopranos.* The slow movement is a favorite for wedding ceremonies.
- Concerto in C Major for 2 Trumpets and Strings, RV 537. The two trumpets play together, often creating echo effects.

George Frideric Handel (1685–1759) wrote many concertos, mostly during his time in England, and many imitating the style of Corelli.

- Concerto Grosso in B-flat Major for 2 Recorders, 2 Oboes, 2 Bassoons, Violin, and Strings, op. 3, no. 1. Handel gives the wind instruments unusually prominent roles in this work.

Johann Sebastian Bach. All six of his Brandenburg Concertos are well worth knowing.

- Concerto no. 1 in F Major, BWV 1046
  There are no true soloists in this concerto; every instrument is treated virtuosically. Written for two horns, three oboes, bassoon, violino piccolo (a type of small violin tuned slightly higher than the standard violin), strings, and basso continuo.

- Concerto no. 3 in G Major, BWV 1048
  For strings alone, with no soloists. But each of the stringed instruments (violins, violas, cellos) is subdivided into three separate parts, creating a nine-voice texture, all above the basso continuo.

- Concerto no. 4 in G Major, BWV 1049
  The soloists are two recorders and violin; the orchestra consists of strings and basso continuo. The finale is a rousing fugue.

- Concerto no. 5 in D Major, BWV 1050
  The soloists are a flute, violin, and—an innovation in this work—a harpsichord, which at times plays as a member of the basso continuo, at times as a true soloist.

- Concerto no. 6 in B-flat Major, BWV 1051
  The scoring is limited entirely to low strings. The soloists are two violas, accompanied by viola da gambas, cellos, and basso continuo.

16

George Frideric Handel
Water Music, selections

 Listen to This

Form

Listen for two distinct sections in each of these two movements. Notice that each section is repeated immediately.

Rhythm

Listen for the regularity of the rhythmic patterns in the music. What is the meter of each movement? Triple or duple? Listen for patterns of accented and unaccented beats: **1**-2-3 | **1**-2-3, or **1**-2 | **1**-2.

Timbre

Listen for the contrasting combinations of instruments used in these two dances, and to the contrast of instruments within the second one in particular (winds vs. strings).

A good party needs good music. Because kings tend to have big budgets, they can hire not only the best bands but also the best composers to write the music. King George I hired the best on July 17, 1717, when he and his entourage traveled by boat down the River Thames from Whitehall to Chelsea and back. An orchestra of 50 musicians traveled along, and George Frideric Handel wrote parts or all of what we now know as his *Water Music* for the occasion. The *Water Music* is a **suite**, a series of some two dozen individual dance movements, two of which are presented here. A suite typically consists of different types of dances, such as minuets, gavottes, and gigues. The variety of dance types—fast vs. slow, lively vs. stately, duple vs. triple—gave composers ample room to juxtapose contrasting moods.

Whether people actually danced to this music varied from place to place and time to time. We do not know if the king and his followers actually danced at the premiere of Handel's *Water Music,* but there can be no doubt that the music was received with great enthusiasm. The music is still beloved by audiences today, and has been featured in several movie and television soundtracks, including *Dead Poets Society, Map of the Human Heart,* and *Moll Flanders.*

Water Music: Rigaudon

A **rigaudon** (pronounced *rig-o-dohn*) is a fast dance in duple meter, invariably cheerful in tone.

Binary Form

Like most dances of the Baroque era, this one is in **binary form**. Binary form takes its name from the fact that it always consists of two sections, both repeated. (The symbol |: :| is used to indicate a unit of music to be repeated.)

Binary Form

	|: First Section	:| |: Second section	:|
Key Area	Primary key (tonic) → Secondary key	Any key except tonic → Tonic	

The pattern of the key areas helps create both unity and variety within any binary form. As shown in the diagram above, the first section of a binary form begins in the primary key or tonic and often **modulates** to a secondary key area. (A **modulation** is a change of key within the course of a movement.) The second section begins in almost any key *except* the tonic and remains harmonically unstable—that is, it moves rapidly through several different key areas without settling on any particular one—before finally returning to the tonic. Without these changes, the music would sound harmonically repetitive. If it did not end in the key in which it began, the music would sound unfinished. This basic pattern of starting and ending in the same key and moving away from it in the middle is basic to binary form and to many other musical forms as well.

Melodically, a binary form often rests on a single basic idea. Composers typically manipulate particular elements of a theme, such as its opening segment or its characteristic rhythm, but rarely do they try to create thematic contrast within a simple binary form. Binary-form movements appear in such genres as sonatas and symphonies as well as suites. Binary form eventually became the basis for sonata form, the most important instrumental form of the Classical era (see chapter 22).

A Regular Rhythm in Two

The regular rhythm of this dance reinforces its duple meter (**1**-2 | **1**-2 | **1**-2). Listen to the way in which notes of varying duration—some long, some short, some in between—invariably conform to the basic framework of units consisting of two beats. The very first note actually falls on a beat *before* the downbeat. This kind of rhythmic pattern is called by various names: a pickup beat, an upbeat, or—borrowing from poetry—an **anacrusis**.

The rhythm of the opening of the "Rigaudon."

Now listen to the "Rigaudon" again, following the Listening Guide.

Water Music: Hornpipe

A hornpipe is a lively dance in triple meter, often associated with sailors, which certainly befits a suite of dances to be played on a boat. Handel directs that this particular dance be performed three times in succession.

Binary Form

Again, the basic framework of this dance is binary form, with two sections, each repeated. The entire unit is played three times in succession.

Handel as a young man, composing at the keyboard. Like many men of the day, he kept his head shaved to better accommodate a wig, which he always wore in public.
© Archivo Iconografico, S.A./CORBIS

A Regular Rhythm in Three

Listen for the regularity of the triple meter (**1**-2 3 | **1**-2-3 | **1**-2-3) offset by the occasional **syncopation**, a moment in which the accent falls on a beat other than the normal downbeat (see Elements, p. 7). One prominent moment of syncopation (at 0:09) happens to coincide with the onset of the harmonic modulation.

Timbre: Winds vs. Strings

Handel himself did not always specify exactly which instruments should perform which parts; instead, he left it up to the performers to create timbral variety by using a different **orchestration** each time the binary form is presented. Orchestration is the manner in which various instruments are assigned to the musical lines. In the performance here, we hear the same musical lines three times in succession, but they sound different because of the different orchestration each time:

Giovanni Canaletto's *View of London and the Thames* shows a procession probably similar to the one for which Handel wrote his *Water Music*.

Bridgeman-Giraudon/Art Resource, N.Y.

1. The first time, we hear the dance played by strings (violins, violas, cellos, and basses) and basso continuo (harpsichord and cello).
2. The second time, we hear the winds (three oboes and, on the bottom, two bassoons) and basso continuo.
3. The third time, we hear all these instruments together: the full ensemble of strings, winds, and basso continuo. The sound thus expands both in variety and volume from beginning to end.

These contrasting timbres are in keeping with the Baroque era's fondness for contrast and extremes. Over time, composers became more and more specific about which instruments should play which parts. By the early nineteenth century, some composers were even writing manuals of how to write for the orchestra, with special attention to the qualities of each instrument.

Now listen to the "Hornpipe," using the Listening Guide.

George Frideric Handel *Water Music: Rigaudon*

→ = begins to modulate (move to a different key)

Time	Form: Section	Harmony: Key Areas	Timbre
0:00	First	G major → begins to modulate at 0:09, arrives in D major at 0:11	Melody carried by violins, doubled by oboes. In this performance, the basso continuo consists of harpsichord and cello.
0:12	First (repeated)	G major → begins to modulate at 0:20, arrives in D major at 0:24	
0:24	Second	Unstable → returns to G major (0:30)	
0:42	Second (repeated)	Unstable → returns to G major (0:48)	

George Frideric Handel *Water Music: Hornpipe*

Time	Statement	Form: Section	Harmony: Key Areas	Timbre
0:00	1	First	F major → C major (0:11)	Winds and basso continuo
0:12		First (repeated)		
0:24		Second	Unstable → returns to F major (0:35)	
0:36		Second (repeated)		
0:47	2	First	F major → C major	Strings and basso continuo
0:59		First (repeated)		
1:10		Second	Unstable → F major	
1:22		Second (repeated)		
1:34	3	First	F major → C major	Strings and winds together, with basso continuo
1:46		First (repeated)		
1:57		Second	Unstable → F major	
2:09		Second (repeated)		

Student FAQs

Why are there so many repeats in the music?

Dance music typically establishes a rhythmic pattern and then repeats it many times. While we often listen to dance music without dancing, its primary function is to make dancing easy. Consider the repetition in today's dance music. Small rhythmic and melodic units repeat, sometimes throughout the entire song, and entire sections often play several times, so it's easy to focus on movement.

Are the dances in this suite in any particular order?

No. A number of later composers have made arrangements of the dances in Handel's *Water Music*, presenting the dances in a fixed sequence, but in the composer's own time, the individual numbers followed no particular progression. Other suites may or may not feature a fixed order of dances.

George Frideric Handel (1685–1759)

THE WELL-TRAVELED COMPOSER

George Frideric Handel and J.S. Bach were born within a month of each other and less than 100 miles apart, but they never met, and their careers as composers could scarcely have been more different. Bach spent his entire life in central Germany, whereas Handel traveled widely throughout Europe. He moved to Italy in 1706 and soon established a name for himself as a composer of operas and oratorios. He returned to Germany as music director for the Elector of Hanover in 1710, but he soon journeyed to England, where his operas won great acclaim.

When the Elector of Hanover ascended the English throne as George I in 1714, Handel was still in his service and thus perfectly positioned to enjoy the new king's patronage and support. Over the course of his long career in England, Handel wrote many operas and oratorios that met with great public success. He abandoned opera altogether in 1741 and turned his attention toward the oratorio.

The music historian Charles Burney, who knew Handel personally, wrote this reminiscence:

> The figure of Handel was large, and he was somewhat corpulent, and unwieldy in his motions; but his countenance, which I remember as perfectly as that of any man I saw but yesterday, was full of fire and dignity; and such as impressed ideas of superiority and genius. He was impetuous, rough and peremptory in his manners and conversation, but totally devoid of ill-nature or malevolence; indeed, there was an original humor and pleasantry in his most lively sallies of anger or impatience, which, with his broken English, were extremely risible. His natural propensity to wit and humor, and happy manner of relating common occurrences, in an uncommon way, enabled him to throw persons and things into very ridiculous attitudes.*

PLAYLIST: HANDEL

Messiah (oratorio). See chapter 18.

Saul (oratorio). One of Handel's many oratorios on a story from the Old Testament. The text deals with the relationship between Saul, King of Israel, and the young David.

Rinaldo (opera). Handel's first operatic hit, premiered in London in 1711.

Giulio Cesare (opera). One of Handel's most enduring operas, the tale of Caesar and Cleopatra in ancient Egypt.

Alexander's Feast (ode). Set to a text by poet and playwright John Dryden, this work for soloists, chorus, and orchestra extols the power of music even over Alexander the Great, ruler of the world's greatest empire in his day.

HANDEL'S WORLD

Although born in the same year and not far from J.S. Bach, Handel traveled widely throughout his life.

* Charles Burney, *An Account of the Musical Performances in Westminster-Abbey . . . in Commemoration of Handel*. London: T. Payne, 1785, pp. 31–32.

The Composer as Cultural Hero

Handel was so beloved by the English public that he was buried in Westminster Abbey, a place of special cultural importance to the nation. Westminster Abbey itself is the church in which the kings and queens of England have been crowned since 1066 and the resting place of many of those monarchs. One particular area of the church, known as "Poets' Corner," contains the graves of such literary figures as Geoffrey Chaucer, Edmund Spenser, John Dryden, Charles Dickens, Alfred Lord Tennyson, Rudyard Kipling, and Thomas Hardy. Handel is buried in that section as well.

What is Handel, a composer, doing in the Poets' Corner? Other composers, like Henry Purcell, had been buried elsewhere in the Abbey, but only because they had worked there. Handel was accorded this esteemed resting place by virtue of the music he had written. The court and public alike saw him as the artistic equal of England's greatest literary figures.

In 1784, a quarter century after his death, Handel was commemorated through a series of enormous concerts in Westminster Abbey, organized by the monarchy with the purpose not only of honoring the composer but also of consolidating a sense of national pride. The concerts were so popular that a similar festival was held annually thereafter until 1791, with the number of participants more than doubling, from around 500 the first year to more than 1,000 in the last.

Handel was one of the first composers to become a cultural hero, a figure who was perceived to have contributed to the broader well-being of society as a whole, not merely the music-loving portion. Over the course of the nineteenth century, civic monuments would be erected to such composers as Bach, Haydn, Mozart, and Beethoven.

EXPAND YOUR PLAYLIST

Baroque Suites

Many Baroque composers wrote multiple series of dances that they gathered into suites that were quite successful commercially.

Elizabeth Jacquet de la Guerre
Suite in D Minor (1707). One of several suites for harpsichord by a woman who was herself an outstanding keyboard virtuoso.

François Couperin
Keyboard Pieces, Book IV, 25th Group (1730). Many of the movements from Couperin's suites for harpsichord bear programmatic titles, including pieces in this group with such intriguing headings as "The Visionary," "The Mysterious One," "The Victorious Muse," and "The Wandering Shadows."

Johann Sebastian Bach
Orchestral Suite No. 3 in D Major, BWV 1068 (ca. 1730). One of four suites for orchestra by Bach, this one includes the celebrated "Air on the G String."

Partita No. 4 in D Major, BWV 828. "Partita" is another term used in the Baroque era for suite, and Bach wrote six partitas for harpsichord. The finale of this one is a fugue based on a theme that sounds like a jig (or gigue, to use the French form of the word).

George Frideric Handel
Royal Fireworks Music (1748). Written in 1749 for a ceremony to celebrate the peace treaty that ended the War of Austrian Succession, this suite originally was scored for a large wind band. Later, it was arranged for a full orchestra.

17

Johann Sebastian Bach
Cantata 140: *Awake, a Voice Calls to Us,* selections

 Listen to This

The selections here are the first and last movements of a **cantata**, a work sung during a service of worship. Listen for the way in which Bach uses the melody of the same hymn tune—also known as a **chorale**—as the basis for both of these movements. To help you recognize the chorale, you may find it easier to listen to the last movement first.

Melody

- *First Movement:* Listen to how the individual phrases of the chorale are separate by long passages of contrasting music.
- *Last Movement:* Listen to how the chorale is presented in a straightforward fashion, with only brief pauses between its individual phrases.

Timbre

- *First Movement:* Listen for the contrast between the chorus and the orchestra.
- *Last Movement:* Listen for the *lack of* contrast between chorus and orchestra.

Texture

- *First Movement:* Listen for the polyphonic texture. The chorale appears in the uppermost voice, but the lower voices present contrasting, important melodic material of their own.
- *Last Movement:* Listen for the homophonic texture, with the melody in the uppermost voice and accompanying voices beneath.

Form

- *First Movement:* Listen for the orchestral ritornello that introduces the chorale and then returns between the chorale's individual phrases.
- *Last Movement:* Listen for the absence of any ritornellos in this movement.

When J.S. Bach became music director at St. Thomas' Church in Leipzig in 1723, he agreed to provide music for the Lutheran worship services each Sunday, and it was in this position that he wrote the vast majority of his more than 200 cantatas. The word "cantata" means simply "that which is sung," and cantatas can range from a single movement for one vocal soloist to an extended cycle of movements for soloists, chorus, and orchestra, such as Cantata 140. Had Bach written these works over the span of his 27 years in Leipzig, the accomplishment would be remarkable enough. But through detailed studies of paper, handwriting, and other evidence, scholars have discovered that Bach actually wrote about 150 cantatas within his first three years in Leipzig, at the rate of roughly one a week.

When one considers the time needed to compose a new work, write down the score, supervise the copying of the parts, rehearse the new work, and then perform it on Sunday—all in addition to his duties as a teacher at St. Thomas's School—Bach's achievement seems almost superhuman. What motivated him to write such elaborate music week after week, year after year? We cannot know for sure, but he clearly embraced the opportunity to express his faith through music. Just as the resident preacher would write a sermon each Sunday expounding on the Biblical readings for that day, Bach would compose a cantata expressing through music the ideas or lessons gleaned from those readings.

Awake, a Voice Calls to Us (Wachet auf, ruft uns die Stimme) was written for the 27th Sunday after Trinity in 1731. The Gospel reading for that Sunday is Matthew 25:1–13, which is the parable of the wise and foolish virgins who attend a wedding. The wise ones are prepared for the bridegroom's arrival: they have brought extra oil for their lamps in case he is late. The foolish ones are unprepared: they must leave to buy oil, and the bridegroom arrives in their absence, at midnight. The message implicit here has to do with the second coming of Christ: Who will be ready?

The Closing Chorale: Movement Seven

Awake, a Voice Calls to Us derives some of its text and a good bit of its musical material—as well as its name—from a hymn tune or **chorale** that was in circulation long before Bach wrote this cantata. In fact, the easiest way to approach this particular cantata is by starting with the last of its seven movements, in which Bach presents the chorale melody in its simplest form. The melody is in the uppermost voice, in a syllabic setting with a four-part harmonization.

The words here are the last stanza of the hymn, but the melody is identical to the one used in the opening movement.

Unified Timbre

The instruments of the orchestra **double** the voices—that is, the instruments play the same notes sung by the chorus: high instruments like the violin, flute, and oboe double the soprano line, while lower instruments (violas, cellos, basses) double the lower voice lines. When instruments double the voices, the contrast between chorus and orchestra is minimized, and the combined forces create a powerful sense of unity, symbolizing the unified belief of the congregation.

A Familiar Melody

The chorale melody is in the uppermost voice, and the lower voices provide a fairly simple harmonization of the tune, one that would have been familiar to every member of Bach's congregation in 1731. It is even possible that worshippers sang along with the chorus in this particular movement. Lutherans, like other Protestants, placed a high importance on the personal connection of each believer to God. Chorale melodies played a role in making this connection, as they were easy to sing and the melodies were memorable, which enabled everyone to participate. Using the vernacular—in this case, German—was another way Protestants aimed to facilitate direct communication between ordinary people and God.

The melody opens with a fanfare-like figure that suits the words of the first stanza ("Sleepers, Awake!"). Notice the contour: the opening phrase (**A**) keeps moving upward before finally settling back down. The individual phrases are brief enough to be sung by untrained singers, and the space between phrases allows the congregation plenty of time to take a good breath. Phrase **A** is sung twice. The contrasting phrase (**B**) that follows has a different contour: it begins high and moves downward before making a long climb to reach the highest point of the melody.

The chorale melody

Bar Form

The movement consists of one verse of the chorale melody, and so the form of the movement reflects the form of the melody: **AAB**. The opening phrase **(A)** is sung twice, and the melody concludes with a contrasting section **(B)**. This pattern is so common that it has its own name: **bar form**. It is sometimes also called **song form** because many popular songs from later eras follow this pattern.

Homophonic Texture: To Hear the Words

The texture is homophonic, with the melody in the uppermost voice and all four parts moving in equal or nearly equal rhythm. The bass voice, which moves at a slightly faster speed, keeps the chorale moving forward and provides rhythmic variety. But the four parts begin their articulation of nearly every word at the same time, which makes the words particularly clear to listeners.

The opening of the chorale, showing all four parts

The Opening Chorus: Movement One

Bach uses this same chorale melody in a spectacular manner in the opening movement of the cantata. Dotted rhythms (LONG-short LONG-short LONG, etc.) and a steady pace suggest a march, the kind of procession described in the cantata's text. Bach's listeners would have heard these dotted rhythms as a reference to the pomp of royalty, as in the French overture (see chapter 10). As in the chorale itself (movement 7), the melody is sung from beginning

St. Thomas's Church in Leipzig, where Cantata 140 ("Awake, a Voice Calls to Us") received its premiere in 1731. Bach is buried inside this church.

AKG-Images

to end by the soprano voices. But instead of a straightforward harmonization, Bach weaves elaborate lines of counterpoint underneath the melody with the other voices and with the instruments of the orchestra.

Melody Interrupted

The melody is sung in the soprano voices, as in the finale, but in this opening chorus, Bach creates substantial pauses after each line and even longer pauses between the main sections (**A** | **A** | **B**). These interruptions in the uppermost voices are filled in by the orchestra (which plays constantly throughout) and by the other voices in the chorus. The music between the sections of the chorale melody thus provides both contrast and commentary.

Like other Protestant composers of his time, Bach often worked chorale melodies into larger, more complex movements. In his Cantata 80, for example, Bach wove the well-known chorale "A Mighty Fortress Is Our God," or some variation of it, into three of the work's eight movements (see Expand Your Playlist). His Cantata 78 (also in the playlist) follows a similar pattern.

Form: The Ritornello Principle

The first movement presents the chorale melody in its entirety in very long note values (in the soprano line), with an instrumental ritornello on each end as well as between major text sections. In this way, the ritornello provides a "frame" for the chorale melody on multiple levels, introducing and concluding the movement, and also introducing and concluding the individual melodic subunits. The ritornello principle here is very similar to the one Vivaldi used in the first movement of "Winter" from *The Four Seasons* (see chapter 14).

Section	Ritornello 1	Chorale A	Ritornello 2	Chorale A	Ritornello 3	Chorale B	Ritornello 4
Timbre	Orchestra	Orchestra & Chorus	Orchestra	Orchestra & Chorus	Orchestra	Orchestra & Chorus	Orchestra

With this in mind, let's now listen to both movements. As suggested earlier, you may find it easier to listen to the last movement first in order to hear the chorale in its simplest, most straightforward form.

Bach's Working Conditions

We have observed how churches and noble patrons competed for the best and brightest musicians, in part because of the influence and prestige the arts could confer. But Bach had a very high estimation of his self-worth, and he was not the easiest of employees. He quarreled almost constantly with his employers about his pay and working conditions no matter where he was. He even spent a month in prison for signing a contract for a new job in Cöthen against the wishes of his then-employer, the Duke of Weimar. In 1730, about six years after moving to Leipzig, Bach wrote to a lifelong friend, venting some of his frustration about his position there:

> Here in Leipzig, by God's will, I am still in service. But as I find that (1) the duties are by far not so agreeable as they were described to me originally; and (2) that quite a few of the bonuses attached to the post have been withdrawn; that (3) the cost of living is very high here; and (4) that the authorities are rather strangely hostile to music; that I have to live in a state of almost constant struggle; that envy prevails and vexations are numerous; I find myself, so help me God, compelled to seek my fortune elsewhere. . . .
>
> My salary here is seven hundred thalers, and when there are more burials than usual, the added fees raise this proportionately higher. But whenever the air is a little more healthful, the loss is great. Last year the fees for common burials showed a deficit of a hundred thalers. With four hundred thalers I could support myself in Thuringia more comfortably than here with twice that amount, for the cost of living in Leipzig is exorbitant.

Source: Letter to Georg Erdmann, 28 October 1730, in *The Pleasures of Music,* trans. Jacques Barzun (Chicago: University of Chicago Press, 1977), pp. 283–84.

 EXPAND YOUR PLAYLIST

Sacred Music of the Late Baroque

Baroque composers wrote vast quantities of music for services of different faiths, including Catholicism and the various Protestant sects. The cantata was used in both Catholic and Protestant services, but it was more important in the latter and more closely connected to the traditions of the chorale. J.S. Bach wrote more than 300 cantatas, of which about 200 survive including:

* *A Mighty Fortress Is Our God (Ein' feste Burg ist unser Gott),* BWV 80, is based on the words and melody of the well-known hymn by Martin Luther. One of Bach's sons later added trumpets and timpani to the score; this version is most often performed today.
* *Praise God in All Lands (Jauchzet Gott in allen Landen),* BWV 51, for soprano solo, trumpet solo, strings, and basso continuo. The two solo parts (one vocal, one instrumental) are spectacular—and spectacularly difficult.

The **motet**, similar to the cantata, was used widely in both Protestant and Catholic services. Here are some examples:

* *Sing Unto God (Cantate Domino)* by **Michel-Richard Delalande** (1657–1726) is a good example of the French motet, for tenor soloist, chorus, and orchestra. The text is in Latin, and the tenor part is highly virtuosic.
* Bach's *Sing Unto the Lord a New Song (Singet dem Herrn ein neues Lied),* BWV 225, is a motet for chorus alone, without soloists or instruments.

The **Mass** is the central liturgical service of the Catholic church, recreating, in symbolic fashion, Christ's Last Supper with his disciples. Although retained in the Protestant service to some extent (usually in the language of the people), the Mass in Latin was associated primarily with the Catholic Church.

* The *Saint Cecilia Mass (Missa Santa Cecilia)* by **Alessandro Scarlatti** (1660–1725) is an elaborate setting of the Mass text, with spectacularly florid parts for the vocalists.
* Though a Lutheran himself, Bach also wrote an important Mass for the Catholic court at Dresden, near Leipzig. The B-Minor Mass, BWV 232, is for chorus, soloists, and orchestra, and it is widely considered the greatest of all Baroque Masses.

The **oratorio** (see chapter 18) is musically very similar to an opera—usually for soloists, chorus, and orchestra—but it is unstaged and is usually based on a sacred topic:

* Giacomo Carissimi's *Jephthe* depicts the story of an Israelite caught between his duty to God and love of his family.
* George Frideric Handel (1685–1759) was the most celebrated composer of oratorios in the Baroque era. In addition to loving his *Messiah* (see chapter 16), audience responded enthusiastically to his other oratorios, including *Samson.*

Listening Guide

CD II · Track 6

GO TO PEARSON mymusiclab for the Automated Listening Guide

Johann Sebastian Bach Cantata 140: *Awake, a Voice Calls to Us*, Movement I

Time	Formal Section	Original German Text	English Translation
0:00	Ritornello 1		
0:28	Chorale A	Wachet auf, ruft uns die Stimme, der Wächter sehr hoch auf der Zinne, wach auf, du Stadt Jerusalem.	"Awake," a voice calls to us, the watchman high in the tower: "Awake, thou city of Jerusalem."
1:32	Ritornello 2		
2:00	Chorale A	Mitternacht heißt diese Stunde, sie rufen uns mit hellem Munde, wo seid ihr klugen Jungfrauen?	Midnight the hour is called; they call to us with bright voices: "Where are you, wise virgins?"
3:04	Ritornello 3		
3:24	Chorale B	Wohlauf, der Bräut'gam kömmt, steht auf, die Lampen nehmt, Alleluia! Alleluia! Macht euch bereit zu der Hochzeit, ihr müsset ihm entgegengehn.	Behold, the bridegroom comes; rise up and take your lamps, Alleluia! Alleluia! Prepare yourselves for the wedding, you must go to meet Him.
5:32	Ritornello 4		

Movement VII

CD II · Track 7

GO TO PEARSON mymusiclab for the Automated Listening Guide

Time	Form	Original German Text	English Translation
0:00	A	Gloria sei dir gesungen, mit Menschen- und englischen Zungen, mit Harfen und mit Zimbeln schon.	Let Gloria be sung to You with mortal and angelic tongues, with harps and even cymbals.
0:24	A	Von zwölf Perlen sind die Pforten, an deiner Stadt sind wir Konsorten der Engel hoch um deinen Thron.	Of twelve pearls the portals are made, in your city we are consorts to the angels high around your throne.
0:47	B	Kein Aug' hat je gespürt, kein Ohr hat je gehört solche Freude, des sind wir froh, io, io, ewig in dulci jubilo.	No eye has ever glimpsed, no ear has ever heard such joy which makes us glad, io, io eternally, with sweet rejoicing!

Melody

Dotted rhythms, march-like feeling

Chorale melody in the highest (soprano) voice, which enters first. "Wachet auf" ("Awake") set to fanfare-like figure (using skips), rather like a trumpet that would awaken a sleeper.

Dotted rhythms; same melody as in Ritornello 1

Same melodic phrase as Chorale A

Same melody as in previous Ritornellos

Chorale melody enters after the other voices, at 3:26.

Same theme as in previous Ritornellos

Melody

Fanfare-like opening (disjunct, upward). Leaps upward again on "mit Menschen" and again on "mit Harfen." Otherwise conjunct motion or repeated notes.

Same music as above, with upward motion at the beginning and leaps upward again on "an deiner Stadt" and "der Engel hoch."

First two lines: Descending conjunct motion. Next line ("solche Freude"): ascends and descends by conjunct motion. "Des sind wir froh" ("which makes us glad"): ascends by conjunct motion to highest pitch of the chorale.

Texture

Homophonic

Student FAQs

What are the other movements of this cantata like?

The second movement is a recitative for tenor and basso continuo; the third movement is a duet for soprano and bass, with a solo violin and basso continuo accompaniment; the fourth movement presents the chorale melody as sung by the tenors of the chorus, with a contrapuntal line weaving around it, played by the violins and violas; the fifth movement is a recitative for bass; and the sixth movement is another duet for soprano and bass, with an oboe solo.

How large was Bach's chorus?

This has been a matter of heated debate among scholars in recent years. Documentary evidence has come to light that indicates that for at least some performances, there was only one singer to a part. But there is no consensus on whether this represented standard practice or an exception. Conductors today must take into account the quality of the singers in their ensemble and the size of the space in which they are performing. There is no one "right" size for a chorus when performing this work.

18

George Frideric Handel
Messiah, selections

Form

Listen to the different style of singing in each of the three formal types: recitative, aria, and chorus. Consider how each allows its text to be projected in a different way and how the three work together to form a dramatic unit.

Word-Music Relationships

Try to identify specific ways the music supports and describes the words.

Melody

Notice that the aria has just one distinctive melody from beginning to end, in keeping with the single-mindedness of the text. By contrast, listen to the multiple melodies in the chorus.

Texture

Listen to the variety of textures, from homophony in the recitative and aria, to a full array in the chorus: homophony, monophony, and polyphony.

Timbre

Listen to the expanding variety of timbres, from (1) solo voice and basso continuo in the recitative, to (2) solo voice, basso continuo, and violins in the aria, to (3) a large group of singers and a large orchestra in the chorus.

Throughout the Baroque era, the church remained deeply ambivalent toward opera. On the one hand, authorities recognized the power of music to move the spirits of the faithful, and a number of composers in the seventeenth century even wrote operas on sacred subjects, such as the lives of particular saints. On the other hand, opera had become such a spectacle—both visual and aural—that the church could not sanction its production during the penitential seasons of Lent and Advent, when the faithful were supposed to give up worldly pleasures and devote themselves to inward contemplation. But if the church were to ban opera altogether for some 30 days in the late fall (Advent, the season before Christmas) and again for some 50 days in early spring (Lent, the season before Easter), even devout music-lovers would have been deeply resentful.

Oratorio:
is a large musical composition
including orchestra, choir & soloist

The new genre of the **oratorio** offered a way out of this impasse. Musically, an oratorio is virtually identical to an opera: it includes recitatives, arias, and choruses, and the singing can be quite elaborate. The key differences are that an oratorio is not staged—there are no costumes, no sets—and is usually based on a sacred topic. The word "oratorio" is the Italian word for "prayer hall," which is where these works were performed in the seventeenth century. The genre soon spread across Europe and became a standard substitute for opera during the penitential seasons.

Most oratorios have characters and a plot, just as in an opera. Handel's *Messiah,* the most popular of all oratorios, is actually somewhat unusual in this regard. There are no characters and no plot, save a general trajectory from prophecy and the birth of Christ (Part 1) to the crucifixion and resurrection (Part 2) to meditations on the eternal life of the soul (Part 3). The text is drawn from various biblical passages, including both Old and New Testaments. Musically, however, *Messiah* is typical in that it uses the basic conventions of opera. The movements presented here include a recitative, an aria, and a chorus.

• Penitential-
- relating 2 penance
- showing or constituting
penance

Messiah: Recitative ("He that dwelleth in heaven") and Aria ("Thou shalt break them")

This pair of joined movements, both for tenor soloist, forms a sequence of recitative and aria that would have been familiar to Handel's original audiences from opera. The brief recitative ("He that dwelleth in heaven"), for tenor and basso continuo alone, introduces the more extended aria, for tenor and a reduced orchestra of violins and basso continuo.

Form: Paired Movements

The declamatory recitative sets up the more musically elaborate recitative that follows. The aria is built on the ritornello principle, in which the ensemble (the orchestra) and the soloist (the tenor) alternate. The text of the aria is also quite brief, but Handel, like a great many composers of his time, spins a few short phrases into an extended aria by repeating the words several times and by writing long melismas on certain key words.

> Thou shalt break them with a rod of iron,
> Thou shalt dash them to pieces like a potter's vessel.
> *(Psalm 2:9, King James Version)*

Word-Music Relationships: Virtuosic Word Painting

Those being "broken" and "dashed" in the text are the heathen, the unbelievers who scorn God. Handel captures the violence of this text from the very start with a back-and-forth shaking figure in the violins, two rapidly alternating notes repeated several times. And he sets the words "dash them" at several points to a large downward leap, a moment of word painting that suggests an object being thrown from a great height. The words "potter's vessel"—that is, a clay pot—receive elaborate melismatic settings at several points: the many notes sung to these words can be heard to represent the many pieces into which these objects will be broken. The elaborate melodic line of the aria interprets the text. It also allows the singer to display his virtuosity as a musician. And it gave audiences the kind of florid singing they would not otherwise have been able to hear during the periods of the year when operatic performances were banned.

The theme of the aria

A Single Melody

The brief text of the aria speaks of one thing and one thing only: destruction. The first half of Psalm 2:9 is about the tool of destruction ("a rod of iron"), and the second half is about the nature of that destruction ("dash them to pieces like a potter's vessel"). Handel responds to this text with a single melodic idea. He does not use any kind of melodic contrast in his music because there is no real contrast within the text itself.

Homophonic Texture

The homophonic texture in both the recitative and aria allows the solo singer to project his words with great clarity. In the aria, the instruments present the "shaking" melody repeatedly so that it is not merely subordinate to the voice. But the voice stands out, particularly in those passages of the aria in which it is accompanied only by the basso continuo.

A Stark Timbre

The recitative is accompanied only by the basso continuo, following standard practice. But when the tenor's aria begins, only the violins join in. This not only falls well short of the full orchestra—Handel is saving that larger sound for the chorus to follow—but it does not even include all the stringed instruments. Moreover, both sections of violins (Violin 1 and Violin 2) play exactly the same notes, which creates a strong single line that contrasts markedly with both the basso continuo and the solo tenor voice. The result is a stark timbre of only three lines: the voice, the violins, and the basso continuo.

Now listen to the recitative and aria again, following the Listening Guide on pages 162–165.

Messiah: Chorus: "Hallelujah"

Just as the recitative introduces the aria, the aria introduces the chorus, the celebrated "Hallelujah." The text now jumps from the Old Testament to the New. The words of this chorus are a compilation of different verses from the Book of Revelations:

> Hallelujah, for the Lord God Omnipotent reigneth, Hallelujah! (*Revelation 19:6*)
> The Kingdom of this world is become the Kingdom of our Lord, and of His Christ;
>   and He shall reign for ever and ever, Hallelujah! (*Revelation 11:15*)
> King of Kings, and Lord of Lords, and He shall reign for ever and ever, Hallelujah!
>   (*Revelation 19:16*)

Sectional Form

Handel allows the form of the text to shape the form of the music. Each verse or half-verse receives its own melodic material so that there are four large sections within the chorus as a whole (labeled **A, B, C,** and **D** in the Listening Guide). After the introductory, narrative singing style of the recitative and the highly ornamented, reflective style of the aria, the clear and mostly syllabic singing style of the culminating "Hallelujah" chorus makes it easy to understand the jubilant and victorious text. It also enhances these joyous words, which provide the conclusion to Part 2 of *Messiah.*

The Same Melody for the Same Words

Even though the text draws on three different biblical verses, there is a lot of repetition among them. All three end with the opening word of the entire chorus ("Hallelujah"), and the phrase "And He shall reign for ever and ever" appears in two of the three verses.

Handel, accordingly, uses the same melodic ideas when these words return later in the text.

Melody 1 consists of short notes that repeat or move in mainly conjunct motion.

Hal - le - lu - jah, Hal - le - lu - jah, Hal-le - lu-jah, Hal-le-lu-jah, Hal-

Melody 2 is a unison line that rises and falls.

for the Lord God Om - ni - po - tent reign - eth,

Melody 3 is a long, descending line with a dramatic leap up at "the Kingdom of our Lord."

The Kingdom of this world is be - come the Kingdom of our Lord and of His Christ, and of His Christ,

Melody 4 is a disjunct line, with several leaps up and down but a generally downward contour.

and He shall reign for ev - er and ev - er,

Melody 5 consists of very long notes in a unison line that rises quite slowly.

King of Kings, _____ and Lord of Lords, _____

Sometimes, melodies appear at the same time. At 0:45, melodies 1 and 2 appear together; at 1:48, we hear both 1 and 5; and at 2:29, melodies 1, 4, and 5 join for a grand polyphonic climax.

Varied Textures

This movement features all three basic textures of music: monophony, homophony, and polyphony. The textures are driven in large part by the text. We hear homophony at the beginning ("Hallelujah"), monophony on the line that emphasizes God's power ("For the

CULTURAL CONTEXT

Why Stand?

If you have ever attended a live performance of Handel's *Messiah,* chances are good that the entire audience stood up for the singing of the "Hallelujah" chorus. It is widely believed that this replicates the actions of King George II, who, during the London premiere of the work in 1743, was moved to rise because of the sheer beauty and majesty of the music. And when the king stands, everyone else stands, too—so the audience rose.

It is a good story, and it may even be true, but the fact is that we have no record of the king having attended any performance of any of Handel's oratorios after 1739. Newspapers and diarists of the time routinely took note of the king's comings and goings, especially to public events, so it seems likely that someone would have recorded this event had George II in fact attended *Messiah* at some point. The first report of the king's response comes to us from 1780, long after the death of not only Handel but of George II (1683–1760) as well.

Yet who is to say whether this actually happened or not? Proving a negative ("King George II never attended a performance of *Messiah*") is virtually impossible. Whatever its origin, the tradition of rising for the "Hallelujah" chorus has grown over time and today symbolizes the emotional connection listeners feel with this music.

A performance of Handel's *Messiah* in Westminster Abbey in 1784, with a massive chorus and orchestra

Lebrecht Music & Arts Photo Library

Lord God Omnipotent reigneth"), and polyphony whenever these texts are combined with other texts. All this contributes to a sense of variety reinforced by the new words, new melodies, and new timbres in each section of the chorus.

Varied Timbres

In the aria immediately preceding this chorus ("Thou shalt break them"), Handel had used a reduced orchestra of only violins and basso continuo. As a result, the full orchestra in this chorus of exaltation ("Hallelujah") sounds even fuller. The timbre also varies within the movement itself. It begins with strings and basso continuo (0:00), which are soon joined by the full chorus and oboes (0:06), and later still by trumpets and timpani (0:29). As the movement progresses, instruments drop out and reenter, building to a climax at the end on the final word, "Hallelujah."

Now listen to the chorus again, following the Listening Guide.

George Frideric Handel *Messiah,* selections

Recitative: "He that dwelleth in heaven"

Time	Text	Texture	Timbre
0:00	He that dwelleth in heaven shall laugh them to scorn; the Lord shall have them in derision.	Homophonic	Tenor (voice) and basso continuo (in this performance, harpsichord and cello)

Aria: "Thou shalt break them"

Time	Form: Ritornello/Solo	Text	Timbre
0:17	Ritornello 1		Sharp contrast between the violins above and the basso continuo below.
0:33	Solo 1	Thou shalt break them with a rod of iron;	The tenor soloist enters.
0:43		Thou shalt dash them in pieces like a potter's vessel.	
1:07	Ritornello 2		Violins and basso continuo alone.
1:14	Solo 2	Thou shalt break them with a rod of iron;	The tenor solo returns. Violins recede or drop out entirely on melismas in this section, exposing the emphasized words still further.
1:29		Thou shalt dash them in pieces like a potter's vessel.	
2:06	Ritornello 3		

Word-Music Relationships	**Melody**
Line goes up to word "heaven," descends on "laugh"	Recitative

Word-Music Relationships	**Melody**
Minor mode and melody establish the violent mood of the text	Theme 1 here and throughout; there is no contrasting melody
Downward leap on "break them"	
Downward leaps on "dash them" and "in pieces." Long melisma on "potter's," evoking the many pieces of a smashed clay pot	
Long melisma on "rod"	
Long melisma on "potter's"	

George Frideric Handel *Messiah,* selections

Hallelujah Chorus

Time	Form: Section	Melody	Text	Texture
0:00	Introduction			Homophonic
0:06	A	Melody 1	Hallelujah,	Homophonic
0:23		Melody 2	for the Lord God Omnipotent reigneth,	Monophonic
0:29		Melody 1	Hallelujah!	Homophonic
0:34		Melody 2	for the Lord God Omnipotent reigneth,	Monophonic
0:45		Melodies 1 & 2 together	Hallelujah, for the Lord God Omnipotent reigneth, Hallelujah!	Polyphonic
1:09	B	Melody 3	The Kingdom of this world is become the Kingdom of our Lord, and of His Christ;	Homophonic
1:26	C	Melody 4	and He shall reign for ever and ever,	Polyphonic (imitative)
1:48	D	Melodies 5 & 1 together	King of Kings, and Lord of Lords, and He shall reign for ever and ever, Hallelujah!	Polyphonic
2:29		Melodies 1, 4, & 5 together	And He shall reign for ever and ever, King of Kings and Lord of Lords, Hallelujah!	Polyphonic

Word-Music Relationships	Timbre
	Strings and basso continuo
Melody 1: Rhythm of music matches two different ways of saying "Hallelujah," either with a long first syllable (HA-le-lu-jah), or with a long third syllable (Ha-le-LU-jah)	The full chorus and oboes join in.
Melody 2: Large leap down and up on "omnipotent," as if to show the range of God's power	
	Trumpets and timpani join in.
	Chorus, strings, bassoons, and basso continuo only
Melodies 1 and 2 together when their texts are combined	Trumpets and timpani join in at 0:51.
Melody 3: Notes moving from high to low suggest the "Kingdom of our Lord" descending to "the Kingdom of this world," that is, earth. The leap upward suggests that earth and heaven are now connected.	
Imitative entries give the impression that this section might continue indefinitely ("for ever and ever")	
"King of Kings" in uppermost (soprano) line, literally above all the other notes, perhaps to parallel God's position in relation to earth. The melodic line reaches its highest point at 2:21.	Trumpets and timpani join in at 1:50.
Melodies 4, 5, and 1 together. Movement ends with the same melodic idea with which it began (1), suggesting the idea of God's eternal power.	Chorus, strings, oboes, bassoon, and basso continuo only. Trumpets and timpani join in at 2:39.

Student FAQs

Is the title of this work The Messiah or Messiah?

Handel called it simply *Messiah*, though the definite article started creeping into accounts of the work almost at once. Everyone would know what you mean if you called the work *The Messiah*, but *Messiah* is the correct title.

Why is this work performed so often around Christmastime?

Part 1 has a definite Christmas theme to it: the prophecy and birth of Christ. But Parts 2 and 3 belong more appropriately to Easter, as they deal with the Crucifixion and Resurrection. But like the tradition of standing for the "Hallelujah" chorus (see box), any tradition, once started, can take on a life of its own.

So the "Hallelujah" is not the end of the work?

No. It's the end of Part 2, and if the work is performed in its entirety, all of Part 3 follows. *Messiah* concludes with an enormous chorus on the word "Amen" that in its own way is as impressive as the "Hallelujah" chorus.

A *Messiah* sing-in at the University of Virginia. Many communities around the country organize public performances of *Messiah* around Christmastime in which anyone—singers and instrumentalists, professional and amateur alike—can participate.

Courtesy of University of Virginia/McIntire Department of Music

---

 EXPAND YOUR PLAYLIST

Covering the "Hallelujah" Chorus

When an artist interprets a song made famous by another artist, we call the new version a "cover." Musicians have been covering the celebrated "Hallelujah" from Handel's *Messiah* since the late eighteenth century, altering the orchestration, the tempo, and even the notes themselves. Here are some examples:

Wolfgang Amadeus Mozart, *Der Messias* (1789). Mozart arranged several of Handel's oratorios for performance in Vienna, using a German translation of the text, lengthening and shortening some numbers, and adding new instruments—flutes, clarinets, bassoons, horns, and trombones.

Johnny Mathis, "Hallelujah Chorus" (1972). A relatively standard version with orchestra and chorus, but with Mathis alone singing the tenor part.

The Roches. "Hallelujah Chorus" (1982). An a cappella version—three voices, no instruments—by an ensemble of three women.

Quincy Jones (producer), *Handel's Messiah: A Soulful Celebration* (1992). A gospel-style rendition of *Messiah* performed by a variety of different artists, this album won the Grammy Award for Best Contemporary Soul Gospel Album in 1992.

Marin Alsop, *Too Hot to Handel* (1993). A gospel-jazz-rock-funk version by a noted conductor who now directs the Baltimore Symphony Orchestra.

Mannheim Steamroller, "Hallelujah" (2004). A purely instrumental version of the chorus, on rock instruments and synthesizers.

Relient K. "Handel's Messiah: The Hallelujah Chorus" (2006). A rock interpretation that adds some counterpoint to the original in places and subtracts it in others.

MAKING CONNECTIONS: Music of the Renaissance and Baroque

	Renaissance	Baroque
Texture	Polyphonic	Polyphonic and homophonic coexist
Melody	Lyrical, rarely virtuosic	Lyrical and declamatory (recitative) coexist; often virtuosic
Rhythm	Relatively smooth and flowing	Wider range of extremes, from smooth and flowing to choppy and irregular
Timbre	No sharp distinction between instrumental and vocal music	Sharp distinction between vocal and instrumental parts
Harmony	Harmony as a by-product of the relationship among polyphonic voices	Harmony as an underlying basis for melody
Form	Primarily sectional	Greater variety of formal principles: sectional form, binary form, theme and variations, ostinato
Word-Music Relationships	Limited use of word painting	Even greater use of word painting. Texture and musical affect strongly support text.

IN REVIEW: Baroque Style

Homophonic Texture. A texture in which one voice predominates and the others support it.

- Monteverdi, *Orpheus* (Chapter 9)
- Strozzi, "Revenge" (Chapter 12)
- Purcell, *Dido and Aeneas* (Chapter 10)

Basso Continuo. The group of instruments accompanying the lead voice in homophonic texture, playing the bass line ("basso") continuously, thereby allowing the solo voice to pursue its own melody, drop out, and return.

- Almost all the works in this part except for Bach's Fugue in G Minor, a purely polyphonic work for organ.

Recitative. A style of singing midway between lyrical song and speech, usually syllabic (one note per syllable).

- Monteverdi, *Orpheus* (Chapter 9)
- Purcell, *Dido and Aeneas* (Chapter 10)
- Handel, *Messiah* (Chapter 18)

Word Painting. While not an entirely new development, word painting—the depiction of specific words through music that imitates the meaning of those words—becomes particularly important in the Baroque era.

- Monteverdi, *Orpheus* (Chapter 9)
- Purcell, *Dido and Aeneas* (Chapter 10)
- Strozzi, "Revenge" (Chapter 12)

- Bach, Cantata 140 (Chapter 17)
- Handel, *Messiah* (Chapter 18)

Ritornello Structure. The regular alternation between sections for contrasting ensembles (soloist vs. orchestra; voices vs. instruments).

- Vivaldi, *The Four Seasons,* "Winter" (Chapter 14)
- Bach, Brandenburg Concerto no. 2 (Chapter 15)
- Bach, Cantata 140 (Chapter 17)

Program Music. Instrumental music that is in some way associated with a story, event, or idea.

- Vivaldi, *The Four Seasons,* "Winter" (Chapter 14)

Binary Form. The most common form for dance movements, consisting of two sections, each repeated in performance.

- Handel, *Water Music* (Chapter 16)

Ostinato. A short repeated pattern of notes.

- Purcell, *Dido and Aeneas* (Chapter 10)
- Mbuti Pygmies, "Marriage Celebration Song" (Chapter 11)

Counterpoint. Two independent melodies, played simultaneously.

- Bach, Fugue in G Minor (Chapter 13)
- Hmong People of Laos: *Gaeng School Song* (Web Bonus Chapter 2)

PART 4 The Classical Era

A classic is something that endures, and the music of what we now call the Classical Era—a period extending from roughly 1750 to 1800—was the first to thrive without interruption long after its composers had died. Joseph Haydn (1732–1809) and Wolfgang Amadeus Mozart (1756–1791), the two leading composers of this era, wrote music that has never really gone out of fashion. The term "classical" also refers to Greek and Roman antiquity, which strongly influenced the arts and architecture of this period. As a new kind of thinking took hold, the Baroque love of ornamentation, virtuosity, and expressive extremes gave way to more classical ideals of balance, clarity, and naturalness.

The eighteenth century as a whole, but particularly the period between about 1720 and 1790, is known as the Age of Enlightenment. Enlightenment thought held that reason could bring humankind to a new age of splendor, freed from the dark superstitions of the past (hence "en*light*enment"). For Enlightenment artists and thinkers, the power to convince lay not in overwhelming displays of opulence, or in larger-than-life drama, or in the expression of a particular effect—all of which aimed to influence the emotions—but rather in critical thinking and reasoned discussion, which aimed to persuade the mind.

The music of the Classical Era reflects these principles of clarity, proportion, and what critics of the day called "naturalness." Classical-Era melodies are on the whole more tuneful, less complicated, and more balanced than those of the Baroque era. More symmetrical melodic phrasing, based on the rhythms of dance music, extended itself across all genres, both

◀ This intriguing image captures the Enlightenment's ideal of the mind—the seat of reason—as the focal point of all perception.
© Bibliothèque des Arts Décoratifs, Paris, France. Archives Charmet/The Bridgeman Art Library

vocal and instrumental. Critics of the day praised homophonic texture for its clarity and grace, and the dense textures of counterpoint became the exception rather than the rule. But this does not mean that music of the Classical Era is somehow simpler, for a typical movement of music from this period features more internal contrasts than its Baroque counterpart. A typical movement in sonata form, the most important new structural innovation of the era (and one used in Mozart's Symphony no. 40 in G Minor), juxtaposes multiple themes that differ markedly in their melody, rhythm, harmony, dynamics, and timbre.

Music as Language

A string quartet such as Joseph Haydn's op. 76, no. 3 was often described as four rational individuals conversing in music. It fits that the string quartet developed in the Classical Era, when instrumental music began to be heard as a language all its own. In the Baroque era and before, the only music thought truly meaningful was that with a sung text; instrumental music was perceived

▲ Joseph Wright, *An Experiment on a Bird in the Air-Pump,* 1768. A scientist demonstrates the effect of a vacuum jar on a small bird. The young boy at the right lowers the cage for the bird, which will be revived when air is reintroduced to the bowl. Empirical science and the application of reason dominated Enlightenment thought.

© National Gallery, London

primarily as a means of entertainment. In the eighteenth century, for the first time, critics described musical structures in terms of language. They recognized that the phrases in a melody corresponded in a general way to the opening and closing phrases in a sentence. Writers of the Enlightenment liked to call music the "language of the heart"—as opposed to verbal language, "the language of the mind"—and in this way, instrumental music moved up a notch in prestige.

▶ Thomas Jefferson's University of Virginia, shown in an early engraving. Jefferson designed the Rotunda after the Pantheon of ancient Rome. Symmetry is important in Classical architecture as well as in the music of the Classical Era, though on closer inspection very few structures—or melodies—prove entirely symmetrical. Each of the large houses for faculty in this "academical village" is slightly different from the others.

Tracy W. McGregor Library of American History, Special Collections, University of Virginia Library

Music and Revolution

The plot of Wolfgang Amadeus Mozart's comic opera *The Marriage of Figaro* (1786) would have been unthinkable only a generation before. Count Almaviva, a nobleman, is outwitted by his servants. This opera captures the growing mood of discontent with the established order of society in the decades leading up to the French Revolution. Basic ideas about human rights ("life, liberty, and the pursuit of happiness," to quote the U.S. Declaration of Independence) won growing acceptance during this time. Enlightenment social critics such as Voltaire (1694–1778) and Jean-Jacques Rousseau (1712–78) argued for the innate goodness of human beings and for the rational pursuit of personal and societal betterment. The U.S. Declaration of Independence is a quintessential document of the Enlightenment, for it recognizes the inherent dignity of the individual. Its principal author, Thomas Jefferson, established the University of Virginia (see image) on the premise that the institution would be "based on the illimitable freedom of the human mind. For here we are not afraid to follow truth wherever it may lead, nor to tolerate any error so long as reason is left free to combat it."

▲ George Washington accepts the surrender of British troops at Yorktown in 1781, marking the end of the Revolutionary War. The military band present at the occasion played "Yankee Doodle" and a tune called "The World Turned Upside Down."
Yale University Art Gallery / Art Resource, NY

The American Revolution (1775–81) established the independence of the United States from Great Britain, and the French Revolution (1789) overthrew the power of what until that time had been the world's most powerful monarchy. The results affected not just the countries immediately involved, but ultimately every nation in the Western world. National independence and democracy, if not always realized in practice, became new ideals of social order. These new ideals, in turn, paved the way for new approaches to education, including the establishment of the first state-run conservatory of music, in Paris, in 1795. The leaders of the new French Republic and the monarchy they had just overthrown agreed on at least one point: that music was an important means of projecting cultural power.

Music and the New Economy

The second half of the eighteenth century witnessed the beginnings of an even more powerful revolution, one that would change everyday life throughout the Western world. Rapid advances in technology—the steam engine, the cotton gin, and the principle of manufacturing based on interchangeable parts, to cite just a few examples—made it possible to produce goods on a far greater scale than ever before. Many national and local economies based on agriculture began to shift toward industry. Cities grew rapidly in size during this period, and this growth in urban populations in turn created new demands for cultural institutions of all kinds, including music.

▶ Musical audiences were more diverse in the late 18th century than they had been in earlier times, when performances were attended largely by the nobility and aristocracy. In this caricature, an amateur music-lover sings along with the soloist on the stage of the opera, much to the consternation of the real performers.
Gerald Coke Handel Collection, Foundling Museum, London / The Bridgeman Art Library

While the churches and royal courts remained important centers of culture, theaters and concert halls open to the paying public began to flourish for the first time on a widespread scale. We see these changes in the careers of both Haydn and Mozart. Haydn worked almost all his adult life in the service of one aristocratic family, composing symphonies, sonatas, and operas according to the desires of his employers. By the 1790s, however, Haydn was lured away to England to write symphonies, including the Symphony no. 102 in B♭ Major, among other works, for a series of public concerts organized by a musical entrepreneur. Mozart left his native Salzburg at the age of 25 to seek his fortune in Vienna. He tried unsuccessfully to land a secure job at the imperial court there, but he managed to support himself reasonably well (for a time, at least) by giving public concerts, by writing operas, and by composing works that could be published and sold to music-loving amateurs. Composers had to write in ways that would appeal to this expanded audience even while maintaining the high standards of their craft. Works like the Piano Concerto in A Major, K. 488, were the perfect lure for audiences intrigued by Mozart's virtuosity both as a composer and as a performer.

The Art of the Natural

Throughout the Classical Era, artists in every field looked to nature as a model. The ideal work of art, according to this view, was one that hid its artifice, that concealed its mechanical elements, and that appeared to be the product of effortless—natural—genius. Composers still had to learn the technique of their craft, to be sure, and they continued to study such topics as harmony and counterpoint with great diligence. But the goal of all this study was not to show off one's art, but to touch the hearts of listeners in a manner that was direct and (seemingly) spontaneous.

This new aesthetic manifested itself in music in many ways. Melodies and ornamentation became less ornate. Textures on the whole tended more toward homophony than polyphony, homophony being the more "natural" of the two textures because it allowed the ear to focus on a single melody. In opera, plots and characters both became decidedly more realistic. Mozart and others devoted great energies to the new genre of **opera buffa** or "comic opera," which portrayed real-life characters and situations, as opposed to the mythological and historical figures that populate so much of Baroque opera. In Mozart's *The Marriage of Figaro*, we can immediately identify with the emotions and actions of the characters because they are presented in a manner that is true to life, in a manner that is, in a word, natural.

▲ A family making music together in late 18th-century England.
Yale Center for British Art/Paul Mellon Collection. The Bridgeman Art Library, NY

The Classical Era: AT A GLANCE

chapter 19

1797

JOSEPH HAYDN
String Quartet op. 76,
no. 3, second movement

GENRE: String Quartet

Chapter highlight:
Classical Chamber Music
The string quartet was primarily for amateurs. Intimate genres were also composed for the newly popular piano, including sonatas, variations, trios, and fantasias. Haydn, Mozart, J.C. Bach, and C.P.E. Bach all contributed to these repertories

KEY CONCEPTS
Theme and variations,
periodic phrase structure, musical appropriation.

chapter 20

1786

MASTER MUSICIANS OF
THE IKUTA-RYU
Cherry Blossom

GENRE: Japanese music

Chapter highlight: .
Theme and Variations
The theme and variations form provides a way to combine repetition, variation, and contrast. It also works particularly well as a basis for improvisation.

KEY CONCEPTS
Theme and variations,
pentatonic scale, tremolo, extramusical content.

chapter 21

1795

JOSEPH HAYDN
Symphony no. 102,
third and
fourth movements

GENRE: Symphony

Chapter highlight:
The Classical Symphony
The symphony, which used strings, winds, and percussion, was the largest, longest, and most prestigious of all instrumental genres in this era. By the end of the eighteenth century, performances of symphonies were decidedly public events.

KEY CONCEPTS
Minuet form, rounded binary form, rondo form, the finale, concert manners and programs.

chapter 22

1788

WOLFGANG AMADEUS
MOZART
Symphony no. 40,
first movement

GENRE: Symphony

Chapter highlight:
Sonata Form
Sonata form was the most important structural convention to emerge from the Classical Era. It is a flexible format in which contrasting themes and harmonic areas are juxtaposed, transformed, and ultimately reconciled.

KEY CONCEPTS
Modulation, contrasting themes and harmonic areas.

---

chapter 23

1786

WOLFGANG AMADEUS MOZART
Piano Concerto K. 488,
first movement

GENRE: Concerto

Chapter highlight:
The Classical Concerto
The concerto of the Classical era combines the ritornello principle of the Baroque with the newer sonata form. A cadenza lets the soloist improvise. Mozart, Haydn, and Marianne von Martinez, among others, wrote concertos for piano, violin, cello, and clarinet.

KEY CONCEPTS
Double-exposition concerto form, the cadenza.

chapter 24

1786

WOLFGANG AMADEUS MOZART
The Marriage of Figaro,
Act 1, selection

GENRE: Comic opera

Chapter highlight:
Classical Opera
Opera remained the most prestigious and lucrative genre and inspired some of the era's greatest music. In addition to providing entertainment, the opera also served as a kind of pressure-valve on social tensions. Mozart and Gluck are generally considered the two greatest composers of opera in the Classical era

KEY CONCEPTS
Opera, drama through music, relationship of dramatic and musical structures (rondo), accompanied recitative.

chapter 25

LISA LU AND THE
BEIJING OPERA COMPANY
The Reunion

GENRE: Chinese opera

Chapter highlight:
Recitative and Aria
In opera of the West and the East, recitative or heightened speech narrates dramatic action, and arias express the lyrical sentiments of the characters.

KEY CONCEPTS:
Opera, language tones, stock characters, pentatonic scale, metabole.

Historical Events

1759
Voltaire publishes *Candide*

1762
Rousseau publishes *Social Contract*

1775
American Revolution

1776
American Declaration of Independence

1789
French Revolution

1789
U.S. Constitution

1793-94
Reign of Terror in France

19

Joseph Haydn

String Quartet in C Major, op. 76, no. 3, second movement

Listen to This

Timbre

Listen to how the sounds of the four instruments both blend together and distinguish themselves. The string quartet consists of two violins, a viola, and a cello. The registers of these instruments range from high (violin) to low (cello), but their sound quality is similar.

Texture

Notice how the melody always appears in one of the instruments and the other three weave around it. Is the texture homophonic or polyphonic? Also listen for the long passage shortly after the beginning in which only two of the instruments—the two violins—are playing.

Melody

Listen for the pauses that break the melody into sections known as phrases. Which phrases sound like the music wants to continue? When do you hear a phrase that sounds conclusive? Which phrases are repeated?

Form

Listen to the way the melody is first presented by one of the violins and then repeated with very little change by each of the other instruments across the course of the movement.

A good melody is worth hearing again and again. But at some point, we also want to hear something different, either a different version of the melody or a different melody altogether. Composers use a combination of repetition, variation, and contrast to satisfy and sustain our interest as listeners. The second movement of Joseph Haydn's String Quartet in C Major, op. 76, no. 3, offers a good example of how music can deliver repetition, variation, and contrast all at the same time. The melody is from a song Haydn himself had written a few months earlier for the birthday of Holy Roman Emperor Franz II, who resided in Vienna. The song, set to the words "God save Franz, the Emperor," was an immediate hit with the public and soon became Austria's unofficial national anthem.

The melody was so closely associated with the emperor that Haydn could not alter the melody itself, for the ideal emperor is steadfast and not subject to change. Haydn created an ingenious solution to this problem by repeating the emperor's theme more or less unchanged four times in succession, varying only the instrument that played it and writing contrasting musical lines to surround the theme. Thus, though the theme remains essentially the same, it stays fresh because the frame around it is constantly changing.

In setting this theme with variations for four instruments of similar timbre, Haydn imposed an additional challenge on himself. Without the full orchestra at his disposal, he could not rely on winds, brass, or timpani to create varieties of sound. This makes his accomplishment—a movement that sustains interest while repeating a melody four times—all the more remarkable.

Haydn was not the first to write string quartets, but he did more than any other composer to establish this new genre's significance from the middle of the eighteenth century onward. Not in spite of its timbral constraints but *because* of them, Haydn, Mozart, and later Beethoven all took up the challenge of writing for the string quartet repeatedly throughout their careers. By the end of the eighteenth century, the string quartet had acquired the reputation of being the most demanding of all musical genres, one that allowed composers to demonstrate their talents more fully.

The quartet is a decidedly intimate genre. In Haydn's time, it was usually performed in the home and only rarely in public concerts. Unlike the concerto, no soloist or small group of soloists stands out; instead, all four instrumentalists operate on an equal footing. Commentators since Haydn's day have repeatedly likened the string quartet to a conversation among four equal participants. The conversational aspect of the genre reinforced the sense that these works were written primarily for the pleasure of the performers. Listeners in private settings sometimes even compared themselves to eavesdroppers.

The typical string quartet of the Classical Era consists of four contrasting movements:

1. The first movement, usually in a fast tempo, is most often written in what came to be known as "sonata form," the most significant new form to come out of the Classical Era. We will take up the sonata form in chapter 22 of this book, with Mozart's Symphony No. 40.
2. The second movement is usually in a slow tempo and in a contrasting key. Slow movements could assume many different forms: sonata form, theme and variations, and **ABA** are the most common. (The movement that we are listening to here is a set of variations on a theme.)

3. The third movement is usually a minuet, a lively, stylized dance in triple meter, in the tonic key. We will take up the minuet in chapter 21 of this book, with Haydn's Symphony No. 102.

4. The fourth movement, also known as the finale, is a somewhat lighter and usually very fast movement. The most common forms used in finales are sonata form and rondo. We will take up the rondo in chapter 21 of this book, with Haydn's Symphony no. 102.

The Timbre of the String Quartet

The string quartet creates an unusually homogeneous timbre, for its instruments are all variants of the same basic instrument. The viola and cello are essentially larger and therefore deeper versions of the violin. Together, these four instruments correspond to the four standard ranges of the singing voice:

HIGHEST	Soprano:	Violin 1
	Alto:	Violin 2
	Tenor:	Viola
LOWEST	Bass:	Cello

Like any good vocal ensemble, the instruments of a string quartet can blend together to sound almost like a single instrument or emphasize their differences. The violin has a sweet, piercing sound, while the cello has a more resonant, richer tone. The viola creates a sound somewhere between these two extremes of high and low. It is particularly easy to compare the differences between the sounds of the individual instruments in this movement because Haydn gives the main theme to each at some point.

A string quartet in performance. From left to right: violin 1, violin 2, viola, and cello.

Zdenek CHRAPEK/Lebrecht Music & Arts Photo Library

Changing Textures

Haydn expands the timbral variety of this movement by changing textures through-out. The theme is first presented in a hymnlike fashion, with the melody in the top voice (Violin 1) and the other instruments supporting it, moving at the same pace, rather like the chorale in the last movement of Bach's Cantata no. 140 (see chapter 17). The texture is homo-phonic. In Variation 1 (1:17–2:27), Violin 2 carries the theme while Violin 1 weaves an intri-cate accompanimental figure around it: this is two-part homophony. In Variation 2, the cello carries the theme, with the three other voices weaving around it. Variation 3 begins with only three voices, with the melody in the viola and the cello silent; when the cello enters, Violin 1 drops out; only later in this variation do we hear all four voices together. Variation 4 features four-part polyphony from beginning to end.

Melody: Periodic Phrase Structure

The melody of this movement is made of five phrases, each marked at the end by a cadence, a brief resting point. The first two phrases (labeled **A**) are the same. They are followed by a phrase that is not repeated (**B**), and then two final phrases (**C**) that are the same.

Neither the **A** phrase nor the **B** phrase sounds complete at the end: with each, we expect the music to continue. Not until the end of the **C** phrase do we feel a sense of conclusion.

The structure of these units (**A, B,** and **C**) can be compared to the elements that make up a sentence. The opening **A** and **B** sections act as **antecedent** phrases (*ante* = before), while **C** functions as a **consequent** phrase (*sequent* = following). As in a sentence, an antecedent phrase sets up a consequent phrase and the two together make a complete sentence.

Antecedent phrase 1	Antecedent phrase 2	Consequent phrase
|If I'm still here tomorrow,|	|and if you're back,|	|I'll stop by your place.|
comma	*comma*	*period*

Neither of the antecedent phrases here is complete: we expect each to continue. In Haydn's melody, neither the **A** nor the **B** phrase of the melody sounds complete because neither finishes on the tonic (home) note of the key. Phrases **A** and **B** both end on the note D, which creates a certain sense of arrival but not closure. These points of arrival are called **half cadences**: they create a moment of punctuation more like a comma than a period. But the melody of the **C** phrase ends on the main note of the tonic key (G), and for that reason, we call it a **full cadence**, and we hear its arrival as a moment of closure.

This kind of phrase structure, with antecedent and consequent units that together make a larger whole, is called **periodic phrase structure**. The term "periodic" comes from the Latin word for sentence—*periodus,* the same word for the mark of punctuation that indicates the end of a sentence—emphasizing the link between musical and linguistic structures. Periodic phrase structure is basic to many melodies from many different eras of music, but is particu-larly associated with music of the Classical Era.

The Theme and Variations Form

The **theme and variations form** was an extremely popular form throughout the Classical Era. It is a basically simple structure: a theme is presented and then altered in some way—through harmony, melody, texture, dynamics, or some combination of these—in a succession of individual variations.

Composers often used well-known themes as the basis of new variations. Mozart, for example, wrote a set of variations on the French song "Ah, vous dirai-je, maman" (better known as "Twinkle, Twinkle, Little Star"; see Expand Your Playlist), and Beethoven later wrote a set on the melody to "God Save the King" (better known in the United States as "My Country 'tis of Thee").

Haydn's unusual move—to keep the theme almost completely intact in each variation, altering only its register (the instrument) and changing the other three voices around the theme—takes on symbolic significance when one considers that the theme began as a birthday melody celebrating the emperor. The constancy of the melody can be heard as a portrait of the constancy of Emperor Franz. Circumstances around him may change, but the emperor remains unchanged.

Now listen to this movement again, using the Listening Guide.

Joseph Haydn (1732–1809)

WRITING TO ORDER

It's hard to imagine any individual having his own orchestra at home nowadays, but that's exactly what Prince Nicholas Esterházy had in the second half of the eighteenth century. And for almost three decades, Joseph Haydn was the prince's music director, responsible for writing new music, conducting the orchestra, and keeping order among the musicians, who could be a rowdy bunch at times. Fortunately for Haydn, Prince Nicholas (known far and wide as "The Magnificent") was willing to spend huge amounts of money on music, and Haydn was thus in charge of one of the very best orchestras in all of Europe. "My Prince was satisfied with all of my works," he told one of his biographers late in life, "and I received applause. As the director of an orchestra, I could make experiments, observe what elicited or weakened an impression, and thus correct, add, delete, take risks. I was cut off from the world, no one in my vicinity could cause me to doubt myself or pester me, and so I had to become original." Haydn wrote whatever works the prince requested: string quartets, operas, sonatas. In fact, his original contract required him to appear in uniform every morning before the prince and receive instructions as to what kinds of works he was to compose.

The death of Prince Nicholas in 1790 opened a new chapter in Haydn's life. He made two extended tours to England, where he composed symphonies, songs, and a number of works for piano. After returning to Vienna for good in 1795, he produced two highly successful oratorios (*The Creation* and *The Seasons*), a handful of Masses, and several of his finest string quartets. The young Ludwig van Beethoven was one of his last composition pupils.

Joseph Haydn, in a portrait done during his years in London in the 1790s.

London, Royal College of Music. AKG London.

PLAYLIST: HAYDN

String Quartet in C Major, op. 76, no. 3 (complete)

String Quartet in D Major, op. 76, no. 5

Symphony no. 45 in F♯ Minor ("Farewell")

Symphony no. 101 in D Major ("Clock")

Piano Sonata in E♭ Major, Hob. XVI: 53

The Creation (oratorio)

Joseph Haydn String Quartet in C Major op. 76, no. 3, second movement

Time	Formal Section	Melodic Phrases	Timbre
0:00	Theme	A (0:00) A (0:15) B (0:31) C (0:47) C (1:03)	Theme in the first violin
1:22	Variation 1	A (1:22) A (1:37) B (1:50) C (2:03) C (2:17)	Theme in the second violin
2:28	Variation 2	A (2:28) A (2:43) B (2:59) C (3:16) C (3:32)	Theme in the cello
3:46	Variation 3	A (3:46) A (4:00) B (4:15) C (4:29) C (4:43)	Theme in the viola
4:58	Variation 4	A (4:58) A (5:15) B (5:31) C (5:48) Now moved to a very high range, the highest in the entire movement C (6:04) In a very high range again.	Theme in the first violin
6:18	Coda	Cadential passage	Cadential material in first violin

Texture

Homophonic. Hymn-like, with all four voices moving at the same speed

Homophonic. The first violin plays a rapid accompanimental figure, while the lower voices (viola and cello) are silent.

Polyphonic. The other three voices are playing lines that have distinctive profiles of their own and are not merely accompanimental.

Polyphonic. As in Variation 2, the other three instruments play lines that have distinctive profiles of their own and are not merely accompanimental.

Polyphonic. Same as in Variations 2 and 3.

Student FAQs

I can't always tell the difference among the four instruments. The cello in Variation 2 and the viola in Variation 3 sound almost the same. Is this a problem?

The three kinds of instruments used in a string quartet all overlap to some degree, so a cello playing in a high range is in fact playing some of the same pitches as a viola, and a viola in its high range covers many of the notes available on the lower end of the violin's range. There is a difference in the quality of sound of the instruments, however, and it is worth listening closely for this difference. If you are able to experience a live performance of this work, or at least watch a video of a live performance of it, the visual cues will help reinforce the individual qualities of the instruments.

Without a conductor, who leads the quartet in performance?

As any string player will tell you, playing in a quartet is very different from playing in an orchestra. A quartet is a collaborative enterprise: the players discuss and agree among themselves in rehearsal about such matters as tempo, phrasing, and dynamics. In performance, the first violinist gives subtle indications to lead the other players, often through a glance, a raised eyebrow, or a slight gesture of the head. But at times other players might give such signals, depending on which instrument leads at any given moment. The longer a group has performed together, the better the individual members know one another's manner of playing, and the more subtle the gestures.

CULTURAL CONTEXT

Musical Appropriation

Music is often used in ways its composers could never imagine. **Musical appropriation** is the use or adaptation of a work to serve something other than its original purpose. The melody Haydn wrote in honor of the Emperor Franz II became so popular that many different poets set new words to it:

• One text praised the people of Hamburg.
• Several praised rulers other than Franz II.
• Another text (in Latin) came from the Book of Psalms.
• Several other texts praised God.

The most famous of all the new texts, though, was "Germany Above All Else" ("Deutschland über alles"), written in 1841 by the German poet August Heinrich Hoffmann von Fallersleben. This song would eventually become the German national anthem, though only the third strophe is used today.

A work setting new words to an established melody is known as a **contrafactum**. Nothing prevents any person or institution—a political party, a nation, a church—from appropriating an existing melody, often in ways that are quite different from the purpose of the original. Often new lyrics turn the original song on its head. The British national anthem, "God Save the King," provided the melody for "My Country, 'tis of Thee," one of the most popular of all patriotic songs in the breakaway colonies of North America. The tune now known as "The Star-Spangled Banner" first accompanied a text that was originally a drinking song.

EXPAND YOUR PLAYLIST

Chamber Music and Solo Keyboard Music of the Classical Era

The second half of the eighteenth century witnessed a tremendous growth in amateur music making at home. New printing technologies had reduced the cost of sheet music, and the fortepiano (a new instrument, the forerunner of the modern-day piano) was less expensive than the harpsichord (the principal domestic keyboard instrument of the Baroque era). The string quartet was one of several genres intended primarily for use in the home.

Joseph Haydn
String Quartet in E♭ Major, op. 33, no. 2 ("The Joke"). Listen to the finale and you will understand the source of its nickname.

String Quartet in E♭ Major, op. 76, no. 6. The first movement is a set of variations on a theme.

Piano Trio in G Major, Hob. XV: 25. The piano trio is an ensemble consisting of a piano, a violin, and a cello. The finale of this particular trio is a rondo "in the Hungarian Style," often called the "Gypsy Rondo."

Wolfgang Amadeus Mozart
String Quartet in C Major, K. 456. The slow introduction to the first movement has so many clashing sounds that the entire quartet is known as the "Dissonance" Quartet.

String Quartet in D Major, K. 575. Includes an unusually prominently cello part; this is one of three quartets Mozart wrote for the King of Prussia, who was a cellist.

Variations on "Ah vous dirai-je, maman," K. 265. A set of variations for piano on the tune known as "Twinkle, Twinkle, Little Star."

Piano Sonata in A Major, K. 331. The finale is a rondo "alla Turca" ("in the Turkish style"), imitating what Mozart thought music from the Ottoman Empire sounded like.

Carl Philipp Emanuel Bach
Fantasia in C Minor, H. 75. A fantasia is a work that follows no formal conventions, guided only by the composer's fantasy. A writer set the words of Hamlet's celebrated monologue "To be or not to be . . ." to this fantasia. C.P.E. Bach (1714–88) was one of several of Johann Sebastian Bach's sons who had distinguished musical careers.

Johann Christian Bach
Keyboard Sonata in D Major, op. 5, no. 2. The young Mozart liked this solo sonata (which could be played on harpsichord or piano) so well that he rearranged it as a piano concerto. J.C. Bach (1735–82), another son of J.S. Bach, was known as the "London Bach" because he lived there for so long.

20

Master Musicians of the Ikuta-ryu
Cherry Blossom

Listen to This

Timbre

Consider how the timbre of the koto differs from that of other string instruments you have heard. Listen for the variety of sounds produced by different plucking and strumming techniques.

Melody

Listen to the three different sections of the melody and to the direction in which each moves.

Form

Identify the melody when it enters, then listen for the ways it is varied throughout the piece.

Texture

Listen to the way the texture changes from homophonic to polyphonic in the middle of the piece, and then back again to homophonic. How many players are there?

The idea of presenting a theme and then repeating it in varied form is basic to the music of many cultures around the world. Japan's Edo Period and the reign of the Tokugawa Shoguns (Japanese rulers), from 1603 to 1867, overlapped the Baroque, classical, and part of the romantic eras in Europe. During that time, in both Europe and Japan, the theme and variations form became well developed. Coincidentally, in the same century in which Joseph Haydn wrote his String Quartet in C Major, op. 76, no. 3 (which we discussed in chapter 19), variations like those on *Cherry Blossom (Sakura)* were composed and performed in Japan.

The koto is a plucked zither with thirteen silk strings stretched over its wooden board. Koto music originated in the Japanese court as early as the eighth century, when a variety of instruments were brought from the Korean Paekche kingdom to the Japanese Fujiwara regent. Early koto music does not survive because it was an oral tradition; that is, it was learned without written notation. The koto was used for the private entertainment of the nobles, and it was also integrated with other court instruments for ceremonies.

THE MONEY TRAIL

Geisha in Japanese Life

The stereotyped image of the geisha as a paid companion who caters to the whims of her male patrons is—like many stereotypes—only partially true. In fact, geisha are more like paid performers than they are servants or—as commonly believed—prostitutes. Geisha are paid for their accomplishments as musicians, dancers, and experts in the tea ceremonies and other ceremonial practices enjoyed by their clients.

It is generally believed that the geisha system was created in the seventeenth century to produce a different order of entertainer from courtesans or prostitutes. To become geisha, young girls were often sold into a kind of indentured service by their parents, and they went through a rigorous training that took years to complete. The final part of this training focused on the traditional arts, and many geisha became renowned for their talents at playing traditional instruments, including the koto or *shamisen* (a kind of plucked lute), and singing and dancing.

Geisha must be single, and they often have a single patron—who himself may or may not be married—who supports them by underwriting their education, clothing, and other expenses. However, the relationship is never sexual, and a geisha must retire if she marries. Many do retire to become music and dance teachers.

As recently as the 1920s, there were estimated to be 80,000 geisha at work in Japan. Today, the number is far smaller and limited to certain special districts.

Yuki Yamada playing the Japanese koto. The long-bodied zither is placed on a table or directly on the floor. Notice how the individual bridges are placed at various places to tune the strings to the correct pitches.

Photograph © 2003 Jack Vartoogian/FrontRowPhotos. All Rights Reserved.

The image of the geisha has varied from one of a sexual slave (in pulp fiction and B movies) to the more accurate and sensitive portrayal in the popular book by Arthur Golden, *Memoirs of a Geisha,* published in 2005.

Popular koto playing is believed to date back to the early seventeenth century, when a blind musician named Yatsuhashi Kengyo learned the art of koto playing from a palace musician. A number of methods for learning koto technique and improvisation developed later. With these schools of playing, known as *ryu,* a notation system developed that uses *kanji* (Chinese-Japanese pictographs) that direct the player but allow for some creativity. This education method is still in use today, and it takes up most of a musician's adolescent and young adult life. Students learn the *ryu* in private institutions and universities throughout Japan, and graduation confers upon the player the title of master.

Through the centuries, koto masters have often been women, many of them geisha— "geisha" translates literally as "arts person" and is both the singular and plural form of the word. The koto is now used in ensembles and for vocal accompaniment as well as for solo works such as *Cherry Blossom.* Modern Japanese composers still compose for it.

The strings of the koto are tightly stretched across the board and are supported by thirteen moveable bridges that are adjusted during tuning. The player wears three ivory *plectra* (picks) on the right thumb and first two fingers for plucking the strings. Traditionally, players used the left hand to the left of the bridge to press a string to raise its pitch, and, conversely, to pull a string to lower its pitch. In the modern technique used in this performance of *Cherry Blossom,* the player's left hand plucks in alternation with the right hand to execute rapid passages.

The Timbre of the Koto

The characteristic focused, penetrating sound of the koto comes from the tension of its strings, which produce few overtone partials. As we saw in the Elements section under "Timbre" (p. 11), partials are frequencies that resonate with the fundamental sound wave to create a richer quality of sound. Western violins and acoustic guitars, for example, produce more partials than the koto and have a correspondingly fuller tone. The tense timbre of the koto is highly valued within traditional Japanese musical culture, and a similarly tense tone may also be heard in Japanese vocal music.

Melody: The Wilt of Sorrow

The word *sakura* means "cherry blossom." The melody is a popular Japanese folk tune with a sad sentiment; cherry blossoms are beautiful but short lived, and the Japanese perceive this as sorrowful. The variations on *Cherry Blossom* portray a cherry blossom's various stages of blossoming and wilting. In a broader sense, they symbolize the human life cycle. Like the *Cherry Blossom* variations, many Japanese melodies have **extramusical** content, which means that the music refers to ideas (such as a dying flower) outside of the sound. "Extramusical" is the term used by ethnomusicologists studying world music to describe what is the equivalent of program music in Western music (see chapter 14). The piece is shaped by its relationship to the title, and a title may be associated with an idea, story, or event. A listener may choose to listen to the piece with the extramusical idea in mind or just listen to the music as it unfolds.

On this recorded example of *Cherry Blossom,* the master musician first plucks through a short section devoted to testing and tuning the instrument's strings. This tuning is considered part of the performance, and it serves as a prelude. After this short prelude, the musician introduces the *Cherry Blossom* melody. It is in the *in* mode, a particularly sorrowful-sounding Japanese tonal sequence similar to the European minor mode. The *in* mode consists of five tones. Five-tone modes, also known as **pentatonic scales**, have long appeared in Asian music and in the folk music of Europe and the Americas, but were not taken up by Western classical music until the nineteenth century.

Form: Theme and Variations

After the theme is played, the master koto musician then performs six variations on it, all with very different plucking and strumming techniques that create rhythmic and timbral variety. Before the final variation, the koto master performs an improvisation around the theme's phrases, **A**, **B**, and **C**. The variations are learned by rote as part of the *ryu,* but the improvised section is freely played from the musician's inner creativity, which is part of being a master.

Textural Variety on the Koto

Although this work is performed by only one musician, the technique of right and left hand alternation results in the performance sounding as though it were played by two musicians, sometimes homophonic and other times polyphonic. The right hand steadily plays the theme's phrases each time they occur, while the left hand creates variations around them.

Now listen to this piece again, following the Listening Guide.

EXPAND YOUR PLAYLIST

Zither-Dee-Dee

The koto is one type of zither; various other types are found around the world.

Japan

* Nanae Yoshimura. *The Art of the Koto, Vol. 1.* Celestial Harmonies B00004X0T4.

This is the first of five CDs showing the development of koto music from the seventeenth century to today.

* Satomi Saeki, koto, and Alcvin Takegawa Ramos, shakuhaci. *Japanese Traditional Koto and Shakuhachi Music.* Oliver Sudden Productions B000CQNIHY.

Traditional pieces played on the low-voiced Japanese flute (shakuhachi) and koto.

China

* Zhiming Han on yangqin and Hsinmei (Cynthia) Hsiang on zheng (Chinese zither). *Celestial Echo: Live Performance on Yangqin—Chinese Butterfly Harp and Zheng.* Plectrum Recordings B000W1MJV0.

Duets on the Chinese hammer dulcimer (or yangqin) and the zheng (a long zither, similar to the Japanese koto).

Austria

* *Anton Karas: First Man of the Zither.* Jasmine Music B00006J9M2.

Played on the Austrian zither, Karas's famous theme for the 1939 thriller *The Third Man,* starring Joseph Cotton and Orson Welles, was a top pop hit in its day.

United States

* *Dulcimer World: Kevin Roth.* Star Gazer Productions B000CAKC3I.

A selection of popular and traditional melodies played on a range of Appalachian dulcimers.

Master Musicians of the Ikuta-ryu *Cherry Blossom*

Time	Form: Section	Melody	Timbre
0:00	Tuning Prelude	Introduction	Penetrating and focused tones plucked melodically throughout the instrument's range.
0:19	Theme	A (0:19) B (0:23) C (0:28) B (0:32) C (0:37) A (0:41) Ending (0:46)	Theme plucked by the right hand with a full timbre. The accompaniment is plucked by the left hand; the tense, higher-register strings create a piercing sound.
0:52	Variation 1	A (0:52) B (0:57) C (1:01)	The right hand plucks the theme in three-note rhythmic groupings. The tones are more connected but accented, creating a stronger timbre.
1:06	Variation 2	A (1:06) B (1:11) C (1:15)	Rapid left-hand variation in four-note rhythmic groupings. The timbre becomes smooth and fuller.
1:20	Variation 3	B (1:20) C (1:24) Slight pause before next variation (1:28)	The tense higher-register strings now sound detached and penetrating.
1:30	Variation 4	A (1:30) B (1:37) C (1:44)	Theme played slowly, with right hand tremolo. The tremolo creates a "shivering" effect (mood).
1:50	Variation 5	A (1:50) B (1:57) Ending (2:01)	Theme with more rapid tremolo, further intensifying the "shivering" effect. There is then an adjusted tuning, giving a different timbre to those changed tones.
2:08	Improvisation	Through-composed variations on phrase fragments.	Rapid, penetrating and focused tones, as the musician plucks with extreme speed.
2:33	Variation 6	A (2:33) B (2:36) C (2:39) A (2:42) B (2:45) C (2:49) A (2:52) B (2:54) Ending (2:27 - 3:06)	Theme played with extreme speed and set by the tempo of the improvisation. Each repetition of the theme is faster.

Monophonic. Strings are individually tested and tuned by both hands in alternation.

Homophonic. The left hand plays an accompanimental figure around the phrases, increasing in speed around the B and C phrases.

Homophonic. The left-hand variation accompanies the theme in rhythm.

Polyphonic. The left-hand variation is independent and moves much faster than before, like flowing water.

Polyphonic. The left-hand variation is in triplets, like raindrops falling.

Homophonic. The left hand strums an accompaniment in rhythm and then plucks a pattern.

Homophonic. The left hand continues to strum in accompaniment to the theme.

Homophonic. The left hand accompanies the right hand improvisation.

Homophonic. The left hand accompanies the theme.

Student FAQs

How does the koto player create the wide vibrato that I hear on this recording?

The strings of the koto are suspended fairly high off the soundboard by passing over a series of footed bridges (see photo). There is considerable play in the string itself; that is, unlike a guitar string, which is kept at a fairly high tension, the koto string can be moved up and down easily by pressing on it with the fretting hand. As the player presses down on the string, the pitch is raised. A talented player can create everything from a slight to a very wide vibrato using this method.

Why does Japanese music sound foreign to me?

Like other forms of world music, Japanese music uses a "gapped" scale; instead of having seven notes, typically Japanese scales have only five notes. (These are also called pentatonic scales.) Western ears are used to hearing melodies based on seven tones, and so these missing notes—or gaps—can make the music sound odd or foreign to us.

Why is the koto so soft compared to Western string instruments?

The koto's strings are made of silk, while the strings on many modern violins are made of gut, a synthetic material such as nylon, or steel. The silk strings are also at a lighter tension than those on the violin, so they don't vibrate as efficiently. The soundboard of the koto is a simple, slightly arched board, which does little to amplify the vibrations of the strings, whereas the violin's sound chamber—the inside of the instrument's body—is very efficient at amplifying the sound of its strings. All these factors combine to make the sound produced by the koto very soft. However, because the koto was designed to be played in small rooms or with only a few other instruments, it was not necessary for

it to be louder. In modern concert halls, the koto's sound is usually amplified by an external microphone.

21

Joseph Haydn

Symphony no. 102 in B-flat Major, third and fourth movements

Listen to This

Timbre

Listen for the breadth of sound from the full orchestra: many strings (first and second violins, violas, cellos, double basses), winds (flutes, oboes, bassoons), brass (horns and trumpets), and percussion (timpani, also known as "kettledrums").

Dynamics

Listen for the frequent changes in dynamics between very loud and very soft.

Form

Listen for the return of the opening idea in each movement.

Listeners hear music against the backdrop of their times. In the middle of World War II, audiences in the United States rejected Igor Stravinsky's unusual harmonization of "The Star-Spangled Banner" for orchestra. Twenty-five years later, in the middle of the Vietnam War, listeners at Woodstock embraced Jimi Hendrix's jarring, distorted rendition of the melody on the electric guitar.

The backdrop in London 1795 was revolution and its aftermath. Among the audience at the premiere of Joseph Haydn's Symphony no. 102 in B♭ Major were French aristocrats fleeing the bloody Reign of Terror that followed the French Revolution. The English press and public were now debating at length how to reconcile the three goals of the French Revolution: "liberty and equality"—personal freedom and democracy—with "fraternity," the need for social order.

Some in Haydn's audience heard this ideal realized in the sound of this symphony. A large number of varied instruments—strings, winds, percussion—contributed uniquely and in equal measure to an all-encompassing harmony. It was a mirror of the ideal society. And unlike chamber music works such as the string quartet, played in small spaces and private homes, the symphony brought large numbers of the public together to hear music give voice to their personal and collective aspirations.

Haydn's London audiences could not get enough of his symphonies. By the time he had finished his two extended visits to the English capital (1791–92, 1794–95), he had written twelve altogether. Each has three or four movements, along the lines of the typical string quartet (see chapter 19). Symphony no. 102 is in four movements:

1. **First movement:** A substantial movement in a fast tempo, usually in what is known as *sonata form* (we will discuss this form on p. 201).
2. **Second movement:** Another substantial movement, but in a slow tempo and in a contrasting key. Slow movements assume many different forms: sonata form, theme and variations, and **ABA** are the most common.
3. **Third movement:** A minuet, a lively, stylized dance in triple meter, in the tonic key. Minuets are always in ternary form (**ABA**), with the **A** and **B** sections each consisting of a binary form. The third movement we are listening to follows this form.
4. **Fourth movement:** A somewhat lighter and usually very fast movement. The most common forms used in the finale are sonata form and rondo. The finale of Haydn's Symphony no. 102 is a rondo.

The Timbre of the Full Orchestra

The size of an orchestra performing a symphony can vary widely, depending on the composer's instructions, the availability of players, and the size of the concert hall. In Haydn's time, a large orchestra would have consisted of strings (about 8–10 first violins, 6–8 second violins, 4–6 violas, 3–4 cellos, and 2 double basses), winds (2 flutes, 2 oboes, 2 bassoons, 2 trumpets, and 2 horns), and percussion (timpani, also known as "kettledrums"). Listen to the ways in which these various instruments and groups of instruments combine and contrast with one another. Haydn uses the full orchestra judiciously. We hear all the instruments playing together at times, but more often we hear smaller groups of instruments: just the strings, or just the winds, or just the winds and percussion. The variety of sound available from the possible combinations is enormous.

The Dynamics of Surprise

Changes in dynamics can help guide our listening. The entire middle section ("trio") of the third movement of Symphony no. 102, for example, is played piano, which helps set it off against the two mostly loud outer sections. Whether we realize it or not, we also have certain expectations about dynamics. When we hear a very soft passage for a long stretch, we begin to anticipate the music getting loud again. Haydn always obliges, but not always when we expect it. Sometimes the music stays unusually soft for much longer than we think it will, such as at the very beginning of the finale (the fourth movement). When the full orchestra comes in, after almost a whole minute, we feel a sense that what we have long anticipated has at last arrived.

While the full orchestra often plays at a very loud volume, as might be expected, dynamics operate independently of the number or combination of the instruments that happen to be playing. Even a large number of instruments playing together can create a soft sound.

The Chamber Orchestra of Philadelphia. An ensemble roughly this size gave the first performance of Haydn's Symphony no. 102 in London in 1795.

Alan Kolc, Courtesy The Chamber Orchestra of Philadelphia

Third Movement: Minuet

The minuet is a courtly, elegant dance, although it often assumes a playful character in Haydn's hands. Like all minuets, this one is in triple meter, with an accent on the first beat of each measure (**1**-2-3, **1**-2-3, etc.).

Minuet Form

In **minuet form**, the opening section, known as the minuet proper (**A**), is followed by a contrasting trio (**B**), which is followed by a repeat of the minuet proper, thus creating the pattern **ABA**. This is called **ternary form**.

A: The minuet proper

- Is in binary form (see p. 141), with two sections, each of which is repeated in performance.
- About halfway through the second section, the opening idea returns in the tonic key, "rounding out" the form. This creates what is known as **rounded binary form**.

B: The trio

- Is also in binary form (two sections).
- The trio provides a contrasting theme and mood to the minuet proper.

- At the end of the trio stands the Italian phrase *da capo*, meaning literally "from the head," or as we would say more colloquially in English, "from the top" or "from the beginning." This indicates that the orchestra is to play the minuet proper again.

A: The return of the minuet proper

- The performers return to the beginning, and the movement as a whole ends with the end of the minuet proper (the **A** section).
- Many modern-day ensembles omit the repetition of these sections the second time around.

This structural pattern—**ABA**—was used frequently in the Classical Era. Composers continued to use it on occasion throughout the nineteenth century and into the twentieth.

Now listen to the third movement of Haydn's Symphony no. 102 again, following the Listening Guide.

Fourth Movement: Finale

The last movement of Haydn's Symphony no. 102—its **finale**—is lighter in tone than the other movements, a "happy ending" to the cycle of the work's four movements. In this respect, it is very typical of the symphonic finale in the Classical Era. Haydn, Mozart, and other composers of the time liked to use the rondo form in the finale of symphonies and other multi-movement works (sonatas, string quartets, etc.) because rondos are jaunty and bright, and their principal melodies are often quite catchy.

Rondo Form

In **rondo form**, an opening theme (**A**) returns repeatedly over the course of the movement, interspersed with contrasting ideas (**B**, **C**, etc.). In this instance, the pattern is **ABACADACA**. In Italian, *rondo* means "round dance," in which any one dancer in a circle of dancers repeatedly moves away from his or her starting point and then returns to it. In a similar fashion, the musical form of the rondo keeps moving away from and returning to its opening idea (**A**).

The main theme (**A**) of a rondo is typically brief and simple, which makes it that much easier to recognize when it returns. The main theme of this particular rondo is almost instantly recognizable because of the distinctive rhythm of its opening (da-da-DUM).

From the listener's perspective, rondos are easy to follow—no matter how intricate the music might be at any given point, even the most casual listener can anticipate and recognize the return of the opening theme. But rondos are not always so simple underneath the surface. Haydn (and later, Beethoven) liked to play with listeners' expectations of the form. In the finale of Symphony no. 102, Haydn repeatedly teases the listener into thinking that the opening theme will return, only to deflect (or delay at least temporarily) this return. The net result is a movement that is at once simple and sophisticated.

Now listen to the fourth movement of this symphony again, following the Listening Guide.

Joseph Haydn Symphony no. 102 in B-flat Major, third movement: Minuet

Time	Formal Section	Subsection	Timbre
0:00	A (minuet proper)	First section: melody is very disjunct.	Full orchestra: the melody is primarily in the first violins.
0:20		Repeat of first section.	
0:39		Second section: begins with three low notes, tossed from cellos and basses to violas, up to the violins; opening idea of minuet returns at 0:56.	
1:27		Repeat of second section; opening idea of minuet returns at 1:44.	
2:16	B ("trio")	First section: melody more lyrical, mostly conjunct.	Reduced orchestra: trumpets and timpani are silent throughout. The melody is carried primarily by the winds (oboes and bassoons).
2:32		Repeat of first section.	
2:48		Second section, with return of the B section's opening idea at 2:56.	
3:12		Repeat of second section, with return of the B section's opening idea at 3:20. Section ends with the instruction "da capo," indicating that the orchestra returns to the beginning of the minuet.	
3:36	A (return of the minuet proper)	Return of first section of minuet proper (this recording does not repeat the first section here)	Full orchestra; the melody is primarily in first violins.
3:55		Return of the second section of the minuet proper; opening idea returns at 4:12 (this recording does not repeat the second section here)	

Dynamics

Frequent alternations between loud and soft.

Entirely soft.

Frequent alternations between
loud and soft.

Joseph Haydn Symphony no. 102 in B-flat Major, fourth movement: Rondo

Time	Section	Melody	Timbre
0:00	A (main theme)	Rapid stepwise motion.	Reduced orchestra (strings and woodwinds alone).
1:00	B	Wide leaps, dotted rhythms.	Full orchestra: horns, trumpets, and timpani join in.
1:26	A	Rapid stepwise motion.	Strings alone.
1:33	C	Meandering melody over a **drone bass**— a single note repeated over and over.	Full orchestra.
2:16	A	Rapid stepwise motion.	Strings and flute, then full orchestra (but softly, starting at 2:25), with back-and-forth between winds and timpani (high) and strings (low).
2:46	D	Leaping melody striding upward.	Full orchestra.
3:25	A	Rapid stepwise motion; note how the theme is interrupted at 3:32.	Strings, alone, then winds join in.
3:40	C	Meandering melody over a drone bass.	Full orchestra.
4:04	A	Rapid stepwise motion; note how Haydn plays with our expectations of how a piece should end.	Winds, then strings, then full orchestra.

Dynamics	Harmony: Key Area
Soft	Tonic (B-flat major)
Loud	
Soft	Not tonic (F major)
Loud/soft/ loud; much contrast of dynamics within this section	
Soft	Tonic (B-flat major)
Loud	Tonic (but in minor mode—B-flat minor), then unstable (moves through various key areas)
Soft	Tonic (B-flat major)
Loud/soft/loud	
Soft/loud	

Student FAQs

Why is there no basso continuo in the orchestra?

Most performances of Haydn's later symphonies dispense with the basso continuo for the simple reason that it's not necessary: the voices are sufficiently full without it. Some ensembles do use a basso continuo, however, for there is evidence that Haydn himself conducted from the keyboard in London. Whether he actually played while sitting at the harpsichord or piano is not clear, but he did write a surprise solo passage for himself into the finale of his Symphony No. 98.

Why does the recording omit the repeats when playing the da capo portion of the minuet proper?

Listeners today tend to be less tolerant of literal repetition than their eighteenth-century counter-parts. When all the repeats are observed, the minuet proper (that is, the opening two sections of the minuet movement, excluding the trio) is heard altogether four times. But repetition was basic to dance music, and Haydn's audiences would not have considered so many repeats unusual in any way.

THE COMPOSER SPEAKS

Haydn in London

Written a week after Haydn arrived in England, this fascinating letter was addressed to Maria Anna von Genzinger, a talented pianist who lived in Vienna. It reminds us of the physical and emotional distance the composer had traveled from his native Austria. When Haydn arrived in London, he was already a celebrity. He granted interviews to three newspapers and received invitations to dine at the highest levels of English society. Only a few months before, he had been going about his daily routine in remote Esterháza, his patrons' palace in the Hungarian countryside.

London/ Arrives 1/2/1791
Dover 1/1/1791
Calais 12/31/1790
Bonn/Late Dec. meets the young Beethoven
Munich
Vienna/Leaves 12/15/1790
Salzburg/ Visits his brother
Esterháza/Summer 1790

N

My arrival caused a great sensation throughout the whole city, and I went the round of all the newspapers for 3 successive days. Everyone wants to know me. I had to dine out 6 times up to now, and if I wished, I could dine out every day; but first I must consider my health, and 2nd my work. . . . I have nice and comfortable, but expensive, lodgings. My landlord is Italian, and also a cook, and serves me 4 very respectable meals; we each pay 1 fl. 30 kr. a day excluding wine and beer, but everything is terribly expensive here. Yesterday I was invited to a grand amateur concert, but I arrived a bit late, and when I showed my ticket they wouldn't let me in but led me to an antechamber, where I had to wait till the piece which was then being played in the hall was over. Then they opened the door, and I was conducted, on the arm of the entrepreneur, up the center of the hall to the front of the orchestra, amid universal applause, and there I was stared at and greeted by a great number of English compliments. I was assured that such honors had not been conferred on anyone for 50 years. After the concert I was taken to a handsome adjoining room, where a table for 200 persons, with many places set, was prepared for all the amateurs; I was supposed to be seated at the head of the table, but since I had dined out on that day and had eaten more than usual, I declined this honor, with the excuse that I was not feeling very well, but despite this I had to drink the harmonious health, in Burgundy, of all the gentlemen present; they all returned the toast, and then allowed me to be taken home.

Source: *The Collected Correspondence and London Notebooks of Joseph Haydn*, ed. and trans. H.C. Robbins Landon (London: Barrie and Rockliff, 1959), pp. 111–113.

Concerts and Concert Manners in the Classical Era

Concerts in Haydn's time were far longer than today, with many of them lasting four hours or more. Unlike nowadays, audiences were not expected to sit as still and silent as statues through the entire performance. Contemporary accounts suggest that sizable portions of the audience used concerts as an occasion for socializing and felt free to converse even while the music was played.

Audiences were also much more open about expressing their reactions to performances, both favorable and unfavorable. Composers could always tell which portion of a particular symphony or concerto an audience liked best, because listeners clapped immediately. Sometimes a movement would even be encored in its entirety.

Contemporary accounts tell us that eighteenth-century audiences could burst into applause even *while* the music was playing—much as what occurs today after a jazz solo, for example. Mozart once described in a letter to his father how he had counted on this custom while composing the finale of one of his symphonies:

> Having observed that all finales as well as opening Allegros begin here [in Paris] with all the instruments playing together and generally in unison, I began mine with two violins only, *piano* [softly] for the first eight measures, followed instantly by a *forte* [loud outburst]. The audience, as I expected, said "hush" at the soft beginning, and when they heard the *forte,* began at once to clap their hands. [letter of 3 July 1778]

In short, concert manners in the late eighteenth century were rather more like concert manners in a rock or jazz concert today. The gap between "serious" art and "popular" entertainment was not nearly as wide in Haydn's time as it is today.

 EXPAND YOUR PLAYLIST

Haydn's Symphonies

Haydn wrote 106 symphonies, and each is distinctive. Here are some of the more famous:

Symphony no. 8 in G Major ("Evening/Le soir")
The third of three programmatic symphonies depicting the times of day (no. 6 is Morning/Le matin; no. 7 is Noon/Le midi). Haydn wrote these works shortly after arriving at the Esterházy court, and he ingratiated himself with the leading members of the orchestra by giving them important solo passages. The evening concludes with a tempest, complete with lightning.

Symphony no. 45 in F♯ Minor ("Farewell")
While the Esterházy castle was still under construction, the musicians had to live some distance away from their families for the whole of the summer. When the prince kept delaying his return to Eisenstadt, Haydn wrote a finale to remind him that the musicians longed to go home. In the finale of this symphony, the players stop playing, one by one, and exit the stage, so that at the end, only two violinists are left. They, too, extinguish their candles and leave the stage.

Symphony no. 94 in G Major ("Surprise")
"I wanted to create a sensation" was Haydn's explanation for the wholly unprepared and—yes—surprising loud chord near the beginning of the slow movement. Everyone remembered this effect, and the symphony received the nickname of "Surprise," which has stuck ever since.

Symphony no. 101 in D Major ("Clock")
This work takes its nickname from the persistent tick-tock rhythm of the slow movement. It is one of the twelve (nos. 93–104) Haydn wrote for London audiences.

22

Wolfgang Amadeus Mozart
Symphony no. 40 in G Minor, K. 550, first movement

Listen to This

Form

Listen for the repeated return of various themes over the course of this movement. Notice, too, the sharp contrast between the character of the themes. The opening is quietly agitated, but within less than a minute, we hear themes that are louder and brighter and still others that are softer and calmer.

Harmony

Listen for the contrast between key areas early in this movement. The change in keys coincides with a change in mode: the opening theme is in the minor mode, the next main theme is in major. Which sounds darker? Which sounds brighter? Which mode predominates in this movement?

Melody

How would you characterize the themes of this movement? What makes them different from each other?

Mozart's Symphony no. 40 in G Minor is one of a group of three symphonies that he wrote in 1788, probably for a concert he organized himself, although no record of the event survives. The symphony has four movements; we are listening to the first.

Even without words, there is real drama in this music. Indeed, if we think of its various themes as characters, this movement features all the essential elements of a good drama: memorable personalities (melodies), conflict (the juxtaposition and transformation of those melodies), and resolution (the restoration of these melodies in their more or less original form). The events of this musical drama unfold in the same kind of logical sequence that we see in a three-act play presented on the stage:

- We meet the main character and the supporting characters ("Act 1").
- We witness their interaction and transformation: they fall in and/or out of love, they fight, they search or struggle for something ("Act 2").
- We experience some kind of resolution in the end: it may be a happy or an unhappy ending, or something in between, but we recognize it as an ending because all the strands of the plot are resolved ("Act 3").

How does Mozart present this drama in purely musical terms? He organizes the first movement of this symphony around a musical structure known as **sonata form**, a form that was new in the Classical Era and that allowed for the presentation, development, and resolution of multiple themes within a single movement. From roughly 1750 to the present day, composers have written literally thousands of movements in sonata form, for it provides a versatile framework for creating a drama without words.

Sonata Form

The three acts of a drama outlined previously correspond to the three parts of sonata form:

Act 1: The **exposition** introduces us to—*exposes* us to—all the movement's thematic ideas. By the end of the exposition, we have met all the musical "characters."

Act 2: The **development** is the middle part of a sonata-form movement, in which the thematic ideas are most intensively *developed,* both thematically and harmonically. Themes are taken apart, combined in different ways, and tried in different keys.

Act 3: The **recapitulation** comes in the last third of the movement. The themes we heard in the exposition are *recapped.* This is the resolution of all we have heard before.

Sonata form emerged around the middle of the eighteenth century as an expansion of a form already well established, **rounded binary form** (see p. 192). Rounded binary form consists of two sections in which the opening idea and the tonic key return simultaneously about a third of the way through the movement. (We saw this structure in the minuet of Haydn's Symphony no. 102, discussed in chapter 21.) In sonata form, two important new elements are added:

1. The first section—the exposition—always modulates, presenting themes in a new, contrasting key area.
2. The theme(s) presented in the new key area in the exposition are repeated in the recapitulation *in the tonic*—that is, in the original key of the movement. This is what helps give a sense of resolution to any sonata-form movement.

Sonata form thus consists of three sections—exposition, development, and recapitulation—that are superimposed on a binary form. The exposition takes up the whole of the first binary section. The development and recapitulation both fall within the second binary section.

Almost by definition, the second binary section is longer than the first, because it develops the themes *and* recapitulates them. Graphically, this form can be represented as follows:

In practice, no two sonata-form movements are entirely alike. Sonata form is a broad and flexible scheme, and composers were extremely adept at manipulating it. There are, however, several predictable features that a listener can recognize:

- There is always a modulation from a primary to a secondary key area in the exposition.
- The first binary section is always repeated; the second binary section may or may not be repeated.
- There is always a departure from these harmonic areas in the development.
- The development moves through various keys and rarely settles on any one of them for very long. This section features bits and pieces of one or more earlier themes, transformed and combined in different ways.
- There is always a return to the primary key area in the recapitulation, and it almost always coincides with the return to the opening idea in its original form. This is the onset of the recapitulation, and it is often a dramatic moment in a sonata-form movement. After the unpredictability and instability of the development, we are now finally back on familiar ground (the opening idea, in the tonic).
- The sequence of themes in the recapitulation usually follows the sequence of themes as presented in the exposition.
- The recapitulation always stays in the tonic throughout.

The first movement of Mozart's Symphony no. 40 in G Minor follows the conventions of sonata form fairly closely:

- It opens with an exposition that modulates from the tonic of G Minor to the contrasting key area of B♭ major. The contrast of mode between the minor mode (the tonic) and the major mode (the new key area) helps make the contrast between the two key areas more audible.
- The development is quite unstable harmonically, and it features an intense manipulation of the movement's opening theme.

- The onset of the recapitulation provides a strong and dramatic sense of return: the music comes back to the tonic, and the opening theme reappears more or less in its original guise.

- Later in the recapitulation, what had been heard outside the tonic in the exposition is now presented in the tonic: again, the contrast of mode (B♭ major in the exposition, G minor in the recapitulation) makes the resolution easier to hear. What we heard in B♭ major in the exposition now returns in G Minor, and the difference is striking.

The movement concludes with a brief **coda**. "Coda" is the Italian word for "tail," and it brings the movement to a close after the recapitulation. Codas stand outside of the sonata-form structure itself and may or may not be present in a sonata-form movement.

Harmony: Minor to Major

To sustain a musical argument across such a long span of time, Mozart uses different key areas to create variety. Harmony also plays an important role in the sonata-form structure, as we have seen. The modulation in this movement from the tonic to the new key area is particularly clear because it also coincides with a change in mode. The first key area is G minor; the mood is dark and brooding. The new key area is B♭ major; here, the music sounds brighter and more optimistic. But when the themes presented in this new key area return in the recapitulation, they are played in G Minor (the tonic), and now they, too, sound dark and brooding. It is as if all the melodies—all the "characters"—have finally come under the spell of the tonic, thereby creating a sense of resolution and closure.

Contrasting Principal Melodies

The dramatic interest of this movement depends not just on forms and harmonies but also on the compelling and contrasting nature of the principal melodies. The music begins with an accompanimental figure in the low strings that sets both a mood (quietly agitated) and a mode (minor). When the first theme enters in the violin soon after, we hear many repetitions of a brief downward step. The melodic line sounds almost like a series of short sighs.

The second principal theme, by contrast, consists of much longer notes, and the agitated accompanimental figure is no longer present. The effect is a mood that is much calmer.

Both themes are constructed around a series of antecedent (opening) and consequent (closing) phrases. But the opening theme (first example, shown previously, Theme 1 in the Listening Guide) stretches out over a much longer span of time, with multiple antecedent phrases. Even though it establishes the tonic key, its restlessness gives it a sense of constant forward motion. The first theme in the new key area, by contrast (second example, shown previously; Theme 3 in the Listening Guide), moves in a slower rhythm and is much more regular and compact.

Throughout this movement, Mozart dismantles and puts back together these two principal melodies, particularly the opening theme and portion of a transitional theme that connects the two (Theme 2 in the Listening Guide). He varies them in multiple ways by presenting them in different keys and by giving them to different instruments or combinations of instruments. In this way, even though Mozart adheres to the conventions of sonata form, he manipulates its content in surprising and unusual ways.

Now listen to this movement again, following the Listening Guide.

The Drama of Sonata Form

If sonata form can be thought of as a drama in three acts, perhaps there are dramas that can be thought of in terms of sonata form. The movie version of *The Wizard of Oz,* for example, bears striking parallels. Think of the characters as themes and the places where the action occurs as the key areas. The black-and-white scenes at the beginning and end of the movie function as the exposition and recapitulation, respectively. In the opening section—before Dorothy is transported to Oz—we meet all the main characters of the story, in two different places: first at home, and then later as Dorothy is running away from home. In the "development"—the bulk of the movie, in color, which takes us through many different places, from Munchkinland, along the Yellow Brick Road, to Oz itself—those same characters are transformed: Miss Gulch becomes the Wicked Witch of the West, the farmhands become the Scarecrow, the Tin Woodsman, and the Lion, and Professor Marvel becomes the Wizard of Oz. When Dorothy returns to Kansas (and the movie returns to black-and-white), all the characters of the exposition (minus Miss Gulch) reappear in their original guises. Even Professor Marvel, whom Dorothy had met away from home, drops by her house to see how she is doing. He is the same person, but now he is in a different place, in Dorothy's home—in musical terms, her tonic key. It is a satisfying conclusion to the whole, in which the characters have all covered a great deal of ground but all return home in the end. All this is laid out in the table here.

Dorothy wakes up in her room toward the end of *The Wizard of Oz.* The characters from the black-and-white "exposition" (Professor Marvel and the three farmhands) who were transformed in the color "development" (into the Wizard of Oz, the Scarecrow, the Tin Woodsman, and the Cowardly Lion) are now reunited in the black-and-white "recapitulation" in their original form on Dorothy's home ground (the tonic or "home key" of the film).
MGM/The Kobal Collection/Picture Desk

Sonata Form Section	Musical Drama	*The Wizard of Oz*
Exposition	The themes of the movement are "exposed" to us.	In the opening black-and-white section, we meet all the major characters of the story.
Tonic	Theme(s) presented in the tonic, the "home" key.	Dorothy at home on her farm; we meet the farmhands and the dreaded Miss Gulch.
→ modulates to	→ modulates to	→ runs away from home
Secondary key area	A new theme or themes are presented in a key area that is not the tonic, away from the "home" key.	Away from home, Dorothy meets a new character, Professor Marvel.
Development	Harmonically unstable. Themes are transformed so that they are different from how we first heard them, yet recognizably the same.	The film turns to color, and all the characters are transformed: Miss Gulch has become the Wicked Witch of the West; the farmhands are now the Scarecrow, the Tin Woodsman, and the Lion; and Professor Marvel has turned into the Wizard of Oz.
Recapitulation	Return to the "home" key of the tonic. All themes heard in the exposition are now presented in the tonic.	Dorothy returns to Kansas and the film returns to black-and-white. The characters of the opening scene (even Professor Marvel, whom Dorothy had met away from home) all reappear in their original form and visit at her bedside.

Wolfgang Amadeus Mozart Symphony no. 40 in G Minor, K. 550, first movement

Time	Sonata Form	Melody
0:00	Exposition	1 = "Sighing" theme, repeated and then interrupted by
0:36		2 = Transitional theme, sudden shift in dynamics (loud) and mode (major); ends with a rapid upward-moving, scale-like figure.
0:55		3 = Calm theme, divided between strings and winds.
1:30		4 = Very similar to opening theme, but now in the new key area and thus conveying a different mood.
2:07	Exposition Repeat	1 = "Sighing" theme.
2:37		2 = Transitional theme.
2:56		3 = Calm theme.
3:35		4 = Similar to opening theme, but in the new key area.
4:10	Development	1 = Opening theme, fragmented and harmonically unstable.
4:24		1 = Fragment of opening theme; highly contrapuntal passage, combining 1 with the rapid upward-moving scale-like figure from theme 2. Winds, high strings, and low strings present different ideas simultaneously.
4:52		3 = Opening theme fragmented and transformed still further. Beginning of a long passage leading back to the recapitulation.
5:25	Recapitulation	1 = Return of the opening theme in the tonic key, with slight alterations in the orchestration (notice the added bassoon part here).
5:58		2 = Transitional theme, but altered here in the recapitulation so as not to modulate.
6:38		3 = Same as theme 3 in exposition, but now in tonic (G minor).
7.25		4 = Same as theme 4 in exposition, but now in the tonic (G minor).
7:45	Coda	1 = Sudden intensification, return of opening theme in tonic, with a full cadence to end the movement.

JEOPARDY!
America's Favorite Quiz Show®

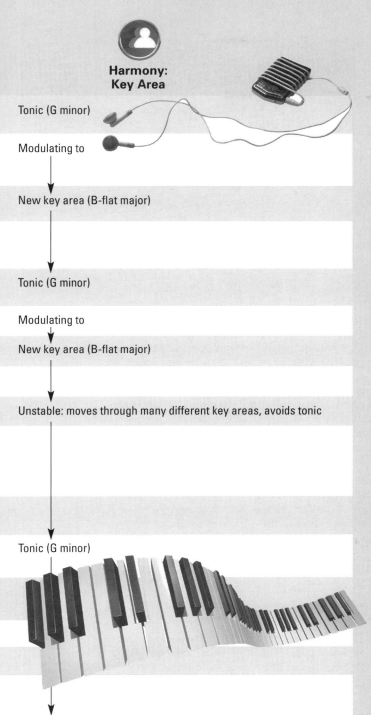

**Harmony:
Key Area**

Tonic (G minor)

Modulating to

↓

New key area (B-flat major)

↓

Tonic (G minor)

Modulating to

↓

New key area (B-flat major)

↓

Unstable: moves through many different key areas, avoids tonic

↓

Tonic (G minor)

↓

Student FAQs

***I don't hear the modulations within the sonata form.
Is that a problem?***

Everyone hears differently, but digital technology makes it easier to
improve your ability to perceive changes in key. For this particular
movement, try listening up to the point just before the recapitulation
begins (at 5:25), then hit the button that takes you back to
the very beginning of the entire movement and listen
through the end of the exposition. What you will have
heard, in effect, is a recapitulation that modulates and
does not end in the tonic; the effect is quite different from
the actual recapitulation, which stays in the tonic throughout.

***What are some other
examples of modulation?***

Modulation—moving from one key to
another—is a very common device in
music. Here are some other examples that
may already be familiar to you, even if you've never thought about
them in these terms:

- Hymns with many stanzas. Organists will often modulate up a step for
  the last stanza to give the music renewed freshness.
- The "Think Music" played in the final round of "Jeopardy!"
  Listen carefully next time you watch this show. The theme is stated
  once in the tonic; the second time around, it is presented in
  a new key.
- Most popular songs. Almost every popular
  song that lasts more than a couple of
  minutes will modulate for the
  sake of variety, usually somewhere near the middle of the song.

Wolfgang Amadeus Mozart (1756–91)

THE COMPOSER AS CHAMELEON

Mozart once observed that he could "write in any style I choose." This wasn't bragging: it was simply the truth. This extraordinary flexibility was due to Mozart's innate genius and his education. His father, Leopold Mozart, a composer of some renown, quickly recognized the musical talent of his young son and took him on a number of extended journeys throughout Europe: to Italy, France, Germany, the Netherlands, and England. At each stop, the Mozarts would meet the local composers, perform in public, and absorb different styles of composition and performance.

The Mozart family, ca. 1780. Leopold Mozart (right) was an accomplished violinist and a composer; Nannerl, the composer's sister, excelled as a keyboard player. Mozart's mother, whose portrait hangs on the wall, had died a few years earlier.
Mozart House, Salzburg, Austria–Erich. Lessing/Art Resource, NY

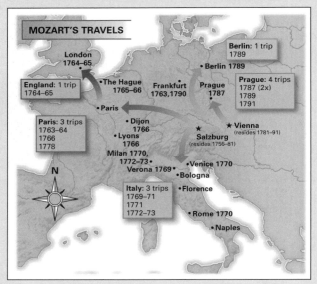

MOZART'S TRAVELS

London 1764–65
Berlin: 1 trip 1789
• Berlin 1789
England: 1 trip 1764–65
• The Hague 1765–66
Frankfurt 1763, 1790
Prague 1787
Prague: 4 trips 1787 (2x) 1789 1791
• Paris
Paris: 3 trips 1763–64 1766 1778
• Dijon 1766
• Lyons 1766
★ Salzburg (resides 1756–81)
★ Vienna (resides 1781–91)
Milan 1770, 1772–73 •
Verona 1769 •
• Venice 1770
• Bologna
N
Italy: 3 trips 1769–71 1771 1772–73
• Florence
• Rome 1770
• Naples

Like many child stars today, Mozart had difficulty in making the transition to adulthood. He found his native Salzburg increasingly provincial, but a series of job searches across Europe proved fruitless. Against his father's wishes, he left Salzburg in 1781 for Vienna without steady employment. He hoped to land a position at the imperial court there but was again unsuccessful. In the meantime, he supported himself and his new wife, Constanze, by giving public performances on the piano, selling his published compositions, and giving lessons in piano and composition. He did fairly well for a time but for reasons that remain obscure—the fickleness of Viennese tastes, hard economic times, or perhaps compulsive gambling—he was in serious debt by the early 1790s and had to borrow money from friends. He died at the age of 35, just when his popularity (and income) seemed to be on the rise again.

Mozart could be eccentric in his behavior, and he refused to play along in the world of Viennese musical politics. He seldom had anything good to say about contemporary composers (Haydn was an exception), and it must have been painful for him to see court appointments go to lesser composers like Antonio Salieri. Although fictionalized to some degree, Peter Shaffer's play *Amadeus* (1980) brilliantly captures the sense of mutual frustration between the competent Salieri and the genius Mozart.

PLAYLIST: MOZART

Mass in C Minor, K. 427. Unfinished, but a magnificent setting for soloists, chorus, and orchestra, with unusually demanding parts for the vocal soloists.

A Musical Joke (Ein musikalischer Spaß), K. 522. A chamber work for string quartet and two horns, this piece is full of intentional mistakes and pokes fun at bad composers.

A Little Serenade (Eine kleine Nachtmusik), K. 525. A suite for strings, among Mozart's most popular works.

String Quintet in G Minor, K. 516. Similar in mood to the Symphony in G Minor (the same key), this work is scored for string quartet plus an additional viola.

Requiem, K. 626. Mozart's last work, a funeral Mass commissioned by a mysterious stranger, a count (not Salieri!) who later tried to pass it off as his own composition.

Mozart's Sister

Maria Anna ("Nannerl") Mozart (1751–1829) was as much a child prodigy on the keyboard as her younger brother. A notice in a German newspaper of the time described her as "a young girl of eleven" who "played with the greatest clarity and an effortlessness scarcely to be believed" the "most difficult sonatas and concertos of the great masters on the harpsichord or on the piano, all with the greatest taste." Their father, Leopold, took both children on concert tours across Europe, and gave her, not Wolfgang, top billing when the family visited London in 1765.

But for reasons that remain unclear, Nannerl eventually stopped traveling with her father and brother. She did not accompany them on two extended tours of Italy in the late 1760s and early 1770s. This may have been by her own choice, her father's choice, or some combination of the two. In any case, Leopold seems to have made a conscious decision to invest his primary energies in the promotion of Wolfgang's career, affording him extensive training in composition as well as performance. All that survives of Nannerl's compositions are a few brief exercises. Professional outlets for women composers were virtually nonexistent in that place and time.

On the other hand, women could and did enjoy successful careers as performers, especially in Vienna. Wolfgang tried to persuade his sister to join him there in 1781: "Believe me, you could earn a great deal of money in Vienna . . . by playing at private concerts and by giving piano lessons. You would be very much in demand—and you would be well paid." Nannerl chose not to pursue a career as a performer, however. Her father arranged for her to marry a baron in 1784, and she bore three children by him—one of whom she named Wolfgang—but she apparently did not perform in public again. After her husband died in 1821, Nannerl returned to Salzburg and gave piano lessons for the rest of her life.

A portrait of Maria Anna ("Nannerl") Mozart. Notice her unusually large hands, which undoubtedly served her well as a pianist.

Dagli Orti (A)/Picture Desk, Inc./Kobal Collection

 EXPAND YOUR PLAYLIST

Mozart's Symphonies

Mozart, like Haydn, seems to have relished the challenge of writing for a large ensemble. Here are some of his better-known symphonies:

Symphony no. 1 in E♭ Major, K. 16. A small-scale work, but nevertheless an impressive accomplishment for an eight-year-old composer.

Symphony no. 25 in G Minor, K. 185. Known as the "Little" G Minor symphony, this work is featured prominently in Milos Forman's film version of Peter Schafer's play *Amadeus.*

Symphony no. 38 in D Major, K. 504. Known as the "Prague" symphony because of its popularity there during Mozart's lifetime. The first movement opens with an extended slow introduction, and the symphony lacks a minuet movement, unlike Mozart's other late symphonies.

Symphony no. 41 in C Major, K. 551. Nicknamed the "Jupiter" symphony sometime after Mozart's death because of its size and exuberant nature. The finale is a remarkable synthesis of fugue and sonata form.

23

Wolfgang Amadeus Mozart
Piano Concerto in A Major, K. 488, first movement

Listen to This

Timbre

Listen to the fluid relationship between the solo instrument—the piano—and the ensemble, an orchestra of strings and winds. Like characters in a drama, they cooperate at times, oppose each other at times, and at times appear by themselves, without the other.

Melody

Listen to the number and variety of the melodies, each with its own distinct character. Notice, too, how these melodies rarely appear in exactly the same guise twice.

Form

Listen for the entrance of the soloist and then later on for the return of the opening idea about two-thirds of the way through the movement, which marks the onset of the recapitulation.

When W.A. Mozart moved to Vienna in 1781, he was determined to make an impression on the Imperial Court and the public, both as a pianist and as a composer. His piano concertos provided him with the ideal vehicle for achieving this dual goal: audiences marveled at the young man's virtuosity at the keyboard and his ingenuity as a composer. Over the span of less than 10 years, Mozart composed 17 piano concertos, including this one from 1786. Like so many of Mozart's works, the Piano Concerto in A Major, K. 488, abounds in melody. Indeed, some critics of the time complained that Mozart's music presented them with too many ideas, and that his melodies moved from one to the next faster than audiences could follow. Yet the ideas themselves seem effortless and natural, clear and unforced.

On closer listening, we can hear that what sounds effortless is in no way simple. In this piano concerto, Mozart explores a variety of moods across three movements, from the serene but passionate first movement to the dark, contemplative second movement, to the rousing, exuberant finale. Here, we are listening to the first movement alone.

Timbre: The Drama of Contrast

The driving force behind any concerto is the inherently dramatic tension between the soloist and the orchestra. The two forces collaborate at times and compete at others; on still other occasions, each appears alone. There are five basic scenarios:

1. Orchestra alone
2. Soloist alone
3. Orchestra supporting the soloist
4. Soloist supporting the orchestra
5. Soloist and orchestra on an equal footing

Listen once through this movement to identify these five different combinations. Here are a just a few examples:

0:00 The orchestra plays by itself for an extended time at the beginning (1).

2:04 When the piano enters for the first time, it plays alone briefly (2).

2:12 When the orchestra reenters, it supports the piano (3).

3:18 The orchestra carries the melody while the piano supports it (4).

3:33 The orchestra and piano engage in dialogue, tossing the theme back and forth between each other (5).

By varying the timbre so frequently and by using so many different combinations, Mozart is able to sustain our interest across a relatively long movement.

Melodic Generosity

One feature that sets Mozart's music apart from that of almost all his contemporaries is the sheer number and variety of musical ideas within a given movement. Where another composer might be satisfied with two different melodies, for example, Mozart provides his listeners with three or four or five. This first movement offers a good example of Mozart's melodic generosity, as well as the way in which he alters the combination of dynamics, texture, and rhythm to create a sense of variety.

Theme 1

The opening idea is serene and balanced, a statement that sets the mood for the movement as a whole. The texture is homophonic, the dynamics soft. The melodic motion is a mixture of conjunct and disjunct, and the contour moves down, then up, ending where it began.

Theme 2

The second idea is more agitated, more propulsive: it moves in a faster rhythm (with shorter note values). The texture is homophonic, the dynamics loud. The melodic motion is marked by prominent upward leaps, and the contour moves largely upward.

Theme 3

This theme also uses shorter note values, but it restores a sense of calm because its many repeated notes help create an impression of not hurrying anywhere. The texture is homophonic, the dynamics soft. The melodic motion is primarily conjunct, and the contour moves largely downward.

Theme 4

This theme is also calm, but the effect comes from the longer note values that make it move more slowly. The texture this time is polyphonic, with some imitation between the voices. The dynamics are soft, and the melodic motion is marked by an initial down contour followed by upward leaps.

Form: Double-Exposition Concerto Form

Like other composers of his time, Mozart adapted sonata form—which was new in the middle of the eighteenth century—to the concerto. But he also retained elements of the contrast between ritornello and solo that was so basic to the Baroque concerto (see chapters 14, 15). Mozart organized the melodic and harmonic structure of the first movement of the Piano Concerto in A Major, K. 488, around a form known as the **double exposition concerto form**. Although based on the same principles as sonata form, double-exposition concerto form differs in several important respects:

Standard Sonata Form	Double-Exposition Concerto Form
• One exposition, repeated literally	• Two different expositions: one for the orchestra, and one for the soloist and orchestra together.
• Exposition modulates from tonic	• The first exposition (for the orchestra alone) stays in the tonic. Only the second exposition (for soloist and orchestra together) modulates to new key area.
• Development avoids the tonic.	• Same.
• Recapitulation	• Same.
• No cadenza.	• At the end of the recapitulation, the soloist plays a *cadenza*—an elaborate improvisation on themes heard earlier in the movement, with no accompaniment at all from the orchestra.

The only entirely new element here is the **cadenza,** a moment when the soloist can display his or her virtuosity to the fullest. Mozart actually wrote down cadenzas for many of his own concertos, but in performance, improvisation was the order of the day. A long trill from the soloist was the standard signal to the orchestra that the cadenza was about to end, and with a gesture from the soloist, the orchestra resumed playing its written parts. Mozart conducted his music from the keyboard; conductors did not arrive on the scene until the early nineteenth century.

Graphically, the double-exposition concerto structure can be represented in this manner:

Double-Exposition Concerto Form

Formal Section	Tutti Exposition (orchestra alone)	Solo Exposition (soloist & orchestra)	Development (soloist & orchestra)	Recapitulation (soloist & orchestra)	Cadenza (soloist alone, improvised)	Coda (orchestra alone)
Key Area	Tonic	Tonic → New key area	Not Tonic (unstable)	Tonic	?	Tonic

☐ Tonic key area   ☐ New key area in exposition   ☐ Unstable key area

Now listen to the first movement of this piano concerto again, following the Listening Guide.

THE MONEY TRAIL

Mozart's Concerts: The Bottom Line

When Mozart moved to Vienna from Salzburg in 1781, he was taking a calculated risk, believing that he could secure a steady position at the Imperial Court or, failing that, earn enough money from concerts, opera commissions, publications, and teaching to support himself (and, after he married, his family).

The actor Tom Hulce in the role of Mozart in *Amadeus* (1984). Mozart was in fact fascinated with the game of billiards, and the image of him composing on a billiard table is entirely plausible.

© Saul Zaentz Company/Courtesy Everett Collection

For a time, at least, Mozart's gamble paid off. His concert series in the years 1783–86 were a great success and attracted many subscribers, including wealthy aristocrats whose opinions could make or break the career of any new musician who had just arrived in Vienna. Mozart kept his expenses down in part by doing almost everything himself. He wrote the music

for his concerts (symphonies and, above all, piano concertos), performed the music himself as soloist and conductor (sometimes filling both functions simultaneously), hired the musicians, and even sold the tickets from his own apartment. (Mozart was affluent enough to afford a servant, and it was presumably the servant, rather than Mozart himself, who actually sold the tickets.)

One reliable recent estimate of Mozart's balance sheet for his 1785 subscription concert series shows that he in fact made a healthy profit on his venture:

Income:

150 subscribers @ 13.5 Gulden ea. for 6 concerts =	2,025 Gulden

Expenses:

Orchestra musicians (estimated):	420 Gulden
Concert hall rental	80
Lighting, printing, and other miscellaneous expenses:	100
Total Expenses:	600 Gulden
Net Profit:	1,425 Gulden

To give some sense of what this meant in terms of purchasing power, the rent for Mozart's apartment at this time was 460 Gulden per year. His subscription series of six concerts thus generated more than three times his annual housing costs. Beyond the subscription concerts, of course, Mozart was also free to give special additional concerts as well.

Source: Mary Sue Morrow, *Concert Life in Haydn's Vienna: Aspects of a Developing Institution* (Stuyvesant, NY: Pendragon Press, 1989), p. 135.

Mozart on Modern Instruments

The recording here presents Mozart played on the instruments that he would have known in his lifetime, all of which have changed somewhat over the years. The stringed instruments of the eighteenth century—violins, violas, cellos, and basses—all used strings made from catgut, not wire; this made their sound warmer, softer, and less penetrating than the sound of modern instruments.

The piano, in particular, has changed considerably since Mozart's day. It is a much longer, heavier, and louder instrument. In Mozart's time, the hammers that struck the strings were covered with leather, not felt, producing a lighter, more percussive sound. The fortepiano, as it was known back then, is a more delicate and intimate instrument than today's grand piano. It produced far less volume, but this was not a drawback, as concert halls in Mozart's time were much smaller than today's. A large number of musicians and listeners prefer the sound of Mozart's music on the kind of instrument he actually wrote for, rather than the larger instrument we know as the piano today.

Which is better? That is entirely a matter of taste. Advocates of the fortepiano argue that we should try to re-create the sound that Mozart had in mind when he wrote his music. Advocates of the modern piano make the case that in proportion to the size of today's concert halls, the modern piano alone creates a sound that fills the space; they also point out that the fortepiano had already begun to grow in size and volume during Mozart's lifetime, and that Mozart himself embraced these developments.

Fortunately, as listeners in today's music world, we have plenty of choices. The following are some good recordings of Mozart's Piano Concerto in A Major, K. 488 on modern instruments:

Alfred Brendel, piano. Academy of St. Martin in the Fields, Neville Marriner, conductor. Philips 000552102.

Murray Perahia, piano. English Chamber Orchestra, Murray Perahia, conductor. Sony 87230.

Ingrid Haebler, piano. London Symphony Orchestra, Witold Rowicki, conductor. Eloquence 468171.

Christian Zacharias plays and conducts a Mozart piano concerto from the keyboard on a modern grand piano. The lid of the piano has been removed to reduce the volume of sound that projects out to the audience. This also improves the sight lines between the soloist-conductor and the members of the orchestra.

Richard Termine/Richard Termine Photography

Ronald Brautigam performs a Mozart concerto on a replica of a fortepiano from Mozart's time. Notice how much smaller the earlier instrument is compared to the modern grand piano.

Courtesy of Ronald Brautigam

Wolfgang Amadeus Mozart   Piano Concerto in A Major, K. 488, first movement

Time	Form: Section	Melody	Timbre
0:00	Tutti exposition (orchestra alone)	1 = lyrical, begins with long notes, downward contour	Strings alone present the theme, which is then repeated by the winds alone.
0:32		2 = more energetic theme, begins with repeated notes but then has several upward leaps and a generally upward contour	Full orchestra.
0:56		3 = another lyrical theme, largely conjunct, downward contour	Strings alone at first, winds join in later
2:04	Solo exposition (soloist and orchestra together)	1 = a more elaborate presentation of the theme	Soloist alone, joined gradually by orchestra
2:32		2 = begins as above, but continues differently so that it modulates, taking the music to a new key area	Orchestra alone, joined by soloist
3:03		3 = as above, but now in the new key area	Soloist alone, joined by the orchestra (at 3:15)
4:27		4 = a new theme, not heard in the tutti exposition; long notes, disjunct motion, generally downward contour	Orchestra (strings alone), joined by soloist (at 4:48)
4:52	Development (soloist and orchestra together)	4 = dialogue between soloist and orchestra on fragments of this theme	Winds alone at first, joined by soloist and strings
6:12	Recapitulation (soloist and orchestra together)	1	Orchestra (with winds now), soloist joins in at 6:27)
6:40		2	Orchestra, then soloist
7:10		3	Soloist, then orchestra
8:12		4	Soloist, then orchestra
8:55		2 (brief return)	Orchestra alone
9:07		4 (brief return)	Orchestra alone
9:20	Cadenza	Improvisation on themes heard earlier in the movement	Soloist alone
10:20	Coda (orchestra alone)	3 (fragment)	Orchestra alone

Harmony: Key Areas

Tonic (A major)

Tonic

→ (modulating to) . . .

New key area (E major)

Unstable: the music moves quickly through many key areas

Tonic: a strong sense of arrival at the beginning of the recapitulation, both to the opening theme and to the opening key

Does not modulate; stays in the tonic

Tonic

Unstable, returns to tonic

Tonic

Student FAQs

Isn't the piano soloist playing very softly with the orchestra in the tutti exposition?

Yes, and you have an extremely good ear if you can hear this. The piano's very discreet (almost inaudible) part here represents a holdover from the days when the keyboard soloist would perform double duty as both a soloist and as a member of the basso continuo. In modern performances that strive to replicate eighteenth-century perform-ance practice (as in the recording here), the soloist helps support the basso continuo in the tutti exposition and at the end, in the coda, fills out harmonies here and there without really calling attention to himself or herself.

How could Mozart have conducted from the keyboard while playing? Didn't he need his arms to conduct?

Yes, but playing the lead on the piano created a basic beat for the musicians to follow. Also, Mozart could use his head and eyes to gesture to the musicians while playing. In those passages in which the orchestra took the lead (as in the tutti exposition), Mozart probably did conduct with one or both arms.

Did Mozart really improvise his cadenzas on the spot?

It's hard to say for sure—even if we could ask him, would we believe his answer? It seems likely, though, that Mozart would have given at least some advance thought to how he might improvise on the themes of a concerto movement, combining those premeditated strategies with genuine improvisation at the moment of performance. Jazz musicians today often do the same thing: to varying degrees, their solo riffs represent a combination of both the planned and the spontaneous.

EXPAND YOUR PLAYLIST

The Classical Concerto

Carl Philipp Emanuel Bach (1714–88), one of J.S. Bach's sons, wrote more than 50 keyboard concertos. The Concerto in G Minor, H. 442, is from the mid-1750s.

Johann Christian Bach (1735–82), like his much older half-brother, Carl Philipp Emanuel Bach, wrote dozens of keyboard concertos. J.C. Bach's Concerto in B♭ Major, op. 7, no. 4 (1770) is written in a more modern style, closer to that of W.A. Mozart.

W.A. Mozart wrote concertos for a variety of different instruments, including not only piano (27 of them) but also violin (5), horn (4), bassoon (1), and flute and harp (1), among others. Some recommendations for further exploration:

- Piano Concerto in D Minor, K. 466. This is one of the darker and more turbulent of the 27 piano concertos Mozart wrote for himself.

- Concerto for Two Pianos in E♭, K. 365. Mozart wrote this to be performed jointly with his sister Nannerl, an accomplished pianist in her own right.

- Sinfonia Concertante in E♭, K. 364. A "concerto-like symphony," grand in scale and sound, for solo violin and viola, with orchestra.

- Clarinet Concerto in A Major, K. 622. Mozart's last concerto for any instrument, written for a friend of his, the clarinetist Anton Stadler.

Joseph Haydn's most celebrated concertos are the Cello Concerto in D Major, Hob. XIIb: 2 and the Trumpet Concerto in E♭, Hob. VIIe:1.

Marianne Martinez (1744–1812), who in her youth studied composition with Haydn, wrote three concertos for piano.

24

Wolfgang Amadeus Mozart
The Marriage of Figaro, Act 1, selection "Cosa sento"

Listen to This

Word-Music Relationships

Listen to the contrasting singing styles of Susanna (soprano), Basilio (tenor), and the Count (bass). The three personalities are shaped not only by the words, but by the way each character sings them.

Form

Much of the drama is in the music itself. Listen to the increasing and decreasing tension of the music over the course of this one selection. These three characters are singing to one another, not just to the audience.

Melody

Listen for the return of the opening melody at various points. In the middle of the excerpt, notice the sudden change in the Count's singing style from lyrical to declamatory.

The dramatic elements of instrumental music become even more apparent when reinforced with a dramatic text. In this trio from Mozart's comic opera *The Marriage of Figaro (Le nozze di Figaro),* words and music combine to create a moment of intense confrontation full of both suspense and humor. The text enriches the music, and the music enriches the text. The scene occurs toward the end of the opera's first act.

The three characters singing in this selection are the following:

- Count Almaviva (bass), who is married to the Countess but has his eyes on Susanna.
- Susanna, the Countess's maidservant. Susanna is engaged to be married to Figaro, the Count's manservant.
- Basilio, the music teacher at the court. He is meddlesome and loves to gossip.

There is actually a fourth character on stage as well, but Cherubino (a page boy) is silent in this scene because he is hiding. When he is discovered, about midway through the selection, he is too mortified to sing.

How did we get into this situation? Cherubino is infatuated with women in general and the Countess in particular. In the scene just prior to this one, Cherubino has been asking Susanna's help in calming the anger of the Count, who the day before has caught him making advances on Barbarina, the young daughter of the gardener. But while Cherubino and Susanna are discussing the matter, the Count arrives unexpectedly, and Cherubino must hide behind a large chair. (The audience, of course, can see everyone on the stage.) In the process of trying to seduce Susanna, the Count is in turn interrupted by the impending arrival of the music teacher, Basilio. So now the *Count* must hide, and he goes to conceal himself behind the very same chair where Cherubino is crouching. Using her quick wits, Susanna steps between the Count and the chair and directs Cherubino to slip onto the seat itself and conceal himself underneath one of the Countess's dresses that happens to be lying there. Just as the Count assumes his position behind the chair, Basilio enters the room. He is a meddlesome creature, and he teases Susanna about the Count's interest in her. He then goes on to tell her about Cherubino's interest in the Countess, which by now has become common knowledge at the court. At this moment an indignant Count bursts out from his hiding place. "I heard that!" he roars ("Cosa sento!"). And with that, our scene begins.

Mozart's *The Marriage of Figaro* is a **comic opera** or *opera buffa,* to use its Italian name. *Buffa* comes from the same root word as "buffoon." The genre uses many of the same conventions as serious opera—arias, recitatives, ensembles, choruses—but the plots do not revolve around mythical or historical figures. Instead, comic operas tend to deal with very believable characters who behave as individuals, not as symbols, and we can relate to all of them to varying degrees. Mozart's music makes them even more believable.

Word-Music Relationships: The Character of Each Voice

Even without music, this is a highly dramatic scene. The witty libretto, by the Italian poet Lorenzo da Ponte (1749–1838), is based on a stage play of the same name by the French dramatist Pierre Augustin Caron de Beaumarchais (1732–99). A great deal happens here within a short span of time. As soon as the Count emerges from his hiding place ("Cosa sento!"—"I heard that!" he exclaims), Basilio backtracks and apologizes, claiming that what he had just been saying about Cherubino and the Countess was merely a suspicion rather than a fact. But the Count is all the more determined now to banish Cherubino from his court. He tells Susanna and Basilio about his encounter with the page the day before and describes exactly how he had discovered Cherubino under the table by lifting the tablecloth. He illustrates his discovery of the previous day by lifting the dress off the chair—only to find Cherubino cringing before him, hiding yet again.

The duplicity and irony of it all is hilarious, for the Count himself had been hiding behind this very same chair only moments before. The Count had come to seduce Susanna (on the day of her wedding!) and yet when he overhears Basilio talking about Cherubino's infatuation with the Countess, he becomes outraged. And just what was the Count doing at Barbarina's house the day before, when he discovered Cherubino there? She was "more flustered than usual," the Count observes; apparently this was not the first time the Count had visited Barbarina.

This scene illustrates Mozart's uncanny ability to capture the essence of individual characters and at the same time move a plot forward through the music. What Mozart's music so beautifully portrays in this brief trio is the fluidity of each character's emotions. We witness the following changes:

1. The Count moves from outrage (on hearing of Basilio's suspicions about Cherubino and the Countess) to astonishment at discovering Cherubino in hiding once again, for the second time in two days.
2. Basilio moves from embarrassment (on realizing that the Count has overheard his gossip about the Countess) to triumph when Cherubino's presence in the Countess's chamber bears out what Basilio had at first called "mere suspicions."
3. Susanna moves through states of increasing humiliation that her reputation has been compromised by the presence of all three male visitors, none of whom should really be where they are and certainly should not be alone with her on the day of her own wedding.

These contrasting emotional states are reflected in the contrasting melodies Mozart gives to each character.

Contrasting Melodies

Mozart associates distinctly different melodies with each of the emotional states of the three characters. The Count's opening theme (Theme 1 in the listening guide, later in this chapter)—a slow, rising line—reflects his determination to banish Cherubino from the court. Basilio's whiny and slightly hesitant descending line (Theme 2) matches his embarrassment at having been overheard repeating malicious gossip about the Countess. Susanna's agitated melody (Theme 3) sounds like it is shaking: it moves up and down, back and forth with a very narrow register, reflecting her personal agitation: she alone knows that Cherubino, who is the object of all this gossip, is still hiding in the room.

Later on (at 2:12), when the Count narrates his encounter with Cherubino the day before, he suddenly shifts to a more syllabic, declamatory style of singing. This is **accompanied recitative**—recitative accompanied by the orchestra, as opposed to the more standard recitative accompaniment of basso continuo alone. This passage stands in marked contrast to the rest of the scene, for it is a narration of something that has already happened.

Dramatic Form, Musical Form

As in any opera, the form of this number is built around its text. Mozart structures the music around a recurring musical theme that reflects the scene's recurring dramatic theme: the Count's resolve to send Cherubino away from the court. We hear some variation of this theme ("1" in the listening guide) three times:

- At the very beginning, when the Count reacts to Basilio telling Susanna about Cherubino's interest in the Countess;
- After Susanna's "fainting" spell, when Basilio apologizes for what he has said about Cherubino and the Countess;
- After the Count discovers Cherubino hiding under a dress on the chair.

These moments are separated by two dramatic interruptions. Susanna pretends to faint to draw attention away from Cherubino. But she has to "revive" quickly so as not to be placed on top of him, for the two men are trying to help her sit down on the chair where he is hiding. The second interruption comes from the Count himself when he narrates the events of the day before, describing how, while visiting Barbarina (another young girl he is pursuing), he had discovered Cherubino hiding under the table. He demonstrates to Susanna and Basilio how he had lifted the tablecloth, using the dress on the chair as a prop to demonstrate his actions of the previous day—only to find Cherubino once again.

This sequence of dramatic events suggests a musical form rather like the rondo (see p. 193). In a rondo, an opening melodic idea returns repeatedly over the course of a movement, and these points of return are separated by contrasting melodic ideas. Mozart seems to have recognized a parallel in the dramatic situation with this particular scene, for he set the action to music in a manner that resembles the rondo form, with the moments of musical and dramatic return and interruption closely coordinated.

Now listen to the *Marriage of Figaro* excerpt again, following the Listening Guide.

Count Almaviva, outraged, uncovers the young page, Cherubino, hiding beneath a dress draped over a chair. Basilio (left) is delighted; Susanna (right) is horrified. The character of the young man Cherubino, who is silent throughout the trio "Cosa sento," is always performed by a woman dressed as a man.

Photo by Susan E. Picinich

Opera in the Classical Era

Opera remained the most prestigious (and lucrative) genre in the Classical Era and inspired some of its greatest music. Mozart and Christoph Willibald Gluck are generally considered the two principal composers of opera in this period. A sampling of their works:

Wolfgang Amadeus Mozart

Don Giovanni, K. 527. The story of Don Juan ("Don Giovanni" in Italian) and his many amorous conquests. The libretto is by Lorenzo da Ponte, who also wrote the text for *The Marriage of Figaro.*

Così fan tutte, K. 588. "All women act that way" is a loose translation of the title. The libretto, again by da Ponte, traces the fate of two couples and a bet by the men that their fiancées will not be unfaithful. The men lose their bets.

The Magic Flute (Die Zauberflöte), K. 620. A fairy-tale *Singspiel*—a play combining spoken text with music—about a prince and his birdlike companion and their search for knowledge (and a princess).

Christoph Willibald Gluck (1714–87)

Gluck was born in what is now Germany but spent much of his life in Italy, England, France, and Austria. He worked to bring a sense of naturalness to opera, avoiding excessive displays of virtuosity.

Orfeo ed Euridice. Another setting of the legend of Orpheus and his use of music to bring his beloved Eurydice back from Hades to the land of the living. Gluck also produced a French-language version of this same opera (*Orphée et Eurydice*).

Alceste. Based on the Greek legend of Queen Alceste, who offers to sacrifice her own life to save that of her husband, King Admetus. The music includes extensive choral numbers and accompanied recitatives as well as arias.

Wolfgang Amadeus Mozart *The Marriage of Figaro*, Act I, selection "Cosa sento"

Time	Character(s) Singing	Original Italian	English Translation	
0:00	Count	Cosa sento! Tosto andate, e scacciate il seduttor!	I heard it all! Go at once and throw the seducer out!	
0:16	Basilio	In mal punto son qui giunto; perdonate, o mio signor.	I have arrived at an unfortunate moment; forgive me, my lord.	
0:25	Susanna *(as if fainting)*	Che ruina! me meschina! Son' oppressa dal dolor!	What a catastrophe! I am ruined! I am oppressed with sadness!	
0:47	Basilio and Count *(supporting Susanna)*	Ah, già svien la poverina, Come, oh Dio, le batte il cor!	The poor child has fainted! My Lord, how her heart is beating!	
		(Basilio and the Count draw Susanna toward the chair to set her down in it—the chair on which Cherubino is hiding under a dress)		
1:05	Basilio	Pian pianin: su questo seggio.	Gently, gently, to this chair.	
1:09	Susanna *(reviving)*	Dove sono? cosa veggio? Che insolenza, andate fuor.	Where am I? What do I see? What insolence, get away.	
		(She frees herself from both of them)		
1:17	Count and Basilio	Siamo qui per aiutarti, [Count]: Non turbarti, o mio tesor. [Basilio]: È sicuro il vostro onor.	We're here to help you, [Count] Don't be alarmed, my dear. [Basilio] Your honor is safe.	
1:34	Basilio *(to the Count)*	Ah del paggio quel ch'ho detto Era solo un mio sospetto!	What I was saying about the page Was merely a suspicion I had!	
1:43	Susanna	È un'insidia, una perfidia, Non credete all'impostor.	It's a snare, a lie; Don't believe this impostor.	
1:53	Count	Parta, parta il damerino!	The young girly-boy must go!	

Form: Parallels to Rondo Form	Melody	Word-Music Relationships
A	(1) Rising contour	This theme recurs whenever the Count reacts to news about Cherubino's amorous advances.
	(2) Falling contour	This theme recurs whenever a character refers to his suspicions about Cherubino's attempted seductions.
	(3) Narrow range, static motion: the melody winds around on itself	The rapid, fluttering notes of this theme reflect Susanna's agitation.
B	(4) New melody, rising contour	This theme recurs whenever the Count and Basilio try to assist Susanna.
		"Faints" in a low register but suddenly starts singing in a high one when she realizes she is about to be put on the same seat where Cherubino is hiding.
	(4) Same as 0:47	Again, the two men assist Susanna.
	(2) Same as 0:16	Basilio apologizes for having suggested that the Countess and Cherubino have been meeting in secret.
	(3) Variant of earlier melody (at 0:24)	Susanna is agitated again; she has barely managed to conceal Cherubino's presence.
A	(1) Return to opening theme	Varied return of the opening theme emphasizes the Count's resolve to banish Cherubino from the court.

Student FAQs

Why are they singing in Italian? Wasn't German the language that was spoken in Vienna?

Yes, but Italian was the international language of opera throughout Europe at this time, even in England. Most of the leading singers of Mozart's day were Italian by birth, as was Mozart's librettist, Lorenzo da Ponte. *Don Giovanni* and *Così fan tutte*, two other librettos he wrote for Mozart, are also in Italian. And although German was the standard language in Mozart's Vienna, many audience members also spoke and understood Italian; those who did not could buy a copy of the libretto—a word whose literal meaning in Italian is "little book"—with parallel texts in Italian and German.

Why is there so much repetition of the text in the singing?

This is standard practice in operas. Music gives added emotional depth to the words, but it can also make those words more difficult to understand. Repetition helps audiences grasp the actual words being sung. This is especially important when two or more characters are singing at the same time. When the Count narrates his discovery of Cherubino from the day before, on the other hand, he does so in recitative, which allows him to present quite a large quantity of text in a short time: because recitative stands halfway between speech and song, it is easier to comprehend its words.

continued

Time	Character(s) Singing	Original Italian	English Translation
1:56	Susanna and Basilio	Poverino!	Poor boy!
2:02	Count	Poverino! Ma da me sorpreso ancor.	Poor boy! But I have found him out yet again.
2:07	Susanna	Come?	How's that?
2:08	Basilio	Che?	What?
2:12	Count	Da tua cugina L'uscio ier trovai rinchiuso, Picchio, m'apre Barbarina, Paurosa fuor dell'uso. Io dal muso insospettito, Guardo, cerco in ogni sito,	At your cousin's yesterday I found the door locked; I knocked, and Barbarina opened it, more flustered than usual. My suspicions aroused, I looked in every corner,
2:31		Ed alzando piano pianino Il tappeto al tavolino, Vedo il paggio!	And lifted, ever so quietly, The tablecloth on the table, And there I saw the page!
2:40	(He illustrates his action of the day before by raising the dress draped over the chair, only to discover Cherubino once again)		
2:47	Count	Ah, cosa veggio!	Ah! What do I see?
2:50	Susanna	Ah, crude stelle!	Ah, cruel fate!
2:52	Basilio (laughing)	Ah, meglio ancora!	Ah, it's getting even better!
2:56	Count	Onestissima signora! Or capsico come va.	O madame of highest virtue, Now I see how things are.
2:58	Susanna	Accader non può di peggio; Giusti Dei! che mai sarà?	Nothing worse could happen now; Ye gods of justice! What will happen?
3:03	Basilio	Così fan tutte le belle Non c'è alcuna novità.	All beautiful women act the same! There's nothing new about this.
3:21	Basilio (to the Count)	Ah del paggio quel ch'ho detto Era solo un mio sospetto!	What I was saying about the page Was merely a suspicion I had!
3:29	Count, Susana, Basilio	(All three repeat their texts from 2:56–3:20)	(All three repeat their texts from 2:56–3:20)

Form: Parallels to Rondo Form	Melody	Word-Music Relationships
		Susanna and Basilio sing a continuation of the Count's theme. (1). For the first time, the two agree on something.
C	(5) Declamatory	Accompanied recitative, not very melodic, as the Count narrates yesterday's events.
	(2)	The "suspicion" theme returns.
A	(1) Opening theme again	The Count reacts again to news of Cherubino.
		Susanna is mortified, the Count feels vindicated, and Basilio gloats over the misfortunes of others.
B	(2)	Basilio repeats his earlier apology, but this time it sounds triumphant: the "suspicion" has turned out to be true.
A	(1)	The Count and Basilio feel vindicated, Susanna feels humiliated. (But she will get her revenge in Act 4!)

Student FAQs

Why do characters sing different texts at the same time? They seem to cancel each other out.

In a play, when two or more characters are talking at the same time, it's almost impossible to understand either one. In opera, however, each character sings in a distinctive vocal range (soprano, tenor, and baritone in this case), which allows listeners to distinguish among the lines more easily. The repetition of texts also helps us understand what is being sung.

Cherubino is silent in this scene. What does he sound like when he's singing?

Cherubino is a young teenager whose voice has not yet broken, and the role is always sung by a woman dressed as a man. This kind of role—a woman playing the part of a young man—is known as a "trousers role."

25

Lisa Lu and the Beijing Opera Company
The Reunion

 Listen to This

Melody

How are the melodies constructed? Do you hear a difference between singing that is more like speech and singing that is more like song?

Timbre

Do certain instruments have a more penetrating sound than others? Do the sounds of the instruments have different purposes?

Texture

Listen to how instruments and voices interact. Are they working together or independently?

Rhythm

Describe how the rhythm changes. How are percussion rhythms used for musical meaning?

The term "opera" (literally "works") has been applied to many forms of sung theater throughout the world. **Jingju** is the principal form of Chinese opera today. Because it developed in China's capital city of Beijing, it came to be known as *jingju* (which means "capital theater") in China, and Peking or Beijing Opera in the West.

Jingju emerged in Beijing in the mid-nineteenth century. At that time, many genres of Chinese theater were performed in the capital city, and *jingju* developed out of these styles into a new, lavish art form. Its first patron was the Empress Dowager (1835–1908), who brought its performance into the Forbidden City (the Imperial Palace, located in the heart of Beijing) and developed a court troupe. The period of *jingju*'s development coincided with the era of European operatic composers such as Giuseppe Verdi and Richard Wagner (see chapters 38 and 39).

Jingju dominated Beijing entertainment for over 100 years, until the Cultural Revolution (1966–76) of Mao Zedong cancelled its performance and exiled its performers. The Communists considered *jingju* as a byproduct of elitist culture. After 1978, the new Chinese government advocated the renewal of old traditions such as *jingju,* and it is now studied in government-supported schools. The Liyuan Theater (Pear Garden Theater) in Beijing still stages *jingju* productions.

There are about 200 plays in the *jingju* repertoire, drawing mainly from popular legends, historical events, narratives, and novels. Characters are stock types distinguished by singing style, costume, makeup, and role. The main roles are male (*sheng*), female (*dan*), painted face (*jing*), and clown (*chou*). These roles are divided into young man (*xiaosheng*), old man (*laosheng*), male warrior (*wusheng*), mature woman (*qingyi*), young lady (*huadan*), old woman (*laodan*), and female warrior (*wudan*). Each character has a specific psychological significance. On stage, there is no scenery, and the action usually takes place in front of a curtain.

Jingju singing includes short phrases and songs that may be compared to recitatives and arias in European opera. Melody in *jingju* is a natural recitative in which the speech tones of spoken Mandarin become musical. In the Mandarin language, the meanings of some syllables change depending on whether they are pronounced in a high, low, rising, or falling tone. Recitative-like phrases and heightened speech narrate dramatic action, and arias express the lyrical sentiments of the characters. The arias are based on modal and rhythmic designs called *ban* (literally, "beat"). By setting a *ban* to a new melody, a new aria is produced. Of the two main types of *ban, erhuang* are for lyrical or tragic scenes of moderate tempo, and have varied tones based on speech. The livelier *xipi,* used to accompany action, feature melodies based on a five-note scale.

The *jingju* instrumental ensemble is divided into two groups: the *wenchang*— the civic, or melodic, group—and the *wuchang*—the military, or percussive, group. The *wenchang* civic ensemble includes strings such as the *jinghu, erhu, yue qin,* and *sanxian,* winds such as the *dizi, sheng,* and *suona,* and a gong, the *yunluo.* This instrumentation accompanies singing and it provides introductions and interludes. The *jinghu,* the lead instrument, is a two-string fiddle. *Jinghu* literally means "capital fiddle," and since it is the major supporting sound to the singing, it must have a strident timbre. The *wuchang* military percussion group provides rhythmic punctuation for singing, movements, entrances, sound effects, and moods. The *wuchang*

Female *huadan* character in a Beijing opera

Liu Ligun/ChinaStock Photo Library

repertory contains over 60 rhythmic patterns, some of which are heard in the Listening Guide later in this chapter.

In the early days of *jingju,* women were banned from the stage to protect them from moral corruption. Men therefore trained to sing women's roles using a falsetto voice. Mei Langfang (1894–1961) was a famous male singer of female roles, and he brought the first Peking Opera troupe to the United States. His granddaughter Lisa Lu (b. 1931) is the *huadan* in this Listening Guide. Here, she plays the Princess Lady Precious Stream and sings of her devotion to her gardener husband.

Painted-face *jing* character in a Beijing opera

Liu Ligun/ChinaStock Photo Library

A Mandarin Word-Melody

The melody is in two parts: the recitative-like phrases in *erhuang* and the metered aria in *xipi.* The melody of this recitative emphasizes the highly elaborate treatment of the Mandarin word-melody. When the *aria* begins at the setting of the *xipi* meter (0:54), the melody follows a **pentatonic** (five-toned) scale (see also chapters 20 and 46). At points in the aria, the singer improvises a countermelody to the *wenchang* melody. For formal contrast, the scale shifts twice to a related mode (at 1:23 and 1:55), and then back to the original mode (at 1:36 and 2:10). The *wenchang* ensemble makes this modal shift by changing one of its pitches, causing the tonal pattern for the singers to drop to a lower register. This type of modal shift has been called **metabole** because it means a change of pitch level.

Jingju and the Cultural Revolution

When Mao Zedong took over the rule of China in 1949, the government changed from a monarchy to the communist system. Under communism in Russia, traditional arts had been transformed to convey the new message of collective life and communist ideology to the common people. China would follow in these footsteps in the famous Cultural Revolution from the mid-1960s to the mid-1970s, led by Mao's wife Chiang Ching. She targeted *jingju* opera in particular for reform, eliminating the older plots and replacing them with messages more appropriate to the revolution.

The new propagandistic plots centered on workers battling the evils of capitalism or happily participating in communal farms and industries. These watered-down productions eliminated many of the favorite characters of the past, including the Monkey King, a sassy jokester who enjoyed creating trouble for trouble's sake. The result was a bland and pedantic art, rather than the rich experience of the original *jingju* productions. Eventually, all but five "model" operas were banned from performance.

Luckily, with the passing of Maoism and a new interest in ties with the West, *jingju* was eventually restored to its original form. New schools were opened, sponsored by the state, and traditional plots and characters were revived.

Timbre and Texture

Because it leads the *wenchang* ensemble, the timbre of the *jinghu* is strident. The *jinghu*'s part mirrors—but is not identical to—the singer during the recitative; this style is known as **heterophony** (two or more parts that are nearly the same sounding simultaneously; see also chapter 4). During the aria, the *jinghu* plays heterophonically with the *wenchang*, which provides a **polyphonic** accompaniment to the singer. In the *wenchang* sections, heterophony is clearly heard between the leading voice, the plucked strings, in contrast with the fiddles. The *wuchang* percussion ensemble provides a textural contrast sometimes with the *wenchang* and sometimes alone when it punctuates musical segments.

Rhythm and Punctuation

The *ban* of the aria is *xipi,* which is in four. It follows the unmetered *erhuang* recitative based on the speech tones. When the *xipi* section begins, the aria has begun. As prescribed in *xipi,* the melody enters on the third beat. In the Listening Guide, once the melody has started, the *gu* (tight drum) strikes on beats 3 and 1 to clarify the *ban*. The *gu* and other *wuchang* instruments, especially the *xiaoluo* (rising gong), punctuate musical segments to mark off sung sections rhythmically.

Now listen to this piece again, following the Listening Guide.

Lisa Lu and the Beijing Opera Company *The Reunion*

Time	Melody	Timbre and Texture	Rhythm
0:00		*Ban* (wooden clapper) punctuates the start of the recitative, followed by one strike on the *gu* (tight drum), and then two *xiaoluo* (rising gong) strikes.	Free
0:04	Recitative announced, in *erhuang*. The voice sings with the *jinghu* a short motive based on word tones of spoken Mandarin.		
0:06	The voice and *jinghu* melodically continue a phrase together based on word tones.	Heterophony	
0:14		A cymbal crash followed by an interlude of the combined *wenchang* and *wuchang* ensembles. Plucked lutes can be heard in the texture.	
0:21		Heterophony; the *wenchang* supports the voice. The *jinghu* timbre is prominent.	
0:46		The *wuchang* punctuates a melodic section. Four *xiaoluo* (rising gong) strikes.	
0:54	*Xipi*—the aria is begun by the *wenchang* on beat 1.	Throughout, the *wenchang* plays a melodic line sometimes in heterophony with the melody and sometimes counter to it. The timbres of the fiddles and plucked lutes are prominent under the voice.	*Xipi*—in four beats
0:56	The singer begins the *xipi* melody on beat 3.		Begins loosely
0:59		The *gu* strikes beat 3 of *xipi* as a time marker.	The steady rhythm of *xipi* is set.
1:00	Pentatonic. The vocal melody is partly improvised according to the rules of *xipi* against the *wenchang* counterpart. The voice sometimes also follows the *wenchang* heterophony.	The *gu* strikes beat 1 of *xipi* to mark the strong beat of the *ban*. Heterophony with polyphony during improvised voice phrases.	*Xipi* in four beats continues throughout.
1:23	Metabole—change of mode to a lower pentatonic mode	The *wenchang* changes tuning.	
1:36	Return to the original mode	The *wenchang* readjusts tuning.	
1:55	Metabole—changes again to the lower pentatonic mode	The *wenchang* changes tuning.	
2:10	Return again to the original mode with much vocal improvisation	The *wenchang* readjusts tuning.	
2:32			Slowing down
2:36		*Wuchang* signals the end of the aria.	
2:41	The aria ends.		

Student FAQs

Why does so much Chinese music sound so different to Western ears?

Chinese and other traditional musical styles often use a five-note (or pentatonic) scale. You can approximate one type of pentatonic scale by playing these notes on the piano keyboard: C-D-E-G-A-C. The gaps in the scale give it a distinctive tonality often associated with Eastern music. Western composers—particularly for films—often use a pentatonic scale when they are trying to imitate Chinese music.

Why do some characters wear masks in jingju?

Masks are often used in dramatic productions to emphasize that a certain character represents a type rather than an actual person. In *jingju,* as we have discussed, there are many character types that appear in the different operas. These characters are not meant to be real human beings but to represent a group of character traits, such as envy or greed. The stylized masks give a visual cue to the audience so that they immediately recognize the character being portrayed.

Why do the musicians sit on stage, in full view of the audience?

The musicians play a key role in *jingju* productions and are in many ways equal to the actors in setting the mood, expressing feelings, and signaling changes in the action. Again, it's important to remember that *jingju* productions are not meant to be realistic in the sense that Western theater is; the lack of sets, the use of masks, and placing the musicians on stage all remind the audience that they are watching an artistic event. The "illusion of reality" that we expect in Western theater productions is not found in many other cultures.

Traditional Chinese Music

Here are some recordings of other types of traditional Chinese music.

Li Xiangting. *Chine: L'Art du Qin,* Ocora 560001
Music played on the traditional Chinese *qin* or zither, similar in style to the Japanese koto.

Wu Man. *Chinese Music for the Pipa,* Nimbus NI-5368
Wu Man is a modern virtuoso of the Chinese *p'ip'a,* or four-string lute. She plays both traditional and modern compositions on this recording.

Zhou Yu. *The Art of the Chinese Erhu,* Arc 1555
The *erhu* is a bowed lute, something like a violin, found in traditional Chinese music. This recording again combines traditional and more modern styles.

Vocal Music of Contemporary China, Vol. 1: The Han People, Folkways Records FW04091

Vocal Music of Contemporary China, Vol. 2: The National Minorities, Folkways Records FW04092

A two-volume set of vocal music in various styles.

Music of Chinese Minorities, King World Music Library 5142
Musical styles of six minority groups from China. These represent various different traditions (Korean, Mongolian, etc.) found within China that are not part of mainstream (i.e., government-sponsored) traditional Chinese music.

PART 4 Summary

	Baroque	Classic
Texture	Polyphonic and homophonic coexist.	Both polyphonic and homophonic, but on the whole more homophonic.
Melody	Lyrical and declamatory (recitative) coexist; often virtuosic.	Growing importance of periodic phrase structure in all genres of music, not just in dance.
Rhythm	Wider range of extremes, from smooth and flowing to choppy and irregular.	More smoothly flowing melodies.
Timbre	Sharp distinction between vocal and instrumental parts.	Establishment of the modern orchestra (strings, winds, percussion).
Harmony	Harmony as an underlying basis for melody.	Harmony becomes increasingly important as a large-scale structural element (tonic/not-tonic/tonic).
Form	Greater variety of formal principles: sectional form, binary form, theme and variations, ostinato.	Theme and variations, minuet (**ABA**), rondo, sonata form, double-exposition concerto form.
Word-Music Relationships	Even greater use of word painting. Texture and musical affect strongly support text.	Word painting still present, but not as prevalent and often more subtle.

IN REVIEW: Classical Style

Periodic phrase structure. Melodies are constructed of antecedent (opening) and consequent (closing) phrases.

- Haydn, String Quartet in C Major, op. 76, no. 3, second movement (Chapter 19)
- Haydn, Symphony no. 102 in B♭ Major, third and fourth movements (Chapter 21)
- Mozart, Symphony no. 40 in G Minor, K. 550, first movement (Chapter 22)

Theme and variations. A modular form, with a theme followed by a series of discrete units, each of which presents a varied restatement of the theme.

- Haydn, String Quartet in C Major, op. 76, no. 3, second movement (Chapter 19)
- Master Musicians of the Ikuta-rya, *Cherry Blossom* (Chapter 20)

Binary form. A structure consisting of two sections, each of which is repeated in performance (**AABB**).

- Haydn, Symphony no. 102 in B♭ Major, third movement (Chapter 21)

Minuet form. A ternary form (**ABA**) with a strong sense of contrast between the **A** and **B** sections, each of which is itself a binary form.

- Haydn, Symphony no. 102 in B♭ Major, third movement (Chapter 21)

Rondo form. A structure in which the opening idea (**A**) returns repeatedly after the presentation of contrasting ideas (**B, C, D,** etc.), creating such patterns as **ABACADA**.

- Haydn, Symphony no. 102 in B♭ Major, fourth movement (Chapter 21)

Sonata form. An expanded type of binary form in which the music modulates to a secondary key area in the first section and then returns to the tonic about midway through the second section. A sonata form movement consists of an exposition, a development, and a recapitulation.

- Mozart, Symphony no. 40 in G Minor, K. 550, first movement (Chapter 22)

Double-exposition concerto form. A type of sonata form often used in concertos of the Classical Era, with two separate expositions, the first for the orchestra (which does not modulate) and the second for the soloist and orchestra together (in which the music does modulate). The development and recapitulation follow the standard pattern of sonata form.

- Mozart, Piano Concerto in A Major, K. 448, first movement (Chapter 23)

The orchestra. An ensemble of strings, winds, and percussion. The orchestra would expand in size and range later in the nineteenth and twentieth centuries, but its nucleus established itself in the second half of the eighteenth century.

- Haydn, Symphony no. 102 in B♭ Major, third and fourth movements (Chapter 23)
- Mozart, Symphony no. 40 in G Minor, K. 550, first movement (Chapter 24)
- Mozart, Piano Concerto in A Major, K. 448, first movement (Chapter 23)

Recitative and aria. Opera uses two basic forms for vocal selections: semi-spoken sections (recitative) and fully sung ones (aria).

- Mozart, *The Marriage of Figaro*, Act 1 "Cosa sento" (Chapter 25)
- Lisa Lu and the Beijing Opera Company, *the Reunion* (Chapter 25)

PART 5 The Nineteenth Century

In the nineteenth century, the rationality of the Enlightenment gave way to a new fascination with imagination, individual emotion, and longing. "Romanticism," as this movement was called, does not refer to a kind of love; it derives its name from a literary genre—the "romance," forerunner of today's novel—that was largely free of structural or narrative conventions. For the Romantic, dreams were as important as the intellect, and art—particularly music, which did not rely on words or the representation of objects—offered access to a realm of ideals beyond the limitations of human reason and the physical world. Romanticism was thus less a new style of art than a new way of thinking about art.

The music of the nineteenth century reflects this increased sense of freedom from convention. Composers felt obligated to develop their own distinctive voices. To make their music original, composers explored musical extremes of all kinds. They wrote for orchestras that were bigger and louder than ever before. They emphasized extreme contrasts of texture between the simple and the complex. They wrote music that ranged from the disarmingly simple to the fiendishly difficult, often within the course of the same work. They gave growing importance to program music, sometimes exploring the darker side of the human psyche in what many of the time considered shocking detail: the "March to the Scaffold" of Berlioz's *Symphonie fantastique* depicts an artist being led to his execution, with music so graphic that we hear the sound his head makes when it falls into the bucket at the base of the guillotine. In short, the range of each musical element available to composers—melody, rhythm, harmony, dynamics, timbre, texture, form—grew exponentially in the nineteenth century.

▲ Caspar David Friedrich's *The Wanderer* (1818) captures the Romantic fascination with dream, contemplation, and the infinite. Hamburg Kunsthalle, Hamburg, Germany. Bridgeman Art Library

"Most Romantic of All the Arts"

On hearing a performance of Beethoven's Fifth Symphony in 1810 (the premiere a year and a half before had all but flopped, with unrehearsed musicians, a cold auditorium, and an exhausting program), critic E.T.A. Hoffmann wrote the longest, most detailed review in the history of music criticism. "Beethoven's music sets in motion the machinery of awe, of fear, of terror, of pain," Hoffmann declared, "and awakens that infinite yearning which is the essence of Romanticism." For Hoffmann music was "the most Romantic of all the arts," for it "opens to mankind an unknown realm, a world that has nothing in common with the outer sensual world that surrounds him." This was particularly true of instrumental music, he felt, because it was unencumbered by words. Hoffmann's review won widespread praise because it articulated a fundamental shift from eighteenth-century thinking, which had held that the verbal arts gave form to the highest expressions of thought.

Composers, once seen as artisans providing musical goods made to order, were now perceived to have a window on the infinite and the spiritual, and their social status rose accordingly. They received invitations to gatherings at the highest levels of society and commanded enormous fees for their performances. They joined the pantheon of painters and poets who gave voice to that which could not be expressed in ordinary language. A famous

The Italian violinist and composer
Nicolò Paganini (1782–1840)

The opera composer
Giacchino Rossini (1792–1868)

The French playwright Victor Hugo
(1802–85), author of *Les Misèrables*

A portrait of the English poet
George Gordon, Lord Byron (1788–1824)

Alexandre Dumas, *père*
(1802–70), author of
*The Count of Monte
Cristo* and *The
Three Musketeers*

A bust of the composer
Ludwig van Beethoven
(1770–1827)

Franz Liszt (1811–86),
pianist and composer

The French novelist
George Sand (1804–76),
whose real name was
Amandine-Aurore-Lucile
Dudevant; she was
Chopin's lover for a time.

Marie d'Agoult (1805–76),
who wrote under the pen
name "Daniel Stern" and
bore three children by Liszt

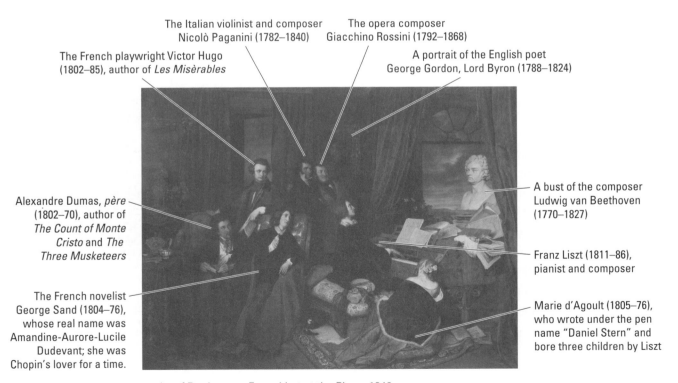

▲ Josef Danhauser, *Franz Liszt at the Piano*, 1840.
Juergen Liepe/Art Resource/Bildarchiv Preussischer Kulturbesitz

▲ An American piano factory in the late 19th century. The scale of production reduced costs and made it possible for most middle-class households to own an instrument.
Photograph courtesy of the Hagley Museum and Library, Wilmington, Delaware

portrait of the composer and pianist Franz Liszt shows him surrounded by a gathering of both writers and musicians, while he himself gazes at a bust of Beethoven, the dominant composer of the early decades of the nineteenth century.

A Piano in Every Home

Today, one is most likely to hear a song like Schubert's "Erlkönig" in the concert hall. A highly trained singer and a skilled pianist perform from the stage for a quiet audience. The song was composed, however, to meet the growing nineteenth-century demand for music that could be played at home. The Industrial Revolution, which had begun in the second half of the nineteenth century, made it possible to manufacture goods on a scale never before imagined. In Mozart's time, a piano maker built instruments one at a time, and only the wealthy could afford them. By the middle of the nineteenth century, pianos and other instruments could be produced in mass quantities in large factories. This made pianos more affordable than ever before, and by 1840, pianos were a fixture of middle-class households. Demand grew for piano compositions, songs, and chamber music.

Music as Political Force

"Leave the dreaming and hesitation behind/Without fatigue, go forward!" With these words, set to music by Clara Schumann in her song "Vorwärts!," the Dresden Choral Society exhorted listeners to work—fight, if necessary—for a united and democratic Germany. This push was

▲ Street fighting in Berlin, 1848. Barricades were constructed by ordinary citizens to block the movement of the royal armies.

Art Resource/Bildarchiv Preussischer Kulturbesitz

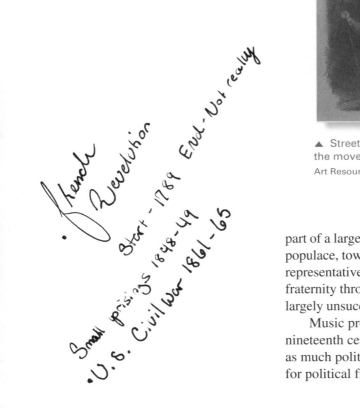

French Revolution
Start - 1789 End - Not really
Small uprisings 1848-49
• U.S. Civil War 1861-65

part of a larger impulse, distributed widely throughout discontented segments of the European populace, toward the goals set out by the French Revolution of 1789: freedom in the form of representative government, equality through the abolition of hereditary class privilege, and fraternity through rights of assembly and association. A series of uprisings in 1848–49 were largely unsuccessful at the time but helped pave the way for later political reforms.

Music proved an important vehicle for expressing political sentiment throughout the nineteenth century. The numerous choral societies that sprang up across the continent were as much political as artistic. Much of the repertory of these groups gave voice to aspirations for political freedoms.

Nationalism

Another political impulse that developed over the course of the nineteenth century was nationalism. More and more peoples began to perceive their social identities on the basis of a shared language and cultural practices in a community that extended far beyond any one locale or region. The idea of the nation as the focal point of social identity became a powerful social and political force. The U.S. Civil War (1861–65) helped change the United States from a plural noun to a singular. Government documents that had once read "The United States are determined to . . ." now read "The United States is determined to. . . ."

But not all groups united by language and culture had their own nation-states. Many ethnic Czechs and Hungarians, for example, were subjects of the Austrian Empire, whose capital (Vienna) and official language (German) were foreign to them. Poles, in turn, fell under the rule of the Prussian or Russian Empires at various times and places. Music proved a powerful outlet for the expression of nationalistic feelings. Without recourse to language, and without the incrimination specific words might bring, composers could express in sound their sense of national pride by using the characteristic melodic and rhythmic elements of their peoples. Chopin, living in Paris, felt deep sympathy for the plight of his native Poland. His Mazurka in B-flat Major, op. 7, no. 1, was one of numerous pieces he wrote using elements of Polish folk music. Chopin's Polonaises, in particular—piano works based on the proud national dance of Poland—were described by a contemporary as "cannons wrapped in flowers."

The Revolution in Transportation

In 1893, Antonín Dvořák was able to travel from New York City to the Czech-American community of Spillville, in northeastern Iowa, in less than three days, where he would compose a string quartet he called "The American." Increased mobility on both land and sea in the nineteenth century fostered commercial and cultural connections that would have been unthinkable only a few generations before. Music publishers could distribute their music on a global basis for the first time. European musicians could tour the United States with ease, and American musicians could tour Europe.

▲ *The End of Poland (Finis Poloniae)* shows a Polish officer comforting two disconsolate soldiers after the Battle of Ostrolenka (1830), in which the Russian army defeated Polish forces. Polish nationalism was a driving force behind the uprising.

Ruth Schacht/Art Resource/Bildarchiv Preussischer Kulturbesitz

▼ This hand-colored photograph shows the ceremony marking the completion of the Transcontinental Railroad in 1869, linking the eastern and western United States by rail for the first time.

The Granger Collection

Populations increased dramatically in the nineteenth century: from 1800 to 1900, the world's major powers grew 150 percent. At the same time, technological innovations including the telegraph, telephone, railroads, and steamships made the world a smaller place. The completion of the transcontinental railroad in 1869 made it possible to travel from New York to San Francisco in only a week. Before, the journey could take as much as six months. On the water, steam-powered engines replaced sails, cutting the travel time from Europe to the United States to as little as six days. Passengers were no longer at the mercy of the winds.

The Nineteenth Century: AT A GLANCE

chapter 26

1805
LUDWIG VAN BEETHOVEN
Symphony no. 5, in C Minor, op. 67
GENRE: Symphony

Chapter highlight:
Nineteenth-century Symphony
Dynamic and timbral contrasts increased. The Fifth Symphony helped redefine the symphony as a genre that carried a meaning beyond the notes themselves. Beethoven's Ninth Symphony includes voices and a text, and his Sixth Symphony ("Pastoral") is programmatic.

KEY CONCEPTS
Orchestral timbre, rhythmic-motivic development, dynamics, sonata form, alternating theme and variations, scherzo, cyclic form.

chapter 27

1815
FRANZ SCHUBERT
"Erlkönig," D. 328
GENRE: Song

Chapter highlight:
Nineteenth-century Song
We often use the German term to identify this genre for voice and piano: Lied. Other German composers include Brahms, Wolf, and Mahler. Composers such as Fauré (French), Mussorgsky (Russian), and Foster (English) contributed to this rich repertory in a variety of languages.

KEY CONCEPTS
Modified strophic form, ballad.

chapter 28

1826
FELIX MENDELSSOHN
Overture to A Midsummer Night's Dream
GENRE: Concert overture

Chapter highlight:
Concert Overture
During the 19th century, many composers wrote music for dramatic performances. The overture was designed to set the mood for the play's action, as well as to highlight its major themes. Many of these overtures became so popular that they were performed on their own, and became known as "concert overtures."

KEY CONCEPTS
Program music, relationship of drama and purely instrumental music, sonata form without exposition repeat.

chapter 29

1830
HECTOR BERLIOZ
Symphonie fantastique, fourth movement "March to the Scaffold"
GENRE: Program symphony

Chapter highlight:
Program Music
Program music became increasingly important during the 19th century as artists sought to integrate purely instrumental music with ideas. Sometimes, composers wrote prose narratives to be distributed at performances. But ambivalence remained about specific meaning in music.

KEY CONCEPTS
The modern orchestra, program music, major vs. minor mode.

---

chapter 33

1862
LOUIS MOREAU GOTTSCHALK
Union
GENRE: Solo piano

Chapter highlight:
Virtuosity
Much 19th-century music lies beyond the ability of the amateur performer. Virtuosos such as Paganini, Liszt, and Paderewski toured with their own compositions and were accorded near-divine status. Nineteenth-century composer-performers took full advantage of the concerto as a vehicle for showing off their talents in both fields at once.

KEY CONCEPTS
Virtuosity, Nationalistic melodies, homophonic vs. polyphonic texture.

chapter 34

RAVI SHANKAR
Raga Sindhi-Bhairavi
GENRE: Indian Music

Chapter highlight:
Indian Music
Perhaps the most highly developed classical music in the world, the concert music of India features a complex set of scale and rhythms. The raga is a multi-movement composition comparable to a Western concerto.

KEY CONCEPTS
Virtuosity, Sitar, tonal pattern and mood, pulse cycles, metered vs. unmetered rhythm, improvisation.

chapter 35

1853
GIUSEPPE VERDI
La Traviata, Act I, selection
GENRE: Opera

Chapter highlight:
Nineteenth-century Opera
Operas written by such composers as Rossini, Bellini, Puccini, Bizet, and von Weber form the core operatic repertory today. Dramatic realism assumed new importance, and long musical units allowed for virtuosity and the expression of strongly contrasting emotions. Wagner attempted to integrate orchestra, singers, and text to create a new kind of unified drama.

KEY CONCEPTS
Integration of recitative and aria, vocal virtuosity, word-music relationships.

chapter 30

WEB BONUS
chapter 3

chapter 31

chapter 32

1846

FANNY MENDELSSOHN HENSEL
Piano Trio, op. 11, third movement
GENRE: Piano trio

↓

Chapter highlight:
Nineteenth-century Chamber Music
Chamber music enjoyed great prestige throughout the 19th century. It also became increasingly public over time, moving into the concert hall, even as it continued to be cultivated in the home. Beethoven, Mendelssohn, and Brahms added much-loved contributions to this genre.

KEY CONCEPTS
Chamber music, a song without words, modified strophic form.

1840

ROBERT SCHUMANN
"Dedication"
GENRE: Song

↓

Chapter highlight:
Ternary Form
Compositions in three main sections, with a variation of the first section returning at the end (ABA'). The second part is often dramatically different in mood and feeling.

KEY CONCEPTS
ABA Form, modulation to a remote key, melodic contour, rhythmic contrasts.

1848

CLARA WIECK SCHUMANN
"Forward!"
GENRE: A cappella choral music

↓

Chapter highlight:
Political Music
The public uprisings that began with the French Revolution of 1789 opened up new ways of connecting music and politics. Communal singing fostered solidarity, and the idea that every nation should have its own national anthem took root. Every mass political movement since then has had its songs.

KEY CONCEPTS
Political music, word-painting, timbre of the a cappella chorus.

1830s

FRÉDÉRIC CHOPIN
Mazurka in B-Flat, op. 7, no. 1
GENRE: Piano character pieces

↓

Chapter highlight:
Nineteenth-century Piano Music
The piano became tremendously popular in the home as well as concert hall. Character pieces, sonatas, variations, and etudes by such composers as Beethoven, Schumann, Liszt, and Brahms suited the 19th century penchant for intense personal expression.

KEY CONCEPTS
Homophonic texture, drone base, scalar melodies, song-like texture, "vocal" melody.

chapter 36

chapter 37

chapter 38

1856

RICHARD WAGNER
The Valkyrie, Act III, selection ("Wotan's Farewell")
GENRE: Opera

↓

Chapter highlight:
Leitmotif
A leitmotif is a brief musical phrase or idea connected dramatically to some person, event, or idea in the drama. Wagner was a master of creating memorable themes that would help his audiences quickly identify a character or situation.

KEY CONCEPTS
Relationship of voices to orchestra, relationship of thematic ideas to the drama (the Leitmotif).

1885

JOHANNES BRAHMS
Symphony no. 4 in E Minor, op. 98, finale
GENRE: Symphony

↓

Chapter highlight:
Theme and Variations
A popular form in the Baroque Era, it is based on the simple idea of taking a short melodic theme and then subjecting it to a series of increasingly complex variations. Brahms updated and revived it by adding new timbres and harmonies available in the 19th century orchestra.

KEY CONCEPTS
Theme and variations and ABA form, orchestral timbre.

1893

ANTONIN DVOŘÁK
String Quartet in F Major, op. 96 ("American"), third movement
GENRE: String quartet

↓

Chapter highlight:
Nationalism
Music became a powerful means of expressing national identity. Composers such as Smetana, Borodin, Chopin, Gottschalk, Chabrier, and Rimsky-Korsakov wrote pieces incorporating folk elements from their own countries or from countries they admired.

KEY CONCEPTS
Call-and-response texture, pentatonic melody, folk-like rhythms, nationalism.

1804
Napoleon crowns himself Emperor of France

1815
Napoleon defeated at Waterloo; territorial boundaries of Europe redrawn

1837
Telegraph invented

1848
Marx and Engels publish *The Communist Manifesto*

1848-49
Revolutions sweep Europe

1859
Darwin publishes *On the Origin of Species*

1860
Italian unification

1861-65
American Civil War

1869
Completion of American transcontinental railroad

1871
Germany unification

1876
Telephone invented

1877
Phonograph invented

1898
Spanish-American War

Historical Events

26

Ludwig van Beethoven
Symphony no. 5 in C Minor, op. 67, first movement

 Listen to This

Rhythm

You may already know the opening motif: "short-short-short-LONG." Listen for how this basic rhythmic idea is varied not only in the first movement, but in all four movements. (NOTE: Movements 2, 3, and 4 Listening Guides are available online.)

Dynamics

Notice the repeated and sudden contrasts between loud and soft.

Timbre

Listen to the how Beethoven varies the sound of the full orchestra by using all of it at times and only a small portion of it at others (just strings, or just winds). Be ready for the addition of new instruments (especially trombones) at the beginning of the finale.

Form

Listen for the variety of forms among the four movements:

- First movement: This is in sonata form
- Second movement: This is a set of variations on two different themes, one soft and one loud.
- Third movement: Listen for the ternary form (**ABA'**), with the return of **A** varied. This movement leads without a break into the next one.
- Fourth movement: This is in sonata form. Listen for the surprise return of material from the third movement just before the beginning of the recapitulation.

The opening of Beethoven's Fifth Symphony is quite possibly both the briefest and best-known theme in all of music: it is instantly recognizable. Generations of listeners around the world have heard this theme as an aural symbol of strength and resolve precisely because it is so simple and so straightforward. Like an acorn that grows into a giant oak tree, this theme provides the basic rhythmic motif for almost every theme in the work. Even though Beethoven gave no indication in the score of an extramusical meaning of this work, critics from his time onward have interpreted it as a progression from struggle (in the first movement) to triumph (in the finale), from the darkness of C minor to the brightness of C major.

Beethoven never wrote a program for the work, but when asked the meaning of this opening idea, is said to have grumbled in response: "Thus Fate pounds at the portal." Whether the report is true or not—it was first published long after the composer's death by a notoriously unreliable witness (see "Fate?," p. 247)—it has been repeated many times over. This symphony does indeed seem to "describe" a process that moves from struggle (in the first movement) to triumph (in the finale).

Beethoven's symphonies—he wrote nine altogether—helped establish his reputation as the greatest instrumental composer of his time. Works like the Fifth Symphony helped redefine the symphony as a genre that carried a meaning that went beyond the notes themselves, without the aid of a sung text or program. Beethoven's last symphony, the Ninth, includes voices and a text in its finale, and his Sixth Symphony ("Pastoral") is programmatic. But in the Fifth Symphony, Beethoven created a work that challenged listeners to create their own sense of meaning.

Rhythm: A Germinal Cell

The Fifth Symphony opens with a distinctive but deceptively simple theme. It consists of only four notes and two different pitches. The texture is monophonic: the instruments play in unison, and we hear no harmony of any kind. The rhythm is what gives this idea its real identity: short-short-short-LONG—that is, three notes of equal length followed by one longer note. One of the things that make this symphony so remarkable is the fact that Beethoven transforms this simple musical idea in so many different ways.

In the first movement, the process of transformation begins almost instantly:

1. 0:00 Opening statement of the *s-s-s-L* figure, with last note held out long (unison texture).
2. 0:03 Restatement of the *s-s-s-L* figure, moved down a step. The texture is still unison, and the rhythm is still the same, but the notes are different.
3. 0:06 Restatement of the *s-s-s-L* figure in different voices in succession (polyphonic texture) and on different pitches. Now the texture *and* the notes are different; only the rhythm remains the same.

This transformation continues throughout all the movements that follow (see the Listening Guide for the first movement in this chapter; Listening Guides for the remaining movements are online). The pitches, harmonies, and textures are constantly shifting, but the same basic rhythmic idea—short-short-short-LONG—remains recognizable from the beginning of the symphony to the very end. Only occasionally does it leave the stage, and when it does, it always comes back.

0:00 **(1)** Opening statement of the *s-s-s-L* motif, with last note held out long (unison texture).

0:03 **(2)** Re-statement of the *s-s-s-L* motif, moved down a step (unison texture).

0:06 **(3)** Re-statement of the *s-s-s-L* motif in different voices in succession and on different pitches (polyphonic texture). Only the rhythm remains the same.

Dynamics: Loud vs. Soft

One of the more striking features of the Fifth Symphony is its treatment of dynamics. The music repeatedly moves without warning from extremely loud to extremely soft and vice versa. The very opening establishes this contrast: the loud unison is immediately followed by a soft passage. These dynamic contrasts are especially prominent at the end of the third movement, where the music remains extremely quiet for a very long time before moving without a break into the finale, which erupts in an explosion of sound. Composers had exploited dynamic contrasts long before the early nineteenth century, but the number of sudden changes, their rapidity, and, above all, the wide extremes of volume in this work were unprecedented.

Timbre: The Orchestra Grows

The contrast in dynamics between the end of the third movement and the beginning of the finale is reinforced by the addition of new instruments at that point. The piccolo and contrabassoon enrich the upper and lower ranges of the orchestra, respectively, and the trombones help create an even fuller sound in the middle ranges.

Already, in the first movement, Beethoven repeatedly contrasts wind instruments (flute, clarinet, oboe, bassoon, horns, and trumpets) against the stringed instruments (violins, violas, cellos, and double basses). The oboe has an unusual and wholly unexpected solo in the recapitulation of the first movement. The double basses have an unusually prominent and difficult passage in the middle (**B**) section of the ternary-form third movement. By using these instruments in such distinctive ways, Beethoven creates an enormous sense of breadth within a small space: the Fifth is among the shortest symphonies he wrote. Later composers of the nineteenth century would extend the range of orchestral timbre still further.

Cyclic Form

When the individual movements of a work are linked in some tangible and distinctive way (usually through the use of a common musical idea) we say that the work as a whole is **cyclic**. In his Fifth Symphony, Beethoven links all four movements through various permutations of the *short-short-short-LONG* figure and by repeating an extended passage of the third movement during the course of the fourth. These devices contribute to the sense of growth across the work as a whole. Other composers of the nineteenth century would follow Beethoven's lead.

With these points in mind, listen again to the entire work, using the Listening Guide in this chapter for the first movement and the Automated Listening Guides online for the last three movements.

CULTURAL CONTEXT

Fate?

According to one story, Beethoven claimed that the powerful opening theme of the Fifth Symphony—the short-short-short-LONG motif—represented "Fate pounding at the portal." But did he really say this?

Over the last decade of his life, Beethoven employed a personal assistant to help him with various chores. One of these assistants was Anton Schindler (1794–1864), who published a lengthy biography of the composer in 1840, 13 years after Beethoven's death. Given Schindler's close contact with Beethoven, this book was long accepted as an authoritative, eyewitness account of the composer's later years. In the last 30 years, however, scholars have discovered that Schindler fabricated evidence on many occasions, so it is not always easy to know which of his stories are true. Schindler is the source of the story about Beethoven's alleged explanation of the Fifth Symphony.

Even if Beethoven really said it, how are we to interpret it? Was he serious? Or was he just trying to get Schindler off his back? Does the statement apply only to the opening of the symphony, the first movement, or the entire work? And can a musical idea really "mean" anything at all?

Winston Churchill, prime minister of Great Britain during World War II, flashes the "V for Victory" sign to a jubilant crowd celebrating the end of the war in Europe in May 1945. The short-short-short-LONG figure that opens the Fifth Symphony happens to correspond to the letter "V" in Morse code (dot-dot-dot-DASH). For the Allies in World War II, "V" was shorthand for "Victory." The opening motif of Beethoven's Fifth soon became an audible icon for the resolve of the allies to achieve victory in Europe: the British Broadcasting Corporation opened its European broadcasts each night with this stirring theme.

Topham/The Image Works

Ludwig van Beethoven Symphony no. 5 in C Minor, op. 67, first movement

First Movement
Tempo: Allegro con brio [Fast, with energy]
Form: Sonata form

Time	Form: Sonata - form section and key area	Melody	Rhythm The short-short-short-LONG motif
0:00 (1:27)	**Exposition** Tonic (C minor)	1: *s-s-s-L* motif in its original form	First in a powerful unison, then in polyphony
0:27 (1:55)	Transition	2: constant motion	In the bass
0:44 (2:11)	Secondary key area (E♭ major)	3: more lyrical	In the beginning by the horn, then in the bass
1:17 (2:44)		4: triumphant	Same as 1, but in a different key and in the major mode)
2:54	**Development** (harmonically unstable)	1	In unison horns, then in many different voices (polyphony)
3:30		3	In unison strings, then polyphonic. The music seems to lose its drive momentarily.
4:17	**Recapitulation** Tonic (C minor)	1	In the theme
4:37		Oboe "cadenza": mournful, slow, rhythmically free	Motif disappears momentarily
4:56		2	In many voices
5:12		3	First unison, then polyphonic
5:51		4	In many voices
5:58	**Coda** Tonic	1	In many voices
6:14		3	In many voices
6:30		New theme	*s-s-s-L* motif absent here
7:00		1	Returns in strings, then full orchestra (unison, 7:05), then polyphonic (7:15) before final cadence

Second time = exposition repeat

Timbre

Strings alone at first, alternating with full orchestra

Full orchestra

Starts with horns; strings and other winds enter gradually; a sense of relative rest after the turmoil of the opening

Full orchestra; a sense of triumph

Full orchestra; a sense of quiet desperation returns

Strings alternate against winds.

Full orchestra in unison; even louder and more powerful than the opening

Solo oboe, a complete surprise

Full orchestra

Starts with bassoons, then full orchestra

Full orchestra

Full orchestra

Student FAQs

Why isn't the short-short-short-LONG motif present in every theme?

It's rarely absent for very long, but Beethoven no doubt wanted to avoid having the theme overstay its welcome. He created sufficient variety by transforming the motif both within and across movements, and also by providing some contrast in the form of themes that don't use the motif at all.

What do the extra musicians who come in at the beginning of the finale do during the first three movements?

Nothing. They must sit quietly and wait their turn. They are nevertheless paid at the same rate as the musicians who have been playing throughout.

Ludwig van Beethoven (1770–1827)

COMPOSING THROUGH DEAFNESS

Deafness was only one of many obstacles Beethoven faced as a composer. He was exploited as a child by his father, a court musician in Bonn (in present-day northern Germany), who lied about his son's age to make the boy's talents as a pianist seem even more remarkable. More seriously, his father's alcoholism forced the young Beethoven to become the principal breadwinner for his family even while still in his mid-teens. But a grant from the Elector of Bonn allowed him to travel to Vienna to study composition with Joseph Haydn (among others), and Beethoven quickly established a reputation both as a piano virtuoso and as a composer. He would spend the rest of his life in Vienna.

When Beethoven began to go deaf in his late 20s, he became increasingly withdrawn from society. It is unclear exactly what caused this deafness, but we know from his letters that it caused him great psychological pain. He eventually had to stop performing in public altogether, and his despair at one point drove him to contemplate suicide. "It was only *my art* that held me back," he confessed in 1802. "Ah, it seemed to me impossible to leave the world until I had brought forth all that I felt was within me."

Beethoven's contemporaries found his music demanding, but he was widely recognized at the time as the greatest living composer of instrumental music, and he enjoyed the financial support of an important group of aristocratic patrons in Vienna. The last 15 years of his life were nevertheless filled with difficulties. He suffered from chronic poor health, his deafness grew even worse, and he became embroiled in a bitter custody battle with his sister-in-law over her son Karl. Beethoven held his sister-in-law in low regard—as did the courts, who awarded him custody of the boy in 1816. But Beethoven was not well prepared to become the single parent of a teenager, and constant struggles over the next decade, both in and out of court, took their toll both emotionally and financially.

When he died in 1827, Beethoven was hailed as a national hero. His funeral was attended by throngs of spectators who wanted to catch a last glimpse of the great composer who called himself a "tone poet," a poet who created with musical sounds rather than words.

Beethoven, ca. 1804–5, as depicted by his friend, the painter J.W. Mähler. Beethoven's pose is similar to that of the Greek character Orpheus (see chapter 9): he holds a lyre in his hand and beckons from the darkness and turmoil behind him to the light and order ahead of him.

Historisches Museum der Stadt Wien/The Bridgeman Art Library

PLAYLIST: BEETHOVEN

Piano Sonata in C♯ Minor, op. 27, no. 2 ("Moonlight")

Piano Sonata in D Minor, op. 31, no. 2 ("Tempest")

Piano Sonata in F Minor, op. 57 ("Appassionata")

Violin Sonata in A Major, op. 47 ("Kreutzer")

String Quartet in F Major, op. 59, no. 1 ("Razumofsky")

Piano Trio in B-flat Major, op. 97 ("Archduke")

Violin Concerto in D Major, op. 61

Piano Concert in E-flat Major, op. 73 ("Emperor")

Beethoven's Other Symphonies

Symphony no. 1 in C Major, op. 21

Symphony no. 2 in D Major, op. 36

Beethoven's first two symphonies are similar in format and scope to Haydn's late symphonies.

Symphony no. 3 in E-flat Major, op. 55

Called the "Eroica" ("Heroic") Symphony by Beethoven himself, this is widely viewed as Beethoven's breakthrough symphony, a work almost twice as long as any previous symphony by any other composer. Beethoven originally intended to dedicate the work to Napoleon but became disillusioned when Napoleon crowned himself Emperor of France. He finally issued it instead "In memory of a great man."

Symphony no. 4 in B-flat Major, op. 60

An energetic work in four movements.

Symphony no. 6 in F Major, op. 68

Called the "Pastoral" by Beethoven, this is the most programmatic of his symphonies.

Symphony no. 7 in A Major, op. 92

A large work in four movements, one of the most popular of all the symphonies. Sarah Brightman's 2000 hit "Figlio Perduto" ("Lost Son") is based on the music of this symphony's second movement.

Symphony no. 8 in F Major, op. 93

A relatively small-scale work and more playful than Beethoven's other symphonies.

Symphony no. 9 in D Minor, op. 125

The finale incorporates vocal soloists and a chorus singing Schiller's "Ode to Joy." This is the symphony that was performed when the Berlin Wall came down in 1989.

27

Franz Schubert
"Erlkönig", D. 328

Form

Listen for the way in which the same basic musical idea is presented in each strophe of the text, but in a new guise each time.

Word-Music Relationships

The song is about a father riding on horseback through the night, holding his ill child. Listen to how the song captures the rhythms of the horse's hooves beating along the road. Notice the way in which the four characters—the narrator, the father, the child, and the Erlkönig, all sung by a single voice—differ from one another in register (high vs. low) and dynamics (loud vs. soft).

Schubert's song "Erlkönig" presents a drama in miniature, using only one singer and a pianist to portray a narrator, three different characters, and one highly emotional series of events. The work opens with a loud, fast, repetitive figure that evokes the sound of a galloping horse. The narrator tells us that a father is carrying his ill child on horseback through the night. We hear a dialogue between father and son: the feverish boy imagines that he hears and sees the malicious Erlkönig, who has come to take him away from the land of the living to the land of spirits; the father tries to comfort the child, telling him that his visions come from the wind and from wisps of cloud. And then we hear the voice of the Erlkönig himself, who at first tries to attract the child with promises of a wonderful realm of games, dance, and beautiful clothing, but who eventually tires of this and resorts to force to carry the child away. At the end, the narrator returns to tell us the aftermath.

The text of Schubert's "Erlkönig" is a poem written in the 1780s by the celebrated German poet Johann Wolfgang Goethe (1749–1832). Goethe's "Erlkönig" is a **ballad**, a poem that tells a story, and Schubert's setting of it is, in effect, his interpretation of the poem. Just as a speaker giving a dramatic reading can shape a poem's sound and meaning by emphasizing certain words, varying the speed of delivery, or altering the register and volume of the voice, so can a composer shape the sound and meaning of the text by manipulating these same elements—rhythm, tempo, register, dynamics—and by incorporating elements unique to music, such as melody and harmony. Schubert's setting is longer and more musically varied than any of the many earlier settings of the poem: the piano part is more important and technically demanding, and the voice part covers a wider range than ever before.

Songs for voice and piano were so widespread and popular in Germany from the late eighteenth century onward that we often use the German term today to identify this genre: *Lied* (pronounced "leet") is the German word for "song" (the plural, **Lieder**, is pronounced like "leader"). Schubert wrote hundreds of *Lieder* for voice and piano during his short life. "Erlkönig" is one of his earliest: he wrote it when he was only eighteen.

Moritz von Schwind, *A Schubert Evening with Joseph von Spaun.* In this scene from a Viennese salon, Schubert plays the piano while the singer sits beside him. The salon was a gathering in a home, where guests conversed, ate, drank, and entertained one another with song, poetry readings, or reenactments of scenes from dramas. During Schubert's lifetime, the *Lied* was a distinctly domestic genre. Only later did it move into the concert hall.

Dagli Orti (A)/Picture Desk, Inc./Kobal Collection.

Modified Strophic Form

Almost every composer who writes a song begins with the text. In this case, Schubert began with Goethe's poem of eight strophes (also known as stanzas). He could have set each strophe to the same music, creating a song in simple strophic form. Or he could have written entirely new music for each strophe. In the end, he chose a middle path: he set each strophe to the same basic melody and rhythms presented in the first strophe, but he varied the music with every subsequent strophe. If there were no words to this song, we would hear, in effect, a set of variations (strophes 2–8) on a theme (strophe 1). But because there are words, we call the form of this song **modified strophic form**. Each strophe, as we shall see, is varied (modified) to fit the text in a particular way.

Word-Music Relationships: Creating Characters

Goethe's poem tells the story of a father riding through the night on horseback, holding his son in his arms. The child is ill, and as he slips ever closer to death, he hears the voice of the Erlkönig, a shadowy figure from the realm of the beyond who, according to legend, is visible only to those who are about to die. (In German, "König" means "king" and "Erl" means "alder," a type of birch tree. But the legend of the Erlkönig originated in Denmark as *ellerkonge,* which means "elf king," and this term was incorrectly translated into German in the eighteenth century as "Erlkönig.") Like any good song composer, Schubert studied the content, meter, and rhyme scheme of the poem very carefully before deciding on an appropriate musical setting, and he used these musical elements to connect the music with the words:

- **Rhythm:** Schubert uses a repetitive rhythmic figure at the very beginning of his setting to capture the constant forward movement of the pair on horseback and the thundering of the horse's hooves.

- **Register:** There are three characters and a narrator in this dramatic poem, all of them sung by a single voice. Schubert differentiates among them by placing each in a particular range or register of the voice. The narrator occupies a neutral space in the middle; the father's words are always sung in the lowest register; and the words of the child and the Erlkönig both sound in the highest range.

- **Dynamics:** Schubert indicates gradations of volume with great care in this song. The father is unchanging: he always sings forte (loud). The child starts softly but grows louder and louder. The Erlkönig starts softly and grows even softer before erupting at the end, when he loses patience and finally seizes the child.

- **Harmony:** Schubert begins and ends in the key of G minor but moves through several different keys in between to provide harmonic variety. He even shifts to the major mode when the voice of the Erlkönig enters.

Now listen to the piece again, using the Listening Guide.

Franz Schubert (1797–1828)

TURNING POETRY INTO MUSIC

Franz Schubert was an astonishingly prolific composer of songs for voice and piano. The most recent recording of all his songs fills no fewer than 37 compact discs—quite an accomplishment for a composer who died so young. In the year 1815 alone, when he was 18, he composed 144 songs, including "Erlkönig." Even more remarkably, each song is distinct.

Schubert was constantly looking for poetry to set to music. Some of his *Lieder* are settings of verse by the greatest writers of the day, like Goethe (for "Erlkönig"); others draw on works by poets who are largely forgotten today. He approached each new text on its own terms, however, trying to interpret, through music, the words he had chosen to set. As if his song output alone were not impressive enough, Schubert composed many other works: nine symphonies, dozens of piano sonatas, and dozens of works for various chamber ensembles. Yet he never achieved widespread fame during his life. He enjoyed a devoted following in Vienna and probably would have attracted a wider audience had he not died at the age of 31 (five years younger than Mozart at the time of his death).

Franz Schubert, ca. 1825, by W. A. Rieder. As in many portraits of composers from this time, he sits near a piano, quill pen in hand.
Lebrecht Music & Arts Photo Library

PLAYLIST: SCHUBERT

"Gretchen at the Spinning Wheel" ("Gretchen am Spinnrade"), a song

"The Trout" ("Die Forelle"), a song

"Death and the Maiden" ("Der Tod und das Mädchen"), a song

The Trout ("Piano Quintet in A Major")

Death and the Maiden ("String Quartet in D Minor")

Piano Sonata in B-flat Major, D. 960

Symphony no. 8 in B Minor ("Unfinished")

Symphony no. 9 in C Major

The first edition of Schubert's *"Erlkönig,"* billed as a "Ballad by Goethe, set to music for a solo voice with piano accompaniment . . . by Franz Schubert." The name of the dedicatee, Count Moriz von Dietrichstein, is considerably larger than the composer's name. The vignette illustration shows the Erlkönig hovering over the father and the son on horseback.

Lebrecht Music & Arts Photo Library

 EXPAND YOUR PLAYLIST

Schubert's Songs

"Erlkönig" is only one of many hundreds of songs written by Schubert. Some others worth exploring include the following:

"Gretchen am Spinnrade" ("Gretchen at the Spinning Wheel"). The song is taken from Goethe's drama *Faust*. Gretchen muses over her agitated state (she is in love), and the music of the piano imitates the motion of her spinning wheel.

"Die Forelle" ("The Trout"). The music of this song imitates the swimming motions of a fish. Schubert used the melody as the theme of a set of variations in his Piano Quintet nicknamed "The Trout" (see Schubert Playlist, on page 254).

"Der Tod und das Mädchen" ("Death and the Maiden"). A dialogue between Death and a young woman. Once again, Schubert used the melody of one of his songs for a set of a variations, this time a string quartet (known as "Death and the Maiden").

"Prometheus." A stirring song set to another text by Goethe, narrated by Prometheus, the god who gave fire to mortals and was punished for his deed.

"Ständchen" ("Serenade"). One of Schubert's best-known melodies, a song from a lover to his beloved.

Franz Schubert "Erlkönig," D. 328

Time	Strophe	Character	Melody: Register	German Original	English Translation
0:00	1	Narrator	Middle	Wer reitet so spät durch Nacht und Wind? Es ist der Vater mit seinem Kind; er hat den Knaben wohl in dem Arm, er fasst ihn sicher, er hält ihn warm.	Who rides so late through night and wind? It is the father with his child; He holds the boy fast in his arms He holds him tightly, he keeps him warm.
0:50	2	Father	Low	Mein Sohn, was birgst du so bang dein Gesicht?	My son, why do you hide your face so anxiously?
1:03		Son	High	Siehst, Vater, du den Erlkönig nicht? den Erlkönig mit Kron und Schweif?	Do you not see, father, the Erlkönig? The Erlkönig with crown and train?
1:20		Father	Low	Mein Sohn, es ist ein Nebelstreif.	My son, it is a streak of clouds.
1:29	3	The Erlkönig	High	"Du liebes Kind, komm, geh mit mir! gar schöne Spiele spiel' ich mit dir; manch bunte Blumen sind an dem Strand, meine Mutter hat manch gülden Gewand."	"You dear child, come with me! Such wonderful games I will play with you; So many beautiful flowers are on the shore, My mother has many a golden robe."
1:50	4	Son	High	Mein Vater, mein Vater, und hörest du nicht, was Erlenkönig mir leise verspricht?	My father, my father, do you not yet hear, What the Erlkönig softly promises me?
2:04		Father	Low	Sei ruhig, bleibe ruhig, mein Kind: in dürren Blättern säuselt der Wind.	Be calm, stay calm, my child: Through the dry leaves rustles the wind.
2:13	5	The Erlkönig	High	"Willst, feiner Knabe, du mit mir gehen? meine Töchter sollen dich warten schön; meine Töchter führen den nächtlichen Reihn und wiegen und tanzen und singen dich ein."	"Will you, dear child, come with me? My daughters shall wait on you well; my daughters dance at night and will cradle and dance and sing to you."

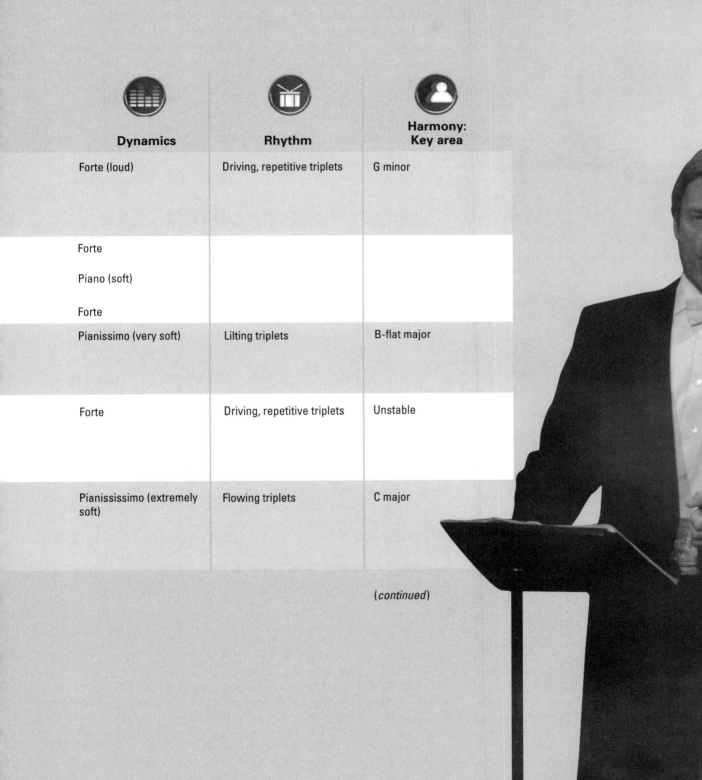

Dynamics	Rhythm	Harmony: Key area
Forte (loud)	Driving, repetitive triplets	G minor
Forte		
Piano (soft)		
Forte		
Pianissimo (very soft)	Lilting triplets	B-flat major
Forte	Driving, repetitive triplets	Unstable
Pianississimo (extremely soft)	Flowing triplets	C major

(*continued*)

Time	Strophe	Character	Melody: Register	German Original	English Translation
2:30	6	Son	High	Mein Vater, mein Vater, und siehst du nicht dort Erlkönigs Töchter am düstren Ort?	My father, my father, do you not see there Erlkönig's daughters in the desolate place?
2:44		Father	Low	Mein Sohn, mein Sohn, ich seh es genau, es scheinen die alten Weiden so grau.	My son, my son, I see it clearly, The old fields appear so gray.
2:55	7	The Erlkönig	High	"Ich liebe dich, mir reizt deine schöne Gestalt, und bist du nicht willig, so brauch ich Gewalt."	"I love you, your lovely form charms me, and if you're unwilling, then I'll use force."
3:11		Son	High	"Mein Vater, mein Vater, jetzt fasst er mich an! Erlkönig hat mir ein Leids getan!"	"My father, my father, now he seizes me! Erlkönig has done me harm!"
3:25	8	Narrator	Middle	Dem Vater grauset's, er reitet geschwind, er hält in Armen das ächzende Kind, erreicht den Hof mit Müh und Not; in seinen Armen das Kind war tot.	The father, filled with horror, rides fast, He holds in his arms the groaning child, Reaches the courtyard with toil and trouble, In his arms the child was dead.

	Dynamics	Rhythm	Harmony: Key area
	Forte	Driving, repetitive triplets	Unstable
	Pianissimo Fortississimo (extremely loud)		D minor
	Forte		G minor

28

Felix Mendelssohn
Overture to A Midsummer Night's Dream

Word-Music Relationships

Mendelssohn's music is an overture to Shakespeare's play *A Midsummer Night's Dream,* and it reflects in music many of the leading characters in that comedy. As you listen for the first time, try to identify which passages might be associated with fairies, kings and queens, lovers, and a donkey. (The last one is particularly obvious!)

Form

This one-movement work is in sonata form, but without a repeat of the exposition. Listen for those elements of the form that you have learned to expect: a modulation to a new key early on, a development section, and a return to the opening idea and key in the recapitulation, about two-thirds of the way through.

M endelssohn's overture to Shakespeare's *A Midsummer Night's Dream,* written when he was just 17, captures the chaotic, magical spirit of an enchanted forest. Shakespeare's play is about the collision between the world of fantasy and the world of reality, and Mendelssohn translates these two worlds into music by using melodies that can be readily associated with the play's principal characters, which range from the real (two pairs of human lovers) to the unreal (fairies) to the real transformed into the unreal (a workman whose head is changed into that of a donkey). The title alone supplies the verbal cue to these links, for in this composition, Mendelssohn creates a purely instrumental work that embodies the spirit of the play, its main characters, and its overall dramatic shape.

This kind of music—a purely instrumental work openly linked in some way to an object, story, or idea outside of the music—is a good example of **program music**. Program music was not new in the nineteenth century (see chapter 14), but it became increasingly important during this time as artists sought to integrate purely instrumental music with ideas.

Mendelssohn originally wrote this overture as a stand-alone work to be performed in the concert hall; but 16 years later, he set to music all the songs in Shakespeare's play (Shakespeare had provided only the poetry, not the music), along with other incidental music—marches, dances, intermezzos, and the like—including the celebrated "Wedding March."

Word-Music Relationships: Creating Characters Through Sound

All the principal thematic ideas in this piece can be linked to characters in Shakespeare's play. The number identifying each theme below is the same as that used in the Listening Guide.

1. The opening five measures, given entirely to the winds, draw us into the enchanted forest that is the setting for much of the play.

2. The scurrying, high-pitched figure in the strings that begins at 0:22 conjures up the kingdom of the fairies, led by Oberon and Titania.

3. This loud, pompous theme (beginning at 1:07) reflects the heavier world of the humans and its ruler, Theseus.

4. The first theme in the secondary key area (beginning at 2:02) corresponds to the two pairs of human lovers who over the course of the play, through magic, fall in and out of love with one another and in various combinations.

Crescendo
(gradually louder)

Decrescendo
(gradually softer)

5. The loud, braying theme at 2:56 is clearly associated with Bottom, the weaver, who figures prominently in Shakespeare's play-within-the-play, when he appears on stage with the head of a donkey.

Accent marks

Hee-haw   Hee-haw

The Drama of Sonata Form

This one-movement work follows the basic conventions of sonata form. Mendelssohn introduces all the principal characters to us in the exposition. In the development section (beginning at 3:44; the exposition does not repeat), the scurrying theme associated with fairies predominates. Mendelssohn captures the sometimes chaotic magical spirit of the midsummer night's forest by having different sections of the orchestra play in simultaneously contrasting dynamics. At 4:19, for example, he brings in the horns fortissimo, "with all force"—even as the strings and high winds maintain their elfin pianissimo—extremely quiet—figure. The recapitulation brings all the main themes back in the tonic, and the coda ends the work as it began, with the sound of long-held notes high in the winds.

Felix Mendelssohn (1809–47)

THE COSMOPOLITAN COMPOSER

Perhaps the most cosmopolitan composer who ever lived, Mendelssohn spoke fluent English, French, and Italian, in addition to his native German, and he could read ancient Greek and Latin with ease. He was as much at home in England as he was in Germany. He even excelled at painting and created a number of watercolors of very high quality.

Mendelssohn was born into a prominent family whose fame was based not on music, but on philosophy and finance. His grandfather, Moses Mendelssohn, was one of the leading philosophers of his day, and his father, Abraham Mendelssohn, was one of Berlin's most successful bankers.

Felix was the greatest child prodigy of his age, both as a composer and as a pianist. As a young child, he traveled across Europe in much the same manner Mozart had half a century before. By the time he was 17, he had already written the Octet for Strings, op. 20, and the *Overture to a* Midsummer Night's Dream, op. 21. He also excelled as a conductor. In 1828, on the hundredth anniversary of its premiere, he led a hugely successful performance of J.S. Bach's *Saint Matthew Passion*, a then-forgotten work he had helped rediscover.

Mendelssohn on one of his many trips to England, painted by James Warren Childe. Mendelssohn was a particular favorite of Queen Victoria.
Ruth Schacht/Art Resource/Bildarchiv Preussischer Kulturbesitz

PLAYLIST: MENDELSSOHN

Complete Incidental Music to *A Midsummer Night's Dream*

Symphony no. 3 ("Scottish")

Symphony no. 4 ("Italian")

Violin Concerto in E Minor

Elijah (oratorio)

A nineteenth century depiction of Felix Mendelssohn's workroom in Leipzig. In the foreground, a square piano is covered with a cloth; by the window, a writing desk is visible where the composer could work on scores.
Lebrecht Music & Arts Photo Library

Felix Mendelssohn *Overture to* A Midsummer Night's Dream

Time	Form: Sonata form section	Melody	Word-Music Relationships Character or Setting
0:00	**Exposition** (tonic)	Theme 1 (long-held notes in winds only)	World of fantasy
0:22		Theme 2 (scurrying figure in strings)	Fairies
1:07	Tonic, with modulation beginning around 1:33	Theme 3 (full orchestra, loud)	Theseus, the ruler of the humans: a loud, pompous theme
2:02	Secondary key area	Theme 4 (lyrical, first in clarinet, then in strings)	The two pairs of human lovers
2:56		Theme 5 (loud, braying sound: full orchestra)	Bottom, the weaver dressed as a donkey
3:27		Theme 3 again, but now in new key area (full orchestra)	Theseus's theme, varied
3:44	**Development** (unstable harmony)	2 (scurrying figure)	Confusion in the dark woods
5:26		4 (lyrical)	Lovers' theme, now in minor; the pairs of lovers become separated.
5:54	**Recapitulation** (tonic)	1 (long-held notes in winds)	Return of the opening theme and key
6:19		2 (scurrying theme)	Fairies again, but now with added winds and timpani
6:55		4 (lyrical)	Lovers' theme, now in the tonic
7:48		5 (braying)	Bottom's theme (the donkey)
8:49		3 (pompous)	Theseus's theme
9:18	**Coda** (tonic)	2 (scurrying)	Fairies
10:07		4 (lyrical)	Lovers' theme, now in major mode and much slower
11:01		1 (long-held notes)	Opening phrase closes the work

Student FAQs

I don't know Shakespeare's play. Can the music still make sense?

Yes. Composers can never really be certain that their listeners will have a program in hand, or in their heads, and so they generally try to write music that can function on its own, in purely musical terms. Mendelssohn's overture is no exception to this pattern. While our understanding of it can be enriched through knowledge of Shakespeare's play, we can enjoy the work even without being aware of its connections to the drama.

Why is there no repeat of the exposition?

By the end of the eighteenth century, it had become common to omit the exposition repetition in opera overtures, and Mendelssohn continues that tradition withthis overture to a spoken play.

THE COMPOSER SPEAKS

Mendelssohn Reflects on his *Overture to A Midsummer Night's Dream*

Mendelssohn never issued a program to accompany this work, but in a letter to his publisher, he explained the relationship between the musical elements of the overture and the drama on the stage. He

In the film version of *A Midsummer Night's Dream* directed by Michael Hoffman, Kevin Kline (Nick Bottom) and Michelle Pfeiffer (Titania) spin out love's sweet dream. The soundtrack uses Mendelssohn's overture and some of the additional incidental music he wrote for the play much later, in 1842. The music Mendelssohn added later includes the celebrated "Wedding March."

© Corbis Sygma

acknowledged broad parallels between his overture and Shakespeare's play, but he stopped short of drawing direct equivalencies between the two. This reflects the feelings of many composers about attaching specific meanings to their music. Clearly, Mendelssohn wanted his listeners to associate his overture with Shakespeare's play—otherwise, he would not have given it the title that he did—but he also wanted listeners to accept the work on its own terms, as music.

The piece is . . . closely associated with the play, and thus it might perhaps be quite appropriate to indicate to the public the main events of the drama. . . . I believe it would suffice to recall how the elf-royalty, Oberon and Titania, appear with all their train throughout the play, at one moment here, at another there; then comes Duke Theseus of Athens, who goes hunting in the forest with his bride-to-be; then the two pairs of tender lovers, who lose and find one another; and finally the troop of clumsy, coarse tradesmen, who pursue their heavy-handed amusements; then the elves once again, who tease all of them—it is precisely out of

all this that the work is constructed. When at the end everything is resolved and the main characters depart fortunate and happy, the elves follow them, bless the house, and disappear as the morning dawns. So ends the play, and my overture too. I would prefer it if on the printed program you . . . nothing further about my music, so that it can simply speak for itself, if it is good; and if it is not good, then no explanation will help at all.

Mendelssohn, *Briefe an deutsche Verleger* (Berlin: de Gruyter, 1968), pp. 25–26.

EXPAND YOUR PLAYLIST

Shakespeare in Music

Many of Shakespeare's plays call for moments of instrumental music, song, or both. A good anthology of settings by Shakespeare's contemporaries is available in *Shakespeare's Songbook*, vols. 1 & 2, ed. Ross Duffin (New York: Norton, 2004).

Hector Berlioz, *Roméo et Juliette.* A symphony consisting of both instrumental and vocal movements for soloists, chorus, and orchestra.

Franz Liszt, *Hamlet.* An orchestral work loosely based on Shakespeare's play.

Giuseppe Verdi, *Macbeth* (1847), *Otello* (1887), and *Falstaff* (1893).

All three are operas. The last of these draws on *The Merry Wives of Windsor* and the *Henry IV* plays for its libretto.

Pyotr Ilich Tchaikovsky, *Romeo and Juliet, Fantasy-Overture.* A work for orchestra.

Sergei Prokofiev, *Romeo and Juliet.* A ballet.

Cole Porter, *Kiss Me, Kate.* A Broadway adaptation of *The Taming of the Shrew.*

Leonard Bernstein, *West Side Story.* A Broadway adaptation of *Romeo and Juliet* (see chapter 52).

29

Hector Berlioz
Symphonie fantastique, fourth movement ("March to the Scaffold")

Listen to This

Timbre

Listen for the massive sound of the orchestra, especially in the brass (trumpets, horns, trombones, and tubas) and percussion (timpani, snare drum, cymbals, and bass drum).

Word-Music Relationships

Berlioz's *Symphonie fantastique* is a work of program music. But listen to this movement at least once before reading the program (caution: plot spoilers below). Can you guess what kind of event this movement might represent?

Form

Listen for the alternation between large sections of music in the minor mode and large sections in major mode. What happens at the very end of the movement?

This "Fantasy-Symphony" re-creates, in music, the thoughts, dreams, and nightmares of an artist. Originally entitled *Episode in the Life of the Artist: Symphonie fantastique,* this work is one of the most celebrated instances of program music in the entire concert repertory. Berlioz himself wrote a detailed prose narrative to be distributed at performances. It is the story of a dream (the "fantasy" in the title) that moves from blissful reverie (in the opening movement) to nightmare (in the fourth and fifth movements). The artist dreams about his beloved and her eventual rejection of him. In the fourth movement, the "March to the Scaffold," presented here, the artist dreams that, having killed his beloved, he is being led up to a large platform (the scaffold), where he is executed by a guillotine. The music is so detailed that we even hear his head plop into the basket beneath the blade.

The *Symphonie fantastique* captures Romanticism's fascination with the world of the gothic and the grotesque. The artist who "dreams" this symphony dreams not of glory, but of his own downfall and death. In this work, Berlioz paints a musical picture of darkness and despair, and he uses the full resources of the orchestra to portray this nightmare in sound.

Timbre: The Modern Orchestra

Berlioz is widely acknowledged as the first great master of **orchestration**, the art of arranging music for the instruments of the orchestra. He came of age at a time when concert halls—and thus orchestras—were becoming larger and larger, and he incorporated a wider variety of instruments into his compositions than anyone before. He achieved novel and spectacular orchestral effects, and even his detractors praised his ability to draw new sounds out of the orchestra by combining the timbres of individual instruments or groups of instruments to create timbres that had never been heard before. The brass section in this particular movement is unusually prominent, and the percussion section (timpani, bass drum, and snare drum) comes to the fore in ways that no one had ever imagined. Berlioz would go on to write an important treatise on orchestration. Then, as now, any composer who wanted to write a work of music for orchestra must know the particular characteristics of every instrument, starting with its range (what notes are within its reach) and extending to what kinds of melodies or figures work best for it.

Word-Music Relationships: The Program

Berlioz wrote a detailed program for his *Symphonie fantastique* and gave each of its five movements a distinctive title. "A young musician of morbidly sensitive temperament and fiery imagination poisons himself with opium in a fit of lovesick despair," he explains in the introduction to his program. "The dose of the narcotic, too weak to kill him, plunges him into a deep slumber accompanied by the strangest visions, during which his sensations, his emotions, his memories are transformed in his sick mind into musical thoughts and images. The loved one herself has become a melody to him, an *idée fixe* as it were, that he encounters and hears everywhere."

This *idée fixe* is a melody whose form changes from movement to movement but which appears at some point in all five, transformed to fit the emotion of the moment. In the fourth movement, presented here, the *idée fixe* is heard only once, just before the end (at 4:14). Its appearance marks the last thought of the artist, a split second before the blade of the guillotine chops off his head.

Here are the titles of all five movements and a summary of the program of each:

1. "Dreams—Passions." The artist fixates on his beloved and imagines her in the form of a melody, the *idée fixe* or "obsessive idea" heard in every movement in one guise or another.

2. "A Ball." The artist imagines he sees his beloved at a ball, during a waltz.

3. "Scene in the Countryside." A slow movement in which the artist dreams he is in the countryside. The scene begins peacefully, but he is soon seized by panic, thinking that his beloved has been unfaithful to him.

4. "March to the Scaffold." Having murdered his beloved for her unfaithfulness, the artist is led to the scaffold, a large elevated platform supporting a guillotine. There, he dreams of her one last time, but her musical image—the *idée fixe*—is interrupted by the fall of the guillotine's blade. The artist dies, at least in his dream.

5. "Dream of a Witches' Sabbath." In this dream within a dream, the artist finds himself "in the midst of a frightful troop of ghosts, sorcerers, and monsters of every kind, gathered for his funeral." The beloved, in the form of her melody, the *idée fixe,* now appears in grotesque form, for in the artist's nightmare, she has become a witch. In the end, evil triumphs over good.

Musical Form, Programmatic Form

The form of this movement is fairly straightforward. It consists of two contrasting sections based on two contrasting themes—the opening **A** section is in the minor mode, the contrasting **B** section is in the major mode. The movement as a whole is framed by an introduction and coda. Graphically, the form of this movement can be represented as:

Introduction A / B / A / B / A Coda

But this tells only half the story of the music's form, which would seem to be dictated every bit as much by the prose of Berlioz's program:

> He [the artist] dreams he has killed his beloved, and that he is condemned to death and led to the scaffold. The procession moves forward to the sounds of a march that is at times gloomy and ferocious, at times solemn and brilliant. Noisy outbursts are followed without pause by the heavy sound of measured footsteps. At the end, the *idée fixe* appears for a moment, like a last thought of love broken off by the fatal blow [of the guillotine's blade].

"At times gloomy and ferocious, at times solemn and brilliant": this description is reflected directly in the form of the music in the alternation between the minor-mode **A** section ("gloomy and ferocious") and the major-mode **B** section ("solemn and brilliant"). The ending is particularly graphic, because the *idée fixe,* the musical image of the beloved, is interrupted—almost literally "cut off"—with the sudden fall of the guillotine's blade represented by a thundering chord played by the entire orchestra.

The guillotine's blade falls here in the "March to the Scaffold," interrupting the *idée fixe*

With these points in mind, listen once again to this movement, using the Listening Guide.

Hector Berlioz *Symphonie fantastique,* fourth movement ("March to the Scaffold")

Time	Form: Section	Harmony (Mode)	Word-Music Relationships: Berlioz's Program	Timbre
0:00	Introduction	Minor	He [the artist] dreams he has killed his beloved, and that he is condemned to death and led to his execution. The procession moves forward to the sound of...	Rumblings in the low strings, low winds, and low brass
0:27	A	Minor	...a march, at times gloomy and ferocious...	March-like theme in low strings, descending by step
1:39	B	Major	...at times solemn and brilliant. Noisy outbursts...	Brass and winds predominate.
2:11	A	Minor	...are followed without pause by the heavy sound of measured footsteps.	March-like theme, descending by step
2:22	B	Major		Brass and winds predominate.
2:53	A	Minor		March-like theme, descending by step
4:14	Coda	Major	At the end, the *idée fixe* appears for a moment [4:14, on the clarinet], like a last thought of love broken off by the fatal blow [of the guillotine's blade, at 4:24].	The severed head falls into the bucket (pizzicato figure at 4:25) and the crowd (the full orchestra) roars its approval (4:27).

Student FAQs

Did audiences in Berlioz's time know about the program?

Sometimes yes, sometimes no. Berlioz once wrote that "at concerts where this symphony is to be performed, it is essential that this program be distributed in advance in order to provide an overview of the dramatic structure of this work." Later in life, however, he felt that the program was actually drawing attention *away* from the music, and he declared that the names of the individual movements would suffice.

Does the program account for everything in the music?

No. As is almost always the case with program music, many details are left to the listener's imagination. As Berlioz himself noted, the purpose of the program was to give listeners "an overview of the dramatic structure of the work," not an explanation of its every detail.

Hector Berlioz (1803–69)

MUSIC AS AUTOBIOGRAPHY

More than any major composer before or since, Berlioz wrote his personal life into his music. The *Symphonie fantastique* mirrors his obsession with Harriet Smithson. He wrote his second symphony, *Harold en Italie (Harold in Italy),* which was loosely based on Byron's epic poem *Childe Harold,* after a two-year stay in Italy. His sequel to the *Symphonie fantastique,* entitled *Lelio; or, The Return to Life,* has often been seen as a thinly veiled marriage proposal to Harriet Smithson.

Berlioz had to struggle to establish himself in music. His father wanted his son to follow in his footsteps and become a doctor, so he sent the young Hector off to Paris to study medicine. But the younger Berlioz was more interested in music: he stopped attending medical classes and began spending more and more time at the national conservatory of music, where he eventually enrolled as a student. His teachers thought him talented but undisciplined; those teachers today are largely forgotten. He had to supplement his income for some time by writing music criticism, and only late in life did he enjoy the accolades of a public that for decades had not quite known what to make of his music.

PLAYLIST: BERLIOZ

Symphonie fantastique (complete).

Harold in Italy (Harold en Italie). A symphony loosely based on Byron's epic poem *Harold in Italy,* with a prominent part for solo viola.

Roméo et Juliette. A symphony based on Shakespeare's play, for soloists, chorus, and orchestra.

Requiem. A mammoth setting of the Catholic service for the dead, requiring multiple choruses and instrumental ensembles.

The Infancy of Christ (L'enfance du Christ). An oratorio for soloists, chorus, and orchestra.

Hector Berlioz in a portrait from 1832, two years after the premiere of the *Symphonie fantastique.* Caricatures invariably exaggerated the composer's dramatic hairstyle (see image p. 272). One contemporary compared Berlioz's hair to a "forest growing on the edge of a steep cliff."

Scala/Art Resource, NY.

How Loud Is Too Loud?

Volume is relative: what is unbearably loud to some seems perfectly acceptable to others. And perceptions of volume have changed over time. In an era before amplified sound, few things were louder than a large orchestra playing with full force. Berlioz's contemporaries were quick to point out the physical pain associated with the volume of sound he could elicit from a large ensemble of instruments.

The decibel is the standard measurement of sound volume: the higher the decibel level, the louder the sound. Most experts consider prolonged exposure to anything over 80 dB as potentially dangerous. Decibels increase logarithmically: an increase of 10 dB, for example, means that a sound becomes 10 times louder. A large orchestra playing at peak volume can reach potentially painful levels, as high as 110 decibels (dB). Ear-buds for portable listening equipment often produce decibel levels of over 120 dB. Hearing damage is a function not only of the decibel level but also of the duration of exposure to that level. As little as 15 minutes of exposure to 100 dB can cause permanent hearing damage.

Berlioz conducts. This caricature reflects the reactions of contemporaries to the sheer level of sound called for in certain passages in Berlioz's music, including the "March to the Scaffold" from the *Symphonie fantastique*. While clearly exaggerated—a cannon spews notes and giant hammers strike the timpani—the reactions of Berlioz's contemporaries are not without foundation.
The Pierpont Morgan Library/Art Resource, NY.

Decibels	Sound Source	Relative Musical Dynamic
150	Jet engine (at 1,000 ft.)	
130	Jackhammer	
120	Rock concert	
110	Large orchestra (full volume)	
100	Piano (loudest peak)	fff
90	Shouting voice	ff
80	Busy street noise	f
60	Speaking voice	mp
50		p
40		pp
30	Whispering voice	ppp

Source: http://sonomatics.com/usf/acoustics/CommonDBLevels.pdf

EXPAND YOUR PLAYLIST

The Music of Dreams

Berlioz's *Symphonie fantastique* is only one of many musical compositions that depict the sequence of a dream.

Franz Schubert, *Nacht und Träume,* D. 827. A song on "Night and Dreams."

Vincenzo Bellini, *La Sonnambula (The Sleepwalker;* 1831). An opera whose plot turns on the heroine's walking in her sleep (she sings, too).

Felix Mendelssohn, *Overture to A Midsummer Night's Dream* (see chapter 28).

Robert Schumann, "Träumerei" ("Dreaming") is one of a group of short pieces for solo piano in a collection called "Scenes from Childhood."

Edward Elgar, *The Dream of Gerontius* (1900). An oratorio for soloists, chorus, and orchestra that traces the fate of a soul from death through purgatory.

Thelonious Monk, *Monk's Dream*. A work created and performed by the jazz pianist.

Elvis Costello, *Il Sogno*. Costello's ballet, based on Shakespeare's *Midsummer Night's Dream,* combines classical and jazz idioms in a work for large orchestra.

30

Fanny Mendelssohn Hensel
Piano Trio in D Minor, op. 11, third movement

Listen to This

Timbre

Listen to the interplay of the three instruments: piano, violin, and cello. How would you describe their relationship? Is any one instrument more important than the others?

Word-Music Relationships

The entire Trio in D Minor is purely instrumental and has no words. But this movement bears the title "Lied" ("Song"), suggesting that the composer conceived of it as a song with a text, even if she gives no hint of what that text might be. What kind of poetic text might fit the mood of this movement?

Melody

There is only one melody in this entire movement, but it returns repeatedly in a varied form. Listen for these differences across the course of the movement.

I n an era before recorded sound, people who wanted to hear music at home had to play it themselves. Pieces for solo piano and songs formed a major part of the domestic repertory. But no medium proved as versatile and wide-ranging as the piano trio. The third movement of Fanny Mendelssohn Hensel's Piano Trio in D Minor, op. 11, offers an excellent example of the genre and invites us to imagine what it must have been like to make music in a nineteenth-century parlor. It is the kind of music families and gatherings of friends would have played in a private setting. And because so many homes had pianos, the piano trio lent itself particularly well to music making in the home. We can hear the intimacy of the setting in the intimacy of the music, which presents a single melody in ever-changing guises.

The Timbre of the Piano Trio

The piano trio—an ensemble consisting of piano, violin, and cello—had been a popular medium ever since the middle of the eighteenth century: Haydn, Mozart, Beethoven, Schubert, and Felix Mendelssohn (Fanny's brother) had all written piano trios. Part of the appeal of this ensemble was the breadth of sound available from only three instruments: the violin and cello are melodic instruments in the high and low ranges, respectively, while the piano can play chords as well as melodies in all registers. Because so many amateur musicians owned and played at least one of these instruments, piano trios enjoyed special popularity in the nineteenth century. Indeed, many musicians and listeners of the time heard the symphonies of Haydn, Mozart, and Beethoven performed more often in the home in an arrangement for piano trio than they heard these works in their original orchestral setting in the concert hall.

In this particular movement, the piano takes the lead from the very beginning, introducing the melody in an extended solo passage and then playing continuously throughout. The violin and cello each has its turn of presenting the melody as well. In the end, the three instruments blend to create a full, rich sound.

A Song Without Words

Fanny Mendelssohn Hensel placed the word "Lied"—"Song"—at the head of this movement. It is a provocative title, for the music has no words. How can a song not have words? Fanny and her brother Felix had in fact already written a number of piano pieces with precisely this title: *Songs Without Words*. These are short, lyrical works that imitate songs, both in their form and in their texture, with a clear melodic line throughout. In this movement, Fanny Mendelssohn Hensel creates a song without words for piano, violin, and cello.

What are we, as listeners, to make of this wordless song? The title serves as an invitation to us to create our own lyrics. What kind of text would best fit the music? Is this song lyrical (describing an emotional state) or is it a ballad (narrating a story)? Are there points at which the "voice" drops out?

This meter is called *trochaic tetrameter.* Trochaic indicates that the basic unit is LONG-short (or TUM-ta); tetrameter means that each line consists of four basic units ("tetra" = "four"). Henry Wadsworth Longfellow's *Song of Hiawatha* is written in this meter, and the words in fact fit the opening theme of this piano trio's movement quite well:

> **By** the **shores** of **Git**che **Gu**mee,
> **By** the **shi**ning **Big**-Sea-**Wa**ter,
> **Stood** the **wig**wam **of** No**kom**is,
> **Daugh**ter **of** the **Moon**, No**kom**is.

Can you think of other texts in this meter that might fit this music, or create your own?

Fanny Mendelssohn Hensel (1805–47)

OVERCOMING OBSTACLES

As a composer, Fanny Mendelssohn faced two major obstacles. The first was the immense fame of her younger brother Felix, who was an international celebrity as both a performer and composer while still in his teens. In spite of her own accomplishments as a pianist and composer, Fanny was inevitably known as "Felix's sister." Only recently have critics and historians begun to discover the full range of her talents as a composer of more than 200 songs, more than 100 works for piano, and more than 24 works for chorus, as well as various works for chamber ensembles.

The second obstacle was her gender. Fanny grew up in an era when musical composition was not considered an appropriate profession for women, and she grew up in a family in which women were not expected to pursue a vocation of any kind. Her father, Abraham Mendelssohn, wrote to her in 1820—she was 15 at the time—that while Felix might pursue a musical career, music "for you will always remain but an ornament; never can or should it become the foundation of your existence." This helps explain why for most of her life, Fanny published her music under her brother's name. Only later—just a year before her death, as it turned out—did she begin issuing compositions under her own name.

Felix and Fanny were extremely close not only in childhood but in their adult years as well, even after Fanny married the painter Wilhelm Hensel in 1829. She shared her brother's interest in the music of J.S. Bach and remained his closest musical confidante until her sudden death at the age of 41. Felix himself died only six months later.

Fanny Mendelssohn Hensel.
ColouiserAL/Lebrecht Music & Arts Photo Library

PLAYLIST: FANNY MENDELSSOHN HENSEL

Gartenlieder, Six Songs for Soprano, Alto, Tenor, and Bass, op. 3
Six Songs, op. 9
Six Songs, op. 10
Four Songs (Without Words) for Piano, op. 2
Four Songs (Without Words) for Piano, op. 6
String Quartet in C Minor
String Quartet in E-flat Major
Prelude in F Major, for organ

Melodic Metamorphosis

This is a song in modified strophic form (see chapter 27). We hear only a single melody, but the composer skillfully alters it each time it returns, changing the notes slightly, changing the instrument in which it appears, or changing the nature of the accompaniment. This creates a satisfying sense of both variety and unity.

Now listen to this trio movement again, following the Listening Guide.

Fanny Mendelssohn Hensel Piano Trio, op. 11, second movement

Time	Melody		Timbre	Word-Music Relationships
0:00	A		Piano alone; violin joins in at 0:14, cello at 0:16	The imagined text is presented in its original form.
0:23	**A1,** more somber, with minor mode inflections		Piano alone at first; cello joins in at 0:30, violin at 0:33	The "text" begins similarly but takes a darker and more circuitous turn
0:50	**A2**		Violin has the melody.	The "text" reappears closer to its original form in the violin and reaches its most intense point toward the end of this section.
1:18	**A3**		Cello has the melody at first, then all three instruments (1:33).	The "text" reappears in its original form, now in the cello, with a confident and affirmative ending.

Student FAQs

Does the piano always have the leading role in piano trios?

The piano is the biggest, loudest, and widest-ranging of the three instruments, and so in fact it usually does play more often than either of the other two. The violin and cello might occasionally have a passage to themselves as soloists or as a duet, but the piano is rarely out of the spotlight for long in a piano trio.

Not all songs have words. What makes the lack of a text here significant?

In English, many people tend to use the word "song" rather loosely to mean any work of music. Technically, however, a song is a piece of music that has a text to be sung. Particularly in German, the word placed at the head of this movement by Fanny Mendelssohn Hensel—"Lied"—strongly suggests the presence of a text, which makes the absence of one here all the more surprising.

Women Composers of the Nineteenth Century

Fanny Mendelssohn Hensel was one of a growing number of women in the nineteenth century who won fame through their compositions. Like women in many other professions of the time, most of these composers struggled to win recognition in a sphere dominated and controlled by men. Women were widely encouraged to sing or play the piano, but rarely were they encouraged to pursue a career in composition.

Maria Szymanowska (1789–1831), born in Warsaw (Poland), toured extensively as a piano virtuoso throughout Europe before settling in St. Petersburg (Russia) in 1827. She wrote primarily for her own instrument, the piano, and was an important precursor of Chopin (also a native Pole), writing mazurkas and nocturnes (see chapter 35).

Louise Farrenc (1804–75) wrote three symphonies, a piano concerto, four piano trios, and many other chamber works, in addition to a large number of works for piano. She was the only woman in the nineteenth century to hold a permanent chair at the Paris Conservatory, where she taught piano.

Clara Wieck Schumann (1819–96). See chapter 31.

Augusta Holmès (1847–1903) was born in France of Irish parents and added the accent to her last name when she became a French citizen in 1871. Her *Triumphant Ode* was commissioned as the musical centerpiece of the 1889 World's Fair, which gave us the Eiffel Tower. It is an enormous work for soloists, chorus, and orchestra, requiring more than 1,000 musicians to perform.

Cecile Chaminade (1857–1944), a native of Paris, achieved both critical and commercial success through her compositions for solo piano, as well as larger-scale compositions like her *Concertstück* for piano and orchestra and her Concertino for flute and orchestra. The French government awarded her the prestigious Order of the Legion of Honor in 1913 for her achievements in music.

Teresa Carreño (1853–1917), born in Venezuela, studied piano with Louis Moreau Gottschalk (see chapter 36). Her piano technique was so powerful that she was known as the "Valkyrie of the Piano." She played in the White House for both Abraham Lincoln (in 1863) and Woodrow Wilson (in 1916); she also sang in and conducted operas. Carreño composed almost exclusively for solo piano.

Amy Marcy Cheney Beach (1867–1944) was born in New Hampshire but spent most of her life in Boston. She performed

Amy Marcy Cheney Beach, ca.1900.
Milne Special Collections and Archives, University of New Hampshire Library

as a piano soloist several times with the Boston Symphony Orchestra, beginning in 1885. After marrying that year, she turned her attention away from performance and toward composition. She wrote in many genres, from chamber music to orchestral music to choral music, and her output includes such works as a piano concerto and a Mass. Her "Gaelic" Symphony (1897) shows the influence of Dvořák and was the first symphony written by an American woman.

EXPAND YOUR PLAYLIST

Chamber Music of the Nineteenth Century

Chamber music enjoyed great prestige throughout the nineteenth century. Composers, performers, and listeners all approached it as a serious and demanding category of music. It also became increasingly public over time, moving more and more into the concert hall, even as it continued to be cultivated in the home.

Ludwig van Beethoven: Piano Trio in B-flat Major, op. 97 ("Archduke").
The most famous of Beethoven's six piano trios, so named because he dedicated it to one of his composition pupils, Archduke Rudolph of Austria.

Ludwig van Beethoven: String Quartet in A Minor, op. 132.
One of Beethoven's "late" quartets, written in the last years of his life. The slow movement is labeled "Song of Holy Thanksgiving from a Convalescent to the Almighty."

Franz Schubert: Piano Trio in B-flat Major, D. 898.
One of two lengthy piano trios by Schubert, as long as many symphonies of the time.

Felix Mendelssohn: Piano Trio in C Minor, op. 66.
One of two piano trios by Fanny's brother Felix. The finale incorporates a sacred chorale (hymn tune).

Johannes Brahms: Piano Quintet in F Minor, op. 35.
Densely textured but richly melodic, this quintet resembles a symphony in its scope and tone.

Johannes Brahms: Clarinet Quintet in B Minor, op. 115.
Brahms became attracted to the clarinet as a solo instrument relatively late in life; this work is one of the few of its kind in the repertory.

31

Clara Wieck Schumann
"Forward!"

Listen to This

Timbre	This work is for chorus without instrumental accompaniment of any kind. Listen for the range of voices from highest (soprano) to lowest (bass).

Melody	Listen for the return of the opening melody at later points in the work, and listen for the way it is varied each time. Also listen for the contrasting melody between these returns of the opening theme.

Word-Music Relationships	Listen for **word painting** in certain passages, in which the melodic contour or texture of the music reinforces the ideas of the text.

This work began as a birthday present. Clara Schumann wrote it as a gift to her husband, Robert Schumann, on his 38th birthday, on June 8, 1848. She even arranged a performance of it on that day in their home, engaging members of the Dresden Choral Society, a group her husband had founded earlier that same year.

But the text of "Forward!" ("Vorwärts!") is political, not personal. The poem was written in 1840 by the poet Emanuel Geibel, and its title was a slogan for those who believed in a united and democratic Germany. What we now think of as Germany was at the time divided into a myriad of large and small states—Prussia, Swabia, Baden, Saxony, etc.—each with its own monarch, laws, and currency. The idea of unifying these various states into a single nation (Germany) with provisions for representative government was the chief goal of the revolutionaries who fought in the streets during the uprisings of 1848 and 1849. These outbreaks of violence were scattered and sporadic and ultimately failed. Not until 1871 did Germany emerge as a united country under the leadership of the former king of Prussia, with a limited form of representative government.

When Clara Schumann wrote this work, in the early summer of 1848, revolution was in the air, and she was well aware of the political implications of "Forward!" Her husband did not participate actively when revolution broke out in Dresden a year later, but he did follow the events closely in the newspapers and even wrote to a colleague in 1849 that he felt a responsibility "to tell, in music, of the sorrows and joys that motivate the times." In "Forward!," Clara Schumann had beaten him to the punch.

A Cappella Timbre

A group of unaccompanied voices is called an **a cappella** chorus. The voices in this particular work are "mixed"—that is, consisting of both women (sopranos, altos) and men (tenors, basses). The practice of a cappella singing goes back to the Middle Ages and Renaissance, so the timbre itself was not new in the nineteenth century, even if the harmonies now moved in a wider range, the rhythms were more jagged and irregular, and the dynamic contrasts were more pronounced. But performances of choral music took on special social significance in German-speaking lands in the nineteenth century, where laws of association strictly regulated and limited large social gatherings of any kind. Choruses of all varieties—men's, women's, and mixed—were permitted on the grounds that they were artistic and not political. In reality, everyone knew that these groups were to some extent political organizations giving voice to what could otherwise not be said in public.

Contrasting Melodies

Clara Schumann's setting of the text follows the form of the poem's five strophes, three of which (1, 3, and 5) begin with or culminate in the word *Vorwärts* ("Forward"). She sets these three strophes to a loud, rhythmically energetic melody, varying it with each strophe. The other two strophes (2 and 4), which speak to the temptations of complacency and fatigue, are set to a very different melody that is softer and more rhythmically smooth. Here, too, the melody is varied when it returns. The contrasting melodies become the basis of contrasting sections, creating a form which approximates that of a rondo (**A B A' B' A"**).

Painting Revolutionary Words

The key word of the text, *Vorwärts* ("Forward"), is a charged word. The composer goes to great lengths to emphasize it at its first appearance, at the end of the first strophe, where it stands out by virtue of its unison texture and trumpet-like melodic line. Passages that speak of calm and peace—the contrasting strophes 2 and 4—are set to a low dynamic (piano). And the music hits its registral high point on the word *Himmel* ("heaven") just before the very end.

Now listen to this work again, following the Listening Guide.

Clara Wieck Schumann (1819–96)

INDEPENDENT SPIRIT

Clara Wieck's father, Friedrich Wieck, was adamantly opposed to the idea of his daughter marrying a musician, particularly a composer of such limited means as Robert Schumann. The situation was complicated by the fact that Wieck was Robert Schumann's piano teacher. The young couple eventually eloped and married against her father's wishes. Clara and her father were estranged for many years, and at one point she had to go to court to recover her piano from him.

This independence of spirit grew even stronger after the death of her husband. Finding herself a widow when only in her mid-thirties, she went on to pursue a highly successful career as a soloist and teacher. Her performances of Beethoven's sonatas and concertos, Chopin's piano pieces, and her husband's compositions were legendary in their time, and critics hailed her as one of the great piano virtuosos of her generation. Her compositional output includes a piano concerto, a piano trio, and many short piano works and songs for voice and piano. Later in life, she edited the first complete edition of her husband's musical works.

PLAYLIST: CLARA SCHUMANN

Three Songs on Texts by Rückert

Three Romances (solo piano)

Variations on a Theme by Robert Schumann (solo piano)

Piano Trio in G Minor

Piano Concerto in A Minor

Clara Schumann
Dagli Orti, courtesy of Picture DeskInc./Kobal Collection

Clara Wieck Schumann "Forward!"

Time	Original German Text	English Translation	Melody
0:00	1. Lass das Träumen, lass das Zagen, Unermüdet wandre fort! Will die Kraft dir schier versagen, "Vorwärts!" ist das rechte Wort.	Leave the dreaming and hesitation behind, Without fatigue, go forward! If you simply run out of energy, "Forward!" is the right word.	1 = rising figure, dotted rhythms
0:16	2. Darfst nicht weilen, wenn die Stunde Rosen dir entgegenbringt, Wenn dir aus des Meeres Grunde Die Sirene lockend singt.	You may not dally, if the day Brings you roses, Or if from the depths of the ocean The siren sings seductively to you.	2 = higher register, leaps up, then moves down
0:29	3. Vorwärts, vorwärts! Im Gesange Ringe mit dem Schmerz der Welt, Bis auf deine heisse Wange Goldner Strahl von oben fällt,	Forward, forward! In song Wrestle with the suffering of the world, Until on your hot cheek A golden ray from above should fall,	1 (varied)
0:42	4. Bis der Kranz, der dichtbelaubte, Schattig deine Stirn umwebt, Bis verklärend überm Haupte Dir des Geistes Flamme schwebt.	Until the crown, thickly woven, wraps itself with shadows around your head, Until above your head transfigured The flame of the spirit hovers before you.	2 (varied)
0:55	5. Vorwärts drum durch Feindes Zinnen, Vorwärts durch des Todes Pein, Wer den Himmel will gewinnen, Muss ein rechter Kämpfer sein!	Forward, then, through the enemy's lines, Forward through the pain of death, Whoever would gain entry to heaven Must be a true fighter!	1 (varied)

Form: Section	Word-Music Relationships
A	Unison trumpet-like figure on the word *Vorwärts!* ("Forward!") (0:10)
B	Soft dynamics for passage of text describing a lack of conflict in life
A′	*Goldner Strahl von oben* ("Golden ray from above") moves from high to low.
B′	Soft dynamics describing the transport of the soul to heaven.
A″	Highest note of the entire work on the word *Himmel* ("heaven") at 1:04.

Student FAQs

How many singers are in an a cappella chorus?

The number can vary. Some a cappella groups have only one or two singers on each part (thus, four to eight singers in total), while others might have as many as eight or ten to a part. In the recording here, we hear a group of about two dozen singers.

Whatever happened to the tradition of a cappella singing?

It continues to this day. Many colleges in the United States feature a cappella groups (men, women, or mixed). The Fisk Jubilee Singers, of Fisk University in Nashville, Tennessee, is one of the oldest groups of this kind. The original members consisted of emancipated slaves, and they broke racial barriers when they began touring with their repertory of spirituals and "slave music" in 1871. Today, it is estimated that there are more that 1,500 a cappella ensembles on U.S. college campuses. Many of these groups specialize in a particular repertory of music, such as classical, popular, gospel, or jazz.

Music and Politics

Music has served political ends for thousands of years. Rulers from all periods and all corners of the world have used it repeatedly to demonstrate their cultural power. To read accounts from Renaissance Italy, one might easily imagine one ruler saying to another: "My court singers are better than your court singers." And in the early nineteenth century, when Beethoven was at one point considering leaving Vienna for good, the city's nobility and aristocracy of Vienna considered it a point of national pride to keep him there, so they raised sufficient funds to persuade him to stay. Beethoven responded by writing a number of works on overtly political texts that glorified Austria.

The public uprisings that began with the French Revolution of 1789 opened up new ways of connecting music and politics. Communal singing became an important means of fostering solidarity among a large and diverse population, and the idea that every nation should have its own national song or anthem took root around this time. Every mass political movement since then has had its songs. In the twentieth century, protesters for and against many different causes used music to galvanize support. Labor unions, supporters of the Civil Rights movement, and opponents of the Vietnam War all developed extensive repertories of songs.

Politicians have also perceived certain kinds of music as threats at various times. Certain types of jazz were prohibited in Nazi Germany and the Soviet Union. Rock music has been banned on state-run media in many countries on many occasions. In 2001, the president of Turkmenistan banned opera and ballet; and in 2005, he outlawed lip synching on the grounds that it exercised "a negative effect on the development of singing and musical art." "Don't kill talents by using lip synching," he argued. "Create our new culture." Bizarre as the law may seem, its roots lie in the recognition of music's power within society.

Martin Luther King Jr. addresses the Civil Rights March on Washington on August 28, 1963. Musical performers at the event included Marian Anderson, Joan Baez, Bob Dylan, Mahalia Jackson (see Web Bonus Chapter 5), and Peter, Paul, and Mary. But the most moving performance, by all accounts, was by the assembled crowd itself singing "We Shall Overcome."

AP Wide World Photos

 EXPAND YOUR PLAYLIST

Political Music

Music has a long history of being used to promote political causes. Some examples:

The French Revolution
"La Marseilles"
"Ça ira"

The Civil War
"The Battle Hymn of the Republic"

The Civil Rights Movement
"The Battle Hymn of the Republic"
"If I Had a Hammer"
"We Shall Overcome"

The Vietnam War
Country Joe and the Fish, "I-Feel-Like-I'm-Fixin'-to-Die Rag" (1965)
Creedence Clearwater Revival, "Fortunate Son" (1969)

32

Frédéric Chopin
Mazurka in B-flat, op. 7, no. 1

 Listen to This

Texture

Notice how clearly the melody stands out in the uppermost voice. The lower voices play a strictly supporting role. This piece is thoroughly **homophonic**.

Melody

Listen for a direct upward path through a series of steps (punctuated by jagged dotted rhythms), which then lead to three leaps downward (also in dotted rhythms). In the quiet, mysterious middle section, do you notice that the melody now moves *downward,* primarily by steps?

Rhythm

Listen carefully to the opening rhythm, which repeats itself many times, and then see if you can tap it out yourself afterward.

Form

In this work, Chopin uses just a few brief melodic ideas to create a larger whole, through repetition, variation, and contrast. Listen for the return of the opening idea and the way in which themes introduced later contrast with the opening.

For many, Frédéric Chopin epitomizes Romanticism. His piano music is passionate and direct. A renowned piano virtuoso, Chopin was able to evoke a wide range of emotions in the works he composed for his instrument. Without recourse to words, he created poetry for the keyboard that still speaks in a profound way to pianists and audiences today. His repertory consists mainly of what are called **character pieces**, relatively short works that capture a particular character—not in the sense of a character in a story, but in the sense of a mood. The titles of these works always provide a clue to the character they seek to establish.

A **mazurka** is a Polish folk dance in triple meter, often with a heavy accent on the second or third beat of each measure (1-**2**-3 | 1-**2**-3 or 1-2-**3** | 1-2-**3**) instead of the usual accent on the first beat (**1**-2-3 | **1**-2-3). Chopin, who was born in Poland but later moved to France, wrote many mazurkas and other types of Polish dances as an expression of his intense national pride for his native land, using the rhythms of folk dances as the basis for miniature works of art. This work is thus an example of musical **nationalism**. Chopin was neither the first nor the last composer to draw on folk music for inspiration, but the particular context of a work like the mazurka—Poland was under Russian occupation at the time—gave this music a sense of political meaning that was quite obvious to his contemporaries, regardless of their nationality.

Texture: The Pianist as Vocalist

Chopin advised young pianists to listen carefully and often to great singers and to imitate at the keyboard their manner of projecting the voice. In composing, he put this advice into practice. He endowed one part with a beautiful melody—as though giving a song to a singer—and created other parts to support and enhance the melody—as though giving the singer a truly inspired and creative accompanist or backup. This homophonic texture worked particularly well on the piano because it is an instrument that can play both lyrical melodies and accompaniment at the same time. In this piece, the right hand carries the melody, in a higher register, while the left hand provides the accompaniment.

About two-thirds of the way through (at "C" in the Listening Guide), the accompaniment changes markedly. It moves from a series of varied chords to a **drone bass**, a single pair of notes repeated over and over, rather like the sound of a bagpipe. This static harmony creates a strong sense of contrast between this section and those before and after. It also reinforces the folk-like origins of the mazurka as a genre, for the bagpipe is an instrument associated almost exclusively with the music of the countryside.

Melody: Scales Going Up, Scales Going Down

If you ever learned to play an instrument or sang in a choir, you probably learned to play or sing scales (or "Do-Re-Mi's"). Maybe you even wondered why you were asked to spend time practicing something other than actual songs. If you have not played or sung much music yourself, you have probably still heard of scales as a building block of music, and wondered what they actually have to do with the music itself. This mazurka is an example of how scales can form important parts of melodies, and also how different scales can create completely different-sounding music.

This mazurka, a very popular one with pianists, opens with a theme that consists quite simply of an ascending scale—a series of steps up. Pianists who have practiced their scales conscientiously will have an easier time playing this scalar melody. Because it is a major scale, it sounds bright and optimistic. (You may come up with slightly different terms, because the quality of a sound remains subjective.) The top note of this scale is marked by a trill (two notes a step apart played in alternation so rapidly it can be difficult for the listener to separate them).

Later, at 1:30, the mood changes to one of perhaps mystery or contemplation, and we hear a scale going downward. But it is not the downward motion that creates this unusual sound with a completely different feel. It is the kind of scale that it is: a variation on a minor scale—which, as we have already heard, imparts a sadder or more somber quality to music. You hear that the dynamics are suddenly very quiet, which enhances the minor mood or mystery.

Between these two melodies, at 0:34, we hear a gentler melody that has neither a long trajectory upward or downward nor wide leaps. It moves within a limited range of notes.

Undulating motion, narrow range

p *legato*

Form: Repetition, Variation, Contrast

Chopin uses just a few brief melodic ideas to create a larger whole. Here, the various sections (**A, B, C**) are restated without significant variation to create a rondo-like pattern, in which **A** returns repeatedly after the interjection of contrasting ideas (**B** and **C**):

A   A   B   A   B   A   C   A   C   A

Rhythm: The Pride of Poland

The rhythm that you hear at the beginning is found in some guise in every mazurka Chopin wrote—and he wrote at least 57. They encompass many different moods, from melancholy to exuberant, but all contain this rhythm typical of Polish folk dance, with an accent on the second beat of a three-beat measure ("2") rather than on the downbeat ("1"):

Now listen to the Mazurka again, following the Listening Guide.

Frédéric Chopin (1809–48)

A POLISH COMPOSER IN FRANCE

The son of a French father and a Polish mother, Chopin never felt quite at home in either land. After early training in his native Poland, he set out on an extended tour of Western Europe and never returned. But Poland was never far from his mind. When Russia annexed all but a tiny portion of the country in 1831, the cause of Polish nationalism burned even brighter in the nation's exile community. Chopin's cultivation of such national dances as the polonaise and mazurka manifests his deep feelings toward his native land.

Thanks in part to the large number of Polish expatriates in Paris, Chopin was able to circulate in the highest levels of society. He made a good living from his teaching and sales of his own music, along with the occasional public concert, though he avoided these as much as he could, especially in his later years. In 1837, he began a decade-long liaison with the novelist Amandine Lucile Aurore Dudevant (1804–76), better known by her pen name, George Sand. In 1838–39, the two wintered on the island of Majorca, off the Spanish coast in the Mediterranean. There, local doctors diagnosed Chopin's growing illness as tuberculosis. In spite of his poor health, Chopin continued to compose steadily until the last few months of his life.

Most of Chopin's music is for solo piano, and even the small number of works that are not—such as songs, concertos, and a piano trio—include the piano.

Chopin was one of the first composers to have been photographed. This daguerreotype was taken only a few months before his death.

Getty Images/De Agostini Editore Picture Library

PLAYLIST: CHOPIN

Solo piano:

Preludes, op. 24

Etudes, op. 10

Ballade no. 1 in G Minor, op. 25

Berceuse in D-flat Major, op. 57

Polonaise in A Major, op. 40, no. 1 ("Military")

Piano with orchestra:

Piano Concerto no. 1 in F Minor, op. 21

Frédéric Chopin, Mazurka in B-flat, op. 7, no. 1

Time	Form/Melody	Texture
0:00	**A** (= a long ascending scale with sudden downward leaps; major mode)	Homophonic throughout
0:17	**A**	
0:34	**B** (= a much narrower range; major mode)	
0:45	**A**	
1:01	**B**	
1:13	**A**	
1:30	**C** (= a downward trajectory; minor mode)	With drone bass
1:44	**A**	
2:02	**C**	With drone bass
2:16	**A**	

Student FAQs

How is the mazurka actually danced?

As a folk dance, the mazurka emphasizes the off-beat accents (on "2" of each measure) by calling on the dancers to click their heels or stamp their feet. More stylized forms of the dance emerged later, allowing the dancers relatively great freedom to improvise steps and gestures of the hands.

Would anyone have actually danced to Chopin's mazurkas?

Probably not, at least not in public. Even though this is dance music, with a steady beat, it was meant to be heard rather than serve as the accompaniment to an actual dance.

Speeding Up and Slowing Down: Robbed Time

Listen carefully to almost any recording of Chopin's solo piano music and you will notice that the performer does not always maintain a strict tempo but instead speeds up and slows down subtly at times. The changes are not dramatic, but they are noticeable and effective. These subtle changes of tempo applied by the performer are known as **tempo rubato**—literally "robbed time"—or simply **rubato**.

Many accounts of Chopin's piano playing mention his use of rubato. One particularly intriguing account has come down to us from one of his students:

> In keeping time Chopin was inexorable, and . . . the metronome never left his piano. Even in his much maligned *tempo rubato,* the hand responsible for the accompaniment would keep strict time while the other hand, singing the melody, would free the essence of the musical thought from all rhythmic fetters, either by lingering hesitantly or by eagerly anticipating the movement with a certain impatient vehemence akin to passionate speech.

The key phrase here is: "akin to passionate speech." Music that imitates singing must capture the flexible declamation that is so characteristic of singers. Just as we speak with varying speeds—speeding up here, slowing down there for emphasis—so, too, do operatic performers vary the pace of their delivery, altering the rhythm of their words to match the emotion. Pianists imitating singers have a corresponding obligation to play this kind of music with a sense of expression, as "passionate speech."

The metronome is a mechanical device developed in the early 19th century for measuring musical time more precisely. By raising or lowering the weight on the stick, the user can increase or decrease the pace of the clicking sound produced by the back-and-forth motion of the pendulum.

© Dorling Kindersley

EXPAND YOUR PLAYLIST

Piano Music of the Nineteenth Century

Many of the nineteenth century's leading composers were themselves pianists, and they wrote extensively for the instrument.

Ludwig van Beethoven

- Piano Sonata in C-sharp Minor, op. 27, no. 2 ("Moonlight")
- Piano Sonata in F Minor, op. 57 ("Appassionata")
- Piano Sonata in B-flat Major, op. 106 ("Hammerklavier")
- Piano Sonata in E Major, op. 109
- Beethoven's 32 piano sonatas, of which these are only a few, remain a staple of the repertory and cover an enormous range of styles and moods.
- 33 Variations on a Waltz by Diabelli, op. 120

Robert Schumann

- *Carnaval,* op. 9
A cycle of small works based on the theme of Carnival, in which party-goers wear masks and behave in unusual ways.

- *Fantasia,* op. 17
A three-movement work comparable to a sonata.

Franz Liszt

- Sonata in B Minor
A central idea is transformed across the entire work.

- *Etudes d'execution transcendentale*
A set of studies or exercises of transcendental difficulty.

Johannes Brahms

- Intermezzo, op. 118, no. 2
One of Brahms's most beloved piano miniatures, it is deceptively simple.

- *Variations and Fugue on a Theme by Handel,* op. 24

33

Louis Moreau Gottschalk
Union

Listen to This

Melody

Listen for the three well-known patriotic tunes in this work: "The Star-Spangled Banner," "Hail, Columbia," and "Yankee Doodle."

Texture

Listen for differences in texture in the way these melodies are presented. "The Star-Spangled Banner" and "Hail, Columbia" are homophonic (melody with accompaniment). But when "Yankee Doodle" is introduced toward the end, it is combined with "Hail, Columbia" to produce a polyphonic texture, two independent melodies played at the same time.

Louis Moreau Gottschalk composed *Union: Concert Paraphrase on National Airs,* a piece for solo piano, in response to the recent outbreak of the U.S. Civil War. Although he was born and raised in New Orleans, Gottschalk was an ardent Unionist who opposed slavery and secession. To express his political convictions, he wrote a work that incorporates three well-known patriotic tunes: "Yankee Doodle," "Hail, Columbia," and "The Star-Spangled Banner." Toward the end of the work, he brings in the latter two simultaneously.

Gottschalk was the first American-born piano virtuoso to achieve international fame. His solo recitals were legendary, and his repertory consisted almost entirely of music he had written himself, because it allowed him to display his technical abilities to greatest effect. He performed *Union* to great acclaim throughout the United States—at least in the North—and in Latin America. Gottschalk noted in his diary that a performance of *Union* in Philadelphia during the Civil War elicited "unheard-of enthusiasm. . . . Recalls, encores, hurrahs, etc.!"[1]

---

[1] Louis Moreau Gottschalk. *Notes of a Pianist.* Ed. Clara Gottschalk, trans. Robert E. Peterson. Philadelphia: Lippincott, 1881, p. 81.

Orchestras around the country featured Gottschalk as a soloist in showpieces he wrote to display his own talents, like the *Grand fantasie triomphale,* a series of brilliant variations on the Brazilian national anthem, or the *Grande tarentelle* for piano and orchestra, based on the traditional Italian dance said to cure the bite of a tarantula. Other nineteenth-century musicians took full advantage of the concerto as a vehicle for showing off their talents as both composers and performers. Franz Liszt wrote two fiendishly difficult piano concertos—he was one of the few musicians of his time who could do justice to them—and Felix Mendelssohn, Frédéric Chopin, and Johannes Brahms also wrote piano concertos in addition to solo piano pieces (see Expand Your Playlist).

Patriotic Melodies Made Virtuosic

The "national airs" that Gottschalk incorporates in this piece—"The Star-Spangled Banner," "Hail, Columbia," and "Yankee Doodle"—were all closely identified with the Union cause. Even though he was from New Orleans, a city in a Confederate state, Gottschalk believed in the preservation of the United States as a single nation. The work presents no original melodies of its own but offers instead, as its title promises, a "paraphrase" on these "national airs." The patriotic melodies themselves are fairly simple, but Gottschalk embellished them in ways that allowed him to demonstrate his abilities as a piano virtuoso. This work is fiendishly difficult to play, and contemporary audiences were probably responding not only to the **nationalism** inherent in the music, but also to the sheer skill it took to perform it. With its rapid runs, large leaps, and complicated rhythms, all played for the most part at a very rapid speed, *Union* is the kind of work that only the most technically skilled pianists can perform convincingly. The virtuosity demanded in this work is in many respects physical, similar in kind to that required by a figure skater to execute a difficult maneuver.

Same Melodies, Different Textures

The texture of this work builds from homophonic at the beginning to polyphonic at the end. The harmonization of "The Star-Spangled Banner" is unusual, but the texture is clearly homophonic: melody above, accompaniment below. When "Yankee Doodle" enters clearly for the first time, however, it is combined not with a simple accompaniment underneath, but with another well-known melody, "Hail, Columbia." Both melodies are clearly audible at the same time. Even more remarkably, Gottschalk proceeds to reverse the relative position of these two "national airs," moving "Hail, Columbia" to the uppermost voice and placing "Yankee Doodle" underneath it. Writing two different melodies that work together is difficult enough; writing two melodies whose positions can be reversed is even harder. (The technical term for this kind of polyphony is "invertible counterpoint.") Even though Gottschalk wrote neither of these melodies, he recognized their compatibility and was thus able to demonstrate his skills as a composer and performer at the same time.

Now listen to this piece again, following the Listening Guide.

Music in the Civil War

Works like Gottschalk's *Union* remind us of the power of music to arouse intense feelings of community spirit, whether for a school, a faith, or a nation. When giving a concert in Maryland—a slave state that had not seceded and whose citizens' loyalties were deeply divided between North and South—Gottschalk realized that he could not play both *Union* and "Dixie" on the same program without risking a riot, so fierce were the sentiments that could be aroused by certain works of music.

Some songs had more universal appeal. "All Quiet Along the Potomac Tonight," for example, was sung on both sides of the conflict. The words had been written as a poem in 1861 by Ethel Lynn Beers, a New Yorker. Two years later, South Carolinian John Hill Hewitt set them to music while living in Georgia. The song speaks to the quiet fate of an enlisted soldier killed by a sniper; the newspapers the following day report no action along the Potomac River—the river separating Virginia from Maryland, South from North—but the soldier's family knows better.

With the advent of war, old tunes received new texts: a newly minted Confederate version of "Yankee Doodle," issued early in the Civil War, begins:

> Yankee Doodle had a mind
> To whip the Southern "traitors,"
> Because they didn't choose to live
> On codfish and potaters.

Several Northern poets, in turn, penned new words to the melody of "Dixie," including these:

> Away down South in the land of traitors,
> Rattlesnakes and alligators,
> Right away, come away, right away, come away.
> Where cotton's king and men are chattels,
> Union boys will win the battles,
> Right away, come away, right away, come away.

Music provided an important emotional outlet for soldiers in the field and their families back home, a source of comfort and inspiration to both. And for the soldiers, music was more than entertainment: every unit had its allotted number of musicians, who conveyed orders across wide distances (through musical signals), mustering the troops, and moving them into position for both drill and battle.

The most common band instruments of the Civil War were trumpets, fifes (a small, high flute, similar to the piccolo), and many different kinds of drums. The large instruments in the front row are saxhorns, a brass instrument named after Adolphe Sax, who also invented the saxophone. Players carried the instrument over their shoulders, with the bell pointing backward, which allowed troops in the rear to hear their music.

Band of the 107th U.S. Colored Infantry at Fort Corcoran, Arlington, Virginia, in 1865.
Courtesy of the Library of Congress

Louis Moreau Gottschalk *Union*

Time	Section	🎵 Melody	Texture	Rhythm: Meter
0:00	A	Fragments of "Yankee Doodle" (in minor mode), beginning at 0:24	Homophonic	Duple
1:36	B	"The Star-Spangled Banner" ("with melancholy")		Triple
3:22	A	Fragments of "Yankee Doodle" in minor mode		Duple
3:39	C	Imitation of trumpets (3:39), followed by "Hail, Columbia" This section begins softly, grows in volume, and recedes, as if played by a band approaching, marching by, and departing. The "drums" become more audible at 5:00, then recede, as if into the distance.		
6:06	D	"Yankee Doodle" (upper voice) and "Hail, Columbia" (lower voice); voices switch positions at 6:22. "Yankee Doodle" returns to its usual major mode in this section.	Polyphonic	
6:29	A	Fanfare-like figure from the beginning	Homophonic	
6:43	D	"Yankee Doodle" (upper voice) and "Hail, Columbia" (lower voice); voices switch positions at 6:58	Polyphonic	

 Student FAQs

Why is "The Star-Spangled Banner" section marked "With melancholy"?

We can't know for certain what Gottschalk had in mind here, but the melody does gradually grow more resolute. Perhaps this reflects the dissolution of the Union at the beginning of the Civil War (April 1861) and the subsequent resolve to preserve it.

I've never heard of "Hail, Columbia" before. Was it well known in Gottschalk's time?

"Hail, Columbia" was widely known in the nineteenth century and served as a kind of unofficial national anthem, along with "The Star-Spangled Banner." For reasons that remain unclear, the tune fell out of use sometime after World War I.

Louis Moreau Gottschalk (1829–69)

THE MUSICIAN AS SHOWMAN

Wherever he performed, Gottschalk won over audiences with a combination of superb piano technique, good looks, and showmanship. He always made a ceremony of taking off his white gloves before performing at the piano, and critics raved about his ability to play even the most difficult passages with ease.

Many of Gottschalk's works incorporate national or ethnic elements. His piano piece *The Banjo,* for example, imitates the sound of that quintessentially American instrument and includes a reference to Stephen Foster's beloved song "Camptown Races." Another of Gottschalk's piano works, *Bamboula,* incorporates the rhythms of African American dances of the mid-nineteenth century.

A native of New Orleans, Gottschalk studied piano in Paris, where his playing was praised by Chopin, Berlioz, and other leading European musicians. He returned to the United States in 1853 and soon became one of the nation's most popular soloists, touring the country extensively and playing almost entirely works he had composed himself. He died of yellow fever in Rio de Janeiro, Brazil, during an extended tour of Latin America.

Louis Moreau Gottschalk, ca. 1860. He had a long-standing business relationship with Chickering, a major piano manufacturer, endorsing their instruments and performing on them whenever possible.
Art Resource/The New York Public Library

PLAYLIST: GOTTSCHALK

The Banjo (solo piano)
Bamboula (solo piano)
Souvenir de Puerto Rico (solo piano)
Symphony no. 1 ("A Night in the Tropics")
Symphony no. 2 ("À Montevideo")

GOTTSCHALK'S CONCERT TOUR, SPRING 1862

CANADA

U.S.A.

Hamilton   Lakeport

Milwaukee   Buffalo

Toledo   Cleveland   Newark   New York City

Pittsburgh   Philadelphia

Cincinnati   Baltimore   Wilmington

Indian Territory   Washington D. C.

N

St. Louis

Louisville

Confederate States of America

Returns to U.S. in Feb. 1862 after 5 years in Latin America, mostly in the Caribbean. Premieres *Union* on Washington's birthday, Feb. 22.

The Nineteenth-Century Virtuoso

Audiences throughout Europe and the United States paid big money to hear the great virtuosos of their time perform, either in one-person recitals or as soloists with an orchestra, in concertos. Virtuosos were part musician, part showman. Many of these individuals, like Gottschalk, wrote and performed their own music.

Nicolo Paganini (1782–1840) was the greatest violin virtuoso of the nineteenth century. He did nothing to dispel rumors that he had made a pact with the devil to achieve his mastery of the instrument.

- *Caprices,* op. 1, no. 24. This is a fiendishly difficult set of variations on a short theme.
  Violin Concerto no. 2 in B Minor, op. 7, finale. The main theme of this rondo sounds like the ringing of bells.

Franz Liszt (1811–86) was the greatest piano virtuoso of the nineteenth century. As a child, he met Beethoven; one of his daughters married the composer Richard Wagner; and he almost single-handedly created the public solo piano recital.

- Hungarian Rhapsody no. 2. This is the most famous of the 19 solo piano works Liszt wrote in a quasi-Hungarian style. Although Liszt was born in present-day Hungary, his native language was German, and he started to learn Hungarian only later in his life.

- Piano Concerto no. 2 in A Major. This is one of two concertos Liszt wrote to perform himself.

- *Grandes etudes de Paganini,* no. 3 in G-sharp Minor ("La Campanella") Liszt's reworking of the finale of Paganini's Violin Concerto no. 2 (see above), for piano, adding extra lines to make the music even more difficult.

Ignacy Jan Paderewski (1860–1941) was famous as a piano performer, composer, and statesman. In later life, he served briefly as prime minister of his native Poland and was active in the Polish government-in-exile during World War II.

- *Humoresques de concert*: Minuet in G Major

34

Ravi Shankar
Raga Sindhi-Bhairavi

 Listen to This

Melody

Listen to the sitar, an Indian plucked lute, and the melodies produced on it from string bending and striking techniques. Are some scale tones more important than others?

Texture

Listen to the texture. How many instruments do you hear? Is it homophonic or polyphonic? How does it change throughout the piece?

Form

Listen for four different sections and the way each section changes in texture and rhythm.

Rhythm

Listen to how the rhythm begins freely but becomes more established throughout. What suddenly marks the fourth rhythmic change?

Virtuosity on an instrument is basic to the music of many cultures around the world. During India's Mughal Period—which lasted from the early sixteenth through the mid–nineteenth centuries—the musician Tansen (1500–89) was brought to the court of Emperor Akbar in Delhi. Tansen introduced the *raga* as a genre of Hindustani

Ravi Shankar is considered to be one of the finest sitarists in the world, and he is certainly the most famous. Shankar was born in 1920 in Benares, India, and his fame spread in the Western Hemisphere after 1956. George Harrison of the Beatles, one of his best-known pupils, learned the sitar and performed on it on the Beatles' albums *Rubber Soul* and *Revolver*. Schools for *raga* performance exist throughout the world today, including in many U.S. and European cities.

David Farrell/Lebrecht Music & Arts Photo Library

(or North Indian) music. **Raga**, which means "mood," "color," or "musical scale," is also the term that refers to an instrumental performance featuring a soloist who played to color the emperor's mood or day. Although this was a century before the Baroque era in Europe, Tansen developed a solo instrumental genre prior to the solo violin sonatas of Arcangelo Corelli, the Italian composer and violin virtuoso (see chapter 13). The dissolution of the Mughal court after 1720 led to the dispersal of Hindustani musicians and *raga* performance throughout northern India at about the same time the *sonata* spread throughout Europe.

The **sitar** is a plucked lute that usually has 18 strings ("tar" is the Indian word for "string"). The strings are arranged in three sets: the playing strings, the drone strings, and the sympathetic strings. The playing strings are fretted and produce the melody. The most important playing string is the *baj tar*. It is played by bending it far across the frets to produce a wide range of pitches. An ornament produced by rapid and varied string bending is called a *gamaka*. One of the drone strings, or *jhala tar*, is struck periodically to resonate with an important tone in the melody. The sympathetic strings, or *taraf tar*, are located under the frets and are played during the melody; they vibrate when a corresponding pitch is sounded (but typically a soloist often strums down across the sympathetic strings at the very beginning and very end of a piece, which can be heard in the accompanying listening example).

The strings are fastened to a wooden neck with pegs. The neck of the sitar is attached at the base to a large gourd resonator, and at the top of the neck is often attached a smaller gourd resonator. For plucking, the player wears a wire plectrum around the index finger of the right hand. Players perform seated (see the photograph of Ravi Shankar above).

Raga (also the plural form of the word) are scalar patterns with distinct melodic shapes and are derived from numerous tones. Each combination of tones has a certain character, or mood, that is believed to affect the universe. North Indian classical music uses far more tones than European classical music does. Theoretically, thousands of *raga* exist; however, seventy-two *raga* are known and performed today. Based on the larger vocabulary of available tones, new *raga* may still be invented.

Melody of the Sunrise

Raga Sindhi-Bhairavi is a morning *raga*. It was created by Shankar, who is also a composer and improvisor. From the sixteenth through mid–nineteenth centuries, a morning *raga* could be performed at the court only at sunrise to regulate the sun's movement over the horizon. A different type of *raga* performed at that time of day, or a morning *raga* played with mistakes, was believed to throw off the entire day because the musical vibrations would be "out of synch" with the vibrations of the universe at that moment. Today, any *raga* can be performed at any

Meet the Sitar

Ravi Shankar was already well known in Western classical and jazz circles when George Harrison first heard his playing in the mid-1960s. The lead guitarist for the Beatles—the most popular group of the day—Harrison first played sitar on their recording of the song "Norwegian Wood." Soon after, Brian Jones of the Rolling Stones played a sitar part on that group's hit single "Paint It Black." Harrison remained deeply devoted to Indian music and philosophy, studying with Shankar and also incorporating Indian tonalities and instruments into several of his songs, most notably "Within You, Without You" on *Sgt. Pepper's Lonely Heart's Club Band*.

Shankar's fame in rock circles grew after he appeared at several major festivals in the late 1960s, including the Monterey International Pop Music Festival in 1967 and the famous Woodstock festival in 1969. His best-known appearance was at the Concert for Bangladesh at New York's Madison Square Garden in 1971. Shankar had approached Harrison after hearing of the devastating floods in the Bangladesh region, situated between India and Pakistan. Harrison enlisted other rock artists—including Bob Dylan, Eric Clapton, and Ringo Starr—to perform at the concert. The concert opened—as did the later three-album record set—with a half-hour performance by Shankar on sitar.

Shankar has continued to perform a mix of traditional *ragas* with his own compositions and to cross genres to work with classical orchestras and jazz and pop ensembles. His daughter, Anoushka, is also a noted sitar artist; another daughter, Norah Jones, is well known as a pop singer, songwriter, and pianist.

British pop musician George Harrison, right, a former member of the Beatles, with seven top Indian instrumentalists, singers, and dancers. Ravi Shankar is third from the right.

Getty Images Inc.—Hulton Archive Photos

time of day because they have become concert pieces. Many European composers have depicted the sunrise in their works as well, and those pieces, too, may be performed in the evening.

At the opening of this performance, Ravi Shankar demonstrates the ascending and descending scales that form the basis of this *raga*. Note that these scales are not identical; the descending scale has more notes than the ascending one and also more up-and-down motion. Note also the small bends and ornaments that he applies to certain notes to give them a distinct flavor; these are also part of the voicing of the scale.

A *raga* solo always begins with the sounding of the tones of the *raga* scale in descending motion. Then, throughout the first three unmetered sections, the soloist freely improvises themes using the tones of this particular *raga*. Each *raga* has scale tones that are more important than others; you can hear during the improvisations that Shankar lingers on certain tones longer, or decorates them with brief upward or downward movements in pitch while basically remaining on the same note. These key notes are the ones that will be used to build the principal melody of the *raga*, known as a *gat* (see below).

A performance of a *raga* features improvisation. Improvisation was also a typical practice in nineteenth-century Europe among virtuoso instrumentalists and composers, such as

Frédéric Chopin, Franz Liszt, and the American artist Louis Moreau Gottschalk (see chapters 35 and 36). The *raga* improvisations gain in intensity throughout and culminate in the statement of the principal theme of the *gat,* which is a short, composed melody.

A Triple Texture

In addition to the texture created by the sitar's numerous strings, Hindustani music requires three players to produce the layers of musical activity: a melodic soloist (sitar or other instrument), a separate drone instrument, and an accompanying drummer. *Raga* performance by a sitarist is always accompanied by two instruments: the *tambura* and the *tabla*. The **tambura** is a plucked lute like the sitar, but it has four to six strings and is used only to provide a drone. When the sitar is playing only over the drone, the texture is considered as **drone harmony**.

The **tabla** is a set of two drums struck with the fingertips. The *tabla* enters in the fourth and final section of the *raga,* when the meter becomes established. After the *tabla* enters, the texture is homophonic when the drumming supports the *gat,* although it can be considered to be polyphonic when the *tabla* makes percussive lines independently of the sitar melodies. The *tabla* player is able to vary the pitch of each drum by pressing his hand against the drum head, creating a sliding sound something like the bending of the melody string on the sitar. So the *tabla* part can combine rhythm and melody, and can "answer" the melodies stated by the sitar.

Form by Four Sections. The improvisation of the *raga* takes place over four sections of music:

1. The *alap* is the introductory section. The soloist is accompanied only by the *tambura.* The *alap* section allows a free-ranging exploration of the *raga* without a regular meter

Ravi Shankar and his daughter, Anoushka.

Mladen Peric/Lebrecht Music & Arts Photo Library

or pulse. It starts out in free rhythm and increases through a series of plateaux until the listener has a sense of a regular rhythmic pulse.

2. The *jor* is the section of the pulsed improvisation that develops from the *alap*. The *jor* tempo is faster than the *alap*, and the density of the rhythm increases.

3. The *jhala* section, the second type of pulsed improvisation, involves repeatedly striking a *jhala* (drone) string on the sitar.

4. The *gat tora* section introduces the meter set by the *tabla* drums. The *gat*, as mentioned above, is a short composed melody, and the primary theme of the song. *Tora* are the alternated, improvised passages between the *gat* statements.

Rhythm from Free to Established

Tala are fixed, repeated cycles of pulses. Certain pulses receive accents and are thus more important than the others. *Tala* is absent from *alap, jor,* and *jhala* sections, because these sections build from free rhythm to a constant unmetered pulse. The *tala* always is established at the *gat tora* section of a *raga*. As Shankar notes, the basic rhythm can be played at various speeds, in this case at a medium and fast tempo.

There are many *tala* patterns. In *Raga Sindhi-Bhairavi*, the *tala* is *tintál*, a 16-beat cycle. The 16 beats are further broken down into groups of four, with the first beat of each grouping receiving extra emphasis: **1**-2-3-4 **5**-6-7-8 **9**-10-11-12 **13**-14-15-16. In the *gat tora*, the soloist and *tabla* player can exchange roles, one improvising for a rhythmic cycle or two, while the other plays the fixed melody or rhythmic pattern.

Now listen to this piece again, following the Listening Guide.

EXPAND YOUR PLAYLIST

Raga

Ravi Shankar

Three Ragas, Angel 67310.
First issued in 1956, this recording captures Shankar at his youthful prime playing three traditional ragas.

At Woodstock, BGO 117.
Three ragas recorded live at the famous 1969 rock festival.

Improvisations, Angel 67049.
Originally released in 1961, this album features Shankar playing with two American jazz musicians, Bud Shank on saxophone and Gary Peacock on bass. It represents an early attempt at "fusion" of North Indian *raga* and American jazz musics.

Anoushka Shankar

Anoushka, Angel 53729.
The 2000 debut album by Ravi's talented daughter is a program of original compositions in the style and spirit of classical *raga*.

Ali Akbar Khan

Khan is a master of the *sarod*, a 25-string fretless lute that features a skin head stretched over the gourd-shaped body. The use of metal strings and neck and the skin head produce a much sharper and louder sound than is heard on the sitar.

Signature Series No. 1: Three Ragas, Aamp 7500.
The "Signature Series" brings onto CD classic recordings by Khan and represents some of his best works. This CD includes the night *raga* "Chandranandan."

George Harrison, Ravi Shankar, and Others

The Concert for Bangladesh, Sony 4688352.
The famous live concert from 1971, featuring a wonderful traditional performance by Ravi Shankar.

Ravi Shankar *Raga Sindhi-Bhairavi*

Time	Melody	Texture	Form
0:00	Shankar demonstrates the *raga's* tones and tells the rhythmic pattern of the piece. In his narration, Shankar refers to "two pieces" of the *raga*: the first piece includes the *alap, jor,* and *jhala,* played in medium tempo; and the second piece is the *gat,* played quickly.		
0:28	After an opening strum down across the sympathetic strings, which are individually tuned to the tones of the *raga*, the piece begins with freely improvised short melodic phrases on the playing strings. Listen to how some phrases lead up to the highest tone of the *raga* while other phrases feature lower tones of the *raga*. Bending of the strings is used in an expressive and decorative style.	Drone harmony. The *tambura* continues providing a soft drone to the freely improvised introduction of the *raga* scale.	*Alap*
4:26	The soloist strikes a string to create a pulse and continues improvising now with a rhythmic pulsation.		*Jor*
4:54	The soloist features a repeatedly struck *jhala* string to build the first part of the piece to a climax.		*Jhala*
5:48	The *gat* theme begins with a brief flourish by the sitar, which is answered by the entrance of the *tabla*.	The drone continues; the introduction of the *tabla* drums creates a homophonic texture when the *tabla* supports the sitar's melodies	*Gat tora*
7:28	More improvisation is featured during this section. Listen to how the melody of the *gat* features more improvised variations as this section continues.	Homophonic	
11:26	Second, faster gat and final section of the raga. Improvisation is more quickly employed in this final section. The faster tempo helps build the performance to a climactic finish.	Homophonic	

Rhythm

Free rhythm

Rhythm established but in unmetered pulsations.

Rhythm continues in unmetered pulsations.

Tintál begins on the first tone of the *gat*. It is a 16-beat cycle. The *tabla* drums enter midway through the rhythm cycle.

Tintál rhythm cycle continues.

Tintál rhythm cycle continues with the final note struck by both the sitar and *tabla* on the first note of the *raga* and beat one of the rhythm cycle. The sitar concludes with a strum down across the sympathetic strings.

Student FAQs

What are sympathetic strings? How do they work?

A sound wave creates physical movement in the air around it. When a string is plucked, its vibrations move through the air; if another string is nearby, even if it is not touched by a pick or finger, it is set into vibration by the original sound. This is described as a "sympathetic vibration," although of course the second string doesn't feel any sympathy for the first!

How are drone strings different from sympathetic strings?

Both sympathetic and drone strings play only one note and are not "fretted" by the sitar player. However, the drone strings are regularly played with the pick to sound throughout the piece. Sympathetic strings are never struck; rather, they simply vibrate on their own when the sound of another string sets them into motion.

How does a sitar player play different ragas if each raga has a different set of scale notes?

The sitar player can adapt his instrument to different scales by moving the frets on the fingerboard. Unlike a guitar, that has frets permanently placed into the neck, the sitar's frets are arched metal pieces attached to the back of the neck by thick twine to stay in place. To play a different scale, it is easy to slide the frets into different positions.

35

Giuseppe Verdi
La Traviata, Act I, selection

)))) *Listen to This*

Melody

Listen to the contrast between the melodic styles of the recitative and the aria. Violetta, a high-class prostitute, thinks she may be falling in love with Alfredo, a young gentleman she has just met at a party. Alone back in her apartment, she moves from recitative at the beginning—simple, declamatory, syllabic—to a virtuosic aria at the end. Her singing is interrupted by Alfredo, whom she hears but does not see singing his own aria to her. At the end of this excerpt, then, we hear two separate melodies—two separate arias—performed simultaneously.

Word-Music Relationships

Listen to the contrast between the introspective nature of the opening recitative and the growing exuberance of the music that leads into the aria. Note in particular Verdi's setting of the key word "*gioir*" ("enjoy"), set melismatically and in an extremely high register. Listen for the changes in tempo and melody later in the aria that reflect Violetta's attraction to Alfredo.

his scene from Verdi's opera *La Traviata* ("The Lost One") takes us on an emotional roller coaster. Violetta, a high-class prostitute in 1840s Paris, has fallen in love with Alfredo, a young gentleman who has also fallen in love with her. But Violetta is already suffering from the consumption (tuberculosis) that will eventually kill her. She knows her days are numbered, and she must decide whether to keep her freedom or commit to one man alone (Alfredo). The music she sings here ranges from uncertainty and fear of abandonment to the ecstasy of freedom to the crippling pain of love.

Verdi projects these profoundly contrasting emotions through a variety of singing styles. In this scene, we hear passages of declamatory, syllabic recitative flowing in and out of more lyrical, aria-like sections. We hear spectacularly virtuosic singing and extremely high notes—the kind that can sometimes break glass—and a moment later, simple, declamatory song. By writing long units of music that encompass both lyrical and declamatory moments, Verdi is able to move the plot forward (through recitative) and at the same time provide plenty of space for both the lyrical and virtuosic singing that opera audiences love so dearly. In this scene, in fact, Violetta's aria becomes a duet, for about halfway through this scene, Alfredo joins in. We do not see him onstage—he is singing his serenade of love to her from the street up to her balcony. This is a melody Alfredo had sung to her earlier in Act 1, and the combined sound of Alfredo's voice and this hauntingly lyrical melody causes Violetta to doubt her own resolve to live freely, alone and independent of anyone else's demands.

Verdi's *La Traviata* exemplifies the best elements of nineteenth-century Italian opera. It showcases the voice and uses the orchestra sparingly but effectively. Above all, it is dramatically realistic—who has not been torn between the desire for freedom and the pull of love?— and musically satisfying. Even if we do not understand the words, we can hear the sound of the emotions expressed by the singers.

Melody: Declamatory, Lyrical, Virtuosic

Verdi uses three distinct types of melody in this brief scene:

- **Declamatory.** Violetta begins her monologue by singing in the declamatory style of accompanied recitative. The melody is syllabic, making the text easy to understand. The melody is quite simple: at one point, Violetta sings the same note repeatedly, as if talking to herself—which, in fact, she is. The focus here is on the text.

- **Virtuosic.** At the exclamation *"Gioir!"* ("Take pleasure!"), the music suddenly becomes melismatic. The text is not so easy to understand at this point, for intelligibility has taken a back seat to virtuosic display. Violetta hits some extremely high notes (at 0:36 and 0:56) and navigates through difficult runs at a rapid pace. When the aria begins (at 1:07), the orchestra introduces the principal melody but then gives way to Violetta, who continues to sing in a highly virtuosic style throughout the aria portion of the scene. When a soprano sings this role well, few things can be more thrilling in the world of opera.

- **Lyrical.** When Alfredo (or to be more precise, Alfredo's voice) enters the scene, we hear a very different kind of singing. The tempo is slower, the notes are longer and smoother, and the declamation is for the most part syllabic. There are no enormous leaps to the extreme end of the tenor's vocal range, no breathtaking runs. The music is sustained and lyrical.

Word-Music Relationships: Signs of Contemplation, Ecstasy, Love

Like every good opera composer, Verdi captures the drama of the text through music. The contrasting styles of singing noted above—declamatory, virtuosic, and lyrical—correspond to the emotional states of the characters singing them. When Violetta is unsure of what to do, she sings in recitative. But at the moment when she decides to devote herself to a life of pleasure, her whole manner shifts quite suddenly. When she sings *"gioir"* ("enjoy"), we can almost feel with her the bodily pleasure she takes in singing the word, lingering over it, repeating it, hitting the highest range of her register. Even if we do not understand the word itself, we know that her emotion is one of ecstasy. She reinforces this sense with the way she goes on to sing the word *"vortici"* ("vortices," in the phrase: "Perish in the vortices of pleasure!"), spiraling downward from a high note to a low one.

Love—emotional love, as opposed to merely physical love—appears in the guise of Alfredo's lyrical melody. Dramatically, the sound of Alfredo's voice derails Violetta's ecstatic singing. She suddenly shifts to her original mood of contemplation and sings in the manner of recitative once again, punctuating the phrases of Alfredo's melody. When she once again rejects the path of emotional commitment and returns to her ecstatic, virtuosic style of singing (2:43), she sings a variation of the aria's opening text and music that is even more spectacular than before. This highly virtuosic moment of intensification is motivated by the drama itself, for Violetta has contemplated her choices (as heard in the sections of accompanied recitative) and opted for pleasure (as heard in her virtuosic singing).

With these points in mind, listen to this scene once again, using the Listening Guide.

The Russian-born soprano Anna Netrebko as Violetta in a production of *La Traviata* at the Salzburg Festival in 2005. New opera productions often update the scenery and staging of the original.
© CORBIS. All Rights Reserved

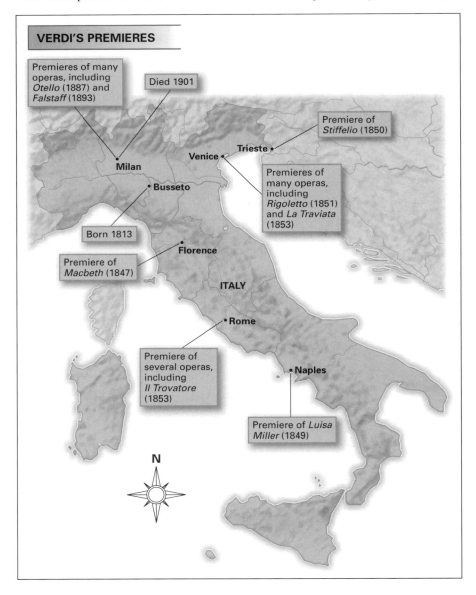

VERDI'S PREMIERES

Premieres of many operas, including *Otello* (1887) and *Falstaff* (1893)

Died 1901

Premiere of *Stiffelio* (1850)

Trieste

Venice

Milan

Premieres of many operas, including *Rigoletto* (1851) and *La Traviata* (1853)

Busseto

Born 1813

Florence

Premiere of *Macbeth* (1847)

ITALY

Rome

Premiere of several operas, including *Il Trovatore* (1853)

Naples

Premiere of *Luisa Miller* (1849)

N

Giuseppe Verdi (1813–1901)

THE COMPOSER AS SOCIAL REFORMER

The story of *La Traviata* mirrors Giuseppe Verdi's own life in certain respects. Audiences were scandalized to see the portrayal of an unwed couple living together, but this is exactly the situation in which Verdi found himself while composing *La Traviata.* He and Giuseppina Strepponi, a soprano, had been living together openly since 1848; they eventually married (in 1859), but Verdi experienced first-hand the same kind of scorn cast at those who, like his operatic characters Violetta and Alfredo, defy social conventions.

Through his art, Verdi sought to reform political conventions as well. Several of his operas incorporate thinly veiled appeals for the unification of Italy, which at the time was still a loose confederation of small states, many of them under the domination of the Austrian Empire. The chorus of captive Israelites in ancient Babylon in Verdi's *Nabucco* (1842) became the unofficial anthem of the simmering Italian uprising that would eventually liberate and unify Italy. Verdi himself was elected to the newly constituted Italian parliament in 1860, though by his own admission he spent little time there. He was too busy fulfilling commissions for new operas from around Europe, including France, Russia, and even Egypt. His *Aïda* (1871), set in ancient Egypt, was written to celebrate the opening of the Suez Canal.

Giuseppe Verdi
Archives Larousse, Paris, France/The Bridgeman Art Library

Julia Roberts and Richard Gere at the opera house in the 1990 film *Pretty Woman.* The opera they are watching is Verdi's *La Traviata,* which provides the basis for much of the plotline of *Pretty Woman.*

For all his accomplishments, Verdi remained a private and modest individual. A few years before his death, he established a home for retired musicians unable to support themselves, and he consigned all royalties for the 30 years after his death to this institution.

PLAYLIST: VERDI

Il Trovatore ("The Troubadour"). An opera about a series of loves and rivalries among a group of gypsies.

Rigoletto. An opera about a hunchback court jester (Rigoletto) and a lascivious duke.

Aïda. An opera commissioned to celebrate the opening of the Suez Canal; the story takes place in ancient Egypt.

Requiem. A Mass for the dead, composed in honor of the Italian writer Alessandro Manzoni, this work is for chorus, soloists, and orchestra. It is quite operatic in its style, despite its being written for the church.

Giuseppe Verdi *La Traviata,* Act I, selection

Time	Character	Original Italian Text	English Translation	Melody Melodic Style
0:00	Violetta	Follie! Delirio vano è questo! Povera donna, sola, abbandonata In questo popoloso deserto Che appellano Parigi, Che spero or più? Che far degg'io?	It's madness! Empty delirium! A poor woman, alone, abandoned In this populated wasteland They call Paris; What can I now hope? What should I do?	Accompanied recitative (syllabic, many repeated notes)
0:26		Gioir! Di voluttà ne' vortici perir!	Take delight! Perish in the vortices of pleasure!	Virtuosic
0:49		Gioir!	Take delight!	
1:07		Sempre libera degg'io Folleggiare di gioia in gioia, Vo' che scorra il viver mio Dei sentieri del piacer.	Always free I must Frolic from pleasure to pleasure, I want to glide through my life Along the paths of pleasure.	Aria
1:31		Nasca il giorno, o il giorno muoia, Sempre lieta ne' ritrovi,	As each day dawns, or as each day dies,	
1:44		A diletti sempre nuovi Dee volare il mio pensier.	I shall always be joyful in discovering Constantly new pleasures that make my spirit soar.	
2:06	Alfredo [underneath the balcony]	Amor è palpito …	Love is the pulse	Aria (to words and a melody Alfredo had sung to Violetta earlier in the opera).
2:14	Violetta	Oh!	Oh!	Accompanied recitative

Word-Music Relationships

Violetta contemplates and sings in declamatory manner.

Resolved to dedicate herself to pleasure, she begins to sing virtuosically.

Continues to sing in a virtuosic fashion

Lyrical melody: long, sustained notes, no high leaps or rapid runs

Violtetta contemplates her options once again, and she returns to a more declamatory style of singing.

(continued)

Time	Character	Original Italian Text	English Translation	Melody Melodic Style
2:15	Alfredo	… dell'universo intero …	… of the entire universe …	Aria
2:22	Violetta	L'amore!	Love!	Accompanied recitative
2:24	Alfredo	Misterioso, altero, Croce e delizia al cor.	Mysterious, proud, The torment and delight of the heart.	Aria
2:43	Violetta	Follie!	It's madness!	Accompanied recitative (resumes)
2:58		Gioir!	Take delight!	Virtuosic
3:14		Sempre libera degg'io Folleggiare di gioia in gioia, Vo' che scorra il viver mio Dei Sentieri del piacer.	Always free I must Frolic from pleasure to pleasure, I want to glide through my life Along the paths of pleasure…	Aria
3:26		Nasca il giorno, o il giorno muoia, Sempre lieta ne' ritrovi,	As each day dawns, as each day dies, I shall always be joyful in discovering	
3:40		A diletti sempre nuovi Dee volare il mio pensier	Constantly new pleasures That make my spirit soar.	
4:02	Alfredo	Amor è palpito … dell'universo intero…	Love is the pulse … of the entire universe… [transl. MEB]	Aria

**Word-Music
Relationships**

Once again, Violettta rejects emotional love and returns to a virtuosic style of singing.

We briefly hear both voices at the same time, each singing in its own way.

Student FAQs

Can high notes like the one in this aria really break glass?

Yes, although crystal is easier to break than glass. If you tap a fine crystal wineglass, you will hear a tone: this is the pitch that corresponds to the structures of the crystals that make up the glass. If a singer hits precisely this pitch and sings loudly enough, the glass can break. The crystals in a normal pane of glass, or in a beer bottle, are irregular enough to resist this kind of breakage.

Are operas amplified with microphones and speakers when they are performed?

Sometimes they are, especially if they're being performed outside or in an extremely large arena. But for the most part, opera companies tend to avoid amplified sound. Opera singers are trained to fill large spaces with their voices, and most opera lovers want to hear voices in their purest form. Even the very best amplification systems distort sound in subtle ways.

CULTURAL CONTEXT

The Diva

"Diva" is an Italian word that means "goddess" and in the world of opera, it is used to describe that small handful of singers in each generation whose voices and personalities together capture the imagination of opera lovers. Some of the great divas of the last 50 years include Maria Callas, Joan Sutherland, Marilyn Horne, and Leontyne Price.

The diva is more than just a singer: she is a phenomenon, a force whose life story fascinates as much as her artistic accomplishments. The soprano Maria Callas (1923–77) attracted an enormous following during her lifetime, and through her recordings, her reputation has grown still greater. She remains one of the top-selling operatic vocalists to this day, more than 30 years after her death.

The voice was spectacular, with an enormous range, a huge variety of colors, and an unmistakable sound that belonged to her and to no other soprano. Her personal life was equally distinctive. She was notoriously temperamental and demanding, and she was romantically linked for many years to Aristotle Onassis, a Greek shipping magnate. But when Onassis abandoned Callas in 1968 to marry Jacqueline Kennedy, widow of the late U.S. president, the diva was once again in the news, even though she had retired from the stage three years before.

There is a male counterpart to the diva—the divo—but the image has not sparked nearly the same response in audiences. The idea of the diva, however, has extended itself beyond the opera house to include any female entertainer who becomes larger than life and whose off-stage persona is as eagerly

American-born Greek soprano Maria Callas as Violetta in a 1958 production of Verdi's *La Traviata*.

followed as her on-stage presence. There is no official roster of divas, but any list of recent ones would have to include such figures as Bette Davis, Joan Crawford, Lucille Ball, Judy Garland, Marilyn Monroe, Elizabeth Taylor, and Cher. Their fans are devoted beyond all measure, and their flamboyant personalities, both on and off screen, sustain a major part of that appeal.

 EXPAND YOUR PLAYLIST

The Art of the Diva

A comparison of different artists performing the same work—here, the excerpt from Verdi's *La Traviata*—quickly reveals the enormous difference singers can make in bringing a work to life. Listen for differences in interpretation—tempo, rhythm, articulation, dynamics—and above all, the quality of the voice itself.

Renata Tebaldi (1922–2004) was widely perceived as the greatest rival of Maria Callas. Like Callas and Sutherland, she excelled in Italian opera. Opera d'Oro 1276.

Joan Sutherland (b. 1926) was one of the great sopranos of her generation until her retirement from the stage in 1990. Born in Australia, she established her reputation singing Italian opera of

the nineteenth century. The Italians dubbed her "La stupenda" ("The stupendous one"). Decca 430491.

Kiri Te Kanawa (b. 1944) began her career in her native New Zealand singing in clubs. She is of both Maori and European descent and was made Dame Commander of The Order of the British Empire in 1982. Philips 464982.

Anna Netrebko (b. 1971) was born in St. Petersburg, Russia, and became an Austrian citizen in 2006. She has entranced audiences around the world with both her voice and striking physical appearance. DG 000692209.

36

Richard Wagner
The Valkyrie, Act III, selection ("Wotan's farewell")

Listen to This

Texture

Listen to the relationship between the voices and the orchestra. In traditional opera, the orchestra supports the voice; in Wagner's operas, the two blend into a single unit.

Word-Music Relationships

Listen for the return of certain musical themes or fragments of themes and their relationship to what is being sung or acted on the stage. Wotan, the chief god in Norse mythology, punishes Brünnhilde, his daughter, by depriving her of her supernatural powers and placing her in a deep sleep, surrounded by a ring of fire.

The excerpt here is the closing scene of *The Valkyrie* (*Die Walküre*), the second opera in a cycle of four operas known as *The Ring of the Nibelungs* (*Der Ring des Nibelungen*). The libretto, by Wagner himself, draws heavily on northern European mythology, including many of the same sources used by J.R.R. Tolkien in his *Lord of the Rings* (see "Wagner and Tolkien: A Tale of Two Rings," p. 319).

Wagner's *Ring of the Nibelungs* traces the fate of a magic ring that has supreme powers of both good and evil. There are many strands running through the plot. In *The Valkyrie,* the principal characters are Wotan, the chief of all gods, and his daughter Brünnhilde, a warrior-like Valkyrie. Against Wotan's explicit command, Brünnhilde has interceded on behalf of a human couple (Siegmund and Sieglinde). Enraged, Wotan condemns his daughter to death. But she pleads for a lesser sentence, and because she is his favorite offspring, Wotan relents. He strips Brünnhilde of her godlike powers, encloses her in a deep sleep, and surrounds her with a ring of fire that can be crossed only by an individual who has no fear of Wotan's spear, an object which represents his authority over the universe. As it turns out, in the next opera of the *Ring* cycle, Brünnhilde will be awakened by Siegfried, who in the meantime has in fact shattered Wotan's spear. For the moment, though, all this still lies in the future. In the scene here, a Wotan full of mixed emotions bids farewell to his beloved Brünnhilde, puts her into a deep sleep, and then summons Loge, a shifty, firelike figure, to create the circle of magic fire that will protect her from ordinary mortals, who would fear the fire.

Texture: The Relationship of Voice and Orchestra

Wagner and Verdi were contemporaries, but the styles of singing in their operas are very different. In Verdi's *La Traviata,* the voices predominate over the orchestra and dazzle with their virtuosic runs, elaborate melismas, and spectacular high notes. Wagner felt that this kind of singing sacrificed the intelligibility of the text (the libretto) for the sake of musical effect. Wagner, in fact, considered conventional opera—by Mozart, Verdi, and others—to be based on a fundamentally false premise: that the words being sung constituted little more than an excuse for virtuosic singing. The "error of opera," Wagner declared, was that "a means of expression"—the music—had become an end in its own right while the goal of that expression—the drama—"had been made a means." Wagner wanted to restore dramatic integrity to opera by creating a style of singing that was at once musically satisfying and readily intelligible. Thus in Wagnerian opera, the vocal writing tends to be more syllabic—one note per syllable of text—and not nearly so virtuosic. There is also very little repetition of text: just as actors in a spoken drama rarely repeat their lines, singers typically sing their words only once. The melodies also tend to be more rhythmically fluid, avoiding any strong sense of periodic phrase structure.

The Valkyrie, Act III: Wotan leaves Brünnhilde asleep within a ring of magic fire; only a hero with no fear of Wotan's spear will brave the flames to awaken her.
Bayreuther Festspiele, Jochen Quast/AP Wide World Photos

In a particularly memorable turn of phrase Wagner called the drama—the events transpiring on the stage—"deeds of music made visible." What happens on the stage, in other words, is a tangible reflection of what is going on in the orchestra pit. Ideally, then, one should be able to follow the course of a Wagnerian music drama through the music alone, without the aid of words, by tracing the fate of its various musical ideas. These musical ideas would eventually come to be known as *Leitmotifs* (see below).

Word-Music Relationships: The Themes and the Drama

Minimizing virtuosity and projecting the text more clearly were only two of Wagner's strategies for integrating text, voices, and instruments. Another important element of Wagnerian opera is the technique of **Leitmotif**, a brief musical phrase or idea connected dramatically to some person, event, or idea in the drama. These "leading motifs" are meant to lead—direct—our minds in such a way as to help us understand what we see happening onstage. A modern example of this technique is found in the Star Wars movies: every time Darth Vader appears on screen, we hear the theme associated specifically with him. In the excerpt here, the bright but constantly shifting music heard at 0:09, 0:31, 1:00, etc., is consistently associated with the character of Loge, who in the world of northern European mythology is half-creature, half-flame, a cunning figure who resists taking on solid shape. The musical *Leitmotif* for Loge reflects this unstable nature: the theme, like the character himself, darts around and avoids any clearly defined shape. Thus, whenever we hear Loge's *Leitmotif*—his "signature tune," as it were—we know that Loge or fire (or both) are about to figure in the plot.

The other *Leitmotifs* heard in this excerpt are the following:

1. **Wotan's spear** (0:00-0:07, 0:27-0:31). This is a steady, confident, downward-striding figure in the brass. The character of this theme captures the solidity and confidence of Wotan's authority, in contrast to the flitting, ever-changing form of Loge's fire-music. All the laws of the world are carved on Wotan's spear; in the excerpt here, it represents Wotan's duty to punish Brünnhilde, who has broken one of these laws.

2. **Sleep** (1:37-1:51). Also a descending line, but this time it is played softly by winds and high strings (as opposed to the loud brass of Wotan's spear). The sleep *Leitmotif* is also highly **chromatic**. This means that it contains many notes that do not naturally occur in the scale or key area on which it is based. These extra notes undermine the sense of a harmonic center or goal. This motif thus gives the impression of gentle falling, as in falling asleep. Even if you don't play the piano, you can produce a chromatic line by

simply playing any series of adjacent notes—both black keys and white keys—in succession. You'll notice that no matter where you stop, there is no sense of closure, no center of melodic or harmonic gravity. This is the essence of chromaticism.

3. **The Sword** (2:01-2:29, 2:32-2:58). The sword is the magic talisman that Siegfried will eventually use to shatter Wotan's spear. The theme is loud, bright, and confident, rather like a fanfare. Wotan sings it to the words "Whoever fears the point of my spear shall never pass through the fire!" Siegfried, brandishing the magic sword, is the one mortal who has no fear of Wotan's spear; thus when Wotan sings this *Leitmotif*, he is (consciously? unconsciously?) anticipating the future. The words do not tell us this, but the music does.

4. **Fate** (3:49-3:55, 3:56-4:02). A brief, open-ended, rather questioning phrase associated throughout the *Ring* with the idea of destiny, of what must be.

"Magic fire" leitmotif
(piccolo, strings, harp)

"Fate"
leitmotif
(brass)

Of particular importance is the way in which these *Leitmotifs* transform themselves and combine with one another. These are not inert themes, but flexible ideas that are developed in much the same way that themes in the development section of a sonata-form movement are developed.

Now listen to this selection again, using the Listening Guide.

CULTURAL CONTEXT

Wagner and Tolkien: A Tale of Two Rings

J.R.R. Tolkien vehemently denied any connection between his *Lord of the Rings* and Wagner's *Ring of the Nibelungs*. "Both rings were round, and there the resemblance ceases," he once declared. But the parallels are too strong for us to accept this assertion at face value. We know, in fact, that Tolkien collaborated on a translation of *The Valkyrie* with his friend C.S. Lewis (author of *The Chronicles of Narnia*); unfortunately, the translation was never finished.

Tolkien may or may not have borrowed directly from Wagner, but both artists drew on the same Nordic myths for

Nikolai Putilin performs as Alberich with the Kirov Opera. Alberich, the dwarf in Wagner's *Ring of the Nibelungs*, owns the magic ring for a brief time; he wins it by renouncing love, but it is later stolen from him.
Photo by Brian Ach/WireImage/Getty Images, Inc.

Gollum (Andy Serkis) holds the Ring in Peter Jackson's film adaptation of Tolkien's *Lord of the Rings*.
© New Line/Everett Collection

their subject matter. Thus the characters, events, and themes of the two works exhibit striking similarities. For example:

1. Each cycle consists of four works, the first of which (Wagner's *Das Rheingold,* Tolkien's *The Hobbit*) serves as a prelude to the central sequence of three.
2. In both cycles, the ring holds great power but also brings grief to any owner who covets that power.
3. The plots center on efforts to own and control the ring.
4. Both cycles begin in a state of innocence (the Rhine; the Shire) that is corrupted and then ultimately restored.
5. Both cycles feature giants, dragons, dwarves who are great metalworkers, a riddling match, and a shattered sword recast into one even more powerful.

Richard Wagner *The Valkyrie*, Act III, selection ("Wotan's farewell")

Time	Original German text	English translation
0:00	*Wotan, having put Brünnhilde into a deep sleep, kisses her on her closed eyes and turns away from her slowly. Then he strides with solemn resolution to the middle of the stage and points his spear toward a massive, rocky cliff.)*	
0:09	Loge, hör'! Lausche hieher! Wie zuerst ich dich fand, als feurige Glut, wie dann einst du mir schwandest, als schweifende Lohe; wie ich dich band, bann ich dich heut'!	Loge, listen! Listen here! As I found you first, a fiery ember, as you once fled from me, a flitting flame; as I tamed you, so I call on you today!
0:33	Herauf, wabernde Loge, umlodre mir feurig den Fels!	Come, flickering glow, Surround the rock for me with flames!
0:48	*(He strikes his spear three times on the rock.)* Loge! Loge! Hieher!	*(He strikes his spear three times on the rock.)* Loge! Loge! Come!
1:00	*A flash of flame comes out of the rock and gradually swells into a glowing fire. Bright flickering erupts. Wotan directs the flame to form a circle around the sleeping figure of Brünnhilde. He then recedes into the background, even as the flames continue to glow.*	
2:01	Wer meines Speeres Spitze fürchtet, durchschreite das Feuer nie!	Whoever fears the tip of my spear shall never pass through the fire!
2:01	*He stretches out his spear as if to cast a spell, then looks with pain back upon the figure of Brünnhilde (2:57) and turns slowly to depart (3:25). He looks back once again (3:46), before disappearing through the fire (4:00). The curtain drops.*	

Word-Music Relationships
Musical Leitmotifs

- Spear (= Wotan's authority) at 0:00
- Loge (= fire) at 0:07

- Loge (= fire) at 0:09
- Spear (= Wotan's authority) at 0:27 on Wotan's command that Loge appear.

- Loge (= fire) at 0:31

- Loge (= fire) at 0:49

- Magic fire music at 1:00 a variant of Loge's Leitmotif, but much brighter and in a higher register, representing the flames that rise up to surround Brünnhilde
- Sleep at 1:37, representing Brünnhilde's sleep within the circle of fire

- The Sword at 2:01, again at 2:32. The music tells us that a sword will in fact eventually destroy Wotan's spear, and that Siegfried will awaken Brünnhilde from her sleep.
- Magic fire music throughout. This Leitmotif, in the high register, plays simultaneously with the one above and throughout this entire section.

- Magic fire music throughout.
- Fate at 3:49, 3:56 Wotan knows what must happen (fate), but it pains him nevertheless.

Student FAQs

How did Wagner's original audience know the meaning of the Leitmotifs when this work was first performed?

Wagner believed that anyone following the plot would associate the music they heard with the action on the stage. Whether they made these associations consciously or unconsciously did not matter to him. He was in fact quite reluctant to attach names to specific musical motifs, and only later did critics begin to compile guides to the *Leitmotifs* in *The Ring*.

Is it true that Brünnhilde is the Fat Lady in the saying "It ain't over 'til the Fat Lady sings"?

Yes. After Siegfried slays the dragon guarding the ring, he awakens Brünnhilde and gives her the ring as a token of his love, not understanding its full power. When Siegfried is killed in the last opera of *The Ring of the Nibelungs*, Brünnhilde sings an enormously long passage, at the end of which she throws the ring back into the Rhine, where it came from in the first place. When she finishes singing, *The Ring*—all four nights of it—is over.

Richard Wagner (1813–83)

THE COMPOSER AS RADICAL

Wagner is easily the most controversial composer who ever lived. Worshipped by some, reviled by others, the man and the music have provoked extreme reactions from the middle of the nineteenth century to the present day. Those who admired him during his lifetime considered him the most progressive composer of his day, advancing the harmonic idiom of music into new and exciting realms. His detractors assailed his music as ear-splitting noise. One caricature from the 1860s captures this sense of pain quite graphically (see image right).

Wagner's influence, moreover, went well beyond the realm of music. His operas are full of social and political ideas. George Bernard Shaw, for one, interpreted the massive *Ring of the Nibelungs* as an allegory on capitalism and communism. *Tristan and Isolde* was seen by many as an impassioned plea for free love, an assault on the institution of marriage. And *Die Meistersinger von Nürnberg* has long been viewed as a monument to German political and cultural nationalism. Drawing on Wagner's well-documented anti-Semitism, the Nazis would later use his music to promote their own racial and social agendas.

Born in Leipzig, Wagner immersed himself in the music of Beethoven and secured a series of increasingly prestigious appointments as a conductor. His participation in the uprisings of 1848, however (see chapter 31) forced him to flee to Switzerland to avoid arrest. After living in exile there for a decade, he won the support of King Ludwig II of Bavaria, who spared no expense to support the composer and his art. The final phase of Wagner's life centered around Bayreuth, a small city about halfway between Munich and Berlin, the respective capitals of Bavaria and Prussia. "Germany" had only recently become a political reality, and it was Wagner's aim to build in Bayreuth a *Festspielhaus*—a "festival drama house"—that would unify Germany culturally as well. Wagner oversaw every detail of the building and the performances to be held within it. Thus, when the *Ring* received its premiere there in 1876, Wagner could legitimately claim not only to have written the libretto and the music but to have built the opera house as well. He died in Venice in 1883, and his descendants still control the *Festspielhaus* in Bayreuth.

Wagner hammers away at the modern ear, using a quarter note to inflict pain.

Leonard de Selva/Corbis/Bettmann

PLAYLIST: WAGNER

The Ring of the Niebelungs (Der Ring des Nibelungen)
   The Rhine Gold (Das Rheingold)
   The Valkyrie (Die Walküre)
   Siegfried
   Twilight of the Gods (Götterdämmerung)
The Flying Dutchman (Der fliegende Holländer)
Tannhäuser
Lohengrin
Tristan und Isolde
Die Meistersinger von Nürnberg
Parsifal

Stations in Wagner's life.

 EXPAND YOUR PLAYLIST

Opera in the Nineteenth Century

Operas written in the nineteenth century form the core repertory of most opera houses. Italian opera (by Rossini, Bellini, Verdi, and Puccini, among others) dominated the stage across all of Europe, but operas in French (by Bizet) and German (by Weber, Wagner, and others) had strong followings as well.

Italian Opera
* Giacchino Rossini: *The Barber of Seville (Il Barbiere di Siviglia)*. Like Mozart's *Marriage of Figaro,* this opera is based on a play by Beaumarchais and even includes many of the same characters (Figaro, the Count, the Countess).

* Vincenzo Bellini: *Norma.* A Romeo-and-Juliet-style story set in ancient Gaul. Norma is a Druid, her lover a Roman.

* Giuseppe Verdi: *La Traviata.* See chapter 35.

* Giaccomo Puccini: *La Bohème.* The story of struggling young artists, set in late nineteenth-century Paris. The Broadway musical *Rent* draws on the plotline of this opera.

* Giaccomo Puccini: *Madama Butterfly.* The story of the relationship between a young American naval officer and the Japanese woman he marries and then abandons.

French Opera
* Georges Bizet: *Carmen.* The story of an enchantress (Carmen) and her ill-fated lover (Don José), who is torn between love and duty.

German Opera
* Carl Maria von Weber: *The Free Shooter (Der Freischütz).* A hunter makes a pact with the devil to win a shooting competition, and with it, the hand of the woman he loves.

English Opera
* Arthur Sullivan: *The Pirates of Penzance.* The most successful operas in English in the nineteenth century were the operettas (literally, "little operas") by Arthur Sullivan and his librettist, W.S. Gilbert. Together, Gilbert and Sullivan created a long series of what we today call musicals: spoken dialogue interspersed with musical numbers (arias, duets, choruses, etc.).

37

Johannes Brahms
Symphony no. 4 in E Minor, op. 98, finale

Listen to This

Form

Listen for the way in which the very brief theme at the beginning—it lasts only 15 seconds—is varied across the entire movement, which is in the form of **theme and variations**. Also listen for the change in tempo (to slow) and mode (to major) in the middle of the movement.

Timbre

Each variation has its own distinctive sound, depending on which instrument or group of instruments predominates. Listen for the ways in which the various groups of instruments—strings, winds, brass, and percussion—at times work independently and at times engage in dialogue with one another. The textures created by these groupings are at times quite thick, at times quite transparent.

The finale of Brahms's Fourth Symphony is a kaleidoscope of emotions. Thirty short variations on a very short theme present a series of constantly shifting moods. The theme makes its first appearance in a majestic, grandiose fashion in the brass. The first variation is subdued and reticent, played by the timpani and low brass. The winds create a new, more wistful mood when they join in for the second variation. The third variation is more rhythmically lively, and the violins take over with a lyrical counter-melody in the fourth variation. The shifting moods continue as each variation establishes its own sound world.

Brahms wrote only four symphonies, but all four are mainstays of today's concert repertory. His Fourth Symphony calls for a large orchestra that reflects the growing size of concert halls in the last decades of the nineteenth century. It also synthesizes the old and new in ingenious ways. Brahms takes both the form and theme of this movement from the Baroque era. Theme and variations form had been popular in Bach's time, and the theme itself is in fact derived from a work by Bach (see below). But Brahms creates harmonies, textures, and timbres that were novel in their day. The harmonies are highly chromatic at times, and the textures tend to be richly layered and dense. The timbre can range from the bright to the dark, but in this movement, more often than not, they veer toward a somber, serious kind of sound that many listeners find lush and—to use a metaphor drawn from the world of food—ripe. Brahms demands our attention when we listen, and his music repays the effort.

Form: Theme and Variations Plus

The theme consists of only eight notes. This type of form—many variations on a very short theme—was tremendously popular during the Baroque era. Purcell had used it in the ostinato bass of Dido's aria in Act I of *Dido and Aeneas* in the late seventeenth century (see chapter 10), and Johann Sebastian Bach had used this kind of structure in a number of works.

Brahms borrowed the theme from Bach's Cantata no. 150, and it is extremely simple. Notes 1–6 move up, step by step, then drop down (note 7), only to end up exactly where the theme had begun. This simplicity works to the listener's advantage, because Brahms subjects the theme to an increasingly complex series of variations. But because the theme itself is so simple, listeners can hear it more easily. This movement represents what might be called compositional virtuosity, for Brahms demonstrates his ability to construct a great deal out of very little.

There is no end of melodic richness in this movement. Each variation uses the eight notes of the theme as a framework for its own counter-themes. The texture throughout is strongly polyphonic, for in many variations we hear the original theme played against a new and different counter-melody. At other times, Brahms adds many additional notes around the theme, so that it is in effect embedded within a new and different theme (as in Variation 12). In still other variations, Brahms distributes the notes of the theme across different instruments.

On a larger scale, Brahms creates a **ternary form (ABA)** by making the middle variations (nos. 10–15) markedly different from the others. They are all slower, and the first three of them (nos. 13–15) are in E major rather than E minor. This creates a strong sense of contrast in the middle of the movement (the **B** section of the **ABA** form), reinforced by the clear return of the opening theme of the movement in variation no. 16 (the second **A** in the **ABA** form).

The Conductor

Exactly what does a conductor do? It's a good question, and the answer is not so obvious, particularly because most concertgoers tend to see only the conductor's back during performances.

Even from the back, however, conductors' styles can vary enormously. Some are like gymnasts on the podium: they jump, twist, crouch. Others are more reserved and seem to move scarcely at all. Some use a baton, others use only their hands.

For all these outward differences, all conductors have a basic responsibility of keeping performers playing together, in time. They do this by beating the basic meter of the music during performance: every player can see the conductor, so all the performers can play together. The more rhythmically complicated the work at hand, the greater the need for a conductor. In the finale of Brahms's Fourth Symphony, for example, Brahms calls on the orchestra to change to a slow tempo at Variation 12. But how slow? That is up to the conductor to decide, and the players follow the conductor's lead.

At a deeper level, conductors also shape the interpretation of the work at hand through such elements as dynamics, rhythm, texture, and timbre. Are the trumpets playing too loud? Are the flutes too soft? Are the violins entering sharply enough? These are just a few of the many questions conductors have to answer when rehearsing with an orchestra. And even in performance, there is room for spur-of-the-moment changes: holding a long note just a fraction of a second longer, slowing down just a little more, making a loud passage even louder.

Marin Alsop conducting. She uses a baton, which many orchestral musicians say helps them see the conductor's beat out of the corner of their eyes, which are otherwise focused on the notated music on their stands.
T Martinot/Lebrecht Music & Arts

No two performers play the same music exactly the same way: each has an individual style. This is true for conductors as well, whose instrument is in effect the orchestra. Listen to multiple recordings of the finale of Brahms's Fourth Symphony—or of any other work in this book, for that matter—and you will immediately realize the enormous freedom performers have in bringing a work of music to life.

Timbre: The Drama of Orchestration

Brahms also used orchestration to create a sense of forward movement and contrast among the 30 different variations. The winds and brass announce the theme together at the very beginning with great force. The focus then moves to the timpani and the plucked low strings (Variation 1), after which the winds join in (Variation 2), followed by the full orchestra (Variation 3). At times, a pair of variations share the same basic orchestration (Variations 5 and 6, Variations 8 and 9), but more often than not, each new variation differentiates itself from the one before through its timbre. The theme itself appears in all the different instruments (except timpani) at one point or another.

This work is remarkable in its emotional range. It embraces an entire sweep of moods that might be described as extending from angry at first, to brooding, energetic, melancholic, docile, pleading, devotional, anxious, triumphant—each listener will find slightly different adjectives. The last movement of Brahms's last symphony sums up an entire century of symphonic composition: its orchestration is rich, its textures varied, its harmonies wide-ranging.

Now listen to this symphony finale again, following the Listening Guide.

Johannes Brahms (1833–97)

THE COMPOSER AS HEDGEHOG

In an age of flamboyant composer-celebrities who wrote and talked endlessly about themselves and their own music, Johannes Brahms was by comparison a recluse. He preferred to let his works speak for themselves and remained an intensely private individual to the end of his life. One particularly revealing caricature of him done during his lifetime shows him walking next to a hedgehog: the prickly composer and prickly animal bear a striking resemblance.

Perhaps Brahms became a bit prickly because of the criticism he received during his lifetime. Part of this can be traced to the unrealistic expectations projected on him by no less a figure than Robert Schumann, editor of one of the leading music journals of the day (the nineteenth-century equivalent of *Rolling Stone* or *Spin*). Brahms was a virtually unknown 20-year-old when Schumann introduced him as the savior of music, a messiah who had arrived on the scene "fully developed," ready to assume the mantel of the deceased Beethoven. This publicity cut both ways for Brahms: he was an instant celebrity, but the public expected more than he was prepared to offer, at least at that point in his career. As in the musical world of today, the best artists can withstand criticism, and Brahms eventually proved that Schumann was right in the end. By the time he died in 1897, Brahms had become the last of the "three B's" of German music—Bach, Beethoven, Brahms—and he would be buried next to Beethoven in Vienna's Central Cemetery.

Brahms's links to Bach and Beethoven rest on more than mere alliteration. He was deeply interested in the music of the past, and in the music of the two other "B's" in particular. He helped edit works by Bach and zealously collected sketches by Beethoven. The finale of the Fourth Symphony, in a sense, represents Brahms's synthesis of the two: he presents Bach's technique of varying a brief theme within Beethoven's most challenging genre, the symphony. Brahms uses this traditional form and genre to create what is nevertheless a thoroughly modern work.

Brahms and the hedgehog. A contemporary caricature by Otto Bohler.
Lebrecht Music & Arts/Lebrecht Music & Arts Photo Library

PLAYLIST: BRAHMS

Symphony no. 1 in C Minor, op. 68

Symphony no. 2 in D Major, op. 73

Symphony no. 3 in F Major, op. 90

Piano Concerto no. 1 in D Minor, op. 15

Piano Concerto no. 2 in B-flat Major, op. 83

Violin Concerto in D Major, op. 77

A German Requiem, op. 45 (for chorus, orchestra, and soloists)

Clarinet Quintet in B Minor, op. 115

Johannes Brahms Symphony no. 4 in E minor, op. 98, finale

Form

Timbre

Time	Theme and Variations	Ternary Form	Timbre
0:00	Theme	**A** (E minor)	Winds and brass
0:15	Variation 1		Pizzicato (plucked) strings, with percussion and low brass
0:30	Variation 2		Winds join in
0:46	Variation 3		Full orchestra
1:01	Variation 4		Strings
1:18	Variation 5		Strings and winds
1:32	Variation 6		
1:48	Variation 7		High strings and winds
2:04	Variation 8		Strings and winds
2:20	Variation 9		
2:36	Variation 10		Strings and winds
2:53	Variation 11		Strings, winds, horns
3:14	Variation 12		Flutes, horn, and strings
3:57	Variation 13	**B** (E major)	Winds and strings in dialogue
4:37	Variation 14		Brass enter with hymn-like sound, all parts moving together in a slow, stately rhythm
5:17	Variation 15		Winds join in

Melody

Theme in high winds; long note values

Theme in pizzicato (plucked) strings

Theme stays in pizzicato (plucked) strings

Theme in violins

Theme in low strings; counter-melody in violins

Theme in low strings; counter-melody in high strings & winds

↓

Theme in low strings; counter-melody of dotted rhythms (short-LONG-short-LONG etc.) in high strings & winds

Theme in low strings; rapid figure in violins

Theme in strings; longer note values give the impression of slowing down

Theme in low strings; syncopated figure in high strings (off the beat)

Theme embedded within flute's counter-melody

Theme distributed among various instruments

Theme distributed among trombones.

↓

Johannes Brahms Symphony no. 4 in E minor, op. 98, finale

	Form		
Time	**Theme and Variations**	**Ternary Form**	**Timbre**
6:03	Variation 16	**A'** (E minor)	Return to opening theme: winds & brass, then strings join in
6:16	Variation 17		Strings (tremolo) and high winds in dialogue
6:28	Variation 18		Full orchestra
6:40	Variation 19		
6:53	Variation 20		
7:05	Variation 21		
7:19	Variation 22		High winds and low strings
7:31	Variation 23		Full orchestra
7:44	Variation 24		
7:57	Variation 25		Full orchestra, strings tremolo
8:11	Variation 26		Full orchestra
8:26	Variation 27		Winds and strings in dialogue
8:40	Variation 28		
8:54	Variation 29		
9:08	Variation 30		Full orchestra
9:29	Coda	Coda (E minor)	Full orchestra

Melody

Theme in high winds; new counter-melody in violins

Theme in syncopated high winds

Theme distributed among high winds

Theme distributed among various instruments; Strings with fast triplet figure (*1*-2-3-*1*-2-3-*1*-2-3)

Theme distributed among various instruments

Theme distributed among various instruments

Theme clearly presented in horns

Theme in high strings

Theme distributed among various instruments

Theme distributed among horns and winds; somewhat calmer

Theme embedded in counter-melody in strings

Theme embedded in counter-melody in winds

Theme embedded in pizzicato strings in syncopation

Theme distributed among various instruments counter-melodies in both strings and winds

Theme clearly stated in brass and winds at the beginning of this section, but the music continues beyond this in a free fashion for the first and only time in the movement.

Student FAQs

I can't always hear the theme. Is that a problem?

No. Brahms's self-imposed challenge was to say the same thing in a different way 30 times in a row. For this reason, he wanted to mask the theme often enough so that it would not become tiresome. Some of the variations in the **B** section (Variations 13-15) hide the theme so well it becomes very difficult to hear. As you become more familiar with the movement, you will probably hear the theme more clearly in most variations with each new listening.

Is there any consistent meter in this movement?

The theme and every variation are always in triple meter, though Brahms creates a good deal of variety by skillfully varying the underlying rhythms and (in the middle of the movement) the tempo.

EXPAND YOUR PLAYLIST

The Art of the Conductor

You can learn more about what goes into leading an orchestra by listening to recordings of the same work by different conductors. Here are some alternative performances of the finale of Brahms's Fourth Symphony. Listen carefully for different approaches to tempo, dynamics, phrasing, and balance among the instruments.

Felix Weingartner (1863–1942) was one of the leading conductors of his day. His style, in a recording made with the London Symphony Orchestra in 1938, reflects a more flexible approach to rhythm and phrasing than would be fashionable later in the century. Centaur 2128.

Arturo Toscanini (1867–1957) was born in Italy but emigrated to the United States in the late 1930s to escape the Fascist government. In New York, NBC created an orchestra expressly for Toscanini, and he made many recordings and radio broadcasts with it. His style of conducting attracted an almost cult-like following. RCA Red Seal 55838.

Leonard Bernstein (1918–90) was the first American-born conductor to lead the New York Philharmonic, one of the premier orchestras in the nation. A composer as well as a conductor, he was known for promoting modern music and the music of other American composers. Sony 61846.

Marin Alsop (b. 1956) is one of a growing number of female conductors who have enjoyed both artistic and commercial success. She is currently director of the Baltimore Symphony Orchestra. Her performance, recorded with the London Philharmonic Orchestra in 2007, combines both flexibility and drive. Naxos 8570233.

38

Antonin Dvořák
String Quartet in F Major, op. 96 ("American"), third movement

Listen to This

Timbre

Listen to the call-and-response of various combinations of the four instruments—two violins (high register), a viola (medium), and cello (low)—at the very beginning of the movement and at later points as well. Listen, too, for extended passages in which only the two highest or the two lowest of the four instruments are playing.

Melody

Listen for the folk-like sound of the various melodies of this movement. What makes this music sound like folk music?

Form

Consider all three principles of form—repetition, variation, and contrast—as you listen for the musical elements above. Can you identify the sections of the piece?

Antonin Dvořák wrote his String Quartet in F Major, op. 96, in Iowa, more than 5,000 miles from his native Prague. He spent the summer of 1893 in Spillville, a small town of about 350 inhabitants, most of them immigrants and children of immigrants from Dvořák's Bohemia. Dvořák was in the United States on a two-year contract as director of the National Conservatory of Music in New York City. His personal assistant, Josef Kovařík, an American of Czech descent, had grown up in Spillville, and he persuaded the composer to spend the summer there. Dvořák welcomed the opportunity for a change of scene.

Shortly after arriving in Iowa, Dvořák set out, by his own account, "to write something really melodious and simple." Of course, writing good melodies is not easy, and what seems simple is often difficult to craft. But he must have been inspired by his new surroundings, for in just a little over two weeks, he completed a four-movement string quartet he called the "American." The selection here is the third movement of this quartet.

Timbre: Call-and-Response Between Strings

Dvořák had been a professional violist earlier in his career, and he knew the instruments of the string quartet from the inside out. In the very opening of this movement, he creates a kind of call-and-response pattern that begins with two instruments (second violin and cello, 0:00) answered by the full ensemble (0:04). The music continues with the upper three instruments (0:07) punctuated by the lowest, the cello (0:08). This kind of back-and-forth between individual instruments or groups of instruments continues throughout the movement and creates timbral variety. Call-and-response is a basic element of many kinds of folk music, particularly in African music (see chapter 11) and music cultivated by the descendants of Africans in the Americas, such as the blues (see chapter 46). In emphasizing this kind of pattern, Dvořák was at the same time emphasizing the folk-like nature of his quartet.

Folk-Like Melodies

The movement features two principal melodies, each of which is based on a limited number of notes. The opening phrases of both melodies use only four different notes, and the consequent phrases introduce only two new ones. Although not strictly **pentatonic** (see chapter 25), these melodies convey a feeling of simplicity because they use fewer than the standard seven notes in the diatonic scale that is so common in Western music. In this way, Dvořák creates a folk-like sound. The clarity of the antecedent-consequent phrase structure (see chapter 21) also contributes to the apparent simplicity of the melodies.

The first part of the second principal theme consists of only *four* notes:

But what is the "folk" in question here? Like other composers of his time, Dvořák felt that composers should draw on the folk or indigenous music of their countries, and he wrote the "New World" Symphony and "American" String Quartet to provide examples for composers of the United States (see "The Composer Speaks"), using pentatonic melodies in both. Dvořák himself once observed that pentatonic melodies were common to music of African Americans, Native Americans, and (remarkably enough) "the music of Scotland." Pentatonic or quasi-pentatonic melodies also figure in the folk music of Dvořák's native Bohemia, so it is hard to say clearly which tradition this quartet represents. In any case, its unmistakably folk-like feel contrasts with the more formal sound of Haydn's string quartet from more than 100 years before.

Scherzo Form: Repetition, Variation, Contrast

This third movement is a **scherzo**. "Scherzo" is the Italian word for "joke," and a musical scherzo is a light-hearted movement in a fast tempo and in triple meter. Over the course of the nineteenth century, the scherzo gradually replaced the minuet (see chapter 21) as one of the internal movements of a four-movement cycle in a symphony, sonata, string quartet, or other similar instrumental work. The scherzo retained the basic **ABA** form of the minuet, but often with the addition of an extra trio section (**ABABA**), as in this particular movement. The overall form can be represented graphically in this way:

A	**B**	**A′**	**B′**	**A**
Scherzo Proper	Trio I	Scherzo Proper (varied)	Trio II (varied)	Scherzo Proper (literal repetition of A)

Dvořák uses all three principles of form in this movement:

- **Repetition**. The scherzo proper is repeated literally ("da capo") at the end of the movement. The movement thus ends with exactly the same section of music with which it began.

- **Variation**. Both the scherzo proper and the trio are subject to variation: **A** becomes **A′**, and **B** becomes **B′**.

- **Contrast**. **A** and **B** differ markedly in their melodies, harmonies (modes), and timbres. The differences in the melodies of **A** and **B** have already been noted above. The two sections are also in contrasting modes: **A** is consistently in F major, while **B** is consistently in F minor. The timbres of the two sections also contrast markedly: The **A** section is quite expansive, covering a wide register, while **B** tends to move in a more narrow range, with the instruments closer together.

Now listen to this movement once again, using the Listening Guide.

Antonin Dvořák String Quartet in F Major, op. 96 ("American"), third movement

Time	Melody	Form: Section	Timbre
0:00	Theme 1 = disjunct, clear antecedent/consequent phrase structure	**A** = Scherzo proper (F major)	Call-and-response interplay between individual instruments and groups of instruments
0:46	Theme 2 = narrow range, begins with only four notes; clear antecedent/consequent phrase structure	**B** = Trio I (F minor)	Passages for two instruments (0:46–0:52; 1:06–1:12) contrast with passages for all four instruments.
1:26	Theme 1, but this time it begins quietly, with the themes in different instruments from the first time around	**A′** = Variation of Scherzo proper: (F major)	
2:15	Theme 2, but this time it begins quietly and in a much higher register than before	**B′** = Trio II (in fact a variation of Trio I) (F minor)	Higher register than before. All four instruments together throughout
2:57	Theme 1	**A** = Literal repeat of Scherzo proper (F major)	

Student FAQs

Did Dvořák ever actually hear any music performed by Native Americans?

He did when he was in Iowa, although it's not entirely clear just what kind of Native Americans were performing, and we should remember that musical styles vary widely from tribe to tribe. We also know that Dvořák read at least one and probably more accounts of Native American music.

Why does the movement end so softly? It doesn't sound like a real ending.

Quiet endings are not all that uncommon, actually. Keep in mind that this is the third movement of a four-movement string quartet, and that a very lively finale begins shortly after this movement ends. By not ending this movement with a bang, Dvořák is able to start the next movement with one.

Antonin Dvořák (1841–1904)

IN SEARCH OF NATIONAL SOUNDS

Even before he arrived in the United States in 1892, Antonin Dvořák was known as a composer who drew widely on the folk music of his native Bohemia (corresponding roughly to today's Czech Republic). As director of the (now defunct) National Conservatory of Music, in New York City, he felt a responsibility to show American composers how to incorporate the characteristic sounds and inflections of the folk music of their own country. He studied with interest the melodies of African Americans—freed slaves and their first-generation descendants—and of Native Americans and discovered that pentatonicism figured prominently in both repertoires. He wrote pentatonic melodies into his next symphony, which quickly became known as the "New World" Symphony. Composers, critics, and audiences took note, for all were eager to find a way by which the United States could establish its own musical sound, distinct from the traditions of European music.

Dvořák was less interested in borrowing from specific African American or Native American songs than he was in seeking an idiom based in the spirit of all those who made music outside the concert hall, outside the traditions of "learned" music. He seems to have been seeking a kind of nationalism that would speak to the varied ethnic backgrounds of the American people, no matter what the color of their skin (see "The Composer Speaks"). In the end, though, in spite of being so closely associated with American music, Dvořák remained true to his own roots. His personal assistant, Josef Kovařík—the man who took him to Iowa—reports the composer as having made himself quite clear on this point:

> So I am an American composer, am I? I was, I am, and I remain a Czech composer. I have only showed them the path they might take—how they should work. But I'm through with that! From this day forward I will write the way I wrote before.*

*Josef Kovařík, quoted in Michael Beckerman, *New Worlds of Dvořák* (New York: Norton, 2003), p. 16.

Dvořák (right) and his family shortly after their arrival in the United States in 1892.
Lebrecht Music & Arts/Lebrecht Music & Arts Photo Library

PLAYLIST: DVOŘÁK

Piano Trio in E Minor, op. 90 ("Dumky")

Piano Quintet in A Major, op. 81

Cello Concerto in B Minor, op. 104

Slavonic Dance for Orchestra, op. 46, no. 8

Symphony in E Minor, op. 96 ("New World")

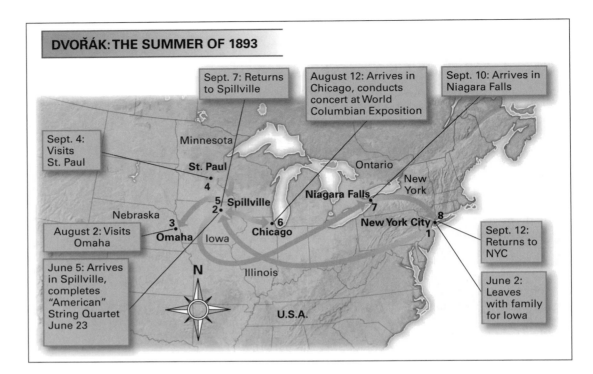

DVOŘÁK: THE SUMMER OF 1893

Sept. 7: Returns to Spillville

August 12: Arrives in Chicago, conducts concert at World Columbian Exposition

Sept. 10: Arrives in Niagara Falls

Sept. 4: Visits St. Paul

Minnesota

St. Paul
4

Ontario

New York

Niagara Falls
7

Spillville
5
2

Nebraska
3

Omaha

Iowa

Chicago
6

New York City
1
8

Sept. 12: Returns to NYC

August 2: Visits Omaha

June 5: Arrives in Spillville, completes "American" String Quartet June 23

N

Illinois

U.S.A.

June 2: Leaves with family for Iowa

Dvořák's travels in America, Summer 1893

The Sources of an American Musical Style

Two years after writing his "American" Quartet, Dvořák wrote an essay entitled "Music in America," published in *Harper's New Monthly Magazine.*

A while ago I suggested that inspiration for truly national music might be derived from the Negro melodies or Indian chants. I was led to take this view partly by the fact that the so-called plantation songs are indeed the most striking and appealing melodies that have yet been found on this side of the water, but largely by the observation that this seems to be recognized, though often unconsciously, by most Americans. All races have their distinctively national songs, which they at once recognize as their own, even if they have never heard them before. When a Tcech [Czech], a Pole, or a Magyar [Hungarian] in this country suddenly hears one of his folk-songs or dances, no matter if it is for the first time in his life, his eyes light up at once, and his heart within him responds, and claims that music as his own. So it is with those of Teutonic or Celtic blood, or any other men, indeed, whose first lullaby mayhap [perhaps] was a song wrung from the heart of the people. . . .

It matters little whether the inspiration for the coming folk songs of America is derived from the Negro melodies, the songs of the creoles, the red man's chant, or the plaintive ditties of the homesick German or Norwegian. Undoubtedly the germs for the best in music lie hidden among all the races that are commingled in this great country. The music of the people is like a rare and lovely flower growing amidst encroaching weeds. Thousands pass it, while others trample it under foot, and thus the chances are that it will perish before it is seen by the one discriminating spirit who will prize it above all else. The fact that no one has as yet arisen to make the most of it does not prove that nothing is there.

Antonin Dvořák, "Music in America," *Harper's New Monthly Magazine,* February 1895, pp. 433–434.

MUSIC IN PERFORMANCE

How to Make a Quartet

Forming a string quartet is really no different from putting together a rock band. Two or more players know one another well and look for others to fill out the group, musicians who can bring their own creative ideas to the table. And like rock bands, string quartets often transform themselves over time. The Juilliard String Quartet, based at the Juilliard Conservatory of Music in New York City, has over the course of more than 60 years featured two different first violinists, five second violinists, two violists, and three cellists.

Artistic collaborations invariably involve artistic differences: quartet members can (and often do) disagree about how to perform a particular work or a passage in a work, but the best groups work through these differences to create performances that are fresh and exciting. There is no conductor in a string quartet: the four players have to agree on just about everything, including where and what to perform. By the same token, a single player who has fundamentally different ideas about how to make music likely will not last very long in a quartet.

Not all quartets play the standard stringed instruments. The Kronos Quartet, formed in 1973 and based in San Francisco, was one of the first to use electronic as well as acoustical instruments and incorporated many special lighting and stage effects into their concerts. In 1991 the group started taking "roadies" on its tours to handle this end of its performances. More recently, bond (the group uses a lower-case "b" to avoid copyright

The group bond performing at the Classical Brit Awards, 2005. The instruments of this string quartet are electric, its repertory eclectic.
C. Christodoulou/Lebrecht Music & Arts

infringements with 007) has moved to exclusively electronic instruments (violins, viola, cello), performing a repertory that ranges from classical to pop to New Age. The group's first album sold more than two million copies. In 2001 bond performed with the tenor Luciano Pavarotti at his annual all-star charity concert and collaborated with the Royal Philharmonic Orchestra on their 2003 album *Classified*.

 EXPAND YOUR PLAYLIST

Nationalism in Nineteenth-Century Music

Dvořák was one of many composers working in the late nineteenth century who sought to infuse at least some of their works with nationalistic elements, though not necessarily from their own countries. Just as Dvořák, a Czech, wrote at times in an "American" style, Brahms (a German) sometimes wrote in a "Hungarian" style, and Chabrier (a Frenchman) wrote in a "Spanish" style.

Biedrich Smetana (1824–84), *The Moldau*. This symphonic poem paints a picture of the most important river in Smetana's native Bohemia (present-day Czech Republic).

Louis Moreau Gottschalk: *Union*. See chapter 33.

Johannes Brahms: *Hungarian Dances*. These piano pieces (later orchestrated by the composer) incorporate characteristic Hungarian rhythms and melodic turns of phrase. Brahms lived most of his life in Vienna, not far from present-day Hungary.

Alexander Borodin (1833–87): *Polovtzian Dances* from the opera *Prince Igor*. Borodin's native Russia extended eastward into Asia, and these dances capture its flavor.

Emmanuel Chabrier (1841–94): *Espana*. This single-movement work for large orchestra reflects the Frenchman Chabrier's fascination with Spain.

Nikolai Rimsky-Korsakov (1844–1908): *Scheherazade*. This suite for orchestra narrates, without words, episodes from a series of stories originating in ancient Persia, *The Book of One Thousand and One Nights*. Rimsky-Korsakov's music evokes many effects associated with music of the Near East.

MAKING CONNECTIONS: Music of the Classical Era and the Nineteenth Century

	Classical Era	Nineteenth Century
Texture	Both polyphonic and homophonic, but on the whole more homophonic	Both homophonic and polyphonic
Melody	Growing importance of periodic phrase structure in all genres of music, not just in dance	Periodic phrase structure continues, but also more fragmented thematic ideas; some use of pentatonic scales. Growing tendency toward virtuosic writing for both voices and instruments
Rhythm	More smoothly flowing melodies	Highly varied, from simple to complex
Timbre	Establishment of the modern orchestra (strings, winds, percussion)	Orchestra continues to grow, with addition of trombones, tubas, piccolos, contrabassoon, and more percussion instruments.
Harmony	Harmony becomes increasingly important as a large-scale structural element (tonic/not-tonic/tonic).	Harmony becomes increasingly chromatic.
Form	Theme and variations, minuet (**ABA**), rondo, sonata form, double-exposition concerto form	Sonata form, ternary forms, theme and variations, modified strophic form
Word-music relationships	Word painting still present, but not as prevalent and often more subtle	Greater importance of program music

IN REVIEW: Nineteenth-Century Style

Program music. Although not new in the nineteenth century, program music took on increasing importance as composers attempted to connected purely instrumental music with the wider world of events and ideas.

* Mendelssohn, *Overture to* A Midsummer Night's Dream (Chapter 28)
* Berlioz, *Symphonie fantastique* (Chapter 29)
* Gottschalk, *Union* (Chapter 33)

Virtuosity. While most composers continued to write for amateur performers in many instances, at least some devoted their energies to writing for performers of exceptional talent, creating music that was notoriously difficult to perform.

* Gottschalk, *Union* (Chapter 33)
* Verdi, *La Traviata* (Chapter 35)
* Ravi Shankar, *Raga Sindhi-Bhairavi* (Chapter 34)

Nationalism. At least some nineteenth-century music expresses the aspirations of national groups united either politically or ethnically.

* C. Schumann, "Forward!" (Chapter 31)
* Chopin, Mazurka, op. 7, no. 1 (Chapter 32)
* Gottschalk, *Union* (Chapter 33)
* Dvořák, String Quartet, op. 96 (Chapter 38)

Song. The song (German: *Lied*) became an important domestic genre, noted for its lyricism and intimacy of tone. These works were mostly for voice and piano, but the style could be applied in almost any medium, including solo piano music or the piano trio.

* Schubert, "Erlkönig" (Chapter 27)
* Hensel, Piano Trio, op. 11 (Chapter 30)
* R. Schumann, "Dedication" (Web Bonus Chapter 3)

The Growth of the Orchestra. The orchestra continued to expand throughout the nineteenth century, growing in both the number and variety of instruments.

* Beethoven, Symphony no. 5 (Chapter 26)
* Mendelssohn, *Overture to* A Midsummer Night's Dream (Chapter 28)
* Berlioz, *Symphonie fantastique* (Chapter 29)
* Brahms, Symphony no. 4 (Chapter 37)

Opera as a Fusion of Music and Drama. Leading composers used different means to integrate music and drama. Verdi created large-scale units that move fluidly between declamatory and lyrical singing; Wagner created even larger units in which the voice and orchestra present ideas on an equal footing.

* Verdi, *La Traviata* (Chapter 35)
* Wagner, *The Valkyrie* (Chapter 36)

PART 6 The Twentieth Century

he pace of musical change—like the pace of life itself—increased dramatically in the twentieth century. Thanks to advances in technology—sound recordings, radio, film, television, and the computer, to name only a few—listeners had more access to more different kinds of music than ever before. Musical styles were changing just as rapidly. By the 1930s, listeners could choose to listen to music that went beyond long-standing principles of harmony, melody, rhythm, and timbre. Many composers created entirely novel approaches to music by writing works without a tonal center and without a clear sense of meter or regular rhythm. Others incorporated sounds from the music of non-Western cultures. Still others opened up the realm of timbre by using the wealth of electronically generated sounds that had only recently become available. And some composers wrote works that called into question the nature of music itself.

But novelty did not always mean a rejection of the past. Twentieth-century listeners could also choose from a wide variety of fresh and innovative music that remained tonally based and rhythmically regular, from the concert hall to the jazz club. Ragtime, jazz, and the blues developed novel ways of applying tonal harmonies and metered rhythms. Indeed, music became such a lucrative business in the twentieth century that many talented composers and musicians earned fortunes writing for a mass-market audience. Jazz, the blues, film music, musicals, and many other new genres of popular music both appealed to and reflected the tastes of a musical public that was now broader and more diverse than ever. The influence of African American and Latin composers and musicians became particularly pronounced in all realms of music, recorded and live, popular and classical.

▶ For some audiences, the pace of musical change in the 20th century was a bit too fast. This cartoon is based on an actual scuffle that occurred at one of Arnold Schoenberg's concerts in 1913 (see chapter 42). Schoenberg continues to conduct, apparently perceiving the noise of the riot as music. The musicians use their instruments as weapons with which to assault listeners. The composer Franz Schubert (see chapter 27) lies sprawled in the center foreground.

Phaidon Press Limited

Modernism

Paris, May 1913: The composer Igor Stravinsky sits expectantly in the auditorium at the premiere of his ballet *The Rite of Spring* (see chapter 43). After the first few bars, some audience members begin to laugh derisively. Stravinsky slips out into the backstage wings and listens with astonishment. "These demonstrations," he later wrote, "at first isolated, soon became general, provoking counter-demonstrations and very quickly developing into a terrific uproar." Before long, the dancers can hardly hear the irregular beats of the music, and they begin to dance out of step with each other. General chaos in the audience ensues, and the next press speaks of a "riot" at the performance.

This scene encapsulates the relationship between many artists and their public in the early decades of the twentieth century. Stravinsky was writing in a new—and to many listeners, shocking—manner. A new spirit, known as modernism, had taken hold in all the arts, and it represented an abolishment of tradition and a quest for novelty that far exceeded any such drive in the past. The public was often quite simply shocked.

Ironically, the work that unleashed a riot at its premiere is now one of the most popular works in today's concert halls, a staple of the orchestral repertory. A similar pattern of shock followed by acceptance can be seen in the other arts as well. Many modernist painters rejected the time-honored idea that a painting had to represent a particular object; abstract art, based on color and form, became a touchstone of modernism. Even artists who created representational images began to do away with the illusion of perspective (depth) in their paintings. Viewers were scandalized at first, but eventually they came to accept and even embrace such new approaches to art. In architecture, modernists rebelled against the imitation of past models, advocating a style of design based on the spirit of contemporary times. Modernist architects eliminated elements of ornamentation and focused on smooth, clean lines. Novelists experimented with such techniques as writing in an unbroken "stream of consciousness," in which readers were often at a loss to decipher any clear story line. While these approaches no longer seem unusual to us today, they were shocking and unsettling in their time.

▲ Wassily Kandinsky, *Improvisation No. 7 (Storm)*, 1910. The Russian modernist Kandinsky was among the first painters to abandon the idea of representation, preferring instead to create images based on forms and colors. Gift of Collection Société Anonyme. 1941.527 Location: Yale University Art Gallery, New Haven, Connecticut, U.S.A./Art Resource, NY. ©2010 Estate of Wassily Kandinsky/ARS Artists Rights Society, NY

◄ Pablo Picasso, *Violin and Grapes* (1912), retains elements of representation—one can recognize certain aspects of both a violin and some grapes—but the sense of perspective is heavily distorted: we see the violin from several different angles all at once. This style of painting is known as cubism.
The Museum of Modern Art, New York, NY, U.S.A. Digital Image © The Museum of Modern Art/Licensed by SCALA/Art Resource, NY. © 2010 Estate of Pablo Picasso/ARS Artists Rights Society, NY

▲ "Little Nipper" listens to "His Master's Voice." This 1899 painting by the English artist Francis Barraud served as the logo for the HMV record label (and later RCA and JVC) for most of the 20th century. The gramophone is playing a 78 rpm shellac disk that contains only about three minutes' worth of music. The machine operated on a windup hand crank; speakers and electrical wiring came only later.

Corbis/Bettmann

Audio Technology

Perhaps the single most remarkable aspect of music in the twentieth century is that for the first time, listeners could hear music when and where they wanted to. We take the portability of music—on radio, CDs, and MP3s—for granted nowadays, but being able to hear music without the physical presence of performing musicians marked a radical change in the history of music. In theory at least, anyone could hear anything at any time, anywhere.

Thomas Edison had invented the cylinder disk in 1877, but the earliest recordings were poor and served only to emphasize the gulf between live and recorded sound. With the advent of 78 rpm (revolutions per minute) disks in 1897, the availability and quality of recorded music began to expand exponentially. For the first time, listeners could hear the same performance more than once, and they could listen to music without any performers present. Radio stations, which first appeared in the early 1920s, radically changed the music industry by broadcasting everything from grand opera to hillbilly music to audiences who had never had the chance to hear those performances live. Eventually, film, television, and the Internet gave listeners even more choices and easier access to far more music than ever before.

This revolution in listening changed the way music was produced. Traditional written notation became irrelevant in many musical styles. With the ready availability of audiotape beginning in the 1940s, composers could for the first time manipulate sound by splicing and re-recording taped sounds. It was now possible to use the recording studio not merely to refine the sound of a recording, but actually to create the work from the ground up. Beach Boy Brian Wilson composed his 1960s hit "Good Vibrations" (see chapter 58) entirely in the studio, in a painstaking process involving the cutting and splicing of several recording sessions into one three-and-a-half-minute song. Only later did the band learn to perform the song live. In 1990, rap group Public Enemy relied on studio manipulation of sounds from other albums to create the musical accompaniment for their lyrics in "Fight the Power" (see chapter 59). Some composers took the classical tradition into a whole new realm of experimental electronic sounds and recording techniques, and some performers gave up live performance completely in favor of the recording studio, where they had complete control over quality.

Social Diversity

When Duke Ellington and his orchestra recorded the swing hit *Cotton Tail* (see chapter 47) in 1940, American society was sharply divided along racial lines. Most institutions, including the military and schools—not to mention housing, restaurants, hotels, and professional sports—were segregated either by law or by practice. And yet in dance halls like New York City's Savoy Ballroom, where Ellington frequently played, whites and African Americans alike thronged to hear the hottest bands and dance the newest steps. By 2000, Americans as a whole were far more accepting of the idea of social diversity than they had been a hundred years before. Over the course of the twentieth century, the image of a social melting pot had given way to the idea of society as a mosaic of different cultures and traditions, each contributing in its own distinctive way toward the larger whole.

Music played an important role in this change. Styles with roots in the traditions of African American culture in particular, helped bridge the divide between the races. As early as the 1930s, whites and blacks were playing together in instrumental ensembles. Ragtime, jazz, rock, and hip hop all became a part of mainstream American culture. But the move across racial and social divides was never easy. At different times, every one of these very same kinds of music erupted as a flashpoint of social conflict. In the 1920s, many white parents expressed open opposition to the sexual overtones in ragtime and jazz. Many of their children, in turn, were shocked in the 1950s when white teenagers began listening (and worse, dancing) to music written in a style traditionally associated with the music of African Americans. Throughout the twentieth century, pop music has been an integral part of social change and protest—gospel in the civil rights movement of the 1950s and 1960s, psychedelia in the anti-war movement of the 1960s and 1970s, punk as an outcry against economic repression in the 1970s and 1980s, hip hop as a statement on racism and discrimination at the end of the century and beyond.

▲ More than any other kind of music, jazz promoted racial integration for audiences and performers alike. Here, the celebrated clarinetist Artie Shaw jams with Duke Ellington and drummer Chick Webb in 1937 while a racially mixed audience listens with obvious pleasure.

Photograph by Charles Peterson, courtesy of Don Peterson

Globalization

It was a revelation for the French composer Claude Debussy when, in 1889, he heard the Javanese musical ensemble known as the gamelan play at Paris's Universal Exposition (the same event that gave us the Eiffel Tower). A gamelan includes many percussion instruments—drums, gongs, and xylophones, among others—and its music has what Western ears often perceive as a floating, nondirectional quality that operates outside the conventions of Western harmony. Debussy was so impressed by this kind of sound that he incorporated elements of it into his *Voiles*, for piano, in 1910 (see chapter 39). In an age before recordings, such cross-cultural musical encounters were rare. Few gamelan ensembles had ever performed outside of what is now Indonesia, and if Debussy had wanted to travel there, it would have taken him several weeks by steamship. Thanks to air travel, gamelan ensembles perform all over the world today, and recordings make their music even more widely available. Indeed, more than 100 gamelan ensembles are now based in the United States alone.

The growing ease of telecommunications and transportation made the world of 2000 a far smaller place than it had been in 1900. Telephones, fax machines, video transmissions, and the Internet made it possible to communicate from almost any point on the globe to almost any other. National economies grew increasingly dependent on one another. Disparate cultures mingled even within individual composers and performers, who often rebelled against the notion that they or their music belonged strictly to one tradition or another. Whether in the concert hall, the jazz club, or on the dance floor, music had become a global phenomenon.

▼ The English violinist Yehudi Menuhin in rehearsal with the Indian sitar player Ravi Shankar in London, 1966. Menuhin and Shankar concertized and recorded widely together, creating a fusion of Eastern and Western styles.

David Farrell/Lebrecht Music & Arts Photo Library

The Twentieth Century: AT A GLANCE

chapter 39

1910
CLAUDE DEBUSSY
Voiles from *Preludes,* book 1
GENRE: Solo piano music

Chapter highlight:
Impressionism
Impressionist composers emphasized timbre over melody; melodic ideas are often fragmentary and unstable. The use of whole-tone and pentatonic scales undermine the sense of a tonal center.
KEY CONCEPTS
Timbre for the piano, whole-tone scale, pentatonic scale.

chapter 40

GAMELAN GONG KEBYAR
OF BELALUAN
Kebyar Ding III,
"Oncang-oncangan"
GENRE: Gamelan music

Chapter highlight:
Harmony and Timbre
The shimmering percussive timbre and hypnotic harmonies of Gamelan music have had a deep influence on twentieth-century composers in the Western classical tradition.
KEY CONCEPTS
Timbre, Homorhythm, ostinato, connection to minimalism.

chapter 41

1908
CHARLES IVES
The Unanswered Question
GENRE: Programmatic work for chamber orchestra

Chapter highlight:
Tonality vs. Atonality
Tonality, the basis of Western music for centuries, no longer seemed adequate in the early years of the twentieth century; several composers searched for a new, atonal language.
KEY CONCEPTS
Consonance, dissonance, layered texture.

chapter 45

1899
SCOTT JOPLIN
Maple Leaf Rag
GENRE: Ragtime

Chapter highlight:
Ragtime
Ragtime incorporates syncopated African American rhythms with straightforward dance forms like marches and cakewalks, laying the groundwork for early jazz.
KEY CONCEPTS
Syncopation, sectional form, compound melodies.

chapter 46

1936
ROBERT JOHNSON
"Terraplane Blues"
GENRE: Downhome blues

Chapter highlight:
Blues
Early blues recordings captured an oral tradition with deep roots in the Mississippi Delta region. In the 1940s, blues musicians changed to electric guitar, and new styles of blues emerged in Chicago, Kansas City, and elsewhere.
KEY CONCEPTS
Twelve-bar blues, blue notes, timbre of vocal blues.

chapter 47

1940
DUKE ELLINGTON
Cotton Tail
GENRE: Big band jazz

Chapter highlight:
Big Band Swing
Dance orchestras of the 1920s evolved into jazz bands that used swing rhythms and featured improvisation. These bands increased in size during the Swing Era.
KEY CONCEPTS
Big-band instrumentation, swing rhythms, standard song form choruses.

chapter 42	chapter 43	chapter 44

1912

ARNOLD SCHOENBERG
"Columbine" from
Pierrot lunaire

GENRE: Song cycle for voice
and chamber ensemble

Chapter highlight:
Expressionism
Expressionism gave priority to truth over
beauty, including the sometimes less-
than-beautiful workings of the human
psyche. Expressionist works were at times
grotesque and surreal.

KEY CONCEPTS
Atonality, Sprechstimme.

1913

IGOR STRAVINSKY
Rite of Spring, **Part One (excerpt)**

GENRE: Ballet

Chapter highlight:
Modernism
Modernist composers pursued a relentless
quest for novelty. The unconventional
nature of modernist music often scandalized
audiences.

KEY CONCEPTS
Polytonality, metrical irregularity,
pentatonic melodies, instruments
of the modern orchestra.

GLOBAL CONNECTION

BERTA WAZA
Greetings by Aba Musa!

GENRE: WAZA

Chapter highlight:
Polytonality
Polytonality is the presence of more than
one tonal center, and it occurs when harmonies that are consonant by themselves
are juxtaposed to create a dissonance.

KEY CONCEPTS
Polytonality, African horns,
interlock, ostinato.

chapter 48	chapter 49	WEB BONUS chapter 4

1946

CHARLIE PARKER
Ornithology

GENRE: Bebop jazz

Chapter highlight:
Bebop Jazz
Jazz music for listening, not dancing, arose
in the mid-1940s. Smaller ensembles, more
emphasis on virtuosic improvisation, and a
serious attitude toward the music characterized bebop.

KEY CONCEPTS
Jazz combo instrumentation, improvisation,
soloist vs. rhythm section.

1930

RUTH CRAWFORD
Piano Study in Mixed Accents

GENRE: Solo piano music

Chapter highlight:
Toward Serialism
Composers who pursued a more modernist
style struggled to break free of the conventions of tonality. Serial composition, in
which no one note in the twelve-note scale
would return until the others had been
heard, gave composers a flexible framework
for writing atonal music.

KEY CONCEPTS
Atonality, register as a structural element.

1927

GERMAINE TAILLEFERRE
**Concertino for Harp
and Orchestra, finale**

GENRE: Neo-classicism

Chapter highlight:
Neo-classicism
Neo-classicism was a response to modernism. Neo-classical works draw on the
idioms of earlier eras but incorporate
modern elements as well. Stravinsky,
Hindemith, Prokofiev, and Shostakovich
also composed neo-classical works.

KEY CONCEPTS
Periodic phrase structure, transparency
of texture, rondo form.

1903
Wright Brothers'
first flight

1914-18
World War I

1920
First commercial
radio station

1927
First films
with sound

1929
U.S. stock market
crash launches the
Great Depression

1939-45
World War II

1948
Cold War begins

1948
LP records
commercially
available

1950-53
Korean War

Historical
Events

The Twentieth Century: AT A GLANCE

chapter 50

1949

WILLIAM GRANT STILL
"A Black Pierrot" from
Songs of Separation

GENRE: Art song

Chapter highlight:
Art song

The art song, for voice and piano, sets serious poetry to music, in the twentieth century, the art song took on the inflections of many different styles, from atonality to the blues.

KEY CONCEPTS

Blues inflections, chromatic harmony, through-composed form.

chapter 51

1942

Aaron Copland
"Hoe-Down" from *Rodeo*

GENRE: Ballet

Chapter highlight:
Nationalism

Copland pioneered a sound evocative of the open spaces of the western United States. Wide spacing of instruments, bright timbres, and energetic rhythms contribute to a distinctively American sound.

KEY CONCEPTS

Populist modernism, traditional folk tunes, "open" orchestration and texture, rondo form.

chapter 52

1957

LEONARD BERNSTEIN
"Tonight" from
West Side Story

GENRE: Musical

Chapter highlight
The Broadway Musical

The Broadway musical is a direct descendent of European operetta, a spoken play with ample quantities of sung music. It is often lighter in tone than standard opera.

KEY CONCEPTS

Additive form, ensembles.

chapter 53

1952

JOHN CAGE
4'33"

GENRE: Aleatory music

Chapter highlight:
Experimental Music

A number of 20th-century composers explored the nature of music. Some incorporated everyday sounds, some manipulated standard instruments or created their own, and some experimented with chance.

KEY CONCEPTS

Aleatory music, what is music?

chapter 56

1961

MARVELETTES
"Please, Mr. Postman"

GENRE: Motown

Chapter highlight:
Motown

This record label found a new way to market black performers to a wider audience by adding slick studio production to R&B music.

KEY CONCEPTS

Close vocal harmonies, doo-wop chord progression, verse-chorus form.

chapter 57

1966

BEACH BOYS
"Good Vibrations"

GENRE: Psychedelia

Chapter highlight:
Sixties Rock

In the mid-sixties, rock music entered a period of great creative innovation. Even the Beach Boys, known for their light surf music, experimented with psychedelic sounds.

KEY CONCEPTS

Composition in the studio, psychedelic sound effects, verse-chorus form with extensions.

WEB BONUS
chapter 6

SEX PISTOLS
"God Save the Queen"

GENRE: Punk

Chapter highlight:
Rebellious Rock

Punk revived earlier rock traditions and combined them with biting social commentary. The do-it-yourself attitude was audible in the music's distorted timbres and simple forms.

KEY CONCEPTS

Irony, distorted rock timbre, extreme vocal techniques.

chapter 58

1990

PUBLIC ENEMY
"Fight the Power"

GENRE: Hip hop

Chapter highlight:
Hip hop

Hip hop emerged from a culture of black, urban artistic expression in dance, graffiti, DJ'ing and MC'ing. Hip hop music relies on sampling and mixing beats, combined with syncopated text delivery.

KEY CONCEPTS

Sampling, quotation and references, scratching, hip hop beats.

1976
PHILIP GLASS
"Knee Play 1" from
Einstein on the Beach
GENRE: Opera

Chapter highlight
Minimalism
Minimalism grows out of multiple repetitions and subtle variations of a few brief ideas. Minimalist techniques have been applied in many different kinds of music, including techno, minimal techno, and microhouse.

KEY CONCEPTS
Drama without a plot,
variation form, ostinato.

1957
CHUCK BERRY
"School Day"
GENRE: Rock 'n' roll

Chapter highlight:
Rock 'n' Roll
Rhythm and blues and honky tonk fused into youth-oriented, reckless, rock 'n' roll. White and black performers found a waiting audience of baby-boom teenagers.

KEY CONCEPTS
Shuffle rhythm, electric guitar solos,
12-bar blues.

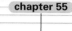

MAHALIA JACKSON
"It Don't Cost Very Much"
GENRE: Gospel

Chapter highlight:
Gospel
Gospel combined vocal techniques from the blues with rousing rhythms and chord progressions from Sanctified church traditions.

KEY CONCEPTS
Piano and organ in a gospel timbre,
free rhythmic phrasing, gospel harmonies.

1986
TANIA LEÓN
A la Par, second movement
("Guaguancó")
**GENRE: Music for percussion
ensemble**

Chapter highlight:
Postmodernism
Postmodernism iintegrates modern idioms with more traditional ones. Postmodern works are often playful in spirit, a reaction against the unrelenting seriousness of much modernist art.

KEY CONCEPTS
Tonal vs. atonal elements,
percussion instruments.

2000
TAN DUN
"Farewell" from
*Crouching Tiger,
Hidden Dragon*
GENRE: Film music

Chapter highlight
Global Music
Tan Dun's score synthesizes elements of traditional Chinese music with the idioms of European-American music.

KEY CONCEPTS
Western and Eastern instruments
juxtaposed, quasi-pentatonic melodies.

1954
Supreme Court outlaws segregation in public schools

1964-65
Civil Rights and Voting Rights Acts

1964-73
Vietnam War

1969
American astronauts walk on the moon

1982
CDs commercially available

1989
Berlin Wall falls;
Cold War ends

1990s
Introduction of Internet to a broad public

1999
Napster and other peer-to-peer file-sharing networks change the way music is shared by fans

Historical Events

39

Rennes • FRANCE
PARIS •
• Bordeaux   Lyon

Claude Debussy
Voiles from *Preludes*, book 1

 Listen to This

Timbre

How would you describe the sound of the piano in this work? How is it different from the sound of other works for piano (for example, the Mazurka by Chopin discussed in chapter 32)?

Melody

How many distinct themes can you identify?

Dynamics

What is the predominant volume of this work? Does it change at any point?

Rhythm

What is the basic meter of this work: duple or triple?

Harmony

Listen for a sense of a harmonic center. Can you hum a note that sounds like home base, or *do* (as in do-re-mi)? Does the music feel at rest anywhere, as though it has arrived?

Form

Listen for the return of the opening idea toward the end of the work.

Debussy's title is deliberately ambiguous: the French word *voiles* (pronounced like "wall" with a "v" immediately before the "w") can mean either "sails" (as in the sails on a boat) or "waves." Thus, even though the work has a programmatic title, we cannot be sure of the exact sense of that title. Interestingly, Debussy placed this title at the end of the written score rather than at the beginning. The music, too, suggests rather than states: the timbre is muted, melodies appear and disappear without development or conclusion, harmonies remain unresolved, and the rhythm never establishes any strong sense of meter.

This quality of suggesting rather than stating is basic to an artistic movement known as **impressionism**. Impressionism was particularly important in the realm of painting (see "Impressionism," p. 359), where artists focused more on sensations, perceptions, and light than on the direct representation of objects. Although paintings by Monet and Renoir are among the most familiar and treasured images in art museums today, at the time of their creation, they met with considerable skepticism. Were the paintings even finished? Critics and viewers wondered. Similarly, the music of Debussy confronted listeners with an entirely new sound that ignored conventions and defied expectations. In this way, Debussy's music was an early manifestation of the modernist impulse, and critics and audiences were often at a loss to understand it.

In literature, a group of French poets known as symbolists (including Stéphane Mallarmé, Arthur Rimbaud, and Paul Verlaine) used comparable techniques with words, avoiding clear syntax and using symbols to suggest rather than articulate ideas. Debussy was drawn to their texts, setting some as songs, and regularly attended readings by his friend Mallarmé.

Timbre: A Nonpercussive Sound

It may surprise some people to learn that the piano is essentially a percussion instrument, but consider its action: the performer strikes a key, which in turn activates a hammer that strikes metal strings, which vibrate and produce sound. When pianists play a melodic line, they must work to make this sound as lyrical and nonpercussive as they can. But Debussy is going even further here and trying to get a completely different kind of sound out of the piano, writing for it as if it were (in his own words) an "instrument without hammers." The ultra-smooth lines and the persistently soft volume create a timbre that is more intimate, more inward than the often bold, crisp sound of the piano.

Where did Debussy come up with such an unusual idea? We happen to know that he was intrigued by the sound of the Javanese ensemble known as the **gamelan**, a large collection of drums, gongs, xylophones, and plucked string instruments. (Java is one of the principal islands of present-day Indonesia.) Debussy had heard a gamelan at the Universal Exposition in Paris in 1889 and was fascinated by the gentle, floating timbres of what is essentially a percussion ensemble. The gongs in a gamelan, in particular, can be set in motion by the softest of touches, and it would seem that Debussy was trying to recreate this kind of sound on the piano. A French composer absorbs and reinterprets the sound of Javanese music: *Voiles* thus reflects the growing globalization of music in the twentieth century.

We also know that Debussy was intent on exploring musical timbre in much the same way that the French symbolist poets—all of them his contemporaries, some of them his friends—explored sound for sound's sake, unconstrained by logic or syntax. Debussy's rich sonic palette particularly inspires performers to listen and make careful choices regarding touch and pedaling, so that the exploration continues with each new performance.

Melody: Fragments

Instead of clear themes, Debussy presents what sound more like fragments of themes than actual self-sufficient themes:

> 1 = a downward contour, ending with a leap upward (first presented at 0:00)

> 2 = a single repeated note in the bass (first presented at 0:10)
> 3 = a slow, rising three-note figure (first presented at 0:15)

4 = a turning figure (first presented at 1:01)

5 = a harp-like glissando figure (first presented at 2:08)

None of these themes has a particularly strong profile: each is as fluid as a wave or a sail, altered slightly every time it returns. The music as a whole avoids any sense of strong direction: we do not feel at any point as if it is moving toward a goal or climax. Instead of a kind of musical narrative, Debussy is presenting something more like a succession of slowly changing images.

Dynamics: Whispering, Hinting

Except for one very brief passage in the middle (2:08–2:20), the entire work is written at the level of *piano* (soft) or *pianissimo* (very soft). This extremely low dynamic reinforces the nonpercussive timbre of the instrument, as the pianist touches the keys lightly, even wiping or caressing them rather than striking them. It also allows the one *forte* (loud) moment to stand out all the more markedly. In this manner, dynamics assume a kind of structural importance, providing a point of contrast against an otherwise unchanging plane of softness.

Rhythm: Where's the Downbeat?

Although notated in duple meter, *Voiles* provides the listener with almost no sense of a fixed metrical pattern. Most music in duple meter would follow a pattern of **1**-2 **1**-2 **1**-2, with a strong accent on the downbeat, but Debussy's music resists any such pattern. Instead, the music seems to float or drift, again evoking the images suggested by the work's title.

The repeated B-flats in the lower register help obscure the meter of the work even more. At times they fall on the beat, at times off it. This repeated note seems to operate in its own little world and never quite synchronizes with the upper voices. It disappears, returns, and then disappears again. It is as unpredictable as a gentle wave or as a sail flapping in a light breeze.

Harmony: A Centerless Center

The piece opens in a relatively high register, but at 0:10, a single, low note—the note B♭—enters in the bass. This B♭ is repeated in various rhythms throughout the entire work until just before the very end (it drops out at 3:29). Yet the constant presence of this one note actually *reduces* the sense of any harmonic center. Because it is always there, it recedes into the background and contributes still further to the sense of floating or drifting created by the timbre, dynamics, and rhythm. It is a little like the sound of waves lapping against the side of a boat, or wind flapping against a sail: we hear these sounds if we listen for them, but after a while, we stop hearing them precisely because they never stop.

Another element that undermines any sense of a harmonic center is the use of the **whole-tone scale**. A scale, as we have seen (see "The Elements of Music," as well as chapter 32), is an ordered arrangement of notes that together make up a kind of palette for melodies. As we saw in "The Elements of Music," the standard Western-music scale, known as the **diatonic scale**, consists of a combination of whole steps and half steps. To recap:

- A **half step** is the smallest distance between two adjacent notes on a piano (white or black), such as C-C♯; it is also the smallest distance you can comfortably sing.
- A **whole step** is a little bigger. An example on the keyboard is C-D, which skips C♯. In other words, one whole step equals two half steps.

- The standard diatonic scale uses a combination of whole and half steps to emphasize the tonal center of any given key. The placement of those half steps tells your ear which note is home base, or the **tonic**.

But a whole-tone scale has no half steps, thereby eliminating a sense of a tonal center.

Debussy's use of the whole-tone scale in *Voiles* helps give the music the sense that it has no tonic, that all notes are equally important. In this way, too, the music may offer an impression of a drifting cloud or a billowing sail. Western listeners tend to associate the whole-tone scale with the music of East Asia. And as noted earlier, Debussy was in fact influenced by certain repertories from this part of the world, particularly the gamelan from Indonesia (see chapter 40).

Debussy was one of several composers working in the early twentieth century who were questioning **tonality**, which for many centuries had been the primary system of organizing pitch. Other composers would take the challenge still further, until it became possible to compose using an entirely nontonal or "atonal" style altogether (see chapters 42 and 49).

Form: Nondirectional

All the elements discussed to this point—timbre, dynamics, rhythm, harmony— combine to create a sense of nondirectional form. The music never seems to be moving toward a particular goal. There is a climax of sorts in the middle, when the music becomes rhythmically more animated and loud for a brief moment before returning to its original tempo and dynamic. This creates a vague sense of an overall **ABA′** form. But even this change in the middle comes as something of a surprise: it simply arrives, one more event in a series of seemingly random events. And thanks to the whole-tone scale, we do not have a sense that the music is moving away from or back toward a tonic key at any point. Even the ending seems inconclusive. The music stops, but it does not convey any strong sense of closure.

With these points in mind, now listen to the work using the Listening Guide.

Claude Debussy *Voiles* from *Preludes*, book 1

Time	Melody	Rhythm	Harmony	Dynamics	Form
0:00	1 (descending line, ending with leap up). Debussy's instructions to the pianist: "Moderately, in a rhythm without rigor and caressingly"	Begins with dotted rhythms	Whole-tone scale is established by the first five notes.	p (*piano*, soft)	**A**
0:10	2 (single low note repeated in bass)	Slow, irregular	Low note is disconnected from harmonies above.	pp (*pianissimo*, very soft)	
0:15	3 (rising three-note figure)	Slow, regular	Octaves imply no harmony at all.		
0:26	1 and 2 and 3 simultaneously, in various combinations		The three voices are seemingly unconnected.		
1:01	4 (turning figure), to be played "very supplely." Combined with 2 (repeated bass note), which continues throughout.	Moderately fast, regular	Based on whole-tone scale		
1:38	3 (rising three-note figure) added to 4 and 2				
2:08	5 (harplike glissando figure). "Becoming more animated." Combined with 3 underneath.	Fast, regular	Based on pentatonic scale (five notes: see chapter 41)	p growing to f (*forte*, loud)	**B**
2:44	5 and 2 and 3. "As at the beginning of the work."			pp	**A'**
3:15	1 returns. "Very calmly and growing increasingly faint from here to the end." Combined with 5; 3 (repeated bass note) drops out for first time.				

Student FAQs

Is this music difficult to play?

Yes and no. It's not difficult to hit the right notes, but it is very difficult to sustain such a quiet sound for this length of time. It's a little like holding one's hand still in midair: it's easy to do it for a short time, but after a while it becomes a challenge. The performer has to pay attention to every subtle nuance in this work, and that requires a high degree of musicianship.

I can't really hear the difference between "piano (soft)" and "pianissimo (very soft)." Is that a problem?

Not all pianists bring out the difference clearly, but most do, and given the limited range of dynamics in this work, it's a difference worth listening for. You should be able to hear the one "*forte* (loud)" moment as quite clearly different, though.

Claude Debussy (1862–1918)

THE PATH LESS TAKEN

Debussy's life straddled two centuries—he was born during the U.S. Civil War and died a few months before the end of World War I—yet he is widely regarded as the first great composer of the twentieth century. The inevitable association of his style with the label of impressionism tends to obscure the wide-ranging novelties of his music: no other single figure of his era did more to expand the possibilities of form, harmony, and timbre.

Debussy was born on the outskirts of Paris and studied piano and composition at the renowned Conservatory of Paris, where he won a prestigious prize in composition. But from that point on, Debussy pursued a highly unconventional career as a composer. He never held a public post of any kind, appeared in public as a pianist or conductor only sporadically, and didn't teach students on any regular basis. Instead, he pushed the boundaries of composition with increasing intensity, exploring new ways of applying the basic elements of music to his works. He rejected many of the conventions of composition and sought to create sounds that had never before been heard. He was a master of orchestration and drew sounds from the orchestra that had never been heard before. But like the impressionist artists and symbolist poets who were his contemporaries, Debussy often worked in obscurity. Works that are now recognized as masterpieces, like *The Afternoon of a Faun,* were initially greeted with indifference—or even scorn.

Ultimately, Debussy was vindicated in his drive to extend the boundaries of music. He had many imitators (*Debussyistes,* as they were known), and his death was widely mourned throughout the musical world. In 1920, a group of prominent composers—Igor Stravinsky, Béla Bartók, Paul Dukas, Manuel de Falla, Maurice Ravel, and Erik Satie—honored his memory with a series of short piano pieces issued in a commemorative volume called *Le tombeau de Claude Debussy* ("The Tomb of Claude Debussy"). Composers after him continued to expand the possibilities of harmony, eventually exploding the very definition of harmony itself.

PLAYLIST: DEBUSSY

Suite bergamasque. A series of movements for piano, including the famous *Clair de lune.*

Claude Debussy in 1911
Lebrecht Music & Arts Photo Library

Préludes, Books 1 and 2. Two collections of works for solo piano, including *Voiles.*

Children's Corner. A suite of dances about childhood, for piano, including the famous *Golliwogg's Cake-Walk,* a quasi-ragtime piece.

Nocturnes. A set of three orchestral movements: "Clouds," "Festivals," "Sirens."

Prélude à l'après-midi d'un faune ("Prelude to the Afternoon of a Faun"). A ballet later made famous by Nijinsky and the Ballets Russes (see chapter 43).

String Quartet in G minor. An early work and Debussy's only string quartet, but a staple of the quartet repertory today.

Pelléas et Melisande. Debussy's only completed opera, based on a drama by Maurice Maeterlink about a doomed love affair in legendary times.

Impressionism

Debussy's music is often associated with **impressionism**, an artistic movement spearheaded by French painters like Claude Monet, Pierre Auguste Renoir, and Edgar Degas in the late 1860s. These artists used an accumulation of short, visible brush strokes instead of a continuous line to produce not so much a representation of an object as the sensation—the impression—produced by it. They were particularly interested in the effects of light on our perception of an object. Color took precedence over line. Because the idea was to capture a moment in time, impressionists worked quickly to reproduce on canvas the fleeting appearance of a scene, and then moved on to the next painting, leading some critics to call their works unfinished.

In music, the impressionist style is similarly based on a blurring of harmonies, rhythms, and forms. It tends to avoid clear cadences and rhythmic patterns, and the music often seems to ebb and flow with a fluid sense of motion. Above all, impressionist composers placed great emphasis on the color (timbre) of sound. Debussy, the leading composer in this style, brought new sounds out of the orchestra and piano alike. Early critics were not so enthralled. One took the composer to task for writing "unprecise harmonies and fleeting phrases." Another said of his opera *Pelléas et Melisande* that "Debussy has definitely discounted all melody. . . . He lets us hear only chords. . . . The score resembles a curiosity shop of tangled harmonies . . . which makes a less disagreeable impression only because it falls on our ears in soft and discreet half fading tones."

Debussy himself intensely disliked the term "impressionism," especially if it was applied to music. He insisted he was more concerned with making "something new—realities—as it

Claude Monet's painting *Impression: Sunrise* (1872) supplied the name of the movement that would later be known as "impressionism." Though a few objects in this painting—two boats and, the sun, for instance—are recognizable, Monet's emphasis is on capturing the mood of early morning on the water.

ARS Artists Rights Society, NY

were." An impression, he maintained, was reality reconstructed in the mind from our sensory perceptions of the world. These mental reconstructions offered, in effect, an alternative reality of ideas to the reality of the physical world.

 EXPAND YOUR PLAYLIST

Impressionism

Debussy is regarded as the great master of impressionism, but other composers wrote in this style as well.

Maurice Ravel, "Mirrors" (*Miroirs*). A suite of movements for piano, including "Sad Birds" and "Valley of the Bells."

Frederick Delius, *Appalachia*. This "American Rhapsody," for orchestra, records the impressions of an English composer who spent considerable amounts of time in the southern United States.

Charles Griffes, *The White Peacock*. This "tone poem" for orchestra is by the leading American composer associated with the impressionist movement.

Manuel de Falla, "Nights in the Gardens of Spain" (*Noches en los jardines de España*). Though often categorized as a composer who expressed nationalist sentiments through his music for his native Spain, de Falla was also influenced in at least some of his compositions by the impressionist idiom, including this work for piano and orchestra.

40

Gamelan Gong Kebyar of Belaluan
Kebyar Ding III, "Oncang-oncangan"

Listen to This

Timbre

How do the tones of the instruments sound? Why do they sound that way?

Melody

What do you notice about the way the melody is put together? Can you identify the individual parts?

Dynamics

When and how does the volume level change?

Form

How are sections marked off? When and why does the speed of the music change? How are the rhythmic pulses marked by the instruments?

Gamelan means "musical ensemble." It is played in Indonesia, traditionally at the Javanese courts. In 1915, Balinese villagers created a new style, *gamelan gong kebyar*, which consists of a number of instruments that play melodies in interlocking patterns. The primary melody instruments are the *gender*, a kind of bronze-keyed vibraphone, and *trompong*, horizontally mounted, bowl-shaped gongs. These instruments are played in pairs, with one set tuned slightly out of tune with the other, creating a shimmering sound. *Gamelan gong kebyar* also involves vertically hung gongs, which are struck to mark off fixed beats within the metric structure of the piece. In Balinese music, this is referred to as *colotomic structure*, where each section of the piece is marked by a hierarchy of gong pulses. There are also a number of drums and smaller percussion instruments in this genre.

Double-headed drum

Trompong

Gender

Small percussion instruments

Gamelan musicians
Steve Vidler/eStock Photography LLC

Gamelan music traditionally was not notated, and the players learned their parts by rote. The music is composed and structured. Today, the music is taught using a numerical notation, with each number representing a corresponding scale step. Gamelans of all types are found in the music departments of many American, Canadian, and British universities.

Gamelan gong kebyar is easily distinguished from the older Javanese gamelan, which was sedate, symbolic of elegance, and performed for princes. The Balinese style is energetic, with many abrupt changes of tempo and dynamics. The word *kebyar* means "explosive." Compositions are built of series of **ostinatos**, which are constantly repeated musical patterns, and each has a different length and is set in a different tempo. The technique of Balinese ostinato composition later influenced American minimalist composers in their repetitions of motives and their developments.

The listening example of *gamelan gong kebyar* in this chapter is from the first historic set of Balinese music recordings made by the German record label Odeon in 1928. They first appeared on 78 rpm (revolutions per minute) discs, and since 78 rpm discs could allow only three minutes of music per side, the work *Kebyar Ding* was divided into six sections for this production. In actual performance, they would be continuous in sequence. The listening example you will study is *Kebyar Ding III: Oncang-oncangan*, the third section. We already know that the term *kebyar* means "explosive," but *ding* means "first tone," and *oncang-oncangan* is an onomatopoeia that sounds like the pounding of rice mortars as grain is husked.

A *gender* (metal-keyed xylophone) player
William Waterfall/PacificStock.com

Its predominant melody is played on *gangsa*, high-pitched *gender*, with the musicians rapidly executing passages in interlock. In the middle of the piece occurs a *ngucek* rhythmic phrase. *Ngucek* literally means "rubbing," and here it refers to the back and forth melodic movement of two closely juxtaposed rhythmic sections, which "rub" against one another.

Shimmering Timbre

The first thing you may notice about the sound of this music is that the timbre of the instruments "shimmers." This effect is intentional and produced by the paired melody instruments being tuned to tones very slightly apart. This effect is called a "beat tone." This shimmering effect is one of the hallmarks of Balinese gamelan music.

A Textured Melody

The melody is played on a group of *gangsa*, the high-pitched *gender*. The interlocking pattern of these instruments forms the basis of a repeated ostinato. *Trompong* enter at points with ostinatos that run counter to the *gangsa* ostinatos. Drumming and gongs marking pulsations add to the textural coloration.

Dynamics and Tempo

Dynamics vary widely in *gamelan gong kebyar* pieces, and they change along with tempo to create different sections. More abrupt changes in tempo occur to mark the end of a section and the start of a new one. This involves loud *kebyar* striking of all the instruments in

Gotta Minimalist?

Gamelan music has had a deep influence on twentieth-century composers in the Western classical tradition, from Debussy's encounter with a gamelan at the famous Paris Expo through composers like Henry Cowell, John Cage, and Lou Harrison, all of whom tried to emulate the percussive sound of gamelan in their compositions, to the minimalists of the 1960s and 1970s, notably Philip Glass (see chapter 58) and Terry Riley. Minimalists were interested in the hypnotic quality of the repeated melodic fragments and interlocking patterns that are created by the gamelan.

In 1975, filmmaker Geoffrey Reggio began working on a film drawing together images of contemporary American life. Using techniques of speeding up and slowing down film, rapid cuts, and unusual camera angles and edits, he wanted to create a kind of montage of what life was like in a highly industrialized society. The result was the film *Koyaanisqatsi*, taken from the Hopi Indian term that means "crazy life" or "life out of balance." Because of the many hypnotic, repetitive images in the film, it seemed natural to invite composer Philip Glass—known for his minimalist scores—to contribute to the work. Glass and Reggio worked an additional three years after the film was completed to carefully fit the music to the imagery. The result was finally issued in 1982, and the film quickly became a favorite on college campuses and in alternative cinemas.

The powerful visual impact of the film is matched by Glass's adventurous score. Although it sounds like an electronic

Philip Glass at the keyboard, 2003

Toby WALES/Lebrecht Music & Arts Photo Library

composition, the work is actually scored for conventional brass instruments, strings, organ, and 6 vocalists. Like many of Glass's works of the period, it consists of short, repeated parts that are layered on top of each other in interlocking patterns, much in the way a gamelan composition is created. The "Vessels" section of the score is sometimes performed separately by small choral ensembles.

the ensemble together. Sometimes the loud *kebyar* is just one struck sound, and sometimes the *kebyar* proceeds briefly in an ensemble **homorhythm**, which means all the instruments are playing in the same rhythm. After a *kebyar* interlude, the following section may be loud or soft, fast or slow, depending on the composition.

Form. The *gamelan gong kebyar* is structured in different sections of ostinatos with varied tempo and dynamics. In this example there are six sections. The fifth section—occurring between 1:22 and 1:38—is the *ngucek*, where the homorhythmic ensemble juxtaposes a triplet rhythm against a long-short rhythm back and forth.

Each section is organized by its colotomic structure. The strongest and most important colotomic pulse is produced on the lowest gong, intermittently, while more regular and secondary pulses are struck melodically on higher gongs between the low gong tones. *Kebyar* explosions and homorhythms mark off the sections, and a subsequent section may be recognized by its tempo change.

Now listen to this piece again, following the Listening Guide.

Gamelan Gong Kebyar of Belaluan *Kebyar Ding III*, "Oncang-oncangan"

Time	Melodic Texture	Tempo	Dynamics	Form
0:00	The *gangsa* state an introductory melodic figure.	Moderate	Soft	Introduction
0:03	The entire *gamelan* strikes simultaneously.		Very loud	*Kebyar*, or "explosion"
0:05	*Gangsa* play high rapid ostinato melody in *kotekan* (interlocking parts).	Moderate pulse, rapid ostinato	Medium	First section. The lowest gong marks the beat of the colotomic structure, (0:05, 0:10) while a higher set of gongs mark colotomic pulses occurring more frequently between the low gong strokes.
0:17	*Gangsa* and drums abruptly play a homorhythmic pattern.	Rapid	Soft to loud (crescendo).	Low gong marks last tone of the colotomic structure of this section.
0:20	New section with a slower ostinato outline played by half of the *gangsa*	Slow	Soft	The sound of a higher gong marks the colotomic structure.
0:21	Interlocking half of the ostinato enters in the other half of the *gangsa*.			Continued colotomic pulses
0:32	*Trompong* gongs are struck to mark a strong point in the structure.		Medium	
0:40	Drumming begins and accelerates.		Soft	
0:42	Higher gongs on the *trompong* enter in an interlocking ostinato.			
0:44	A short rhythmic break and homorhythmic pattern	Stopping		Lull in activity

(continued)

Time	🎵 Melodic Texture	Tempo	Dynamics	🏛 Form
0:46	Continued *gangsa* interlock now with *trompong* interlock to the *gangsa* interlock added.	Resumption of tempo		Third section. Resumption of colotomic pulses. Lowest gong strikes colotomic pulse (0:52).
1:01				Lowest gong tone
1:07	Drumming again begins and accelerates.			
1:10	Another homorhythmic break of the ensemble		Very loud	*Kebyar*
1:12	Continuation of interlocking melodic ostinato in a much faster tempo	Fast	Loud	Fourth section. Colotomic structure
1:22	Ensemble begins a prolonged homorhythmic passage			Fifth section. Preparing the *ngucek.*
1:24	The ensemble homorhythm becomes grouped by three quick pulses.			Setting the triplet rhythm of the *ngucek*
1:34	Ensemble homorhythm becomes grouped by LONG-short patterns.			Juxtaposed LONG-short rhythm of the *ngucek*
1:36	Homorhythm is the *ngucek* "rubbing" of patterns against each other, triplet feel to LONG-short feel.			*Ngucek*
1:38	Drum roll	Break	Soft	Lull in activity
1:39	The *gangsa* start a new, slow, melody over a slow colotomic structure and drum accompaniment. The *gangsa* are struck by one mallet per tone together.	Slow	Soft	Final section. Slow colotomic structure.
1:58	*Trompong* enter in interlocked ostinato softer than the *gangsa* melody.			Lowest gong again marks the colotomic structure.

(continued)

Time	Melodic Texture	Tempo	Dynamics	Form
2:02	*Trompong* discontinue. *Gangsa* continue the slow melody.			Lowest gong tone
2:18	*Trompong* again enter in ostinato.			Lowest gong tone
2:21	*Trompong* discontinue. *Gangsa* continue the slow melody.			Lowest gong tone
2:31	*Gangsa* begin to accelerate the melody.	Beginning to get quicker	Beginning to get louder	*Trompong* begin marking the colotomic structure in the background.
2:33	Rapid *gangsa* interlocking melody gradually resumes.			Low gong tone; at 2:38, low gong strikes more regularly
2:41	*Gangsa* interlocking becomes more rapid.	Getting faster	Getting louder	*Trompong* clearly mark the colotomic structure.
2:43	Drumming enters and accelerates. The *gangsa* accelerate to the end.	Faster to the end	Louder to the end	Colotomic structure faster to the end
2:53	Ensemble marks the end of the piece in a *kebyar* homorhythm.			
2:54	Final drum strike marks the end.			

Student FAQs

How hard is it to play this music?

While the overall piece is complex, each individual part is not that hard to learn. Each player has to play a short phrase that is usually repeated many times through a composition. Most Balinese gamelan musicians are not professional and perform in this orchestra only on specific holidays.

Who organizes a gamelan?

Originally, gamelans were sponsored by the Javanese courts and were heard only by the nobility. However, in this century, local villages and clubs have taken over the sponsorship of these ensembles.

When was the gamelan first introduced in the West?

The Paris Exposition (or World's Fair) of 1889 is noted as one of the first times that a gamelan was heard in Western Europe. French composer Claude Debussy (see chapter 39) heard the ensemble there, and it greatly influenced his compositions that followed.

EXPAND YOUR PLAYLIST

Gamelan Music

Golden Rain: Balinese Gamelan Music, Nonesuch Explorer 72028. First released in the early 1970s, this was one of the first recordings of Balinese gamelan to be readily available in the United States. The group works in the same *kebyar* style in playing both traditional and recent compositions.

Gamelan Semar Pegulingan, Nonesuch Explorer 79720. In *Semar Pegulingan,* the rhythmic changes are less abrupt than in the *kebyar* style, with more lyrical melodies although equally complex rhythms.

Javanese Court Gamelan, Nonesuch Explorer 72044. This offers an opportunity to compare the Javanese gamelan with the Balinese style. Note the use of the *rebab* (a bowed string instrument), along with zithers, flutes, and vocalists, as well as the xylophones and gongs heard in the Balinese ensemble.

Lou Harrison: Gamelan Music, Music Masters 67091. Contemporary classical compositions using the gamelan, written by one of the twentieth century's most innovative composers.

Philip Glass. *Koyaanisqatsi,* Elektra 79506. An edited version of the soundtrack for the influential film. The film is also available on DVD.

41

Charles Ives
The Unanswered Question

Listen to This

Timbre | Listen for the distinctive sound of three different groups of instruments: strings, solo trumpet, and a quartet of wind instruments (two flutes and two clarinets). |
|

Texture | Listen for the layered texture of these instruments. Notice that the strings play continuously, while the trumpet and the quartet of winds come and go. |
| **Harmony** | Which group plays the most conventional-sounding musical harmonies? Which plays the most unconventional musical harmonies? |

"Please don't try to make things nice. All the wrong notes are right," Charles Ives once implored a scribe he had hired to copy some of his music. But what makes notes "wrong" or "right"? Ives, along with many other modernists working in the early twentieth century, was trying to change conventional notions of musical correctness. Nowhere is this struggle between old and new styles more evident than in *The Unanswered Question.*

Contrasting Timbres

The music is performed by three contrasting groups of instruments:

- **Strings:** A small string orchestra of violins, violas, cellos, and double basses plays throughout the entire work from beginning to end, without pause.
- **Solo trumpet:** A single trumpet interjects what Ives called "The Unanswered Question" at five different points over the course of the piece.
- **Wind quartet:** An ensemble of four wind instruments (two flutes and two clarinets) responds to the trumpet's "question," each time with a different "answer."

Layered Texture

Many composers had used contrasting groups of instruments before—think of Vivaldi's "Winter" from *The Four Seasons* (violin vs. string orchestra, chapter 14) or Mozart's Piano Concerto, K. 488 (piano vs. full orchestra, chapter 23)—so the idea of having two groups of instruments in dialogue with one another was certainly not new. What is unusual here is the manner in which the strings seem utterly oblivious to the dialogue taking place between the two groups of wind instruments (the solo trumpet and the flute quartet). The result is a kind of layered texture in which three blocks of sound—the strings, the solo trumpet, and the winds—are moving completely independently of one another.

Atonal vs. Tonal Harmony

Ives uses these contrasting timbres and textures to highlight, in microcosm, the conflict between two very different harmonic languages: **tonal** and **atonal**.

- Tonal music establishes a harmonic center of gravity, a central note (the tonic) that provides a strong sense of resolution and closure. We have talked about the role of the tonic in chapters 14 and 39, for example. There is an experiment that you can use to help clarify the significance of the tonic. When we sing the end of "The Star-Spangled Banner" (". . . home of the *brave*"), the note for "brave" is the tonic, also known as the "tonal center," of the melody. Try singing the last phrase but not the last note ("O'er the land of the free, and the home of the . . .": if you end on the word "the," you will immediately sense the strength and pull of the tonic note in tonal music. You want to go there!
- Atonal music, by contrast, has no harmonic center of gravity. No single note exerts the kind of force, the attraction, that we find in the tonic note in tonal music. Or, to put it more positively, all notes in atonal music are of equal weight: no particular note is more important than any other. Without a tonal center, everything our ears have come to expect notes to do, in the music we have listened to so far in this book and in the music we hear most often in the world around us, simply does not happen. Not only do notes not follow other notes the way we expect, but notes do not line up together the way we expect to hear them, and often

they sound like they clash—like they are wrong. This sound is called a **dissonance**. (The opposite sound, the one our ear finds naturally right, is called a **consonance**.) A dissonance gives us the sense that something has not quite been finished or resolved.

In *The Unanswered Question*, the strings play in a decidedly tonal fashion, moving in a slow, measured pace, almost as if playing a very slow hymn. What little dissonance we hear is carefully resolved afterward: nothing is left open-ended or unresolved.

The solo trumpet, by contrast, repeatedly poses a five-note figure that implies no harmonic center at all. The instruments of the wind quartet are even more tonally diffuse and grow rhythmically more independent as the work progresses. The music of all these instruments is atonal.

The contour of the Question

In his foreword to the score of *The Unanswered Question*, Ives hinted at the symbolism behind these contrasting elements of tonal (strings) and atonal (trumpet, wind quartet) writing:

> The strings play *ppp* [*pianississimo*—extremely quietly] throughout with no change in tempo. They are to represent "The Silence of the Druids—Who Know, See and Hear Nothing." The trumpet intones "The Perennial Question of Existence," and states it in the same tone of voice each time. But the hunt for "The Invisible Answer" undertaken by the flutes and other human beings, becomes gradually more active, faster and louder through [a section marked] *animando* [animatedly] to [one marked] *con fuoco* [with fire]. This part need not be played in the exact time position indicated. It is played in somewhat of an impromptu way; if there be no conductor, one of the flute players may direct their playing. "The Fighting Answerers," . . . after a "secret conference," seem to realize a futility, and begin to mock "The Question"—the strife is over for the moment. After they disappear, "The Question" is asked for the last time, and "The Silences" are heard beyond in "Undisturbed Solitude."[1]

It is revealing that Ives should choose to represent this metaphysical debate through a simultaneous contrast of the musical old (conventional harmony and regular rhythms within a single tempo) and the musical new (unconventional harmony and irregular rhythms across shifting tempos). Like other modernist composers of the early twentieth century, Ives was trying to shock listeners out of what he perceived to be their all-too-comfortable habit of listening to "beautiful" music—listeners who, like the Druids of *The Unanswered Question*, are content within themselves and oblivious to all that is around them. Ives elsewhere wrote that

> . . . beauty in music is too often confused with something that lets the ear lie back in an easy chair. Many sounds that we are used to do not bother us, and for that reason we are inclined to call them beautiful. Frequently—possibly almost invariably—analytical and impersonal tests will show, we believe, that when a new or unfamiliar work is accepted as beautiful on its first hearing, its fundamental quality is one that tends to put the mind to sleep. A narcotic is not always unnecessary, but it is seldom a basis of progress—that is, wholesome evolution in any creative experience.[2]

Now listen to this work once again, using the Listening Guide that follows.

---

[1]Quotation from Charles Ives, Foreword to the score of *The Unanswered Question* (New York: Southern Music Publishing, 1953), p. 2. Published by Southern Music for Peer International. International copyright secured. Used by permission. All rights reserved.

[2]Charles Ives, "Essays Before a Sonata" (1920), in *Essays before a Sonata and Other Writings,* ed. Howard Boatwright (New York: Norton, 1962), pp. 97–8.

Listening Guide

Charles Ives *The Unanswered Question*

Time	Timbre		Texture	Harmony
0:00	Strings		Homophonic throughout by themselves	Strings tonal throughout
1:08		Trumpet	Monophonic by itself; polyphonic when heard against strings throughout	Trumpet atonal throughout
1:27		Wind quartet	Polyphonic by itself; more densely polyphonic when heard against strings	Wind quartet atonal throughout
1:42		Trumpet		
1:54		Wind quartet		
2:14		Trumpet		
2:26		Wind quartet		
2:46		Trumpet		
2:56		Wind quartet		
3:15		Trumpet		
3:27		Wind quartet		
3:39		Trumpet		
3:47		Wind quartet		Strings land on final (tonic) chord at 4:10 and sustain to the end.
4:14		Trumpet		

Student FAQs

What does Ives mean by the strings representing "The Silence of the Druids"?

Druids were Celtic priests in pre-Christian Britain and Ireland. It's not entirely clear what Ives meant by this remark, but the Druids are (or were) mystical figures of the distant past who practiced ancient rituals—which seems consistent with the role Ives assigns to the strings in this work: tonal, brooding, slow-moving, unchanging.

How did early critics respond to this work?

Remarkably, *The Unanswered Question* did not receive its first performance until 1946, almost 40 years after it was written. By that point, critics had begun to realize just how far ahead of his time Ives really was, and they responded positively. Had it been performed at the time of its composition, the work would probably not have been received nearly as well.

Charles Ives (1874–1954)

AGAINST THE GRAIN

Ives both absorbed and rebelled against almost every musical tradition of his time. The son of a Civil War bandmaster, he grew up in Danbury, Connecticut, where he learned many different kinds of music: the orchestral repertory of the concert hall, church hymns, band music, and popular songs in the parlors of the town's homes. Ives worked all of these idioms into his own music, often in the same work.

As a composer, Ives's career path also went against the grain. If a composer "has a nice wife and some nice children," he once asked, "how can he let them starve on his dissonances?" His "day job" was in insurance, and as it turned out, Ives did quite well for himself. He composed in his spare time, but his music was rarely performed or published during his lifetime. Declining health forced him to more or less give up composition after 1918. Only toward the end of his life did critics and performers begin to take note of his music. By the time he died, he was recognized as a pioneer who had challenged convention and gone against the grain well before other American composers would take up the cause of modernism.

Charles Ives in his study, ca. 1947.

Corbis/Bettmann

PLAYLIST: IVES

Piano Sonata no. 2: Concord, Mass., 1840–60. A solo sonata with movements devoted individually to Emerson, Hawthorne, the Alcotts, and Thoreau.

String Quartet no. 2. In Ives's own words, this work depicts "four men who converse, discuss, argue . . . fight, shake hands, shut up—then walk up the mountainside to view the firmament."

Three Places in New England. A series of orchestral movements based on specific locales. The second is "Putnam's Camp," about the dream of a small boy who falls asleep during a Fourth of July celebration at the site of a Revolutionary War camp.

Symphony no. 2. This piece uses thematic material derived from patriotic tunes, Stephen Foster melodies, gospel hymns, and a college song.

 EXPAND YOUR PLAYLIST

Tonal versus Atonal

Ives was not the only composer of his generation to write music that openly contrasts tonal and atonal blocks of sound.

Arnold Schoenberg, *Pierrot lunaire,* op. 21, no. 1, "O alter Duft." The music of the finale of this song cycle (see chapter 42), which has been entirely atonal to this point, becomes surprisingly tonal.

Arnold Schoenberg, String Quartet no. 2, op. 10. The third movement includes a distorted version of the children's folksong "O du lieber Augustin" (known in English as "The More We Get Together" or "Did You Ever See a Lassie?").

Alban Berg, Violin Concerto, finale. Berg quotes a well-known chorale melody "Es ist genug" ("It is enough") in the finale, along with J.S. Bach's harmonization of it, in an otherwise atonal work.

Béla Bartók, String Quartet no. 5, third movement. This Scherzo "Alla bulgarese" ("In the Bulgarian Style") juxtaposes an intentionally cheap-sounding melody against music that while not atonal, is not clearly tonal, either.

42

Arnold Schoenberg
"Columbine" from *Pierrot lunaire*

Listen to This

Timbre

How would you describe the vocalist's sound? Is it singing? Speech?

Harmony

Does the music feel at rest anywhere, or as though it finds resolution in a certain place? In other words, do you hear a tonal center?

Word-Music Relationships

How does the music capture the meaning of the words?

Can anguished thoughts be expressed through beautiful music? "Columbine," one of a set of 21 songs for soprano and a small ensemble of instruments from Arnold Schoenberg's *Pierrot lunaire*, offers one answer. The music is certainly not beautiful in any conventional sense. Schoenberg purposely set this anguished text to music that is equally tormented. He saw no point in trying to project pain through beauty. Instead, his music captures pain itself.

Schoenberg's *Pierrot lunaire* represents **expressionism**, a broad artistic movement that flourished in music, painting, and literature in the early decades of the twentieth century. Expressionist painters used exaggerated imagery and sometimes garish colors to create art that was not so much beautiful as probing. Their concern was not with the representation of external objects, but rather with the representation—the expression—of inner moods and thoughts. Expressionism sought to give voice (expression) to the unconscious, to make manifest humanity's deepest and often darkest emotions. In Freudian terms, expressionist art bypasses the ego—the conscious self—and aims straight for the id, the unconscious repository of basic instincts and drives. Expressionist art rejects conventional techniques of representation, favoring instead devices that exaggerate and distort. Psychological truth takes precedence over beauty, and inner emotion takes precedence over any sense of external reality. Widely dismissed by more conservative critics in its time, expressionist art has since come to be recognized as one of the most important manifestations of modernism in the twentieth century.

Pierrot is the pale, moonstruck clown of the *commedia dell'arte,* a type of improvisational theater that originated in the Renaissance in Italy but eventually spread across Europe. Its stock characters include such figures as Harlequin and Punch and Judy. These figures always behave according to type: the cunning Harlequin is constantly playing tricks; the anarchic Punch is constantly swinging at other characters with his stick; and the lovesick Pierrot is forever pining away, unduly influenced by beams of moonlight ("lunaire" = "lunar"). Pierrot's view of life is darkly tragic yet at the same time laughable: he can scarcely control his own emotions and takes himself so seriously that we alternately sympathize with and scorn him.

Pierrot was in this sense the perfect vehicle for expressionist art, which sought to remove all inhibitions on personal expression. Schoenberg was drawn to the surreal, violent, and eerie imagery in Albert Giraud's *Pierrot lunaire,* a cycle of poems that had recently been translated from their original French into German. The text of the selection here, the second of the 21 songs in Schoenberg's cycle, concerns Columbine or Columbina, another character from the commedia dell'arte. She is a sharp-witted maidservant and is usually linked romantically to Harlequin. Here, Pierrot laments that Columbine has rebuffed him; he sings the lament of a rejected lover.

A recent Pierrot. The facial expression captures the character's sense of longing and anxiety. Pierrot's mood is subject to sudden and unpredictable changes—exuberant one moment, lugubrious the next. Like a true expressionist, he wears his heart on his sleeve.

Darren Matthews/Alamy Images

Timbre: The *Sprechstimme*

Throughout *Pierrot lunaire,* Schoenberg calls on the soprano to sing in a manner that is halfway between speech and song. He called this device *Sprechstimme,* which means literally "Speech-Voice," with "voice" understood here in the sense of "singing voice." Everyday speech has its own notes, but we do not sustain those notes. In *Sprechstimme,* Schoenberg calls for the singer to hit—but not sustain—precise pitches. Thus when the singer hits the note, she drops her voice. This creates an eerie, disassociated sort of sound that fits well with the eerie, disassociated texts of *Pierrot lunaire.*

Sprechstimme is similar to the recitative of earlier eras (see chapters 9, 10, 24, and 35) in some respects but different in important ways. Like conventional recitative, it is syllabic, which makes it more like speech and less like lyrical song. But in *Sprechstimme,* the notes are delivered slowly enough so that the sound of the voice actually tails off at the end of each word, creating something that sounds like someone talking in an exaggeratedly slow fashion. The vocalist has to sustain the tone to connect the words, but the tone is not sustained as it would be in conventional singing: the vocalist hits the specified pitch but then lets go of it almost at once, without, however, falling silent. The effect is eerie and somehow surreal.

Harmony: Atonality

Debussy had used the whole-tone scale in *Voiles* (see chapter 39) to create a harmonic idiom in which all notes are of equal weight and no single note forms a center of attraction (a "tonic"). Ives, similarly, had explored the possibility of writing melodies or melodic fragments also lacking a tonal center. Yet both composers had kept one foot squarely in the tonal universe: Debussy by using a single tone underneath the entire work to ground it all, Ives by playing off the atonal trumpet and wind instruments against the thoroughly tonal strings. In *Pierrot lunaire,* Schoenberg breaks all ties with the tonal tradition to create a work that is thoroughly **atonal**, without any sense of a tonal center, without any sense of resolution or harmonic closure. Many listeners found (and continue to find) this kind of writing jarring and unpleasant; but others found (and continue to find) in it a powerful means of expression. How better to convey the agony of rejection? How better to convey Pierrot's overwhelming sense of alienation from the world, from everything around him that is "normal"?

Word-Music Relationships: Expressing Anguish

Pierrot is suffering from an inability to express his emotions through action. He wants to scatter white rose petals on Columbine's hair but lacks the courage to pluck even a single rose. He sings in mostly very short notes, often broken by short pauses, creating a sense of breathlessness. One repeated phrase comes in for special treatment: whenever he sings of the "miraculous white roses," the music makes large leaps or descends to the very lowest range of the singer's register, or both.

When Pierrot begins to describe the way in which he would pluck the petals off the roses and strew them in Columbine's hair, the music makes a sudden shift: the flute and clarinet, silent up until this point, enter with a repeated three-note figure that seems to mimic the sound of petals dropping. The music is as quietly desperate as Pierrot himself.

With these points in mind, listen again to this selection, using the Listening Guide.

Arnold Schoenberg (1874–1951)

THE COMPOSER AS OUTSIDER

Schoenberg was a tortured soul, an outsider who longed to be accepted yet never felt comfortable regardless of his place in the world. Widely perceived as a musical radical, he considered himself a traditionalist who was extending the heritage of Bach, Beethoven, and Brahms. Born Jewish, he converted to Christianity but later went back to Judaism. An Austrian by birth, he moved back and forth between Vienna and Berlin, finally immigrating to the United States when the Nazis assumed power in Germany. (It was in the United States that he changed the spelling of his name from Schönberg to Schoenberg.) He eventually moved to Los Angeles and bought a home in Brentwood, across the street from Shirley Temple and only a few doors down from what would become O.J. Simpson's house.

As composers challenged tonality and then finally pushed beyond it entirely, Schoenberg began a relentless search for a new system for organizing music. What he came up with, in the 1920s, completely altered the way composers thought about their craft. Twelve-tone composition, as his system was called, organized pitches into rows of 12 different notes. Each of the 12 tones had equal weight, and none was repeated before all the others had been played. We will take a closer look at the principles of 12-tone composition when we look at the work of Ruth Crawford (chapter 49).

In 1935 Schoenberg was appointed to the faculty of the University of Southern California; he later taught at UCLA, and he became an American citizen in 1941. He had many pupils in the United States and exerted a powerful influence. Every subsequent generation of composers has studied Schoenberg's music carefully, and in this sense he stands as one of the most influential composers of the entire century—maybe *the* most influential.

PLAYLIST: SCHOENBERG

Chamber Symphony no. 1 in E Major, op. 9. One of Schoenberg's last works to bear a key designation ("E Major"), but it is highly dissonant nevertheless.

Variations for Orchestra. A 12-tone work that is a series of variations on a 12-tone theme.

Erwartung. A "monodrama" for soprano and orchestra, a stream-of-consciousness monologue from a woman who discovers the corpse of her lover in the woods.

"Gaze" by Arnold Schoenberg, 1910.
© Belmont Music Publishers, Los Angeles, © VBK, Vienna.

Arnold Schoenberg, ca. 1920. Notice the similarity of this photographic portrait by Man Ray with Schoenberg's painting "The Gaze."

© 2010 Estate of Man Ray/Artists Rights Society.

A Survivor from Warsaw. A cantata for narrator, male chorus, and orchestra, based on a report of Jews being shipped to the gas chambers in World War II bursting into the *Shema Yisrael*, a sung prayer.

Moses und Aron. An opera based on Moses and the Israelites in the wilderness.

Arnold Schoenberg "Columbine" from *Pierrot lunaire*

Time	Original German Text	English Translation	Timbre	Word-Music Relationships
0:00	Des Mondlichts bleiche Blüten, Die weißen Wunderrosen, Blühn in den Julinächten— O bräch ich eine nur!	Moonlight's pale blossoms, The miraculous white roses, Blossom in the nights of July Oh, if I could pluck just one!	Vocal soloist (*Sprechstime*), piano, and violin, which alternates between bowed and plucked (pizzicato) passages	Conjunct motion for most words except those describing the "miraculous white roses," which are set to large leaps. Notes are short, broken, breathless.
0:27	Mein banges Leid zu lindern, Such ich am dunklen Strome Des Mondlichts bleiche Blüten, Die weißen Wunderrosen.	To still my anxious suffering, I seek alongside the dark stream Moonlight's pale blossoms, The miraculous white roses.		The notes of "the miraculous white roses" go extremely deep in the singer's range.
0:52	Gestillt wär all mein Sehnen, Dürft ich so märchenheimlich, So selig leis —entblättern Auf deine braunen Haare Des Mondlichts bleiche Blüten!	All my longing would be stilled If I could, in fairy-tale fashion, Secretly and softly—pluck onto your brown tresses Moonlight's pale blossoms!	Vocal soloist (*Sprechstime*), flute and clarinet enter for the first time at 1:13, on the word *entblättern* ("pluck").	Repetitive three-note pattern in the wind instruments, beginning at 1:13, reflects the image of Pierrot dropping the white rose petals onto Columbine's brown hair.

© Arnold Schoenberg Center, Vienna

Student FAQs

Why would anyone want to listen to such ugly music?

"Ugly" is in the ear of the listener. Besides, works of art don't always have to be beautiful to be moving. For many listeners, a work like Schoenberg's is appealing not because it is beautiful, but because it is true, because it confronts the reality of the mind and doesn't try to sugar-coat things.

Why Sprechstimme?

Schoenberg probably felt that normal singing would sound too, well, normal. So he settled on a technique that would make the voice seem stylized and distorted, the sonic counterpart of expressionist painting and (later) expressionist film (see "Expressionist Film").

Konzert-Bureau Emil Gutmann, Berlin W. 35

Choralionsaal Mittwoch, 16. Oktober, abds. 8 Uhr

Uraufführung

Arnold Schönberg "Pierrot Lunaire"

Deutsch von A. Giraud, übertragen von Otto Erich Hartleben.

3 Mal sprechit für eine Sprechstimme und kleines Kammerorchester.

Albertine Zehme (Rezitation)

Eduard Steuermann (Klavier), Jakob Malinjak (Violin, Bratsche), Hans Kindler (Violoncello),
H. W. de Vries (Flöte), C. Essberger (Klarinette).

© Arnold Schoenberg Center, Vienna

CULTURAL CONTEXT

Expressionist Film

Expressionism came of age in the years just after World War I, when filmmaking was becoming a serious art form. A number of prominent directors around this time, especially in Germany, made movies that reflect the expressionist outlook. These films tend to be dark, severe, and highly stylized. They are often gruesome and surreal. The plots of these movies rarely involve action and revolve instead around issues of insanity and the psychologically abnormal.

Fritz Lang (1890–1976) is widely regarded as the greatest of all expressionistic directors. Like Schoenberg, he immigrated to the United States because of his Jewish ancestry. Lang's most famous films, *Metropolis* (1927) and *M* (1931), won international acclaim and still hold their own in moviehouses today. The tradition of expressionist film lives on in the work of such modern-day directors as Tim Burton (*Batman Returns, Edward Scissorhands*) and David Lynch (*Eraserhead, Lost Highway*).

A still from *The Cabinet of Dr. Caligari*, an early (1920) German expressionist film about the head of an insane asylum who is himself a serial murderer. Notice the distorted use of perspective, the grotesque costumes and makeup, and the stylized decor of the room.

The Museum of Modern Art/Film Stills Archive

 EXPAND YOUR PLAYLIST

Expressionism

Schoenberg was the leading composer of the expressionist movement, but others followed his lead and developed their own personal varieties of expressionism.

Anton Webern. Six Bagatelles, op. 9. These aphoristic works for string quartet, by an Austrian protégé of Schoenberg, are highly atonal and intense. The title ("Little Trifles") is ironic. These works are anything but trifles, in spite of their size.

Anton Webern. *Five Pieces for Orchestra,* op. 10. Like all Webern's works, these are brief but concentrated. Webern's music does not "scream" in the same way that some of Schoenberg's does, but it can be quietly desperate.

Alban Berg. *Wozzeck*. This expressionist opera, by another Austrian disciple of Schoenberg, is a mainstay of the operatic repertory today; its story, about the fate of a poor soldier, still exerts a powerful effect on audiences around the world.

Alban Berg. *Lulu*. Another highly successful expressionist opera, this one about the rise and fall of a *femme fatale*.

Ernst Křenek. *Jonny spielt auf! (Johnny Strikes Up the Band)*. This opera, by an Austrian composer of Czech ancestry, mixes jazz idioms with atonal expressionism.

43

Igor Stravinsky
Rite of Spring, Part One

 Listen to This

Harmony

Are the harmonies here tonal or atonal? Do you hear a harmonic center of gravity?

Melody

Listen for the fragmentary nature of the melodies, which seem to start and stop suddenly, without warning.

Rhythm

What is the meter of this work? Can you tap a regular pattern of beats? Are some sections more regular than others?

Timbre

The enormous size of the orchestra for this ballet was virtually without precedent. Listen for the variety of sounds in all families of instruments: woodwinds, brass, strings, and percussion.

Word-Music Relationships

The dancers present through movement and gesture the storyline of the ballet. What images or events or moods come to mind as you listen to this music?

Stravinsky's ballet *The Rite of Spring (Le Sacre du printemps)* was so controversial at its premiere in 1913 that it caused a riot. Many in the Paris audience found the harmonies, melodies, and rhythms to be beyond the limits of the acceptable, and they let their feelings be known (see "The Audience Riots"). Yet within a few years *The Rite of Spring* had become an audience favorite around the world. Tastes were changing rapidly, and what had been on the cutting edge in 1913 was hardly modern a decade later.

The work was commissioned by Sergei Diaghilev for his Ballets Russes (The Russian Ballet), a company of largely Russian dancers whose home base was in Paris. The score follows the scenario of a ballet Stravinsky himself recalls as having first conceived in "a fleeting vision which came to me as a complete surprise. . . . I saw in my imagination a solemn pagan rite. Sage elders, seated in a circle, watched a young girl dance herself to death. They were sacrificing her to propitiate the God of Spring. I heard and I wrote what I heard. I am the vessel through which *Le Sacre* passed." In the end, the scenario for the ballet was drawn up by Stravinsky and Nikolai Roerich, a leading expert in Russian folklore and ancient ritual. Originally called *The Great Sacrifice,* the ballet was eventually divided into two parts: (1) The Adoration of the Earth; and (2) The Sacrifice.

Polytonal Harmonies

Does Stravinsky's *The Rite of Spring* lack a tonal center, as Schoenberg's *Pierrot lunaire* and parts of Ives *Unanswered Question* do? Is this atonal music? No, it is not. The reason the harmonies of *The Rite of Spring* sound different, and the reason the tonal center is hard to find, is not because there isn't one, but because at any given moment there is

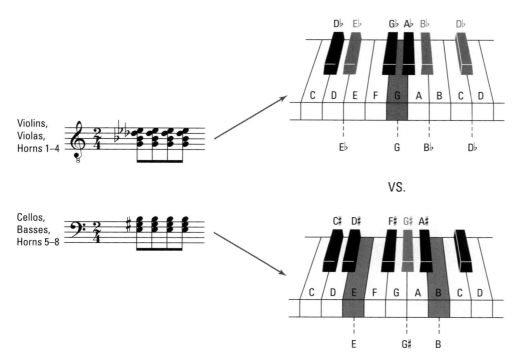

often *more* than one. The repetitive chords at 3:36, for example, juxtapose two conventional harmonies in a way that creates a new dissonance of its own. Each of the two chords is tonal in its own right, but when combined, they clash. This kind of harmony is called **polytonal**.

To hear this clash of tonalities, ask someone who knows how to play the piano to play an E-major chord with the left hand. Then ask that person to play an E-flat seventh chord with the right hand. Separately, the two chords sound perfectly consonant. Finally, ask the person to play the two chords together. Simultaneously, they sound dissonant. This is **polytonality**.

Pentatonic Melodies

Many of the melodies in *The Rite of Spring* are built on the **pentatonic scale**. As its name implies ("pent" = "five," as in the word "pentagon"), this scale consists of five notes instead of the conventional seven. An example of a melody based on a pentatonic scale may be found at the beginning of the "Spring Round Dance" (8:22).

Like Dvořák before him (see chapter 38), Stravinsky was trying to capture a folk-like sound. The setting of this ballet, after all, is "Pagan Russia," before the arrival of Christianity there in the tenth century. In the context of this ballet, the pentatonic melodies—some of which Stravinsky found in transcriptions of Russian folksong—give the work an exotic, even modern sound, very different from that of the musical traditions of Western Europe. The melodies tend to be brief and full of repetitions—small fragments repeated and varied many times in succession—and they always seem to arrive and depart without warning.

A recent production of *The Rite of Spring,* performed by the Kirov Ballet.
Laurie Lewis/Lebrecht Music & Arts Photo Library

Ostinato Rhythms

One of the most novel elements of this music is its use of extremely irregular rhythms at times. Notice, for example, how the melody at the beginning of the "Spring Round Dance" (see musical example above) changes meter three times within three measures: the first measure has five beats, the second has seven, and the third has six. This kind of rhythmic irregularity is offset by the frequent use of **ostinato** figures, in which a single rhythmic or rhythmic-melodic gesture is repeated over and over again, many times. Listen, for example, to the ostinato in the low strings beginning at 8:48. This figure repeats itself no fewer than 32 times over the next two-and-half minutes. Similar extended ostinato patterns can be found through the work.

The Mega-Orchestra

The orchestra for Brahms's Fourth Symphony (1885) seems like a chamber ensemble by comparison to the orchestra of Stravinsky's *The Rite of Spring,* which calls for an ensemble consisting of the following:

Woodwinds:
1 piccolo
3 flutes, 1 doubling on second piccolo
1 alto flute
1 English horn
4 oboes, 1 doubling on second English horn
1 E♭ clarinet
3 clarinets, 1 doubling on second bass clarinet
1 bass clarinet
4 bassoons, 1 doubling on second contrabassoon
1 contrabassoon

Brass:
8 French horns, 2 doubling on tenor tubas
1 high trumpet (D trumpet)
4 trumpets
1 bass trumpet
3 trombones
2 tubas

Percussion: Timpani, bass drum, cymbals, gong, guero ("scraper"), tambourine, triangle

Strings: Violins 1 & 2, violas, cellos, double basses

Percussion · Horns · Woodwinds (flutes, clarinets, oboes, bassoons) · Trumpets · Trombones · Tuba

First violins · Second violins · Conductor · Violas · Cellos · Double basses

Unsung Words: The Scenario

In ballet, the dancers present, through their movement, a story line known as the **scenario**. The words of the scenario are not sung, but they shape the form of the music directly. In the fall of 1913, a few months after the work's premiere, Stravinsky drew up the following description of the ballet's scenario:

> *The Rite of Spring* is a musical choreographic work. It represents pagan Russia and is unified by a single idea: the mystery and great surge of creative power of Spring. The piece has no plot, but the choreographic sequence is as follows:

Part One: The Adoration of the Earth

The Spring celebration. The pipers pipe and young men tell fortunes. The old woman enters. She knows the mystery of nature and how to predict the future. Young girls with painted faces come in from the river in single file. They dance the Spring dances. Games start. The Spring *Khorovod* [a stately dance]. The people divide into two opposed groups. The holy procession of the wise old men. The oldest and wisest interrupts the Spring games, which come to a stop. The people pause trembling before the Great Action. The old men bless the earth. The Kiss of the Earth. The people dance passionately on the earth, sanctifying it and becoming one with it.

Part Two: The Great Sacrifice

At night the virgins hold mysterious games, walking in circles. One of the virgins is consecrated as the victim and is twice pointed to by fate, being caught twice in the perpetual circle of walking-in-rounds. The virgins honor her, the Chosen One, with a marital dance. They invoke the ancestors and entrust the Chosen One to the old wise men. She sacrifices herself in the presence of the old men in the Great Sacred Dance, THE GREAT SACRIFICE.[1]

In writing *The Rite of Spring,* Stravinsky gave each of these scenes its own distinctive music. The form of the work is **through-composed**. There is very little repetition of music between individual sections.

With these points in mind, listen once again to Part One of Stravinsky's *The Rite of Spring,* using the Listening Guide.

---

[1]Vera Stravinsky and Robert Craft, *Stravinsky in Pictures and Documents* (New York: Simon & Schuster, 1978), p. 75.

Igor Stravinsky (1882–1971)

"MODERNSKY"

Like many of today's pop artists—Bob Dylan, David Bowie, Madonna—Stravinsky was constantly reinventing himself. The son of a famous operatic bass singer, he was born in St. Petersburg, and many of his early works, including *The Rite of Spring*, reflect his Russian ancestry. By 1917, he was at the forefront of a new movement, neoclassicism, which turned its back on the huge orchestras and complex textures of his own earlier music. In this period, Stravinsky wrote music that was more clearly tonal, using forms and rhythmic patterns that owed much to the music of the eighteenth century. Many other composers followed his lead.

With the advent of World War II, Stravinsky continued his westward migration, settling in Los Angeles in 1939 and becoming a U.S. citizen in 1945. Late in life, to everyone's astonishment, he began writing 12-tone music, the most intellectually rigorous and severe form of atonal music. Even at an advanced age, the old composer could learn new tricks.

From the 1920s onward, Stravinsky was widely regarded as one of the century's two greatest composers, together with Arnold Schoenberg (who had fled his native Austria and also settled in Los Angeles). Unlike Schoenberg, however, Stravinsky found a relatively wide following among concertgoers. In spite of his avowed modernism (one clever critic dubbed him "Modernsky"), he was able to connect with audiences. He had no direct students, but his influence on subsequent generations of composers has been profound.

PLAYLIST: STRAVINSKY

Petrouchka. A ballet written for Diaghilev shortly before *The Rite of Spring,* also based on Russian themes.

Pulcinella. A ballet in the Neoclassical style, again for Diaghilev, based in part on actual melodies from the eighteenth century.

Stravinsky (seated) visiting Claude Debussy, a composer whose works he admired enormously, ca. 1912. Like Debussy, Stravinsky sought to expand the vocabulary of music.

Corbis/Bettmann

Symphony in Three Movements. Another neoclassical work that includes a fugue.

The Rake's Progress. An English-language opera set to a libretto by the English poet W.H. Auden, tracing the decline and fall of a libertine.

Canticum sacrum. A late, 12-tone work for tenor, baritone, chorus, and orchestra.

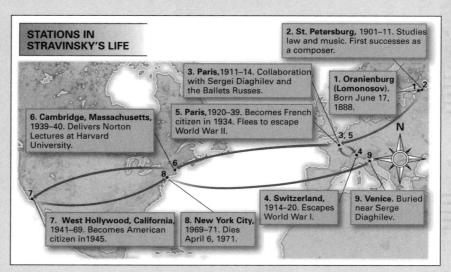

STATIONS IN STRAVINSKY'S LIFE

1. Oranienburg (Lomonosov). Born June 17, 1888.

2. St. Petersburg, 1901–11. Studies law and music. First successes as a composer.

3. Paris, 1911–14. Collaboration with Sergei Diaghilev and the Ballets Russes.

4. Switzerland, 1914–20. Escapes World War I.

5. Paris, 1920–39. Becomes French citizen in 1934. Flees to escape World War II.

6. Cambridge, Massachusetts, 1939–40. Delivers Norton Lectures at Harvard University.

7. West Hollywood, California, 1941–69. Becomes American citizen in 1945.

8. New York City, 1969–71. Dies April 6, 1971.

9. Venice. Buried near Serge Diaghilev.

Igor Stravinsky *Rite of Spring*, Part One (excerpt)

Time	Word-Music Relationships The Scenario	Timbre	Rhythm
0:00	**Introduction** (the curtain remains down). Stravinsky later said that this introduction "should represent the awakening of nature" after a long Russian winter, "the scratching, gnawing, and wiggling of birds and beasts."	Wind instruments predominate. Each instrument seems to function independently of the others, from the solo on the bassoon at the opening through the gradual addition of horns, clarinets, English horn, oboes, and flutes.	Free
3:14	*The Spring celebration. The pipers pipe and young men tell fortunes. The old woman enters. She knows the mystery of nature and how to predict the future.*	The entrance of the fortuneteller (3:14) is signaled by the appearance of an ostinato motif in the violins (pizzicato).	
3:36	**The Harbingers of Spring; Dances of the Adolescents.** *Young girls with painted faces come in from the river in single file. They dance the Spring dances.*	Full orchestra. Strings enter in force for the first time.	Same chord repeated many times, but with no predictable pattern of accent
6:56	**Game of Abduction.** *The games start.*	Full orchestra, including heavy beating of timpani and bass drum.	Frenzied pace, fast rhythm
8:22	**Spring Round Dance.** *The Spring Khorovod (a traditional Russian circle dance).*	High winds introduce the main melody, played on clarinets.	A slow, stately dance, which transforms the preceding mood of frenzy into one of calm. Ostinato bass begins at 8:48.
12:16	**Games of Rival Tribes.** *The people divide into two opposed groups.*	Percussion and low brass open this section.	Another energetic section based on a succession of ostinato patterns.
14:16	**Procession of the Sage.** *The holy procession of the wise old men. The oldest and wisest interrupts the Spring games, which come to a stop.*	Steady drum beat, with prominent brass parts	Another section based on a slow, steady, ostinato pattern. Comes to a sudden and extremely abrupt stop.
14:58	**Adoration of the Earth.** *The people pause trembling before the Great Action. The old men bless the earth. The Kiss of the Earth.*	Sustained low winds, with high notes on double bass, punctuated by timpani	For the first time, the forward momentum of the music stops.
15:20	**The Dance of the Earth.** *The people dance passionately on the earth, sanctifying it and becoming one with it.*	Full orchestra	Ostinato pattern in bass.

Melody

Fragments are mostly based on a pentatonic scale. Several of the melodies are based on Russian folk tunes that Stravinsky knew from a published source.

The ostinato figure that occurs here will come back later.

Ostinato figure throughout (3:46, 4:01, 5:02, etc.); melodic fragments above and below

Short fragment running up and down, repeated many times

Pentatonic melody at 8:22. The theme sounds extremely simple at first but becomes more complicated as it progresses.

Many thematic fragments simultaneously, in layers of the orchestra

Again, many fragments in layers of the orchestra

The "kiss" is an eerily quiet chord played on a group of 14 solo string instruments (violins, violas, cellos, double basses).

The "kiss" unleashes a frenzy of motion. Once again, the music builds over a sustained ostinato pattern. And once again, the music comes to an abrupt halt.

Student FAQs

Is this work always performed as a ballet?

No. In fact, ballet performances are fairly rare. Stravinsky's *The Rite of Spring* has become a staple of the concert hall, where it is enjoyed without the added dimension of dance.

Why did the first audience riot?

There were many reasons. Some were sincerely offended by the unconventional nature of the music. Others found the choreography preposterous: ballet dancers, by convention, had always emphasized grace in their movements, and Vaslav Nijinsky's choreography called for the dancers to do many decidedly ungraceful moves, like a rapid series of standing vertical leaps. And there is speculation that Sergei Diaghilev, the director of the dance company, may have actually encouraged a scandal at the opening. A scandal meant publicity, and publicity meant ticket sales, not only for this ballet, but for others being produced by the Ballets Russes.

The Business of Dance

Sergei Diaghilev (1872–1929) had a great eye for talent. As director of the Ballets Russes in Paris, he encouraged the still relatively unknown Igor Stravinsky to write music for his company. In addition to Stravinsky, he engaged groundbreaking composers such as Claude Debussy, Maurice Ravel, Erik Satie, Richard Strauss, Sergei Prokofiev, and Francis Poulenc. And he worked with an equally impressive array of artists on set designs, including Pablo Picasso, Leon Bakst, and Juan Gris. Many of the dancers and choreographers in his company became legends in their own right, including Vaslav Nijinsky (chief choreographer for *The Rite of Spring*), Anna Pavlova, and Georges Balanchine (1904–83), the last of whom became a leading force in the world of American ballet.

Diaghilev combined his sense of taste with the skills of a businessman. The early years of the Ballets Russes, from its founding in 1909 until the outbreak of World War I in 1914, were the most financially successful. The musical repertory consistently included new works by promising young composers, which were always a topic of conversation among the Parisian elite. Even the riot at the premiere of *The Rite of Spring* produced excellent press for the company. As a result of the scandal, subsequent performances attracted supporters, detractors, and those who were just plain curious, and all of them paid to see the show.

Sergei Diaghilev, the Russian impresario who found great success in Paris through his collaborations with Stravinsky, Picasso, and others.
Lebrecht Music & Arts Photo Library

"The Elect" from Stravinsky's *Rite of Spring* in the original 1913 production. The innovative costumes and masks were by Russian designer N. K. Roerich and were part of what made the original production so shocking to audiences.
Lebrecht Music & Arts

The years after the war were less rewarding. Cultural life did not return to its earlier level for several years, and Diaghilev had to use great ingenuity to keep his company afloat. The revival of *The Rite of Spring* in 1920 offers a case in point. The work was in great demand—audiences *wanted* to hear the work now, not shout it down—but the orchestra demanded by the score was enormous, almost twice the size of the company's normal ensemble, and all 97 musicians had to be paid. Diaghilev turned to the fashion designer Gabrielle ("Coco") Chanel for help, and she contributed a large sum of money that made the production possible. After Diaghilev's death, the Ballets Russes struggled, changing its name and locale at various times but never recreating the success it had enjoyed under its founder.

MUSIC IN PERFORMANCE

The Audience Riots

The audience at the premiere of *The Rite of Spring* in Paris in May 1913 was scandalized by the music and the dancing, which by the composer's own account was seriously out of step with the music. As Stravinsky later recalled:

> The complexity of my score had demanded a great number of rehearsals, which [Pierre] Monteux had conducted with his usual skill and attention. . . . During the whole performance I was at [the choreographer Vaslav] Nijinsky's side in the wings. He was standing on a chair, screaming "sixteen, seventeen, eighteen"— they had their own method of counting to keep time. Naturally, the poor dancers could hear nothing by reason of the row in the auditorium and the sound of their own dance steps. I had to hold Nijinsky by his clothes, for he was furious, and ready to dash on to the stage at any moment and create a scandal. [The impresario Sergei] Diaghilev kept ordering the electricians to turn the lights on or off, hoping in that way to put a stop to the noise. That is all I can remember about that first performance. Oddly enough, at the dress rehearsal, . . . everything had gone off peacefully, and I was very far from expecting such an outburst.[1]

[1]"Igor Stravinsky, *Stravinsky: An Autobiography* (New York: Simon and Schuster, 1936), pp. 72–3."

The noted Parisian critic Pierre Lalo spoke for many of his contemporaries when he characterized the work in these terms:

> *Le Sacre du Printemps* is . . . the most dissonant and the most discordant composition that has ever been written. . . . Never before has the system and cult of the wrong note been applied with such industry, zeal, and obstinacy. From the first measure of the work to the last, whatever note one expects is never the note that follows. . . . Whatever the previous chord, the chord one actually hears, and this chord and this note are used expressly to produce the impression of falseness that is acute and almost excruciating. When two themes are superimposed, the composer scarcely uses themes that might work together; quite to the contrary, he chooses themes whose superimposition produces the most irritating friction and grating that can be imagined.[2]

But the riot soon turned to Stravinsky's advantage. Within a few short months, audiences across Europe were greeting *The Rite of Spring* with great enthusiasm, and the initial rejection of the work served to rally all artists of modernist tendencies. They saw in this incident a vindication of artistic vision in the face of conservative public tastes. Audiences, in turn, became increasingly tolerant of modernism in general.

[2]"*Le Temps*, Paris, June 3, 1913. Transl. MEB (author)."

 EXPAND YOUR PLAYLIST

Ballet Music

Ballet can be danced to almost any kind of music, but from the middle of the nineteenth century onward, a number of prominent composers have written works expressly to be danced onstage.

Adolph Adam. *Giselle.* One of the earliest (1841) full-length ballets to establish itself in the repertory. A love story, full of intrigues and disguises.

Leo Delibes. *Coppélia.* An intricate plot centered around a pair of lovers. It premiered in 1870 at the Paris Opera.

Pyotr Illich Tchaikovsky. *The Nutcracker, Swan Lake, Sleeping Beauty.* Tchaikovsky's ballets, especially these three most famous works, are standards of the repertory today.

Francis Poulenc. *Les biches.* Commissioned by Diaghilev and the Ballets Russes in 1922, the scenario of this ballet (whose title translates awkwardly as "The Female Deer") takes place at a fashionable party in contemporary Paris. Poulenc was a member of the French group of composers who called themselves "Les Six" (see Web Bonus Chapter 4).

Sergei Prokofiev. *Romeo and Juliet.* This 1935 score, commissioned by the Kirov Theater of Leningrad (St. Petersburg), follows the basic outline of Shakespeare's tragedy.

44

Berta Waza
Greetings by Aba Musa!

Listen to This

Melody

Listen for the melody. How is it distributed throughout the instrumental parts?

Harmony

How do the tones blend together?

Texture

How is the sound of this ensemble built up? How would you describe the sound?

Rhythm

Listen for the beat. How many beats are in the cycle? Find the first beat of the cycle.

The waza trumpet ensemble is performed by the Berta people of the Blue Nile province in southern Sudan. It consists of 12 trumpets made from gourds, the instruments ranging in length from approximately 1.5 to 6 feet (0.45 to 1.8 meters). To make a trumpet, several gourds are attached to form a tube; bamboo splits, tied on by ropes, are used to join the gourds and help to keep the instrument straight. Each trumpet can produce only one tone. Five of the trumpeters, while blowing a trumpet held in the left hand, tap an angled wooden crook called a *bali,* draped over their right shoulder, with a cow horn held in the right hand. The taps set the rhythm for the trumpet ensemble.

Like the Mbuti Pygmies of central Africa (see chapter 11), the *waza* ensemble creates a single melody through **interlocking** parts. Each musician has an individual part to perform simultaneously with all the others. The full ensemble then creates a melody out of these many individual parts. The individual parts occur within a repeated rhythmic cycle, or pattern, and together melody and rhythm form an ostinato. A *waza* ensemble's song also has words that are sung by women.

The *waza* belongs to older African musical traditions that were performed especially for chiefs. The original Berta chiefs were called *mek,* but they were displaced in the nineteenth century by Muslim rulers from the northern Sudan. The *waza* still performs for Islamic chiefs, but the musicians remain ethnic Berta. Songs may be in either the Berta language or Arabic. Today the *waza* is also played at public and communal events and is not just reserved for chiefs.

Waza is always performed after sunset, and it is never played for funerals or during the rainy season. The trumpets are believed to contain spirits that are brought to life by having a burning torch set against them. In the old animist practice, the torches were then thrown in one of the four compass directions, depending on the season of the year. This listening example is music for a boy's circumcision ceremony.

A *waza* orchestra is divided into two parts: trumpets 1–5, which are the shorter trumpets, and trumpets 6–10, the longer. Typically, the trumpet 1, called the *wazalu,* begins the song alone on his tone in his rhythmic pattern, and then trumpet 2, called the *waza moshang,* plays a cross rhythm on his tone. Then, trumpets 1–5 play the song melody in interlock, while trumpets 6–10 double their parts in the lower register, also in interlock. The trumpets, however, are not exactly tuned, so when the doubled parts are played simultaneously the result is **polytonality**.

Two short trumpets called *mashair* have been added to reinforce the sounds of the high-pitched lead and second trumpets. These two additional trumpets are neither exactly tuned to the *wazalu* nor to the *waza mushang,* and their harmonizations are also polytonal.

Polytonality in *waza* happens quite naturally. Tones do not have to be exact, just a relative degree higher or lower to create the melodic line. The rhythm of the interlocking patterns is of primary importance; tones are secondary and may be varied as long as they are proportional to the melody. It is a natural polytonality, because the 12 differently pitched *waza* trumpets create literally "many tones." While the polytonality created is conventional in Berta music, it is unconventional in European orchestral music. Twentieth-century composers such as Igor Stravinsky created a similar effect by contrasting tones played within a pulsing, rhythmic framework. You may compare this *waza* performance to Stravinsky's *The Rite of Spring* (chapter 43).

Melody

An introductory melody is sung by the women. Then the trumpet players enter separately in cross rhythms on their single pitches. When all the trumpets have entered and are playing in interlock, they outline the melodic contour of the actual song the women begin to sing. They do not reproduce the *exact* tones, just relative steps. The women sing the melody over the trumpets, while the trumpets render the melody in what may be described as a polytonal accompaniment to the song.

Melodic contour of *Aba Musa Iadoiya* in ostinato

1 2 3 4   5 6 7 8 9 10 11 12

Harmony

The trumpets' tones create a polytonal texture under the sung tones of the women. The trumpets' tones are relative to the sung pitches because they are relative to the melodic contour. The importance of the *waza* tones is in their relative relation. The tones are polytonal, however, and these polytones occur throughout the ostinato.

Texture

Each individual player has his own rhythmic pattern that interlocks with all the others. Once established, the song repeats in ostinato; the structure of the music is built up by all the parts repeating over and over.

Rhythm

The song is in a fast cycle of 12 beats. All the trumpet parts play the 12-beat cycle but begin at different points in the cycle, creating cross rhythms. The cross rhythms are timed to create the melodic line and accompanying texture. Once the cycle is established, the singers and the *waza* trumpets perform the song over and over in ostinato, clearly heard beginning at 0:42 and 0:49. The songs, of which "Greetings by Aba Musa!" ("Aba Musa Iadoiya!") is an example, are short and simple, and are about everyday matters that reflect Berta values. Note that in the cycle, the melody extends through beat 8, and from beats 9 through 12, the interlocking trumpets maintain the rhythmic and harmonic texture.

Now listen to this piece again, following the Listening Guide.

Polytonality in Jazz

Jazz music weds European and African influences. While African instruments like the *waza* trumpet have been replaced by the European valved trumpet, the idea of an ensemble playing a melody simultaneously but not exactly identically carried over from African ensembles to early New Orleans jazz. In what is called polytonality or heterophony, the musicians do not attempt to play exactly the same parts but rather interact dynamically with each other, creating a melodically and rhythmically rich texture.

The greatest example of New Orleans–style polytonality was achieved in the recordings of Louis Armstrong's Hot Five and Hot Seven (the number varied by the actual size of the group on each individual recording). In the ensemble part, the lead instruments—Armstrong's trumpet, Johnny Dodd's clarinet, and Kid Ory's trombone—did not play the exact same melodic part. The differences were often subtle and could vary in terms of tonality (such as attack or vibrato), rhythm (such as placement of the note against the beat), or variation (such as Dodds occasionally taking off on a clarinet riff that broke free of the constraints of the melody itself).

However, Armstrong's groups differed in the fact that Armstrong himself was such a great virtuoso that his solo playing often was featured, with the ensemble merely vamping in the background. One of the most famous of all moments in early jazz is the amazing solo introduction to "West End Blues," where the unaccompanied Armstrong plays a breathtaking cadenza culminating in a lip-blistering high C.

Louis Armstrong and his Hot Five, 1926. Left to right: Louis Armstrong at piano holding trumpet, Johnny St. Cyr with banjo, Johnny Dodds, Kid Ory, Lil Hardin Armstrong.
JAN PERSSON/Lebrecht Music & Arts Photo Library

While the swing era (see chapter 50) led to more arranged, carefully harmonized ensemble playing, polytonality would never completely disappear from jazz. With free jazz, jazz rock/fusion, and other later styles, the idea of ensembles playing nearly the same melody simultaneously would return with many interesting variations.

Listening Guide

Berta Waza *Greetings by Aba Musa!*

Time	Melody	Texture	Harmony
0:00	Women sing an introductory melody.	Heterophonic singing with a definite leader	Monophonic or heterophonic
0:15	Singing stops.	(Silence)	(Silence)
0:17	The *wazalu* lead trumpet begins its rhythmic pattern, the player also tapping on the *bali* to set the pulse.	Solo Trumpet	Monophonic
0:19	The *waza moshang* trumpet begins its rhythmic pattern.	The first interlocking part begins.	Parts set for polytonal texture.
0:21	A lower trumpet begins its rhythmic pattern.	The second interlocking part begins.	
0:23	Introductory melody sung again by the women over the *waza* as it builds the interlocking patter from the many trumpet parts. This section is like an extended introduction to the actual song.	Interlocking builds up	
0:26	A high trumpet enters in its rhythmic pattern.		
0:30	A low trumpet begins its rhythmic pattern.		
0:34	A higher trumpet enters in rhythm with another.	Reinforcement of interlocking parts	Polytonal harmony prominent
0:35	Singing stops again.		
0:36	Another trumpet enters, doubling a part.		
0:37	Other trumpets begin to enter and double parts.		
0:41	The high *mashair* trumpet plays a strong tone.	Interlock fully established	Polytonal
0:42	The *waza* interlocking melody is fully established on the first beat of the ostinato cycle.		
0:49	Women begin the song's words on beat 1 of the third established cycle.	Interlock of the trumpets and sporadic call and response of the lead singer to the chorus	Polytonal texture within the trumpets' parts, and a polytonal relationship of the trumpets to the sung melody
3:17	The *waza* ends and the women sing an ending melody.	Heterophonic Singing	Heterophonic

Rhythm

Freely

(Silence)

Pulse set by the *bali* wood crook; the cycle not yet established

The two trumpets are in cross rhythm and creating the cycle.

Three-trumpet cross rhythms

Four-trumpet cross rhythms

Five-trumpet cross rhythms

Cycle almost fully established

The *mashair* enters on beat 12 to demark the conclusion of the introduction and the beginning of the song's cycle on the next beat. The *mashair* continues to play this strong tone on beat 12 in every recurrence of the ostinato cycle. The high tone can be clearly heard on beat 12, sometimes in variations but still on 12.

A 12-beat cycle. The *waza* play the cycle twice before the singers reenter.

Ostinato of 12 beats fully established with the singers and trumpets.

Ends

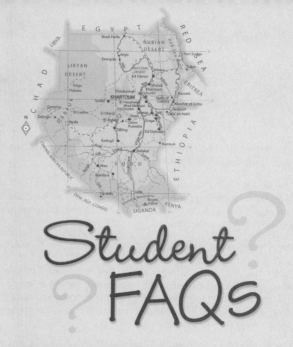

Student FAQs

Why are these instruments called trumpets?

The term "trumpet" doesn't just apply to the European, brass-bodied, valved instrument. A trumpet is technically a wind instrument that requires the player to vibrate his or her lips together to create the sound. This buzzing-like technique breaks up the air flow into pulses that are transmitted through the tube of the instrument to create the basic tone.

Why does each trumpet play only one note?

The modern orchestral trumpet is able to play all the notes of the scale thanks to the introduction of keyed valves in the nineteenth century. When a valve is opened, an additional length of tubing is open to the flow of air created by the trumpeter's blowing into the mouthpiece of the horn. The longer the airstream, the lower the pitch is. Each valve adds length and can be combined with the others to create any note desired. On the other hand, the *waza* trumpet is called a "natural" trumpet because it has no valves or extra tubing. A single tube can play only one note strongly (**harmonics**, or further subdivisions of the primary vibrating column of air, may be heard more faintly). Therefore, to play additional notes, other trumpets of varying lengths are needed.

Why is the women's role limited to singing while the men are allowed to play musical instruments?

In different traditional cultures, men's and women's roles are strictly defined. Music making is one area where men traditionally are given a broader role than women because of the perceived power of music to affect the spiritual and earthly world. Even in Western cultures, women have traditionally played a secondary role in music making, although this has been changing rapidly in modern times.

Come Blow Your Horn!

Here's a list of recommended African and other traditional recordings featuring trumpets or horns.

African Music, Folkways FW08852.
Early field recordings (made in the late 1930s) by pioneering ethnomusicologist Laura Boulton in Africa demonstrating various instruments, including horns.

Por Por: Honk Horn Music of Ghana, Smithsonian/Folkways SFW40541.
Performed by The La Drivers Union Por Por Group, this wonderful record shows how Africans have taken the tradition of interlocking parts to modern times. The ensemble uses car horns, tire rims, and other "found" industrial objects to create complex interlocking melodies and rhythms.

Best of Mariachi, Dorchester Classics 9010.
Mexican mariachi bands prominently feature trumpets, usually in pairs, that play both melody and interspersed harmonic accompaniments to the soaring vocals. This recording features three of the best-known contemporary mariachi bands: Mariachi Sol, Mariachi Azteca, and De Norte a Sur y Amigos.

Music of New Orleans, Vol. 2: Music of the Eureka Brass Band, Folkways FW02462.
Traditional brass band music of New Orleans, predating jazz but showing group polytonality in its performance.

The Best of Louis Armstrong: Hot Fives and Hot Sevens, Columbia Legacy 593590.
This "official" reissue has superior sound quality and notes compared to the many other (less expensive) sets available. Armstrong is at the height of his powers, and his sidemen, including Johnny Dodds, Kid Ory, Earl Hines (on some tracks), and Lonnie Johnson (on some tracks), are wonderful.

45

Scott Joplin
Maple Leaf Rag

Listen to This

Rhythm

Find the basic beat of the piece, and then listen for rhythmic accents. Do they occur on the beat or off the beat? Are some sections of the recording more rhythmically active than others?

Melody

Can you identify any melodies that contain wide leaps? If you were asked to sing back the melody of the piece, what would you sing? Are there ever multiple melodies audible at the same time?

Form

Do you hear discrete musical sections? Do any of them repeat or return later in the recording? How long are the sections?

When Scott Joplin published *Maple Leaf Rag* in 1899, the piece became an enormous hit, selling thousands of copies of sheet music during its first few years in print and inspiring countless musicians to perform it and to create new arrangements of it. The money Joplin earned from the piece encouraged him to dedicate more time and energy to composing and publishing his music. Over the span of his career, he published approximately 80 pieces, including several of the best-known ragtime works.

Ragtime was a style of music that emphasized rhythmic **syncopation** (regularly spaced musical accents that occur off the beat) while continuing many of the characteristics of marches, cakewalks, two-steps, and popular songs from the late nineteenth century. Ragtime music during the first decade of the twentieth century included solo piano pieces, songs (with lyrics), and pieces for small dance ensembles, but most listeners today know the piano solos best.

The style originated in the Midwest when musicians improvised catchy rhythmic variations of popular songs, a technique known as "ragging" a tune. In 1893, Chicago hosted the World's Columbian Exposition, which drew musicians and performers from around the country. African American musicians excluded from the official entertainment performed outside the exposition in countless venues, exchanging musical ideas and learning each other's styles. Musical developments at these and similar gatherings brought ragtime into existence. The first pieces titled "Ragtime" or "Rag" appeared in 1897 in Chicago, and the style spread rapidly across the country.

In the first years of the twentieth century, ragtime was perceived as a threat to the "moral, spiritual, mental, and even physical well being" of the nation (as historian Edward Berlin explained).[1] One reason was that the music was associated with saloons, brothels, and illicit establishments, all of which frequently hired ragtime pianists to entertain customers. Furthermore, the music used rhythmic patterns that were associated with African American musical traditions. During those years, racist perceptions of African American musical practices in many communities meant that ragtime was seen as undermining the more genteel, socially appropriate, and proper (i.e., white) cultural forms. Finally, ragtime was dance music, and dance music invoked sexual interpretations that again threatened the social decorum of the era. Although older generations mostly disapproved of the music, ragtime became immensely popular with the young people. Its rhythms, melodies, and performance traditions provided one of the foundations of jazz, and it became known as a quintessentially American musical style.

Rhythmic Syncopation

The piece is in duple meter, and one can easily count "one-and-two-and-one-and-two-and" along with the music. Notice that every other high note in the opening few measures falls between those counted moments.

While it is easy to hear the beat in *Maple Leaf Rag* and tap along with it, many of the rhythmic accents, such as those high notes in the first few measures, do not fall on the beat. Instead, they occur at regularly spaced intervals that oppose the underlying beat. This rhythmic technique is called "syncopation." It occurs in Western classical music as well as in many other traditions around the world, but its pervasive use in ragtime makes it a primary identifier of the style.

The syncopation in *Maple Leaf Rag* occurs because the music's accompaniment consists of notes that are evenly spaced two rhythmic pulses apart, while the melody uses patterns that are three rhythmic pulses long. (In music notation, these rhythmic pulses are sixteenth notes;

[1]Edward A. Berlin, *King of Ragtime: Scott Joplin and His Era* (New York: Oxford University Press, 1994), p. 87.

see example below.) The rhythmic relationship between the melody and accompaniment creates the following pattern, where "x's" represent rhythmic accents:

| Melody: | X O O X O O X O O X O O... |
| Accompaniment: | X O X O X O X O X O X O... |

To hear this pattern of syncopation, tap your foot in a steady beat of one tap for every "x" or "o" in the chart. Have one person clap on the "x's" in the accompaniment pattern, while a classmate claps on the "x's" in the melody pattern.

This particular type of syncopation, where patterns of "2's" occur at the same time as patterns of "3's," is identified as **hemiola**. Hemiola is a more complex type of syncopation than what is found in many other ragtime compositions. Its use in *Maple Leaf Rag* helps the piece stand out from the hundreds of other ragtime publications from the same time period.

Another type of syncopation in the piece occurs when the melody sounds like it jumps in "early" in relation to the accompaniment. Listen to the repeated notes in the melody at 0:16–0:18. The first and the last of the melody's repeated notes come in before the metric downbeat, and sooner than the steady pulse of the pattern would indicate.

Joplin also writes rhythmically straight passages so that the syncopated patterns sound fresh in contrast. Like most effective rhythmic techniques, if syncopation were used continuously, it would lose its magic.

Hidden Melodies and Stride Bass

Listen to the melody that begins at 0:44. If you focus on all the notes that the pianist is playing in the higher register, the melody sounds jumpy and disjointed.

The red line on this score excerpt shows the leapy contour of the melody.

However, the notes that form the peaks of this contour are all close in pitch. This passage uses a technique known as "compound melody," in which a single melody has additional pitches from other melodies woven between its notes. We can hear the main melodic line by focusing only on the notes that move down by half steps. The performer's task is to differentiate these notes from those of the other melody lines.

The connected melodic line is marked with circles and a red line:

At 1:48, we can identify three distinct registers in the music: a high melody, a low bass line which is played in octaves, and some chords in the middle register. There is a significant distance between the lowest notes and the chords in the middle of the piano. If we could watch the pianist play this passage, we would see his left hand jump from the bottom section of the piano keyboard for the bass notes to the middle section for the chords, and back again in rapid motion. This physical movement of the hand "striding" up and down the keyboard led to the term "stride bass." The stride bass pattern occurs throughout most of *Maple Leaf Rag* and was extremely common in ragtime piano compositions.

Here is the stride bass:

The stride bass pattern from ragtime became the foundation for an entirely new style of music known as stride piano. Stride piano developed in Harlem after World War I, and combined a stride bass pattern with an increasingly virtuosic and blues-influenced set of melodies and flourishes for the pianist's right hand. It was one of the ways in which ragtime contributed significantly to later jazz styles.

Sectional Form

There are four distinct musical sections in *Maple Leaf Rag*. The juxtaposition of discrete units of music to create the complete piece is known as sectional form, and in this book we have also encountered it in chapter 7, William Byrd's "Sing Joyfully." Every section in *Maple Leaf Rag* is 16 measures long, which is standard for ragtime compositions, and every section is composed of phrases and subphrases in 2-, 4-, or 8-measure lengths.

Scott Joplin (1868–1917)

THE KING OF RAGTIME

Scott Joplin is widely known as the King of Ragtime, but he always wanted to be respected as a classical composer. During his lifetime, there was a wide gulf between the two musical worlds, and in spite of his best efforts, Joplin never succeeded in obtaining recognition for his classical works.

Little is known for sure about the first decades of Joplin's life. He learned to play the piano, violin, guitar, and mandolin in his early teens, and shortly thereafter, he left his family's home in Texarkana, Arkansas, for St. Louis to pursue a musical career. In 1894, he moved to Sedalia, Missouri, and built a career as a pianist at local social clubs. These performances gave Joplin ample opportunity to hone his ragtime skills. Five years later, he began a long-term business association with John Stark, an ambitious businessman who agreed to publish *Maple Leaf Rag* in spite of his reservations that the piece was too difficult for amateur pianists. Sales were slow at first, but after a decade, the piece was selling approximately 15,000 copies a year, turning a healthy profit for both Stark and Joplin.

Joplin and Stark called his pieces "classic rags" in an attempt to make them sound more sophisticated, refined, and cultured than other ragtime pieces. While he made most of his money from ragtime hits, including "The Entertainer" (made famous again in 1973 when it was used for the soundtrack to the movie *The Sting*, starring Robert Redford), "The Easy Winners," and "Pine Apple Rag," Joplin spent much of his life seeking critical acceptance as a composer of art music. He published a theater tableau piece for narrator and dancers, "The Ragtime Dance," and two operas, *Guest of Honor* (for which the score and libretto have been lost) and *Tremonisha*. Joplin spent his last years in New York

Scott Joplin
Art Resource/The New York Public Library for the Performing Arts

composing prolifically and trying desperately to get a full production of *Tremonisha* staged. Sadly, he never succeeded in getting the opera produced during his lifetime, and modern audiences still know him best for his ragtime compositions.

PLAYLIST: JOPLIN
(all for piano solo)

"The Easy Winners"
"The Entertainer"
"Pine Apple Rag"
"Solace"

The complete form is represented graphically below. The third section ("C") is known as the "Trio," an idea borrowed from ternary forms in the Western classical tradition (see chapters 19 and 22). It features a change of key and a change of texture.

TIME:	0:00	0:44	1:26	1:48	2:31			
	0:21 (repeat)	1:06 (repeat)		2:09 (repeat)	2:52 (repeat)			
FORM:	‖: **A** :‖	**B** :‖	**A**	‖: **C**	:‖: **D**	:‖		
KEY:	A♭			D♭	A♭			

Now listen to this piece again, following the Listening Guide.

Scott Joplin *Maple Leaf Rag*

Time	Form	Rhythm	Melody
0:00	**A**	Syncopation, with the hemiola pattern at the beginning	Static, with emphasis on the same pitches and attention focused more on rhythm than on melody
0:21	**A** repeats.		
0:44	**B**	Syncopation continues.	Compound melody, with a chromatic descending line
1:06	**B** repeats.		
1:26	**A** returns again.		
1:48	**C**, in a new key (D♭ major). Also known as the Trio section.		High melody uses more chords (a different texture) than the previous sections. Clear stride bass in the accompaniment.
2:09	**C** repeats.		
2:31	**D**, in the original key (A♭ major)	Simplicity and straight (nonsyncopated) rhythms at the beginning of this section	Complex interactions between inner voice melodies and bass-line melodies at the end of this section
2:52	**D** repeats.		

Student FAQs

Why does this piece remind me of Charlie Chaplin?

During the era of silent films, theater orchestras, organists, or pianists performed live music to accompany movies, an old-fashioned version of today's soundtracks. Ragtime was frequently used, partly because theater pianists knew the songs and audiences liked them. *Maple Leaf Rag* was certainly one of most popular. Chaplin chose to include it in the music to accompany his 1928 film *The Circus*.

Is there anything in the music that unites the A, B, C, and D sections?

There are some abstract motivic relationships between the sections, but basically, the melodies are different—that's what makes it sectional form.

MUSIC IN PERFORMANCE

Should You Play the Notes in the Score?

When Joshua Rifkin, a musicologist and classically trained pianist, recorded an album of Scott Joplin's rags in 1970, he very carefully followed the printed music and played the pieces as cleanly as possible. That recording, which includes a version of *Maple Leaf Rag,* was nominated for a Grammy Award and contributed to the revival of ragtime. However, Rifkin's approach was not necessarily the same one that pianists took during Joplin's era.

The recording used for the Listening Guide is the only evidence we have of how Joplin might have played the piece. In 1916, Scott Joplin recorded *Maple Leaf Rag* on a piano roll (a long strip of paper) designed to be played on a player piano (see image at right). In the years before record players were commonly available, families purchased player pianos as a means of hearing the latest hits. The piano roll had holes punched in it to represent each note in the performance. The paper was placed in the player piano, where a mechanized device translated the holes in the paper back into sounds. The keys moved, the hammers struck strings, and it looked as though the piano was playing itself. On the piano roll he cut for "Maple Leaf Rag," Joplin adds extra bass, arpeggios, and flourishes throughout the piece that are not in the notated score. He also plays the melody in some sections an octave higher than it is written in the score. These types of alterations are typical for a musician who is used to improvising and is not concerned with strict adherence to the score.

Whether Joplin actually played all the notes on the piano roll is subject to debate. Many piano rolls were edited after they were recorded, and additional embellishments were added simply by punching holes in the correct places on the paper. By this technique, elaborate performances were created, sometimes with so many additional notes that it would have been physically impossible for a live pianist to play them all.

Regardless, the existence of Joplin's piano-roll performance of *Maple Leaf Rag* hints that indeed the ragtime pianists of his day did not adhere strictly to the score. Furthermore, many of the most famous ragtime pianists from Joplin's era could not

An Aeolian player piano, c. 1925. The piano roll (with the holes cut out for each note in the piece) sits in the front panel area, and the "performer" pumps the pedals to power the pneumatic mechanisms in the instrument.

Richard Booth/Lebrecht Music & Arts Photo Library

read music and learned the tunes by ear before recreating them in personalized versions. One of the traditions during that time was "cutting" contests, in which two ragtime pianists attempted to outplay each other by adding virtuosic embellishments. Furthermore, in the 1920s and 1930s, jazz musicians frequently used ragtime melodies as the starting point for entirely new, improvised performances (such as Jelly Roll Morton's and Marcus Roberts's versions of *Maple Leaf Rag*—see "Expand Your Playlist"). In subsequent decades, attitudes toward the importance of the score in ragtime have varied. Thus, a performer today might stick to the score or embellish it in any number of ways, and either approach is historically justified.

THE MONEY TRAIL

Making Money on a Hit

John Stark, publisher of *Maple Leaf Rag,* was continually looking for new pieces. Sheet music was one of the most lucrative parts of the music business at the end of the nineteenth century. Long before most households owned a record player, live musical performance was the primary way most Americans enjoyed their entertainment. Touring musicians and theater performers presented new songs to their audiences, and amateur enthusiasts then purchased the sheet music, usually for a few cents, to perform those songs at home.

Songwriters and composers of popular music often sold their music to publishing firms for a flat fee of $25 or $50. The publisher registered the copyright for the piece and then retained all the profits on the sales. A popular song might sell several thousand copies a year, netting a handsome sum for the publisher. The composer, on the other hand, not only received no royalties but might not even have his or her name appear on the published sheet music.

Joplin signed a very different contract when he agreed to publish *Maple Leaf Rag* with Stark's firm. Their contract specified that Joplin's name would appear as the composer. It also guaranteed the minimum retail price for the music ($.25) and assigned to Joplin a royalty of $.01 per copy sold—a reasonable rate for 1899. A decade after the piece's initial publication, those royalties netted Joplin approximately $600 per year, according to biographer Edward Berlin's calculations, which was sufficient to cover most of Joplin's basic living expenses quite handily.

Sheet music sales plummeted in the years after World War II, with the rise of recordings and the popularity of new styles of music that were not as easily notated. Songwriters and composers today still sign contracts with publishing firms, however,

The cover for the first printing of *Maple Leaf Rag.*
Courtesy David A. Jasen

who administer each song's royalties from a variety of licenses required by copyright law. Today, publishers receive $.095 per copy of a CD, record, or digital download for a short song. The contract between the songwriter and publisher determines how much of that money goes to the songwriter and how much to the publisher. Another source of royalties is the fee that businesses pay for the right to play recorded music in their establishments. Performance rights organizations collect these fees and distribute them to the publishers. The two major performance rights organizations are the American Society of Composers, Authors, and Publishers (ASCAP; founded in 1914) and Broadcast Music Incorporated (BMI; founded in 1939). When you go to a restaurant or nightclub, or listen to a radio station that plays recorded music, look at the business's window: you will likely see stickers confirming that the business has licenses with both ASCAP and BMI.

 EXPAND YOUR PLAYLIST

Rooted in Ragtime

These pieces illustrate various piano styles that had their roots in ragtime.

James P. Johnson, "Carolina Shout" (1921). Johnson's recording transformed basic musical ideas from ragtime into the style known as Harlem Stride Piano.

Zez Confrey, "Kitten on the Keys" (1921). Confrey's composition was one of the most successful "Novelty Piano Pieces," which followed after ragtime faded from popularity. Novelty pieces were showy bits of entertainment that featured stride bass patterns under lengthy scalar passages and glitzy arpeggios.

Jelly Roll Morton, "Maple Leaf Rag" (1938). Morton played the piece at the Library of Congress for collector Alan Lomax, and his version was heavily improvised and different from the published version of the piece.

Meade "Lux" Lewis, "Honky Tonk Train Blues" (1938). One of the next virtuosic styles of piano jazz to emerge was the boogie woogie style of Lewis, best demonstrated on his biggest hit.

Marcus Roberts, *Maple Leaf Rag* (1998). This is a contemporary jazz pianist's improvisation derived from Joplin's classic and shows the incredible diversity of musical styles the piece can support.

46

Robert Johnson
"Terraplane Blues"

Listen to This

Melody

Listen for notes that are indistinct and slide from one pitch to another.

Timbre

Listen for the wide variety of sounds and syllables the singer utters. Listen also for the extra sound effects made on the guitar. Finally: what makes this recording sound different from today's recordings?

Form

Within each separate text verse, what pattern of repetition, variation, and contrast do you hear? Do any of the verses follow a different pattern?

Word-Music Relationships

How might this text, which is nominally about a car, be interpreted metaphorically? Can you understand all the words? Are the expressions familiar to you?

Mississippi blues musician Robert Johnson made this recording in 1936, only a few years before his death. That same year, he recorded 16 blues tunes, and the subsequent year an additional 13; altogether, his recordings include some of the most influential examples of early "downhome blues" recordings ever made. It took decades for many of his other recordings to become popular, however, and "Terraplane Blues" was Johnson's only hit during his lifetime.

The **blues** is a musical genre derived from African American performance traditions that uses "blue notes" in its melodies and tells first-person stories of hard knocks and love gone wrong. It was originally transmitted orally, without any formal notation. The earliest recordings of blues were made in 1920, when record companies began sending producers and recording teams to different cities to capture folk traditions and local styles that they had previously ignored. These "city blues" or "vaudeville blues" usually featured a female singer with a small instrumental ensemble including a piano and sometimes a trumpet, cornet, clarinet, or saxophone. The first female singer to have a major hit was Gertrude "Ma" Rainey, but the most popular of these singers was Bessie Smith, who recorded prolifically through the 1920s.

About three years later, record companies began to send producers and small teams of sound engineers with portable equipment to more rural regions. Many of the most successful trips were to the deep South, where a very different style of blues records were made. These recordings, often called "country blues," "delta blues," or "downhome blues," featured solo male singers accompanying themselves on guitar. Throughout the 1920s and 1930s, the Mississippi Delta and Texas in particular produced many of the most famous blues musicians.

A Blue-Note Melody

One of the most significant musical features of downhome blues recordings is the use of **blue notes**, particularly in the melody. Blue notes are pitches that are performed flatter (lower) than the standard major scale; usually these notes occur as substitutes for the third and seventh (and occasionally the fifth) notes of the scale. These blue notes are not necessarily exactly a half step lower. Instead, a singer or instrumentalist lowers the note as much as the mood and emotional inflection indicates. An extension of this style is the incorporation of notes that are indistinct or slide between several different pitches. In the first line of "Terraplane Blues," the text is "When I feel so lonesome you hear me when I moan." Johnson uses exaggerated blue notes for the words "when," "so," "hear," and "moan." At 0:42, the word "flash" is sung over a wavering and changing pitch, another use of this blue-note technique.

Historic Blues Timbre

What may strike you first about this recording is that it sounds old. There is continuous hiss and white noise in the background, and the recording is monophonic, which means that the left and right speakers play the same thing. Some contemporary listeners value blues recordings more if they sound old because the recording's timbre—raw, authentic, and noisy—invokes a sense of time and place before the music became fully commercial. Other listeners are bothered by the scratchy sounds. Consider for a moment how your response is affected by the timbre.

Many of the words Johnson sings are difficult to understand, sometimes because they are no longer common vocabulary or phrases, sometimes because his Mississippi accent blurs the syllables, and sometimes because of the poor quality of the recording. For instance, at 0:57, Johnson sings "I'm going to hoist your hood, mama . . . ," but many of the individual syllables are missing, merged together, or altered with different vowel sounds. Johnson's vocal style encompasses a variety of techniques that convey the song's emotional meaning even when the individual words are hard to understand: he sings some words in his regular voice, but he also speaks some words, sings other words in a high, hollow falsetto tone, adds a growl to his voice at times, and occasionally utters generic syllables instead of words. Note, for instance, the spoken interjection at 0:37, "Somebody's been running my batteries down on this machine." Here, Johnson takes on the role of commenting on his own song. The falsetto high notes, such as those heard when Johnson is "crying" at 1:30–1:32, convey the emotion of the text. At 1:46, he adds a vocal growl to the word "Highway" that evokes the gritty realism of the blues. When Johnson half-sings and half-speaks "and I'm booked and I got to go" at 2:05, the change in vocal timbre conveys both the casual nature of the performance and the sense that the singer is revealing his most sincere thoughts to the listener.

His guitar also offers a range of timbres that are as varied and expressive as those Johnson provides with his voice. At key moments, Johnson presses a short bar against the strings on the instrument to produce a wavering tone (a technique known as slide guitar), always on a long note in the middle of the guitar's pitch register. Listen for this at 0:26, 0:51, 1:14, 1:40, and several times later in the song.

12-Bar Blues Form

Each verse of "Terraplane Blues" contains three vocal phrases:

- The first line of text
- The first line repeated, sometimes with slight variation or additional commentary
- The second line of text, often a response or reaction to the situation described in the first line

The first verse begins at 0:06 and ends at 0:31, with the following text in the three-line pattern:

> And I feel so lonesome, you hear me when I moan.
> When I feel so lonesome, you hear me when I moan.
> Who been drivin' my Terraplane for you since I been gone?*

This text pattern is typical of verses in the **12-bar blues**, the best-known and most commonly used model for blues songs. The model is not strict: instead, it describes the underlying patterns from which individual songs and performers frequently deviate. Each three-line unit forms one verse of the song, and the overall form of the 12-bar blues is strophic, which means that it consists of a series of verses (strophes), each set to essentially the same music.

*Excerpt from lyrics to "Terraplane Blues" by Robert Johnson. Reprinted by permission of MCPA.

Although there are some typical text patterns, the 12-bar blues is first and foremost a musical form, not a textual one. Each verse consists of just that: 12 bars (measures) of music—although in many instances, musicians either stretch or compress the basic pattern a bit. The three lines of text each receive four measures of music. The singer typically finishes singing the words in the beginning of the third measure, leaving time for the guitar or other accompaniment to add a **fill**, or short, instrumental response that occupies the time between the singer's phrases. Each musical phrase has a predetermined chord progression, or pattern of harmonies, although musicians frequently add variations or substitutions. The three chords used in the 12-bar blues pattern are built on the first, fourth, and fifth scale degrees, represented in the chart below as roman numerals (I, IV, and V).

                        vocal phrase

          First line of text.   (instrumental response)
          I   I   I   I
measure: 1   2   3   4

                        vocal phrase

          First line of text repeats. (instrumental response)
          IV   IV   I   I
measure: 5   6   7   8

                        vocal phrase

          Verbal response.   (instrumental response)
          V   V *   I   I
measure: 9   10   11   12

*Some blues songs substitute a IV chord here.

Like most downhome blues artists, Robert Johnson seldom sings a verse that follows the 12-bar blues pattern exactly. His most common variation is to shorten the third phrase to less than four full measures of music. In the first verse, for instance, "Who's been drivin' my Terraplane since I been gone?" is three beats shorter than the 12-bar blues model predicts.

In the fourth verse, Johnson uses a different text pattern that became important to later generations of musicians. Instead of the usual three lines of text, he sings four lines, or a quatrain consisting of a pair of rhymed couplets:

> Now, you know the coils ain't even buzzin', little generator won't get that spark;
> Motor's in a bad condition, you gotta have these batteries charged;
> But I'm cryin', plee-ease, plee-ease don't do me wrong.
> Who been drivin' my Terraplane now for you since I been gone?*

*Excerpt from lyrics to "Terraplane Blues" by Robert Johnson. Reprinted by permission of MCPA.

The musical pattern of chords (harmonies) and musical phrases remains the same as in the other verses. Two of the lines of text are sung rapidly during the first four-measure musical phrase, with the other two lines of text placed over the second and third musical phrases as follows:

This four-line text pattern is only one of many used with the 12-bar blues (see chapter 56 for a different text pattern). It also is a common pattern in the blues-based recordings from the 1950s that were made by rockabilly artists in Memphis.

Word-Music Relationships: Metaphors and the Vernacular

"Terraplane Blues" is ostensibly about a car—the Terraplane was an affordable automobile built by the Hudson Motor Company in the 1930s—but in the vernacular tradition of the blues, the car is merely a risqué metaphor for sexual troubles and an unfaithful woman.

Blues performances, particularly in the types of road houses and bars where Johnson played, were often lively events where audiences responded to the singer's tales of romantic woe not with depressed sympathy but with a humor-filled empathy. Blues lyrics occasionally relate to social protest, personal misery, depression, or discrimination; however, the vast majority of downhome blues songs address romantic relationships, almost always with some sexual undertones and usually where love has gone wrong. Listeners familiar with the blues anticipated these topics, and had no trouble interpreting the double meanings and hearing the wry humor.

Now listen to this song again, following the Listening Guide.

Listening Guide

Robert Johnson "Terraplane Blues"

Time	Text	**Form**	**Melody**
0:00		Introduction	
0:06	And I feel so lonesome . . . . . . since I been gone?	Verse 1: three lines of text in a 12-bar blues form, with the length of the last phrase altered	Basic melody for the blues tune is introduced. Blue notes on "when," "so," and "hear."
0:32	I'd said I flash your lights, mama . . . . . . it's way down below.	Verse 2.	Melody is similar to the one used in Verse 1, but slightly varied. Wavering blue-note tone on "flash." Johnson's voice trails off to indistinct low notes at the end of the verse.
0:57	I'm gon' h'ist your hood, mama . . . . . . down in Arkansas.	Verse 3: the metaphoric interpretation of the text becomes more explicit.	
1:20	Now, you know the coils ain't even buzzin . . . . . . since I been gone?	Verse 4: the form of the text changes to a four-line (quatrain) structure. This verse is a point of contrast in the middle of the recording.	Vocal melody changes to a very repetitive pattern that emphasizes just two notes.
1:45	Mr. Highway Man . . . . . . I'm booked and I got to go.	Verse 5: the form of the text returns to the standard three-line pattern.	Vocal melody is a new variation on the first melody.
2:11	Mmm . . . . . . since I been gone?	Verse 6.	Vocal melody is quite similar to Verse 1.
2:35	I'm gon' get deep down in this connection . . . . . . your spark plug will give me fire.	Verse 7.	Vocal melody is quite similar to Verse 3.

Excerpt from lyrics to "Terraplane Blues," by Robert Johnson. Reprinted by permission of MCPA.

Timbre

Solo guitar, playing in a Delta, Mississippi, downhome blues style

Johnson's voice slides between several notes, matching the sound of the slide used on the guitar (at 0:26).

At 0:37, spoken comment interjected.
Johnson introduces a brief falsetto exclamation at 0:52, and there is a guitar slide.

Johnson uses the wooden body of the guitar to add percussive sounds. At 1:14, there is a guitar slide.

Johnson's falsetto expression on "Plea—, please" matches the meaning of the words.
Guitar slide at 1:40.

Vocal growl on the word "Highway." At the end of this verse, Johnson adopts a speechlike pattern for the last few words.

At 2:46, Johnson uses a long falsetto utterance that mimics a pattern earlier blues artists used.

Student FAQs

Were all blues singers black?

There were plenty of white blues musicians during this time period. Record companies, however, kept two separate catalogs of recordings, sorted by the race of the performer, because the white musicians' recordings were not marketed the same way. Many early country musicians, including Jimmie Rodgers, recorded lots of blues tunes.

Did the blues musicians know about the 12-bar blues model?

They learned the style from other performers. Although they intuitively knew what patterns did and did not work in the style, they were not consciously trying to use a particular formal model, nor were they concerned with how many measures each phrase lasted. We use models like the 12-bar blues as analytical tools to help understand musical developments and styles.

What are the percussive noises at 1:08?

Johnson is tapping the wooden body of his guitar to add rhythmic energy to the performance.

Robert Johnson (1911–38)

A DEAL WITH THE DEVIL

For modern audiences, the legend of Robert Johnson making a deal with the devil is the most famous aspect of Johnson's entire career. According to the story, Johnson traveled at midnight to a deserted crossroads, where he met with the devil and traded his soul in exchange for the ability to play blues guitar. One of Johnson's blues recordings was titled "Cross Road Blues," and became associated with the legend.

The story first appeared in print in 1966 (nearly three decades after Johnson's death), based on a vague recollection from one of Johnson's contemporaries. The same year, a southern preacher gave an interview in which he described in great detail a bluesman's fateful deal with the devil, but this interview was about a musician named Tommy Johnson, not Robert. In subsequent years, the story gained credence merely through the telling, and in 1986, it appeared in a popular movie called *Crossroads*. By the 1990s, when Johnson's complete recordings were reissued on CD, the legend was inextricably linked to him in spite of the tale's sketchy sources. Part of its appeal is the story's similarities to the tale of Faust, a character in German legend who made a deal with the devil in exchange for knowledge, power, or happiness (in various versions of the tale). Faust has been a popular theme for countless literary, musical, and artistic works.

One reason the deal with the devil has been such an appealing story about Robert Johnson is that relatively little is known about his biography. He was born in Hazlehurst, Mississippi, and became interested in music at a young age. He traveled throughout Arkansas, Mississippi, and Tennessee, learning from and playing with the best blues musicians he could find. In 1936, a salesman working for a record label put Johnson in touch with Don Law, a well-known producer. Law arranged a recording session for Johnson in San Antonio, Texas, and a second session in Dallas. Several of his recordings were released, but only "Terraplane Blues" was a hit.

In 1938, Johnson traveled to Greenwood, Mississippi, and booked two performances at a jook joint, a roadside tavern that featured rowdy carousing and dancing (the term "jukebox" derives from the fact that coin-operated phonographs were installed in jook joints). He took up with a local woman, who—as misfortune

Robert Johnson
© 1986 Delta Haze Corporation. All Rights Reserved.
Used by Permission.

would have it—was married to the owner of the joint. How exactly Johnson died has never been conclusively determined, but most evidence indicates that he was poisoned at the second of his performances, possibly by a bottle of tainted whiskey supplied by the cuckolded owner. He died a few days later.

PLAYLIST: JOHNSON

"Cross Road Blues"

"I Believe I'll Dust My Broom"

"Sweet Home Chicago"

"Hellhound on My Trail"

"Love in Vain"

MUSIC IN PERFORMANCE

Who Wrote the Blues?

With "Terraplane Blues," we regard Robert Johnson as both composer and performer, which is different than how we think about music in the European classical tradition. Even though other musicians have recorded "Terraplane Blues," the complete song as Robert Johnson conceived it consists of much more than just words, melody, and chords, and in the down-home blues tradition, the nuances of each person's performance are considered part of the song.

Frequently, blues musicians borrowed rhymed couplets or verses from each other, and sometimes they lifted almost entire songs for their own use—Robert Johnson sometimes refused to play facing his audience, not due to shyness but because he didn't want other guitarists to figure out the fingerings for his signature motives and styles. Even in songs as unique in their use of images and metaphors as "Terraplane Blues," stock phrases appear that are common to many downhome blues songs. For instance, one can find variations on the phrases "since I been gone" and "I got a woman" in countless other blues songs. These common phrases tie together the many different songs and performers into a single tradition.

The blues tradition was one in which music was both shared broadly and occasionally protected as personal. Thus, while we talk about Robert Johnson as both composer and performer—and he certainly put his own signature on his songs—it is essential to bear in mind that blues, and, indeed, most oral musical traditions, are also the product of many different musicians.

Son House, blues performer who knew Robert Johnson in 1960

Photo by Estate of Raeburn Flerlage/Michael Ochs Archives/Getty Images

---

 EXPAND YOUR PLAYLIST

The Blues in Different Styles

Once you learn to recognize the 12-bar blues form, it is easy to spot in many different recordings. During the 1920s and early 1930s, female blues singers like Bessie Smith and "Ma" Rainey were incredibly popular, far more than country blues singers like Johnson.

- Bessie Smith, "St. Louis Blues" (1925). This classic blues written by W.C. Handy in 1912 is one of the most popular of all blues styles and illustrates the 12-bar blues form. Smith's recording is considered the classic version.

In the 1960s, many British and American rock musicians drew inspiration from Robert Johnson's recordings and covered his songs. Listen to some of the cover versions to see how his blues tunes sound in different musical styles:

- Cream, "Crossroads" (1968). This is a live performance, featuring Eric Clapton.
- Rolling Stones, "Love In Vain" (1969).
- Fleetwood Mac, "Hellhound on My Trail" (1971).

47

U.S.A.

Los Angeles

Washington D.C.

HOLLYWOOD

Duke Ellington
Cotton Tail

 Listen to This

Harmony

Listen for patterns of chords that repeat frequently in the piece. Listen also for chords that consist of many notes and are sonically dense.

Texture

Notice how the different instrumental groups fill different roles of melody and accompaniment as the piece unfolds. Listen, too, for sections where groups of instruments engage in musical dialogue with each other.

Rhythm

The tempo of this piece is extremely fast. See if you can also hear the uneven (long-short-long-short) rhythmic quality in the quick notes played by the lead instruments. What is it that gives this piece its momentum, or "swing" quality?

Form

Try to identify the beginning of each new section. How does the ending of the piece relate to the opening?

n 1940, Duke Ellington and his Famous Orchestra were in peak performance. Having already toured extensively through both Europe and the United States, the ensemble was now on the West Coast. Ellington's lineup for this recording session included 15 stellar players: two trumpets, one cornet, three trombones, five saxophones (one of whom doubled on clarinet), guitar, bass, drums, and Ellington himself at the piano. Victor Recording Company released *Cotton Tail* on a 78-rpm record as a "swing classic." Swing was a highly danceable style of jazz that emerged in the early 1930s, featuring large ensembles known as big bands. Swing music found widespread popularity with many different audiences, and the years it flourished, from the start of the Great Depression through World War II, are often described as the swing era.

Jazz is a musical genre that evolved out of many styles, including ragtime, dixieland, and blues. Its earliest practitioners were mostly black, and its earliest forms did not rely on musical notation. Jazz made heavy use of rhythmic innovations like syncopation (a major characteristic of ragtime) and swing rhythms, which are discussed below. Improvisation, in which a performer makes up the melody while playing it, is another key feature of most styles of jazz. Improvisation also alters the concept of the "composer." With *Cotton Tail*, Ellington wrote the main melody and many of the detailed instrumental sections, but the bulk of the recording is a saxophone solo improvised by Ben Webster. Thus, while we talk about Ellington as the composer, in a certain way the soloist composed many of the notes we hear.

Harmony: Rhythm Changes

The harmonic progression used in *Cotton Tail* was written by American composer George Gershwin for his song "I Got Rhythm," which he used in his 1930 Broadway musical *Girl Crazy*. *Cotton Tail* is only one of dozens of tunes that have borrowed Gershwin's pattern. It has three significant characteristics:

• A "circle-of-fifths" progression, a series of chords whose roots are all five notes below the previous chord. This chord progression is one of the most common chord patterns in big band jazz. The progression moves at a quick speed, with only two beats per chord. We hear the pattern twice in the first four seconds (0:00–0:02 and 0:03–0:04), then again at 0:08–0:10 and 0:10–0:12.

• A bass line that steps down chromatically (by half steps) from the first degree of the scale. You can hear this beginning at 0:04.

• A **sequence**, a short musical motif that repeats at successively higher or lower pitches. The sequential pattern occurs several times in the recording, but is particularly clear at 2:20. Listen to the musical pattern where the saxophones ascend, then descend (2:20–2:23). That same musical material is then repeated (2:24–2:27), but starting one note lower.

At 1:32, the trumpets, cornet, and trombones create dense harmonies in the jazz idiom. Unlike classical, tonal music, in which the harmony is based mainly on three-note chords, jazz chords are often stacks of many more than three pitches. Ellington makes frequent use of multinote chords, and in this arrangement he uses what are known as close, tight **voicings**. The term "voicing" refers to the spacing of the individual notes in a chord, and a close voicing is one in which as many individual notes of a chord as possible are played within the same octave. The result of a close, or "tight," voicing is a dense, colorful, and bright sound, which is heard again at 2:04 in the saxophone section and at 2:50 from the whole band.

Contrasting Textures

When we refer to a **section** of an orchestra, choir, or band, we are referring to a group of instruments or voices with similar timbres or the same role within the ensemble.

Ellington generates excitement throughout the recording by using the different sections of his band to create striking contrasts in texture, in part by letting them trade roles in melody and accompaniment. At 0:45, the trumpets and tenor saxophone set up a **call-and-response** texture, in which the brass instruments offer a short musical motif and the saxophone improvises an answer. Within big band arrangements, call-and-response textures act as a form of musical conversation, moving the focal point of the music back and forth. The call-and-response at 2:35 is known as a "shout" chorus, because the trumpets are playing long, attention-getting harmonies in an extremely high register. In many jazz pieces, the last section is a shout chorus because that brings the piece to an exciting conclusion.

Swing Rhythms

The fast notes throughout the recording alternate between slightly longer and slightly shorter durations, creating a rhythmic **groove** known as **swing**. Swing rhythms generate internal momentum because the shorter notes continually propel the music toward the longer ones. Musicians resist attempts to define the rhythmic pattern according to any fixed ratio, however, in most instances, it approximates 2:1. Notated jazz music uses regular "straight," or even, notes on the page, and musicians intuitively know how to alter them to produce the effect of swing.

32-Bar Standard Song Form

Composers of Broadway show tunes and popular songs from the Tin Pan Alley era through the 1930s wrote many of their songs in the same musical form: a short verse that set up the characters and the scene, followed by a 32-measure "chorus" that followed a

A major component of the swing groove is Jimmy Blanton's "walking bass" line, which connects one chord to the next smoothly by moving stepwise, one note per beat. Ellington uses contrast between heavily syncopated rhythms played by some instruments, and "square" rhythms played on the beat by other instruments, to give his arrangement of *Cotton Tail* its energized, swing character.

predictable form. The 32 measures were divided into four phrases as follows:

Section	Duration	Melody
A	Eight measures	First melody
A	Eight measures	First melody, with slight variation
B	Eight measures	New melody that used a musical sequence
A	Eight measures	Return of the first melody, with slight variation

This pattern of **AABA** is known as "Standard Song Form" because it was so pervasive among the "standards" or popular hits of the 1920s and 1930s. When jazz musicians borrowed the harmonic progressions (or sometimes even the melodies themselves) from these songs, they discarded the comparatively forgettable opening verse and simply repeated the more memorable 32-bar chorus several times. In "I Got Rhythm," the chorus is the part most people have heard, beginning with the title of the song, whereas the verse is seldom performed today at all.

Cotton Tail uses six iterations of the chorus, and the first chorus presents the main tune, which is called the **head**. However, Ellington subtly manipulates this structure. In the opening chorus, we expect to hear 32 measures that follow the form **AABA**. However, the fourth unit (starting at 0:25) is shortened to only half its expected length, and instead of the opening melody, we hear a bold passage played by the trumpets. The sixth chorus (2:35) begins as a bold shout chorus, and we expect it to finish with the same high-energy, high-volume style with which it begins. However, its final **A** section reverts to the opening texture and timbre and presents the first melody exactly as we had anticipated at 0:25. Ellington delays the sense of closure through the recording by moving the first chorus's expected conclusion to the very end of the whole piece!

Now listen to this song again, following the Listening Guide.

Duke Ellington *Cotton Tail*

Time	Form	Harmony	Texture
0:00	First Chorus: **A** section (head)	Characteristic descent of the rhythm changes are audible at 0:04 in the upright bass.	The head (main melody) is introduced by trumpet and tenor saxophone, accompanied by the rhythm section.
0:08	**A** section		Opening melody repeats, accompanied by both rhythm section and trombones.
0:17	**B** section		Improvised trumpet solo over thick saxophone accompaniment
0:25	**A** section (shortened to half its typical length, and featuring loud trumpets).		Full ensemble plays the melody; saxophone solo provides a countermelody.
0:29	Second Chorus: **A** section (improvised solo begins).	Harmonies are *implied,* mainly by the walking bass line, with only occasional chords from guitar and piano supporting them.	Thin texture of solo (tenor saxophone) accompanied by bass and drums, with occasional piano and guitar chords added
0:37	**A** section		
0:45	**B** section	Solo incorporates a bit of the Gershwin song "I Got Rhythm."	High trumpets create a call-and-response texture with the tenor saxophone solo.
0:53	**A** section		Solo accompanied by rhythm section
1:01	Third Chorus: **A** section	The piano interrupts the expected harmonic progression and plays a single chord as a means of building dramatic tension.	
1:09	**A** section	Expected chord progression returns.	
1:16	**B** section	Chord sequence is punctuated by band.	
1:24	**A** section		
1:32	Fourth Chorus: **A** section (new melodic material features the brass instruments)	Tight, close voicings in the trumpets emphasize jazz harmonies.	Homophonic section with brass instruments playing a new melody in close harmony

Rhythm

Swing groove is established at the beginning of the tune.

Contrast between melody's rhythms (heavily syncopated) and trombone chords (on the beat)

Long, sustained chords in the saxophone

Exaggerated off-beat rhythms in trumpets

Long, sustained note in the saxophone solo at the beginning of this section adds rhythmic drama. Staccato trumpets at 0:58 punctuate the end of this chorus.

Trumpets' chords on the beat contrast with the off-beat and syncopated solo.

(continued)

Duke Ellington *Cotton Tail*

Time	Form	Harmony	Texture
1:41	**A** section		
1:48	**B** section	Baritone saxophone solo, accompanied by prominent, sustained piano chords	
1:56	**A** section		Piano solo in a stride style, accompanied by the rhythm section
2:04	Fifth Chorus: **A** section (new melodic material features the saxophones)	Tight, close voicings in the saxophone chords	Homophonic section with saxophones playing a new melody.
2:11	**A** section		
2:20	**B** section	Sequence is clearly audible.	
2:27	**A** section		
2:35	Sixth Chorus: **A** section (shout chorus)		Call-and-response between "shout" trumpets and saxophone section, which plays a variation of the original melody
2:43	**A** section	Horn harmonies.	
2:50	**B** section	Close jazz voicings create a harmonic climax for the tune.	Homophonic brass section create a thick texture.
2:59	**A** section (return of the head).		Tenor saxophone plus trumpet play the opening melody again.

Rhythm

Piano solo emphasizes the downbeats, rather than off-beats.

Long, sustained trumpet chords contrast rhythmically with the active melody from the saxophones.

Student FAQs

Why does the trumpet have a strange timbre in its solo at 0:17?

Cootie Williams played this trumpet solo with a plunger mute—literally the rubber end of a bathroom plunger—which he held near the bell opening of the trumpet. By adjusting the angle and the distance between the mute and the trumpet, he was able to add "wah-wah" effects that imitate speech.

What instrument is playing the opening melody?

The head is played by both a trumpet and tenor saxophone at the same time. The combination of instruments creates a unique timbre. Ellington was known for composing with interesting combinations of instruments, thereby creating new timbres.

Duke Ellington (1899–1974)

COMPOSING JAZZ AND BEYOND

Edward Kennedy "Duke" Ellington is widely revered as the greatest American jazz composer, but his musical ambitions reached far beyond any one genre. He was a major bandleader in the swing era of the 1930s and the big band era of the 1940s, and wrote hundreds of tunes that have become jazz standards. Yet he also wrote film scores for Hollywood, concertos and concert pieces, and works for theater, which influenced the development of many young jazz artists. His greatest compositional innovations include his use of unusual combinations of instruments and careful control of timbre in his orchestrations. He was also intimately aware of the strengths and styles of his individual band members and exploited those personal abilities to great effect.

Born and raised in Washington, D.C., Ellington found his big break as house bandleader at New York City's Cotton Club, an upscale nightclub in Harlem where celebrities, tourists, and New York's high society went to hear the hottest music and see a spectacular stage show (see "The Swing Revival," following). Here he gained crucial experience working with stage performers, which served him well later when he began to compose for film.

Ellington's unorthodox compositional approaches manifested his desire to write great music unbounded by any genre or category. He never left behind his love of jazz, but he appropriated musical forms of Baroque suites, classical concertos, and other larger concert works for his own compositions. Public reception of these works never rivaled that of his shorter big-band tunes, but those compositions challenged the idea that

Duke Ellington
Corbis/Bettmann

jazz and classical music should be perceived and treated as two different types of art.

PLAYLIST: ELLINGTON

"It Don't Mean a Thing (If It Ain't Got That Swing)"

"Satin Doll"

"Take the 'A' Train"

"Mood Indigo"

Black, Brown, and Beige

CULTURAL CONTEXT

The Swing Revival

In the 1920s and 1930s, New York's Harlem was home to a new movement in art, literature, and music. Historians have dubbed that era the Harlem Renaissance, and New Yorkers, both white and black, were captivated by the new jazz sounds emanating from New York's nightclubs. The Cotton Club featured some of the greatest bands of the swing era, but it was the Savoy Ballroom that hosted the best dancing.

Unlike the whites-only Cotton Club, the Savoy Ballroom opened its doors in the 1930s to white and black patrons alike, who came to hear hot swing bands engage in battles of musicianship and showmanship. On the floor, a group of young, black dancers began to improvise a new social dance that borrowed from the Charleston, and other popular dances of the day. The new dance, called the Lindy hop in celebration of Charles Lindbergh's heroic transatlantic flight, matched the high-energy swing rhythms of the bands with its footwork, including "breakaways," in which one partner flings the other out for a few solo steps, along with acrobatic jumps, throws, and kicks.

Herbert "Whitey" White, who worked as a bouncer at the Savoy, recognized the commercial potential in the new dance and assembled a performance troupe of the best Lindy hoppers. Whitey's group was hired to dance not only in stage shows but in Hollywood films. White and black dancers alike took up the Lindy hop during the 1940s, with new variations evolving on the West Coast. By the end of the decade, the Lindy hop began to fade from popularity.

In the 1980s, a new generation discovered the Lindy hop. Several of Whitey's Lindy Hoppers were still alive, and they

Dancers from the "Burn the Floor," a dance extravaganza. A group of 44 of the world's most talented dancers from 11 countries toured, performing a mix of styles, including the Lindy hop.
Gerry Penny/Agence France Presse/Getty Images

began to teach their old footwork to young fans. In 1992, director Spike Lee featured an extensive Lindy hop scene in his biographical film *Malcolm X.* By the mid-1990s, the dance fad had grown into a full revival, which renewed interest not only in the dancers but also in the old bands, clothes, styles, and slang expressions from the 1930s and 1940s.

 EXPAND YOUR PLAYLIST

Rhythm Changes in Jazz

Jodi Benson, "I Got Rhythm" (1992). This track from the original Broadway cast recording of *Crazy for You* features a lively version of Gershwin's song in a contemporary recording. *Crazy for You* was a reworked revival of Gershwin's original musical, *Girl Crazy* (1930), and Benson performs it in a traditional Broadway style.

Count Basie, "Lester Leaps In" (1939). Saxophonist Lester Young played with the famous, hard-swinging Count Basie Orchestra from 1936 until 1940. This recording, which is set to the rhythm changes, features one of his most famous solos.

Dizzy Gillespie Sextet, "Dizzy Atmosphere" (1945). Gillespie's group (including saxophonist Charlie Parker, see chapter 48) was a

significant force in the birth of bebop, audible in the style of the solos here. This tune uses rhythm changes at a slightly faster tempo than *Cotton Tail.*

Miles Davis Quintet, "Oleo" (1956). This tune, by saxophone legend Sonny Rollins, follows rhythm changes with understated, cool-jazz soloing from trumpeter Miles Davis.

Ella Fitzgerald, *Cotton Tail* (1957). Fitzgerald recorded this version with Duke Ellington's band. It features vocal scat (nonsense syllables) on the melody, as well as memorable improvised jazz solos on violin and guitar.

48

U.S.A.

Los Angeles · Washington D.C.

← HOLLYWOOD

Charlie Parker
Ornithology

 Listen to This

Timbre

Listen as the instruments blend for the opening melody and then introduce themselves separately with short solos. Notice the different sounds the drums make in different sections of the piece.

Melody

Listen for melodies that rise and fall rapidly, for sustained dissonant pitches, and for short motifs that repeat.

Texture

Notice the clear melodic line throughout, and its rhythmic accompaniment.

Form

Listen for timbre changes that mark the beginning of new sections. Listen also for repeating chord progressions.

Alto saxophonist Charlie Parker's recording of *Ornithology* captures the musical craze known as bebop, which infiltrated the jazz world immediately after World War II. A group of young jazz musicians working in New York nightclubs during those years developed a new style of playing that used small groups of typically five to seven players, called "jazz combos," rather than the larger big band ensembles that had been so popular in the 1930s (and that still played the big dance halls).

The instrumentalists who created bebop wanted jazz to be treated as serious music for listening. Bebop was considered the new, modern jazz, and the attitude of its proponents matched the serious, postwar developments in other arts as well. The main emphasis of bebop was improvisation: spontaneously created solos. Improvisation, the musicians believed, was the ultimate means of self-expression that reflected an individual's experience in the moment. The musicians devised a new approach to improvisation that emphasized fast, virtuosic playing. Bebop soloists used more dissonant notes, more extreme highs and lows, and a tone quality that was more intense and less sweet than their swing predecessors. They also developed a simple approach to musical form: they composed new melodies that were angular, dissonant, and challenging to the performer. These melodies, or "heads," were the core of a piece. The lead instruments (usually trumpet and saxophone) played the head through once and then took turns soloing. The piece ended with another rendition of the head.

Fans who were accustomed to big band swing music found bebop difficult to listen to. The music was strikingly dissonant, favored very fast tempos, and used radical new harmonies that added more notes to each chord. Drummers frequently played with irregularly spaced accents, while pianists inserted chords in rhythmically sporadic patterns.

In 1946, Charlie Parker traveled to California with trumpet player Dizzy Gillespie's quintet for an engagement at a Los Angeles club. Parker remained on the West Coast for several months, during which time trumpet player Miles Davis headed to California to play with Parker. This recording of *Ornithology* was made by Parker, Davis, and a backup group at that time.

Jazz Combo Timbre

The recording opens with an attention-grabbing drum solo. The lead instruments then fuse into a single timbre to play the head—much as the tenor saxophone and the trumpet had joined their sounds in Ellington's "Cotton Tail" (see chapter 47). In this case, we hear the alto saxophone and trumpet play a unison line while the tenor saxophone plays the same notes an octave lower.

After the head, the instruments take turns introducing themselves with a short triplet motif, while the drums and bass remain in a supporting role. At the end of the song (2:50–2:57), each instrument plays the triplet motif alone once again, in a parting musical comment.

The extended solos feature some unique timbres that give the recording personality and intimacy. For example:

- At 1:13–1:46, the trumpet plays with more buzz than a typical trumpet. Davis used a mute, which changed the timbre of his instrument.
- At 2:10–2:14, as the tenor sax concludes its solo by moving into its upper register; it is possible to hear a faint whistling-wind sound above the notes.

Timbral changes, particularly in the drums, also mark new sections of the piece. In choruses 2 and 4 (0:39–1:12 and 1:47–2:20), we hear a high-frequency shimmer. The drummer is using his ride cymbal extensively. In chorus 3 (1:13–1:46), we hear a distinct change. The drummer has switched to more hi-hat and less cymbal.

From Improvisation to Melody

The head for *Ornithology* has three different melodic segments, each with different basic contours:

- First segment (0:04–0:09): alternates rising and falling lines and presents the basic melodic idea for the tune
- Second segment (0:10–0:13): a short, descending fragment that is then **sequenced**, or repeated starting on a different note
- Third segment (0:14–0:17): an ending or **cadential** motif, followed by a triplet motif that repeats the same notes over and over (0:15–0:17)

All three of those segments then repeat for the second half of the head (0:21–0:38), with only slight variations in the exact pitches.

The head of *Ornithology* comes from a famous solo that Parker had improvised four years earlier, on a recording called "The Jumpin' Blues." For the harmony, Parker borrowed the chord progression from a popular song called "How High the Moon." Borrowing the chord progressions, or "changes," from popular songs was common practice in bebop and other styles of jazz (see also chapter 47). "How High the Moon," shares not only its chord progression but also its opening melodic motif with the new composition.

Each new instrumental solo begins with a melodic fragment that loosely echoes the music preceding it. In this way, the soloists more easily transfer the focus of the song from one player to the next. The solos reveal some signature features of the bebop style:

- Angular melodic lines, from high to low and with jagged motion
- A squeezed, forced sound as players reach the highest ranges of their instruments
- Prolonged dissonant notes (notes outside the prevailing harmony)

Texture: Rhythm Section Plus Soloist

The rhythm section, comprising bass, drums, and piano, creates a steady foundation and groove for the tune. Together, the piano and bass articulate the chords of the song, over which the other instruments solo. The texture features a single-line melody even at the beginning when all the instruments are playing, because the head is presented in unison and octaves. The only instrument that moves between the roles of soloist and accompanist is the piano, which emerges briefly to provide **fills**, or very brief solos that occupy musical gaps between sections (2:35–2:38, for instance).

Sectional Form

In *Ornithology,* the lead instrument changes with each of the five major sections, or choruses (0:04, 0:39, 1:13, 1:47, 2:21). Each is different except the last, which is a repetition of the opening chorus. Bebop compositions typically use this sectional form, with the head providing the first and last chorus and the number of iterations dependent on the number of soloists and how many choruses each soloist wishes to play.

Improvisation

When Charlie Parker improvised, his musical decisions were informed both by the chord progression of the song and by an extensive catalog of musical formulas he spent a lifetime collecting. In some styles of improvisation, the solo is essentially a variation on the song's main melody. In bebop, however, only occasionally did the musicians quote from the original melody. Instead, they devised a system in which certain scales were determined to match certain chords. When those chords appeared in the song, the musicians used fragments of the matching scale, along with arpeggiations of the chord itself, to build a new melody. The musicians also spent hours working on short motifs that they could play rapidly starting on successive pitches to create a melodic sequence. They even borrowed short motifs from books on technique for violinists, pianists, and clarinetists.

Once the musicians had a catalog of motifs, scales, and arpeggios that they could play fluently in any key, they used this musical vocabulary to construct their new improvised solos. Thus, one can find the same motifs and musical fragments in many different Charlie Parker tunes.

In the decade after Parker's best known bebop recordings, jazz musicians pushed the concept of improvisation to the point where it became the very structure of the music itself. This became known as free jazz.

Tommy Potter, Charlie Parker, Dizzy Gillespie, and John Coltrane in 1951 at the New York City club Birdland, which was named for Parker.
Frank Driggs Collection

Each chorus, is 32 measures long—the typical length for early twentieth-century popular songs. Unlike many others, however, including "I Got Rhythm" (see chapter 47), "How High the Moon" does not follow the "Standard Song Form" of **AABA**. Instead, it uses a two-part form, **A A'**. The tick-mark next to the second **A** means it is a variant of the first **A**: it has a slightly different ending. Each section is divided into two phrases, "a" and "b."

Ornithology retains the **A A'** form of "How High the Moon," but the two-part division (a–b) within each section becomes a three-part division, as we saw above under "Melody." The head's second melodic segment begins during the chords from the first phrase of the original tune and continues over part of the second phrase.

Melodic Segments and Chord Progression			
Melodic segments in *Ornithology*	First segment (0:04–0:09)	Second segment (0:10–0:13)	Third segment (0:14–0:17)
Chord progression from "How High the Moon"	"a" phrase		"b" phrase

The five choruses of this recording are vaguely similar in concept to a theme and variations movement (see chapters 20 and 34). However, because a different individual shapes each improvised solo, there is no large-scale plan or progression of the "variations." Furthermore, in the bebop performance practice, unlike in classical themes and variations, the last section revisits the opening melody in its original form.

Now listen to this song again, following the Listening Guide.

Charlie Parker *Ornithology*

Time	🏛 Form	〽 Timbre	🎵 Melody
0:00	Introduction	Drum solo	
0:04	First Chorus (Head): **A** section.	Trumpet and alto sax playing in unison, with the tenor sax one octave below	First segment of the head
0:10			Second segment of the head
0:15			Third segment of the head. During the piano's fill (0:17–0:21), the pianist arpeggiates the chords, alternating ascending and descending runs.
0:21	First Chorus: **A'** section.		First segment
0:27			Second segment
0:33			Third segment
0:39	Second Chorus	The drummer uses lots of ride cymbal, which adds a high-frequency shimmer to this section.	The first three notes of the alto sax solo are the same triplet figure that ended the previous section. Note the emphasized dissonance (0:53). The contour of his improvised melody spans extreme highs and lows in almost every measure (especially 1:08–1:13).
1:13	Third Chorus	Trumpet player uses a mute, which adds additional complexity to the timbre of the trumpet. Drummer shifts to more hi-hat.	This solo emphasizes repeated notes and pairs of notes (e.g., 1:32–1:33, 1:35–1:37). The climax of the solo is one high registral section (1:38). The trumpet player emphasizes dissonant pitches at several places (e.g. 1:48).
1:47	Fourth Chorus	Drummer switches back to heavy use of the ride cymbal. When the tenor saxophone is playing in the highest register (2:10–2:14), the instrument makes faint but audible whistling-wind sounds.	Tenor sax uses his highest register, allowing the melody to become pinched (2:01, 2:03, 2:06). At the end of the solo, the sax player arpeggiates the chords, alternating ascending and descending lines (2:16–2:19).
2:21	Fifth Chorus (repeats the head): **A** section		
2:38	**A'** section	All instruments except bass and drums play the final triplet motif in turn (trumpet, alto, tenor, guitar, and piano).	

OOP BOP SH-BAM
BE-BOP (THE NEW JAZZ)
DIZZY GILLESPIE
Series of PIANO SOLOS

Texture

Melody plus accompaniment (homophony), separating the rhythm section from the lead instruments

The lead instruments pause, allowing the piano to provide the fill.

Each lead instrument repeats the same triplet motif: trumpet, then alto sax, then tenor sax, then guitar, with a piano fill afterward.

Alto sax solo. Notice the piano plays chords in a free and asymmetric rhythmic pattern in the rhythm section.

Trumpet solo

Tenor sax solo

The head is played in unison. At 2:33–2:34, the trumpet plays the triplet motif as a solo, and the pianist fills the remainder of that phrase (2:35–2:38) with a short solo.

Piano becomes more active within the rhythm section (2:46–2:50).

Student FAQs

Where did the term "bebop" come from?

The term "bebop" came from the nonsense syllables that jazz vocalists used in their solos. The singers strung together syllables in interesting phonetic patterns that helped them sing the elaborate, improvised melodies.

What is the difference between a tenor and an alto saxophone?

A tenor saxophone is larger and plays lower notes than an alto sax. Saxophones are transposing instruments, which means that the notes we hear a saxophone play are different than the pitches notated on a saxophone player's music. The pitch C written on a piece of music would sound as an E♭ on an alto saxophone and a B♭ on a tenor saxophone. Although this may seem unnecessarily confusing, it allows performers to switch more easily between playing instruments in the same family.

I found a recording of **Ornithology** by Charlie Parker, but it sounds completely different. Is it still the same piece?

Jazz musicians play a song differently almost every time they perform it, sometimes transforming even the head itself. Every recorded version of the piece captures a specific time, place, and moment in musical history, and jazz fans frequently talk not about a song (i.e., *Ornithology*), but instead about a specific recording, simply because they're all so different.

Charlie Parker (1920–55)

THE SELF-DESTRUCTIVE ARTIST

Charlie "Yardbird" Parker left behind a legacy as a jazz innovator of profound musical genius troubled by a lifetime of drug addiction, a series of failed relationships, and a frustrating inability to control his professional life. He was raised in Kansas City, Missouri, when that city's nightlife was hopping with innovative jazz musicians who gathered in open jam sessions. Parker honed his craft by sitting in with those local bands and practicing obsessively. In 1939, he moved to New York City and sought out the best jam sessions in Harlem. In the jazz clubs there, Parker developed a style of virtuosic soloing that used complex harmonies, lightning-fast technique, and dissonance. With those innovations, bebop was born.

At the same time he was crafting new styles of jazz, Parker was sinking deeper into his drug addiction and either failing to turn up at performances or showing up in such a state that he could barely play. As Parker's career progressed, it was pockmarked with arrests, emotional breakdowns, the failure of four relationships, and declining health. He lost his license to perform in New York City nightclubs because of his arrest record and, by 1955, was at a state of physical collapse and entertaining thoughts of suicide. He passed away a recluse, living alone at the apartment of a jazz patron. Unlike his collaborator Miles Davis, Parker never shook off the demons of his addiction. But the music he created astounded listeners. Parker's name, his solos, his compositions, and his recordings are revered among jazz fans, who sometimes wonder if they came to fruition only through the same destructive yet mind-altering forces that ultimately cost him his life.

Charlie Parker in 1947.
Frank Driggs Collection

How he acquired his nickname of "Yardbird" is hotly debated. The Birdland jazz club in New York opened in 1949 as a tribute to him, and even the title *Ornithology* paid homage.

PLAYLIST: PARKER

"Shaw 'Nuff"

"Ko Ko"

"Scrapple from the Apple"

"Night in Tunisia"

"Embraceable You"

 EXPAND YOUR PLAYLIST

From Bebop to Free Jazz

Sonny Rollins, "Strode Rode" (1956). This bebop recording mixes variety in the rhythm section's playing with Rollins's tenor saxophone solo. Note the extended section where the saxophone plays just with the bass.

Miles Davis, "So What" (1959). Davis's solo is an example of modal jazz, in which melodic development becomes more important than adhering to tonal chord changes.

Ella Fitzgerald, "How High the Moon" (1960). Fitzgerald uses vocal "scat" in one of her most memorable solos. Notice that she quotes Parker's *Ornithology* in her solo.

John Coltrane, "Giant Steps" (1960). Coltrane's famous tune demonstrates the furthest reaches of bebop.

Ornette Coleman, "Free Jazz" (1960). Coleman's recording is nearly 40 minutes long and illustrates simultaneous improvisation in the absence of a predetermined form or chord progression.

49

Ruth Crawford
Piano Study in Mixed Accents

 Listen to This

Rhythm	What is the meter of this piece? Can you tap the beats? Are some notes long and some short, or are they all even?
Texture	Do you hear one melodic line played at a time, or more than one? Do you hear a melody plus accompaniment?
Harmony	Can you find a tonal center? What helps establish it, or what prevents it from being established?
Melody	What makes this melody interesting?
Form	How is this piece divided into sections? Can you identify what makes sections similar or different? Can you identify an overall shape to the piece?

Writing in a new style means avoiding old styles, and in her *Piano Study in Mixed Accents,* Ruth Crawford made a conscious effort to avoid using some of the most basic elements of music—harmony, melody, and rhythm—in any conventional sort of way. Instead, she used a new, modern idiom in music, freed from the constraints of conventional harmony, melody, and rhythm.

Crawford was an American composer who in 1930 had just become the first woman ever to be awarded a prestigious Guggenheim Fellowship in composition. She used the funds to travel to Europe, where she spent most of her time in Berlin, one of the liveliest cultural cities in the world and a hotbed of modernism. For a brief time in the 1920s and early 1930s, there was an "Anything Goes" mentality in the arts there: painters, playwrights, poets, and musicians were all exploring new ways of expressing themselves. Crawford did not study with Arnold Schoenberg or any of the other modernist composers in Berlin at the time; instead, she forged her own brand of modernism by working under a series of self-imposed limitations that helped her avoid such basic elements as meter, tonality, and patterned rhythms. The result is like no work of music ever heard before: its forward drive is relentless, and the absence of a tonal center has the effect of liberating the entire spectrum of notes.

Mixed Rhythms

These notes go by very fast, so it may be hard to tell at first, but they are all of equal value. Is the meter duple or triple? The answer is neither. The music establishes absolutely no sense of meter or fixed pattern of rhythms. Instead, we hear a series of small units. The music is organized into groupings of anywhere between two and eight notes, with the first note of each unit accented. The very opening of the work, for example, consists of a series of units consisting of 6, 5, 5, 5, 3, 6, and 4 notes:

These irregular groupings create a series of what Crawford called "mixed accents." As you listen, there is no way of knowing in advance how many notes will be in any given unit. This unpredictability of rhythmic organization helps distance this work from the fixed metrical and rhythmic patterns that characterize more conventional music.

Monophonic Texture

Again, it may be difficult to tell at first because of the rapidity of the notes, which linger in our ear and mind even as the next ones are being played, but there is in fact only one melodic line. Texture is thus another way in which Crawford succeeded in separating this work from more conventional approaches to music: we haven't heard much monophony since the Middle Ages. Here, the pianist plays the same melodic line simultaneously in the right and left hands: only the register differs. The first three notes of the work in the right hand, for example, are D-F-E. The first three notes in the left hand are also D-F-E, played at exactly the same time and in the same rhythm, but an octave lower on the keyboard. (An octave is the distance between two different notes with the same name, like D and D, one higher than the other.) There is no accompaniment (as in homophony), and there is no interplay of equal melodic lines (as in polyphony).

An Absence of Harmony

The monophonic nature of the music means that there is, by definition, no harmony. But even a melody alone can imply a harmony because a conventional melodic line implies a tonal center. We can usually sense when a melody has landed on the note that is central to its key area—in other words, its tonic. When we hear "brave" at the very end of "The Star Spangled Banner" (in the phrase "home of the brave"), for example, we have a sense that the melody has concluded not simply because we know from experience that this is the end of the melody, but because we hear the note for "brave" as the tonic note. One reason we hear it this way is because of the position of half and whole steps in the scale on which the melody is based (see Elements and chapters 39 and 41). Another reason we hear this particular note as the central one is that we have heard it early and often: "Oh, say . . ." "twilight's last gleaming" "Whose broad stripes . . ." "gallantly streaming" "O'er the land of the free and the home of the brave."

The melodic line in Crawford's *Piano Study in Mixed Accents,* by contrast, projects no sense of any such tonal center. In other words, it is **atonal**. Notes do not play specific roles based on a particular scale, and no one note returns more often than any other. Crawford avoids repeating any one note until nine, ten, or eleven other different notes have sounded. By avoiding repetition or repeated returns to any particular note, Crawford reinforces the essential equality of all notes in this work. In this way, she creates a very modern sound.

Let's look once again at the very opening of the *Piano Study in Mixed Accents*: we can see that although "D" is the first pitch we hear, we do not hear it again until we have heard eleven other pitches—every other pitch, in fact, except one (G#).

Registers of Melody

Without certain notes being more important than others or having roles to play based on a tonal scale, it is difficult to create a melody that is easy for a listener to follow, remember, or understand in the usual ways. Crawford creates interest and variety by giving unusual prominence to the melodic element of **register**, the range in which the music is presented. The melodic line never makes very large leaps, but it does move gradually from its opening low range to a very high register in the middle of the work and then back down again at the end, finishing very close to where it had begun. This attention to register helps give the work a strong sense of shape, with a beginning, a middle, and an end. It also draws attention to the differing sounds of the piano in its low, middle, and high ranges. The growling rumble of the low bass gives way to the more delicate sounds of the upper range in the middle of the work, but the journey ends back where it began, in the bass.

Sectional Form

The music is punctuated by a few brief but important moments of silence—musical rests—that help divide the work into five large-scale sections. The proportions of these sections combine with the rise and fall of the melodic register to create a strong sense of symmetry. The musical timeline below represents visually what you heard. Notice how the work begins by setting out two relatively short sections of eight and nine seconds each, then expands into a large section in the middle (which is almost as long as the other four combined), then shrinks back down into two very brief sections (nine and six seconds) on the other side. There is a kind of rough formal symmetry to the architecture of this work.

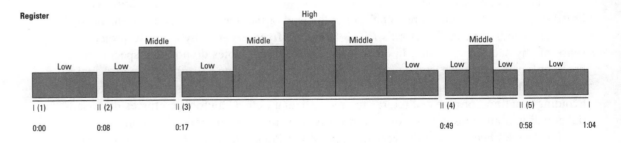

With these points in mind, listen now to the work once again, using the Listening Guide.

Ruth Crawford (1901–53)

MODERNIST COMPOSER AND FOLKSONG ARRANGER

Ruth Crawford is known today in two fields of music that might at first seem wholly incompatible. She was an uncompromising modernist composer (as is evident in her *Piano Study in Mixed Accents*), and she was also an important collector and arranger of American folksongs. Her early career focused on composition. Born in Ohio (East Liverpool) and raised in Indiana (Muncie) and Florida (Jacksonville), she studied composition with Charles Seeger, whom she married in 1932. From that point onward she published her work under the name Ruth Crawford Seeger. In 1930, she became the first woman ever to win a Guggenheim Fellowship in musical composition. While in Europe, she observed firsthand the cutting edge of musical modernism, and she continued her search for a new idiom different from that of the musical past.

After her return to the United States, Crawford continued to compose, but she began to devote more and more of her attention to collecting, editing, and arranging American folksongs. Part of the drive behind this was musical—folksongs have captured the imagination of composers and music lovers in many countries for generations—but another element behind her interest in this repertory was social and political. Folk music, as she observed in 1948, "knows and tells what people have thought about the ways of living. It bears many fingermarks. It has been handled roughly and gently. It has been used. . . . It is not 'finished' or crystallized—it invites improvisation and creative aliveness. . . . It invites participation." Her children, Mike Seeger and Peggy Seeger, along with her stepson Pete Seeger, would later become major recording artists of folksong.

Ruth Crawford, ca. 1930.

Fernand de Guidre/Judith Tick

Ruth Crawford *Piano Study in Mixed Accents*

Time	Form: Section	Melody: Register	Texture
0:00	1	Low	Monophonic
0:08	2	Low → Middle	
0:17	3	Low → High → Low	
0:49	4	Low → Middle → Low	
0:58	5	Low	

Student FAQs

Is there any way to slow this piece down? It's almost too fast to hear what's going on.

The speed is part of what makes this piece so challenging and exciting. Don't fight it: accept it on its own terms and let it carry you along. It might help to think of this work as a piece that travels through the dimension of space, starting low, moving upward, and returning back to where it started. Multiple listenings will help, too.

Is it all right to think up a storyline to go with this music? It almost sounds like the soundtrack to a scene in a movie.

Absolutely. You're free to associate whatever you hear with whatever you wish at any time, keeping in mind that the associations will be sharper and more meaningful if you attend to the musical elements of the work as well.

Twelve-Tone Composition

Ruth Crawford's efforts to avoid giving prominence to any one particular note in a melodic line is typical of those modernist composers determined to cut all ties to conventional notions of tonality. The most widely used means for avoiding such repetition was developed in the 1920s by Arnold Schoenberg (see chapter 42). He called this system "Twelve-Tone Composition" because its fundamental basis is a series ("row") of the twelve notes in the chromatic scale (A-A#-B-C-C#-D, etc., up through G#). Here is the row for one of Schoenberg's early twelve-tone works, the Suite for Piano, op. 25:

Row starting on E

Same row starting on B♭

E F G D♭ G♭ E♭ A♭ D B C A B♭

Rows could be written forward or backward, or even inverted (a sort of "mirror" image of the row) or inverted *and* backwards. Rows could also be transposed to start on different pitches. All these variables allowed the composer considerable freedom but helped ensure that the music written in this system would not betray any unintentional vestiges of tonality.

Twelve-tone composition (or serial composition, as it is sometimes called) was at the cutting edge of Western art music for the middle decades of the twentieth century. Even composers who did not write in this system experimented with it at times. By the 1970s, however, the system had begun to lose its grip on compositional thought, though all student composers continue to learn it as one of many different approaches to writing music.

 EXPAND YOUR PLAYLIST

Women Composers of the Twentieth Century

The opportunities for women composers expanded enormously over the course of the twentieth century. In addition to Ruth Crawford, Germaine Tailleferre (Web Bonus Chapter 4), and Tania León (chapter 60), these women composers achieved renown:

Thea Musgrave (b. 1928), born in Scotland, has lived in the United States since the 1970s. Some of her best-known works are the operas, *Mary, Queen of Scots* and *Pontalba*.

Pauline Oliveros (b. 1932), a native of Houston, has been at the forefront of American experimental music. Her *Sound Patterns,* for a cappella chorus, uses phonetic sounds rather than words.

Joan Tower (b. 1938) teaches composition at Bard College in her native New York. Her *Fanfares for the Uncommon Woman* are a response to Aaron Copland's *Fanfare for the Common Man.*

Ellen Taaffe Zwilich (b. 1939), born in Miami, was the first woman composer to win the Pulitzer Prize in music (in 1983), which she received for her *Three Movements for Orchestra (Symphony No. 1).*

Libby Larsen (b. 1950) was the first woman to serve as resident composer with a major orchestra (the Minnesota Orchestra). She has written in many genres, including opera (*Frankenstein*) and song (*Songs from Letters: Calamity Jane to Her Daughter Jamey*).

Jennifer Higdon (b. 1962) teaches composition at the Curtis Institute of Music, in Philadelphia. Her *Blue Cathedral,* a one-movement work for orchestra, has won wide praise from critics.

50

William Grant Still
"A Black Pierrot" from *Songs of Separation*

Listen to This

Harmony

Does the music sound tonal, atonal, or somewhere in between?

Melody

Listen for the changes in register throughout. Where is the highest note of the vocal line? Can you identify any passages in the song that suggest the style of the blues?

Form

Does the same music appear with each strophe, or is there new music for each strophe?

William Grant Still's "A Black Pierrot" is an **art song**—that is, a song set to serious poetry, usually for solo voice and piano, in the tradition of the German *Lied* (see chapter 27 and Web Bonus Chapter 3). The text takes up the same imagery Arnold Schoenberg had used in *Pierrot lunaire* (see chapter 42), but with a twist. In this text by the African American poet Langston Hughes (1902–67), the quintessentially pale-white figure of Pierrot is black. As in Schoenberg's "Columbine," Pierrot has also been rejected, but instead of seeking more whiteness, he creeps away into the night ("and the night was black, too") to "seek a new brown love."

Still's setting of this imagery also parallels Schoenberg's, but again with a twist. "A Black Pierrot" conveys a profound sense of insecurity and quiet desperation—Pierrot is never successful in his amorous pursuits—but Still achieves this effect by using a tonal style inflected with melodic turns borrowed from the blues. The "Black Pierrot" expresses himself in an idiom that at once mixes traditions of the Western classical art song (by composers such as Schubert and Schumann) with traditions more closely associated with African American music (for example, Robert Johnson—see chapter 46). In a similar fashion, art song and popular song coexisted throughout the twentieth century. As an art song, Still's "A Black Pierrot," along with the other *Songs of Separation,* the larger collection in which it appeared, did not receive the kind of widespread exposure many popular songs enjoyed. This repertory deserves to be better known.

Chromatic Harmony

From the very first puzzling, unsettled chord in the piano, we suspect this piece won't offer much comfort in the way of a home key. The octave notes that follow do little more to establish a tonic. When the voice enters, it starts in a low register with a simple statement ("I am a black Pierrot"), but it moves in wholly unpredictable directions. It wavers between major and minor and seems to change its mood constantly. And yet interspersed throughout this first, searching strophe, we do hear sounds that we recognize and chords that give us moments of harmonic stability, even if they are only brief ones.

The style of harmony Still employs here is called **chromatic**: it is tonal, but it has strong inflections that make the tonic less powerful (see also chapter 36, Wagner). A chromatic scale consists entirely of half steps.

It therefore implies no tonal center. (In the same way, a scale consisting entirely of whole steps implies no tonal center—see Debussy, chapter 39.) To create a tonic sound, a scale must contain both half and whole steps—as, for example, the familiar major and minor scales do. Still bases this song on a major scale, but he uses extra half steps from the chromatic scale to obscure the tonic and continually move the music away from it.

We hear the tonic center infrequently enough in this song for it to stand out. It appears most strongly in the middle of the second stanza and again at the end (see the Listening Guide). Listen to the contrasting sense of tonal stability in these passages compared with the chromatic instability of the others.

The harmonizations at the end of the song are particularly intense when the last two lines of text are presented three times in succession. The first two times (1:42–1:59), the voice and the piano harmonize the tonic together. The third time (2:00–2:23), only the voice stays in the tonic, while the piano harmonizes the melodic line in highly chromatic fashion, using lots of half steps to pointedly avoid the tonic. Even the very last harmony of the work—normally a tonic—is a chromatic inflection of the tonic, not a pure resolution to the home key.

Melody: A Touch of Blue

The melody, always in the voice, is chromatic throughout, wandering and weaving around the notes of the chromatic scale. Like the harmony, it rarely establishes a firm sense of arrival, and when it does land on a point of stability, it does not stay there very long. Only at the end of the song do we hear an extended point of arrival (". . . a new brown love").

The melody also shows certain affinities at points to the blues; this is, after all, the song of a rejected lover. When the music finally lands squarely on the tonic for the first time, for example (on the word "black" in "black Pierrot" at 0:40), we hear what sounds rather like a "blue note," a note that is slightly lower than its given pitch in a standard scale; see p. 410). The accompanimental figures at several subsequent points (0:48, 1:11) aid the melody in evoking the spirit of the blues, at least indirectly, with the walking bass line and the off-beat chords in the piano.

Still also uses changes of register in the vocal line to emphasize important moments in the text. The first strophe moves gradually from a low to a high register, the second occupies a middle range, and the third moves from high to low and back to high again, hitting the highest note of the entire song at the very end, by the musical and emotional climax of the song.

Through-composed Form

In spite of a good deal of textual repetition between strophes—each strophe begins with the same two lines, and the first word of the third line ("So") is also the same—there is very little repetition or even variation of musical ideas in this song. Instead, each strophe receives its own musical setting. This type of form is called **through-composed**, in which the composer uses distinctly new music from beginning to end. Through-composed form differs from strophic form (same music for each strophe) and modified strophic form (a variation of the same music for each strophe—see chapter 27).

Through-composed form was not new in the twentieth century: composers had been using this approach to setting texts for centuries. But it is one of the devices that tends to distinguish the art song repertory from that of popular song, which tends to use strophic or modified strophic form.

With these points in mind, listen to this song once again, using the Listening Guide.

William Grant Still (1895–1978)

A CAREER OF FIRSTS

In an age when the world of the American concert hall was still largely closed to African American composers and musicians, William Grant Still compiled a remarkable record of "firsts." He was the first African American composer to have a symphony performed by a major orchestra (*Afro-American Symphony,* Rochester Philharmonic, 1931), the first to conduct a major American orchestra (the Los Angeles Philharmonic, in 1936), and the first to have an opera performed by a major American opera company (*Troubled Island,* New York City Opera, 1949).

Born in Woodville, Mississippi, Still was raised in Little Rock, Arkansas. After attending Wilberforce University, he studied composition at Oberlin Conservatory and the New England Conservatory of Music. (This was not a first: these schools, and others like them north of the Mason-Dixon line, had been accepting African American students for many decades, even if not in great numbers.) Still worked in New York City throughout the 1920s, arranging music for jazz bands and dance orchestra while launching his career as a composer. He moved to Los Angeles in the early 1930s and spent the rest of his life there, composing and arranging music for films and writing works for the stage and concert hall. In many of his works, he sought to create an idiom that blended such African American idioms as spirituals or the blues into more traditionally European genres like the symphony, the opera, and the ballet.

William Grant Still and the poet Langston Hughes are only two of the many African American artists associated with a movement known as the "Harlem Renaissance." During the 1920s, Harlem—in upper Manhattan, in New York City—emerged as a kind of cultural capital of African American arts, including literature, painting, and music. Other artists associated with the Harlem Renaissance include the novelists Zora Neale Hurston and Wallace Thurman, the entertainers Josephine Baker and Paul Robeson, and the composer-musician Duke Ellington (see chapter 47). Many works by these artists, including Langston Hughes's poem "A Black Pierrot," openly celebrated African American identity. In many ways, the Harlem Renaissance brought African American art into the American mainstream.

Culture and politics, never too distant from one another, were closely allied in the Harlem Renaissance. Artists and public alike recognized that the production of art by African American artists could help promote

William Grant Still, ca. 1930.
Lebrecht Music & Arts Photo Library

the struggle for racial equality. The poet James Weldon Johnson (author of the lyrics to "Lift Ev'ry Voice and Sing") was a longtime activist in the National Association for the Advancement of Colored People (NAACP); the singer Paul Robeson would later become an important leader in the civil rights movement.

PLAYLIST: STILL

Songs of Separation. The complete cycle of songs for voice and piano.

Africa. For piano.

Symphony no. 1 (*Afro-American Symphony*). Uses blues progressions.

Troubled Island. An opera.

And They Lynched Him on a Tree. For chorus.

William Grant Still "A Black Pierrot" from *Songs of Separation*

Time	Text	Harmony	Melody
0:00	I am a black Pierrot: / She did not love me, / So I crept away into the night / And the night was black, too.	Avoids landing on the tonic clearly	Voice line moves from a low to high register
0:37	I am a black Pierrot: / She did not love me, / So I wept until the dawn / Dripped blood over the eastern hills / And my heart was bleeding, too.	Establishes tonic clearly finally at 0:48, but then starts moving away from it again after 0:58.	The voice line stays in the middle register.
1:16	I am a black Pierrot: / She did not love me, / So with my once gay-colored soul / Shrunken like a balloon without air, / I went forth in the morning / To seek a new brown love.	The last two lines are repeated three times, with the voice and piano both in the tonic the first two times, but only the voice in the tonic the third time (from 2:00 onward), with the piano harmonizing against and not with the tonic key.	Moves from high to low and back to high again, reaching the highest note of the entire song at the very end

Langston Hughes: I am a Black Pierrot from Vintage Hughes. © 2004 Vintage, a division of Random House, Inc. and Harold Ober Associates, Incorporated.

Student FAQs

Schoenberg's Pierrot is sung by a female, Still's by a male. Why is that?

Still's setting preserves the male persona of Pierrot. Schoenberg's creates an even greater sense of distance between the character (Pierrot, a male) and the singer (a female). Which approach is more effective in setting texts like these? That is a matter of debate.

Did Langston Hughes and William Grant Still collaborate on these settings?

No. While the two were acquainted, Still set a text that Hughes had written more than twenty years before. It is also worth remembering that Still would have paid royalties to Hughes for the use of these texts in his new songs.

EXPAND YOUR PLAYLIST

Twentieth-Century African American Composers in the Western Classical Tradition

In addition to William Grant Still, Scott Joplin (see chapter 45), Duke Ellington (see chapter 47), and Tania León (see chapter 60), many African American composers have established their place in the concert hall, writing in genres and idioms associated with the Western classical tradition.

- Florence Beatrice Price (1887–1953) was born in Little Rock, Arkansas, and studied at the New England Conservatory. A number of her works incorporate Negro spirituals, including her *Mississippi River Suite.*

- Henry T. Burleigh (1866–1949) was born in Erie, Pennsylvania. He taught the Czech composer Antonín Dvořák about the music of African Americans during Dvořák's years in the United States (see Chapter 38). He wrote many art songs that use melodies from Negro spirituals, including *Deep River.*

- Margaret Bonds (1913–72), although born in Chicago, spent most of her life in New York City. She was a friend of Langston Hughes and set many of his texts to music, including *Three Dream Portraits.*

- George Walker (b. 1922), born in Washington, D.C., studied composition at Oberlin College and the Eastman School of Music. He was the first African American composer to win the Pulitzer Prize in music (in 1996), for his *Lilacs,* a work for voice and orchestra.

- Keith Jarrett (b. 1945), born in Allentown, Pennsylvania, performs and composes in many different styles, including jazz, gospel, and classical. His *Elegy for Violin and Strings,* written for his Hungarian grandmother, uses idioms often associated with gypsy music.

51

Aaron Copland
"Hoe-Down" from *Rodeo*

Listen to This

Melody — How long before you hear something in this work that actually sounds like a real melody? And when it finally arrives, what is it like? Is it conjunct or disjunct—that is, does it move by steps or by leaps? What about other melodies that come in later on?

Timbre — This work is for a large orchestra, but how often do you actually hear all the instruments playing? Listen for long passages with smaller groupings of instruments within the orchestra.

Rhythm — Listen to the way the meter is simple at times, complex at others. Some sections are in straightforward duple meter, while others are full of syncopation (off-beat accents).

Form — Listen for the repeated return of the opening section's main idea and the contrast with sections based on other melodies. This movement is a **rondo**.

How do you create through sound alone, without words, the sense of a place? Aaron Copland did just that in his *Rodeo* (pronounced "ro-DAY-oh") when he captured the sound of the American West. He composed this ballet at the request of the dancer Agnes de Mille, who choreographed the ballet and danced the lead role.

The story takes place somewhere in the American West and centers on the Cowgirl, who is determined to win the heart of the Head Wrangler. The Head Wrangler is unimpressed with the Cowgirl's prowess with ropes and horses. Not until the concluding Hoe-down—the big Saturday night dance—does she succeed in catching his eye (and his heart), having traded her cowboy outfit for a dress. De Mille jokingly described the scenario as "The Taming of the Shrew—cowboy style." Shortly after completing the ballet, Copland extracted four scenes to be played in concert settings, of which "Hoe-Down" is the last.

Copland creates an identifiably American sound in this movement by using actual folk tunes that are rhythmically vigorous and cover a wide range. He also orchestrates his music in an extremely open fashion—that is, he uses the full range of registers from highest to lowest and leaves as much space as possible between groups of instruments. This "open scoring," as musicians refer to it, creates a kind of sonic counterpart to the open spaces of the American West.

Folk Melodies

The opening melody—and the one that keeps returning in this movement—is a traditional fiddle tune called "Bonaparte's Retreat." Copland found this melody, transcribed by Ruth Crawford Seeger (see chapter 49), in a 1941 collection of American folk music called *Our Singing Country* (see "Using Hoe-Down"). He introduces the theme gradually by first presenting only a small portion of it at the very beginning, followed by the sounds of a square-dance band tuning up. Only later do we hear the main melody in its full form. The music stays squarely in the tonic in this opening section, in keeping with the mood of a folk dance.

The jaunty, disjunct melody in the middle of the movement (**C** in the Listening Guide) is also based on a traditional fiddling tune. Copland found this melody, called "McLeod's Reel," in another published anthology of American folk tunes. Like "Bonaparte's Retreat," it contributes to the identifiably American sound of "Hoe-Down."

Timbre: Smaller Ensembles Within the Orchestra

Copland creates variety within this movement by varying the orchestration throughout. At times we hear the full ensemble—a big orchestra, with a large percussion section of timpani, piano, xylophone, snare drum, bass drum, cymbal, and wood block—and at other times we hear a reduced ensemble of only a few instruments. The piano is a relative newcomer to the orchestra; Copland uses it sparingly but to good effect by imitating the sound of a piano one would typically hear in a Western dance-hall.

The timbres are noticeably bright and transparent. Even though Copland is writing for a large orchestra, he allows the individual instruments or groups of instruments to come through clearly because he writes in what might be called sonic layers, with each instrumental grouping projecting its own identity. Listen to the groups of sounds at the very opening: the strings are clearly divided into low and high groupings that are distinct from each other and distinct yet again from the brass instruments, which themselves are clearly divided into high and low groupings. This kind of writing helps reinforce the contrast of sound between these layers. And like many twentieth-century composers writing for orchestra, Copland also gives unusual prominence to the percussion instruments. The notion of giving a fiddle tune to a xylophone (at 0:34, for example) creates a particularly penetrating sound.

Dance Rhythms

A hoe-down is an energetic, duple-meter dance that has come to be associated particularly with the tradition of Western square-dancing, and Copland maintains duple meter throughout. But he varies the beat by presenting some sections in clearly demarcated duple meter while introducing a high degree of syncopation into other sections. Consider the opening melody ("Bonaparte's Retreat"): Copland accents the highest notes of the tune whenever it leaps upward. Or listen to the main melody when first presented by the full orchestra: the brass instruments come in consistently off the beat, and this creates a sense of forward momentum that would otherwise be lacking.

Rondo Form

Copland constructs this dance in the form of a **rondo**. The main theme (**A**), or at least parts of it, alternates with contrasting melodic ideas. The opening is particularly clever: Copland captures the spirit and even the sequence of events in a Western-style dance by having the orchestra "tune up" early on, and by presenting accompanimental patterns but no real melodies until about half a minute into the piece: the ensemble is getting ready, but it takes a little while for it to get into the full swing of things. Only with the first return of the **A** section do we hear the main theme in its entirety for the first time. We've been anticipating it, and the orchestra has been hinting at it, but only now do we actually hear it.

Now listen to this music again, following the Listening Guide.

The American dancer Agnes de Mille in the role of the Cowgirl in the premiere of Copland's *Rodeo* (1942). De Mille also choreographed this production, which blended modern ballet with square dancing. She later choreographed a number of Broadway musicals, including *Oklahoma!* (1943), *Carousel* (1945), *Brigadoon* (1947), and *Paint Your Wagon* (1951).

© 2008 Ronald Seymour, Inc. Photo: Maurice Seymour

Aaron Copland (1900–90)

POPULIST MODERNIST

Born in Brooklyn, Aaron Copland came of age in the 1920s and 1930s, and was consumed with the idea of writing "American music." Like so many of his contemporaries, he was trained in the European tradition, and he could also write in the style of cutting-edge modernists. Yet he was politically and emotionally a populist at heart, and he never lost touch with his American roots, using actual folk tunes in such works as *Rodeo* and *Appalachian Spring*. He also wrote music for a number of Hollywood films, including *Our Town* and *Of Mice and Men*. The appeal of Copland's music transcends generations. The filmmaker Spike Lee used several of his works in the soundtrack to *He Got Game* (1998). "When I listen to Copland's music," Lee explained, "I hear America, and basketball is America. It's like he wrote the score for this film."

In addition to his work as a composer, Copland was also a superb lecturer and writer on music. His *What to Listen for in Music* remains a model of its kind.

PLAYLIST: COPLAND

Fanfare for the Common Man. A short but memorable work, often used (like "Hoe-Down") in commercials.

Appalachian Spring. A ballet written for Martha Graham, celebrating the virtues of frontier life.

Billy the Kid. Another American-themed ballet.

Aaron Copland and Nadia Boulanger, 1972. In the 1920s, Copland studied composition with Boulanger (1887–1979) in her native France. Her later pupils included such prominent American composers as Roy Harris, Walter Piston, Virgil Thomson, and Elliott Carter.
Douglas Lyttle

Lincoln Portrait. For narrator and orchestra, using Lincoln's own words as a spoken text.

Twelve Poems of Emily Dickinson. For solo voice and piano.

CULTURAL CONTEXT

Using "Hoe-Down"

The principal melody of "Hoe-Down" started life as a country fiddle tune known as "Bonaparte's Retreat." Alan Lomax, a folklorist, recorded a version of it by "Fiddler Bill" Stepp (1875–1957) in eastern Kentucky in 1937. Ruth Crawford Seeger (see chapter 49) transcribed the recording for Alan and John Lomax's book *Our Singing Country* (1941). Copland found the melody in this book (called "Bonyparte" there), orchestrated it, and incorporated it into the larger movement he called "Hoe-Down." Here are some of the many ways this tune has been used:

1. The British rock group Emerson, Lake, and Palmer recorded their version of the tune, called "Hoedown," on the 1972 album *Trilogy*. The album reached number 5 on Billboard's chart at one point.

2. In the early 1990s, the National Cattlemen's Beef Association and Beef Board began using Copland's version of the tune as the musical backdrop for a series of television commercials with the tagline "Beef: It's What's for Dinner."

3. The director Spike Lee used Copland's version in the soundtrack to the 1998 film *He Got* Game.

4. In 2000, the bluegrass-jazz group Béla Fleck and the Flecktones recorded their own version of the tune on *Outbound*.

5. The opening ceremony of the 2002 Winter Olympics, in Salt Lake City, used Copland's version from *Rodeo* as a backdrop to an enormous hoe-down with hundreds of dancers.

6. In 2006, Bob Dylan used a recording of Copland's "Hoe-Down" for his stage entrance at live performances.

Aaron Copland "Hoe-Down" from *Rodeo*

Time	Form: Section	Melody	Timbre	Rhythm
0:00	A	Fanfare-like figure in the brass, swirling figures in the strings; then (0:04) an imitation of instruments being tuned in the strings, but no real melody yet	Full orchestra	No clear sense of meter, much syncopation
0:18	B	Dancelike accompaniment, but still no clear melody	Piano bass line, wood blocks, imitation of a dance-hall double bass in the lower strings	Clear duple meter
0:40	A'	Same swirling figure as in **A**, but now it continues to present the main melody of the movement, a rapid, energetic theme that swoops down and then up.	Violins play the melody as if it were being played on a country fiddle (0:48). Prominent parts for oboe (1:08) and xylophone (throughout).	Duple meter, but with syncopation in some voices
1:39	C	Jaunty, disjunct melody with large upward leap	Solo trumpet (1:39), solo oboe (1:47), solo violin (1:51), then the full orchestra (1:56)	Duple meter, no syncopation at first; then increasing syncopation as brass enter (2:04) and grow stronger
2:25	B'	Dancelike accompaniment, again without any clear melody.	Piano bass line, wood blocks (2:28); trombone (2:34); strings and celesta (2:48)	Duple meter, no syncopation. Tempo gradually slows down, as if the music is running out of energy
2:50	A"	Main melody returns	Full orchestra	Tempo returns to its original fast pace. Duple meter with much syncopation.

Student FAQs

What was Agnes de Mille's choreography of Rodeo like?

From still pictures, her notes, and eyewitness accounts, we know that de Mille's choreography combined the free movements of modern dance with more traditional elements of folk dancing and square-dancing. Unfortunately, we have no film version of how she and her troupe performed this ballet.

OH, WHAT A BEAUTIFUL MORNIN'

OKLAHOMA!

This music is used so often and in so many places (see "Using Hoe-Down"). Who gets the royalties today?

The royalties go to Aaron Copland's estate, which funds a program that allows individual composers to spend six weeks in residence at the house in which Copland lived for the last 30 years of his life, in Cortlandt, New York, in Westchester County, just north of New York City.

"Are You Now or Have You Ever Been...?"

It is ironic that Aaron Copland, whose music has been so strongly identified with America, was the most prominent composer brought before Congress to testify in the McCarthy hearings of the early 1950s. Sen. Joseph McCarthy was convinced that Communists and Communist sympathizers had infiltrated the U.S. government. The arts of all kinds, including music, were part of the Cold War effort to fight the influence of the Soviet Union, and Copland was an ideal ambassador for American culture. But he had also belonged to several musical groups that fostered contacts between American and Soviet composers, and this brought him—and many other artists—under the suspicion of being a "Communist sympathizer."

Copland protested strenuously that participation in such groups was based entirely on his "concern with cultural and musical affairs. I had no knowledge or reason to believe, from my own experience, that any such organization was subversive or communistic. . . . As one who has benefitted so greatly from the unique opportunities that America offers its citizens, not only on a financial but also on a spiritual and artistic level, I am far too grateful for the privilege of being an American to become a member of any organization that I believed was merely a forum for Communist propaganda."*

But the taint of association lingered, and Copland had trouble securing a passport to travel abroad for several years. When his *Lincoln Portrait* was performed on television's *Ed Sullivan Show* in 1956, Ed Sullivan pointedly failed to identify the

Copland's subpoena to testify before Congress on May 25, 1953. He received this telegram on May 22.

composer of the work. With time, however, Copland regained his status as an iconic American composer. In 1986, the same Congress that had investigated him 30 years earlier awarded him the Congressional Gold Medal, its highest civilian honor.

*Quotation found online in an unpublished essay by Ryan Patrick Jones called "La forme fatalé: Aaron Copland and the Allure of Opera," Brandeis graduate Journal 2004, volume 2.

EXPAND YOUR PLAYLIST

The Sound of the American West

Rodeo was one of several works by Copland to evoke the American West, and other composers were quick to follow his lead in using sonic layers to create an open sound reflecting the open spaces of the region.

Aaron Copland, *Billy the Kid.* A ballet commissioned by the choreographer Lincoln Kirsten in 1938.

Aaron Copland, *The Red Pony.* A film score to the 1949 movie, starring Robert Mitchum and Myrna Loy, based on the short story by John Steinbeck.

Ferde Grofé, *Grand Canyon Suite.* A suite for orchestra, composed in 1931. Each of the five movements paints in sound a scene from the Grand Canyon.

Dmitri Tiomkin, *High Noon.* The film score won an Academy Award both for best song ("Do Not Forsake Me, Oh My Darlin'") and for best soundtrack. Tiomkin was a Ukrainian who did not arrive in the United States until the age of 31.

Elmer Bernstein, *The Magnificent Seven.* The main title theme has been used in innumerable commercials and is instantly recognizable as a sonic icon of the Old West.

Enrico Morricone, *The Good, the Bad, and the Ugly.* One of the Italian composer's many scores for "spaghetti Westerns," so called because the films were produced and often directed by Italian artists (in this case, Sergio Leone). Morricone received a Lifetime Achievement Award at the 2007 Oscars ceremony for his film scores.

52

NEW YORK CITY

Los Angeles · Washington D.C. · U.S.A.

Leonard Bernstein
"Tonight" from *West Side Story*

 Listen to This

Melody	Listen for the two contrasting melodies in this scene. How are they different? Who sings which?
Texture	Listen for the growing complexity of texture, from the homophonic beginning (one singer with accompaniment) to the polyphonic ending (five different vocal lines).
Form	Listen for the way in which the scene grows from a series of sections sung by individual singers (solos) to a trio (three different singers) to a quintet. Also listen for the way in which the two main themes are varied and eventually combined.
Word-Music Relationships	The key word in this scene is "Tonight." Listen for the way in which it is sung consistently (but very differently) in each of the two melodies. Notice, too, how all the singers arrive at this one word together from different routes at the very end of the scene.

eonard Bernstein's *West Side Story* is a modern-day retelling of the story of Romeo and Juliet. The feuding "families" in this case are urban gangs: the Jets (whites) and Sharks (Puerto Ricans). When Tony, a Jet, falls in love with Maria, whose brother Bernardo is leader of the Sharks, the stage is set for a tragic ending.

West Side Story is a **musical**, a spoken drama with a substantial amount of singing. Unlike opera, which is sung from beginning to end, the musical is essentially a spoken drama with extended musical interjections. The idea of working songs into spoken plays goes back to Shakespeare and even before. But the genre in which music becomes more extensive and important than the spoken parts first arose in Europe in the eighteenth century—Mozart even wrote a few (the German term is *Singspiel*, or "song-play")—and flourished in the operetta tradition of the nineteenth century, particularly in the works of Johann Strauss (*Die Fledermaus*) and Gilbert and Sullivan (*Pirates of Penzance, H.M.S. Pinafore, The Mikado*). These **operettas**—literally "small operas"—were invariably comic and lighthearted, often sentimental. They were also enormously popular and profitable. Transplanted to the United States, the operetta reached new heights, where it became known as the musical or the "Broadway musical," in honor of the street in New York City with the greatest concentration of musical theaters. In the hands of such American composers as Jerome Kern (*Show boat*), Richard Rodgers (*Oklahoma!*), and Allen Jay Lerner (*My Fair Lady*), the Broadway musical soon developed into an institution that would be exported throughout the world.

Bernardo (George Charkiris) leads two of his Sharks down the street. Jerome Robbins's choreography, both for the 1957 Broadway production and for the 1961 film, was widely acclaimed.
Mirisch-7 Arts/United Artists/The Kobal Collection

West Side Story was an instant hit when it premiered on Broadway in 1957. Bernstein's music uses elements of jazz, both in its orchestration and in its syncopated rhythms. The characters in the scene here are:

- Riff, leader of the Jets
- Bernardo, leader of the Sharks
- Chorus of Jets
- Chorus of Sharks
- Anita, a Puerto Rican, the girlfriend of Bernardo
- Tony, a Jet in love with Maria
- Maria, the sister of Bernardo, in love with Tony

All of them have big plans for "tonight." The Jets and Sharks are planning a rumble (fight). Anita readies herself for a night of passion with Bernardo. And Tony and Maria plan to see each other when it is dark, for they cannot carry on their romance in the light of day.

Representative Melodies

There are two opposing emotions in this scene: hate (between the Jets and the Sharks) and love (between Tony and Maria). Bernstein gives each a representative melody. The opening of the scene sets out a choppy, fast-paced melody over an ostinato bass (marked as "1" in the Listening Guide) with strong syncopations. Though they are rival gangs, the Jets and Sharks both want the same thing, a fight, and we hear this in their music: their words are

Maria (Natalie Wood) and Tony (Richard Beymer) in the 1961 film adaptation of *West Side Story*. The "balcony scene" from Shakespeare's *Romeo and Juliet* has been transferred to a fire escape.
Mirisch-7 Arts/United Artists/Picture Desk, Inc./Kobal Collection

different, but both gangs sing the same melody. Tony and Maria also want the same thing—to be together—and we hear this in the very different music the two of them sing ("2," below), a soaring, lyrical melody. This melody ("Tonight") is one they had sung earlier in the show in the "balcony scene." (The balcony in this urban setting was a fire escape.)

Anita occupies an interesting position here. She is more worldly than Maria, and her interest in Bernardo seems largely physical ("Anita's gonna get her kicks tonight"). She sings words of passion ("Don't matter if he's tired, As long as he's here") to the same melody sung by the Jets and Sharks in anticipation of their rumble.

Additive Form

The scene introduces the characters one by one and brings them all together (musically, at least) in the following order. The principal themes (1 and 2) are shown in parentheses.

1. **Chorus:** The Jets (led by Riff) and Sharks (led by Bernardo) each lay out their grievances with the other group. The two gangs occupy opposite ends of the stage and do not interact, even though they are singing the same music together and at times even the same words (1).
2. **Solo (Anita).** Anita sings the same melody in anticipation of her evening with Bernardo, after the fight (1).
3. **Solo (Tony).** Tony sings a new melody in anticipation of his evening with Maria (2).

4. Solo (Maria). Maria sings the same melody as Tony, anticipating her evening with him.
5. Chorus (Jets). The Jets approach Tony.
6. Trio (Maria, Tony, Riff). Maria continues Tony's lyrical melody (2). But instead of echoing her, Tony agrees to Riff's demands (1). We hear both themes simultaneously.
7. Quintet (Maria, Tony, Anita, Jets, Sharks). All the characters sing at once: Tony and Maria sing their melody (2) while all the others sing theirs (1). Everyone lands on the same word—"tonight"—at the very end.

By using just two basic melodies and distributing them among different characters, Bernstein is able to create a kind of **additive form** in which nothing disappears, but new layers are constantly added. This is a technique Bernstein had learned from the world of opera, in which the music in a given scene often becomes more layered—and the stage more populated—as the action progresses.

Increasingly Complex Textures

Closely related to the scene's additive form are its increasingly complex textures, which move from homophonic at the beginning (one melodic line with accompaniment), to a trio (three voices), to a quintet (five voices). What we hear at the end is, in effect, five monologues performed simultaneously. This reveals one of the advantages of sung drama over spoken drama. If these same characters were merely speaking their parts, we would comprehend none of them, and it would all sound like mere babble. Because we hear the characters singing their parts, we can differentiate among the contrasting melodies and emotions and experience them simultaneously.

Word-Music Relationships: "Tonight," Two Ways

The contrasts in the setting of this one word capture the basic conflict between the world of Tony and Maria and the world of the Jets and Sharks. Those anticipating the physical side of things—Riff and the Jets, Bernardo and the Sharks, and Anita—sing the word to a menacing-sounding figure that sounds impatient and pressed (see notation example above). Tony and Maria sing the same word very differently, leaping up or down to a long, sustained note (see notation example above).

We would, of course, expect lovers to be singing the same melody to each other: in opera, this is one sure-fire indication that a couple is really in love, and it often marks a major moment in an onstage relationship. Bernstein plays off this convention by having the two lovers sing separately, in simultaneous monologues. He applies the same device to the two warring gangs: they are not singing to each other, either, and the fact that they share a common melody makes the whole situation that much more ironic, for in the end, the two gangs are not really all that different on a personal, human level. It is only their races that separate them.

With these points in mind, now listen to this scene again using the Listening Guide.

Listening Guide

CD V · Track 10 GO TO PEARSON mymusiclab for the Automated Listening Guide

Leonard Bernstein "Tonight" from *West Side Story*

Time	Form	Character(s)	Text	Melody
0:00	Chorus	**JETS**	The Jets are gonna have their day—Tonight. The Jets are gonna have their way—Tonight. The Puerto Ricans grumble: "Fair fight." But if they start a rumble, We'll rumble them right.	1 = choppy melody with ostinato bass
0:22		**SHARKS**	We're gonna hand 'em a surprise—Tonight. We're gonna cut 'em down to size—Tonight We said, "O.K., no rumpus, No tricks." But just in case they jump us, we're ready to mix—Tonight.	
0:40		**JETS**	We're gonna rock it tonight, We're gonna jazz it up and have us a ball!	
0:45		**SHARKS**	They're gonna get it tonight; The more they turn it on the harder they'll fall!	
0:52		**JETS / SHARKS**	Well, they began it! Well, they began it!	
0:54		**ALL**	And we're the ones to stop 'em once and for all—Tonight!	
1:02	Solo	**ANITA**	Anita's gonna get her kicks—Tonight. We'll have our private little mix—Tonight. He'll walk in hot and tired, poor dear! Don't matter if he's tired, as long as he's here—tonight.	1 = variant of same melody
1:18	Solo	**TONY**	Tonight, tonight, won't be just any night, Tonight there will be no morning star. Tonight, tonight, I'll see my love tonight. And for us, stars will stop where they are.	2 = lyrical melody
1:42	Solo	**MARIA**	Today, the minutes seem like hours, the hours go so slowly, And still the sky is light. Oh moon, grow bright, And make this endless day endless night!	
2:12	Group	**JETS**	The Jets are comin' out on top—Tonight. We're gonna watch Bernardo drop—Tonight. That Puerto Rican punk'll go down. And when he's hollered "Uncle," we'll tear up the town!	1 = choppy melody

Texture	Word-Music Relationships
Homophonic	The word "tonight" stands out because it is sung smoothly to the same upward-moving figure each time. The Jets and Sharks are leaders of opposing gangs, but they have the same ideas (and music) about what will happen "tonight."
	Both gangs sing in unison; they have agreed that there will be a fight tonight.
	Anita is also singing of her (very different) plans for what will happen "tonight," using a variant of the same melody sung by the gangs.
Homophonic	A new melody, lyrical rather than choppy. The ostinato bass gives way to a flowing accompaniment. This is the return of a melody sung by Tony and Maria earlier in the show in their "balcony scene."
Homophonic	

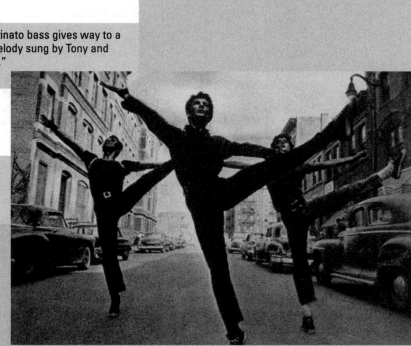

(continued)

Listening Guide (continued)

Time	Form	Character(s)	Text	Melody
2:27	Trio	**MARIA**	Tonight, tonight, won't be just any night, Tonight there will be no morning star . . .	2
		RIFF	We'll be in back of you, boy?	1
		TONY	All right.	
		RIFF	We're gonna flatten him good.	
		TONY	All right.	
		RIFF (spoken)	One, two, three!	
		TONY (spoken)	One, two, three!	
		RIFF	And then we'll have us a ball:	
		TONY	Tonight . . .	
2:40	Quintet	**MARIA**	Tonight, tonight, I'll see my love tonight. And for us, stars will stop where they are.	2
		JETS/SHARKS	We're gonna rock it tonight! We're gonna jazz it tonight! They're gonna get it tonight.	1
		MARIA AND TONY	Today the minutes seem like hours. The hours go so slowly, And still the sky is light. Oh moon, grow bright, And make this endless day endless night,	2
		ANITA	Tonight, late tonight We're gonna mix it tonight. Anita's gonna have her day, Bernardo's gonna have his way, tonight.	
		JETS/SHARKS	They began it, they began it, they will watch. We'll stop 'em once and for all. The Sharks are gonna have their way, the Sharks are gonna have their day, We're gonna rock it tonight. Tonight!	
3:12		**ALL**	Tonight!	

Texture	**Word-Music Relationships**
Polyphonic: both (1) and (2) at the same time	Maria sings Tony's melody (2) while Riff reminds Tony that he has to be at the fight tonight (1); Tony agrees (1).
Polyphonic	The climax of the scene, presenting the emotions of all the characters at once.
	Maria and Tony sing the same music together for the first time in this scene

Student FAQs

What's the difference between music that is sung in an opera and music that is sung in a musical?

The two styles of writing overlap considerably—both genres have their arias, ensembles, choruses—so it's impossible to make hard-and-fast distinctions between the styles of the two. In general, the vocal parts in musicals tend to be somewhat less demanding from a technical point of view, though there are plenty of musically challenging roles on Broadway. There is perhaps more of a difference in styles of singing. Singers with a "Broadway voice" often project with a bigger, brassier kind of voice and in a manner that is more declamatory; they certainly have to be better actors than singers in a standard operatic production.

Why are the lyrics in the stage version slightly different?

The 1961 movie version "cleaned up" the lyrics at several points to conform to the standards for Hollywood productions of the time. In the original stage production, for example, Anita sings: "He'll walk in hot and tired / So what? / Don't matter if he's tired / As long as he's hot."

What happens in the fight?

That would be a plot-spoiler. The movie version of *West Side Story* won many Academy Awards and is well worth seeing in its entirety.

Leonard Bernstein (1918–90)

FOUR LIVES IN ONE

Shortly after Leonard Bernstein died in 1990, the composer Ned Rorem observed that he had not died at the age of 72, but 288. Why? Because "Lenny led four lives in one." And indeed, Bernstein achieved what for many musicians would amount to four lifetimes' worth of accomplishments:

- As a conductor, he was the first American-born musician to lead a major symphony orchestra, the New York Philharmonic. He made his debut with the group in 1943 and served as its music director from 1958 to 1969. He was chosen to conduct the performance of Beethoven's Ninth Symphony in Berlin in 1989 that celebrated the fall of the Berlin Wall.

- As a composer, Bernstein wrote for the stage (*West Side Story, Candide*), the concert hall (three symphonies), the screen (*On the Waterfront*), and the ballet (*Fancy Free*).

- As a pianist, he collaborated with such prestigious groups as the Juilliard String Quartet, the Vienna Philharmonic, and the New York Philharmonic.

- As an educator, Bernstein worked tirelessly to expand audiences for classical music. His "Young People's Concerts," televised nationwide between 1958 and 1972, exposed millions to a repertory they might otherwise never have heard.

Bernstein in rehearsal in 1947 with the American soprano Marian Anderson (1897–1993).

Estate of Ruth Orkin Photo Archive

PLAYLIST: BERNSTEIN

On the Town. Bernstein's first Broadway hit (1944).

Candide. Another musical, based on Voltaire's satirical novel.

Chichester Psalms. A setting of Psalms for chorus and orchestra, commissioned by the dean of Chichester Cathedral, England.

Mass. A "theater piece" for dancers, singers, and orchestra, commissioned to inaugurate the opening of the Kennedy Center, Washington, D.C. (1971).

    EXPAND YOUR PLAYLIST

Broadway's Social Conscience

West Side Story stands in a long tradition of musicals that combine entertainment with social commentary.

- *Show Boat* (1927, music by Jerome Kern, lyrics by Oscar Hammerstein II). The first major musical to tackle the issue of racial bigotry.
- *South Pacific* (1948, music by Richard Rodgers, lyrics by Oscar Hammerstein II). One of the plot strands deals with prevailing prejudices against interracial love; the story is set against the backdrop of World War II.
- *My Fair Lady* (1956, music by Frederick Loewe, lyrics by Alan Jay Lerner). Based on George Bernard Shaw's play *Pygmalion,* this musical tackles serious issues—poverty and social mobility—in

a humorous but moving manner, focusing on language and speech as weapons of class warfare.

- *Les Misérables* (1980, music by Claude-Michel Schönberg, lyrics by Alain Boublil). An adaptation of Victor Hugo's novel of the same name, this French musical (translated into English in 1982) explores the nature of poverty.
- *Miss Saigon* (1989, music by Claude-Michel Schönberg, lyrics by Richard Maltby, Jr., and Alain Boublil). Based loosely on Puccini's *Madame Butterfly,* this musical considers the aftermath of the U.S. military involvement in Vietnam.
- *Rent* (1996, music and lyrics by Jonathan Larson). A reinterpretation of Puccini's opera *La Bohème* (1897), *Rent* confronts issues of sexual orientation, drug addiction, and AIDS.

53

NEW YORK CITY

Los Angeles   Washington D.C.

U.S.A.

John Cage
4'33"

Listen to This

There is no recording of this work. It consists of three movements in which the performer plays nothing for as long as he or she wishes. But is the result silence? What do you actually hear during any span of time? Is this music?

A rguably the most controversial work of music ever written, John Cage's *4'33"* has polarized listeners from the start. Its admirers find it endlessly fascinating, while its detractors dismiss it as a mere gimmick—and not even music, at that. Many critics have dismissed *4'33"* as a prank, a clever joke but nothing more. Others, however, have defended it for raising fundamental questions about the very nature of music, the way we make music, and above all, the way we listen to music.

4'33" is often said to consist of four minutes and thirty-three seconds of silence. This description is inaccurate on both counts. Neither the length of the work nor the "silence" is quite so straightforward. Cage's score notes simply that the work lasted *4'33"* when it was first performed in Woodstock, New York, on August 29, 1952. The real title of the work, as Cage notes, "is the total length in minutes and seconds of its performance," which can vary from performance to performance; for, as Cage goes on to indicate in the score, "the work may be performed by any instrumentalist or combination of instrumentalists and last any length of time." Thus even the one element of the work that might seem constant—its length—is in fact subject to variability.

And is there really such a thing as silence? There are always sounds around us. When we listen to a "silent" work, we become acutely aware of what we otherwise try *not* to hear: breathing, coughing, a room's ventilation system, a dog barking in the distance. Whether we like it or not, these kinds of sounds are always a part of the listening experience, and if we choose to shut them out, it is only because we have been conditioned to do so.

According to Cage, *4′33″* was inspired by the "white paintings" created by one of his friends, the artist Robert Rauschenberg (b. 1925). These "blank" canvases are never truly blank, of course. Every canvas has its own unique color and textures even before any paint is applied, and each canvas is constantly changing because of the way it reflects the light of its surroundings. But as viewers, we have been conditioned not to notice such details or to mentally compensate for them. In much the same way, Cage's *4′33″* challenges the notion that there is such a thing as silence, the musical equivalent of a "blank" canvas.

Cage's *4′33″* is an example of **aleatory music**, music of chance. The word "aleatory" comes from the Latin *alea* ("die," the singular of "dice"), and aleatory music involves—at least metaphorically—a "roll of the dice." The idea of writing music by chance, even by a literal throw of the dice, was by no means new in the twentieth century. Mozart and other composers of the Classical Era were fascinated by the possibility of creating works based on modular units chosen at random from an extensive array of possibilities. But aleatory music came into its own in the middle of the twentieth century, and Cage led the way. In his *Imaginary Landscape No. 4* (1951), for 12 radios, 24 players, and a conductor, he specified elements of rhythm and dynamics with great precision but left the sound content entirely to chance. The score calls for two performers on each radio, one controlling the frequency, the other the volume, with the conductor giving cues for each. The duration of the work, the volume, and the points of entry are all fixed, but what is actually heard at any given moment from any of the twelve radios is entirely unpredictable, from rock to talk to classical to static.

Robert Rauschenberg's "Portrait of Iris Clert" (1961). Is a work of art a work of art because the artist says so?
Jurg Dontasch/ Robert Rauschenberg Studio/Untitled Press Inc. Art © Robert Rauschenberg/Licensed by VAGA, New York, NY

John Cage (1912–92)

WHAT IS A COMPOSER?

"Everything we do is music," Cage once declared. He did not see himself as a high priest of art but rather as a facilitator between listeners and sounds. Profoundly influenced by Zen Buddhism and its renunciation of striving and the will, Cage maintained that his "purpose is to eliminate purpose," and many of his works from the late 1940s on seem to avoid or challenge the traditional stance of the composer as an omnipotent creator of a small musical world.

Born in Los Angeles, Cage studied composition with Arnold Schoenberg but soon moved on to composing in a manner even more radically modern than that of his teacher. In the 1940s, Cage began writing a series of works for "prepared piano," a piano whose strings were outfitted with such everyday objects as screws, rubber bands, and coins, producing a range of timbres as oddly familiar as they are strange. In the 1950s, he became interested in the possibilities of electronic music and multimedia art, combining word, music, and movement, often mixing live and recorded sounds and images. Cage and his music consistently polarized listeners. Most of the audience at New York's Lincoln Center walked out of his *Atlas eclipticalis* (whose notated score superimposes transparent staff paper on star charts to determine pitches) when it was first presented by the New York Philharmonic in 1964; even members of the orchestra hissed the composer. But Cage's provocative music and writings remained fresh over time, and toward the end of his life he was showered with honors. He delivered the prestigious Charles Eliot Norton lectures at Harvard University in 1988, continuing in the tradition of other composers before him, including Igor Stravinsky, Aaron Copland, and Leonard Bernstein. Some saw genius in his works, others charlatanism, but all were provoked by them to rethink the nature of music and its relationship to the world around us.

John Cage gathering wild greens in Rockland County, New York, May 1971. He was an acknowledged authority on mushrooms and won a large cash prize on a quiz show on Italian television in 1958 for answering a series of questions about them.

James Klosty

PLAYLIST: CAGE

Sonata and Interludes. A series of pieces for what Cage called "prepared piano," a piano with various screws, bolts, and pieces of felt placed strategically on the strings inside a piano, thereby creating a radically different sound from the instrument.

Fontana Mix. A work for magnetic tape.

Roaratorio: An Irish Circus on Finnegans Wake. For magnetic tape and live performers, based on James Joyce's novel.

0' 00". The performer is instructed to perform "a disciplined action," sonically amplified to the greatest possible degree.

THE COMPOSER SPEAKS

John Cage on *4'33"*

When the composer and writer William Duckworth interviewed John Cage in the late 1980s, the conversation turned, almost inevitably, to Cage's best-known work.

◆◆◆

DUCKWORTH: Let me ask you a few questions about *4'33"*. Is it true that it was actually conceived of in the late forties and just not presented until the fifties?

CAGE: Yes. I knew about it, and had spoken about the possibility of doing it, for about four years before I did it. . . . I knew that it would be taken as a joke and a renunciation of work, whereas I also knew that if it was done it would be the highest form of work. Or this form of work: an art without work. I doubt whether many people understand it yet.

DUCKWORTH: Well, the traditional understanding is that it opens you up to the sounds that exist around you and . . .

CAGE: . . . to the acceptance of anything, even when you have something as the basis. And that's how it's misunderstood.

DUCKWORTH: What's a better understanding of it?

CAGE: It opens you up to any possibility *only* when nothing is taken as the basis. But most people don't understand that, as far as I can tell.

DUCKWORTH: Is it possible that instead of being taken as too foolish, it's now taken too seriously?

CAGE: No. I don't think it can be taken too seriously.

DUCKWORTH: What I mean is that it's approached too intellectually. My own feeling is that it's not a piece to approach intellectually, maybe not even a piece to approach, in the traditional sense.

CAGE: Well, I use it constantly in my life experience. No day goes by without my making use of that piece in my life and in my work. I listen to it every day. Yes I do.

DUCKWORTH: Can you give me an example?

CAGE: I don't sit down to do it; I turn my attention toward it. I realize that it's going on continuously. So, more and more, my attention, as now, is on it. More than anything else, it's the source of my enjoyment of life.

DUCKWORTH: But it seems to me that when you focus on that piece it becomes art silence rather than real silence. And that the understanding of real silence is what that piece is about. But that the only way you can get to real silence is through artistic silence. Is that accurate?

CAGE: Thoreau came to this same attitude of mind and use of his faculties without my being anywhere around.

DUCKWORTH: Yes, but you'd be hard-pressed to name another one who came to that attitude, wouldn't you?

CAGE: Well, I would think quite a lot of people in India feel that music is continuous, it is only we who turn away. This is a cliché in Indian thinking and, surely, in Indian experience. My affirmation of this is within the context of twentieth-century art music. But the important thing, surely, about having done it, finally, is that it leads out of the world of art into the whole of life. . . .

Listening Guide

John Cage, *4'33"*

Student FAQs

Is this work ever actually performed in concert?

Yes, and it always provokes a response from audiences because it's a very different experience to actually hear this work than to imagine what it would be like to hear it. Videos of concert performances are occasionally available on the Internet and are worth watching.

Is this really music?

Good question.

Paying for Silence

On September 23, 2002, cnn.com ran the following story:

Composer Pays for Piece of Silence

LONDON, England—A bizarre legal battle over a minute's silence in a recorded song has ended with a six-figure out-of-court settlement.

British composer Mike Batt found himself the subject of a plagiarism action for including the song "A One Minute Silence" on an album for his classical rock band The Planets.

He was accused of copying it from a work by the late American composer John Cage, whose 1952 composition "4'33"" was totally silent.

On Monday, Batt settled the matter out of court by paying an undisclosed six-figure sum to the John Cage Trust.

Batt, who is best known in the U.K. for his links with the children's television characters The Wombles, told the Press Association: "This has been, albeit a gentlemanly dispute, a most serious matter and I am pleased that Cage's publishers have finally been persuaded that their case was, to say the least, optimistic.

"We are, however, making this gesture of a payment to the John Cage Trust in recognition of my own personal respect for John Cage and in recognition of his brave and sometimes outrageous approach to artistic experimentation in music."

Batt credited "A One Minute Silence" to "Batt/Cage."

Before the start of the court case, Batt had said: "Has the world gone mad? I'm prepared to do time rather than pay out. We are talking as much as £100,000 in copyright.

"Mine is a much better silent piece. I have been able to say in one minute what Cage could only say in four minutes and 33 seconds."

Batt gave a cheque to Nicholas Riddle, managing director of Cage's publishers Peters Edition, on the steps of the High Court, in London.

Riddle said: "We feel that honour has been settled.

"We had been prepared to make our point more strongly on behalf of Mr Cage's estate, because we do feel that the concept of a silent piece—particularly as it was credited by Mr Batt as being co-written by 'Cage'—is a valuable artistic concept in which there is a copyright.

"We are nevertheless very pleased to have reached agreement with Mr Batt over this dispute, and we accept his donation in good spirit."

"A One Minute Silence" has now been released as part of a double A-side single.

Source: http://archives.cnn.com/2002/SHOWBIZ/Music/09/23/uk.silence/

 EXPAND YOUR PLAYLIST

Experimental Composers of the Twentieth Century

A number of important twentieth-century composers confronted audiences with basic questions about the nature of music. John Cage is the most famous, but he was by no means alone.

Henry Cowell (1897–1965), a native of California, was one of John Cage's teachers. *The Banshee* calls for the performer to manipulate the strings inside the piano, which creates an eerie, otherworldly sound.

Harry Partch (1901–74), a native Californian who sometimes wrote under the name "Paul Pirate," designed and constructed his own new instruments capable of playing music based on unusual tuning systems, with as many as 55 notes in the span of conventional octave. *O Frabjous Day!* is a setting of the poem from Lewis

Carroll's *Alice in Wonderland* for voice and an ensemble of original instruments.

Moondog was the pseudonym of Louis Thomas Hardin (1916–99), a blind American composer and musician who by his own choice lived on the streets of New York City for almost twenty years. *Bird's Lament,* written in memory of the saxophonist Charlie Parker, was later sampled by the deejay Mr. Scruff for "Get a Move On" and eventually reused in a television commercial for the Lincoln Navigator SUV.

Lejaren Hiller (1924–94) taught at the University of Illinois, where he wrote the *Illiac Suite* in 1957, the first work of music composed by means of a programmed computer.

54

NEW YORK CITY

Los Angeles   Washington D.C.

U.S.A.

Philip Glass
"Knee Play 1" from *Einstein on the Beach*

Listen to This

Timbre

Listen for three layers of sound: (1) the bass line (the organ), (2) the chorus of voices that sing above it, and (3) the two speaking parts that operate seemingly independently of the music.

Harmony

Listen for the simple and strongly tonal harmonic progression that is repeated over and over in this scene.

Form

Listen for the repeated pattern in the bass line (the organ) that continues from beginning to end. Try to identify variations in the basic rhythmic and melodic patterns of the voices. Finally, be aware of the added elements (new voices, both singing and speaking) that emerge over the course of the scene as a whole.

An opera with very little singing and no plot: this is the world of Philip Glass's *Einstein on the Beach*. Although a good deal of text is recited, only small portions of it are sung, and the text that is sung is limited to the counting of numbers ("One, two, three," etc.) or solfege syllables (do-re-mi-fa-so-la-ti). There is no plot in the conventional sense. Instead, the opera is built around a series of recurring images: a train, a trial, a spaceship in a field. A character resembling Einstein appears at several points playing the violin (the real Einstein was in fact an amateur violinist). The four acts, performed without intermission, are introduced and connected by a series of "Knee Plays." According to Glass himself, the term "Knee Play" takes its name from the joining function of the human knee. The first of these Knee Plays—the opening number of the opera—is presented here.

Glass worked closely with the director and playwright Robert Wilson (b. 1941) to develop this radical new form of opera. "It never occurred to us that *Einstein on the Beach* would have a story or contain anything like a plot," Glass would later explain. "The title merely provided an occasion for which a theatrical/visual work could be constructed. . . . In a sense, we didn't need to tell an Einstein story because everyone who eventually saw our *Einstein* brought their own story with them." The work premiered in France in July 1976. "In the four months that we toured *Einstein* in Europe," Glass noted, "we had many occasions to meet with our audiences, and people occasionally would ask us what it 'meant.' But far more often people told us what it meant to *them*. . . . The point about *Einstein* was clearly not what it 'meant' but that it was *meaningful* as generally experienced by the people who saw it."*

Glass's music for *Einstein on the Beach* is written in a style known as **minimalism**, in which a brief musical idea or group of ideas is repeated and varied incrementally over a long span of time, with a relatively slow rate of change. Minimalist music, in spite of its name, tends to unfold across long periods and relies on the passage of time to create an almost trance-like state in the mind of the listener. Indeed, there is so much repetition that as listeners, our scale of perception changes, so that even a slight variation in the rhythm becomes a major event. "Knee Play 1" is typical of minimalist music in its use of fairly simple melodic, harmonic, and rhythmic building blocks.

Minimalism began in the visual arts, with the repetition of a single image varied across space. This is Andy Warhol's 1964 depiction of Marilyn Monroe.

Tate Gallery, London, Great Britain/Art Resource, NY. © 2003 The Andy Warhol Foundation for the Visual Arts/ARS, New York. ™2002 Marilyn Monroe LLC under license authorized by CMG Worldwide Inc., Indianapolis, Indiana 46256 USA www.MarilynMonroe.com.

Layered Timbres

The musical forces performing in this opening scene are quite modest: an electronic organ, a small chorus of mixed voices (soprano, alto, tenor, bass), and two speakers (both women). The organ and chorus move in close coordination, while the spoken voices enter and drop out in a manner that seems to be random. Glass allows for considerable latitude in the score, leaving it up to performers how many times they will repeat a certain section or exactly when the spoken texts will be recited and at what speed.

Simple Harmony

The organ and chorus outline a standard harmonic progression, one often heard in cadences in tonal music. The chords used are those built on the fourth, fifth, and first scale degrees (IV, V, and then I, in musical terms). The 12-bar blues chord progression, for example, makes exclusive use of these three chords (see chapters 46 and 56), and these are the same three chords that, according to some learn-how-to-play-music advertisements, will allow you to perform a thousand songs. By making the harmony so simple and by repeating it so often, Glass is able to draw our attention toward other elements of change, such as the varied rhythms of the melody and the gradual addition of new performing forces.

*Music by Philip Glass by Philip Glass; edited and with supplementary material by Robert T. Jones. New York: Harper & Row, 1987, p. 32.

Variation Form

The form of this scene is actually quite simple: it is a series of variations on a series of short melodic fragments, with the music unfolding over a constantly repeated bass, an **ostinato** (see chapters 10, 40, and 43). The rhythm of the theme and each of its variations remains essentially constant from beginning to end, with the singers counting the beats they sing out loud to some variation of this basic pattern:

1 2 3 4 | 1 2 3 4 5 6 | 1 2 3 4 5 6 7 8 |

Glass repeats this basic unit, with its three subunits of four, six, and eight beats, many times, but often with subtle variations. He creates variety in three ways:

1. **Altered rhythms:** Certain beats at the beginning of each subunit drop out in no predictable pattern. For example, at 1:03 we hear:

   1 2 3 4 | [pause] 2 3 4 5 6 | 1 2 3 4 5 6 7 8 |

   and at 1:45 we hear:

   [pause] 2 3 4 | 1 2 3 4 5 6 | [pause] 2 3 4 5 6 7 8 |

   Glass uses these and other rhythmic permutations throughout, eliminating the "1" beat in one or more of the three subunits of 4, 6, and 8 that make up the basic rhythmic unit.

2. **Divided voices.** At 2:06, the two vocal lines we have heard up to this point—sopranos and altos singing the upper line together, tenors and basses singing the lower line—split into four parts. Sopranos now sing "do re mi" to the same notes as the altos, who continue to sing as before, but the sopranos sing these syllables at a much slower rhythm. The tenors do the same (on the syllables "la so do") with the basses underneath.

3. **Added spoken voices.** Glass makes no distinction between speech or song: all become a part of the sonic landscape. At 1:03, we hear the first of two women's voices recite (in speech) some of the numbers being sung by the chorus. At 1:24, these voices begin to recite their own independent texts. This text (by the poet Christopher Knowles) is itself full of internal repetitions and is not meant to make sense syntactically. Here, for example, is the opening (beginning at 1:03):

   > Will it get some wind for the sailboat. And it could get for it is.
   > It could get the railroad for these workers. And it could be were it is.
   > It could Franky it could be Franky it could be very fresh and clean.
   > It could be a balloon.
   > Oh these are the days my friends and these are the days my friends.
   > It could get some wind for the sailboat. And it could get for it is.
   > It could get the railroad for these workers. It could get for it is were.
   > It could be a balloon. It could be Franky. It could be very fresh and clean.*
   > All these are the days my friends and these are the days my friends.
   > It could be those ways.

With these points in mind, listen to the scene once again using the Listening Guide.

*Excerpt of lyrics from "Einstein on the Beach," music by Philip Glass, lyrics by Christopher Knowles.

Listening Guide

CD V · Track 11
GO TO PEARSON mymusiclab for the Automated Listening Guide

Philip Glass "Knee Play 1" from *Einstein on the Beach*

Time	Form: Section (each section is stated twice)	Timbre	Rhythm	Spoken Text
0:00	1	Organ only	Ostinato figure: long, slow notes	
0:21	2	Sopranos and altos sing the upper line; tenors and basses sing the lower line.	1 2 3 4 1 2 3 4 5 6 1 2 3 4 5 6 7 8	
0:42	3		1 2 3 4 1 2 3 4 5 6 [pause] 2 3 4 5 6 7 8	
1:03	4		1 2 3 4 [pause] 2 3 4 5 6 1 2 3 4 5 6 7 8	First voice enters, speaking numbers with the sung chorus, seemingly at random.
1:24	5		[pause] 2 3 4 1 2 3 4 5 6 1 2 3 4 5 6 7 8	First voice begins to recite the text ("Will it get some wind for the sailboat," etc.).
1:45	6		[pause] 2 3 4 1 2 3 4 5 6 [pause] 2 3 4 5 6 7 8	Second voice enters to join in reciting the text.
2:06	7	Two lines in chorus divide to become four. The sopranos now sing the same pitches in longer notes to "do-re-mi," and the tenors sing the same pitches in longer notes to "la so do."	1 2 3 4 1 2 3 4 5 6 [pause] 2 3 4 5 6 7 8	
2:27	8		1 2 3 4 [pause] 2 3 4 5 6 [pause] 2 3 4 5 6 7 8	
2:48	9		[pause] 2 3 4 [pause] 2 3 4 5 6 [pause] 2 3 4 5 6 7 8	
3:09	10		1 2 3 4 [pause] 2 3 4 5 6 1 2 3 4 5 6 7 8	
3:30	11		[pause] 2 3 4 1 2 3 4 5 6 [pause] 2 3 4 5 6 7 8	

Student FAQs

Don't people get tired of so much repetition?

Some do, but to call this music repetitious reminds us that the term is relative. Like John Cage before him (see chapter 53), Glass challenges listeners to reconsider the basic premises of how they listen. Listening to a minimalist work is a little like looking at something under the microscope: we begin to see (hear) things that we sometimes take for granted.

The spoken text makes no sense. What does it add?

As Glass suggests (see his comments above), the point is not so much what the opera "means" as what listeners hear in it. The text means whatever listeners think it means.

Philip Glass (b. 1937)

PROLIFIC MINIMALIST

Philip Glass stands out among contemporary composers for having become so famous that he is mentioned in no fewer than three episodes of *The Simpsons* and is satirized in an episode of *South Park*. He was born and raised in Baltimore, where he studied flute at the Peabody Conservatory of Music. He went on to study composition at the Juilliard School of Music in New York City, after which he worked in Paris with Nadia Boulanger, who 40 years before had been Aaron Copland's teacher (see p. 447). He traveled widely in Asia as well, studying Indian music with the legendary sitar player Ravi Shankar. He returned to New York in the mid-1960s convinced that modern music needed to reach out to audiences more directly, and so he established the Philip Glass Ensemble, a group of musicians who still tour the country on a regular basis and draw consistently large audiences to concerts of new music.

Glass is an astonishingly prolific composer. In addition to 10 operas, he has written large quantities of vocal and instrumental music, as well as soundtracks for a number of mainstream films, including *The Illusionist*, *The Secret Garden*, *The Truman Show*, and *Candyman*.

PLAYLIST: GLASS

Etudes. A series of technical studies for piano.

Violin Concerto. A work written for violin and orchestra, in three movements.

The Hours. Film score, one of three for which Glass was nominated for an Academy Award, along with his music for *Notes on a Scandal* and *Kundun.*

A Descent into the Maelstrom. A dance theater piece inspired by Edgar Allen's Poe short story of the same name.

Akhnaten. An opera set in ancient Egypt.

Philip Glass at the electronic organ, ca. 1976
Richard Pasley Photography

Lucinda Childs (left) and Sheryl Sutton in "Knee Play 1" from *Einstein on the Beach*, at the Brooklyn Academy of Music Opera House, Brooklyn, New York.

Minimalism

Terry Riley, *In C.* A series of 53 brief thematic fragments that can be played "by any number of instruments of any kind." Each performer plays all 53 fragments but may repeat each as often as he or she likes, so the length of the work can vary enormously in performance. One recent recording runs for 43 minutes, another for 76 minutes.

Steve Reich, *Three Tales.* A video opera made in collaboration with Beryl Korot, the composer's wife. The first of the three scenes revolves around the crash of the dirigible *Hindenburg* in Lakehurst, N.J., in 1937; the second centers on the testing of an atomic bomb in the South Pacific in 1946; and the third focuses on the sheep named Dolly, who in 1996 became the world's first successfully cloned mammal.

John Adams, *Short Ride in a Fast Machine.* A brief work for orchestra that has proven extremely popular with concert audiences. The composer has said of the title: "You know how it is when someone asks you to ride in a terrific sports car, and then you wish you hadn't?"

The Beatles, "Tomorrow Never Knows." A drone-based composition influenced by Indian raga. The backdrop changes only minimally through the piece.

Peter Gabriel, "This Is the Picture." A synthesized backdrop repeats a simple melodic figure, very much in the style of African traditional music, as Gabriel sings the lyric above it.

55

Chuck Berry
"School Day"

Listen to This

Rhythm — Tap along with the beat and try to identify the rhythmic patterns that appear most frequently. Listen for the moments when the entire band stops together.

Timbre — Notice the aggressive tones of the guitar that cut through the sound of the rest of the instruments. Listen for the high notes in the piano that are present throughout almost all the recording.

Texture — Notice the alternation between voice and guitar.

Form — Listen for individual verses. Try to identify the length (number of measures) and harmonic pattern of each verse.

During the mid-1950s, Chuck Berry, along with Elvis Presley, Little Richard, Buddy Holly, Fats Domino, and Jerry Lee Lewis, blended the musical styles of jump blues and honky-tonk with an edgy attitude to create a new genre known as rock 'n' roll. It was music aimed at a teenage audience, produced mainly by independent record labels and marketed by hip deejays to youngsters, both white and black. Among those six musicians, Berry stands out because he not only sang but also played the guitar in a unique style and wrote the majority of his hits.

Rock 'n' roll capitalized on the youth culture of the baby boom generation, who had more disposable income, more free time, and more technological access to entertainment than any previous generation. The 1950s were a time of social contradictions for American youth. The idyllic domestic life portrayed on television shows like *Leave It to Beaver* and the relative prosperity of the middle class provided unprecedented material wealth and freedom to teenagers. Yet at the same time, the burgeoning civil rights movement brought change and even violence to many regions of the country. Tensions of the Cold War and McCarthy-era communist paranoia further fueled social unrest. Rock 'n' roll music offered escape from adult concerns and serious issues. It provided teenagers with music that openly defied their parents' artistic sensibilities. And it blended white and black art forms with dancing, partying, and barely disguised metaphors for sex—deejay Alan Freed co-opted the phrase "rock 'n' roll" from a black slang phrase for sex.

Two years before "School Day" was released, the movie *Blackboard Jungle* portrayed high school students as rebels obsessed with sex and delinquent behavior of all sorts, set to the rock 'n' roll sounds of "(We're Gonna) Rock Around the Clock" (see Expand Your Playlist). One scene in the film depicted teens breaking treasured old jazz records, and the theme song was reputed to have sparked riots and hoodlum behavior. The same year *Blackboard Jungle* appeared, James Dean brought the angst-ridden world of teen pop culture to the silver screen in *Rebel Without a Cause*. Although Chuck Berry was 30 years old when he recorded "School Day," his lyrics captured the attitude of his young fans perfectly.

Shuffle Rhythm and Stop Time

The rhythmic elements of this song provide the core of its appeal. At several points, the melody consists of a single note or chord repeated many times, and here it is the rhythm that creates a sense of excitement. At other points, the rhythmic patterns come to a sudden and dramatic stop, leaving a wide open space for the singer or soloist to enter.

The introduction (0:00–0:02) mimics the ringing of a school bell with 13 attacks on the same guitar chord. With these 13 chords, Berry establishes what is known as a **shuffle groove**, a mid-tempo rhythmic pattern, typically in quadruple meter, in which each beat is subdivided into three pulses. The shuffle groove for "School Day" is based on four beats per measure, as follows:

```
Beats:          1     2     3     4
Guitar chords:  x x x  x x x  x x x  x x x
```

The shuffle groove was used frequently in earlier rhythm and blues (R&B) recordings by artists like Fats Domino (see Expand Your Playlist). In most shuffle grooves, the bass player and drummer do not play all three subdivisions of the beat. Instead, they play only the first and the third. The first note occupies two-thirds of the beat, and the second note occupies the last third of the beat, forming a LONG-short-LONG-short rhythmic pattern similar to swing rhythms (see chapter 47). You can hear this pattern in the bass when it first enters (0:04).

The poetic meter of the lyrics follows the pattern of the shuffle groove. For instance, "Workin' your fingers right down to the bone" (0:17) places accented syllables on the beats, and three syllables in each beat:

Syllables:	*Work*-in' your	*fin*-gers right	*down* to the	*bone*
Beats:	X	X	X	X

Six times in the song, the shuffle rhythm comes to an abrupt halt. The instruments that provide the basic accompaniment strike a single note on a downbeat of a measure together and then remain silent for the rest of the measure. This is known as **stop time**. These moments punctuate the end of individual sections, simultaneously opening up rhythmic space for the singer or soloist to launch a new section. Once one has gotten a sense of how the verses flow, it is relatively easy to anticipate where these moments of stop time will occur.

During each stop-time moment, Berry enters with lyrics for the next verse. The beginning vocal phrase of each verse corresponds to beats 2, 3, and 4, and then concludes on the downbeat:

Time:	2:14				
Beats:	1	2	3	4	1
	(stop time)				(band enters)
Lyrics:		Hail,	hail	Rock 'n'	**roll**
		(pick-up notes, or anacrusis)			
	(downbeat)				

Notes that begin a phrase before the downbeat are known as an **anacrusis**, or "pick-up notes." Anacrusis is a significant rhythmic feature of "School Day."

Rock 'n' Roll Timbre

Chuck Berry's recordings highlighted his electric lead guitar. "School Day" features Fred Below on drums and Willie Dixon on bass. Guitarist Hubert Sumlin recalls playing on the recording as well, although his name is not listed in the session's paperwork. Although he is difficult to hear on this particular recording, pianist Johnnie Johnson, Berry's musical partner since 1952, added a signature sound to the band that was particularly important in live performances and that helped the whole band come together in the tight rhythmic grooves his audiences loved. On "School Day," Johnson's left hand plays boogie-shuffle patterns in the lower notes of the piano and his right hand plays continuous fills, featuring melodic counterpoint and decorations. You can hear him particularly well during the guitar solo at 1:32, after the words "days of old . . ." at 2:20, and while Berry sings "the beat of the drum . . ." at 2:25.

Fans can recognize most of Chuck Berry's hit records from just their short guitar introductions. The most famous of these is the introduction to "Johnny B. Goode" (see Berry Playlist). Although Berry's brief introductions are indelibly linked to him, he often borrowed or adapted them from other artists and earlier recordings. The opening of "Johnny B. Goode," for

Chuck Berry (b. 1926)

MUSICAL RECIPE FOR ROCK 'N' ROLL

Chuck Berry grew up on a blend of blues, hillbilly, and western swing tunes in his native St. Louis. As a high school student, Berry borrowed a four-string guitar and cultivated his musical ambitions. Those plans were derailed, however, when in 1944 Berry and a few friends were involved in an automobile theft. The accompanying shenanigans landed him in prison for three years. He was released on his 21st birthday and bounced from odd job to odd job for a few years before rekindling his interest in performing. In 1950, Berry purchased an electric guitar and a reel-to-reel recorder and began to pursue music with a new sense of purpose.

Berry quickly established himself as a multitalented musician whose guitar work was unforgettable and whose songwriting ability connected with youth culture. On stage, Berry's charisma won over teen audiences, and he developed a distinctive performance gimmick known as the "duck walk," in which he crouched on one leg, stuck the other out in front of him, and scooted across the stage, pecking his head back and forth at the same time.

The heyday of rock 'n' roll was short-lived, from Elvis Presley's first rockabilly recordings in 1954 to the "day the music died" (a fateful plan crash that claimed the lives of Buddy Holly, Ritchie Valens, and The Big Bopper) in 1959. By the end of the decade, troubles plagued many of the first stars of the genre. Elvis had been drafted; Jerry Lee Lewis married his 13-year-old cousin in a scandal that sank his reputation; and Chuck Berry was convicted of transporting a minor across state lines for immoral purposes and began another prison sentence. Berry later recorded more hits (including the novelty number "My Ding-a-Ling" and toured successfully for many decades, but the rock 'n' roll craze was over.

Chuck Berry performs his signature "duck walk" on stage, ca. 1958.
Michael Ochs Archives Ltd./Getty Images Inc.—Los Angeles

PLAYLIST: BERRY

"Johnny B. Goode"

"Memphis"

"Sweet Little Sixteen"

"Roll Over Beethoven"

instance, is almost identical to the introduction Carl Hogan played on Louis Jordan's recording "Ain't That Just Like a Woman." Pianist Johnnie Johnson came up with the introduction for "School Day," which he borrowed from a piano-boogie recording of "Honky-tonk Train Blues" by Meade "Lux" Lewis. With these short introductions, Berry's recordings pay tribute to his musical influences and connect his rock 'n' roll recordings to the traditions that came before him.

Call-and-Response Texture

After each vocal phrase, the guitar loosely echoes the singer's melody, in a type of call-and-response texture (see also chapter 47). Compare "Ring, ring goes the bell" at 0:24 to the guitar's phrase that follows it at 0:26. This echo pattern allows the singer to take a breath and pause between each phrase, while the gritty tones of the electric guitar continue the energy and melodic momentum of the song. Berry's guitar playing follows the general contour of the vocal melody for each phrase, but it includes slight variations and flourishes that add the characteristic twang and energy to the rock 'n' roll recording.

12-Bar Blues Form

"School Day" is a strophic song (see also chapter 46). The recording consists of a short introduction, followed by six verses and a guitar solo that follows the same musical form as the verses. There is no separate chorus or bridge. Each verse consists of the same 12-measure chord progression, known as the 12-bar blues (see chapter 46 for another example). The 12-bar blues uses just three different chords, built on the first, fourth, and fifth scale degrees. Unlike downhome blues performers like Robert Johnson, rock 'n' roll performers tended to use the 12-bar blues without any variations. To follow the 12-bar blues progression, count four beats per measure, starting at where the bass enters, and listen for when the bass player changes notes: these moments represent changes to a new chord. Timings and reference points in the text for the first verse are shown here:

Time:	0:04		... rule	
Lyrics:	... school			
Chords:	I	I	I	I
Time:	0:11		0:15	
Lyrics:	... math		... pass	
Chords:	IV	IV	I	I
Time:	0:19		0:22	
Lyrics:	... bone		... alone	
Chords:	V	V	I	I

The guitar solo is one of the most exciting moments in the recording. Berry begins a repetitive guitar pattern at the end of the fourth verse (1:29). Other verses conclude with a stop-time moment and a break in the music. Here, however, the guitar pattern continues right into the guitar-solo section—also a 12-bar blues chord progression (beginning at 1:32)—building momentum and dramatic tension by bridging the gap between verse and instrumental solo.

Now listen to this song again, following the Listening Guide.

Television and the Rise of Rock 'n' Roll

In the 1940s, televisions were a novelty item that few Americans had seen. By 1954, more than 55 percent of all American households had a television, and the major broadcasting networks were vying to create the most successful programs. Variety shows hosted by established stars were common. Steve Allen, Milton Berle, Arthur Godfrey, and Ed Sullivan were a few of the entertainers who had their own shows.

Television also captured the inherent tensions between the conservative older generation and their children. Adults were outraged when Elvis Presley gyrated his hips during his televised performances, while the younger generation swooned over the hot, young star. In 1956, a reported 60 million viewers saw his famous debut on the Ed Sullivan Show. At the end of his third performance, Sullivan offered, "This is a real decent, fine boy." With this endorsement from the show's famous host, Presley began his transformation from short-lived teen star to lasting cultural icon.

In 1952, a Philadelphia television station launched a staged version of the type of Saturday-night dance most teenagers regularly attended in their hometowns. The show's host introduced hit musicians and showed youngsters dancing in the most popular styles. In 1956, Dick Clark was invited to host the show, which was picked up for national distribution and christened *American Bandstand* in 1957. The show spread new records, new artists, and new dance styles across the country.

Dick Clark, at the podium in the upper left, surrounded by teenage fans on his nationally televised dance show *American Bandstand* in 1958.

AP Wide World Photos

 EXPAND YOUR PLAYLIST

Styles of Early Rock 'n' Roll

While there are many commonalities in early rock 'n' roll recordings, the first generation of musicians all had distinctive individual styles. The musicians listed here include both black and white performers who drew equally frequently from R&B and honky-tonk musical sources.

Elvis Presley, "Blue Moon of Kentucky" (1954). Bluegrass pioneer and mandolinist Bill Monroe wrote and recorded this song in 1946. When Presley covered it, he changed its style from a moderate waltz to a hard-driving rockabilly number, using only the minimalist instrumentation of electric guitar, acoustic guitar, and bass.

Bill Haley and His Comets, "(We're Gonna) Rock Around the Clock" (1954). This song's appearance in the soundtrack to *Blackboard Jungle* brought the new sound of rock 'n' roll to an enormous audience.

Buddy Holly, "That'll Be the Day" (1957). Holly combined rockabilly sounds with Texas swing in many of his hits, including this one. Holly's distinctive voice is the central focus of this recording.

Jerry Lee Lewis, "Great Balls of Fire" (1957). This recording uses 12-bar blues and features Lewis's distinctive piano style and flourishes, along with lots of reverb and echo effects, in an eight-to-the-bar boogie groove.

Fats Domino, "Ain't It a Shame" (1955). Frequently mislabeled by the song's lyrics, "Ain't *that* a shame," this recording features a shuffle groove and a saxophone solo that illustrates one of the more mid-tempo, mellow sides of early rock 'n' roll.

Little Richard, "Tutti Frutti" (1955). Named for the nonsense-syllable introduction to the stop-time moments at the end of each chorus, this recording mixes blues lyric couplets with heavy drums, twelve-bar blues progressions under the chorus, and a raging saxophone solo.

Chuck Berry "School Day"

Time	Text	Form	Rhythm
0:00		Introduction	The repeated chords establish the shuffle groove.
0:02	Up in the mornin'...	Verse 1: the vocal phrase begins as the anacrusis to the 12-bar blues section.	Poetic meter of the text matches the shuffle groove.
0:04	...school...	The 12-bar blues pattern for Verse 1 begins.	Bass enters, with LONG-short-LONG-short rhythm.
0:24	Ring, ring goes the...	Verse 2: the vocal phrase begins.	
0:26	...bell...	The 12-bar blues pattern for Verse 2	
0:46	Soon as three o'clock rolls... *The text's narrative continues chronologically through the day.*	Verse 3: vocal phrase begins.	
0:48	...around...	The 12-bar blues pattern for Verse 3.	
1:08	Drop the quarter right into the...	Verse 4: vocal phrase begins.	
1:10	...slot...	The 12-bar blues pattern for Verse 4	
1:29		End of the 12-bar blues pattern for Verse 4	Repeated guitar chords are the final phrase of Verse 4, but continue into the next section of the recording.
1:32	(guitar solo)	The 12-bar blues pattern under the guitar solo	While the guitar continues the same chords as the end of Verse 4, a new twelve-bar section begins as the piano enters.
1:52	Drop the quarter right into the...	Verse 5 (repeating the lyrics of Verse 4): vocal phrase begins.	
1:54	...slot...	Twelve-bar blues pattern for Verse 5.	
2:14	Hail, hail rock 'n'...	Verse 6: vocal phrase begins.	
2:16	...roll...	The 12-bar blues pattern for Verse 6	

Texture

Solo electric guitar

Stop time

Call-and-response texture. The vocalist sings his phrases before the downbeat of each section, and the guitar echoes the singer.

Stop time

Call-and-response texture

Stop time

Call-and-response texture continues.

Stop time

Call-and-response texture continues.

No stop time at the end of Verse 4

Guitar solo with full accompaniment

Stop time

Call-and-response pattern between . guitar and vocals resumes

Stop time

Call-and-response texture

Student FAQs

How does Berry get his unique guitar sound?

The unique timbre of Berry's solos is characteristic of the specific electric guitar he played (a Gibson ES350TN for the first several years of his career), combined with the type of amplifiers used in 1956. The specific R&B motives he borrowed from earlier styles also contributed, but his equipment was the primary determinant of his sound.

If the chord progression is the same throughout this song, why doesn't the music sound boring?

There are many styles of music, both classical and popular, that rely on repeated chord progressions. In these styles, listeners focus on the melodic variations, the lyrics (if there are words), the embellishments, and the rhythmic groove. Listeners also generally like some aspect of their music to include repetition because that sets up subconscious expectations for what is coming next, and then the music can either reward or surprise.

56

DETROIT →
Los Angeles   Washington D.C.
U.S.A.

The Marvelettes
"Please, Mr. Postman"

Listen to This

Timbre

Listen for hand-claps. Pay attention to the tone quality of the backup vocal quartet. How does the rhythm section contribute to the overall sound?

Harmony

Do you recognize the basic, repeating chord progression?

Form

Do any sections repeat? Do you hear slight variations in those sections? How does the song end?

I n 1961, five high-school girls from Inkster, a suburb of Detroit, recorded a new song for a startup rhythm and blues label called Tamla Motown. The record company badly needed a new hit. Nearly a year had passed since Smokey Robinson and the Miracles' "Shop Around" had reached number one on the R&B charts (which tracked music played on black radio stations for a mostly black audience).

The young Marvelettes—Gladys Horton, Katherine Anderson, Juanita Cowart, Georgeanna Tillman, and Wanda Young—provided that hit. "Please Mr. Postman" reached the top of both the R&B charts and the pop charts (tracking a mostly white audience), indicating widespread success that crossed conventional boundaries of race and audience. The song's gold-record sales assured the continuation of "Motown," as the label was more commonly known, and established the Marvelettes among its early stars.

"Please Mr. Postman" was released during a period in music history caught between the early rock 'n' roll innovations of the mid-1950s and the popular-music revolution of 1964 brought about by four young men from Liverpool. In the years before this "British Invasion," as the Beatles' success in America became known, black rhythm and blues ensembles such as the Coasters and the Shirelles reached new audiences by melding rhythmically innovative pop songs with blues idioms. Motown took advantage of the burgeoning popularity of R&B, cultivating its danceable grooves into an instantly recognizable musical style. By the mid-1960s, the Motown sound had evolved into the mature, pop sounds of groups like Diana Ross and the Supremes, and the Temptations (see Motown Playlist), and Motown had become a major contributor to American popular music.

Timbre: The "Motown Sound"

Recordings made for the Motown label had an instantly recognizable, highly polished and slick sound. The way the instruments were played and mixed in the studio produced a timbral sheen far different than the grittier, rougher sounds coming out of other R&B labels at the time. By the mid-1960s, Motown had made solid inroads into popular music, and its musical arrangements routinely featured strings and horns (especially extended saxophone solos), lots of rhythmic sound effects from claps, snaps, and tambourines, and a tight rhythmic groove from the bass and drums. Motown vocals used close harmony from backup singers behind a featured lead singer, and the musical arrangements often used sophisticated techniques like modulation (changing keys) and phrase expansions to make the titles of the songs more memorable. "Please Mr. Postman" was recorded before that formula was fully established, and so it contains only a fledgling version of the Motown sound:

- **Hand-claps.** These set up a **hook**, or a short, catchy motif that forms the memorable core of the song, right at the beginning. Hand-claps were common throughout the R&B hits of the 1950s like The Coasters' "Smokin' Joe's Cafe" (see "Expand Your Playlist"). They mark "Please Mr. Postman" as a recording in the up-tempo R&B tradition.

Rhythmic pattern for the hand-claps.

Songs like "My Guy" (Mary Wells), "The Way You Do the Things You Do" (The Temptations), or "Baby Love" (The Supremes), from the Motown Playlist, also use hand-claps.

- **Close, female vocal harmony.** Close harmony from female voices was a common R&B formula that launched a new style of music in the late 1950s and early 1960s featuring "girl groups," such as the Chantelles and Shirelles. Throughout "Please Mr. Postman," the backup singers provide a full, brassy layer of sound that supports the lead singer. What makes this sound so clear and penetrating is the tight spacing of pitches within chords, combined with generally stepwise motion from chord to chord. The chords are arranged in brief, repetitive and memorable fragments ("wait, wait for you")—like the hand-claps, generating another musical hook for the song.

- **A tight, rehearsed groove.** The Funk Brothers were the house band at Motown studios, and it was their perfectly coordinated rhythm section that compelled Motown fans to move. The rhythmic groove emphasized the back beats (1 **2** 3 **4**) and combined rhythmic patterns with strong ties to dance traditions.

Harmony: Descending Thirds

The basic progression of chords in "Please Mr. Postman" may sound familiar to you. These four chords were used in countless popular songs during the 1950s and 1960s, like "Blue Moon," "Earth Angel," "Johnny Angel," "Duke of Earl," and "Those Magic Changes" (from the musical *Grease*). They are the progression for "Heart and Soul," which children often like to play as a duet on the piano. The progression and its variants also show up in classical music quite frequently—even Pachelbel's famous *Canon in D* uses something closely related.

The four chords are sometimes called the "doo-wop" chord progression. Doo-wop was a style of R&B and precursor of Motown, popular in the 1950s, that relied heavily on nonsense syllables (including the syllables "doo-wop"), sung by backup vocalists to accompany the lead singer. The doo-wop chord progression is also called a "descending thirds" progression because for the first few chords, the bass moves down three notes (a distance of a third) from one chord to the next. The last chord in the pattern carries with it a strong sense of tension requiring resolution: after hearing it, the listener naturally would like to hear the first chord again. The progression therefore creates the sense of an endless loop.

Chord progression: **I**   **vi**   **IV**   **V**

Chord numbers are represented in roman numerals; the vi is lowercase because it is a minor chord.

Verse-Chorus Form with a Twist

"Please Mr. Postman" opens with a chorus, a savvy move for a song that was marketed toward a radio audience because it puts the catchiest and most memorable part at the very beginning. The song's core structure is

Chorus-Verse-Verse-Chorus-Verse-Chorus.

Verse-chorus is one of the simplest models of form in popular music. The chorus contains the main idea of the song, usually incorporating the title as well. When the chorus returns, it keeps the same text and music. The verses, on the other hand, advance the plot. Each different verse uses the same music but different texts, as building blocks in the story. Verse-chorus form can use any combination of verses and choruses, although the last unit will always be a chorus.

Verse-chorus form relies on repetition, and the chord progression is repetitious as well. The piece nevertheless builds in excitement and variety as the basic form is augmented by a few subtle yet important features:

- **A vamp section at the end.** After the last chorus, the singers and band **vamp**, or repeat a basic section of the music, while the lead singer improvises on a single motif ("wait a minute, wait a minute"). A vamp section builds energy and allows a song an infinitely expandable length. In this case, the producers kept three of the vamp sections at the end of the song, although more were recorded in the studio.

- **Best for last.** The lead singer does not sing the main text of the chorus until its third appearance, and the audience subconsciously waits for this last, most exciting iteration.

- **Intensifying hooks.** The backup singers intensify their contributions to each verse, as the song progresses, with more elaborate parts. The hooks become successively longer.

Backup singers, verse 1:	You, for you.
Backup singers, verse 2:	You, wait, wait for you.
Backup singers, verse 3:	You, wait Mr. Postman.

Listen for the expanded verse-chorus structure as you follow the Listening Guide.

Listening Guide

The Marvelettes "Please, Mr. Postman"

Time	Text	Form	Harmony
0:00	*Wait* Woh yes, wait a minute...	Introduction	The close vocal harmony of the background singers appears right at the beginning (after a single drum-hit).
0:09	*Please Mr. Postman...*/Woh yeah *Is there a letter...*/Please, please Mr. Postman...	First chorus	One complete "doo-wop" (descending thirds) progression accompanies each verse.
0:25	You.../There must be... For you.../From my boyfriend...	First verse: backup singers use their shortest phrase, "for you," between the lead's lines.	Complete descending thirds chord progression
0:40	You.../I've been standin'... Wait, wait for you...	Second verse: backup singers use a longer, syncopated phrase, "wait, wait for you."	Etc.
0:56	Please.../*Please*... Oh yeah/*Is there a letter...* (1:04) Mr. Po-wo-wo-wostman...	Second chorus	
1:12	You.../So many days... Wait, Mr. Postman, you/You saw the tears...	Third verse: backup singers use longest phrase of any verse, "wait, Mr. Postman, you."	
1:28	Please Mister Postman,.../ *Postman, postman* Is there a letter... *Postman, postman.../*You know it's... *Postman, postman.../* Yeah, since I heard...	Third chorus: lead singer sings complete chorus for the first time.	
1:43	You better wait... Wait, wait a minute... ...Please check and see...	Extended vamp 1: repetitive pattern builds energy, prolongs the song, and creates space for vocal improvisation.	
1:59	You better wait... Wait, wait... ...Deliver dee letter...	Extended vamp 2	
2:15	You better wait... Wait, wait....	Extended vamp 3 to a fade-out	

*The backup vocalists' text is shown in italics)

Timbre

Rhythmic hand-claps, the loud presence of the drums, the R&B-style bass and piano, and the close vocal harmony

Brassy, high sounds from the backup singers contrast sharply with the bluesy lead singer.

The lead singer's voice incorporates a bluesy growl (0:50–0:55).

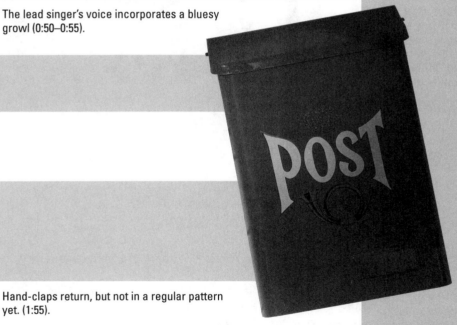

POST

Hand-claps return, but not in a regular pattern yet. (1:55).

Hand-claps are still present, now in their regular rhythmic pattern.

Student FAQs

Why doesn't this recording sound as slick as the Motown recordings that are more famous?

Keep in mind that this was done very early in Motown's timeline, and the label's fully mature sound had not yet been established. Also, even though three Motown staff musicians worked on the song, it was the product of amateur songwriters in the first place, so its basic musical structure was less sophisticated than later Motown songs.

What can I do to hear the doo-wop chord progression more clearly?

Listen to some of the other songs mentioned in this chapter that use the progression. If you hear it in different contexts, it will likely become easier to recognize.

The Making of "Please Mr. Postman"

AN ORCHESTRATED COLLABORATION

The question of who wrote "Please Mr. Postman" is not a simple one. Five people are credited with writing the song, but their work does not account for all we hear on the record. The creative contributions for any recording include the work of each arranger, each musician who played or sang, and each producer and sound engineer who worked on the mix.

When the teenage quintet who became the Marvelettes auditioned for Motown's record label, they sang hit songs by the Chantels and the Shirelles, both famous girl groups. Motown signed the Marvelettes but asked them to come back with original songs. Georgia Dobbins, at that time a member of the group, asked William Garrett, a local pianist and friend, for help. He gave her a blues number he had written, which Dobbins then reworked into an R&B girl-group piece. The Marvelettes took it to Motown, where staff songwriters Brian Holland and Robert Bateman, plus singer Freddie Gorman, edited it further. "Please Mr. Postman" then went back to the Marvelettes, who recorded it with the record label's house band. In the studio, the musicians worked out the final details of the arrangement themselves.

The piece was then turned over to the producers and sound engineers, who mixed the various tracks from the recording session into the final 45 revolution-per-minute (rpm) vinyl single. They determined the balance between the instruments, background vocals, and lead singer; when to fade out the recording; and even how many of the verses in the extended vamp at the end to include. "Please Mr. Postman" was co-produced by Holland and Bateman, working under the name "Brianbert."

Motown released a new version of "Please Mr. Postman" in 2005 that illustrates the impact producers and sound engineers have on the music we hear. For the new release, a different team of sound engineers and producers remixed the original recording session. The new track is longer, in stereo, and balanced differently so that the listener hears different fragments of melody, different parts of the rhythm section, and even an extra verse (with different lyrics) that had been cut out of the extended vamp.

The Marvelettes, ca. 1970. From left: Gladys Horton, Wanda Young, Georgeanna Tillman, and Katherine Anderson. Juanita Cowart had left the group by the time this photo was taken.
Michael Ochs Archives/Getty Images, Inc.

PLAYLIST: MOTOWN

"Shop Around," Smokey Robinson and the Miracles (1960)

"(Love Is Like a) Heat Wave," Martha & The Vandellas (1963)

"The Way You Do the Things You Do," The Temptations (1964)

"Baby I Need Your Loving," Four Tops (1964)

"Baby Love," The Supremes (1964)

"Ain't No Mountain High Enough," Marvin Gaye and Tammi Terrell (1967)

THE MONEY TRAIL

Reading Labels

When listeners in the 1960s picked up a record with the Motown label, they had a pretty good idea what they would be getting.

Motown was the brainchild of Berry Gordy, a Detroit native who, in 1959, founded Tamla Motown Records to produce black R&B musicians from the area. His "assembly-line" style of musical production has led to comparisons with the auto industry, quite apropos given that the label's name, "Motown," derives from "Motor Town," a reference to Detroit's main business. Gordy's methods also guaranteed that the records shared certain sonic qualities (a "Motown" sound), and that the artists shared aspects of image and style.

Gordy sought widespread distribution for his singers in an era when many black artists had a difficult time obtaining a fair record deal or getting sufficient promotion to place their songs on the pop charts. To compete, Gordy assembled a stable of the best songwriters and session musicians and used them to create almost all the hits that Motown enjoyed in the 1960s. He also invested in a professional choreographer and an "artist development department," responsible for teaching the young artists how to comport themselves, give interviews, and present a polished social image.

Gordy's approach was extremely successful: not only did his artists top the R&B charts, but they also regularly scored number one hits on the pop charts. By the early 1970s, Motown

Motown's headquarters, ca. 1970. Smokey Robinson is standing on the right.

Michael Ochs Archives/ Stringer/Getty Images

Records was the largest African American–owned business in the United States.

Other record labels also have cultivated an easily recognizable sound. For instance, producer Sam Phillips started Sun Records in Memphis in the 1950s, which developed the raw rockabilly sound that Elvis Presley and Johnny Cash used on their first recordings. Also located in Memphis, Stax Records used in-house musicians to create the Southern soul sounds of Otis Redding in the 1950s and 1960s. Other artists who recorded in the Stax studios, including Wilson Pickett, ended up with the same, readily identifiable "Stax Sound" on their records.

 EXPAND YOUR PLAYLIST

Close Harmony in Different Styles

Close vocal harmony was the hallmark of the 1960s girl groups, but it is an important feature of many other styles of popular music. Here is a sampling from five different decades:

The Chords, "Sh'Boom" (1954). This doo-wop classic predates the girl groups and Motown songs that were popular in the 1960s. The Chords' recording features the best of close vocal harmony, clearly displayed in the introduction.

The Coasters, "Smokin' Joe's Cafe" (1955). Often called "Smokey Joe's Cafe," this recording features the hand-claps popular in R&B hits and close vocal harmony using similar chord structures to the Marvelettes. The chord progression, though, uses the 12-bar blues pattern for the song's main sections.

The Beatles, "Please Mr. Postman" (1963). Prior to their arrival in the United States, the Beatles covered many U.S. artists' songs, including this Marvelettes' recording for their album *With the Beatles.* The primary differences are the timbre of the ensemble, which lacks

Motown's bluesy blend of instruments, including the piano; the gendered elements of the lyrics, which are changed from female to male; and the groove, which lacks the emphasis on rhythmic hooks.

Manhattan Transfer, "Java Jive" (1975). The sweet jazz harmonies of this song are presented in tight, close vocal harmony, but in a style very different from that of the girl groups that topped the pop charts the previous decade.

Dolly Parton, Emmylou Harris, and Linda Ronstadt, "Wildflowers" (1987). These three country superstars collaborated on an album with acoustic, old-time influences. This recording highlights their close vocal harmony on the chorus.

*NSYNC, "God Must Have Spent A Little More Time on You" (1998). The boy bands of the 1990s, of which *NSYNC was one of the best known, brought close vocal harmony and R&B grooves to the top of the pop charts. Listen to the close harmony in the chorus, in particular, where the lead vocal is blended into the background vocals.

57

LOS ANGELES
Chicago
Washington D.C.
U.S.A.

Beach Boys
"Good Vibrations"

 Listen to This

Harmony

Listen to the minor quality of the first chord. Notice the sections where the same music is played at successively higher or lower pitches.

Texture

Listen for the addition and subtraction of polyphonic layers.

Timbre

Listen for unusual instruments and sound effects. Pay attention to the close vocal harmony and the sound of the individual vocal lines.

Form

Listen for three sections in the second half of the recording that interrupt the standard verse-chorus form and introduce very different material.

"Good Vibrations" was part of the psychedelic movement in rock music, which emerged in the mid-1960s on the West Coast of the United States and in London. Psychedelia began with the idea that music could create a hallucinogenic trip for the listener, transporting the mind to a freer, higher consciousness.

Many of the musicians in this scene became interested in Eastern philosophies and meditation. They experimented with instruments that had not been used in rock music before, and their lyrics were increasingly abstract and cryptic. Although psychedelic music originated in conjunction with the hippie movement, which denounced established middle-class society, the music itself became widely accepted in mainstream culture.

In a songwriting process that was essentially backwards—normally, live performance precedes recording—Beach Boy Brian Wilson created "Good Vibrations" during seven separate recording sessions held in four studios over several months. Wilson recorded individual sections of the song as separate modules. After the instrumental sections were complete, Wilson and fellow Beach Boy Mike Love wrote the lyrics.

"Good Vibrations" was unusually long for a single record in 1966. Three minutes was the industry standard. However, Wilson crafted a longer, more formally complex song that encapsulated a mind-expanding journey for its listeners. His project was successful: when it was released in October 1966, "Good Vibrations" quickly topped both the U.S. and U.K. charts and became one of the most discussed rock singles ever.

Minor Chords and a Shaped Harmonic Progression

The first chord progression establishes the key as minor—uncommon in rock music at the time. The minor mode in this section adds to the exotic and unusual quality of the recording and ties it to the sonic world of psychedelia.

The bass guitar, foundation of the harmony, gives us an immediate taste of the kind of harmonic motion we will hear throughout the song. From 0:00 to 0:12, we hear the same motif four times, on successively lower pitches. This chord progression is called a "descending tetrachord," which means the chords move down successively by steps on four different pitches. It was used extensively in Western classical music, beginning in the seventeenth century, and shows up in other pop music as well.

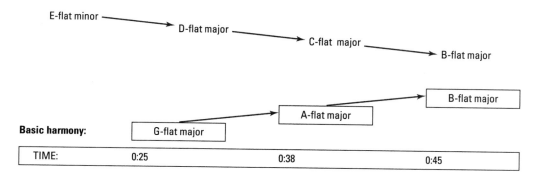

By contrast, in the chorus that follows, the music hoists itself twice to a higher set of pitches, increasing the musical tension and excitement. At 0:38 and 0:45, Brian Wilson repeats the same musical motif but sets it one chord higher, creating this underlying harmonic shape:

The second chorus follows the same pattern. The third time the chorus appears, however, the progression is reversed so that the music's harmonic shape descends:

Basic harmony:

B-flat major		
	A-flat major	
		G-flat major

TIME:	2:57	3:04	3:10

The harmonic ascent in the first two choruses builds up the energy in the piece, while the descent in the third chorus helps bring the piece toward its conclusion.

In the final section (3:13–3:36), the music ascends and then descends, creating a miniature version of the shape that governs the entire rest of the piece:

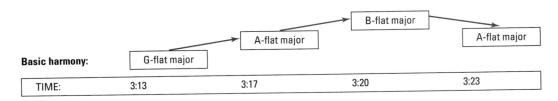

		B-flat major	
	A-flat major		A-flat major
G-flat major			

Basic harmony:

TIME:	3:13	3:17	3:20	3:23

The climax occurs immediately before the third chorus, in one of the most recognizable moments in the entire recording. The vocal lines blend into a single, thick-textured chord, sung on "Ah" (2:54), which is held for a full measure and then continues ringing through the rest of the band's silence.

A Layered, Polyphonic Texture

When the chorus begins (0:25), there is only one vocal line ("I'm pickin' up good vibrations . . ."), sung by the bass in a low register. A new vocal layer, consisting of two voices in harmony, is added at 0:32 ("ooh, bop-bop . . ."). A third vocal layer is added at 0:38 ("good, good, good, good vibrations . . ."). Instrumental melodies contribute more layers to the texture.

This additive polyphonic technique appears elsewhere in the piece as well. At 2:14, the section opens with only an organ and maracas. Every two measures, the pattern repeats, with the addition of a new polyphonic layer: at 2:21, a vocal line is added, followed by the bass and a new line of vocal harmony (2:28), and a high-pitched motif (2:36). The vocals then fade out of the texture, leaving only the instrumental polyphony.

The reverse process occurs at 2:57: the section starts with three layers of vocal polyphony over a full instrumental texture. The voices then fade out, beginning at 3:08, and the last motivic statement in this section is reduced to just a few distinct instrumental layers.

There are also abrupt changes in texture. Two of the most striking occur at 0:51, when the piece moves from the full polyphony of the chorus back to a single vocal line over accompaniment, and at 2:57, when the full ensemble comes in suddenly.

Psychedelic Timbres

The high, ghostly, howling sound in the choruses and at the very end is an electro-theremin. The theremin was one of the earliest electronic instruments, and it allowed the performer to slide from one pitch to the next, creating eerie and other-worldly tones. The electro-theremin was a modified version that employed a small slider, making it comparatively easy to play specific melodic motifs.

The electro-theremin in particular evoked the topic and title of the song—the vibrations Wilson imagined exist around all of us in an extradimensional plane. But other unusual instruments also connected powerfully to the ideology of musical psychedelia and fueled the imaginations of listeners in the late 1960s: a tack piano, whose tinny sound is created by adding metal tacks to the hammers; a buzzing jews harp; and sleigh bells.

A number of timbres and musical fragments reveal Brian Wilson's influences:

- **Phil Spector's "wall of sound."** Producer Phil Spector, who produced hits such as the Ronettes' "Be My Baby" and the Righteous Brothers' "You've Lost That Lovin' Feeling" in the 1960s, was famous for bringing huge ensembles into his studio to create one dense timbre for his monophonic recordings. Wilson borrowed heavily from this production style.

- **George Gershwin's *Rhapsody in Blue*.** Wilson was fascinated with the hybrid blend of classical and jazz elements in this famous work from 1924. The orchestration he used for "Good Vibrations" was inspired by the concept of bridging boundaries between a rock band and a classical orchestra.

- **Rhythm and blues.** This style is particularly evident in the bass line at 2:28.

- **Doo-wop.** The close vocal harmony on nonsense syllables at the end of the piece (3:13) reflects the 1950s doo-wop tradition, as does the "Ah" chord at 2:54.

- **Motown.** The chorus, with its layered vocals, could easily have been a Motown recording (see chapter 52). Brian Wilson was also very much attuned to the rhythmic grooves that characterized Motown's biggest hits.

Verse-Chorus Plus Sectional Form

The first half of the song consists of a typical alternation between verses and choruses. The second half incorporates three unique musical extensions—the product of Brian Wilson's modular compositional method. Where Wilson spliced together individual modules, we hear noticeable shifts in texture, timbre, and even tempo, similar to the contrasts that characterize multi-movement works in the Western classical tradition. Wilson described "Good Vibrations" as a "pocket symphony," a term that captures its condensation of different moods, themes, tempos, and orchestrations in a single piece.

Now listen to this song again, following the Listening Guide.

Listening Guide

Beach Boys "Good Vibrations"

Time	Text	Form	Harmony
0:00	I, I love the colorful clothes she wears . . .	Verse 1	First harmony is minor. Chord progression descends through four different harmonies (0:00–0:12), then repeats.
0:25	I'm pickin' up good vibrations. . .	Chorus	The chorus's main motif appears twice on one chord, then moves up a step (0:38), and finally up another step (0:45).
0:51	Close my eyes . . .	Verse 2	Repetition of the chord progression from verse 1
1:16	I'm pickin' up good vibrations . . .	Chorus	Same chord progression as in first appearance of the chorus
1:42	. . . ta-tions . . . I don't know where but she sends me there . . .	Extension 1. There is a sense of time slowing down because the bass plays longer notes, but the tempo does not change.	Very static chord progression
2:14	Gotta keep those lovin' good vibrations A happenin' with her . . .	Extension 2. The tempo is noticeably slower in this section.	Chords change more rapidly than in Extension 1. Harmonic climax at 2:54.
2:57	Good, good, good, good vibrations . . .	Chorus. Tempo is the same as in the previous choruses (noticeably faster than in Extension 2).	The chorus's main motif appears twice on one chord, then moves *down* a step to a lower chord (3:04), and finally down another step (3:10).
3:13	Na na na . . .	Extension 3.	The chord progression here moves up twice (3:17 and 3:20), then back down (3:23).

Texture	Timbre
Vocal solo over instrumental accompaniment	Lead vocal line is multi-tracked with lots of reverb.
Complex polyphony begins with a bass vocal motif (0:25), on top of which background harmonies are layered (0:32—"ooh, bop-bop . . ."), and finally a third vocal layer (0:38—"good, good, good, good vibrations . . .").	The cellos play a rapidly repeating note in the low register; the tambourine adds shimmer, and the electro-theremin adds the ghostly howling sound in the high register.
Instant change in texture back to the original vocal line plus accompaniment.	
	The splice at 1:16 is audible as a fraction of a second of silence before the chorus begins.
Extremely thick instrumental texture under layered vocals	Tack piano plus jews harp, bass harmonica, and rhythm section create an unusual timbre. The vocal harmony enters on "ah . . ." (1:55), followed by sleigh bells and new, abstract lyrics (2:01).
Texture starts very simply, builds up through the gradual addition of new layers, and then reverses the process as the vocals fade out.	Organ plus maracas (shakers) open the section. Bass enters at 2:28, using an R&B style.
Texture moves from many layers to only a few.	Full ensemble is gradually reduced to just cellos, bass, drums, and tambourine.
The first part of this section (3:13–3:27) is complex vocal polyphony with many different lines.	The first part of this section (3:13–3:27) borrows close vocal harmony on nonsense syllables.

Student FAQs

Why does the lead singer's voice sound thicker and more resonant than most vocals?

Carl Wilson sang the same melody more than once in the recording studio, and those "takes" were layered together in a technique known as "multitracking." When two recordings of the same melody are combined, the two sets of sound waves exhibit tiny differences, which give the final version a more robust timbre. Multitracking occurs through most of "Good Vibrations."

How did Brian Wilson combine different recordings to make this song?

Before digital technology was available in the recording studio, producers used razor blades and tape to cut and splice the magnetic recording tape from different takes. Different splicing techniques created different effects; for instance, cross-fading could be done by slicing the tape at an angle.

The Beach Boys

MAKING THE ALBUM THAT NEVER WAS

"Good Vibrations" was slated to be part of a Beach Boys album called *Smile*, the intended masterpiece of the group's most prolific composer, Brian Wilson (b. 1942). The Beach Boys began in 1961 as a surf-rock band with brothers Brian, Carl, and Dennis Wilson plus the boys' cousin Mike Love and their friend Al Jardine. Brian combined the basic style of rock 'n' roll, the ensemble's remarkable vocal abilities, and lighthearted lyrics to create early hits for the quintet, including "Surfer Girl," "Surfin' U.S.A.," "Fun, Fun, Fun," and "409."

In the mid-1960s, while the rest of the Beach Boys embarked on live concert tours, Brian Wilson stayed home to cultivate his ambitions as a composer and producer. The money he earned from the band's "surf rock" hits allowed him unprecedented freedom in the recording studio. His extensive drug use and mental illness contributed to occasional wild eccentricities. He once had a full symphony orchestra wear plastic fireman's hats and sit around a burning bucket of kindling to inspire their recording of a musical "Fire" module. He had a sandbox built around the piano in his home so he could simultaneously compose and experience the beach. Such creative compositional approaches laced his vision for a radical new album called *Smile* that he hoped would revolutionize popular music.

Unfortunately, the rest of the band was less enamored with the new music, neither Brian's record company nor his fans shared his vision, and the project stalled. In place of *Smile*, the band released a haphazardly recorded substitute version called *Smiley Smile*. Nothing the group did after that attained the same recognition as their earlier work, however, and the Beach Boys eventually returned to playing their original surf rock hits.

For decades, fans speculated about the sound of the original *Smile* album. In 2004, Brian Wilson finally reentered the recording studio and finished the project, but by that time, both Carl and Dennis had passed away, and the original Beach Boys had splintered contentiously into separate groups. None of them were involved in the album's completion. Thus, though Brian released *Smile* to critical acclaim, the album never came to light in the way it was originally conceived.

The album that "Good Vibrations" foreshadowed was to be the swan song of a band finally maturing past their surf-rock roots. It was intended to stand on

The Beach Boys pose around a dragster in London's West End. From left: Carl Wilson, Brian Wilson, Dennis Wilson, Mike Love, and Al Jardine.
Getty Images Inc.—Hulton Archive Photos

equal footing with the Beatles' *Sgt. Pepper's Lonely Hearts Club Band*, revolutionize American rock, and declare unconditionally that rock was serious art music. Instead, it became the most famous album in all rock history that no one ever heard.

PLAYLIST: BEACH BOYS

"Surfer Girl" (1963)

"Little Deuce Coupe" (1963)

"California Girls" (1965)

"Wouldn't It Be Nice" (1966)

"God Only Knows" (1966)

"Heroes and Villains" (1967)

"Kokomo" (1988)

CULTURAL CONTEXT

The Summer of Love

"Good Vibrations" helped launch a wave of unprecedented musical development and hippie celebration known as the Summer of Love. In January 1967, the first "Human Be-In" took place in San Francisco's Golden Gate Park, when 20,000 hippies gathered to revel in their outlook on life. The following summer, a musician from San Francisco's psychedelic scene collaborated with a number of businessmen to host the Monterey International Pop Festival, a three-day outdoor celebration of rock's newest musical styles. Historians estimate that well over 50,000 people came to hear the biggest bands of the day as well as up-and-coming stars, all of whom agreed to perform for free. The Beach Boys had been invited to headline the Monterey festival, but at the last minute they withdrew. Although their hit single "Good Vibrations" had been a major factor in mainstream acceptance of psychedelic music, they feared the band's image and the rest of their set list was far too straitlaced and old-fashioned for the new generation of fans.

Just a few weeks before the festival, the Beatles' concept album *Sgt. Pepper's Lonely Hearts Club Band* was released to wild critical acclaim. The Grateful Dead, Jefferson Airplane, and The Byrds also supplied their fans with new musical highs that summer. Jimi Hendrix, who first caught fans' attention when he set his guitar ablaze after a stunning performance at Monterey, ushered in a new era of virtuosic rock guitar. From the United Kingdom, bands from London's psychedelic underground scene (including Pink Floyd) added their hits to the U.S. charts. *Rolling Stone* published its first issue in late 1967, and in several

A crowd demonstrating against the war in Vietnam
Michael Abramson/Black Star

cities, FM radio stations began to program more experimental styles of rock music.

The Summer of Love cultural movement culminated in August 1969, when nearly half a million hippies gathered in Bethel, New York, for Woodstock, unquestionably the most famous of the outdoor music festivals. By then, however, the dark realities of Vietnam had shaken the optimism of the hippie movement's "flower power." Later that year, at a music festival at Altamont Speedway in California, the era of the idealistic rock festival came to a sudden end when a fan was tragically killed.

 EXPAND YOUR PLAYLIST

Psychedelia

The late 1960s spawned some of the most influential rock recordings of any decade. After the Beach Boys' album *Pet Sounds* paved the way, the Beatles released *Sgt. Pepper's Lonely Hearts Club Band*, a concept album that allowed the Beatles to recreate themselves as this fictional performing group.

Byrds, "Eight Miles High" (1966). The timbres in this recording, especially the 12-string guitar and the haunting, open-fifth harmonies in the vocals, have led historians to identify it as one of the earliest fully psychedelic recordings.

Beatles, "Tomorrow Never Knows" (1966). The song features a sitar (see chapter 34), as well as processed sound effects on the vocals and tape effects created by reversing (running the tape backwards), particularly on the guitar solo.

Jefferson Airplane, "White Rabbit" (1967). The lyrics on this San Francisco band's recording borrow heavily from drug culture.

Notice the echoing reverb on the vocals and the intensification of the dynamics and texture as the song reaches its climax.

Pink Floyd, "Flaming" (1967). British groups began experimenting with psychedelic music in an underground scene several years before it became part of the mainstream American sound.

Beatles, "Lucy in the Sky with Diamonds" (1967). Notice the dramatic differences in timbre, tempo, groove, and texture in the individual sections of this recording.

Brian Wilson, "Good Vibrations" (2004). When Wilson rerecorded the song for his *Smile* album, he used the original lyrics he had commissioned from collaborator Tony Asher but then discarded for the 1966 version. Wilson also inserted an additional section and mixed the recording in stereophonic sound.

58

Public Enemy
"Fight the Power"

LOS ANGELES
Chicago
Washington D.C.
U.S.A.

Listen to This

Timbre

Listen for many different layers of sound and for fragments taken from other recordings. Notice the reverberation on the low bass and drums.

Form

Listen for obvious changes in timbre, rhythm, and lyrics that divide the song into sections. Notice that some sections repeat with slight variations.

Rhythm

Be aware of repetition in the rhythmic groove. Feel the steady pulse. Listen to the rhythmic pattern of the lyrics and how it creates tension against the accompaniment's meter.

World-Music Relationships

Notice references to other artists, historical figures, and songs.

Public Enemy recorded "Fight the Power" for film director Spike Lee, who used it as the theme song for *Do the Right Thing* (1989). The movie's plot centers on racial tension in a Brooklyn neighborhood, and Public Enemy's abrasive rap recording vividly conveyed the film's sentiments. Publicity from the movie helped the recording reach number one on *Billboard*'s rap chart. Public Enemy also released it as the last track on their 1990 album *Fear of a Black Planet,* which is the version discussed here. (Several different versions of the song were released at the time.)

Rap music is an art form that combines rhymed speech patterns with hip hop beats. Within hip hop culture, "beat" refers not to a simple pulse but to a complete rhythmic groove constructed from many different sounds repeated in complex patterns. When Public Enemy were recording in the late 1980s, the sounds used to create hip hop beats were **sampled**, or recorded from existing albums—often funk and soul albums from the 1960s and 1970s. Rap musicians took short excerpts—sometimes only a fraction of a second of sound—then programmed their drum machines and synthesizers to play the sounds back in various repetitive patterns, while manipulating their pitch, duration, and timbre. Those patterns provided the rhythmic and musical accompaniment for the rapper's lyrics.

A Layered, Sampled Timbre

The lengthy sample from Dr. King's speech sets the political tone for the song. The speaker's pitch and dynamic levels build up for the first few seconds, then drop off with the phrase "refuse to fight." This pattern of rise and fall creates a wave of rhetorical energy and is often used when delivering sermons.

An opening gesture, which catches the listener's attention but does not start the song's rhythmic groove, follows at 0:16. We hear faint vocals repeating the words "pump it" in a syncopated rhythmic pattern. This short fragment of text is taken from a band called Trouble Funk. It is layered densely with other samples, including a harsh snare drum that defines the pulse of the song. Most significantly, these samples contain audible fuzz and distortion because the sampling process then in use reduced the fidelity of the original recording. The resulting timbre evokes the sound of a boom box playing cassette tapes, obscures the origins of the samples, and makes the rap vocals stand out more because of their relative clarity.

The timbre most strongly identified with hip hop beats is "scratching." Listen for the high-pitched sounds that appear at 2:26, 2:29, 2:31, and 2:33. This scratch technique, originally developed by Grandwizard Theodore (Theodore Livingston), Grandmaster Flash (Joseph Saddler), and Kool Herc (Clive Campbell) in the early 1980s, involves rapidly rotating a vinyl record on a turntable (record player) back and forth while the record is playing. The sound of the scratch is determined by the music on the record at that particular place, as well as the techniques used by the deejay (see Hip Hop's Elements).

Verse-Chorus Form

"Fight the Power" uses a verse-chorus form found in many different genres of popular music, but it also features a lengthy opening section, verses and choruses that vary, instrumental sections, and an epilogue.

• **Extensive opening section.** This consists of the spoken prologue, the musical gesture with "pump it," and the more typical introduction, where the rhythmic groove begins.

- **Expanding verses.** The three verses in this song are different lengths, which is unusual in popular music. The first verse is 12 measures long; the second is 16 measures long; the third is 18. Listeners are probably not consciously aware that each verse is a bit longer than the previous one, but the tension builds as the listener waits longer and longer for the climax of each verse and the arrival of the chorus.

- **Repeating hook in a chorus.** At 1:13, there is a noticeable change in the song's rhythmic groove, which signals the beginning of the chorus. That chorus occurs five times, but the last two appearances omit some lines and alter the rhythmic groove slightly, preventing monotony.

- **Instrumental breaks.** There are two long "breaks," in which the singers are silent while the rhythmic groove takes the stage. The break at 2:25 features scratching as an instrumental solo. The other break, at 4:00, is where other mixes feature Branford Marsalis's solo. This version continues instead with many of the samples from the chorus's accompaniment. At 4:10, a segment of the rhythmic groove repeats in short, syncopated rhythmic patterns, building up the energy level right before the final chorus begins.

- **Epilogue.** At the end of the recording, we hear fragments of an interview asking the band about the future of Public Enemy. These short excerpts are cut off before we hear the band's answer, which suggests that the band's future was uncertain. Indeed, this album appeared during a media firestorm over a band member's apparently anti-Semitic comments, and this epilogue provides a cryptic response to both fans and detractors.

A Repetitive Rhythmic Groove with Syncopated Lyrics

The rhythmic character of "Fight the Power," like most rap recordings, consists of three elements:

- A steady, throbbing pulse that does not change during the song
- A complicated set of rhythmic patterns that repeat to create a unique groove, or hip hop beat
- Syncopated lyrics that create tension in relation to the accompanying groove

The basic pulse of this rap recording is 106 beats per minute, and the tempo does not change during the song. Listen carefully to the groove that is established at 0:23. There is a high-pitched, ringing, electronic sound in the left channel of the stereophonic recording that occurs at the beginning of each four-beat measure. However, the sound is not placed exactly on the downbeat. Instead, it occurs a fraction of a second after the downbeat. The exact placement of each sample in relation to the music's meter gives a particular groove its character. If the samples in this groove were shifted even a fraction of an instant in relation to the meter, the hip hop beat would have a fundamentally different musical flavor.

Syncopation plays a significant role in the rhythmic profile of rap music, particularly when conflicting accents occur between the text and the accompanying groove's meter. Another important layer of syncopation occurs when a rhythmic phrase is repeated, but the second time it occurs, it lines up differently with the underlying pulse. The technique generates conflicting accents in the music: the accents from the metric downbeats, and the accents at the beginning of repeated text phrases. The phrase "Fight the power," which is the hook of the song, starts on the downbeat at the beginning of the chorus (1:13). When it repeats two seconds later, the rhythm of the phrase is the same, but its relationship with the meter has shifted so it starts on the second beat of the measure. The text's phrases repeat after five beats, but the song is clearly in quadruple meter, creating a large-scale syncopation:

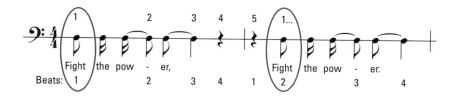

Word-Music Relationships: Politically Charged Hip Hop Rhymes and References

"Fight the Power" used quotations and references from late 1980s hip hop culture to connect with its audience. In the first verse, for instance, the singer says, "funky drummer" and "I know you got soul," both of which are titles of songs that are sampled in the accompaniment, and both of which were popular with other deejays who were laying down hip hop beats during those years. The song cites Bobby McFerrin's hit "Don't Worry Be Happy" in a derogatory statement on the quality of contemporary black music. Both Elvis Presley and John Wayne, entertainers from earlier decades, are mentioned as tokens of white culture and, according to the rap lyrics, its disregard for black role models. At 1:58, Public Enemy also includes a reference to their own first album to compel their audience to join their political crusade for black nationalism. "Yo! bum rush the show," in hip hop slang, means to run full speed ahead into something with reckless abandon.

Now listen to this song again, following the Listening Guide.

Public Enemy   "Fight the Power"

Time	Text	Form	Timbre
0:00	Yet our best-trained . . .	Prologue	Male voice preaching. Audience noise; monophonic, low fidelity recording
0:16		Opening gesture	Sampled sounds, overlaid at 0:18 with a sampled snare drum
0:23	Get it, get, get. . .	Introduction	Amplified bass frequencies, ringing high frequencies, sampled fragments of text
0:45	1989 . . . Sound of the. . . I know . . .	Verse 1	Male rapping, with second voice adding commentary
1:13	(Lemme hear you say . . .) Fight the power . . .	Chorus	Additional reverberation on low bass and drum sounds; new collection of samples create a deeper resonance.
1:31	As the rhythm's designed . . . Yo! Bum rush the show . . .	Verse 2	Return to the first verse's hip hop beat.
2:07	Fight the power: fight the power . . .	Chorus	Same accompaniment as the first chorus
2:25		Break	Scratching featured throughout the solo; heavy-metal guitar sample at 2:41.
2:43	Fight the power . . .	Chorus	Same accompaniment as the first chorus
3:01	Elvis was a . . . Nothing but rednecks. . . 'Don't worry, be happy' was a . . .	Verse 3	Guttural vocal insertions punctuate the rap ("huh" at 3:03; "yeah" at 3:05; "huh" at 3:08).
3:42	Fight the power . . .	Chorus (variant)	New accompaniment under this chorus
4:00		Break	Break extracts parts of the groove from the first chorus but omits some of the samples.
4:19	What we got to say, yeah, fight the power . . .	Chorus (second variant)	Samples and rhythmic grooves from the first verse are combined with vocals from the chorus.
4:37		Epilogue	Three distinct male voices, separated in the stereo mix

Rhythm

Tension is built through the pace of the text's delivery.

Harsh articulation of the beat at 0:18

Text fragments repeated to create syncopated rhythmic patterns.

Regular, steady pulse under a repetitive four-bar rhythmic pattern. Vocals create syncopated patterns against the underlying groove.

Changing metric placement of the hook phrase, generating large-scale syncopation

This verse is four bars longer than the first verse.

Constantly changing rhythmic patterns in the scratching

Rhythmic repetition of opening phrase emphasizes lyrics. Verse is two bars longer than the second verse.

Sampled vocal becomes rhythmic focal point.

First half of the break preserves the rhythmic patterns from the first chorus. Then, at 4:10, a tiny fragment from 4:00 is recast in a more intense and active rhythmic pattern.

Vocals and accompaniment are rhythmically in sync.

Groove ends abruptly; dialogue uses the free rhythms of casual speech.

Student FAQs

Is there a list somewhere of all the samples used in this recording?

There are partial lists, but in interviews, Public Enemy has explained that they aren't even sure exactly what they used. Unlike today, in the first decade of rap recordings, artists frequently used samples without documenting their original sources and with little regard for copyright issues. The original sounds were also often altered beyond recognition. Thus, it is sometimes impossible to identify the samples' sources.

With so many different mixes of this song available, which is the official version?

With a song like this one, there isn't any one version that is considered either original or official. Each mix was done for a specific purpose, and so the more interesting question to ask is, How does each version fit its purpose?

Public Enemy (1986–)

POLITICS AND MUSIC

When Public Enemy began to make records, they brought a powerful, abrasive, and unapologetically radical social agenda to hip hop on the East Coast. In contrast to popular mid-1980s artists who rapped about partying and romance, Public Enemy incited controversy with their politicized lyrics and outspoken commentary on such topics as racism, civil rights, and AIDS. They found a welcome audience for their messages and emerged as major stars during the genre's explosive growth period.

Chuck D (Carlton Douglas Ridenhour) entered the world of hip hop as a graphic artist who designed flyers for parties. There, he met musicians in Long Island's growing rap scene and began to hone his skills as an MC—a hip hop "Master of Ceremonies" (see Hip Hop's Elements). In 1984, he and collaborator Flavor Flav (William Jonathan Drayton Jr.) made a tape called "Public Enemy #1" to answer a challenge from a local rapper, and that tape found its way into the hands of producer Rick Rubin, who founded Def Jam Records with Russell Simmons. Rubin heard tremendous commercial potential in Chuck D's tape and immediately wanted to sign the artist to Def Jam, which was growing into the most significant record label in hip hop. In June 1986, Chuck D finally agreed to a record contract under the name Public Enemy.

As a condition of the contract, Chuck D insisted that he be allowed to assemble an ensemble in the style of hip hop's earliest crews like Grandmaster Flash and the Furious Five, rather than sign as a solo artist. Public Enemy became a self-contained production and entertainment unit. It consisted of Flavor Flav, DJ Terminator X (Norman Rogers), Professor Griff (Richard Griffin) in the role of "minister of information" (essentially a sidekick member of the entourage), an onstage security team known as S1W, plus the "Bomb Squad" production team: Hank Shocklee, his brother Keith Shocklee, and Eric "Vietnam" Sadler. Public Enemy's success had much to do with their production team's talent. The Bomb Squad had a unique ability to create hip hop beats that were sonically dense, heavily layered, and musically chaotic. These timbres and grooves reinforced the serious themes of Public Enemy's lyrics with a musical aggression that cut through the waves of hip hop recordings during that era.

Public Enemy
Michael Ochs Archives Ltd./Getty Images Inc.—Los Angeles

Public Enemy was not the only hip hop ensemble to write politically charged lyrics laced with expressions of black nationalism. During the same era, West Coast rap artists were lashing out with raps about race, poverty, and oppression, most notably N.W.A.'s *Straight Outta Compton* (1988). The media's attention to West Coast rap and the ensuing rise of gangsta rap threatened to overshadow Public Enemy's role in transforming rap into a politically charged musical genre. However, their first three albums were seminal in that process and are widely regarded as groundbreaking by hip hop fans.

PLAYLIST: PUBLIC ENEMY

"Public Enemy #1"

"Don't Believe the Hype"

"911 Is a Joke"

"Fight the Power"—Soundtrack version from *Do the Right Thing*

"Can't Truss It"

Hip Hop's Elements

Hip hop music grew out of an environment in which graffiti, deejaying, emceeing, and break dancing were equally significant forms of cultural expression. In predominantly black neighborhoods of New York City, graffiti was a visual art that let the individual lay claim to space, property, and a public identity through his or her "tags," or graffiti signatures. Deejaying involved manipulating records on turntables to mix and repeat sections of songs, usually drum breaks or solos, in innovative ways, and emceeing involved calling out improvised rhymes to entertain a crowd and keep a party lively; this became rap. Break dancers, known as b-boys and b-girls, responded to the deejay's selection of drum breaks with acrobatic moves. Aspects of fashion and rhetoric were also woven into hip hop culture.

Harsh economic conditions, gang violence, and a sense of despair motivated the first generation of hip hop artists to find a creative outlet through their music, but record executives quickly saw the potential to transform this culture of self-expression into a highly commercial genre that, in its early days, did not espouse strongly politicized messages. With records, radio shows, and growing media coverage, hip hop quickly spread beyond its original neighborhoods. And yet despite many pockets of interest, mainstream acceptance of hip hop was slow in coming. The day before Def Jam Recordings released *Fear of a Black Planet, Newsweek magazine* published a scathing critique of hip hop culture that described its music as a "thumping, clattering, scratching assault." Accusations

Public Enemy's
Fear of a Black Planet album cover
© Dorling Kindersley

abounded that the music was merely noise and that the artists were not really musicians, given that they did not play instruments and rapping was different than singing. The artists also faced harsh criticism and the occasional lawsuit for their sampling practices. Over time, however, those controversies faded as new, legal accountability became the norm, and as fans and writers alike acknowledged that the manipulation of pre-recorded sound was also a form of musical composition.

 EXPAND YOUR PLAYLIST

Musical References in "Fight the Power"

The lyrics to "Fight the Power" quote phrases and titles from several different songs and refer to historical figures both directly and through the use of samples.

Elvis Presley, "Hound Dog" (1956). Recorded by black blues legend Big Mama Thornton three years before Presley, this song is often cited by critics who accuse Presley of appropriating black music. However, this overlooks the fact that the song was written for Thornton by the white songwriting team of Lieber and Stoller.

Sly and the Family Stone, "Sing a Simple Song" (1968). The line "Lemme hear you say" comes from this funk song. It brings an authentic funk voice into the text of "Fight the Power."

James Brown, "Funky Drummer" (1969). Listen to Brown's lyrics that give the instrumentalists instructions. The drum solo toward the end of the recording has been sampled and used in countless hip hop recordings, especially in the late 1980s.

Bobby Byrd, "I Know You Got Soul," (1971). Byrd worked as James Brown's second vocalist for many years, and this song was a favorite source for hip hop samples. Listen to the growls and gravelly quality in Byrd's voice that support the emotional tenor of Public Enemy's message.

Public Enemy, "Yo! Bum Rush the Show" (1987). The phrase "bum rush" is part of hip hop slang; it is also the title of the band's first album and one of its tracks. By using this phrase again in "Fight the Power," Public Enemy invoked their own pioneering role in bringing political messages into rap albums.

Bobby McFerrin, "Don't Worry Be Happy" (1988). This song won the Grammy for Best Song of the Year right before "Fight the Power" was released. The recording uses vocal *a cappella* techniques to create all the rhythmic sounds.

59

Tania León
A la Par, second movement (*Guaguancó*)

Listen to This

Timbre

This piece is written entirely for percussion instruments. Listen for the contrast between those that play specific pitches (like the piano, the vibraphone, and the bongo drums) and those that make only percussive sounds that cannot be tied to any specific pitch (like the cowbell, the cymbals, and the snare drum).

Rhythm

Listen for the repeated melodic and rhythmic figure in the lower register of the piano. This kind of figure is typical of the Afro-Cuban dance known as the *guaguancó*.

Harmony

Listen for the mixture of tonal and atonal harmonies in this work.

Form

The movement divides into two very different sections. Where does the change occur?

What happens when modernism confronts popular music in the same work? *A la par* offers one possible scenario, for it mixes the rhythms of a Cuban popular dance with atonal harmonies. The composer, Tania León, has said that this work reflects her own attempt "to express the dichotomy between the folk-music traditions of my native Cuba and the Classical European training I received at the Havana Conservatory." In this particular movement, the repeated melodic-rhythmic figure in the bass line can be heard as representing the vernacular idioms of Cuban dance, while the other instrumental lines reflect the idiom of European modernism.

The Spanish title *A la par* translates loosely as "at the same time as" or "on the same level as," and it is a fitting description of the relationship between popular and modernist styles. Even though they are often quite distinct—each goes its own way—they nevertheless complement one another to create a whole larger than the sum of its parts. Every instrument seems to occupy its own space, yet in the end, everything is indeed *a la par.*

This musical style in which modern and traditional elements are combined is often called **postmodernism**. Postmodernism is a style of modernism—no one would think of León's music as old-fashioned—but it embraces tonality as well as atonality, rhythmic predictability as well as unpredictability. Postmodern works are often playful in spirit, a reaction against the unrelenting seriousness of much modernist art. As a work of postmodernism, León's *A la par* is both tonal and atonal, rhythmically regular and irregular, serious and playful.

Percussion Timbres

A percussion instrument is one that produces sound by being struck or shaken, and all the instruments in this work belong to the percussion family, including even the piano (a finger strikes the key, which activates a hammer, which strikes a string). Some percussion instruments (like the piano or certain kinds of drums) produce specific pitches, while others do not. In the second movement of *A la par,* León uses both kinds of instruments. The timings in the list below indicate examples of when you can hear these individual instruments. Notice that not all the instruments are played the same way all the time. The player striking the timbales (a pair of small drums), for example, sometimes hits the side of the instrument with a stick and sometimes hits the membrane surface on the top. The conga player sometimes uses the hand, sometimes a stick.

Pitched Instruments

- **Piano:** 0:00 and throughout.
- **Timbales** (a small drum): 0:06 and throughout. In this particular movement, the player most often uses a stick to strike the side of the instrument, but at other times strikes the membrane on top of the drum (as at 0:28–0:30), which is the more standard way of playing the instrument.
- **Tom-toms** (a pair of large drums): 0:35–0:40.
- **Bongos** (a pair of very small hand drums): 0:50–0:52.
- **Snare drum** (a medium-sized drum): 0:23–0:25.

- **Marimba** (a xylophone-like instrument with tubular resonators under each bar): 1:55–end.
- **Vibraphone** (an electrified marimba with motorized controls that can produce different degrees of vibrato, a wavering-like sound, for each pitch): 1:50–end.

Non-Pitched Instruments

- **Conga** (a long, narrow drum): 0:05, very briefly, then again at 0:12–0:15, played first with the hand and then with a stick
- **Cowbell** (struck with a stick): 0:43–0:45.
- **Suspended cymbal** (a single cymbal, struck with a stick): 0:34.
- **Cachiche** (a maraca-like "shaker"): 1:02–1:08.

A couple in Havana dances the *guaguancó*; drummers are visible in the background.

Rebecca Bodenheimer, PhD

Male and Female Rhythmic Lines

In the lower register of the piano, we hear a syncopated figure over and over, the kind of rhythmic pattern to which Cuban dancers could dance the *guaguancó*. The central element of this rumba-style dance is the *vacuno,* a pelvic thrust by the man toward the woman, who both encourages and avoids these thrusts. Listen to the way in which the repeated figure in the bass suggests a physical thrust and how the voices around it—all the other percussion instruments, including the piano in its middle and upper ranges—seem to both encourage and resist this repeated thrusting figure.

Parallel (Non-) Harmonies

The repeated figure in the lower register of the piano is chromatically inflected but squarely tonal: it keeps landing over and over on the same note, so we feel that the music—or at least this portion of the music—has a tonal center. It has some notes that sound slightly dissonant (because they are chromatic), but the repeated note is so prominent that our ear hears this note as a harmonic foundation. Everything else—all the pitches around this bass line—is less centered, including even the higher notes on the piano. The other pitched instruments are insistently atonal. (The non-pitched percussion instruments cannot play a role in the harmony, and function in a purely rhythmic fashion.) This movement thus combines elements of both tonality (the repeated *guanguacó* figure) and atonality.

Sectional Form

The contrast between the last third of the movement and all that has gone before is sudden and obvious: the steady rhythmic figure disappears, the tempo shifts suddenly from fast to slow, almost all the percussion instruments drop out, and two new instruments, the marimba and the vibraphone, enter for the first time. On closer listening, we realize that the first quarter or so of this movement is an introduction of sorts, for while it presents the basic *guanguacó* figure, it does so only sporadically. Only after a short break in the music (at 0:39) does this figure become an ostinato. The movement thus divides into three sections: an introduction, the central *guanguacó*, and a coda. The first two sections are closely related, while the third is quite different.

With these points in mind, now listen to the second movement of this work again, using the Listening Guide.

Tania León (b. 1943)

RESISTING LABELS

"I have a lot of trouble with labels," the composer Tania León recently confessed. "I'm totally anti-label. . . . Everybody has called me so many things. . . . How do they see me? Do they see me? Do they hear me? Do they watch me? Every time I read a different article, I have a different category. Now, the latest thing is Afro-Cuban. The first time that I heard that term, I was announced to an audience by a colleague of mine. I was totally surprised that this colleague of mine chose to say something like that. What is this all about?"

León's music indeed defies easy categorization: it synthesizes a great many traditions, from Cuban dance to atonality and many other styles in between. In this respect, it reflects León's exposure to a great many musical traditions, not only in her native Cuba, where she studied to become a pianist, but also in the United States, where she turned her attention more and more toward composing and conducting. Shortly after immigrating to the United States in 1967, she became the first music director of the Dance Theater of Harlem in 1969 and has taught composition at Brooklyn College since 1985. She has received commissions from throughout the world for works in a variety of genres, including operas and several works for orchestra. As a conductor, she has performed with such prestigious ensembles as the Gewandhaus Orchestra of Leipzig and the New York Philharmonic.

Cuban-born composer Tania León in 1996, conducting one of her compositions in a concert at the New School, in New York City
Jack Vartoogian/Front Row Photos

PLAYLIST: LEÓN

Rituál. For piano.

Pueblo mulato. Three songs to texts by the Cuban poet Nicolás Guillén, for soprano, oboe, guitar, double bass, percussion, and piano.

Indigena. For chamber orchestra.

Scourge of Hyacinths. An opera based on a radio play by the Nobel Prize–winning Nigerian author Wole Soyinka.

Listening Guide

Tania León *A la Par*, second movement ("Guaguancó")

Time	Form: Section	Rhythm	Timbre	Harmony
0:00	(1) Introduction (fast)	Guaguancó rhythm in lower register of piano, but not continuously. The upper register of the piano and all the other instruments weave around this recurring figure.	Piano, percussion instruments	No sense of tonality at first, but the melodic figure in the bass (starting at 0:11) establishes its lowest note as the central tone.
0:39	(2) Ostinato (fast)	The rhythmic figure now becomes an ostinato in the bass, repeated without a pause.		Non-ostinato pitches are atonal; ostinato figure centers on its lowest note.
1:33	(2) Coda (slow)	Guaguancó rhythm drops out for the first time. Piano plays a disjunct, atonal line its place.	Reduced instrumentation and new instruments: Piano, cowbell (briefly), then the vibraphone and marimba enter for the first time.	Wholly atonal; no sense of a tonal center at all.

Student FAQs

How many performers does it take to perform this work?

In a percussion ensemble, one player usually covers multiple instruments, switching from, say, marimba to vibraphone to claves (wooden sticks) as the score demands. The number of performers is optional, but the score determines how many are needed at a minimum. The excerpt given here would require at least four percussionists.

What's the difference between postmodernism and neo-classicism?

The two are related but not the same. Both make reference to earlier idioms, though neoclassicism is generally associated with the 1920s and 1930s, whereas postmodernism is a phenomenon of the late twentieth century. Postmodern music, unlike neoclassicism, embraces modernism as one of many legitimate approaches to artistic expressions, whereas neoclassicism rejects the extremes of modernism. In the end, the terms are labels whose applicability to any given work or artist can be debated.

CULTURAL CONTEXT

Postmodern Architecture

The spirit of postmodernism is perhaps most readily apparent in the field of architecture. For many decades in the middle of the twentieth century, modernist architecture dominated the scene. The typical modernist building favored clean, straight lines with little or no hint of ornamentation.

Advocates of modernist architecture praised its emphasis on functionality and its break with traditions of the past. But in the second half of the twentieth century, more and more critics came to see this style as cold and impersonal. Postmodern architects began adding elements to building that were not driven entirely by function. The curved walls of the Walt Disney Theater in Los Angeles (2004) capture the more playful spirit of postmodernism.

With its symmetrical design and clean, straight lines, the John F. Kennedy Center for the Performing Arts, in Washington, D.C. (1971), exemplifies modernist architecture.

Bill Helsel/Alamy Images

The fanciful, irregular shape of the Walt Disney Concert Hall in Los Angeles (2004) reflects the more recent style of postmodern architecture.

© Lara Swimmer/Esto

EXPAND YOUR PLAYLIST

Postmodern Music

George Rochberg (1918–2005), String Quartet no. 6. A postmodern work by a composer who was an avowed modernist in his early career. The slow movement is a set of variations on Pachelbel's celebrated Canon.

William Bolcom (b. 1938), *Songs of Innocence and Experience*. A setting of texts by William Blake, this cycle of songs juxtaposes a wide range of musical idioms, including atonal and tonal, jazz, gospel, blues, ragtime, and rock.

Luciano Berio (1925–2003), *Sinfonia*. The second movement of this work for orchestra and eight amplified voices uses the second movement of Gustav Mahler's Second Symphony as its basis, with samplings from works by many other com-

posers superimposed on it, along with a text by Samuel Beckett.

Alfred Schnittke (1934–98), *Carmen Suite*. This is a reworking of themes from Georges Bizet's well-known *Carmen* (1875), rewritten and reorchestrated in such a way as to create an arresting mixture of nineteenth- and twentieth-century idioms.

John Zorn (b. 1953), *The Big Gundown: John Zorn Plays the Music of Ennio Morricone*. This album, released in 1985, superimposes idioms of jazz, soul, and other genres on the film scores of a composer who specialized in creating soundtracks for films set in the American West (*A Fistful of Dollars, Once Upon a Time in the West*).

NEW YORK CITY

Los Angeles

Washington D.C.

U.S.A.

60

Tan Dun
"Farewell" from *Crouching Tiger, Hidden Dragon*

 Listen to This

Timbre

Listen for the complementary sounds of the deeply resonant cello and the eerily human Chinese erhu, both string instruments. Listen for additional layers of sound from the hand drums and from the Western-style string orchestra.

Melody

The principal melody, in the cello, is presented eight times, each time in a slightly different form. Listen to the cello and the erhu "slide" into and around their notes. Also listen for the way in which the cello ends each statement of the melody on the same note until the very last time, when the ending is not so clear.

Texture

The texture is polyphonic throughout, with three independent lines: the cello, the erhu, and the orchestra, which plays quietly throughout in the background. Notice the way the melody in the erhu weaves around the melody in the cello.

The music for the 2000 film *Crouching Tiger, Hidden Dragon,* by the Chinese-American composer Tan Dun (b. 1957), unites Western and non-Western timbres and melodic styles to create a soundtrack that won the Academy Award in 2001 for Best Music in an Original Score, as well as a Grammy Award in 2002 for Best Score Soundtrack Album. The film, directed by Ang Lee, is set in eighteenth-century China and tells the story of two couples whose lives are overshadowed by fate. The plot revolves around a legendary sword known as the Green Destiny, and the film includes spectacular fight scenes. But the music of the selection here comes after the bittersweet end of the movie, during the credits. Its central theme is one that has been associated with the two love stories throughout the movie. Tan Dun's score at this point is a purely musical commentary on the sweetness and brevity of love and life.

Eastern and Western Timbres

When Ang Lee first approached Tan Dun about writing the score to this film, the composer recalls, "We started to talk about the high and low cultures, east and west, world instruments and the western symphony orchestras, all those types of things we wanted to use in the score."* In the end, it was agreed that the music would draw on both European and Chinese instruments. The Chinese-American cellist Yo-Yo Ma (b. 1955) proved to be the bridge between these worlds of sound. In "Farewell," the solo cello is matched with the erhu, a traditional Chinese instrument with two strings (made of silk) and a small, octagonal sound box covered with snakeskin. For two instruments that produce sound in such a similar fashion—a bow drawn across strings—the timbres are strikingly different. The cello plays in a lower register and owes its deep sound to the resonance of wood in a large instrument, while the erhu plays in a higher register, produces a smaller sound (because the resonating surface of the instrument is so small), and creates a tone remarkably like the human voice. Further layers of sound can be heard in the string orchestra (a Western ensemble) and the more Eastern-sounding group of hand drums.

Fluid Melody

Stringed instruments like the cello and the erhu can produce sounds that are far more flexible and fluid than those of instruments that can play only fixed pitches, like the piano. On a piano, one key can produce only one note. The cello and erhu, played by fingers moving along strings, can "bend" their notes, sliding up or down in fluid fashion, like a voice. Indeed, both instruments in this selection, particularly the erhu, have a strongly vocal quality. Tan Dun himself has acknowledged that the style of playing he calls for from these instruments was influenced by styles of singing in Chinese opera, in which singers frequently slide into and out of pitches (see chapter 25). This style of playing helps give the music a distinctively non-Western sound, even when played on a Western instrument like the cello. Yet the melody itself is not pentatonic (that is, based on five notes), which is the kind of melody often associated with music of the Far East. It begins as a pentatonic melody, but the dramatic leap upward introduces a sixth note that gives the line a more Western sound.

*Source: [Adapted from] *Tan Dun's Cultural Evolution*, National Public Radio Morning Edition, June 15, 2006.

Xiaohui Ma plays the erhu. A graduate of the Shanghai Conservatory of Music, Xiaohui Ma has concertized throughout the world and recorded more than 40 albums, including the soundtrack for *Crouching Tiger, Hidden Dragon* with the cellist Yo-Yo Ma.
Courtesy of Chia-Chi Charlie Chang and Burnett Thompson Music

The repeated return to the tonic note demarcates the end of each statement of the brief melody. This might seem like a recipe for a choppy, fragmented work. But the composer skillfully uses the erhu to bridge the gaps between each of the cello's statements of the theme. Thus the melody is both clearly demarcated (by the repeated return to the tonic, in the cello) and constantly in motion (thanks to the erhu).

At the very end of this selection—the last statement of the melody—the cello lands on the tonic but does not stop there. Instead, it wavers between two notes, the tonic and the note immediately below it. The music does not resolve to the tonic. Instead, it simply fades away, suggesting that the love of the two couples never ceases.

Symbolic Texture

The registers of the two principal instruments here, the cello and the erhu, correspond roughly to the registers of the voices of a man and a woman. The way the two lines differ yet wrap themselves around each other wistfully can be heard as representing the relationship between both pairs of lovers at the end of the movie. This "Farewell," after all, is a purely musical commentary on the loves of two couples, both of which have ended in sorrow.

With these points in mind, listen to this selection again using the Listening Guide.

Tan Dun "Farewell" from *Crouching Tiger, Hidden Dragon*

Time	Timbre	Melody	Texture
0:00	Cello, orchestra, drums; erhu joins in at 0:12 and continues throughout; the instruments all gradually grow louder until the very end, when they fade out.	1. Cello lands on tonic at 0:16. The erhu bridges the gap to the next statement of the theme, here and at the end of all subsequent statements of the theme.	Polyphonic throughout, first between the cello and the orchestra, then additionally with the erhu.
0:18		2. Cello lands on tonic at 0:30.	
0:34		3. Cello lands on tonic at 0:46.	
0:50		4. Cello lands on tonic at 1:02.	
1:05		5. Cello lands on tonic at 1:18.	
1:21		6. Cello lands on tonic at 1:34.	
1:38		7. Cello lands on tonic at 1:50.	
1:53		8. Cello lands on tonic at 2:07 but then wavers back and forth between tonic and the note below it, fading into unresolved silence.	

Student FAQs

Is the soundtrack on the film the same as the soundtrack on the CD?

Not in the case of *Crouching Tiger, Hidden Dragon,* and usually not with other films, either. Almost invariably, the two are different. Take any movie you know very well and watch it sometime paying attention only to the music. You'll probably be amazed at how often music is present, and you may discover that the CD of the soundtrack is actually quite selective.

How does a composer get commissioned to write a soundtrack?

Getting a commission to compose a soundtrack is like getting any other kind of commission. People go on the basis of what you've already written. So a well-known film composer like John Williams can pick and choose his commissions, while an aspiring young composer will feel fortunate to get a request from a low-budget film. But even John Williams had to start out with writing music for a television series called *Playhouse 90.*

Tan Dun (b. 1957)

COMPOSER IN TWO WORLDS

Born in Hunan Province, in southern China, Tan Dun was forced to work on a commune during the Great Cultural Revolution of the 1970s, planting and harvesting rice. It was during this time that he began to collect folksongs and other music of the Chinese countryside and, though he was only a teenager, to organize his coworkers into musical ensembles. When Beijing's Central Conservatory of Music reopened in the late 1970s, Tan Dun began his formal studies in composition. But a second wave of cultural repression banned performances of his music, and he eventually immigrated to the United States, where he continued his studies, receiving a Doctor of Musical Arts degree from Columbia University in 1993.

As a composer, Tan Dun has always drawn inspiration from the music of his Chinese ancestry, combining it with the traditions of Western classical music. He was twenty years old before he heard a note of Bach, and he was overwhelmed. "You are standing on the ruins," he recently recalled of growing up during the Great Cultural Revolution. "Everything's been destroyed. Family's been destroyed, culture [has] been destroyed. And nobody [was] allowed to touch anything Western or ancient. And suddenly you heard Bach. It's like a medicine curing everything you were suffering."

"An artist's creation more or less always comes from his life experiences, his imagination comes out this way. My imagination always comes out from my experiences in life. I've been living in the United States for fifteen years, but I was living in China for more than twenty years. All those experiences crossing together is what comes out of my music. So of course yes, in all my early experiences I was trained in Chinese theatre and music, this has somehow become very interesting because it comes out of my music today."

Director Ang Lee (left), cellist Yo-Yo Ma (center), and composer Tan Dun (right) during the recording of the soundtrack to *Crouching Tiger, Hidden Dragon.*

© Reuters/Sam Mircovich/CORBIS All Rights Reserved

PLAYLIST: TAN DUN

The First Emperor. An opera, premiered by the Metropolitan Opera of New York City in December 2006; the tenor Plácido Domingo sang the title role.

The Banquet. Another film score, this one for a re-interpretation of Shakespeare's *Hamlet.*

The Map. A work for cello, orchestra, and video recording, based on the composer's return to China to record folk music of his native land.

Symphony 1997. A large-scale work for orchestra, cello soloist, bells, and children's choir, commissioned to celebrate the transfer of Hong Kong from British to Chinese sovereignty.

"Source: Music from the Movies 31132 (Winter 2001). [online at http://www.tandunonline.com/encounter/?id=5]"

Matching Images with Sound

In the era of silent films—before 1927—the only way to provide a musical soundtrack was to have live musicians perform at every showing of a film. The organ was the favorite instrument for providing such music, in part because it is so versatile and can produce so many different timbres; some older theaters today have preserved or reconstructed their organs from days of silent film.

In 1927, Warner Brothers released *The Jazz Singer,* the first feature film with synchronized sound. Not coincidentally, the main character in the film—played by Al Jolson—is a singer who has the opportunity to sing several songs. From that point onward, synchronized sound became the standard in Hollywood. The technology has grown increasingly sophisticated over the years, but the basic process has remained unchanged:

1. The composer develops ideas based on the general outline of the story and genre: a science-fiction film will have a different kind of sound from a Western, which in turn will be different from a romantic comedy, and so on. Using these basic ideas, the composer refines them and develops them into a score based on the edited film, giving close attention to exactly how much time is needed for any given action in any given scene. For example, a composer will know in advance that a scene requires "10.4 seconds of music to accompany a chase," followed by "3.5 seconds of music to accompany a close-up of a character out of breath."

2. The orchestra rehearses the score.

3. The orchestra records the score. The conductor and the performers all have visual access to some projection of the

The noted film composer Hans Zimmer scoring a sequence for *Stallion of the Cimarron* in 2002
© DreamWorks/Everett Collection

scene they are recording in order to ensure precision of timing. Performers often wear earpieces that provide "click tracks," low clicking noises that help players make shifts from one tempo to another with maximum precision. Audio engineers play a vital role in determining the placement of microphones, the balance of the instruments, and the overall shape of the final sound.

4. The music editor superimposes the recorded soundtrack onto the film.

5. The editor makes final adjustments based on the final cut of the film.

 EXPAND YOUR PLAYLIST

Film Music

Film music was an entirely new genre in the twentieth century, and many composers were drawn to Hollywood.

Max Steiner, *Gone With the Wind.* Steiner (1888–1971) wrote operettas in his native Austria before immigrating to the United States in 1914. His soundtrack for *Gone With the Wind* (1939) captured the sound of the antebellum American South.

Erich Wolfgang Korngold, *The Adventures of Robin Hood.* Korngold (1897–1957) was a successful composer of operas before moving to the United States in 1934. He won an opera Academy Award for this 1938 score.

Bernard Hermann, *Psycho, North by Northwest, Taxi Driver.* Hermann (1911–75), a native New Yorker, collaborated with Alfred

Hitchcock on some of the director's greatest movies. He also supervised the eerie avian sound effects in Hitchcock's *The Birds.*

John Williams, *E.T., Star Wars, Jurassic Park,* and the first two *Harry Potter* films. The most successful and prolific of all film music composers, John Williams has an uncanny ability to alter his style to capture the mood of many different kinds of films.

Jerry Goldsmith, *Planet of the Apes, The Omen, Patton, Hoosiers.* Goldsmith (1929–2004) was born in Los Angeles and became one of the most productive film composers of his generation.

Howard Shore, *Lord of the Rings.* This Canadian composer (b. 1946) won Academy Awards in 2002 and 2004 for his music to different installments of *Lord of the Rings.*

PART 6 Summary

	Nineteenth Century	Twentieth Century
Texture	Full spectrum between homophonic and polyphonic	Same
Melody	Longer, more complex melodies, often with wider range, often quite technically demanding	Both tonal and atonal, with or without metrical structure
Rhythm	Wider range of extremes, from balanced to irregular; use of folk rhythms occasionally	Full range of possibilities, from regular to irregular, predictable to unpredictable
Timbre	Emergence of the modern orchestra with large brass and percussion sections	Even greater possibilities of sound from new techniques for playing old instruments, increased use of percussion instruments, and audio technology
Harmony	Increasingly chromatic, undermining a sense of a tonal center	Tonal and atonal, both with and without a sense of a harmonic center
Form	Earlier forms, plus new emphasis on cyclic form (in instrumental music) and larger basic units of construction (in opera)	All earlier forms continue; emergence of aleatory music based on chance
Word-Music relationships	Greater use of program music; intense cultivation of the song as a genre	Continued use of program music; new techniques of singing (*Sprechstimme*)

IN REVIEW: The Twentieth Century

Genres

Ballet. A staged work that presents a drama through dance.
- Stravinsky, *Rite of Spring* (Chapter 43)
- Copland, *Rodeo* (Chapter 51)

Song. A relatively short work for a singer and accompanying instruments.
- Still, "A Black Pierrot" (Chapter 50)
- Johnson, "Terraplane Blues" (Chapter 46)
- Jackson, "It Don't Cost Very Much" (Web Bonus Chapter 5)

Aleatory music. A work whose structure is determined to some degree by chance.
- Cage, *4′33″* (Chapter 53)

Minimalist music. Music based on the frequent repetition (with slight variations) of a small musical idea.
- Glass, *Einstein on the Beach* (Chapter 54)

Musical. A spoken play with ample sung numbers (arias, ensembles, choruses).
- Bernstein, *West Side Story* (Chapter 52)

Film music. Music written expressly for a film.
- Tan Dun, "Farewell" (Chapter 60)

Jazz. Popular music style that weds African American rhythms with European influences.
- Ellington, *Cotton Tail* (Chapter 47)
- Parker, *Ornithology* (Chapter 48)

Rock and Roll. Dominant popular music of the second half of the 20th century.
- Berry, "School Day" (Chapter 55)
- Marvelettes, "Please, Mr. Postman" (Chapter 56)
- Beach Boys, "Good Vibrations" (Chapter 57)
- Sex Pistols, "God Save the Queen" (Web Bonus Chapter 6)

Rap. African American popular music style, combining rhymed recitations with complex recorded accompaniments.
- Public Enemy, "Fight the Power" (Chapter 58)

Stylistic Developments

Impressionist music. Music that emphasizes timbre (color) at the expense of line (melody).
- Debussy, *Voiles* (Chapter 39)
- Gamelan Gong Kebyar, *Kebyar Ding III*, "Oncang-oncangan" (Chapter 40)

Atonality. A style of writing without a tonal center.
- Ives, *The Unanswered Question* (Chapter 41)
- Schoenberg, "Columbine" from Pierrot lunaire (Chapter 42)
- Berta Waza: *Greetings by Aba Musa!* (Chapter 44)
- Crawford, *Piano Study in Mixed Accents* (Chapter 49)

Neo-classicism. A style of writing that embraces the harmonic, rhythmic, and formal styles of the past (specifically, those of the eighteenth century), with limited modernist inflections.
- Tailleferre, Concertino for Harp and Orchestra, finale (Web Bonus Chapter 4)

Postmodernism. A style of writing that integrates modernism with other idioms.
- León, *A la Par* (Chapter 59)

Syncopation. A rhythmic style that emphasizes the off-beat.
- Joplin, *Maple Leaf Rag* (Chapter 45)

PART 7 Music Today

You will be the author of the final chapter. The purpose of this section is to help you construct an interpretive analysis of a short recording of your choice. You will first listen to the recording, taking preliminary notes. Second, you will research the piece to learn about its history, context, and setting. Third, you will explore each musical element in the recording, drawing on your research to help explain various features. Fourth, you will integrate the elements, historical information, and cultural context of the recording into a cohesive analysis.

These guidelines lead to an analysis of the recording consisting of:

1. An introduction to the piece, explaining when and where it was created, who the composer(s) and performer(s) are, and what its social context is
2. An integrated discussion of the key musical elements of the recording and how those features are part of the style, genre, and traditions of the piece and its creators
3. A listening guide that compiles the key features and elements in a time-chart

There is no such thing as one true analysis of a recording. Two students might write very different analyses of the same recording based on the interaction of musical elements each found most interesting. However, there are several questions we can ask to differentiate good analyses from poor ones:

1. Is the piece represented in a detailed and accurate way so that there is musical evidence for every point the author makes?
2. Did the author locate the historical and social context of the piece to create a more informed description and interpretation of its musical elements?
3. Did the author explore the piece's genre and identify similarities and differences with others of the same type?
4. Does the analysis help the reader to hear the recording in a new, interesting, and more active way?

Choose a piece you know well or one that intrigues you. Make sure it is short enough to be manageable (a few minutes is a good guideline). The point is to listen more carefully than you have before, and, in the process of preparing others for the listening experience, to uncover fresh aspects of the music that will enhance your hearing of it as well.

Data Collection: Listen First

The process must begin with close, attentive, and repeated listening. Use the best possible recording, equipment, and listening location:

- **Find the Right Format.** Make sure the recording is in a format that makes it easy to play the piece many times and to start and stop the recording at any point. If your recording is on an LP or a cassette tape, you may wish to digitize it so that you can listen repeatedly without wearing out the original.
- **Keep Source Info.** If you found the recording on a digital download site (iTunes, Rhapsody, or somewhere similar), write down as much detailed information as possible about the album or source to assist you in locating the same recording later and in gathering research materials.
- **Find the Right Location.** Choose a listening location that has both speakers and headphones available, and use the best quality equipment you can. When you expose your ears to the recording in several different ways, your cognitive processes will allow you to pick out different features of the music more easily.
- **Listen and Take Notes.** The first time you play the piece, write down what aspects of the music catch your attention. You might hear a favorite moment, or you might have an emotional response to part of the piece. You might hear references to other music. Do you associate the piece with a particular time, place, film, or feeling? Pull together as many ideas as you can. Note any questions you have about quotations, sounds you don't recognize, unusual timbres or effects, and anything else that might be explained when you research the piece. This free-form list will also contain nuggets that you can explore later when we focus on the musical elements.

What Are the Words?

If your recording involves lyrics, the next step is to transcribe the text onto a working time-chart. Never rely on the lyrics that are printed in the album's liner notes or posted on a Web site. Those lyrics may provide a helpful starting point, but they may not represent what is actually sung on your recording. If your recording is based on or refers to a text, even if lyrics are not present (such as Mendelssohn's *A Midsummer Night's Dream,* chapter 28), find that text and study it, too.

Text Layout

When you transcribe the lyrics, you are making a number of implicit analytic decisions about form and poetic structure, simply by how you choose to lay the words out on the page. Think carefully about how best to represent the text visually. Where should the line breaks fall? Where should each stanza end? What criteria do we use to make these decisions?

Consider the first few lines of "The Star-Spangled Banner." If we transcribe the text so that each line matches one measure of music, it looks like this:

O,
Say can you
See by the

Dawn's early
Light? What so
Proudly we
Hailed at the
Twilight's last
Gleaming? Whose broad
Stripes and bright
Stars through the
Perilous fight, O'er the . . .

This is a perfectly accurate transcription of the words, using a logical process for parsing the text into individual lines (one line per musical measure). But obviously, this is not a particularly helpful visual display of the text for most purposes!

There are several different criteria you can use to determine the form and layout of the text. These include the singer's phrasing, the accompaniment's phrasing, the grammatical construction of the text, and the rhyme scheme.

Using rhyme scheme and the singer's phrasing, we might transcribe the same lyrics as follows:

Text	*Rhyme Scheme*
O, say can you see by the dawn's early light	a
What so proudly we hailed at the twilight's last gleaming?	b
Whose broad stripes and bright stars through the perilous fight,	a
O'er the ramparts we watched were so gallantly streaming?	b
And the rockets' red *glare*, the bombs bursting in *air*,	c
Gave proof through the night that our flag was still there.	c
Oh, say does that star-spangled banner yet wave	d
O'er the land of the free and the home of the brave?	d

Notice that with this transcription, there is an internal rhyme in line 5 (glare/air) that is not shown on our layout. Because every verse of the song preserves that rhyme, we might want to make note of that as a feature of the text's form.

Whatever criteria you use to transcribe the text, make sure that you apply it consistently throughout the recording. Otherwise, you might think the form is different for different verses, when in fact you merely transcribed the piece inconsistently.

Translating a Foreign Language

If the text is in a foreign language, there are two different kinds of translations that will be useful. The first is a word-by-word translation. This type is not particularly prosaic, nor does it necessarily make the overall narrative easy to understand, but it does make it possible to see how individual, important words are portrayed musically (consider our discussions of word painting throughout the book). The second type of translation is a regular, prosaic, and grammatically correct translation, which conveys the meaning of the text but may not match individual words to their English equivalents. This type is very useful for understanding the overall text, its meaning, and its emotional impact. For many classical pieces, professional translations of both types are readily available in reference books and online. Locate both for your recording. This excerpt from Schubert's "Erlkönig" (chapter 27) illustrates the difference: use the word-by-word translation to examine how the composer sets individual words, and the prosaic one for larger gestures and moods.

Text:	*"Mein Sohn, was birgst du so bang dein Gesicht?"*
Word-by-word:	my son why hide you so fearfully your face?
Prosaic:	My son, why do you hide your face so anxiously?
Text:	*"Siehst, Vater, du den Erkkönig nicht?"*
Word-by-word:	see father you the Erl-King not
Prosaic:	Do you not see, father, the Erlking?

Add Timings and Rhyme Scheme

Finally, listen to the piece again and add the timings from the recording to the transcription of the lyrics, along with the rhyme scheme for each stanza or verse and any additional observations. You don't have to record the time for every line as is shown here, but the more detailed your chart, the easier it will be to complete the project. Separate the text into sections if you can tell where the divisions occur. This creates a working time-chart on which you will assemble your notes as you continue to work.

Sample: Working Time-Chart for Text, Schubert, "Erlkönig" (chapter 27)

Time	German Original	Rhyme Scheme	English Translation	Notes
0:24	Wer reitet so spät durch Nacht und Wind?	a	**Narrator:** Who rides so late through night and wind?	0:00–0:22 Dramatic instrumental intro First verse
	Es ist der Vater mit seinem Kind;	a	It is the father with his child;	
	er hat den Knaben wohl in dem Arm,	b	He holds the boy fast in his arms	
	er fasst ihn sicher, er hält ihn warm.	b	He holds him tightly, he holds him warm.	
0:56	Mein Sohn, was birgst du so bang dein Gesicht?	c	**Father:** My son, why do you hide your face so anxiously?	0:50–0:56 brief instrumental interlude Second verse
	Siehst, Vater, du den Erlkönig nicht?	c	**Son:** Do you not see, father, the Erlking?	
	den Erlkönig mit Kron und Schweif?	d	The Erlking with crown and train?	
	Mein Sohn, es ist ein Nebelstreif.	d	**Father:** My son, it is a streak of clouds.	
1:28	"Du liebes Kind, komm, geh mit mir!	e	**The Elf-King:** "You dear child, come with me!	1:25–28; quiet instruments Third verse Softer/gentler accompaniment
	gar schöne Spiele spiel' ich mit dir;	e	Such wonderful games I will play with you;	
	manch bunte Blumen sind an dem Strand,	f	So many beautiful flowers are on the shore,	
	meine Mutter hat manch gülden Gewand."	f	My mother has many a golden robe."	

Doing the Research

You have now listened to the recording several times, you have notes on your first responses to the piece, and if your recording has words, you have a working time-chart with a transcription of the text and translation. The next step toward generating an analysis and listening guide is to do some research beyond the recording itself.

This research has two purposes:

1. Produce a short introduction (probably a few paragraphs) that explains the historical and social context of the work. Tell how, when, and where the piece was created, by whom, and for what purpose. Were there any interesting circumstances surrounding its composition or recording?
2. Provide interpretive clues about the key elements of the recording. Are the features typical of a particular genre or style? Are there aspects of the recording that are signatures of one composer or songwriter? Is there an unusual sound in the recording that you can identify through extra research? Is there some aspect of the performance that arises from a particular tradition?

Who Are the Creators?

The recording that you heard was the product of many individuals' artistic efforts. The composer is of particular importance, but so are the performers, and possibly the conductor, producer(s), and arranger(s). There also may be earlier works on which the composer drew, and the composers of those works are also creators of the music.

Start by identifying the composer (or songwriter). For popular music, this information is often available in the liner notes of the recording or on the artist's Web site. For contemporary works that are still under copyright, you can locate the copyright owner at *http://www .copyright.gov*. The copyright owner might not be the composer, however. Keep in mind, too, that in casual conversation, fans often talk about a popular song's singer as the primary creator but seldom mention the songwriter. For instance, "Hound Dog" is known as an "Elvis Presley tune," even though it was actually written by Jerry Lieber and Mike Stoller, two professional songwriters.

For contemporary works, the composer will likely have registered with one of the major performing rights organizations (ASCAP or BMI), and their Web sites also contain public search engines that list songwriters.

Regardless of who wrote the piece or when the composer lived, the actual sounds you heard on the recording are the artistic output of the performer(s). You can often find out who played on the recording from liner notes or the artist's own Web site. Basic music- information sites like *http://www.allmusic.com* list additional information about individual recordings.

The record's producer may have also contributed to the sound of the recording in substantial ways. In contemporary popular music, the producer may have made decisions about the arrangement (or even hired an arranger to work on the piece), instrumentation, form, and timbre. In these ways, the producer is also a contributing member of the creative musical team. Even the record company may have some bearing on the sound of the recording, so consider extending your research into that area as well.

Once you have your list of creators, you can research their biographies, their time periods, and the social and historical context of their work. When, how, where, and why was the work created? What styles are the creators known for? Is this work typical or atypical of their other output? For instance, the year that Gottschalk wrote *Union* (chapter 33) provides insight into his quotations of patriotic tunes; the low-frequency resonance for which the Bomb Squad is famous is a key feature of Public Enemy's "Fight the Power" (chapter 58); Stravinsky's orchestrations (how the instruments in the orchestra are used and combined) are a product of his Russian musical education (chapter 43); research on the compositional principles of a fugue will help explain the texture that we hear in Bach's Fugue in G Minor (chapter 13).

To Wiki or Not to Wiki: Basic Research Suggestions

Today, most students begin their research on the Internet with public encyclopedia sites (like Wikipedia). Your professor may have specific guidelines about what kinds of resources you should use in your coursework, but some general principles are worth considering.

To gather reliable information about composers, performers, and producers, a researcher needs reference materials that (1) explain the sources of their information and (2) clearly identify the author and the type of information he or she provides. Modern Internet sites sometimes lack those two features: articles and posts are not signed (or are signed only with user names), and sources are not cited. There is nothing inherently wrong with conducting research on Internet sites, but sources and citations are essential for the integrity and accuracy of your own work.

Ask your librarian for information on searching online databases of newspapers, scholarly journals, and digitized reference materials (like the *New Grove Dictionary of Music and Musicians*). Most of those resources are available electronically, and they provide a valuable pool of information with clear authorship and citations.

Once you locate several sources that address your topic, evaluate each source. Do you know who wrote it, and what the author's credentials are? Do you know if the source was checked for accuracy and edited carefully by someone knowledgeable? Most importantly, does the source tell you where the author got his or her information in the first place (via footnotes, a bibliography, a citation list, or other details)? Take a moment to evaluate the range of sources you have, too. Ideally, you should have several different types, such as encyclopedia articles, biographies, liner notes, newspaper articles, and published interviews with the creators.

Remember that it is essential to cite your sources in your listening guide and analysis and to make sure you refrain from plagiarizing the prose or ideas of another author. Keep a complete bibliography and discography as you work with the essential information on each source.

Using Your Sources

The information you are searching for will vary depending on your recording—you are primarily trying to understand the features of one unique piece and performance. A few general suggestions, however, will be relevant to most recordings:

- **Genre.** It is likely that you already knew something about your recording's genre before you listened to it. The modern music industry relies heavily on genre classifications for marketing music, so the section of the record store where you bought the album or the subheading on the digital download site identified the music's genre. However, these marketing classifications (like "Latin Jazz" or "Hip Hop" or "Classical String Quartet") are merely a starting point for exploring musical genre.

As you research your piece, consider what characteristics of instrumentation, style, groove, and historical context best describe it. What other pieces are similar in these ways to your recording? This method of determining genre is more refined than merely adopting the marketing category. Once you have a good description of the recording's genre, you can do additional research on it, including looking at similarities and differences between your piece and others. If the piece is called a "rondo," what does that mean? If the piece was recorded by a band whose style is described as "western swing," what will you likely be hearing in instrumentation, form, tempo, rhythm, and melody?

- **Politics and conflict.** Look for historical context that might explain motivations and meanings in the piece. Was the work written during a time of war? Was the work commissioned for a political event? Did the composer talk about the intended social meaning of his or her work? This information will allow you to interpret various types of references or quotations you might hear in your recording.
- **Setting and context.** Knowing when and where the piece was created (both composed and recorded) can be extremely useful in making sense of the sounds you hear. Was it a live concert setting? Why was this particular work on the program? Was it created in a digital studio? Was it performed on historical instruments? Any of this information will have direct relevance for understanding the timbres, sound effects, and sonic artifacts that you hear.
- **Versions and comparisons.** Are there multiple interpretations, recordings, or versions of your piece? If so, what are the features of your recording that are shared with other versions, and what is different? This information will likely merge with data you have found on the setting and context of the work, but it will also be useful in differentiating between the piece as composed and the particular recording you are studying.

Data Collection: Melody, Rhythm, Harmony

Now it's time to return to your recording. In a scientific experiment, researchers often collect lots of data first, and then decide what data is relevant to the question they are investigating. Music analysts do the same thing: they gather lots of detailed information about a piece first and decide what analytic narrative to construct afterward. Your first listening impressions were helpful in guiding your research, but now you need to assemble charts containing detailed data for each element. After you have collected this data, you can select the few elements that are most salient in this recording and use them to create an informative listening guide.

Melody

Using your original notes, both from your first listening and from your research, as a guide, ask what the most significant aspects of the melody are. Does the melody quote other music, or is it borrowed from another source? Does the melody help define the recording's genre? If so, how? Is it noteworthy for its leaps, its connectedness, its simplicity, its complexity?

If your recording has words, you already have a working time-chart for the piece to which you can add. If not, you need to create one. In one column, list various time-points in the piece where identifiable moments occur. You will add additional time-points as necessary when you add columns for each element.

On your working time-chart, add a new column for melody. Listen to the piece carefully and add information to the time-chart about the melody and melodic phrases that stand out. Provide descriptive adjectives (smooth, leapy, choppy, lyrical), but also keep track of melodies that repeat and places where distinctive new melodies enter. For instance, look at chapter 52, Bernstein's "Tonight" from *West Side Story*, and notice how the Listening Guide's "Melody" column describes the melody at various points as choppy or lyrical, then identifies the return of an earlier melody.

Rhythm

Rhythm is one of the strongest ways composers have of conveying the genre and style of their piece. It is also an opportunity to refer to other works, styles, and historical periods. Finally, rhythm connects a piece to various performance traditions and, at times, dancing. Listen to your recording again, and add a column to your working time-chart that describes any rhythmic features that stand out. For instance, look at chapter 45, Joplin's *Maple Leaf Rag*, and notice how the Listening Guide's rhythm column records times when there is a lot of syncopation and other times when there is very little. In chapter 51, Copland's "Hoe-Down" from *Rodeo,* the rhythm column describes where the meter is clearly discernible and where it is obscured. In Web Bonus Chapter 5, Mahalia Jackson's "It Don't Cost Very Much," the rhythm column describes where the tempo of the song changes.

Harmony

Now listen to the recording again, concentrating only on the harmony. Some students assume that unless they can read musical notation or play an instrument, they can't hear chord progressions accurately, and therefore they neglect thinking about harmony. Harmony, however, is one of the most expressive musical elements and deserves close attention, even if you must rely on descriptive prose, not musical terminology or notation, to discuss it.

Add a column to your working time-chart for harmony. Ask yourself the following questions as you fill in that column:

1. **General characteristics.** Is the harmony primarily tonal, with a clear tonic and resolution, or atonal and abstract? Start with those very general descriptions, and then add as much more detail as you can. For instance, do individual sections of the music sound finished or unfinished (half or full cadences)? Are there noticeable uses of minor chords? Are the harmonies simple (only a few notes per chord) or complex (jazz harmonies with many notes per chord)?
2. **Harmonic rhythm.** Do the chords change at the same rate throughout the piece, or are there sections where the chords are more static or more active? This information may help you define the form of the piece later, as well as being useful for describing the harmony.
3. **Harmonic references.** Is the chord progression one you recognize, either from another piece (like Duke Ellington's use of the chords from "I Got Rhythm," chapter 47), or from a common pattern (like the progression from Pachelbel's Canon that shows up in doo-wop, and specifically in "Please, Mr. Postman," chapter 56), or tradition (like the 12-bar blues used by both Robert Johnson and Chuck Berry, chapters 46 and 55).
4. **Noteworthy chords.** Are there individual moments in the piece where an unusual chord catches your attention? For instance, in "Good Vibrations," (chapter 57), at 2:54 there is a chord that is so distinctive that it encapsulates the whole piece. Are there specific moments in the piece where there is a dramatic and unexpected change in the harmony, either through a modulation or a sudden insertion of a new chord? For instance, in "God Save the Queen" (Web Bonus Chapter 6), the guitar solo at 2:02 begins with chords that are completely different than the few chords that have been used up to that point in the piece.

Data Collection: Texture, Timbre, Dynamics

While melody, rhythm, and harmony often remain essentially the same from one recording of a piece to another, especially in classical music, texture, timbre, and dynamics are all features of a particular arrangement and performance. These elements are heavily determined by the instrumentation and by decisions that the producers of the recording make. Consider the differences between Bach's Fugue in G Minor as played on the organ and as played in Stokowski's orchestral arrangement (see chapter 13). We also heard several different arrangements of Handel's "Hallelujah Chorus," including synthesizer, rock, and gospel versions (chapter 18). With the Brahms symphony (chapter 37), we noted differences in performances with different conductors. With Robert Johnson's "Terraplane Blues," (chapter 46), the timbre is unique to both his performance and the recording technology of the 1930s.

Furthermore, these three elements are heavily interrelated. A change in dynamics will produce a change in timbre; a change in texture will change both dynamics and timbre. All three elements are determined heavily by the piece's instrumentation. These elements are often altered through the studio recording, mixing, and mastering process as well, so the role of the producer may be key.

What Is the Instrumentation?

Both timbre and texture are affected by what instruments are used on the recording and the way the instruments relate to each other. It is sometimes difficult to find out what instruments are used on a particular recording, especially when synthesizers and effects boxes can alter the basic timbre of most instruments until they are almost unrecognizable. Begin by listing instruments you can identify by ear. Then search the album's liner notes for additional information, and comb through your research materials for more clues.

What Role Did the Producer Play?

Texture, timbre, and dynamics may be heavily determined by the producer of the recording. Check the record label and your research notes to see if the record label, choice of studio, or choice of producer may have affected the sound of the recording. Review the ideas presented in the "Reading Labels" box in chapter 56 on the roles of different labels and producers in defining musical styles and recognizable sounds. For instance, in the 1960s, Phil Spector used a technique known as "wall of sound," layering and doubling many instruments in the studio in a monophonic recording, to create thick, blended textures and Motown records all shared a particular timbral similarity.

Dynamics: Special Considerations

At the most basic level, you control the dynamics of your recording when you adjust the volume level on your audio system. Thus, discussions of dynamics are most useful when they center on contrast, not absolutes. However, even the contrasts between loud and soft may have been digitally altered on your recording: many contemporary recordings of popular music use a process called "audio compression," in which the loud and soft parts of a performance are adjusted electronically so that the amplitude of the sound waves remains essentially constant throughout the entire song. This technique is used in lots of Top-40 popular music, and most commercial CDs of popular music feature extensive audio compression.

It is not so different from what many people do while watching a movie on television—turning up the volume during moments of quiet dialogue, and turning down the volume during the chase scenes (or during the advertisements, which are often broadcast at a higher decibel level) to achieve a more consistent volume. As you listen to any recording, you can adjust the volume as you like so that the actual amplitude of the sound waves coming out of the speakers or headphones varies very little. But, as the graphic below shows, an instrument played loudly has a different timbre (literally, a different shape of sound wave) than the same instrument played softly, and we recognize those differences, regardless of the volume. For instance, we explored how the dynamics levels of piano and pianissimo in Debussy's *Voiles* (chapter 39) affect the timbre that we hear from the instrument. Dynamics are thus inextricably linked to texture, timbre, and the studio process, in any recording.

(loud synthesizer)   (soft synthesizer)

Wave forms of a "loud synthesizer" and a "soft synthesizer," showing the difference in wave form (timbre) rather than just amplitude (volume).

Add to Your Chart

As you did for the elements of melody, rhythm, and harmony, return to the recording and add columns for texture, timbre, and dynamics to the working time-chart (practically speaking, you may wish to make a separate chart for these elements so you don't have to manage as many columns on one page).

- **Texture.** Remember that the basic categories are monophonic (one melody line), homophonic (one melody plus accompaniment), and polyphonic (multiple melodies).
- **Timbre.** Descriptions should account for both the instrumentation and the style in which those instruments are played. For instance, a singer's vocal timbre in a classical aria may be sweet, clear, resonant, and full, whereas in a gospel song, it may be raspy, gravelly, brassy, and approximating speech.
- **Dynamics.** Descriptions of dynamics should focus on changes that occur within the piece.

Form

Musical form encapsulates the way we, as listeners, comprehend a piece of music as it is played. Our cognitive processes like to break the piece into a handful of units (usually between three and seven), which we perceive as the basic formal structure. Very rarely is a piece through-composed without any identifiable formal divisions. In most compositions, large units are composed of smaller units. It is often possible to identify several layers in a piece's form, beginning with large sections and moving through phrases down to very small patterns.

To map out the form of your piece, ask yourself the following questions as you listen:

- Are there contrasting sections? How many?
- How often does each section return?

A Few Commonly Used Forms in Popular Music

Form	Description	Example
Strophic form	Many verses	Robert Johnson, "Terraplane Blues," chapter 46
12-bar blues	A special case of strophic form where each verse follows the chord progression and phrase structure for 12-bar blues.	Chuck Berry, "School Day," chapter 55
Standard Song Form	**AABA**, commonly used in Tin Pan Alley songs, Broadway songs, and some jazz, country, and ballad recordings.	Common examples (not in our book) include George Gershwin's "I Got Rhythm" and Hank William's "Your Cheatin' Heart"
Verse-chorus form	Any combination of verses and a chorus, typically arranged in patterns like CVCVC, VVCVC, or VVCVCVC.	Marvelettes, "Please, Mr. Postman," chapter 56
Verse-chorus-bridge form	A song with verses and a chorus, with a contrasting section placed approximately two-thirds of the way through the song. Typical patterns include VCVCBC and VCVCBVC.	This form is extremely common in contemporary songwriting, although none of the chapters in our book illustrate it. Well-known songs in this form include "Long Time Gone" (Dixie Chicks) and "Since U Been Gone" (Kelly Clarkson).

- How long is each section?
- What function does each section appear to serve? For instance, does one section provide a sudden contrast, or does a different section sound open-ended and inconclusive?
- How does each section relate to the text, if there is one?
- Within each section, do you hear music that is repeated? Are there pairs of lines or phrases, for example? What patterns can you detect for smaller units? (You will have already made some discoveries, based on your data-gathering for the other elements.)

Incorporate your observations about the form into the time-chart. You may find it easiest to begin by labeling sections with letters—identify all the sections that share similar melodies and harmonies with the letter **A**, then use **B** for the next set, etc. Based on all you have learned, you may then find certain patterns emerge for which there are official terms.

With the basic historical context and genre of your recording in mind, you can review chapters in the textbook and your research materials to figure out what the likely musical forms might be. Do any of these match the way you have mapped out your piece? See the tables displayed here for some common forms. Remember that most pieces employ a musical form that is typical for their genres, but those forms often show up with slight variations. Forms are models that describe commonalities, not rules that prescribe how composers write music. Therefore, don't be surprised if your recording does not match a strict musical form exactly.

Once you have determined the form of your piece, refine your working time-chart to include appropriate terminology and/or letters. There are many examples for your review

A Few Commonly Used Forms in Classical Music

Form	Description	Example
Sectional form	Discrete sections that do not follow any particular order, although they may be governed by the form of the text.	Byrd, "Sing Joyfully," chapter 7
Simple binary form	**AB**	Tielman Susato, *Moorish Dance*, web bonus chapter 1
Rounded binary form	**ABA'**, where the first section returns at the end of the piece, but in some variant and usually shorter.	Haydn, Symphony no. 102, third movement, chapter 21
Ternary form	**ABA**, where each of the three sections is relatively independent and complete on its own.	Beethoven, Symphony no. 5, third movement, chapter 26
Theme and variations	A short musical work is repeated several times, with embellishments and modifications on each variation.	Haydn, String Quartet op. 76 no. 3, second movement, chapter 19
Ritornello form	A short segment, played by the full orchestra, returns over and over again, separated by short segments played by a soloist.	Vivaldi, *Four Seasons*: "Winter," first movement, chapter 14
Rondo form	**ABACA** or **ABACABA**, where the first section (the "refrain") keeps coming back, alternating with different contrasting sections.	Tailleferre, Concertino for Harp and Orchestra, fourth movement, web bonus chapter 4
Sonata form	Exposition-Development-Recapitulation, where the exposition and recapitulation each consist of two contrasting themes.	Mozart, Symphony no. 40, first movement, chapter 22
Through-composed, text-based, or programmatic	Repetition and contrast are based on a narrative, either the lyrics for the piece or an external text. With through-composed pieces, there is no structural repetition.	William Grant Still, "A Black Pierrot," chapter 50

throughout this book. Nearly every piece has its form mapped out in the Listening Guide, although it is entirely likely that the form of your piece will be slightly different.

Word-Music Relationships

Now that you have explored the rhythm, melody, harmony, texture, timbre, dynamics, and form of your recording in detail, go back to your transcription (and translations, if relevant) of the text and focus on how the music paints the picture of the text. Sometimes this happens quite literally; such as with "skip" in Thomas Weelkes, "Since Robin Hood" (chapter 6) Sometimes the music creates characters or sets scenes; for instance, in Franz Schubert's

Listening Guide

Time	Melody	Rhythm	Harmony

"Erlkönig" (chapter 27), the pianist's rhythm becomes the thundering of the horse's hooves, and the three different registers of the same voice become the father, the son, and the Erlking.

As you have seen in several chapters, the poetic meter and form also relate to musical meter and form, sometimes in complex and interesting ways. For instance, in "Fight the Power" (chapter 58), Public Enemy's lyrics are almost continually in syncopated rhythms, creating the rhythmic contrast between the hip-hop beat and the text; in "School Day" (chapter 55), Chuck Berry's lyrics have the same poetic meter as the music's shuffle groove.

This part of the analysis is where your creativity and insight come into play. Students often ask how they know when a word-music relationship is too far-fetched. If the musical evidence and cultural context makes the relationship plausible, then you should include it in your analysis. Most students err by sticking only to literal interpretations of the text and explicit musical connections, but the metaphoric interpretations and nuanced musical connections are often far more revealing about a piece's artistry.

Add one final column to your working time-chart for word-music relationships. Make entries for word painting, for gestures that link the text to other elements, for relationships between the text's rhythms and the musical setting, and for any interpretations of the text that inform the way you hear the music.

Creating Your Own Analysis

You now have gathered all the necessary data to construct a listening guide and analysis of your recording. Your goal is to assemble your findings into an interesting narrative that explains the most significant elements. Not everything you have explored should be in your final project.

Go back to the very first impressions that you wrote down about your recording. Based on those impressions and your subsequent findings about all the elements, select the three or four elements that you believe capture the essence of your recording. Using those elements as the focus of your analysis, combine your working time-chart with your research notes to produce the following:

1. A short introduction to the piece: its place, time, style, genre, and motivating factors
2. A discussion of the key elements in your recording and how those elements relate to the historical and cultural contexts of your piece.
3. A listening guide that presents the information on the elements you chose from your working time-chart in a clear and organized structure

To write the discussion of your recording's key elements, ask yourself what information from your research explains the features that you noted on your working time-chart. Then explore how the historical, social, and cultural contexts of the work might relate to its specific musical elements. For instance, Duke Ellington's "Cotton Tail" (chapter 47) used a swing rhythm and a shout chorus. Those musical features related to the way that fans danced to the music. The Sex Pistols' "God Save the Queen" (Web Bonus Chapter 6) had harsh, ironic musical settings of the text, which reflected the socio-economic conditions from which the band emerged. Ruth Crawford's adventurous use of register and minimalist treatment of pitch reflect her modernist ideology as a composer (chapter 49). Mozart's Symphony no. 40 uses sonata form in its first movement, which identifies the work as a mainstream composition from the Classical Era, when such forms were the norm (chapter 22). Jimi Hendrix's arrangement of "The Star Spangled Banner" ("The Elements of Music") infused the piece with a radical spirit of political protest partly because of where he was when he played it (Woodstock).

When you are finished, your complete project will tell the story of a specific recording by connecting the elements we hear in the music to their historical and cultural connections. The art of an analysis is its ability to inspire the reader to new awareness when listening to a piece of music. Put your complete analysis to the test by playing your recording one final time. As the elements of music come together in the piece, emotion and meaning emerge. How we listen to music can move our senses and sensibilities, and therein lies the power and magic of the art form.

Glossary

a cappella   sung without instrumental accompaniment of any kind.

accompanied recitative   recitative accompanied by the orchestra, as opposed to by basso continuo alone.

acoustics   the science of sound: how it is produced, transmitted, and received.

additive form   a compositional technique in which nothing disappears, but new layers are constantly added.

aleatory music   music composed using elements of chance.

amplitude   the size of a sound wave; determines volume.

anacrusis   a starting note that falls on a beat before the downbeat. Also called a pick-up beat or an upbeat.

anapestic   a poetic meter of short-short-LONG.

antecedent phrase   in periodic phrase structure, an opening phrase, which sets up the consequent phrase to follow.

anthem   an English sacred choral work.

aria   Italian for "air" or "melody"; any lyrical movement or piece for solo voice, usually with some kind of instrumental accompaniment.

art song   a song set to serious poetry, usually for solo voice and piano, in the tradition of the German Lied.

atonal   a style of writing that establishes no harmonic or melodic center of gravity; without a tonic, all notes are of equal weight and significance.

ballad   a poem or song that tells a story.

bar form   a melodic form in which the opening phrase is sung twice and a contrasting phrase follows (**AAB**). Also called song form.

basso continuo   "continuous bass"; a small ensemble, widely used in music of the Baroque, that plays throughout a work and provides an underlying bass line and harmonies. It consists of two instruments: one that can sustain long notes (such as a bass viol, a cello, or a bassoon), and one that can play chords (such as a lute or a harpsichord).

bebop   new jazz style of the late 1940s/early 1950s that developed in response to the popularity of big band music. Bebop is characterized by fast tempos, short bursts of melodic phrases, heavy and unexpected rhythmic accents, and virtuosic soloing.

big band music   a style of jazz popular in the 1930s and 1940s in which instruments were grouped into sections by function, with carefully constructed arrangements. Many of these arrangements featured call-and-response between the sections, often based on repeated, short melodic riffs.

binary form   a musical structure consisting of two repeated halves (**AABB**).

binary song form   a form common in popular song in the early twentieth century. The basic pattern (**AABB**) is 32 bars long, with each of the four sections occupying 8 bars of music.

blue note   a pitch performed flatter (lower) than the standard major scale would indicate; usually blue notes occur as substitutes for the third and seventh (and occasionally the fifth) notes of the standard major scale.

blues   a musical genre derived from African American performance traditions that uses blue notes (flattened pitches) in its melodies and tells first-person stories of hard knocks and love gone wrong.

cadence   a point of arrival signaling the end of a musical unit.

cadenza   in a concerto, an elaborate improvisation by the soloist on themes heard earlier in the movement, with no accompaniment from the orchestra. It occurs near the end of the recapitulation.

call-and-response   a technique in which one musician or group sings or plays an opening motive, and another musician or group sings or plays an answer.

cantata   a type of vocal genre typically sung during a service of worship. In Italian: "that which is sung," as opposed to *sonata*, "that which is played."

chamber music   instrumental music for a small ensemble, with only one player to each part.

character piece   a relatively short work, usually for piano solo, that captures a particular mood ("character").

chorale   a hymn tune.

choral music   vocal music with more than one singer to a part.

chord   three or more notes played or sung at the same moment.

chorus   an ensemble with multiple singers to a part; "chorus" is also the name for the musical number or movement sung by this ensemble. In Baroque opera, the chorus comments on the action and emotions unfolding onstage.

chromatic   a type of harmony or melody that incorporates many more notes than occur naturally in the scale or key area on which a work is based. A chromatic scale is produced by playing all half steps. On the piano, this would mean all adjacent keys—black or white.

coda   Italian for "tail." A section at the end of a musical work or movement that stands outside any formal structure and brings the whole to a close.

comic opera   in Italian, *opera buffa*. A genre that uses many of the same conventions as serious opera—arias, recitatives, ensembles, choruses—but with plots revolving around believable, everyday characters rather than mythical or historical figures.

concerto   an instrumental genre for a soloist (or sometimes more than one soloist) and a larger ensemble.

concerto grosso   Italian for "big concerto"; a concerto with multiple soloists.

conjunct motion   melodic motion of pitches by step.

consequent phrase   in periodic phrase structure, a closing phrase that follows an antecedent phrase and creates a sense of musical completion.

consonance   the sound of notes together that our ear finds naturally right. Like dissonance, consonance is a relative concept that can change over long periods of time.

contrafactum   a work setting new words to an established melody.

counterpoint   a style of writing in which every voice is a melody and all voices work together; from the Latin word *contrapunctum*, or "note-against-note." Counterpoint is basic to polyphonic texture.

cyclic form   a form in which individual movements are linked in some tangible and distinctive way, usually through the use of a common musical idea.

da capo   Italian for "from the head"; a direction to go back and play from the very beginning of the piece.

da capo aria   an aria that opens with two contrasting sections, **A** and **B**; at the end of the **B** section, the singer and orchestra return to the beginning of the **A** section, following the direction in the score of "da capo"—literally, "from the head." When the singer performs this **A** section a second time, he or she embellishes it heavily.

development   the section within a sonata-form movement that thematically and harmonically manipulates ("develops") the movement's themes most intensively.

diatonic scale   a scale consisting of whole and half steps.

disjunct motion   melodic motion of pitches by leap.

dissonance   the sound of notes that clash, either harmonically or melodically, and do not seem to belong together. Dissonance is a relative concept: what was dissonant in one era is later perceived as consonant.

dotted rhythm   consistent alternation between long and short notes.

double   to play or sing the same musical line in multiple voices or on multiple instruments; most often used to describe an instrument playing the same line being sung by a voice.

double-exposition concerto form   a structure based on sonata form but with two expositions, one for the orchestra alone and one for the soloist and orchestra together. It also includes, near the end of the recapitulation, a cadenza for the soloist.

drone bass   a single long note held underneath the melodic line.

drone harmony   a texture in which a melodic instrument plays over a constant repeated pattern of only a few tones.

duple meter   an underlying pattern of rhythm in which each unit (measure) consists of one accented (strong) beat followed by one unaccented (weak) beat (**1**-2 | **1**-2 | **1**-2 | etc.) or some multiple of two (such as four or eight). A unit of four beats per measure, for example, in which the first is the strongest and the third is the next-strongest (**1**-2-**3**-4, **1**-2-**3**-4, **1**-2-**3**-4, etc.), is a type of duple meter.

dynamics the volume of sound, determined by the size (amplitude) of each sound wave.

elide to begin a new line of text and music before the previous one has come to a complete stop.

episode in a fugue, a passage in which the subject is not present.

exposition the section within a sonata-form movement that introduces ("exposes") all of the movement's themes.

expressionism a broad artistic movement that flourished in music, painting, and literature in the early decades of the twentieth century, in which psychological truth took precedence over beauty, and inner emotion took precedence over any sense of external reality.

extramusical referring to an idea outside the sound. This term is used by ethnomusicologists to describe the equivalent of program music, in Western music.

fill in jazz and popular styles, a short, instrumental response between a singer's phrases, or a brief solo occupying a musical gap between sections of a piece.

finale a last movement of a multimovement work.

form the structure of a musical work; the way in which its individual units are put together.

French overture an overture common in French Baroque opera, usually consisting of a slow introduction with dotted rhythms, followed by a fast section frequently employing imitation.

frequency the number of sound-wavelengths in one second.

fugal exposition the opening section of a fugue, in which all the voices enter with the main subject.

fugue a polyphonic work based on a central theme and employing imitation.

full cadence a musical point of arrival that creates a strong sense of closure.

gamelan an Indonesian musical ensemble consisting primarily of a variety of pitched gongs and xylophones. The conductor or leader of the ensemble often plays a double-headed drum.

genre the category of a work, determined by a combination of its performance medium and its social function.

glissando a continuous ("gliding") melodic motion up or down that goes by so fast we almost cannot hear the individual notes.

gospel music religious-themed music that borrows from R&B, blues, and other popular styles in its vocal and instrumental styles.

Gregorian chant monophonic vocal music in the medieval church, designed to project religious texts. So called because it was alleged to have been written mostly by Pope Gregory I, in the late sixth century.

groove in popular and jazz styles, the underlying rhythmic pattern of a song.

ground bass another name for an ostinato in the bass part.

half cadence a point of musical arrival that is not yet closure. If thought of as punctuation, a half cadence is like a comma, whereas a full cadence is like a period.

half step the smallest distance between two adjacent notes on a piano (white or black), such as C–C#.

harmonics further subdivisions of the primary vibration producing a sound, resulting in additional faintly heard pitches.

harmony the sound created by multiple voices playing or singing together.

head in jazz, the main melody of the song.

hemiola a type of syncopation in which patterns of twos occur at the same time as patterns of threes.

heterophonic texture (heterophony) the simultaneous playing or singing of two or more versions of a melody.

hip hop a cultural movement of the late 1970s through the turn of the century that included fashion, dance (break dancing), art (graffiti), and music (rap). Hip hop music is characterized by semi-spoken lyrics that are recited against an accompaniment often consisting of short, repeated melodic fragments set against a heavily rhythmic beat.

hocket a form of polyphony consisting of two or more rhythmically interlocking voices.

homophonic texture (homophony) a musical texture in which a melody is performed with a supporting accompaniment.

homorhythm all instruments playing in the same rhythm.

honky tonk music a country style of the late 1940s/early 1950s that originally developed in the small bars (known as honky tonks) that catered to rural and working-class audiences. Honky tonk is characterized by a small ensemble, usually featuring a vocalist-guitarist, fiddler, steel guitarist, bass player, and sometimes drums. Themes of lost love and the effects of heavy drinking predominate.

hook a short, catchy motive that forms the memorable core of the song.

humanism an early-Renaissance intellectual and cultural movement that explored human interests and values through the pursuit of science, philosophy, literature, painting, sculpture, and music, particularly vocal music.

iambic a poetic meter of short-LONG, short-LONG, short-LONG, short-LONG.

imitation a shortened form of the term "imitative counterpoint": the same theme introduced by different instruments or voices in succession.

imitative counterpoint a particular type of counterpoint in which in which one voice introduces a new theme and is answered ("imitated") by other voices that enter in succession shortly afterward, even as the first voice continues to sing or play.

impressionism an artistic movement focused more on sensations, perceptions, and light than on the direct representation of objects. In music, the term was used by critics of the early twentieth century to describe harmonies, melodies, and forms they considered indistinct.

interlock a technique in which one voice fills the spaces left by another's rests to complete a melodic unit.

intonation in Bahamian rhyme singing, as well as in other African-influenced musical cultures: a melody line consisting of words spoken in tones.

jingju in Chinese, "capital theater." The principal form of opera in China today. Characters are stock types distinguished by singing style, costume, makeup, and role. On stage, there is no scenery, and the action usually takes place in front of a curtain.

key the central note and mode on which a melody or piece is based.

Leitmotif a brief musical phrase or idea connected dramatically to some person, event, or idea in the drama.

Lied (plural Lieder) German for "song." A genre for voice and piano, popular from the late eighteenth century onward, particularly in Germany but in many other countries as well.

madrigal a musical setting of a text in a single strophe (stanza).

major mode a type of scale produced by singing "do-re-mi-fa-so-la-ti-do," or by playing the white keys of the piano between C and C, in which half steps occur between notes 3 and 4 and notes 7 and 8. The sound of the major mode is often described as "bright" or "happy," in contrast to the minor mode.

mazurka A Polish folk dance in triple meter, often with a heavy accent on the second or third beat of each measure.

measure a rhythmic unit, indicated by bar lines in notated music, that presents one complete statement of the meter.

melisma a syllable of text sung to many notes.

melismatic a style of setting a text to music so that there is more than one note per syllable.

melodic motion the movement of pitches within a melody up or down, either by step (conjunct motion) or by leap (disjunct motion).

melody a single line of notes heard in succession as a coherent unit.

metabole a change of pitch level.

meter (of music) an underlying pattern of beats that maintains itself consistently throughout a work. See also "duple meter"; "triple meter."

meter (of poetry) a poem's basic rhythmic unit.

middle entries in a fugue, later entries of the subject, after the exposition.

minimalism in music, a style in which a brief musical idea or group of ideas is repeated and varied incrementally over a long span of time, with a relatively slow rate of change.

minor mode a type of scale produced by playing the white keys on the piano between A and A, in which half steps occur between notes 2 and 3 and notes 5 and 6, but often with the seventh note raised so that a half step also occurs between notes 7 and 8. The sound of the minor mode is often described as "dark" or "sad," in contrast to the major mode.

minuet form a ternary form (**ABA**) in which the opening section, known as the minuet proper (**A**), is followed by a contrasting trio (**B**), which is followed by a repeat of the minuet proper. The minuet is always in triple meter and its individual units—the minuet proper and the trio—are each in binary form.

modernism a spirit that took hold in all the arts, in the early twentieth century, representing a quest for novelty that far exceeded any such drive in the past.

modified strophic form a form in which each strophe is modified musically to fit the text in a particular way.

modulate to move to a different key area. (Noun: "modulation.")

monophonic texture (monophony) a musical texture consisting of a single melodic line.

motet in the Renaissance, a sacred choral work for the Roman Catholic Church.

musical a spoken drama with a substantial amount of singing.

musical appropriation the use or adaptation of a work to serve something other than its original purpose.

nationalism in music, the use of melodies, rhythms, harmonies, or instruments that reflect the musical practices of a particular nation.

neoclassicism a style of composition in the years after World War I that, although distinctly modern, drew on older (particularly eighteenth-century) uses of melody, harmony, rhythm, and form.

nocturne "night piece." Originally a vocal serenade from lover to beloved. Later, an instrumental work that imitates, though its homophonic texture, such a song.

opera a drama sung from beginning to end.

opera buffa Italian for "comic opera"; a genre that uses many of the same conventions as serious opera—arias, recitatives, ensembles, choruses—but with plots revolving around believable, everyday characters rather than mythical or historical figures.

opera seria Italian for "serious opera"; Italian Baroque opera on a serious subject, typically consisting of alternating recitatives and da capo arias.

operetta Italian for "small opera." A nineteenth-century stage work that incorporated both singing and spoken dialogue, typically on a comic, lighthearted, or sentimental subject. A precursor to the American musical.

oral tradition one passed down without the aid of written words or notated music.

oratorio a work musically similar to an opera but not staged, and usually on a sacred topic.

orchestration the manner in which various instruments are assigned to the musical lines.

ostinato a short pattern of notes repeated over and over.

overture a purely instrumental opening movement that introduces a longer work, often for voices (as an opera).

pentatonic scale a scale consisting of five tones.

percussion instrument an instrument that produces sound when it is struck.

periodic phrase structure a musical structure in which antecedent and consequent phrase units make up a larger whole.

phrase a brief musical statement.

pitch the position of a sound on a range from very low to very high, determined by the frequency of its sound waves.

plainchant monophonic vocal music in the medieval church designed to project religious texts.

polyphonic texture (polyphony) a musical texture consisting of multiple lines of equal importance.

polytonality the juxtaposition of two conventional harmonies in a way that creates a new dissonance.

postmodernism a style in music and the other arts, beginning in the mid-twentieth century, in which modern and traditional elements are combined.

powwow an intertribal gathering where Native Americans of mixed tribes express their mutual bond and identity.

program music an instrumental work that is in some way associated with a story, event, or idea.

psychedelia music influenced by the hippie movement of the late 1960s/early 1970s, with its emphasis on mind-expanding drugs, brightly colored fashions, and spiritual and social freedom.

punk popular music of the mid-1970s that originally arose in reaction to the increasingly commercial and corporate rock of the era. Punk emphasized a do-it-yourself (DIY) attitude. Musical or vocal skills were downplayed; lyrics expressed anger at the failings of the economic and social systems. Fashions included torn T-shirts, body piercings, brightly dyed hair, and other "anti-fashion" looks.

raga in the music of India, a mood, color, or musical scale that forms the basis of a musical composition.

ragtime a style of music from the early twentieth century that emphasizes rhythmic syncopation while continuing many of the characteristics of marches, cakewalks, two-steps, and popular songs from the late nineteenth century.

recapitulation the third and final section within a sonata-form movement, in which all the themes presented in the exposition return, all in the tonic key.

recitative a style of singing that lies somewhere between lyrical song and speech; also, the operatic number that is sung in this style.

refrain the same words with the same basic melody recurring at regular intervals over the course of a work.

register the range of a pitch or series of pitches, usually described as high, middle, or low.

rhyme in a Bahamian rhyme singing group, the lead singer.

rhythm the ordering of music through time.

ritornello Italian for "little return"; name for the statement and return of the full ensemble, in a work alternating between the orchestra and soloist or soloists.

ritornello principle the formal design of alternating ritornello and solo sections.

rock 'n' roll a style of music that evolved in the mid-1950s out of R&B and country styles. Rock 'n' roll is teenage music, expressing the concerns of mid-century young people (romance, cars, dancing). The typical rock group consisted of electric guitar, bass, and drums, with the occasional addition of piano or saxophone.

rondo form a form in which an opening theme (**A**) returns repeatedly over the course of the movement, interspersed with contrasting ideas (**B**, **C**, etc.). An example of the resulting pattern would be **ABACA**.

rounded binary form a binary form in which the opening idea returns in the tonic key about halfway through the second section, "rounding out" the form.

sample to record music or sound from an existing album.

scale a series of notes that provide the essential pitch building blocks of a melody.

scenario the story line of a ballet.

scherzo in Italian, "joke." A musical scherzo is a lighthearted movement in a fast tempo and in triple meter, similar in form to the minuet.

section in a musical ensemble, a group of instruments or voices with similar timbres or roles.

sectional form a form in which each verse or half verse receives its own material (for example, **ABCD**).

sequence a short musical motive that repeats at successively higher or lower pitches.

serialism a style of writing in which notes are drawn not from a scale, but from a predetermined series of notes. Serial composition flourished between ca. 1920 and 1980. See also "twelve-tone composition."

shuffle groove (or, shuffle rhythm) a mid-tempo rhythmic pattern, typically in quadruple meter, in which each beat is subdivided into three pulses.

sonata a type of instrumental genre; literally, a work that is played, as opposed to sung ("cantata").

sonata da camera in the Baroque period, a "chamber" sonata, to be performed for entertainment in the home.

sonata da chiesa in the Baroque period, a "church" sonata, to be performed during sacred services to provide devotional music.

sonata form a musical structure consisting of an exposition, development, and recapitulation, allowing for the presentation, development, and resolution of multiple themes within a single movement. Sonata form was widely used throughout the Classical Era and the nineteenth century.

sound wave the vibration through air that produces sound.

Sprechstimme in German, "speech-voice." A style of singing halfway between speech and lyrical song, in which the singer hits precise pitches and then allows them to tail off, rather than sustaining them, as in lyrical singing.

standard song form a common form for the choruses of "standards" or popular hits of the 1920s, 1930s, and 1940s. It consists of 32 measures divided into four phrases in the pattern **AABA**.

stanza a verse of poetry, or the music corresponding to that verse (see also "strophe").

stop time a kind of musical punctuation between sections, in which the instruments that provide the basic accompaniment strike a single note on a downbeat of a measure together, then remain silent for the rest of the measure.

string instrument   an instrument that produces sound when a taut string is plucked or stroked with a bow.

strophe   a verse of poetry, or the music corresponding to that verse (see also "stanza").

subject   the central theme of a fugue.

suite   a series of individual dance movements, typically in a variety of types such as minuets, gavottes, and gigues, and a variety of characters such as fast vs. slow, lively vs. stately, duple vs. triple.

surrogate speech   the use of musical tones as a replacement for words.

swing   a rhythmic pattern of long and short notes approximating a two-to-one ratio, but varying from piece to piece and performer to performer.

swing music   the name given generally to the popular jazz of the 1930s and 1940s that prominently featured a swing rhythm.

syllabic   a style of setting a text to music so that there is one note per syllable.

syncopation   a type of rhythm in which the notes run against the regular pulse of the musical meter, with accents on beats other than the ones usually accented.

syncretism   the combination of different forms of belief and practice.

tag   in popular styles, a closing section that relies on extensive repetition of a short motive.

tempo rubato   in Italian, "robbed time." Subtle changes of tempo (speeding up and slowing down) applied by the performer, with expressive intent.

ternary form   a form consisting of three parts, labeled **ABA**.

terraced   having a melody that moves up or down through a series of stages, remaining in one general area a while before moving to the next.

texture   the number and general relationship of musical lines or voices to one another.

theme and variations form   a form in which a theme is presented and then altered in some way—through harmony, melody, texture, dynamics, or some combination of these—in a succession of individual variations.

through-composed   a form in which each section has its own music, with very little or no repetition between sections.

timbre   the character or quality of a sound.

tonal   a style of writing that establishes a central note (the tonic) as a harmonic and melodic center of gravity, which in turn creates the potential for a strong sense of resolution and closure.

tonality   a system of organizing pitches (both melodies and harmonies) around a central note, as opposed to atonality, a system with no tonal center. See also "tonal" and "atonal."

tonic   the note that establishes a key, based on its distinctive relationship with a particular set of harmonies or other notes in the underlying scale. Also, the chord based on the first scale degree.

tremolo   rapid repeated notes that produce a shivering or trembling sound.

trio sonata   a work for two high-ranged instruments (such as two violins, or two oboes, or two flutes) and basso continuo.

trio-sonata texture   a texture consisting of three main voices: two in the soprano range and one in the bass (the basso continuo).

triple meter   an underlying pattern of rhythm in which each unit (measure) consists of one accented (strong) beat followed by two unaccented (weak) beats (**1**-2-3, **1**-2-3, **1**-2-3, etc.).

trochaic   a poetic meter of LONG-short, LONG-short, etc.

tutti   Italian for "all": the full ensemble (as opposed to a soloist).

twelve-bar blues   a common model for blues songs, in which each verse consists of three lines of text over twelve measures of music. Each line receives four measures in a predetermined harmonic pattern using chords built on the first, fourth, and fifth scale degrees.

twelve-tone composition   a type of serial composition in which twentieth-century composers manipulated a series ("row") consisting of all twelve notes of the chromatic scale, not repeating any one of these notes until all other eleven had been sounded, thereby effectively avoiding any sense of tonality.

unison   more than one performer playing or singing the same pitch or pitches at the same time.

vamp   to repeat a basic section of the music in order to fill time or provide a basis for improvisation.

verse-chorus form   one of the simplest models in popular music. The chorus contains the main idea of the song, usually incorporating the title as well. When the chorus returns, it keeps the same text and music. Verses advance the plot, using the same music each time but different texts. Verse-chorus form can use any combination of verses and choruses, although the last unit will always be a chorus.

vocables   meaningless sung syllables that take the place of song lyrics.

voicing   the spacing of the individual notes in a chord.

wavelength   the distance between peaks of sound waves.

waza   an ensemble performed by the Berta people of the Blue Nile Province in southern Sudan, consisting of twelve trumpets made from gourds.

whole step   two half steps. On the piano, a whole step skips exactly one key, white or black.

whole-tone scale   a scale with only whole steps, no half steps; this eliminates any sense of a tonal center.

wind instrument   an instrument that produces sound when air passes through it.

word-music relationships   the way a text influences our hearing of the music, and the way music affects our perception of the words.

word painting   music that imitates, describes, or conjures images of the text being sung.

Index

AAB, 151
AABA, 417
ABA, 34, 45, 191, 193, 244, 325, 335, 355
ABAA, 39
ABABA, 335
ABBB, 105
A cappella choral music, 67
  "Forward!" (C. Schumann), 243, 279–283
  number of singers in, 283
Accompanied recitative, 221
Acoustics
  of melody, 6
  of timbre, 13
Adam, Adolph, 389
Adams, John, 101, 131, 469
Additive form, 452–453
Affect, 82, 97
African music
  Greetings by Aba Musa! (Berta waza)
    347, 390–395
  "Marriage Celebration Song" (Pygmies-
    Mbuti), 86, 102–107
A la Par, second movement ("Guaguancó")
    (León), 349
  form, 502, 504
  harmony, 502, 504
  listening guide, 506
  rhythm, 502, 504
  timbre, 502, 503–504
Aleatory music
  defined, 460
  4'33" (Cage), 348, 459–463
Alfonso el Sabio
  background of, 44, 47
  genre and key concepts, 21
  Songs to the Virgin Mary no. 249, "He
    Who Gladly Serves" ("Aquel que de
    volontade"), 19, 21, 43–46
Alsop, Marin, 166, 332
American Bandstand, 475
American music
  See also Twentieth century, music in
  Civil War, 295
  Dvořák on, 338
  of the West, 444–449
American Society of Composers, Authors, and
    Publishers (ASCAP), 404
Amplitude, 6
Anacrusis, 141, 472
Anapestic meter, 62
Antecedent phrases, 177
Anthems, "Sing Joyfully" (Byrd), 50, 53, 66–70
Arcadelt, Jacob, 65
Aria, 95, 96, 109, 157, 236
Armstrong, Louis, 12, 393
Art song
  "Black Pierrot, A" from *Songs of
    Separation* (Still), 348, 438–442
  defined, 438

Atonal, 369–371, 373, 376, 433
Audience riots, 387, 389
Austrian zither, 187

Bach, Carl Philipp Emanuel, 123, 182, 218
Bach, Johann Christian, 123, 182, 218
Bach, Johann Sebastian
  background and works of, 123, 124, 138,
    147, 153
  Brandenburg Concerto no. 2 in F Major,
    84–85, 86, 132–137
  Cantata no. 140 ("Awake, A Voice Calls
    to Us"), 83–84, 87, 148–155
  Fugue in G Minor, 83, 87, 117–122
  genre and key concepts, 86, 87
  trio-sonata texture, 111
Bach, Wilhelm Friedemann, 123
Bagley, E. E., 8
Bahamian music, 78
  "My Lord Help Me to Pray," 53, 73–76
Ballad, "Erlkönig" (Schubert), 242, 252–259
Ballata, 38–41
Ballet
  composers, 389
  "Hoe-Down" from *Rodeo* (Copland), 348,
    444–448
  Rite of Spring, The (Stravinsky), 343,
    347, 380–389
Ballets Russes, 381, 387, 388
Bar form, 151
Baroque era
  background information, 81–82
  churches, splendor of, 83–84
  timeline, 87
Baroque music
  Brandenburg Concerto no. 2 in F Major
    (Bach), 84–85, 86, 132–137
  bridge between Renaissance and, 94
  Cantata no. 140 ("Awake, A Voice Calls
    to Us") (Bach), 83–84, 87, 148–155
  chamber music, 116
  compared to classical music, 235
  compared to Renaissance music, 167
  concertos, 138
  Dido and Aeneas (Purcell), 86, 95–100
  female composers, 114, 115
  Fugue in G Minor (Bach), 83, 87, 117–122
  Messiah (Handel), 84, 87, 153, 156–166
  opera, emergence of, 81, 83, 84
  oratorio, 81, 84
  organ, 124
  Orpheus (Monteverdi), 86, 88–93
  "Revenge" (Strozzi), 84, 87, 109–115
  sacred, 153
  suite composers, 147
  summary of, 168
  virtuoso singers, 84–85
  Water Music (Handel), 82, 86, 139–145
  "Winter" from *Four Seasons* (Vivaldi),
    84, 86, 125–129
Baroque song, "Revenge" (Strozzi), 84, 87,
    109–115
Bartók, Béla, 373
Basie, Count, 423
Basso continuo, 89, 93, 116, 137, 197
Battle sounds, 59

Beach, Amy Marcy Cheney, 277
Beach Boys, 58, 64
  background and works of, 492
  genre and key concepts, 348
  "Good Vibrations," 348, 486–493
Beatles, the, 469, 485, 493
Beaumarchais, Pierre Augustin Caron de, 220
Bebop
  origin of term, 425, 429
  Ornithology (Parker), 347, 424–429
Beethoven, Ludwig van
  background and works of, 250–251, 278,
    292
  genre and key concepts, 242
  program music, 131
  symphonies by, 245, 251
  Symphony no. 5 in C Minor, op. 67 (Fifth
    Symphony), 242, 244–249
"Behold, Spring" ("Ecco la Primavera")
    (Landini), 19, 21
  form, 37, 39
  listening guide, 41
  melody, 37, 39
  rhythm, 37, 39
  texture, 37, 38
  word-music relationships, 37, 40
Bellini, Vincenzo, works of, 272, 323
Bembo, Antonia, 82
Benson, Jodi, 423
Berg, Alban, 373, 379
Berlioz, Hector, 131
  background and works of, 266, 271–272
  genre and key concepts, 242
  Symphonie fantastique, 237, 242,
    267–272
Bernstein, Elmer, 449
Bernstein, Leonard
  background and works of, 266, 332, 458
  genre and key concepts, 348
  "Tonight" from *West Side Story*, 348,
    450–457
Berry, Chuck
  background and works of, 473
  genre and key concepts, 349
  "School Day," 349, 470–477
Binary form, 140, 141, 236, WB1-4
Bird sounds, 59
Bizet, Georges, 323
"Black Pierrot, A" from *Songs of Separation*
    (Still), 348
  form, 438, 440
  harmony, 438, 439–440
  listening guide, 442
  melody, 438, 440
Blondie, WB6-9
Blue-note melody, 406
Blues
  development of, 406
  singers, 406, 413
  "Terraplane Blues" (Johnson), 346,
    405–413
  12-bar blues form, 407–409, 411, 474
  whites as musicians, 411
Boccaccio, Giovanni, 19, 38
Bonds, Margaret, 443
Book of the Courtier, The (Castiglione), 51

Borodin, Alexander, 339
Brahms, Johannes
  background and works of, 278, 292, 327,
    339
  genre and key concepts, 243
  Symphony no. 4 in E Minor, op. 98, 243,
    324–331
Brandenburg Concerto no. 2 in F Major
    (Bach), 84–85, 86
  form, 132, 133
  listening guide, 136–137
  texture, 132, 133–134
  timbre, 132, 133
Britten, Benjamin, 101
Broadcast Music Inc. (BMI), 404
Broschi, Carlo, 84
Brown, James, 501
Buddhist chants, 30
Burleigh, Henry T., 443
Buxtehude, Dietrich, 124
Byrd, Bobby, 501
Byrd, William
  background and works of, 63, 71
  genre and key concepts, 53
  Psalmes, Sonets, & Songs, 72
  "Sing Joyfully," 50, 53, 66–70
Byrds, 493

Caccini, Francesca, 115
Cadences, 2, 39
  elided, 68
  full, 177
  half, 177
Cadenza, 213, 217
Cage, John
  background and works of, 461–462
  4'33", 348, 459–463
  genre and key concepts, 348
Call-and-response, 74, 77, 104, 105, 333, 334,
    416, 474
Callas, Maria, 314
Calypso, 78
Cantata, 116, 148
Cantata no. 140 ("Awake, A Voice Calls to Us")
    (Bach), 83–84, 87
  form, 148, 151, 152
  listening guide, 154–155
  melody, 148, 150, 152
  texture, 148, 151
  timbre, 148, 149
Canterbury Tales (Chaucer), 19
Caribbean
  music of the, 78
  "My Lord Help Me to Pray" (Rhyming
    Singers of the Bahamas), 53, 73–76
  reggae, 74
Carissimi, Giacomo, 153
Carreño, Teresa, 277
Cars, The, WB6-9
Castiglione, Baldassare, 51
Castrati, 85
Cavalli, Pier Francesco, 94, 115
Chabrier, Emmanuel, 339
Chamber music
  Baroque composers, 116
  nineteenth century, 278

number of performers, 113
Piano Trio, op. 11 (Fanny Mendelssohn), 243, 273–276
"Revenge" (Strozzi), 84, 87, 109–115
use of term, 109–110
Chamber music, classical
composers of, 182
String Quartet in C Major, op. 76 (Haydn), 173, 174–181
Chaminade, Cecile, 277
Chants
Native American, 31–36
types of, 30
Chaplin, Charlie, 402
Character pieces, 285–286
Charpentier, Marc-Antoine, 101
Chaucer, Geoffrey, 19
Cherry Blossom (Ikuta-Ryu), 173
form, 183, 186
listening guide, 188–189
melody, 183, 185–186
texture, 183, 186
timbre, 183, 185
Chinese music
composers of music for zither and dulcimer, 187
cultural revolution, impact of, 229, 231
jingju, 229–233
masks, wearing of, 233
opera, *Reunion, The* (Lisa Lu and the Beijing Opera Co.), 173, 228–233
recordings of traditional, 234
Choirs, all-male, 69
Chopin, Frédéric
background and works of, 289
genre and key concepts, 243
Mazurka in B-flat Major, op. 7, no. 1, 241, 243, 285–290
Chorale, 149
Chord, 8
Chords, The, 103, 485
Chorus, 95, 96, 97
"Hallelujah," 159, 161, 164–165, 166
Christian plainchants, 30
Chromatic harmony, 439–440
Chromaticism, 317–318
Cipriano de Rore, 65
Civil War, music in the, 295
Clark, Dick, 475
Classical era
background information, 169–170
nature, role of, 172
new economy and, 171–172
revolutions, 171, 190
timeline, 173
Classical music
compared to Baroque music, 235
compared to nineteenth-century music, 340
concerts and concert manners, 199
keyboard and chamber music composers, 182
Marriage of Figaro, The (Mozart), 171, 172, 173, 219–227
operas, 171
periodic phrase structure, 177–178
Piano Concerto in A Major, K. 488 (Mozart), 172, 173, 210–217
string quartet, development of, 170
String Quartet in C Major, op. 76 (Haydn), 173, 174–181
summary of, 236

Symphony no. 40 in G Minor, K. 550 (Mozart), 173, 200–207
Symphony no. 102 in B-flat Major (Haydn), 172, 173, 190–197
Coasters, The, 485
Coda, 203
Coldplay, 58
Coleman, Ornette, 430
Coltrane, John, 44, 430
"Columbine" from *Pierrot lunaire* (Schoenberg), 347
harmony, 374, 376
listening guide, 378
timbre, 374, 375–376
word-music relationships, 374, 376
Comic opera, *Marriage of Figaro, The* (Mozart), 171, 172, 173, 219–227
Concertino for Harp and Orchestra, finale (Tailleferre), 347, WB4-1 to WB4-5
Concerto, 81
Baroque composers, 138
defined, 125
"Winter" from *Four Seasons* (Vivaldi), 84, 86, 125–129
Concerto, classical
composers of, 218
Piano Concerto in A Major, K. 488 (Mozart), 172, 173, 210–217
Concerto grosso
Brandenburg Concerto no. 2 in F Major (Bach), 84–85, 86, 132–137
defined, 132
Concert overture, Overture to A Midsummer Night's Dream (Mendelssohn), 242, 260–266
Concerts and concert manners, classical music and, 199
Concert Variations on "The Star-Spangled Banner" (Paine), 11
Conductors
famous, 332
role of, 326
Confrey, Zez, 404
Conjunct motion, 3
Consequent phrase, 177
Consonance, 370
Contrafactum, 182
Contrast, 335, 416
Copland, Aaron
background and works of, 447, 449
genre and key concepts, 348
"Hoe-Down" from *Rodeo*, 348, 444–448
Corelli, Arcangelo
trio-sonata texture, 111
works of, 116, 138
Cornetto, WB1-2
Costello, Elvis, 272, WB6-9
Cotton Club, 423
Cotton Tail (Ellington), 344, 346
form, 414, 416–417, 416–417
harmony, 414, 415
listening guide, 418–421
rhythm, 414, 415, 416
texture, 414, 416
Counterpoint, 55, WB2-2
imitative, 67–68, 119
Couperin, François, 147
Cowell, Henry, 463
Crawford, Ruth
background and works of, 432, 435, 437
genre and key concepts, 347

Piano Study in Mixed Accents, 347, 431–436
"Cricket, The" (Josquin des Prez), 52, 53
form, 54, 56
listening guide, 58
texture, 54, 55
word-music relationships, 54, 56
Cyclic form, 247

Dance music
See also Ballet; Rock 'n' roll
hoe-down, 446
hornpipe, 141
Lindy hop, 423
Mazurka in B-flat Major, op. 7, no. 1 (Chopin), 241, 243, 285–290
medieval, 19
minuet form, 192–193
Moorish Dance (Susato), 52, 53, WB1-1 to WB1-6
Morris, 61
Rigaudon, 140–145
swing, 414–423
Davis, Miles, 423, 425, 430
Dead Kennedys, WB6-9
Debussy, Claude
background and works of, 358
genre and key concepts, 346
Voiles, 345, 346, 350–357
Decameron (Boccaccio), 19, 38
Declamatory melody, 307
"Dedication" from *Crouching Tiger, Hidden Dragon* (Dun), 349, 508–511
De Falla, Manuel, 359
Delalande, Michel-Richard, 153
Delibes, Leo, 389
Delius, Frederick, 359
De Mille, Agnes, 446, 448
Development, 201
Diaghilev, Sergei, 381, 387, 388
Diatonic scale, 354–355
Dido and Aeneas (Purcell), 86
form, 95, 96–97
listening guide, 98–99
word-music relationships, 95, 97
Disjunct motion, 3
Dissonance, 370
Divas, 314
Domino, Fats, 475
Doo wop, 103
Dorsey, Thomas A., WB5-5
Double exposition concerto form, 213–214, 236
Drone bass, 45, 286
Drone harmony, 302
Drums, 46
Dulcimers, 187
Dun, Tan
background and works of, 512
"Farewell" from *Crouching Tiger, Hidden Dragon*, 349, 508–511
genre and key concepts, 349
Duple meter, 8, 26, 62
Dvořák, Antonin
background and works of, 337–338
genre and key concepts, 243
"Music in America," 338
String Quartet in F Major, op. 96, 243, 333–336
Dynamics, 1, 6, 12–13
classical, 190, 191–192
nineteenth-century, 244, 246
twentieth-century, 350, 354

Eagle Dance (San Ildefonso Indians), 21
background of, 32
form, 31, 33
listening guide, 35
melody, 31, 34
texture, 31, 32
word-music relationships, 31, 33
Elgar, Edward, 272
Elided cadences, 68
Elizabeth I, 71
Ellington, Duke
background and works of, 414–415, 422
Cotton Tail, 344, 346, 414–421
genre and key concepts, 346
English, operas in, 101, 323
Enlightenment, Age of, 169
Episodes, 119, 134
"Erlkönig" (Schubert), 242
form, 252, 253
listening guide, 256–259
word-music relationships, 252, 253–254
Experimental music
composers of the twentieth century, 463
4'33" (Cage), 348, 459–463
Exposition, 201
Expressionism, 374–375, 379
Extramusical, 185

Falsetto, 58, 64
Fantasia, 122
"Farewell" from *Crouching Tiger, Hidden Dragon* (Dun), 349
listening guide, 511
melody, 508, 509–510
texture, 508, 510
timbre, 508, 509
Farinelli, 84
Farrenc, Louise, 277
Females
Alsop, Marin, 166, 332
blues singers, 406, 413
composers of the nineteenth century, 277
composers of the twentieth century, 437, 443
conductors, 332
Crawford, Ruth, 347, 431–437
divas, 314
Jackson, Mahalia, 349, WB5-1 to WB5-7
jazz singers, 423, 430
León, Tania, 349, 502–506
Marvelettes, 348, 478–484
Mendelssohn, Fanny, 243, 273–276
playing the part of boys, 227
Schumann, Clara, 243, 279–283
Strozzi, Barbara, 84, 87, 109–115
Tailleferre, Germaine, 347, WB4-1 to WB4-5
Fifth Symphony. *See* Symphony no. 5 in C Minor, op. 67 (Beethoven)
"Fight the Power" (Public Enemy), 348
form, 494, 495–496
listening guide, 498–499
musical references in, 501
rhythm, 494, 496–497
timbre, 494, 495
word-music relationships, 494, 497
Fill, 408, 426
Film, expressionist, 379
Film music
composers of, 513
"Farewell" from *Crouching Tiger, Hidden Dragon* (Dun), 349, 508–511
soundtracks, creating, 513

Finale, 193
Firenze, Lorenzo da, 42
Fitzgerald, Ella, 423, 430
Folk music/melody, 445
Form
    additive, 452–453
    bar, 151
    Baroque, 95, 96–97, 109, 110–111, 125,
      126–127, 132, 133, 139, 140, 148, 151,
      152, 156, 157, 159
    binary, 140, 141, 236, WB1-4
    classical, 174, 190, 191–192, 193, 200,
      201–203, 210, 213–214, 219, 222
    defined, 1, 14
    double exposition concerto, 213–214, 236
    medieval, 31, 33, 37, 39, 43, 45, 49
    minuet form, 192–193, 236
    modified strophic form, 253, 275
    nineteenth-century, 244, 252, 253, 260,
      262, 267, 269, 285, 288, 324, 325,
      333, 335
    Renaissance, 54, 56, 66, 68
    ritornello principle, 126–127, 132, 133, 152
    rondo, 193, 236, 444, 446
    rounded binary, 192, 201
    scherzo, 335
    sonata, 191, 201–203, 205, 207, 213, 236,
      244, 262
    song, 151
    ternary, 56, 192, 244, 325, WB3-1,
      WB3-2
    theme and variations form, 178, 186, 236,
      324, 325
    through-composed, 384, 440
    32-bar standard song, 416–417
    12-bar blues, 407–409, 411, 474
    twentieth-century, 350, 355, 397,
      400–401, 405, 407–409, 411, 414,
      416–417, 424, 426–427, 431, 434,
      438, 440, 444, 446, 450, 452–453,
      464, 466, 470, 474, 478, 480–481,
      486, 489, 494, 495–496, 502, 504
Fortepiano, 182
"Forward!" (C. Schumann), 243
    listening guide, 282–283
    melody, 279, 280
    timbre, 279, 280
    word-music relationships, 279, 280
4'33" (Cage), 348, 459–463
Fourth Symphony. *See* Symphony no. 4 in E
    Minor, op. 98 (Brahms)
French opera, 323
French overture, 96
Frequency, 6
Fugal exposition, 119, 134
Fugue
    Brandenburg Concerto no. 2 in F Major
      (Bach), 84–85, 86, 132–137
    defined, 117
    Fugue in G Minor (Bach), 83, 87
    listening guide, 121–122
    melody, 117, 119
    texture, 117, 119–120
    timbre, 117, 118–119

Gabriel, Peter, 469
Gabrieli, Giovanni, 94
Gaeng School Song (Hmong), 87, WB2-1 to
    WB2-7
Gamelan music, 351
    composers, 367
    gamelan gong kebyar, 346, 360–366

listening guide, 364–366
    musical instruments, 360–361
Gaye, Marvin, 10, 58
Geisha, 184
Genre, 1, 15–16
George I, 82
George II, 161
German opera, 323
Gershwin, George, 131, 415
Gibson, Tweedie, 74
Gillespie, Dizzy, 423
Girl Crazy, 415
Glass, breaking by singers, 313
Glass, Philip, 101
    background and works of, 363, 367, 468
    genre and key concepts, 349
    "Knee Play 1" from *Einstein on the
      Beach*, 349, 464–467
Glissando, WB4-3, WB5-3
Gluck, Christoph Willibald, 223
"God Save the Queen" (Sex Pistols), 348,
    WB6-1 to WB6-8
Goethe, Johann Wolfgang, 252
Goldsmith, Jerry, 513
"Good Vibrations" (Beach Boys), 348
    form, 486, 489
    harmony, 486, 487–488
    listening guide, 490–491
    texture, 486, 488
    timbre, 486, 489
Gordy, Berry, 485
Gospel
    "It Don't Cost Very Much" (Jackson), 349,
      WB5-1 to WB5-7
    recordings of, WB5-8
Gottschalk, Louis Moreau, 9
    background and works of, 297
    genre and key concepts, 242
    Union, 242, 293–296
Green, Bruce, 74
Green, Clifton, 74
Greetings by Aba Musa! (Berta Waza), 347
    harmony, 390, 391, 392
    listening guide, 394–395
    melody, 390, 391
    rhythm, 390, 392
    texture, 390, 392
Gregorian chant, 17, 24
Gregory, pope, 17, 20, 24
Griffes, Charles, 359
Grofé, Ferde, 449
Groove, 416
Ground bass/ground, 96
Guaguancó, *A la Par*, second movement
    (León), 349, 502–506

"Hail, Columbia," 293, 294, 296
Haley and His Comets, Bill, 475
"Hallelujah" chorus, 161, 164–165, 166
Hammond, Laurens, 121
Handel, George Frideric
    background and works of, 138, 146, 147
    genre and key concepts, 86, 87
    Messiah, 84, 87, 153, 156–166
    operas, 101
    trio-sonata texture, 111
    Water Music, 82, 86, 139–145
Harlem Renaissance, 423
Harmony
    atonal versus tonal, 369–371, 373, 376,
      433
    chromatic, 439–440

classical, 200, 203
    defined, 1, 8–9, 49
    drone, 302
    illegal, 10
    polytonal, 381–382, 391, 393
    twentieth-century, 350, 354–355, 368,
      369–371, 374, 376, 380, 381–382,
      414, 415, 431, 433, 438, 439–440,
      464, 465, 478, 480, 486, 487–488,
      502, 504
    vocal, 485
Harrison, George, 301, 303
Harrison, Lou, 363, 367
Haydn, Joseph, 169
    background and works of, 179, 182,
      198–199, 218
    concertos by, 218
    genre and key concepts, 173
    String Quartet in C Major, op. 76, 173,
      174–181
    symphonies by, 199
    Symphony no. 102 in B-flat Major, 172,
      173, 190–197
Head, 417
Hemiola, 399
Hendrix, Jimi, 10, 190
Hermann, Bernard, 513
Heterophony, 43, 45, 104, 231
"He Who Gladly Serves" ("Aquel que de
    volontade") (Alfonso el Sabio), 19, 21
    form, 43, 45
    listening guide, 45
    timbre, 43, 44–45
    texture, 43, 45
Higdon, Jennifer, 437
Hildegard von Bingen
    background and works of, 27
    debate over music, 30
    genre and key concepts, 21
    notation, 20
    Play of Virtues (Ordo virtutum), 18, 21,
      22–29, 51
Hiller, Lejaren, 463
Hindemith, Paul, WB4-6
Hindu chants, 30
Hip hop
    elements, 501
    "Fight the Power" (Public Enemy), 348,
      494–501
Hmong, *Gaeng School Song*, 87, WB2-1 to
    WB2-7
Hockets, 104, 107
"Hoe-Down" from *Rodeo* (Copland), 348
    applications of, 447
    form, 444, 446
    listening guide, 448
    melody, 444, 445
    rhythm, 444, 446
    timbre, 444, 445–446
Hoffman, E.T.A., 238
Holly, Buddy, 475
Holmés, Augusta, 277
Homophony, 10, 45
    Baroque, 81, 88, 89–90, 151, 158, 160
    classical, 177
    nineteenth-century, 285, 286
Homorhythm, 363
Hook, 479
Horne, Marilyn, 314
Hornpipe, 141
Horns, 396
House, Son, 413

Hughes, Langston, 442
Humanism, 50

Iambic meter, 61–62
Imitative counterpoint (imitation), 67–68, 96,
    119
Impressionism, 351, 359
Improvisation, 415, 425, 427
Indian music, *Raga Sindhi-Bhairavi*
    (Shankar), 242, 299–305
Instrumental music
    "He Who Gladly Serves" ("Aquel que de
      volontade") (Alfonso el Sabio), 19,
      21, 43–46
    of the Middle Ages, 21, 48, 49
    Moorish Dance (Susato), 52, 53, WB1-1
      to WB1-6
    of the Renaissance, 53, WB1-8
Instruments
    See also type of
    pitched versus non-pitched, 503–504
    used in the Middle Ages, 48
    used in the Renaissance, 51
Interlocking voices, 104
Interval, 3–4
Intonations, 75
Islamic chants, 30
Italian madrigals, 65
Italian operas, 225, 323
"It Don't Cost Very Much" (Jackson), 349,
    WB5-1 to WB5-7
Ives, Charles
    background and works of, 373
    genre and key concepts, 346
    Unanswered Question, The, 346, 368–372

Jackson, Mahalia
    background and works of, WB5-5
    genre and key concepts, 349
    "It Don't Cost Very Much," 349, WB5-1
      to WB5-7
Jacquet de la Guerre, Elisabeth, 82, 115, 147
Jamaican music, 78
Japan, geisha in, 184
Japanese music
    composers, 187
    koto and *Cherry Blossom* (Ikuta-Ryu),
      173, 183–189
Jarrett, Keith, 443
Javanese music, gamelan, 351, 360–366
Jazz
    composers and performers, 406, 413, 423,
      430
    Cotton Tail (Ellington), 344, 346, 414–421
    development of, 415
    Ornithology (Parker), 347, 424–429
    polytonality in, 393
    swing, 414–423
Jefferson Airplane, 493
Jewish chants, 30
Jingju, 229–233
Johnson, James P., 404
Johnson, Robert
    background and works of, 405–406,
      412–413
    genre and key concepts, 346
    "Terraplane Blues," 346, 405–413
Jones, Quincy, 166
Joplin, Scott
    background and works of, 401, 404
    genre and key concepts, 346
    Maple Leaf Rag, 346, 397–402

Josquin des Prez
  background and works of, 57
  "The Cricket," 52, 53, 54–59
  genre and key concepts, 53

Kahn, Ali Akbar, 303
Kemp, William, 60–61
Key area, 126, 129
Keyboard music, composers of, 182
Keys, 5
"Knee Play 1" from *Einstein on the Beach* (Glass), 349
  form, 464, 466
  harmony, 464, 465
  listening guide, 467
  timbre, 464, 465
Korngold, Erich Wolfgang, 513
Koto, *Cherry Blossom* (Ikuta-Ryu), 173, 183–189
Křenek, Ernst, 379
Kronos Quartet, 339
Kuhnau, Johann, 131

Landini, Francesco
  background and works of, 40
  "Behold, Spring" ("Ecco la Primavera"), 19, 21, 37–41
  genre and key concepts, 21
  notation, 20
Lang, Fritz, 379
Langfang, Mei, 230
Laotian music, *Gaeng School Song* (Hmong), 87, WB2-1 to WB2-7
Larsen, Libby, 437
La Traviata (Verdi), 242
  listening guide, 310–313
  melody, 306, 307
  word-music relationships, 306, 307–308
León, Tania
  A la Par, second movement ("Guaguancó"), 349, 502–506
  background and works of, 505
  genre and key concepts, 349
Leonarda, Isabella, 115
Letimotifs, 316–319, 321
Lewis, Jerry Lee, 475
Lewis, Meade "Lux," 404
Lied (lieder), "Erlkönig" (Schubert), 242, 252–259
Liszt, Franz, 239, 266, 292, 298
Little Richard, 475
Lord of the Rings (Tolkien), 319
Lorenzo da Ponte, 220, 225
Loudness, 272
Louis XIV, 82
Lu, Lisa, *Reunion, The*, 173, 228–233
Lully, Jean-Baptiste, 82, 101
Luther, Martin, "A Mighty Fortress Is Our God," 50, 72, 153
Luzzaschi, Luzzasco, 65
Lyrical melody, 307

Machaut, Guillaume de, 42
Madrigals
  composers of Italian, 65
  "Since Robin Hood" (Weelkes), 52, 53, 60–64
Major mode, 5
Manhattan Transfer, 485
Mannheim Steamroller, 166
Manuscripts, producing medieval, 42
Mao Zedong, 229, 231

Maple Leaf Rag (Joplin), 346
  form, 397, 400–401
  listening guide, 402
  melody, 397, 399–400
  recording of, 403
  rhythm, 397, 398–399
Marais, Marin, 116, 131
Marenzio, Lucca, 65
Marley, Bob, 74
Marlowe, Christopher, 51
"Marriage Celebration Song" (Pygmies-Mbuti), 86
  form, 102, 105, 222
  listening guide, 106–107
  rhythm, 102, 105
  texture, 102, 104–105
Marriage of Figaro, The (Mozart), 171, 172, 173
  form, 219
  listening guide, 224–227
  melody, 219, 221
  word-music relationships, 219, 220–221
Martinez, Marianne, 218
Marvelettes
  formation of, 478, 484
  genre and key concepts, 348
  "Please, Mr. Postman," 348, 478–484
Masses, 42, 67, 153
Mathis, Johnny, 166
Mazurka in B-flat Major, op. 7, no. 1 (Chopin), 241, 243
  form, 285, 286
  listening guide, 290
  melody, 285, 286–288
  rhythm, 285, 286
  texture, 285, 286
Mbuti Pygmies. *See* Pygmies (Mbuti)
McFerrin, Bobby, 501
Measure, 7
Melisma (melismatic), 25–26, 40, 49
Melodic motion, 3
Melody
  acoustics of, 6
  Baroque, 109, 110, 117, 119, 148, 150, 152, 156, 158, 159–160
  blue notes, 406
  classical, 174, 177–178, 200, 203–204, 210, 211–213, 219, 221
  components of, 2–6
  declamatory, 307
  defined, 1, 2
  intonations, 75
  lyrical, 307
  medieval, 22, 24–25, 31, 34, 37, 39, 49
  nineteenth-century, 273, 275, 279, 280, 285, 286–288, 293, 294, 306, 307, 333, 334–335
  terraced, 31, 34
  twentieth-century, 350, 352–353, 380, 382, 397, 399–400, 405, 406, 424, 426, 431, 434, 438, 440, 445, 450, 451–452, 508, 509–510
  virtuosic, 307
Mendelssohn, Fanny
  background and works of, 275
  genre and key concepts, 243
  Piano Trio, op. 11, 243, 273–276
Mendelssohn, Felix
  background and works of, 263, 272, 278
  genre and key concepts, 242
  Overture to A Midsummer Night's Dream, 242, 260–266

Messiah (Handel), 84, 87, 153
  Christmastime and, 165
  form, 156, 157, 159
  "Hallelujah" chorus, 159, 161, 164–165, 166
  listening guide, 162–165
  melody, 156, 158, 159–160
  texture, 156, 158, 160–161
  timbre, 156, 159, 161
  title of, 165
  word-music relationships, 156, 158
Metabole, 230
Meter
  anapestic, 62
  defined, 7, 61
  duple, 8, 26, 62
  iambic, 61–62
  triple, 7, 39, 60, 62
  trochaic, 62, 274
Metronome, 291
Middle Ages
  background information, 17
  timeline, 21
Middle Ages, music in
  "Behold, Spring" ("Ecco la Primavera") (Landini), 19, 21, 37–41
  for dancing, 19
  Eagle Dance (San Ildefonso Indians), 21, 31–36
  for entertainment, 18–19
  "He Who Gladly Serves" ("Aquel que de volontade") (Alfonso el Sabio), 19, 21, 43–46
  instrumental, 48
  oral and written transmittal of, 20, 42
  Play of Virtues (Ordo virtutum) (Hildegard von Bingen), 18, 21, 22–29
  sacred, 18
  summary of, 49, 79
Middle entries, 119, 134
Midsummer Night's dream, A (Shakespeare), *Overture* to A Midsummer Night's Dream (Mendelssohn), 242, 260–266
Milhaud, Darius, WB4-6
Minimalism
  composers, 469
  defined, 465
  "Knee Play 1" from *Einstein on the Beach* (Glass), 349, 464–467
Minor mode, 5
Minuet form, 192–193, 236
Modified strophic form, 253, 275
Modulate, 133, 140
Modulation, 140, 207, WB3-2
Monk, Thelonious, 272
Monkey sounds, 59
Monophony, 10, 22, 24, 31, 32, 45, 49, 160–161, 433
Monteverdi, Claudio, 65
  background and works of, 91
  genre and key concepts, 86
  Orpheus, 86, 88–93
  reasons for turning down a job offer in Mantua, 94
Moondog (Louis Thomas Hardin), 463
Moorish Dance (Susato), 52, 53, WB1-1 to WB1-6
Morality plays, 23–24
Morricone, Enrico, 449
Morris dance, 61
Morton, Jelly Roll, 404
Motet, 67, 153

Motown
  composers and performers, 484
  formation of, 485
  "Please, Mr. Postman" (Marvelettes), 348, 478–484
Mozart, Leopold, 208, 209
Mozart, Maria Anna ("Nannerl"), 209
Mozart, Wolfgang Amadeus, 169
  background and works of, 182, 208–209, 214, 218, 223
  concertos by, 218
  as a conductor, 217
  Der Messias, 166
  genre and key concepts, 173
  improvisation, 217
  Marriage of Figaro, The, 171, 172, 173, 219–227
  music of, played on modern instruments, 215
  operas by, 223
  Piano Concerto in A Major, K. 488, 172, 173, 210–217
  symphonies by, 209
  Symphony no. 40 in G Minor, K. 550, 173, 200–207
Musgrave, Thea, 101, 437
Musical appropriation, 182
Musicals
  defined, 451
  description of some, 458
  "Tonight" from West Side Story (Bernstein), 348, 450–457
Musicians as spies, 65
"My Lord Help Me to Pray" (Rhyming Singers of the Bahamas), 53
  form, 73
  listening guide, 76–77
  melody, 73, 75
  texture, 73, 74
  word-music relationships, 73, 75

National Emblem (Bagley), 8
Nationalism, 240–241, 286, 294, 339, 341
Native American music, 336
  San Ildefonso Indians, *Eagle Dance*, 21, 31–35
Neoclassicism
  composers, WB4-6
  Concertino for Harp and Orchestra, finale (Tailleferre), 347, WB4-1 to WB4-5
Netrebko, Anna, 314
Nineteenth century
  background information, 237
  nationalism, 240–241, 286, 294, 339, 341
  Romanticism, 237, 238–239
  timeline, 243
  transportation, impact of, 241
Nineteenth century, music in
  chamber music, 278
  Civil War, 295
  compared to classical music, 340
  compared to twentieth-century music, 514
  "Dedication" (R. Schumann), 243, WB3-1 to WB3-7
  "Erlkönig" (Schubert), 242, 252–259
  female composers, list of, 277
  "Forward!" (C. Schumann), 243, 279–283
  La Traviata (Verdi), 242, 306–313
  Mazurka in B-flat Major, op. 7, no. 1 (Chopin), 241, 243, 285–290
  opera, 323

Overture to A Midsummer Night's Dream
    (Felix Mendelssohn), 242, 260–266
piano music, list of composers and music,
    292
pianos, mass production of, 239
Piano Trio, op. 11 (Fanny Mendelssohn),
    243, 273–276
politics and role of, 240–241, 284
String Quartet in F Major, op. 96
    (Dvořiák), 243, 333–336
summary of, 341
Symphonie fantastique (Berlioz), 237,
    242, 267–272
Symphony no. 4 in E Minor, op. 98
    (Brahms), 243, 324–331
Symphony no. 5 in C Minor, op. 67
    (Beethoven), 242, 244–249
Union (Gottschalk), 242, 293–296
Valkyrie, The (Wagner), 243, 315–321
virtuosos, 298
Notes, 2
'N SYNC, 485

Octave, 3
Oliveros, Pauline, 437
Opera buffa, *Marriage of Figaro, The*
    (Mozart), 171, 172, 173, 219–227
Operas
    amplification of, 313
    classical, 223
    divas, 314
    in Italian, 225
    "Knee Play 1" from *Einstein on the
        Beach* (Glass), 349, 464–467
    La Traviata (Verdi), 242, 306–313
    Marriage of Figaro, The (Mozart), 171,
        172, 173, 219–227
    nineteenth-century composers, 323
    Reunion, The (Lisa Lu and the Beijing
        Opera Co.), 173, 228–233
    Valkyrie, The (Wagner), 243, 315–321
Operas, Baroque
    composers, list of, 101
    Dido and Aeneas (Purcell), 86,
        95–100
    emergence of, 81, 83, 84
    in English, 101
    oratorio compared to, 157
    Orpheus (Monteverdi), 86, 88–93
Operas, Chinese
    jingju, 229–233
    Reunion, The (Lisa Lu and the Beijing
        Opera Co.), 173, 228–233
Operettas, 451
Oral traditions, "Marriage Celebration Song"
    (Pygmies-Mbuti), 86, 102–108
Oratorio, 81, 84, 153
    compared to opera, 157
    Messiah (Handel), 84, 87, 156–166
Orchestra
    classical, 236
    growth of, 341, 383
    section, 416
Orchestration, 142, 268, 326
Organs, 118–119
    Baroque composers, 124
    airflow, 121
Organum, 38
Ornithology (Parker), 347
    form, 424, 426–427
    listening guide, 428–429
    melody, 424, 426

texture, 424, 426
timbre, 424, 425
Orpheus (Monteverdi), 86
    listening guide, 92–93
    texture, 88, 89–90
    word-music relationships, 88, 90
Ostinatos, 96, 466
    Dido and Aeneas (Purcell), 86, 95–100
    gamelan gong kebyar, 361, 363
    "Marriage Celebration Song" (Pygmies-
        Mbuti), 86, 102–108
    rhythms, 382–383
Overture, 95, 96
Overture to A Midsummer Night's Dream
    (Mendelssohn), 242
    form, 260, 262
    listening guide, 264–265
    word-music relationships, 260, 261–262

Pachelbel, Johann, 116
Paderewski, Ignacy Jan, 298
Paganini, Nicolo, 298
Paine, John Knowles, 11
Palestrina, Giovanni Pierluigi da, 67, 72
Parker, Charlie
    background and works of, 427, 430
    genre and key concepts, 347
    Ornithology, 347, 424–429
Partch, Harry, 463
Pentatonic scales, 186, 189, 230, 233, 334, 382
Percussion ensemble, *A la Par*, second
    movement ("Guaguancó") (León),
    349, 502–506
Percussion instruments, 43
Periodic phrase structure, 177–178, 236
Perotin, 38, 42
Phrases, 2
Piano Concerto in A Major, K. 488 (Mozart),
    172, 173
    double exposition concerto form,
        213–214
    form, 210, 213–214
    listening guide, 216–217
    melody, 210, 211–213
    recordings of, 215
    timbre, 210, 211
Piano, solo
    Piano Study in Mixed Accents
        (Crawford), 347, 431–436
    Union (Gottschalk), 242, 293–296
    Voiles (Debussy), 345, 346, 350–357
Pianos
    mass production of, 239
    Mazurka in B-flat Major, op. 7, no. 1
        (Chopin), 241, 243, 285–290
    nineteenth-century music and composers,
        292
Piano Study in Mixed Accents (Crawford),
    347
    form, 431, 434
    harmony, 431, 433
    listening guide, 436
    melody, 431, 434
    rhythm, 431, 432
    texture, 431, 433
Piano Trio, op. 11 (Fanny Mendelssohn),
    243
    listening guide, 275–276
    melody, 273, 275
    timbre, 273, 274
    word-music relationships, 273, 274
Pink Floyd, 493

Pitch, 6
Plainchant, 17, 20, 29
    Play of Virtues (Ordo virtutum)
        (Hildegard von Bingen), 18, 21,
        22–29
Play of Virtues (Ordo virtutum) (Hildegard
    von Bingen), 18, 21, 51
    listening guide, 28–29
    melody, 22, 24–25
    as a morality play, 23–24
    rhythm, 22, 26
    texture, 22, 24
    word-music relationships, 22, 25–26
"Please, Mr. Postman" (Marvelettes), 348
    form, 478, 480–481
    harmony, 478, 480
    listening guide, 482–483
    timbre, 478, 479–480
Politics, music and, 240–241, 284
Polyphony, 231
    Baroque, 160, 161
    call-and-response, 74, 77
    classical, 177
    defined, 10–11
    Middle Ages, 22, 38, 42, 49
    Renaissance, 54, 55, 60, 61, 67–68
Polytonal harmony, 381–382
Polytonality, 382, 391, 393
Porter, Cole, 266
Postmodernism
    A la Par, second movement
        ("Guaguancó") (León), 349, 502–506
    architecture, 507
    composers, 507
Poulenc, Francis, 389
Powwows, 32, 33
Presley, Elvis, 475, 501
Price, Florence Beatrice, 443
Price, Leontyne, 314
Prima prattica, 90
Printing press, impact of, 52, WB1-7
Programmatic work, *Unanswered Question,
    The* (Ives), 346, 368–372
Program music
    composers, 131
    Overture to A Midsummer Night's Dream
        (Mendelssohn), 242, 260–266
    Symphonie fantastique (Berlioz), 237,
        242, 267–272
    Union (Gottschalk), 242, 293–296
    "Winter" from *Four Seasons* (Vivaldi),
        84, 86, 125–129
Prokofiev, Sergei, 266, 389, WB4-6
Psalmes, Sonets, & Songs (Byrd), 72
Psychedelia
    composers and performers, 493
    development of, 486–487
    "Good Vibrations" (Beach Boys), 348,
        486–493
Public Enemy
    background and works of, 500
    "Fight the Power," 348, 494–501
    genre and key concepts, 348
Puccini, Giacomo, 323
Punk
    "God Save the Queen" (Sex Pistols), 348,
        WB6-1 to WB6-8
    groups, WB6-9
Purcell, Henry
    background and works of, 100
    Dido and Aeneas, 86, 95–100
    genre and key concepts, 86

Pygmies (Mbuti)
    background information on, 103–104,
        108
    "Marriage Celebration Song," 86, 102,
        104–108

Quartet. *See* String quartet

Raga, 299–300
    composers of, 303
Raga Sindhi-Bhairavi (Shankar), 242
    form, 299
    listening guide, 304–305
    melody, 299, 3, 30300–302
    rhythm, 299
    texture, 299, 302–303
Ragtime
    composers, 404
    development of, 398
    Maple Leaf Rag (Joplin), 346, 397–402
Rainey, Gertrude "Ma," 406, 413
Rainforest cultures, 108
Rameau, Jean-Philippe, 101
Ramones, The, WB6-9
Rap, 77
Ravel, Maurice, 359, WB4-6
Recapitulation, 201
Recitative, 90, 93, 95, 97, 157, 221, 236
Recorders, WB1-2
Reed instruments, 47
Refrain, 111
Reggae, 74
Register, 26, 434
Reich, Steve, 469
Relient K., 166
Renaissance
    background information, 50–52
    individuality, 51–52
    timeline, 53
Renaissance, music during the
    compared to Baroque music, 167
    compared to medieval music, 79
    "The Cricket" (Josquin des Prez), 52, 53,
        54–59
    economic growth and impact on, 50–51
    Moorish Dance (Susato), 52, 53, WB1-1
        to WB1-6
    playing and singing, 59
    printing of, 52
    religious, 50, 72
    "Since Robin Hood" (Weelkes), 52, 53,
        60–64
    "Sing Joyfully" (Byrd), 50, 53, 66–70
    summary of, 80
Repetition, 335
Reunion, The (Lisa Lu and the Beijing Opera
    Co.), 173
    listening guide, 232–233
    melody, 228, 230
    rhythm, 228, 231
    texture, 228, 231
    timbre, 228, 231
"Revenge" (Strozzi), 84, 87, 109–115
    form, 109, 110–111
    listening guide, 112–113
    melody, 109, 110
    timbre, 109, 111
Rhyme singing
    development of, 73
    "My Lord Help Me to Pray" (Rhyming
        Singers of the Bahamas), 53,
        73–76

Rhythm
  Baroque, 139, 141, 142
  defined, 1, 7–8
  medieval, 22, 26, 37, 39, 49
  nineteenth-century, 244, 245–246, 285, 286
  Renaissance, 60, 61–62
  twentieth-century, 350, 354, 380, 382–383, 397, 398–399, 414, 415, 416, 431, 432. 444, 446, 470, 471–472, 494, 496–497, 502, 504
Rifkin, Joshua, 403
Rigaudon, 140–145
Riley, Terry, 469
Rimsky-Korsakov, Nikolai, 339
Ring of the Nibelungs (Wagner), 319, 322
Rite of Spring, The (Stravinsky), 343, 347
  harmony, 380, 381–382
  listening guide, 386–387
  melody, 380, 382
  rhythm, 380, 382–383
  timbre, 380
  word-music relationships, 380, 384
Ritornello, 126
Ritornello principle, 126–127, 132, 133, 152
Roberts, Marcus, 404
Roches, The, 166
Rock 'n' roll
  composers and singers of, 475
  origin of term, 471
  "School Day" (Berry), 349, 470–477
  television and, 475
Rollins, Sonny, 430
Romanticism, 237, 238–239
Rondo form, 193, 236, 444, 446
Rossini, Giacchino, 323
Rounded binary form, 192, 201
Rousseau, Jean-Jacques, 171
Rubato, 291

Sackbuts, WB1-2
Sacred music
  of the late Baroque, 153
  of the Renaissance, 72
San Ildefonso Indians, *Eagle Dance*, 21, 31–35
Saxophone, difference between tenor and alto, 429
Scales, 3–5
  diatonic, 354–355
  pentatonic, 186, 189, 230, 233, 334, 382
  whole-tone, 354–355
Scarlatti, Alessandro, 153
Scenario, 384
Scherzo form, 335
Schindler, Anton, 247
Schoenberg, Arnold, 437
  background and works of, 373, 377
  "Columbine" from *Pierrot lunaire*, 347, 374–378
  genre and key concepts, 347
"School Day" (Berry), 349
  form, 470, 474
  listening guide, 476–477
  rhythm, 470, 471–472
  texture, 470, 474
  timbre, 470, 472–473
Schubert, Franz
  background and works of, 254–255, 272, 278
  "Erlkönig," 242, 252–259

genre and key concepts, 242
  songs by, 255
Schumann, Clara, 239, WB3-5
  background and works of, 281
  "Forward!," 243, 279–283
  genre and key concepts, 243
Schumann, Robert
  background and works of, WB3-5
  "Dedication," 243, WB3-1 to WB3-7
  genre and key concepts, 243
  works of, 272, 292
Schütz, Heinrich, 94
Scriptoriums, 20
Seconda prattica, 90
Section, 416
Secular music
  "Behold, Spring" ("Ecco la Primavera") (Landini), 19, 21, 37–41
  "The Cricket" (Josquin des Prez), 52, 53
Sequence, 415, 426
Sex Pistols
  background and works of, WB6-8
  genre and key concepts, 348
  "God Save the Queen," 348, WB6-1 to WB6-8
Shakespeare, William, 51, 63
  Overture to A Midsummer Night's Dream (Mendelssohn), 242, 260–266
  works set to music, 266
Shankar, Anoushka, 303
Shankar, Ravi
  background and works of, 301, 303
  genre and key concepts, 242
  Raga Sindhi-Bhairavi, 242, 299–305
Shawms, 43, 44–45, 46, 47
Sheet music, 404
Shore, Howard, 513
Shuffle groove, 471–472, WB5-3
"Since Robin Hood" (Weelkes), 52, 53
  listening guide, 64
  rhythm, 60, 61–62
  texture, 60, 61
  word-music (word painting) relationships, 60, 63
"Sing Joyfully" (Byrd), 50, 53
  form, 66, 68
  listening guide, 70
  texture, 66, 67–68
  word-music (word painting) relationships, 66, 68
Sitar, 300
Sly and the Family Stone, 501
Smetana, Biedrich, 339
Smith, Bessie, 406, 413
Sonata
  da camera, 116
  da chiesa, 116
  defined, 116
  form, 191, 201–203, 205, 207, 213, 236, 262
  trio, 111, 116
Song
  "Columbine" from *Pierrot lunaire* (Schoenberg), 347, 374–378
  "Dedication" (Schumann), 243, WB3-1 to WB3-7
  "Erlkönig" (Schubert), 242, 252–259
  form, 151
  Piano Trio, op. 11 (Fanny Mendelssohn), 243, 273–276
  32-bar standard song form, 416–417

Songs to the Virgin Mary no. 249. *See* "He Who Gladly Serves" ("Aquel que de volontade") (Alfonso el Sabio)
Sound(s)
  loudness, decibel levels, 272
  as music, 59
  wave, 6
South City Voices, 9
Sprechstimme, 375–376, 378
Squarcialupi, Antonio, 42
Squarcialupi Codex, 42
Stanzas, 39
"Star-Spangled Banner, The," 190, 293, 294, 296
  dynamics, 12
  form, 14
  genre, 16
  harmony, 8–9
  melody, 2–6
  rhythm, 7–8
  texture, 10–11
  timbre, 11–12
  word-music relationship, 14–15
Steiner, Max, 513
Still, William Grant
  background and works of, 441
  "Black Pierrot, A" from *Songs of Separation*, 348, 438–442
  genre and key concepts, 348
Stokowski, Leopold, 122
Stop time, 472
Stradivarius, Antonio, 131
Stravinsky, Igor, 10, 190
  background and works of, 385, WB4-6
  genre and key concepts, 347
  Rite of Spring, The, 343, 347, 380–389
String quartet
  development of, 170
  how to form, 339
  movements in classical, 175–176
  who leads, 181
String Quartet in C Major, op. 76 (Haydn), 173
  form, 174
  listening guide, 180–181
  melody, 174, 177–178
  texture, 174, 177
  theme and variations form, 178
  timbre, 174, 176
String Quartet in F Major, op. 96 (Dvořák), 243
  form, 333, 335
  listening guide, 336
  melody, 333, 334–335
  timbre, 333, 334
Strings, sympathetic versus drone, 305
Strophes, 39
Strozzi, Barbara
  background and works of, 114
  genre and key concepts, 87
  "Revenge," 84, 87, 109–115
Suites
  Baroque composers, 147
  Water Music (Handel), 82, 86, 139–145
Sullivan, Arthur, 323
Summer of Love, 493
Surrogate speech, WB2-2
Susato, Tielman
  background and works of, WB1-5
  genre and key concepts, 53
  Moorish Dance (Susato), 52, 53, WB1-1 to WB1-6

Sutherland, Joan, 314
Sweelinck, Jan Pieterszoon, 124
Swing, 414–421
Syllabic, 25, 40, 49
Symphonie fantastique (Berlioz), 237, 242
  form, 267, 269
  listening guide, 270
  timbre, 267, 268
  word-music relationships, 267, 268–269
Symphony no. 4 in E Minor, op. 98 (Brahms), 243
  form, 324, 325
  listening guide, 328–331
  timbre, 324, 326
Symphony no. 5 in C Minor, op. 67 (Fifth Symphony) (Beethoven), 242
  dynamics, 244, 246
  form, 244, 247
  listening guide, 248–249
  rhythm, 244, 245–246
  sonata form, 244
  ternary form, 244
  timbre, 244, 246–247
Symphony no. 40 in G Minor, K. 550 (Mozart), 173
  form, 200, 201–203
  harmony, 200, 203
  listening guide, 206–207
  melody, 200, 203–204
  sonata form, 201–203, 205, 207
Symphony no. 102 in B-flat Major (Haydn), 172, 173
  dynamics, 190, 191–192
  form, 190, 192–193
  listening guide, 194–197
  minuet form, 192–193
  movements, 191, 192–193
  rondo form, 193
  timbre, 190, 191
Syncopation, 62, 142, 398–399
Syncretism, 74
Szymanowska, Maria, 277

Tabla, 302
Tailleferre, Germaine
  background and works of, WB4-5
  Concertino for Harp and Orchestra, finale, 347, WB4-1 to WB4-5
  genre and key concepts, 347
Tala rhythm, 303
Tallis Thomas, 72
Tambura, 302
Tansen, 299–300
Tchaikovsky, Pyotr Illich, 266, 389
Tebaldi, Renata, 314
Te Kanawa, Kiri, 314
Tempo rubato, 291
Ternary form, 56, 192, 325, WB3-1, WB3-2
Terraced melody, 31, 34
"Terraplane Blues" (Johnson), 346
  form, 405, 407–409, 411
  listening guide, 410–411
  melody, 405, 406
  timbre, 405, 406–407
  12-bar blues form, 407–409, 411
  word-music relationships, 405, 409
Texture
  Baroque, 88, 89–90, 117, 119–120, 132, 133–134, 148, 151, 156, 158, 160–161
  call-and-response, 74, 77, 104, 105, 333, 334, 416, 474

classical, 174, 177
defined, 1, 10–11
homophony, 10, 45, 81, 88, 89–90, 151, 158, 160, 177, 285, 286
medieval, 22, 24, 31, 32, 37, 38, 43, 45, 49
monophony, 10, 22, 24, 31, 32, 45, 49, 160–161, 433
nineteenth-century, 285, 286, 293, 294, 315, 316
polyphony, 10–11, 22, 38, 42, 49, 55, 60, 61, 67–68, 74, 160, 161, 171, 231
Renaissance, 54, 55, 60, 61, 66, 67–68
trio-sonata texture, 111
twentieth-century, 368, 369, 414, 416, 424, 426, 431, 433, 450, 453, 470, 474, 486, 488, 508, 510
Theme and variations form, 178, 186, 236, 324, 325
32-bar standard song for,, 416–417
Through-composed, 384, 440
Timbre
acoustics of, 13
Baroque, 109, 111, 117, 118–119, 125, 126, 132, 133, 139, 142, 148, 149, 156, 159, 161
classical, 174, 176, 190, 191, 210, 211
defined, 1, 11–12
medieval, 43, 44–45
nineteenth-century, 244, 246–247, 267, 268, 273, 274, 279, 280, 324, 326, 333, 334
twentieth-century, 350, 351–352, 368, 369, 374, 375–376, 380, 405, 406–407, 424, 425, 444, 445–446, 464, 465, 470, 472–473, 478, 479–480, 486, 489, 494, 495, 502, 503–504, 508, 509
Tiomkin, Dmitri, 449
Tolkien, J.R.R., 319
Tomás Luis de Victoria, 72
Tonality, 355, 369–371, 373
Tonic, 9, 126, 355
"Tonight" from West Side Story (Bernstein), 348
form, 450, 452–453
listening guide, 454–457
melody, 450, 451–452
texture, 450, 453
word-music relationships, 450, 453
Toscanini, Arturo, 332
Tower, Joan, 437
Trains, in music, 59
Trio sonata, 111, 116
Triple meter, 7, 39, 60, 62
Trochaic meter, 62, 274
Trumpets
Baroque versus modern, 135

Cotton Tail (Ellington), 344, 346, 414–421
Greetings by Aba Musa!, Wasa, 347, 390–395
recordings of, 396
Tutti, 126
12-bar blues form, 407–409, 411, 474
Twelve-tone composition, 377, 437
Twentieth century
background information, 342
globalization, 345
modernism, 343
social diversity, 344–345
technology, impact of, 344
timeline, 347, 349
Twentieth century, music in
A la Par, second movement ("Guaguancó") (León), 349, 502–506
"Black Pierrot, A" from Songs of Separation (Still), 348, 438–442
"Columbine" from Pierrot lunaire (Schoenberg), 347, 374–378
compared to nineteenth-century music, 514
Concertino for Harp and Orchestra, finale (Tailleferre), 347, WB4-1 to WB4-5
Cotton Tail (Ellington), 344, 346, 414–421
"Farewell" from Crouching Tiger, Hidden Dragon (Dun), 349, 508–512
"Fight the Power" (Public Enemy), 348, 494–501
4'33" (Cage), 348, 459–463
"God Save the Queen" (Sex Pistols), 348, WB6-1 to WB6-8
"Good Vibrations" (Beach Boys), 348, 486–493
"Hoe-Down" from Rodeo (Copland), 348, 444–448
"It Don't Cost Very Much" (Jackson), 349, WB5-1 to WB5-7
"Knee Play 1" from Einstein on the Beach (Glass), 349, 464–467
Maple Leaf Rag (Joplin), 346, 397–402
Ornithology (Parker), 347, 424–429
Piano Study in Mixed Accents (Crawford), 347, 431–436
"Please, Mr. Postman" (Marvelettes), 348, 478–484
Rite of Spring, The (Stravinsky), 343, 347, 380–389
"School Day" (Berry), 349, 470–477
summary of, 515
"Terraplane Blues" (Johnson), 346, 405–413
"Tonight" from West Side Story (Bernstein), 348, 450–457

Unanswered Question, The (Ives), 346, 368–372
Voiles (Debussy), 345, 346, 350–357
Unanswered Question, The (Ives), 346
harmony, 368, 369–371
listening guide, 372
texture, 368, 369
timbre, 368, 369
Union (Gottschalk), 9, 242
listening guide, 296
melody, 293, 294
texture, 293, 294
Unison, 10, 39

Valkyrie, The (Wagner), 243
listening guide, 320–321
texture, 315, 316
word-music relationships, 315, 316–319
Vamp, 481
Variation, 335
Verdi, Giuseppe
background and works of, 266, 308, 309, 323
genre and key concepts, 242
La Traviata, 242, 306–313
Violins, making, 131
Virtuosic melody, 307
Virtuosos, 84–85
nineteenth-century, 298, 341
Vivaldi, Antonio
background and works of, 130, 138
genre and key concepts, 86
"Winter" from Four Seasons, 84, 86, 125–129
Vocables, 33
Voicings, 415
Voiles (Debussy), 345, 346
dynamics, 350, 354
form, 350, 355
harmony, 350, 354–355
listening guide, 356–357
melody, 350, 352–353
rhythm, 350, 354
timbre, 350, 351–352
Voltaire, 171
Volume, words used to refer to, 13

Wagner, Richard
background and works of, 319, 322–323
genre and key concepts, 243
Ring of the Nibelungs, 319, 322
Valkyrie, The, 243, 315–321
Walker, George, 443
Walter, Johann, 72
Water Music (Handel), 82, 86
form, 139, 140, 141
listening guide, 143–144

rhythm, 139, 141, 142
timbre, 139, 142
Wavelength, 6
Waza
description of, 390–391
Greetings by Aba Musa!, 347, 390–395
Weber, Carl Maria von, 323
Webern, Anton, 379
Weelkes, Thomas
background and works of, 63
genre and key concepts, 53
"Since Robin Hood" (Weelkes), 52, 53, 60–64
Weingartner, Felix, 332
Whole-tone scale, 354
Williams, John, 513
Wilson, Brian, 486–493
Wind instruments, 43
"Winter" from Four Seasons (Vivaldi), 84, 86
form, 125, 126–127
listening guide, 128–129
timbre, 125, 126
word-music relationships, 125, 127
Wizard of Oz, The, 205
Word-music relationships
Baroque, 88, 90, 95, 97, 125, 127, 156, 158
classical, 219, 220–221
defined, 1, 14–15
medieval, 22, 25–26, 31, 33, 37, 40, 49
nineteenth-century, 252, 253–254, 260, 261–262, 267, 268–269, 273, 274, 279, 280, 306, 307–308, 315, 316–319
Renaissance, 54, 56, 60, 63, 66, 68
twentieth-century, 374, 376, 380, 384, 405, 409, 450, 453, 494, 497
Word painting
Cantata no. 140 ("Awake, A Voice Calls to Us") (Bach), 83–84, 87, 148–155
"Cricket, The" (Josquin des Prez), 52, 53, 54–59
Dido and Aeneas (Purcell), 86, 95–100
"Forward!" (C. Schumann), 243, 279–283
Messiah (Handel), 84, 87, 153, 156–166
Orpheus (Monteverdi), 86, 88–93
"Revenge" (Strozzi), 84, 87, 109–115
"Since Robin Hood" (Weelkes), 52, 53, 60–64
"Sing Joyfully" (Byrd), 50, 53, 66–70

"Yankee Doddle," 293, 294, 296

Zimmer, Hans, 513
Zithers
koto, Cherry Blossom (Ikuta-Ryu), 173, 183–189
types of, 187
Zwilich, Ellen Taaffe, 437